EXPERT SYSTEMS

Principles and Programming

EXPERT SYSTEMS
Principles and Programming
Third Edition

Joseph Giarratano

University of Houston–Clear Lake

Gary Riley

Calico Technology

PWS Publishing Company

An International Thomson Publishing Company

Boston • Albany • Bonn • Cincinnati • London • Madrid • Melbourne • Mexico City • New York
Paris • San Francisco • Singapore • Tokyo • Toronto • Washington

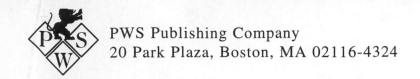

PWS Publishing Company
20 Park Plaza, Boston, MA 02116-4324

I(T)P ™

International Thomson Publishing
The trademark ITP is used under license.

For more information, contact:

PWS Publishing Company
20 Park Plaza
Boston, MA 02116-4324

International Thomson Publishing Europe
Berkshire House 168–173
High Holborn
London WC1V 7AA
England

Thomas Nelson Australia
102 Dodds Street
South Melbourne, 3205
Victoria, Australia

Nelson Canada
1120 Birchmount Road
Scarborough, Ontario
Canada M1K 5G4

Printed and bound in the United States of America.

98 99 00 01—10 9 8 7 6 5 4 3 2 1

Sponsoring Editor: Mike Sugarman
Market Development Manager: Nathan Wilbur
Editorial Assistant: Kathryn Schooling
Production Editor: Pamela Rockwell
Cover Art: Ray Paul, 1993, "Tablet," acrylic collage on canvas
Cover Design: Eileen Hoff Studio
Manufacturing Manager: Andrew Christensen
Text Printer: Quebecor-Fairfield
Cover Printer: Phoenix Color Corp.

International Thomson Editores
Campos Eliseos 385, Piso 7
Col. Polanco
11560 Mexico C.F., Mexico

International Thomson Publishing GmbH
Königswinterer Strasse 418
53227 Bonn, Germany

International Thomson Publishing Asia
221 Henderson Road
#05–10 Henderson Building
Singapore 0315

International Thomson Publishing Japan
Hirakawacho Kyowa Building, 31
2-2-1 Hirakawacho
Chiyoda-ku, Tokyo 102
Japan

Library of Congress Cataloging-in-Publication Data
Giarratano, Joseph C.
    Expert systems : principles and programming / Joseph Giarratano,. Gary Riley. — 3rd ed.
        p.   cm.
    Includes bibliographical references and index.
    ISBN 0-534-95053-1
        1. Expert systems (Computer science) I. Riley, Gary, 1962–
    II. Title.
QA.76.76.E95G53 1998
006.3'3—dc21   97-31814

Contents

PREFACE   xi

FOREWORD TO THE FIRST EDITION   xv

CHAPTER 1: INTRODUCTION TO EXPERT SYSTEMS   1

1.1   Introduction   **1**

1.2   What Is an Expert System?   **1**

1.3   Advantages of Expert Systems   **4**

1.4   General Concepts of Expert Systems   **5**

1.5   Characteristics of an Expert System   **8**

1.6   The Development of Expert Systems Technology   **10**

1.7   Expert Systems Applications and Domains   **15**

1.8   Languages, Shells, and Tools   **21**

1.9   Elements of an Expert System   **23**

1.10 Production Systems   **28**

1.11 Procedural Paradigms   **32**

1.12 Nonprocedural Paradigms   **38**

1.13 Artificial Neural Systems   **43**

1.14 Connectionist Expert Systems and Inductive Learning   **49**

1.15 Summary   **50**

CHAPTER 2: THE REPRESENTATION OF KNOWLEDGE   57

2.1   Introduction   **57**

2.2   The Meaning of Knowledge   **57**

2.3   Productions   **60**

2.4   Semantic Nets   **63**

2.5   Object-Attribute-Value Triples   **66**

2.6   PROLOG and Semantic Nets   **67**

2.7   Difficulties with Semantic Nets   **72**

2.8   Schemata   **73**

2.9   Frames   **74**

2.10 Difficulties with Frames   **77**

2.11 Logic and Sets   **78**

2.12 Propositional Logic   **81**

2.13 The First Order Predicate Logic   **86**

2.14 The Universal Quantifier   **87**

2.15 The Existential Quantifier   **88**

2.16 Quantifiers and Sets   **90**

2.17 Limitations of Predicate Logic   **91**

2.18 Summary   **91**

CHAPTER 3: METHODS OF INFERENCE   97

3.1   Introduction   **97**

3.2   Trees, Lattices, and Graphs   **97**

3.3   State and Problem Spaces   **101**

3.4   And-Or Trees and Goals   **106**

3.5   Deductive Logic and Syllogisms   **109**

3.6   Rules of Inference   **114**

3.7   Limitations of Propositional Logic   **122**

3.8   First Order Predicate Logic   **124**

3.9   Logic Systems   **125**

3.10 Resolution   **128**

3.11 Resolution Systems and Deduction   **131**

3.12 Shallow and Causal Reasoning   **133**

3.13 Resolution and First Order Predicate Logic   **137**

3.14 Forward and Backward Chaining   **143**

3.16 Metaknowledge   **156**

3.17 Summary   **157**

CHAPTER 4: Reasoning Under Uncertainty   165

4.1   Introduction   **165**

4.2   Uncertainty   **165**

4.3   Types of Error   **166**

4.4   Errors and Induction   **168**

4.5   Classical Probability   **169**

4.6   Experimental and Subjective Probabilities   **173**

4.7   Compound Probabilities   **175**

4.8   Conditional Probabilities   **178**

4.9   Hypothetical Reasoning and Backward Induction   **183**

4.10 Temporal Reasoning and Markov Chains   **186**

4.11 The Odds of Belief   **191**

4.12 Sufficiency and Necessity   **193**

4.13 Uncertainty in Inference Chains   **195**

4.14 The Combination of Evidence   **200**

4.15 Inference Nets   **207**

4.16 The Propagation of Probabilities   **216**

4.17 Summary   **220**

CHAPTER 5: INEXACT REASONING   **227**

5.1   Introduction   **227**

5.2   Uncertainty and Rules   **227**

5.3   Certainty Factors   **233**

5.4   Dempster-Shafer Theory   **243**

5.5   Approximate Reasoning   **256**

5.6   The State of Uncertainty   **300**

5.7   Summary   **301**

CHAPTER 6: DESIGN OF EXPERT SYSTEMS   **309**

6.1   Introduction   **309**

6.2   Selecting the Appropriate Problem   **309**

6.3   Stages in the Development of an Expert System   **311**

6.4   Errors in Development Stages   **313**

6.5   Software Engineering and Expert Systems   **315**

6.6   The Expert System Life Cycle   **317**

6.7   A Detailed Life Cycle Model   **320**

6.8   Summary   **325**

CHAPTER 7: INTRODUCTION TO CLIPS 327

    7.1 Introduction   **327**

    7.2 CLIPS   **328**

    7.3 Notation   **328**

    7.4 Fields   **330**

    7.5 Entering and Exiting CLIPS   **333**

    7.6 Facts   **334**

    7.7 Adding and Removing Facts   **337**

    7.8 Modifying and Duplicating Facts   **340**

    7.9 The Watch Command   **341**

    7.10 The Deffacts Construct   **342**

    7.11 The Components of a Rule   **344**

    7.12 The Agenda and Execution   **346**

    7.13 Commands for Manipulating Constructs   **350**

    7.14 The Printout Command   **353**

    7.15 Using Multiple Rules   **353**

    7.16 The Set-Break Command   **355**

    7.17 Loading and Saving Constructs   **357**

    7.18 Commenting Constructs   **358**

    7.19 Summary   **359**

CHAPTER 8: PATTERN MATCHING 365

    8.1 Introduction   **365**

    8.2 Variables   **365**

    8.3 Multiple Use of Variables   **366**

    8.4 Fact Addresses   **367**

    8.5 Single-Field Wildcards   **370**

    8.6 Blocks World   **371**

    8.7 Multifield Wildcards and Variables   **376**

    8.8 Field Constraints   **382**

    8.9 Functions and Expressions   **385**

    8.10 Summing Values Using Rules   **389**

    8.11 The Bind Function   **391**

    8.12 I/O Functions   **392**

    8.13 Summary   **398**

CHAPTER 9: ADVANCED PATTERN MATCHING   **405**

9.1   Introduction   **405**

9.2   The Game of Sticks   **405**

9.3   Input Techniques   **405**

9.4   Predicate Functions   **407**

9.5   The Test Conditional Element   **407**

9.6   The Predicate Field Constraint   **410**

9.7   The Return Value Field Constraint   **411**

9.8   The Sticks Program   **412**

9.9   The *OR* Conditional Element   **413**

9.10 The *AND* Conditional Element   **415**

9.11 The *NOT* Conditional Element   **417**

9.12 The *EXISTS* Conditional Element   **419**

9.13 The *FORALL* Conditional Element   **422**

9.14 The *LOGICAL* Conditional Element   **424**

9.15 Utility Commands   **428**

9.16 Summary   **430**

CHAPTER 10: MODULAR DESIGN AND EXECUTION CONTROL   437

10.1 Introduction   **437**

10.2 Deftemplate Attributes   **437**

10.3 Salience   **445**

10.4 Phases and Control Facts   **448**

10.5 Misuse of Salience   **453**

10.6 The Defmodule Construct   **456**

10.7 Importing and Exporting Facts   **459**

10.8 Modules and Execution Control   **463**

10.9 Summary   **471**

CHAPTER 11: EFFICIENCY IN RULE-BASED LANGUAGES   477

11.1 Introduction   **477**

11.2 The Rete Pattern-Matching Algorithm   **477**

11.3 The Pattern Network   **480**

11.4 The Join Network   **483**

11.5 The Importance of Pattern Order   **486**

11.6 Ordering Patterns for Efficiency **492**

11.7 Multifield Variables and Efficiency **493**

11.8 The Test CE and Efficiency **493**

11.9 Built-In Pattern-Matching Constraints **495**

11.10 General Rules versus Specific Rules **496**

11.11 Procedural Functions **498**

11.12 Simple Rules versus Complex Rules **500**

11.13 Loading and Saving Facts **503**

11.14 Summary **504**

CHAPTER 12: EXPERT SYSTEM DESIGN EXAMPLES 509

12.1 Introduction **509**

12.2 Certainty Factors **509**

12.3 Decision Trees **513**

12.4 Backward Chaining **526**

12.5 A Monitoring Problem **538**

12.6 Summary **554**

APPENDIX A: SOME USEFUL EQUIVALENCES 557

**APPENDIX B: SOME ELEMENTARY QUANTIFIERS
AND THEIR MEANINGS 559**

APPENDIX C: SOME SET PROPERTIES 561

APPENDIX D: CLIPS SUPPORT INFORMATION 563

APPENDIX E: CLIPS COMMAND AND FUNCTION SUMMARY 565

APPENDIX F: CLIPS BNF 579

INDEX 585

Preface

Expert systems have experienced tremendous growth and popularity since their commercial introduction in the early 1980s. Today, expert systems are used in business, science, engineering, manufacturing, and many other fields.

This book is meant to educate students about expert systems theory and programming. The material is written at the upper-division/graduate level suitable for majors in computer science, computer information systems, engineering, and other fields who are interested in expert systems. New terminology is shown in boldface and immediately explained. Numerous examples and references help clarify the meaning of the text and provide guidance for supplementary reading.

Expert Systems: Principles and Programming is divided into two parts. Chapters 1–6 cover the theory behind expert systems and how they fit into the scope of computer science; that is the logic, probability, data structures, AI, and other topics that form the theory of expert systems. Chapters 7–12 cover programming in expert systems. While a previous course in artificial intelligence (AI) is helpful, this·book provides a self-contained introduction to AI topics that are appropriate for expert systems.

We have tried to explain the theory behind expert systems so that the student may make an informed decision regarding the appropriate use of expert system technology. The important point we emphasize is that like any other tool, expert systems have both advantages and disadvantages. The theory also explains how expert systems relate to other programming methods, such as conventional programming. Another reason for discussing theory is to prepare the student to read current research papers in expert systems. Because expert systems draw from so many diverse fields, it is difficult for a beginner to read papers without some grounding in theory.

The second part of this book is an introduction to the CLIPS expert system tool. This part is a practical introduction to expert system programming that serves to reinforce and clarify the theoretical concepts developed in the first part. As with the theory part of the book, the programming part can be understood by students with some programming experience in a high-level language. Students learn the practical problems associated with expert system development using CLIPS, a modern, powerful expert system tool developed by NASA at the Johnson Space Center. Today, CLIPS is used for real-world projects in government, business, and industry. It is available on virtually every type of computer including IBM-PC and clones, VAX, HP, Sun, Macintosh, and Cray. Code developed in CLIPS runs very fast and is very portable. The CD-ROM included with this book contains CLIPS executables for MS-DOS, Windows 3.1/Windows 95, and MacOS; the *CLIPS Reference Manual* and *CLIPS User's Guide*; and the C source code for CLIPS.

Some expert systems courses include a term project. A project is an excellent way to develop skills in expert systems. Students usually complete small expert systems of 50 to 150 rules in a semester project of their choice. A few projects that have been done by students using CLIPS include automobile diagnosis, taxi scheduling, personnel scheduling, computer network management, weather forecasting, stock market prediction, consumer buying advice, and diet advice.

The suggested plan for a one-semester course is as follows.

1. Cover Chapter 1 to provide a quick introduction to expert systems. In particular, assign Problems 1, 2, and 3.

2. Cover Chapters 7–10 to introduce the syntax of CLIPS. It is helpful for students to recode Problem 2 of Chapter 1 to contrast the expert system approach with the language they originally used in Chapter 1. This contrast is very useful in pointing out the differences between a rule-based language like CLIPS and LISP, PROLOG, or whatever the original language used for Problem 2.

3. Chapters 11 and 12 may be covered for a stronger programming emphasis in the course. Chapter 11, on efficiency in rule-based languages, is not essential to an introductory course. It may be discussed if there is interest in building large expert systems or if efficiency is important. Chapter 12 presents a collection of topics that illustrate interesting problems solved using CLIPS.

Alternatively, after Chapter 10 the instructor may return to the theory section. If students have strong backgrounds in logic and PROLOG, most of Chapters 2 and 3 may be skipped. Students who have had a LISP-based introductory AI course or none at all will benefit from Chapters 2 and 3 if a strong emphasis on logic and the fundamental theory of expert systems is desired. If students have strong backgrounds in probability and statistics, the material in Chapter 4 up to Section 4.11 can be skipped.

4. Sections 4.11 to the end of Chapter 4 and Chapter 5 discuss advanced topics in expert systems concerning methods of dealing with uncertainty. These topics include probabilistic inference, certainty factors, Dempster-Shafer theory, and fuzzy theory. Students will gain an understanding of these methods in sufficient detail so they can read current papers in the field and start doing research, if desired.

5. Chapter 6 discusses the software engineering of expert systems and is meant for those students planning to work on large expert systems. It is not necessary to discuss this chapter before assigning term projects. In fact, it would be best to cover this chapter last so that the student can appreciate all the factors that go into building a quality expert system.

A manual with solutions to the odd-numbered problems and some of the even-numbered programs and another manual of the tables and figures contained in the book suitable for viewgraphs is available from the publisher.

Contributors to CLIPS

We'd like to thank all of the people who contributed in one way or another to the success of CLIPS. As with any large project, CLIPS is the result of the efforts of numerous people. The primary contributors have been: Robert Savely, Chief Scientist of Advanced Software Technology at JSC, who conceived the project and provided overall direction and support; Chris Culbert, Branch Chief of the Software Technology Branch, who managed the project and wrote the original *CLIPS Reference Manual*; Gary Riley, who designed and developed the rule-based portion of CLIPS, co-authored the *CLIPS Reference Manual* and *CLIPS Architecture Manual*, and developed the Macintosh interface for CLIPS;

Brian Donnell, who designed and developed the CLIPS Object-Oriented Language (COOL), coauthored the *CLIPS Reference Manual* and *CLIPS Architecture Manual*, and developed the previous MS-DOS interfaces for CLIPS; Bebe Ly, who developed the X Window interface for CLIPS; Chris Ortiz, who developed the Windows 3.1 interface for CLIPS; Dr. Joseph Giarratano of the University of Houston–Clear Lake, who wrote the *CLIPS User's Guide*; and Frank Lopez, who wrote the original prototype version of CLIPS.

Many other individuals contributed to the design, development, review, and general support of CLIPS including Jack Aldridge, Carla Armstrong, Paul Baffes, Ann Baker, Stephen Baudendistel, Les Berke, Ron Berry, Tom Blinn, Marlon Boarnet, Dan Bochsler, B. L. Brady, Bob Brown, Barry Cameron, Tim Cleghorn, Major Paul Condit, Major Steve Cross, Andy Cunningham, Dan Danley, Mark Engelberg, Kirt Fields, Ken Freeman, Kevin Greiner, Ervin Grice, Sharon Hecht, Patti Herrick, Mark Hoffman, Grace Hua, Gordon Johnson, Phillip Johnston, Sam Juliano, Ed Lineberry, Bowen Loftin, Linda Martin, Daniel McCoy, Terry McGregor, Becky McGuire, Scott Meadows, C. J. Melebeck, Paul Mitchell, Steve Mueller, Bill Paseman, Cynthia Rathjen, Eric Raymond, Reza Razavipour, Marsha Renals, Monica Rua, Tim Saito, Gregg Swictek, Eric Taylor, James Villarreal, Lui Wang, Bob Way, Jim Wescott, Charlie Wheeler, and Wes White.

Acknowledgements

In writing this book, a number of people have made very helpful comments. These include Chris Culbert, Dan Bochsler, Tim Dawn, Ted Leibfried, Jack Aldridge, Bob Lea, Chet Lund, Andre de Korvin, Arlan DeKock, Terry Feagin, and the anonymous reviewers. We appreciate the excellent cooperation and facilities of the Desktop Publishing Center in the AV Center at the University of Houston–Clear Lake. Thanks also to Phillip Johnston, Kwok–Bun Yue, Naveed Quraishi, Jenna Giarratano, Anthony Giarratano, and Andrew Griffin, Ph.D.

Foreword to the First Edition

When AI was born in the mid-fifties, its primary concerns were centered on game playing, planning, and problem solving. In the environment of that era, it would have been very difficult to predict that three decades later the most important application areas of AI would be centered on knowledge engineering and, more particularly, on expert systems.

Expert systems as we know them today have their roots in the pioneering work of Feigenbaum, Lederberg, Shortliffe, and Buchanan at Stanford University in the late sixties and early seventies. What is remarkable about this work—and MYCIN in particular—is that it still serves as a paradigm for much of the current activity in expert and, more generally, knowledge-based systems.

During the past few years, demonstrable successes of expert systems in specialized application areas such as medical diagnosis and computer system configuration have led to an explosion of interest in a much wider variety of applications, ranging from battle plan management and optimal routing to fault diagnosis, optimal portfolio selection, and the assessment of creditworthiness of loan applicants.

The mushrooming of applications has generated two distinct needs: (a) the development of a better understanding of how to deal with the key problems of knowledge representation, inference, and uncertainty management; and (b) the development of expert system shells and/or programming languages which minimize the effort needed for constructing a knowledge representation system and an inference engine for a particular application.

The book written by Joseph Giarratano and Gary Riley is the only book at this juncture which addresses both of these needs. Its first part deals authoritatively with the basic issues underlying the representation of knowledge, logical inference, and the management of uncertainty. In this part, particularly worthy of note are the chapters on reasoning under uncertainty, which present a wealth of information on the basic approaches which are in use today. Included in these chapters are insightful descriptions of the techniques employing classical probability theory, certainty factors à la MYCIN and PROSPECTOR, the Dempster-Shafer theory, and fuzzy logic. No other text offers such a wide coverage.

The second part presents a detailed account of CLIPS, an expert system programming language written in C which is intended to serve as a versatile tool for the development and implementation of expert systems. CLIPS is related to OPS5 and ART and has a capability for inference under uncertainty.

In combination, the two parts provide an up-to-date and comprehensive account of the principles of expert systems and their practice. To write a book of this kind is clearly a difficult task and the reader has to be prepared to invest a substantial amount of effort to assimilate the wealth of information presented by the authors. As one of the most sophisticated and most important areas of AI, the theory and practice of expert systems contain many complex and as yet not fully understood problems. Joseph Giarratano and Gary Riley deserve the thanks of all of us for undertaking a difficult task and making an important contribution to a better understanding of the fundamentals of expert systems and their application to real-world problems.

Lotfi A. Zadeh
Berkeley, CA. (January, 1989)

CHAPTER 1
Introduction to Expert Systems

1.1 INTRODUCTION

This chapter is a broad introduction to expert systems. The fundamental principles of expert systems are introduced. The advantages and disadvantages of expert systems are discussed and the appropriate areas of application for expert systems are described. The relationship of expert systems to other methods of programming are discussed.

1.2 WHAT IS AN EXPERT SYSTEM?

The first step in solving any problem is defining the problem area or **domain** to be solved. This consideration is just as true in artificial intelligence (AI) as in conventional programming. However, because of the mystique formerly associated with AI, there is a lingering tendency to still believe the old adage "It's an AI problem if it hasn't been solved yet." Another popular definition is that "AI is making computers act like they do in the movies." This type of mind set may have been popular in the 1970s when AI was entirely in a research stage. However, today there are many real-world problems that are being solved by AI and many commercial applications of AI.

Although general solutions to classic AI problems such as natural language translation, speech understanding, and vision have not been found, restricting the problem domain may still produce a useful solution. For example, it is not difficult to build simple natural language systems if the input is restricted to sentences of the form noun, verb, and object. Currently, systems of this type work well in providing a user-friendly interface to many software products such as database systems and spreadsheets. In fact, the parsers associated with popular computer text-adventure games today exhibit an amazing degree of ability in understanding natural language.

As Figure 1.1 shows, AI has many areas of interest. The area of **expert systems** is a very successful approximate solution to the classic AI problem of programming intelligence. Professor Edward Feigenbaum of Stanford University, an early pioneer of expert systems technology, has defined an expert system as "an intelligent computer program that uses knowledge and inference procedures to solve problems that are difficult enough to require significant human expertise for

1

their solutions." (Feigenbaum 82). That is, an expert system is a computer system that **emulates** the decision-making ability of a human expert. The term *emulate* means that the expert system is intended to act in all respects like a human expert. An emulation is much stronger than a simulation, which is only required to act like the real thing in some respects.

Although a general-purpose problem solver still eludes us, expert systems function well in their restricted domains. As proof of their success, you need only observe the many applications of expert systems today in business, medicine, science, and engineering, as well as all the books, journals, conferences, and products devoted to expert systems.

Artificial Intelligence

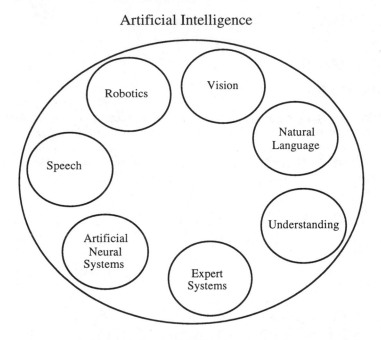

Figure 1.1 Some Areas of Artificial Intelligence

Expert systems is a branch of AI that makes extensive use of specialized knowledge to solve problems at the level of a human **expert**. An expert is a person who has **expertise** in a certain area. That is, the expert has knowledge or special skills that are not known or available to most people. An expert can solve problems that most people cannot solve or can solve them much more efficiently (but not as cheaply). When expert systems were first developed in the 1970s, they contained expert knowledge exclusively. However, the term *expert system* is often applied today to any system that uses expert system technology. This expert system technology may include special expert system languages, programs, and hardware designed to aid in the development and execution of expert systems.

The knowledge in expert systems may be either expertise or knowledge that is generally available from books, magazines, and knowledgeable persons. The terms *expert system*, **knowledge-based system**, or **knowledge-based expert system** are often used synonymously. Most people use the term expert system simply because it's shorter, even though there may be no expertise in their expert system, only general knowledge.

Figure 1.2 illustrates the basic concept of a knowledge-based expert system. The user supplies facts or other information to the expert system and receives expert advice or **expertise** in response. Internally, the expert system consists of two main components. The knowledge base contains the knowledge with which the **inference engine** draws conclusions. These conclusions are the expert system's responses to the user's queries for expertise.

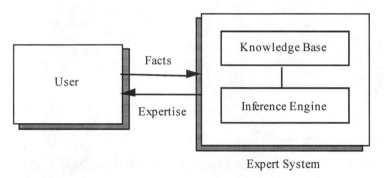

Expert System

Figure 1.2 Basic Concept of an Expert System Function

Useful knowledge-based systems have also been designed to act as an intelligent assistant to a human expert. These intelligent assistants are designed with expert systems technology because of the development advantages. As more knowledge is added to the intelligent assistant, it acts more like an expert. Thus, developing an intelligent assistant may be a useful milestone in producing a complete expert system. In addition, it may free up more of the expert's time by speeding up the solution of problems. Intelligent tutors are another new application of artificial intelligence. Unlike the old computer-assisted instruction systems, the new systems can provide context-sensitive instruction (Giarratano 91a).

An expert's knowledge is specific to one **problem domain**, as opposed to knowledge about general problem-solving techniques. A problem domain is the special problem area such as medicine, finance, science, or engineering, and so forth that an expert can solve problems in very well. Expert systems, like human experts, are generally designed to be experts in one problem domain. For example, you would not normally expect a chess expert to have expert knowledge about medicine. Expertise in one problem domain does not automatically carry over to another.

The expert's knowledge about solving specific problems is called the **knowledge domain** of the expert. For example, a medical expert system designed to diagnose infectious diseases will have a great deal of knowledge about certain symptoms caused by infectious diseases. In this case, the knowledge domain is medicine and consists of knowledge about diseases, symptoms, and treatments. Figure 1.3 illustrates the relationship between the problem and knowledge domain. Notice that this knowledge domain is entirely included within the problem domain. The portion outside the knowledge domain symbolizes an area in which there is not knowledge about all the problems.

One medical expert system usually does not have knowledge about other branches of medicine such as surgery or pediatrics. Although its knowledge of infectious disease is equivalent to a human expert, the expert system would not know anything about other knowledge domains unless it was programmed with that domain knowledge.

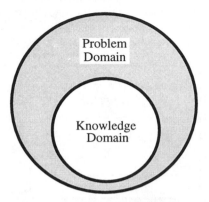

Figure 1.3 A Possible Problem and Knowledge Domain Relationship

In the knowledge domain that it knows about, the expert system reasons or makes **inferences** in the same way that a human expert would infer the solution of a problem. That is, given some facts, a conclusion that follows is inferred. For example, if your spouse hasn't spoken to you in a month, you may infer that he or she had nothing worthwhile to say. However, this is only one of several possible inferences.

As with any new technology, we still have a lot to learn about expert systems. Table 1.1 summarizes the differing views of the participants in a technology. In this table, the technologist may be an engineer or software designer and the technology may be hardware or software. In solving any problem, these are questions that need to be answered or the technology will not be successfully used. Like any other tool, expert systems have appropriate and inappropriate applications. As our experience with expert systems grows, we will discover what these applications are.

Person	Question
Manager	What can I use it for?
Technologist	How can I best implement it?
Researcher	How can I extend it?
Consumer	How will it help me?
	Is it worth the trouble and expense?
	How reliable is it?

Table 1.1 Differing Views of Technology

1.3 ADVANTAGES OF EXPERT SYSTEMS

Expert systems have a number of attractive features:

> • *Increased availability*. Expertise is available on any suitable computer hardware. In a very real sense, an expert system is the mass production of expertise.

- *Reduced cost.* The cost of providing expertise per user is greatly lowered.
- *Reduced danger.* Expert systems can be used in environments that might be hazardous for a human.
- *Permanence.* The expertise is permanent. Unlike human experts, who may retire, quit, or die, the expert system's knowledge will last indefinitely.
- *Multiple expertise.* The knowledge of multiple experts can be made available to work simultaneously and continuously on a problem at any time of day or night. The level of expertise combined from several experts may exceed that of a single human expert (Harmon 85).
- *Increased reliability.* Expert systems increase confidence that the correct decision was made by providing a second opinion to a human expert or break a tie in case of disagreements by multiple human experts. Of course, this method probably won't work if the expert system was programmed by one of the experts. The expert system should always agree with the expert, unless a mistake was made by the expert. However, this may happen if the human expert was tired or under stress.
- *Explanation.* The expert system can explicitly explain in detail the reasoning that led to a conclusion. A human may be too tired, unwilling, or unable to do this all the time. This increases the confidence that the correct decision is made.
- *Fast response.* Fast or real-time response may be necessary for some applications. Depending on the software and hardware used, an expert system may respond faster and be more available than a human expert. Some emergency situations may require responses faster than a human and so a real-time expert system is a good choice (Hugh 88; Ennis 86).
- *Steady, unemotional, and complete response at all times.* This may be very important in real-time and emergency situations, when a human expert may not operate at peak efficiency because of stress or fatigue.
- *Intelligent tutor.* The expert system may act as an intelligent tutor by letting the student run sample programs and by explaining the system's reasoning.
- *Intelligent database.* Expert systems can be used to access a database in an intelligent manner (Kerschberg 86; Schur 88).

The process of developing an expert system has an indirect benefit also since the knowledge of human experts must be put into an explicit form for entering into the computer. Because the knowledge is then explicitly known instead of being implicit in the expert's mind, it can be examined for correctness, consistency, and completeness. The knowledge may then have to be adjusted or re-examined, which improves the quality of the knowledge.

1.4 GENERAL CONCEPTS OF EXPERT SYSTEMS

The knowledge of an expert system may be represented in a number of ways—it can be encapsulated in rules and objects. One common method of representing knowledge is in the form of IF . . . THEN type–**rules**, such as

```
IF the light is red THEN stop
```

If a fact exists that the light is red, this matches the pattern "the light is red." The rule is satisfied and performs its action of "stop." Although this is a very simple example, many significant expert systems have been built by expressing the knowledge of experts in rules. In fact, the knowledge-based approach to developing expert systems has completely supplanted the early AI approach of the 1950s and 1960s, which tried to use sophisticated reasoning techniques with no reliance on knowledge. Some types of expert system tools such as CLIPS allow **objects** as well as rules. Rules can pattern match on objects as well as facts. Alternatively, objects can operate independently of the rules.

Today, a wide range of knowledge-based expert systems have been built. Large systems containing thousands of rules, such as the XCON/R1 system of Digital Equipment Corporation, know much more than any single human expert on how to configure computer systems (McDermott 84). Many small systems for specialized tasks have also been constructed with several hundred rules. These small systems may not operate at the level of an expert, but are designed to take advantage of expert systems technology to perform knowledge-intensive tasks. For these small systems the knowledge may be in books, journals, or other publicly available documentation.

In contrast, a classic expert system embodies unwritten knowledge that must be extracted from an expert by extensive interviews with a **knowledge engineer** over a long period of time. The process of building an expert system is called *knowledge engineering* and is done by a knowledge engineer (Michie 73). Knowledge engineering refers to the acquisition of knowledge from a human expert or other source and its coding in the expert system.

The general stages in the development of an expert system are illustrated in Figure 1.4. The knowledge engineer first establishes a dialog with the human expert in order to elicit the expert's knowledge. This stage is analogous to a system designer in conventional programming discussing the system requirements with a client for whom the program will be constructed. The knowledge engineer then codes the knowledge explicitly in the knowledge base. The expert then evaluates the expert system and gives a critique to the knowledge engineer. This process iterates until the system's performance is judged by the expert to be satisfactory.

The expression *knowledge-based system* is a better term for the application of knowledge-based technology, which may be used for the creation of either expert systems or knowledge-based systems. However, like the term artificial intelligence, it is common practice today to use the term expert systems when referring to both expert systems and knowledge-based systems, even when the knowledge is not at the level of a human expert.

Expert systems are generally designed differently from conventional programs because the problems usually have no algorithmic solution and rely on inferences to achieve a reasonable solution. Note that a reasonable solution is about the best we can expect if no algorithm is available to help us achieve the optimum solution. Because the expert system relies on inference, it must be able to explain its reasoning so that its reasoning can be checked. An **explanation facility** is an integral part of sophisticated expert systems. In fact, elaborate explanation facilities may be designed to allow the user to explore multiple lines of "what if" or **hypothetical reasoning** questions and even to translate natural language into rules.

Some expert systems even allow the system to learn rules by example, through **rule induction**, in which the system creates rules from tables of data. Formalizing the knowledge of experts into rules is not simple, especially when the expert's knowledge has never been systematically explored. There may be inconsistencies, ambiguities, duplications, or other problems with the expert's knowledge that are not apparent until attempts are made to formally represent the knowledge in an expert system.

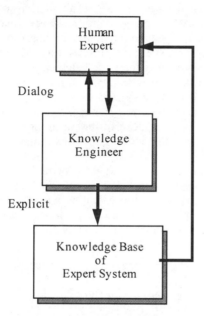

Figure 1.4 Development of an Expert System

Human experts also know the extent of their knowledge and qualify their advice as the problem reaches their **limits of ignorance**. A human expert also knows when to "break the rules." Unless expert systems are explicitly designed to deal with uncertainty, they will make recommendations with the same confidence even if the data they are dealing with are inaccurate or incomplete. An expert system's advice, like that of a human expert, should degrade gracefully at the boundaries of ignorance.

A practical limitation of many expert systems today is lack of **causal knowledge**. That is, the expert systems do not really have an understanding of the underlying causes and effects in a system. It is much easier to program expert systems with **shallow knowledge** based on empirical and heuristic knowledge than with **deep knowledge** based on the basic structures, functions, and behaviors of objects. For example, it is much easier to program an expert system to prescribe an aspirin for a person's headache than to program all the underlying biochemical, physiological, anatomical, and neurological knowledge about the human body. The programming of a causal model of the human body would be an enormous task and, even if successful, the response time of the system would probably be extremely slow because of all the information the system would have to process.

One type of shallow knowledge is **heuristic knowledge** (*heuristic* is Greek and means "to discover"). Heuristics are not guaranteed to succeed in the same way that an algorithm is a guaranteed solution to a problem. Instead, heuristics are rules of thumb or empirical knowledge gained from experience that may aid in the solution but are not guaranteed to work. However, in many fields, such as medicine and engineering, heuristics play an essential role in some types of problem solving. Even if an exact solution is known, it may be impractical to use because of cost or time constraints. Heuristics can provide valuable shortcuts that can reduce both time and cost.

Another problem with expert systems today is that their expertise is limited to the knowledge domain that the systems know about. Typical expert systems cannot generalize their knowledge by using **analogy** to reason about new situations the way people can. Although rule induction helps, only limited types of knowledge can be put into an expert system this way. The customary way of building an expert system, by having the knowledge engineer repeat the cycle of interviewing the expert, constructing a prototype, testing, interviewing, and so on, is a time-consuming and labor-intensive task. In fact, this problem of transferring human knowledge into an expert system is so major that it is called the ***knowledge acquisition bottleneck***. This is a descriptive term because the knowledge acquisition bottleneck constricts the building of an expert system like an ordinary bottleneck constricts fluid flow into a bottle.

In spite of their present limitations, expert systems have been successful in dealing with real-world problems that conventional programming methodologies have been unable to solve, especially those dealing with uncertain or incomplete information. The important point is to be aware of the advantages and limitations of this new technology so that it can be appropriately utilized.

1.5 CHARACTERISTICS OF AN EXPERT SYSTEM

An expert system is usually designed to have the following general characteristics:

- *High performance*. The system must be capable of responding at a level of competency equal to or better than that of an expert in the field. That is, the quality of the advice given by the system must be very high.
- *Adequate response time*. The system must also perform in a reasonable amount of time, comparable to or better than the time required by an expert to reach a decision. An expert system that takes a year to reach a decision compared to an expert's time of one hour would not be too useful. The **time constraints** placed on the performance of an expert system may be especially severe in the case of real-time systems, when a response must be made within a certain time interval.
- *Good reliability*. The expert system must be reliable and not prone to crashes or it will not be used.
- *Understandable*. The system should be able to explain the steps of its reasoning while executing so that it is understandable. Rather than being just a "black box" that produces a miraculous answer, the system should have an explanation capability in the same way that human experts can explain their reasoning. This feature is very important for several reasons.

One reason is that human life and property may depend on the answers of the expert system. Because of the great potential for harm, an expert system must be able to justify its conclusions in the same way a human expert can explain why a certain conclusion was reached. Thus, an explanation facility provides an understandable check of the reasoning for humans.

A second reason for having an explanation facility occurs in the development phase of an expert system to confirm that the knowledge has been correctly acquired and is being correctly used by the system. This is important in debugging because the knowledge may be incorrectly entered by typos or be incorrect due to misunderstandings between the knowledge engineer and the expert. A good explanation facility allows the expert and the knowledge engineer to verify the correctness of the knowledge. Also, because of the way typical expert systems are constructed, it is very difficult to read a significant program listing and understand its operation.

An additional source of error may be unforeseen interactions in the expert system, which may be detected by running test cases with known reasoning that the system should follow. As we will discuss in more detail later, multiple rules may apply to a given situation about which the system is reasoning. The flow of execution is not sequential in an expert system so that you cannot just read its code line by line and understand how the system operates. That is, the order in which rules have been entered in the system is not necessarily the order in which they will be executed. The expert system acts much like a parallel program in which the rules are independent knowledge processors.

- *Flexibility.* Because of the large amount of knowledge that an expert system may have, it is important to have an efficient mechanism for adding, changing, and deleting knowledge. One reason for the popularity of rule-based systems is the efficient and modular storage capability of rules.

Depending on the system, an explanation facility may be simple or elaborate. A simple explanation facility in a rule-based system may list all the facts that made the latest rule execute. More elaborate systems may do the following:

- *List all the reasons for and against a particular hypothesis.* A hypothesis is a goal that is to be proved, such as "the patient has a tetanus infection" in a medical diagnostic expert system. In a real problem there may be multiple hypotheses, just as a patient may have several diseases at once. A hypothesis can also be viewed as a fact whose truth is in doubt and must be proved.
- *List all the hypotheses that may explain the observed evidence.*
- *Explain all the consequences of a hypothesis.* For example, assuming that the patient does have tetanus, there should also be evidence of fever as the infection runs its course. If this symptom is then observed, it adds credibility that the hypothesis is true. If the symptom is not observed, it reduces the credibility of the hypothesis.
- *Give a **prognosis** or prediction of what will occur if the hypothesis is true.*
- *Justify the questions that the program asks of the user for further information.* These questions may be used to direct the line of reasoning to likely diagnostic paths. In most real problems it is too expensive or takes too long to explore all possibilities, and some way

must be provided to guide the search for the correct solution. For example, consider the cost, time, and effect of administering all possible medical tests to a patient complaining of a sore throat.

- *Justify the knowledge of the program.* For example, if the program claims that the hypothesis "the patient has a tetanus infection" is true, the user could ask for an explanation. The program might justify this conclusion on the basis of a rule that says that if the patient has a blood test that is positive for tetanus, then the patient has tetanus. Now the user could ask the program to justify this rule. The program could respond by stating that a blood test positive for a disease is proof of the disease.

In this case, the program is actually quoting a **metarule**, which is knowledge about rules (the prefix *meta* means "above" or "beyond"). Some programs such as Meta-DENDRAL, have been explicitly created to infer new rules (Buchanan 78). A hypothesis is justified by knowledge, and the knowledge is justified by a **warrant** that it is correct. A warrant is essentially a meta-explanation that explains the expert system's explanation of its reasoning.

Knowledge can easily grow **incrementally** in a rule-based system. That is, the knowledge base can grow little by little as rules are added so that the performance and correctness of the system can be continually checked. If the rules are properly designed, the interactions between rules will be minimized or eliminated to protect against unforeseen effects. The incremental growth of knowledge facilitates **rapid prototyping** so that the knowledge engineer can quickly show the expert a working prototype of the expert system. This is an important feature because it maintains both the expert's and management's interest in the project. Rapid prototyping also quickly exposes any gaps, inconsistencies, or errors in the expert's knowledge or the system so that corrections can be made immediately.

1.6 THE DEVELOPMENT OF EXPERT SYSTEMS TECHNOLOGY

AI has many branches concerned with speech, vision, robotics, natural language understanding and learning, and expert systems. The roots of expert systems lie in many disciplines. In particular, one of the major roots of expert systems is the area of human information processing called **cognitive science**. *Cognition* is the study of how humans process information. In other words, cognition is the study of how people think, especially when solving problems.

The study of cognition is very important if we want to make computers emulate human experts. Often experts can't explain how they solve problems—the solutions just come to them. If the expert can't explain how a problem is solved, it's not possible to encode the knowledge in an expert system based on explicit knowledge. In this case the only possibility is programs that learn by themselves to emulate the expert. These are programs based on induction and artificial neural systems, which will be discussed later.

Human Problem Solving and Productions

The development of expert systems technology draws on a wide background. Table 1.2 is a brief summary of some important developments that have converged in modern expert systems. Whenever possible, the starting dates of projects are given. Many projects extend over several years. These developments are covered in more detail in this chapter and others. The single best reference for all the early systems is the three-volume *Handbook of Artificial Intelligence* (Feigenbaum 81).

Year	Event
1943	Post production rules; McCulloch and Pitts Neuron Model
1954	Markov Algorithm for controlling rule execution
1956	Dartmouth Conference; Logic Theorist; Heuristic Search; "AI" term coined
1957	Perceptron invented by Rosenblatt; GPS (General Problem Solver) started (Newell, Shaw, and Simon)
1958	LISP AI language (McCarthy)
1962	Rosenblatt's *Principles of Neurodynamics* on perceptions
1965	Resolution Method of automatic theorem proving (Robinson)
	Fuzzy Logic for reasoning about fuzzy objects (Zadeh)
	Work begun on DENDRAL, the first expert system (Feigenbaum, Buchanan, et al.)
1968	Semantic nets, associative memory model (Quillian)
1969	MACSYMA math expert system (Martin and Moses)
1970	Work begins on PROLOG (Colmerauer, Roussell, *et al.*)
1971	HEARSAY I for speech recognition
	Human Problem Solving popularizes rules (Newell and Simon)
1973	MYCIN expert system for medical diagnosis (Shortliffe, *et al.*) leading to GUIDON, intelligent tutoring (Clancey)
	TEIRESIAS, explanation facility concept (Davis), and
	EMYCIN, first shell (Van Melle, Shortliffe, and Buchanan)
	HEARSAY II, blackboard model of multiple cooperating experts
1975	Frames, knowledge representation (Minsky)
1976	AM (Artificial Mathematician) creative discovery of math concepts (Lenat)
	Dempster-Shafer Theory of Evidence for reasoning under uncertainty
	Work begun on PROSPECTOR expert system for mineral exploration (Duda, Hart, *et al.*)
1977	OPS expert system shell (Forgy), used in XCON/R1
1978	Work started on XCON/R1 (McDermott, DEC) to configure DEC computer systems
	Meta-DENDRAL, metarules, and rule induction (Buchanan)
1979	Rete Algorithm for fast pattern matching (Forgy)
	Commercialization of AI begins
	Inference Corp. formed (releases ART expert system tool in 1985)
1980	Symbolics, LMI founded to manufacture LISP machines
1982	SMP math expert system; Hopfield Neural Net;
	Japanese Fifth Generation Project to develop intelligent computers
1983	KEE expert system tool (IntelliCorp)
1985	CLIPS expert system tool (NASA)

Table 1.2 Some Important Events in the History of Expert Systems

In the late 1950s and early 1960s, a number of programs were written with the goal of general problem solving. The most famous of these was the **General Problem Solver**, created by Newell and Simon and described in a series of papers culminating in their monumental 920-page work on cognition, *Human Problem Solving* (Newell 72).

One of the most significant results demonstrated by Newell and Simon was that much of human problem solving or **cognition** could be expressed by IF . . . THEN–type **production rules**. For example, IF it looks like it's going to rain THEN carry an umbrella, or IF your spouse is in a bad mood THEN don't appear happy. A rule corresponds to a small, modular collection of knowledge called a **chunk**. Chunks are organized in a loose arrangement, with links to related chunks of knowledge. One theory is that all human memory is organized in chunks. An example of a rule representing a chunk of knowledge is

```
IF the car doesn't run and
    the fuel gauge reads empty
THEN fill the gas tank
```

Newell and Simon popularized the use of rules to represent human knowledge and showed how reasoning could be done with rules. Cognitive psychologists have used rules as models to explain human information processing. The basic idea is that sensory input provides stimuli to the brain. The stimuli trigger the appropriate rules of **long-term memory** which produce the appropriate response. Long-term memory is where our knowledge is stored. For example, we all have rules such as

```
IF there is a flame THEN there is a fire
IF there is smoke THEN there may be a fire
IF there is a siren THEN there may be a fire
```

Notice that the last two rules are not expressed with complete certainty. The fire may be out, but there may still be smoke in the air. Likewise, a siren does not prove that there is a fire, since it may be responding to a false alarm. The stimuli of seeing flames, smelling smoke, and hearing a siren will trigger these and similar types of rules.

Long-term memory consists of many rules having the simple IF...THEN structure. In fact, a grand master chess expert may know 50,000 or more chunks of knowledge about chess patterns. In contrast to the long-term memory, the **short-term memory** is used for the temporary storage of knowledge during problem solving. Although long-term memory can hold hundreds of thousands or more chunks, the capacity of working memory is surprisingly small—four to seven chunks. As a simple example of this, try visualizing some numbers in your mind. Most people can see only four to seven numbers at one time. Most people can memorize many more than four to seven numbers. However, those numbers are kept in long-term memory.

One theory proposes that short-term memory represents the number of chunks that can be simultaneously active and considers human problem solving as a spreading of these activated chunks in the mind. Eventually, a chunk may be activated with such intensity that a conscious thought is generated and you say to yourself, "Hmm . . . something's burning."

The other element necessary for human problem solving is a **cognitive processor**. The cognitive processor tries to find the rules that will be **activated** by the appropriate stimuli. But not just any rule will do. For example, you wouldn't want to fill your gas tank every time you heard a siren. Only a rule that matched the stimuli would be activated. If multiple rules are activated at one time, the cognitive processor must perform a conflict resolution to decide which rule has the highest priority. That rule will be executed, for example, if both of the following rules are activated:

```
IF there is a fire THEN leave
IF my clothes are burning THEN put out the fire
```

Then the actions of one rule—with the higher priority—will be executed before the other. The **inference engine** of modern expert systems corresponds to the cognitive processor.

The Newell and Simon model of human problem solving in terms of long-term memory (rules), short-term memory (working memory), and a cognitive processor (inference engine) is the basis of modern rule-based expert systems.

Rules like these are a type of **production system**. Today rule-based production systems are a popular method of implementing expert systems. The individual rules that comprise a production system are the **production rules**. In designing an expert system an important factor is the amount of knowledge or **granularity** of the rules. Too little granularity makes it difficult to understand a rule without reference to other rules. Too much granularity makes the expert system difficult to modify, because several chunks of knowledge are intermingled in one rule.

Until the mid-sixties, a major quest of AI was to produce intelligent systems that relied little on domain knowledge and more on powerful methods of reasoning. Even the name General Problem Solver illustrates the concentration on machines that were not designed for one specific domain but were intended to solve many types of problems. Although the methods of reasoning used by general problem solvers were powerful, the machines were eternal beginners. When presented with a new domain, they had to discover everything from first principles and were not as good as human experts, who relied on domain knowledge for high performance.

An example of the power of knowledge is the game of chess. Although computers now rival humans, people play well despite the fact that computers can do calculations millions of times faster. Studies have shown (Chase 73) that human expert chess players do not have super powers of reasoning but instead rely on knowledge of chess piece patterns built up over years of play. As mentioned previously, one estimate places an expert chess player's knowledge at about 50,000 patterns. Humans are very good at recognizing patterns such as pieces on a chessboard. Instead of trying to reason ahead ten or twenty possible moves for every piece, as a computer might, the human analyzes the game in terms of patterns that reveal long-term threats while remaining alert for short-term surprise moves.

Although domain knowledge is powerful, it is generally limited to the domain. For example, a person who becomes an expert chess player does not automatically become an expert at solving math problems or even an expert at checkers. While some knowledge may carry over to another domain, such as the careful planning of moves, this is a skill rather than genuine expertise.

By the early 1970s, it had become apparent that domain knowledge was the key to building machine problem solvers that could function at the level of human experts. Although methods of reasoning are important, studies have shown that experts do not primarily rely on reasoning in problem solving. In fact, reasoning may play a minor role in an expert's problem solving. Instead, experts rely on a vast knowledge of heuristics and the experience they have built up over the years. If an expert cannot solve a problem based on expertise, then he or she must reason from first principles and theory (or, more likely, ask another expert). The reasoning ability of an expert is generally no better than that of an average person in dealing with a totally unfamiliar situation. Early attempts at building powerful problem solvers based only on reasoning have shown that they are crippled if they must rely solely on reasoning.

The insight that domain knowledge was the key to building real-world problem solvers led to the success of expert systems. The successful expert systems today are thus knowledge-based expert systems rather than general problem solvers. In addition, the same technology that led to the development of expert systems has also led to the development of knowledge-based systems that do not necessarily contain human expertise.

While expertise is considered knowledge that is specialized and known only to a few, knowledge is generally found in books, periodicals, and other widely available resources. For example, the knowledge of how to solve a quadratic equation or perform integration and differentiation is widely available. Knowledge-based computer programs such as MACSYMA and SMP are available to automatically perform these and many other mathematical operations on either numeric or symbolic operands. Other knowledge-based programs may perform process control of manufacturing plants. Today the terms *knowledge-based programming* and *expert systems* are often used synonymously. In fact, expert systems is now considered an alternative programming model or **paradigm** to conventional algorithmic programming.

The Rise of Knowledge-based Systems

With the acceptance of the knowledge-based paradigm in the 1970s, a number of successful prototype expert systems were created. These systems could interpret mass spectrograms to identify chemical constituents (DENDRAL), diagnose illnesses (MYCIN), analyze geologic data for oil (DIPMETER) and minerals (PROSPECTOR), and configure computer systems (XCON/R1). The news that PROSPECTOR had discovered a mineral deposit worth $100 million and that XCON/R1 was saving Digital Equipment Corporation (DEC) millions of dollars a year triggered a sensational interest in the new expert systems technology by 1980. The branch of AI that had started off in the 1950s as a study of human information processing had now grown to achieve commercial success by the development of practical programs for real-world use.

The MYCIN expert system was important for several reasons. First, it demonstrated that AI could be used for practical real-world problems. Second, MYCIN was the testbed of new concepts such as the explanation facility, the automatic acquisition of knowledge, and the intelligent tutoring that are found in a number of expert systems today. The third reason that MYCIN was important is that it demonstrated the feasibility of the expert system **shell**.

Previous expert systems such as DENDRAL were unique systems in which the knowledge base was intermingled with the software that applied the knowledge, the inference engine. MYCIN explicitly separated the knowledge base from the inference engine. This was extremely important to the development of expert system technology because it meant that the essential core of the expert system could be reused. That is, a new expert system could be built much more rapidly than a DENDRAL–type system by emptying out the old knowledge and putting in knowledge about the new domain. The part of MYCIN that dealt with inference and explanation, the shell, could then be refilled with knowledge about the new system. The shell produced by removing the medical knowledge of MYCIN was called EMYCIN (essential or empty MYCIN).

By the late 1970s, the three concepts basic to most expert systems today had converged, as shown in Figure 1.5. These concepts are rules, the shell, and knowledge.

By 1980 new companies had started to bring expert systems out of the university laboratory and produce commercial products. Powerful new software for expert system development was introduced, including the Automated Reasoning Tool (ART) by the Inference Corp., the Knowledge Engineering Tool (KEE) by IntelliCorp, and Rulemaster by Radian Corp. In addition, specialized new hardware was developed to run the software with greater speed than ever before. Companies such as Symbolics and LMI introduced computers referred to as LISP machines because they were designed for LISP, the underlying base language of the expert systems development software. In LISP machines the native assembly language, operating system, and all other fundamental code were created in LISP.

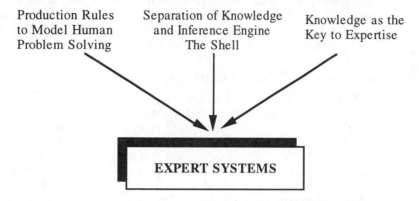

Figure 1.5
Convergence of Three Important Factors to Create the Modern Rule-based Expert System

Unfortunately, this high technology also commanded a high price. Although a single-user LISP machine was much more powerful and productive than a general-purpose machine running LISP, the single-user machine and a single-user software license together cost $100,000. Establishing an AI lab with a half-dozen programmers could easily cost $500,000.

These objections were overcome in the mid-1980s by the introduction of powerful development software such as CLIPS by NASA. CLIPS is written in C for speed and portability, and also uses a powerful pattern matching called the Rete Algorithm. CLIPS is free to government users and government contractors. It is available at a nominal cost to other users from COSMIC, which distributes NASA-developed software; universities can obtain it at half price. CLIPS is royalty free and may be freely distributed by anyone who obtains a legitimate copy from COSMIC.

CLIPS can be installed on any C compiler that supports the standard Kernigan and Richie C language. It has been installed on the IBM-PC and compatibles, VAX, Hewlett-Packard, Sun, Cray, and many other makes of computers. Versions for Macintosh Windows and others are available from COSMIC.

1.7 EXPERT SYSTEMS APPLICATIONS AND DOMAINS

Conventional computer programs are used to solve many types of problems. These problems generally have algorithmic solutions that lend themselves well to conventional programs and programming languages such as FORTRAN, Pascal, Ada, and so on. In many application areas such as business and engineering, numeric calculations are of primary importance. By contrast, expert systems are primarily designed for symbolic reasoning.

While languages such as LISP and PROLOG are also used for symbolic manipulation, they are more general purpose than expert system shells. This does not mean that it is not possible to build expert systems in LISP and PROLOG. In fact, many expert systems have been built with PROLOG and LISP. PROLOG especially has a number of advantages for diagnostic systems because of its built-in backward chaining. However, it is more convenient and efficient to build large expert systems with shells and utility programs specifically designed for expert system building. Instead of "reinventing the wheel" every time a new expert system is to be built, it is more efficient to use specialized tools designed for expert system building rather than general purpose tools.

Applications of Expert Systems

Expert systems have been applied to virtually every field of knowledge. Some have been designed as research tools while others fulfill important business and industrial functions. One example of an expert system in routine business use is the XCON system of Digital Equipment Corp. (DEC). The XCON system (originally called R1) was developed in conjunction with John McDermott of Carnegie-Mellon University. XCON is an expert configuring system for DEC computer systems (McDermott 84).

The **configuration** of a computer system means that when a customer places an order, all the right parts—software, hardware, and documentation—are supplied. For large systems, the customer's system is set up or configured at the factory and tested to insure that it meets the customer's requirements. Unlike with the purchase of a TV set or a home computer, there are many options and interconnections possible with a large computer system. In putting together a large system, it's not enough to ship the requested number of CPUs, disk drives, terminals, and so forth. The proper interconnections and cabling must also be supplied and the system checked to verify that it is working correctly.

The XCON system is probably one of the most successful expert systems in routine use and saves DEC millions of dollars a year, reduces the time to configure the orders, and improves the accuracy of orders. XCON can configure an average order in about two minutes, which is fifteen times faster than a human. Also, whereas the humans configured orders correctly 70 percent of the time, XCON has an accuracy of 98 percent. These are important concerns because configuring a complex computer system at the factory involves considerable effort. It is expensive to partially configure a system and then find out that the system cannot meet the customer's requirements or that other components are needed and shipment will be delayed until the parts arrive.

Hundreds of expert systems have been built and reported on in computer journals, books, and conferences. This probably represents only the tip of the iceberg since many companies and military organizations will not report their systems because of proprietary or secret knowledge contained in the systems. Based on the systems described in the open literature, certain broad classes of expert systems applications can be discerned, as shown in Table 1.3.

Examples of some expert systems are shown in Tables 1.4 through 1.9 (Waterman 86), and in the historical bibliography at the end of this chapter.

Class	General Area
Configuration	Assemble proper components of a system in the proper way.
Diagnosis	Infer underlying problems based on observed evidence.
Instruction	Intelligent teaching so that a student can ask *Why*, *How,* and*What If -*type questions just as if a human was teaching.
Interpretation	Explain observed data.
Monitoring	Compare observed data to expected data to judge performance.
Planning	Devise actions to yield a desired outcome.
Prognosis	Predict the outcome of a given situation.
Remedy	Prescribe treatment for a problem.
Control	Regulate a process. May require interpretation, diagnosis, monitoring, planning, prognosis, and remedies.

Table 1.3 Broad Classes of Expert Systems

Name	Chemistry
CRYSALIS	Interpret a protein's 3-D structure
DENDRAL	Interpret molecular structure
TQMSTUNE	Remedy Triple Quadruple Mass Spectrometer (keep it tuned)
CLONER	Design new biological molecules
MOLGEN	Design gene-cloning experiments
SECS	Design complex organic molecules
SPEX	Plan molecular biology experiments

Table 1.4 Chemistry Expert Systems

Name	Electronics
ACE	Diagnose telephone network faults
IN-ATE	Diagnose oscilloscope faults
NDS	Diagnose national communication net
EURISKO	Design 3-D microelectronics
PALLADIO	Design and test new VLSI circuits
REDESIGN	Redesign digital circuits
CADHELP	Instruct for computer-aided design
SOPHIE	Instruct circuit fault diagnosis

Table 1.5 Electronics Expert Systems

Name	Medicine
PUFF	Diagnose lung disease
VM	Monitor intensive-care patients
ABEL	Diagnose acid-base/electrolytes
AI/COAG	Diagnose blood disease
AI/RHEUM	Diagnose rheumatoid disease
CADUCEUS	Diagnose internal medicine disease
ANNA	Monitor digitalis therapy
BLUE BOX	Diagnose/remedy depression
MYCIN	Diagnose/remedy bacterial infections
ONCOCIN	Remedy/manage chemotherapy patients
ATTENDING	Instruct in anesthetic management
GUIDON	Instruct in bacterial infections

Table 1.6 Medical Expert Systems

Name	Engineering
REACTOR	Diagnose/remedy reactor accidents
DELTA	Diagnose/remedy GE locomotives
STEAMER	Instruct operation—steam powerplant

Table 1.7 Engineering Expert Systems

Name	Geology
DIPMETER	Interpret dipmeter logs
LITHO	Interpret oil well log data
MUD	Diagnose/remedy drilling problems
PROSPECTOR	Interpret geologic data for minerals

Table 1.8 Geology Expert Systems

Name	Computer Systems
PTRANS	Give prognosis for managing DEC computers
BDS	Diagnose bad parts in switching net
XCON	Configure DEC computer systems
XSEL	Configure DEC computer sales orders
XSITE	Configure customer site for DEC computers
YES/MVS	Monitor/control IBM MVS operating system
TIMM	Diagnose DEC computers

Table 1.9 Computer Expert Systems

Appropriate Domains for Expert Systems

Before starting to build an expert system, it is essential to decide if an expert system is the appropriate paradigm. For example, one concern is whether an expert system should be used instead of an alternative paradigm, such as conventional programming. The appropriate domain for an expert system depends on a number of factors:

- *Can the problem be effectively solved by conventional programming?* If the answer is yes, then an expert system is not the best choice. For example, consider the problem of diagnosing some equipment. If all the symptoms for all malfunctions are known in advance, then a simple table lookup or decision tree of the fault is adequate. Expert systems are best suited for situations in which there is no efficient algorithmic solution. Such cases are called **ill-structured problems** and reasoning may offer the only hope of a good solution.

As an example of an ill-structured problem, consider the case of a person who is thinking about travel and visits a travel agent. While most people have a destination and plans, there are exceptions. Table 1.10 lists some characteristics of an ill-structured problem as indicated by the person's responses to the travel agent's questions.

Although this is probably an extreme case, it does illustrate the basic concept of an ill-structured problem. As you can see, an ill-structured problem would not lend itself well to an algorithmic solution because there are so many possibilities. In this case, a default option should be exercised when all else fails. For example, the travel agent could say, "Ah ha! I have the perfect trip for you: a round-the-world cruise. Please fill out the following credit card application and everything will be taken care of."

Travel Agent's Questions	Responses
Can I help you?	I'm not sure.
Where do you want to go?	Somewhere.
Any particular destination?	Here and there.
How much can you afford?	I don't know.
Can you get some money?	I don't know.
When do you want to go?	Sooner or later.

Table 1.10 An Example of an Ill-structured Problem

In dealing with ill-structured problems, there is a danger in that the expert system design may accidentally mirror an algorithmic solution. That is, the development of the expert system may unknowingly discover an algorithmic solution. An indication that this has happened is if a solution that requires a rigid **control structure** is found. That is, the rules are forced to execute in a certain sequence by the knowledge engineer explicitly setting the priorities of many rules. Forcing a rigid control structure on the expert system cancels a major advantage of expert system technology, which is dealing with unexpected input that does not follow a predetermined pattern (Parrello 88). That is, expert systems react opportunistically to their input, whatever it is. Conventional programs generally expect input to follow a certain sequence. An expert system with a lot of control often indicates a disguised algorithm and may be a good candidate for recoding as a conventional program.

- *Is the domain well-bounded?* It is important to have well-defined limits on what the expert system is expected to know and what its capabilities should be. For example, suppose you wanted to create an expert system to diagnose headaches. Certainly the medical knowledge of a physician would be put in the knowledge base. However, for a deeper understanding of headaches, you might also put in knowledge about neurochemistry, then its parent area of biochemistry, then chemistry, molecular biophysics, and so forth perhaps on down to subnuclear physics. Other domains such as biofeedback, psychology, psychiatry, physiology, exercise, yoga, and stress management may also contain pertinent knowledge about headaches. The point: when do you stop adding domains? The more domains, the more complex the expert system becomes.

In particular, the task of coordinating all the expertise becomes a major task. In the real world we know from experience how difficult it is to have coordinated teams of experts working on problems, especially when they come up with conflicting recommendations. If we knew how to program well the coordination of expertise, then we could try programming an expert system to have the knowledge of multiple experts. Attempts have been made to coordinate multiple expert systems in the HEARSAY II and HEARSAY III systems. However, such coordination is a complex task that should be viewed more as research rather than as producing a deliverable expert system product.

- *Is there a need and a desire for an expert system?* Although it's great experience to build an expert system, it's rather pointless if no one is willing to use it. If there are many human experts already, it's difficult to justify an expert system based on the reason of scarce human expertise. Also, if the experts or users don't want the system, it will not be accepted even if there is a need for it.

Management especially must be willing to support the system. This is even more critical for expert systems than for conventional programs because expert systems is a new technology. This means that there are few experienced people and more uncertainty about what can be accomplished. However, the area of expert systems deserves more support because it attempts to solve the problems that cannot be solved by conventional programming. The risks are greater, but so are the rewards.

- *Is there at least one human expert who is willing to cooperate?* There must be an expert who is willing, and preferably enthusiastic, about the project. Not all experts are willing to have their knowledge examined for faults and then put into a computer. Even if there are multiple experts willing to cooperate in the development, it might be wise to limit the number of experts involved. Different experts may have different ways of solving a problem, such as requesting different diagnostic tests. Sometimes they may even reach different conclusions. Trying to code multiple methods of problem solving in one knowledge base may create internal conflicts and incompatibilities.
- *Can the expert explain the knowledge so that it is understandable by the knowledge engineer?* Even if the expert is willing to cooperate, there may be difficulty in expressing the knowledge in explicit terms. As a simple example of this difficulty, can you explain in words how you move a finger? Although you could say it's done by contracting a muscle in the finger, the next question is, how do you contract a finger muscle? The other difficulty in communication between expert and knowledge engineer is that the knowledge engineer doesn't know the technical terms of the expert. This problem is particularly acute with medical terminology. It may take a year or longer for the knowledge engineer to even understand what the expert is talking about, let alone translate that knowledge into explicit computer code.
- *Is the problem-solving knowledge mainly heuristic and uncertain?* Expert systems *are* appropriate when the expert's knowledge is largely heuristic and uncertain. That is, the knowledge may be based on experience, called **experiential knowledge**, and the expert may have to try various approaches in case one doesn't work. In other words, the expert's knowledge may be a trial-and-error approach, rather than one based on logic and algorithms. However, the expert can still solve the problem faster than someone who is not an expert. This is a good application for expert systems. If the problem can be solved simply by logic and algorithms, it is best handled by a conventional program.

1.8 LANGUAGES, SHELLS, AND TOOLS

A fundamental decision in defining a problem is deciding how best to model it. Sometimes experience is available to aid in choosing the best paradigm. For example, experience suggests that a payroll is best done using conventional procedural programming. Experience also suggests that it is preferable to use a commercial package, if available, rather than writing one from scratch. A general guide to selecting a paradigm is to consider the most traditional one first—conventional programming. The reason for doing this is because of the vast amount of experience we have with conventional programming and the wide variety of commercial packages available. If a problem cannot be effectively done by conventional programming, then turn to nonconventional paradigms such as AI.

Although expert systems is a branch of AI, there are specialized languages for expert systems that are quite different from the commonly used AI languages such as LISP and PROLOG. Although many others have been developed, such as IPL-II, SAIL, CONNIVER, KRL, and Smalltalk, few are widely used except for research (Scown 85).

An expert system language is a higher-order language than languages like LISP or C because it is easier to do certain things, but there is also a smaller range of problems that can be addressed. That is, the specialized nature of expert system languages makes them suitable for writing expert systems but not for general purpose programming. In many situations, it is even necessary to exit temporarily from an expert system language to perform a function in a procedural language.

The primary functional difference between expert system languages and procedural languages is the focus of representation. Procedural languages focus on providing flexible and robust techniques to represent data. For example, data structures such as arrays, records, linked lists, stacks, queues, and trees are easily created and manipulated. Modern languages such as Modula-2 and Ada are designed to aid in **data abstraction** by providing structures for encapsulation such as modules and packages. This provides a level of abstraction that is then implemented by methods such as operators and control statements to yield a program. The data and methods to manipulate it are tightly interwoven. In contrast, expert system languages focus on providing flexible and robust ways to represent knowledge. The expert system paradigm allows two levels of abstraction: data abstraction and **knowledge abstraction**. Expert system languages specifically separate the data from the methods of manipulating the data. An example of this separation is that of facts (data abstraction) and rules (**knowledge abstraction**) in a rule-based expert system language.

This difference in focus also leads to a difference in program design methodology. Because of the tight interweaving of data and knowledge in procedural languages, programmers must carefully describe the sequence of execution. However, the explicit separation of data from knowledge in expert system languages requires considerably less rigid control of the execution sequence. Typically, an entirely separate piece of code, the inference engine, is used to apply the knowledge to the data. This separation of knowledge and data allows a higher degree of parallelism and modularity.

In choosing a language, a basic question should be whether the problem is knowledge or intelligence intensive. Expert systems rely on a great deal of specialized knowledge or expertise to solve a problem, whereas AI emphasizes a problem-solving approach. Expert systems often rely on a pattern matching within a restricted knowledge domain to guide their execution whereas AI generally concentrates on searching paradigms in less restricted domains.

The customary way of defining the need for an expert system program is to decide if you want to program the expertise of a human expert. If such an expert exists and will cooperate, then an expert system approach may be successful.

The road to selecting an expert system language is paved with confusion. A few years ago the choice of an expert system language was fairly straightforward. There were only about a half dozen languages available, and they were generally free or cost a nominal amount payable to the universities where they were developed.

However, with the explosive commercial growth in the expert systems field since the 1970s, the selection of a language is no longer so simple. Today there are dozens of languages available, ranging in price up to $75,000. Although it is still possible to obtain some of the older languages such as OPS5 free or at a nominal cost from the universities where they were developed, there is a price to pay in terms of efficiency, lack of modern features, and support.

Besides the confusing choice of the many languages available today, the terminology used to describe the languages is confusing. Some vendors refer to their products as "tools," while others refer to "shells" and still others talk about "integrated environments." For clarity in this book, the terms will be defined as follows:

- **Language**: A translator of commands written in a specific syntax. An expert system language will also provide an inference engine to execute the statements of the language. Depending on the implementation, the inference engine may provide forward chaining, backward chaining, or both. Under this language definition, LISP is not an expert system language but PROLOG is. However, it is possible to write an expert system language using LISP and to write AI in PROLOG. For that matter, you can even write an expert system or AI language in assembly language. Questions of development time, convenience, maintainability, efficiency, and speed determine which language software is written in.
- **Tool**: A language plus associated utility programs to facilitate the development, debugging, and delivery of application programs. Utility programs may include text and graphics editors, debuggers, file management, and even code generators. Cross-assemblers may also be provided to port the developed code to different hardware. For example, an expert system may be developed on a DEC VAX and then cross-assembled to run on a Motorola 68000. Some tools may even allow the use of different paradigms such as forward and backward chaining in one application.

In some cases a tool may be integrated with all its utility programs in one environment to present a common interface to the user. This approach minimizes the need for the user to leave the environment to perform a task. For example, a simple tool may not provide facilities for file management and so a user would have to exit the tool to give operating system commands. An integrated environment allows easy exchange of data between utility programs in the environment. Some tools do not even require the user to write any code. Instead, the tool allows a user to enter knowledge by examples from tables or spreadsheets and generates the appropriate code itself.

• **Shell**: A special-purpose tool designed for certain types of applications in which the user must supply only the knowledge base. The classic example of this is the EMYCIN (empty MYCIN) shell. This shell was made by removing the medical knowledge base of the MYCIN expert system.

MYCIN was designed as a backward chaining system to diagnose diseases. By simply removing the medical knowledge, EMYCIN was created and could be used as a shell to contain knowledge about other kinds of consultative systems that use backward chaining. The EMYCIN shell demonstrated the reusability of the essential MYCIN software such as the inference engine and the user interface. This was a very important step in the development of modern expert system technology because it meant that an expert system would not have to be built from scratch for each new application.

There are many ways of characterizing expert systems such as representation of knowledge, forward or backward chaining, support of uncertainty, hypothetical reasoning, explanation facilities, and so forth. Unless a person has built a number of expert systems, it is difficult to appreciate all of these features, especially those found in the more expensive tools. The best way to learn expert systems technology is to develop a number of systems with an easy-to-learn language and then invest in a more sophisticated tool if you need its features.

1.9 ELEMENTS OF AN EXPERT SYSTEM

The elements of a typical expert system are shown in Figure 1.6. In a rule-based system the knowledge base contains the domain knowledge needed to solve problems coded in the form of rules. While rules are a popular paradigm for representing knowledge, other types of expert systems use different representations, as discussed in Chapter 2.

An expert system consists of the following components:

• **user interface**—the mechanism by which the user and the expert system communicate.
• **explanation facility**—explains the reasoning of the system to a user.
• **working memory**—a **global database** of facts used by the rules.
• **inference engine**—makes inferences by deciding which rules are satisfied by facts or objects, prioritizes the satisfied rules, and executes the rule with the highest priority.
• **agenda**—a prioritized list of rules created by the inference engine, whose patterns are satisfied by facts or objects in working memory.
• **knowledge acquisition facility**—an automatic way for the user to enter knowledge in the system instead of having the knowledge engineer explicitly code the knowledge.

The knowledge acquisition facility is an an optional feature on many systems. In some expert system tools like KEE and First Class the tool can learn by rule induction through examples and can automatically generate rules. However, the examples are generally from tabular or spreadsheet-type data better suited to decision trees. General rules constructed by a knowledge engineer can be much more complex than the simple rules from rule induction.

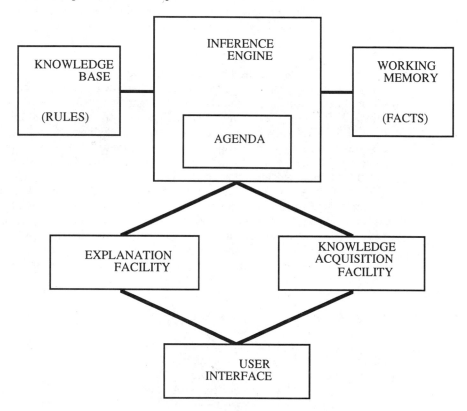

Figure 1.6 Structure of a Rule-based Expert System

Depending on the implementation of the system, the user interface may be a simple text-oriented display or a sophisticated, high-resolution, bit-mapped display. This high-resolution display is commonly used to simulate a control panel with dials and displays.

The knowledge base is also called the **production memory** in a rule-based expert system. As a simple example, consider the problem of deciding to cross a street. The productions for the two rules are as follows, where the arrows mean that the system will perform the actions on the right of the arrow if the conditions on the left are true.

```
the light is red → stop
the light is green → go
```

The production rules can be expressed in an equivalent pseudocode IF...THEN format as:

```
Rule: Red_light
IF
        the light is red
THEN
        stop

Rule: Green_light
IF
        the light is green
THEN
        go
```

Each rule is identified by a name, followed by the IF part of the rule. The section between the IF and THEN parts of the rule is called by various names including the **antecedent**, **conditional part**, **pattern part**, or **left-hand-side** (**LHS**). The individual condition

```
the light is green
```

is called a **conditional element** or a **pattern**.

Some examples of rules from real systems are:

MYCIN system for diagnosis of meningitis and
bacteremia (bacterial infections)
```
IF
        The site of the culture is blood, and
        The identity of the organism is not known with
            certainty, and
        The stain of the organism is gramneg, and
        The morphology of the organism is rod, and
        The patient has been seriously burned
THEN
        There is weakly suggestive evidence (.4) that
            the identity of the organism is pseudomonas
```

XCON/R1 for configuring DEC VAX computer systems
```
IF
        The current context is assigning devices to
            Unibus modules and
        There is an unassigned dual-port disk drive and
        The type of controller it requires is known and
        There are two such controllers, neither of
            which has any devices assigned to it, and
        The number of devices that these controllers
            can support is known
```

```
THEN
      Assign the disk drive to each of the
          controllers, and
      Note that the two controllers have been
          associated and each supports one drive
```

In a rule-based system, the inference engine determines which rule antecedents, if any, are satisfied by the facts. Two general methods of inferencing are commonly used as the problem-solving strategies of expert systems: **forward chaining** and **backward chaining**. Other methods used for more specific needs may include means-ends analysis, problem reduction, backtracking, plan-generate-test, hierarchical planning and the least commitment principle, and constraint handling.

Forward chaining is reasoning from facts to the conclusions resulting from those facts. For example, if you see that it is raining before leaving home (the fact) then you should take an umbrella (the conclusion).

Backward chaining involves reasoning in reverse from a hypothesis, a potential conclusion to be proved, to the facts that support the hypothesis. For example, if you have not looked outside and someone enters with wet shoes and an umbrella, your hypothesis is that it is raining. In order to support this hypothesis you could ask the person if it was, in fact, raining. If the response is yes, then the hypothesis is proved true and becomes a fact. As mentioned before, a hypothesis can be viewed as a fact whose truth is in doubt and needs to be established. The hypothesis can then be interpreted as a goal to be proved.

Depending on the design, an inference engine will do either forward or backward chaining. For example, OPS5 and CLIPS are designed for forward chaining whereas EMYCIN performs backward chaining. Some types of inference engines, such as ART and KEE, offer both. The choice of inference engine depends on the type of problem. Diagnostic problems are better solved with backward chaining whereas prognosis, monitoring, and control are better accomplished by forward chaining.

The working memory may contain facts regarding the current status of the traffic light such as "the light is green" or "the light is red." Either or both of these facts may be in working memory at the same time. If the traffic light is working normally, only one fact will be in memory. However, it is possible that both facts may be in working memory if there is a malfunction in the light. Notice the difference between the knowledge base and working memory. Facts do not interact with one another. The fact "the light is green" has no effect on the fact "the light is red." Instead, our knowledge of traffic lights says that if both facts are simultaneously present, then there is a malfunction in the light.

If there is a fact "the light is green" in working memory, the inference engine will notice that this fact satisfies the conditional part of the green light rule and will put this rule on the agenda. If a rule has multiple patterns, then all of its patterns must be simultaneously satisfied for it to be placed on the agenda. Some patterns may even be satisfied by specifying the absence of certain facts in working memory.

A rule whose patterns are all satisfied is said to be **activated** or **instantiated**. Multiple activated rules may be on the agenda at the same time, in which case the inference engine must select one rule for **firing**. The term *firing* comes from neurophysiology, the study of the nervous system. An individual nerve cell or neuron emits an electrical signal when stimulated. No further amount of stimulation can cause the neuron to fire again for a short time period. This phenomenon is called *refraction*. Rule-based expert systems are built using refraction in order to prevent trivial loops. That is, if the green light rule kept firing on the same fact over and over again, the expert system would never accomplish any useful work.

Various methods have been invented to provide refraction. In one type of expert system language called OPS5, each fact is given a unique identifier called a **timetag** when it is entered in working memory. After a rule has fired on a fact, the inference engine will not fire on that fact again because its time stamp has been used.

Following the THEN part of a rule is a list of **actions** to be executed when the rule fires. This part of the rule is known as the **consequent** or **right-hand side** (**RHS**). When the red light rule fires, its action, stop, is executed. Likewise, when the green light rule fires, its action is go. Specific actions usually include the addition or removal of facts from working memory or printing results. The format of these actions depends on the syntax of the expert system language. For example, in OPS5, ART, and CLIPS the action to add a new fact called "stop" to working memory would be (assert stop). Because of their LISP ancestry, these languages were designed to require parentheses around patterns and actions.

The inference engine operates in **cycles**. Various names have been given to describe the cycle such as **recognize-act cycle**, **select-execute cycle**, **situation-response cycle**, and **situation-action cycle**. By any name for a cycle, the inference engine will repeatedly execute a group of tasks until certain criteria cause execution to cease. The tasks of a cycle for OPS5, a typical expert system shell, are shown in the following pseudocode as **conflict resolution**, **act**, **match**, and **check for halt**.

WHILE not done

> **Conflict Resolution**: If there are activations, then select the one with the highest priority else done.
>
> **Act**: Sequentially perform the actions on the RHS of the selected activation. Those that change working memory have an immediate effect in this cycle. Remove the activation that has just fired from the agenda.
>
> **Match**: Update the agenda by checking whether the LHSs of any rules are satisfied. If so, activate them. Remove activations if the LHSs of their rules are no longer satisfied.
>
> **Check for Halt**: If a halt action is performed or a break command given, then done.
>
> END-WHILE
>
> **Accept a new user command**

Multiple rules may be activated and put on the agenda during one cycle. Also, activations will be left on the agenda from previous cycles unless they are deactivated because their LHS is no longer satisfied. Thus the number of activations on the agenda will vary as execution proceeds. Depending on the program, an activation may always be on the agenda but never selected for firing. Likewise, some rules may never become activated. In these cases, the purposes of these rules should be re-examined because either the rules are unnecessary or their patterns were not correctly designed.

The inference engine executes the actions of the highest priority activation on the agenda, then the next highest priority activation, and so on until no activations are left. Various priority schemes have been designed into expert system shells. Generally all shells let the knowledge engineer define the priority of rules.

Agenda conflicts occur when different activations have the same priority and the inference engine must decide on one rule to fire. Different shells have different ways of dealing with this problem. In the original Newell and Simon paradigm, those rules entered in the system first had the highest default priority (Newell 72, p. 33). In OPS5, rules with more complex patterns have higher priority. In ART and CLIPS, rules have the same default priority unless assigned different ones by the knowledge engineer.

At this time, control is returned to the **top-level** command interpreter for the user to give further instructions to the expert system shell. The top-level is the default mode in which the user communicates with the expert system and is indicated by the task "Accept a new user command." It is the top-level that accepts the new command.

The top-level is the user interface to the shell while an expert system application is under development. More sophisticated user interfaces are usually designed for the expert system to facilitate its operation. For example, the expert system may have a user interface for control of a manufacturing plant that shows a block diagram of the plant with a high-resolution, bit-mapped color display. Warnings and status messages may appear in flashing colors with simulated dials and gauges. In fact, more effort may go into the design and implementation of the user interface than in the expert system knowledge base, especially in a prototype. Depending on the capabilities of the expert system shell, the user interface may be implemented by rules or in another language called by the expert system.

An explanation facility will allow the user to ask how the system came to a certain conclusion and why certain information is needed. The question of how the system came to a certain conclusion is easy to answer in a rule-based system because a history of the activated rules and contents of working memory can be maintained in a stack. Sophisticated explanation facilities may allow the user to ask "What If"-type questions to explore alternate reasoning paths through hypothetical reasoning.

1.10 PRODUCTION SYSTEMS

One of the most popular types of expert systems today is the rule-based system. Rules are popular for a number of reasons.

- *Modular nature*. This makes it easy to encapsulate knowledge and expand the expert system by incremental development.
- *Explanation facilities*. It is easy to build explanation facilities with rules because the antecedents of a rule specify exactly what is necessary to activate the rule. By keeping track of which rules have fired, an explanation facility can present the chain of reasoning that led to a certain conclusion.
- *Similarity to the human cognitive process*. Based on the work of Newell and Simon, rules appear to be a natural way of modeling how humans solve problems. The simple IF...THEN representation of rules makes it easy to explain to experts the structure of the knowledge you are trying to elicit from them. Other advantages of rules are described in Hayes-Roth (85).

Rules are a type of production whose origins go back to the 1940s. Because of the importance of rule-based systems, it is worthwhile to examine the development of the rule concept. This will give you a better idea why rule-based systems are so useful for expert systems.

Post Production Systems

Production systems were first used in symbolic logic by Post, who originated the name (Post 43). He proved the important and amazing result that any system of mathematics or logic could be written as a certain type of production rule system. This result established the great capability of production rules for representing major classes of knowledge rather than being limited to a few types. Under the term **rewrite rules**, they are also used in linguistics as a way of defining the grammar of a language. Computer languages are commonly defined using the Backus-Naur Form (BNF) of production rules.

Post's basic idea was that any mathematic or logic system is simply a set of rules specifying how to change one string of symbols into another set of symbols. That is, given an input string, the antecedent, a production rule could produce a new string, the consequent. This idea is also valid with programs and expert systems in which the initial string of symbols is the input data and the output string is some transformation of the input.

As a very simple case, suppose the input string is "patient has fever," the output string might then be "take an aspirin." Note that there is no meaning attached to these strings. That is, the manipulations of the strings is based on syntax and not on any semantics or understanding of what *fever, aspirin*, and *patient* represent. A human knows what these strings in terms of the real world mean but a Post production system is just a way of transforming one string into another. A production rule for this example could be

```
Antecedent → Consequent
person has fever → take aspirin
```

where the arrow indicates the transformation of one string into another. We can interpret this rule in terms of the more familiar IF...THEN notation as

```
IF person has fever THEN take aspirin
```

The production rules can also have multiple antecedents. For example,

```
person has fever AND
        fever is greater than 102 → see doctor
```

Note that the special connective AND is not part of the string. The AND indicates that the rule has multiple antecedents.

A Post production system consists of a group of production rules, such as the following (the numbers in parentheses are for purposes of this discussion):

```
(1)    car won't start → check battery
(2)    car won't start → check gas
(3)    check battery AND battery bad → replace
       battery
(4)    check gas AND no gas → fill gas tank
```

If there is a string "car won't start," the rules (1) and (2) may be used to generate the strings "check battery" and "check gas." However, there is no control mechanism that applies both these rules to the string. Only one rule may be applied, or both, or none. If there is another string "battery bad" and a string "check battery," then rule (3) may be applied to generate the string "replace battery."

There is no special significance to the order in which rules are written. The rules of our example could also have been written in the following order, and the system would be the same system:

```
(4)    check gas AND no gas → fill gas tank
(2)    car won't start → check gas
(1)    car won't start → check battery
(3)    check battery AND battery bad → replace
       battery
```

Although Post production rules were useful in laying part of the foundation of expert systems, they are not adequate for writing practical programs. The basic limitation of Post production rules in programming is lack of a **control strategy** to guide the application of the rules. A Post system permits the rules to be applied on the strings in any manner because there is no specification given on how the rules should be applied.

As an analogy, suppose you go to the library to find a certain book on expert systems. At the library, you start randomly looking at books on the shelves for the one you want. If the library is fairly large, it could take a very long time to find the book you need. Even if you find the section of books on expert systems, your next random choice could take you to an entirely different section, such as on French cooking. The situation becomes even worse if you need material from the first book to help you determine the second book you need to find. A random search for the second book will also take a long time.

Markov Algorithms

The next advance in applying production rules was made by Markov, who specified a control structure for production systems (Markov 54). A **Markov algorithm** is an ordered group of productions that are applied in order of priority to an input string. If the highest priority rule is not applicable then the next one is applied, and so forth. The Markov algorithm terminates if either (1) the last production is not applicable to a string or (2) a production that ends with a period is applied.

Markov algorithms can also be applied to substrings of a string, starting from the left. For example, the production system consisting of the single rule

```
AB → HIJ
```

when applied to the input string GABKAB produces the new string GHIJKAB. Since the production now applies to the new string, the final result is GHIJKHIJ.

The special character ∧ represents the **null string** of no characters. For example, the production

```
A → ∧
```

deletes all occurrences of the character A in a string.

Other special symbols represent any single character and are indicated by lowercase letters a, b, c, and so forth. These symbols represent single-character variables and are an important part of modern expert system languages. For example, the rule

$$AxB \rightarrow BxA$$

will reverse the characters A and B.

The Greek letters α, β, and so forth are used for special punctuation of strings. The Greek letters are used because they are distinct from the alphabet of ordinary letters.

An example of a Markov algorithm that moves the first letter of an input string to the end is shown following Elson (73). The rules are ordered in terms of highest priority (1), next highest (2) and so forth. The rules are prioritized in the order in which they are entered.

$$(1) \quad \alpha xy \rightarrow y\alpha x$$
$$(2) \quad \alpha \rightarrow \wedge$$
$$(3) \quad \wedge \rightarrow \alpha$$

The execution trace is shown in Table 1.11 for the input string ABC.

Rule	Success or Failure	String
1	F	ABC
2	F	ABC
3	S	αABC
1	S	BαAC
1	S	BCαA
1	F	BCαA
2	S	BCA

Table 1.11 Execution Trace of a Markov Algorithm

Notice that the α symbol acts analogously to a temporary variable in a conventional programming language. However, instead of holding a value, the α is used as a placeholder to mark the progression of changes in the input string. Once its job is done, the α is eliminated by rule 2. The program then ends when rule 2 is applied because there is a period after rule 2.

The Rete Algorithm

Notice that there is a definite control strategy to Markov algorithms, with higher priority rules ordered first. As long as the highest priority rule applies, it is used. If not, the Markov algorithm tries lower priority rules. Although the Markov algorithm can be used as the basis of an expert system, it is highly inefficient for systems with many rules. The problem of efficiency is of major importance if we want to create expert systems for real problems containing hundreds or thousands of rules. No matter how good everything else is about a system, if a user has to wait a long time for a response, the system will not be used. What is really needed is an algorithm that knows about all the rules and can apply any rule without having to try each one sequentially.

A solution to this problem is the **Rete algorithm** developed by Charles L. Forgy at Carnegie-Mellon University in 1979 for his PhD thesis on that institution's OPS (official production system) expert system shell. The Rete algorithm is a fast pattern matcher that obtains its speed by storing information about rules in a network. Instead of having to match facts against every rule on every recognize-act cycle, the Rete algorithm looks only for changes in matches on every cycle. This greatly speeds up the matching of facts to antecedents since the static data that don't change from cycle to cycle can be ignored. (This topic will be discussed further in the chapters on CLIPS.) Fast pattern-matching algorithms such as the Rete completed the foundation for the practical application of expert systems. Figure 1.7 summarizes the foundations of modern rule-based expert system technologies.

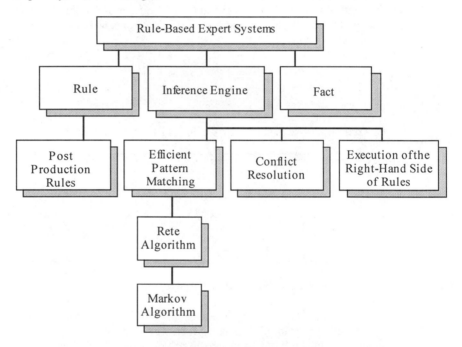

Figure 1.7 Foundations of Modern Rule-based Expert Systems

Different versions of the OPS language and shell have been developed including OPS2, OPS4, and OPS5. A newer commercial version developed by Forgy is OPS83, a very fast shell. However, OPS83 has a significantly different syntax from the OPS5 style and is partly procedural for faster execution.

1.11 PROCEDURAL PARADIGMS

Programming paradigms can be classified as procedural and nonprocedural. Figure 1.8 shows a **taxonomy** or classification of the procedural paradigms in terms of languages. Figure 1.9 shows a taxonomy for nonprocedural paradigms. These figures illustrate the relationship of expert systems to other paradigms and should be considered only as general guides rather than strict definitions. Some of the paradigms and languages have characteristics that may place them in more than one class. For example, some consider functional programming procedural whereas others consider it declarative (Ghezzi 87).

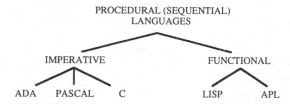

Figure 1.8 Procedural Languages

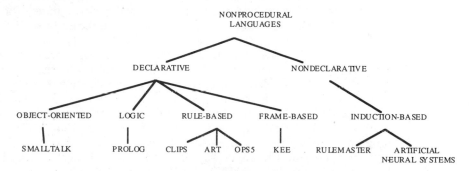

Figure 1.9 Nonprocedural Languages

An **algorithm** is a method of solving a problem in a finite number of steps. The implementation of an algorithm in a program is a **procedural program**. The terms *algorithmic programming*, *procedural programming*, and *conventional programming* are often used interchangeably to mean non-AI-type programs. A common conception of a procedural program is that it proceeds sequentially, statement by statement, until a branch instruction is encountered. Another often used synonym for a procedural program is a **sequential** program. However, the term *sequential programming* implies too much constraint since all modern programming languages support recursion and so programs may not be strictly sequential.

The distinguishing feature of the procedural paradigm is that the programmer must specify exactly *how* a problem solution must be coded. Even code generators must produce procedural code. In a sense, the use of code generators is **nonprocedural** programming because it removes most or all of the procedural code writing from the programmer. The goal of nonprocedural programming is to have the programmer specify what the goal is and then let the system determine how to accomplish it.

Imperative Programming

The terms **imperative** and **statement-oriented** are used synonymously. Languages such as FORTRAN, Ada, Pascal, Modula-2, COBOL, and BASIC all have the dominant characteristic that statements are imperatives or commands to the computer telling it what to do. Imperative languages developed as a way of freeing the programmer from coding assembly language in the von Neumann architecture. Consequently, imperative languages offer great support to variables, assignment operations, and repetition. These are all low-level operations that modern languages attempt to hide by providing features such as recursion, procedures, modules, packages, and so forth. Imperative languages are also characterized by their emphasis on rigid control structure and their associated **top-down** program designs.

A serious problem with all languages is the difficulty of proving the correctness of programs. From the AI standpoint, another serious problem is that imperative languages are not very efficient symbol manipulators. Because the imperative language architecture was molded to fit the von Neumann computer architecture, there are languages that can support number-crunching very well but can't support symbolic manipulation. However, imperative languages such as C and Ada have been used as the underlying base language to write expert system shells. These languages and the shells built from them run more efficiently and quickly on common general-purpose computers than the early shells built using LISP.

Because of their sequential nature, imperative languages are not very efficient for directly implementing expert systems, especially rule-based ones. As an illustration of this problem, consider the problem of encoding the information of a real-world problem with hundreds or thousands of rules. For example, the XCON system used by DEC to configure computer systems currently has about 7000 rules in its knowledge base. Early unsuccessful attempts were made to code this program in FORTRAN and BASIC before settling on the successful expert systems approach. The direct way of coding this knowledge in an imperative language would require 7000 IF...THEN statements or a very long CASE. This style of coding would present major efficiency problems since all 7000 rules need to be searched for matching patterns on every recognize-act cycle. Note that the inference engine and its recognize-act cycle would also have to be coded in the imperative language.

The efficiency of the program could be improved if rules were ordered so that those most likely to be executed were put at the beginning. However, this would require considerable tuning of the system and would change as new rules were added or old ones were deleted and modified. A better method for improving efficiency would be to build a tree of the rule patterns to reduce search time in determining which rules should be activated. Rather than making the programmer manually construct the tree, it would be preferable to have it built automatically by the computer based on the pattern and action syntax of the IF . . . THEN rules. It would also be helpful to have an IF . . . THEN syntax that was more conducive to representing knowledge and had powerful pattern-matching tests. This requires the development of a parser to analyze input structure and an interpreter or compiler to execute the new IF . . . THEN syntax.

When all of these techniques for improving efficiency are implemented, the result is a dedicated expert system. If the inference engine, parser, and interpreter are removed to provide easy development of other expert systems, they comprise an expert system shell. Of course, instead of doing all of this development from scratch, today it is much easier just to use an existing shell that is documented and extensively tested.

Functional Programming

The nature of **functional programming**, as exemplified by languages such as LISP and APL, is different from statement-oriented languages, with their heavy reliance on elaborate control structures and top-down design. The fundamental idea of functional programming is to combine simple functions to yield more powerful functions. This is essentially a **bottom-up** design, in contrast to the common top-down designs of imperative languages.

Functional programming is centered around **functions**. Mathematically, a function is an **association** or rule that maps members of one set, the **domain**, into another set, the **codomain**. An example of a function definition is

```
cube(x) ≡ x*x*x, where x is a real number and
cube is a function with real values
```

The three parts of the function definition are:

(1) the association, $x*x*x$
(2) the domain, real numbers
(3) the codomain, real numbers

of the cube function. The symbol ≡ means "is equivalent to" or "is defined as." The following notation is a shorthand way of writing that the cube mapping is from the domain of real numbers, symbolized as $\Re$, to the codomain of real numbers.

```
cube: ℜ → ℜ
```

A general notation for a function f that maps from a domain S to a domain T is $f{:}S{\rightarrow}T$ (Gersting 82). The **range** of the function f is the set of all **images** $f(s)$ where s is an element of S. For the case of the cube function, the images of s are $s*s*s$ and the range is the set of all real numbers. The range and the codomain are the same for the cube function. However, this may not be true for other functions such as the square function, x*x, with domain and codomain of real numbers. Since the range of the square function is only nonnegative real numbers, the range and the codomain are not the same.

Using set notation, the range of a function can be written as

```
R ≡ {f(s) | s ∈ S}
```

The **curly braces** ({ }), denote a **set**. The **bar** (|) is read as "where." The above statement can be read that the range R is equivalent to the set of values $f(s)$ where every element s is in the set S. The association is a set of ordered pairs (s,t), where $s \in S$, $t \in T$, and $t{=}f(s)$. Every member of S must have one and only one element of T associated with it. However, multiple t values may be associated with a single s. As a simple example, every positive number n has two square roots, $\pm \sqrt{n}$

Functions may also be defined recursively as in

```
factorial(n) ≡ n*factorial(n-1)
          where n is an integer and
          factorial is an integer function
```

Recursive functions are commonly used in functional languages such as LISP.

Mathematical concepts and expressions are **referentially transparent** because the meaning of the whole is completely determined from its parts. No synergism is involved between the parts. As an example, consider the functional expression $x+(2*x)$. The result is obviously $3*x$. Both $x+(2*x)$ and $3*x$ give the same result no matter which values are substituted for *x*. Even when other functions are substituted for **x**, the result is the same. For example, let *h(y)* be some arbitrary function. Then *h(y)* + (2 * *h(y)*) would still be equivalent to 3*h(y)*.

Now consider the following assignment statement in an imperative computer language such as Pascal:

```
sum := f(x) + x
```

If the parameter *x* is passed by reference and its value is changed in the function call, *f(x)*, what value will be used for *x*? Depending on how the compiler is written, the value of *x* might be the original value if it was saved on a stack, or the new value if *x* was not saved. Another source of confusion occurs if one compiler evaluates expressions right to left while another evaluates left to right. In this case, *f(x)+x* would not evaluate the same as *x+f(x)* on different compilers even if the same language were used. Other side effects may occur due to global variables. Thus, unlike mathematical functions, program functions are not referentially transparent.

Functional programming languages were created to be referentially transparent. Five parts make up a functional language:

- **data objects** for the language functions to operate on
- **primitive functions** to operate on the data objects
- **functional forms** to synthesize new functions from other functions
- **application operations** on functions that return a value and
- **naming procedures** to identify new functions.

Functional languages are generally implemented as interpreters for ease of construction and immediate user response.

In LISP (LISt Processing), data objects are **symbolic expressions** (S-expressions) that are either **lists** or **atoms**, whereas in **APL** (A Programming Language) the objects are arrays. Examples of lists are

```
(milk eggs cheese)
(shopping (groceries (milk eggs cheese) clothes
(pants)))
()
```

Lists are always enclosed in matching parentheses with spaces separating the elements. The elements of lists can be atoms, such as milk, eggs, and cheese, or embedded lists such as (milk eggs cheese) and (pants). Lists can be split up but atoms cannot. The **empty list**, ( ), contains no elements and is called **nil**.

There must be some primitive functions provided by the language as a basis for building more complex functions. In the original version of LISP, created by John McCarthy in 1960, there were few primitives, as shown in Table 1.12. Primitives CAR, CDR, CPR, and CTR are acronyms named after the specific hardware registers in the first machine to run LISP. CPR and CTR are now obsolete but the others have remained. Also shown are the **predicates** of LISP. Predicates are special functions that return values representing true and false.

The original version of LISP was called "pure" LISP because it was purely functional. However, it was also not very efficient for writing programs. Nonfunctional additions have been made to LISP to increase the efficiency of writing programs. For example, SET acts as the assignment operator, while LET and PROG can be used to create local variables and to execute a sequence of S-expressions. Although these act like functions, they are not functional in the original mathematical sense.

Function	Predicates
QUOTE	ATOM
CAR	EQ
CDR	NULL
CPR	
CTR	
CONS	
EVAL	
COND	
LAMBDA	
DEFINE	
LABEL	

Table 1.12 Original LISP Primitives and Functions

Since its creation, LISP has been the leading AI language in the United States. Many of the original expert system shells were written in LISP because it is so easy to experiment with. However, conventional computers do not execute LISP very efficiently and are even worse at executing the shells built using LISP. In order to circumvent this problem, several companies offer machines specifically designed to execute LISP code. These LISP machines use it completely, even as their assembly language. However, the LISP machines cost considerably more than conventional machines and are for single users.

This problem of high cost has an impact on both the development and the **delivery problem**. It is not enough just to develop a great program if it cannot be delivered for use because of high cost. A good development workstation is not necessarily a good delivery vehicle due to speed, power, size, weight, environmental, or cost constraints. Some applications may even require that the final code be placed in ROM for reasons of cost and nonvolatility. Putting code into ROM can be a problem with some AI and expert systems tools that require special hardware to run. It's better to consider this possibility in advance rather than having to recode a program later.

An additional problem is that of embedding AI with conventional programming languages such as C, Ada, Pascal, and FORTRAN. For example, certain applications that require extensive number-crunching are best done in conventional languages rather than in LISP, or in expert systems languages written in LISP or PROLOG.

Unless special provisions are made, expert systems which are written in LISP are generally difficult to embed in anything other than LISP programs. One major consideration in selecting an AI language should be the language in which the tool is written. For reasons of portability, efficiency, and speed, many expert systems tools are now being written in or converted to C. This also eliminates the problem of requiring expensive special hardware for LISP-based applications.

1.12 NONPROCEDURAL PARADIGMS

Nonprocedural paradigms do not depend on the programmer's giving exact details for how a problem is to be solved. This is the opposite of the procedural paradigms, which specify *how* a function or a statement sequence computes. Recall that in nonprocedural paradigms the emphasis is on specifying what is to be accomplished and letting the system determine how to accomplish it.

Declarative Programming

The **declarative paradigm** separates the **goal** from the methods used to achieve the goal. The user specifies the goal while the underlying mechanism of the implementation tries to satisfy the goal. A number of paradigms and associated programming languages have been created to implement the declarative model.

Object-oriented Programming

The **object-oriented** paradigm is another case of a paradigm that can be considered partly imperative and partly declarative. The term *object-oriented* today is used in two different ways. The expression **object-oriented design** is growing in popularity as a programming methodology in imperative programming languages such as Ada and Modula-2. The basic idea is to design a program by considering the data used in the program as objects and then implementing operations on those objects. This is the opposite of top-down design, which proceeds by stepwise refinement of a program's control structure. In fact, object-oriented design is essentially what used to be called bottom-up design. Unfortunately, the term *bottom-up* never sounded quite as impressive as *object-oriented*.

As an example of object-oriented design, consider the task of writing a program to manage a charge account with an interactive menu (Riley 87). The important data objects are current balance, amount of charge, and amount of payment. Various operations can be defined to act on the data objects. These operations would be add charge, make payment, and add monthly interest. Once all data objects, operations, and the menu interface are defined, coding can begin. This object-oriented design methodology is well suited to a program that has a weak control structure. It would not be as suitable in a program that requires a strong control structure, such as a payroll application. For the payroll case there is a definite sequence of steps to follow.

1. Obtain time-card data
2. Account for sick leave and vacation time
3. Multiply hours worked × rate of pay
4. Multiply overtime hours × overtime rate
5. Add bonus or sales commissions, if applicable
6. Subtract deductions for taxes, insurance, dues, and retirement
7. Issue paycheck

Object-oriented design requires no special language features. It can be done in FORTRAN, BASIC, C and so on. Languages such as Ada and Modula-2 support object-oriented design because these languages have features to encapsulate data in modules and packages.

The term *object-oriented programming* was originally used in reference to languages such as Smalltalk, which was specifically designed for objects. The term is now often used to refer to programming of an object-oriented design even in a language that has no true object support.

Smalltalk has features to support objects built into the language. In fact, Smalltalk has a programming environment built entirely using objects. Smalltalk is descended from SIMULA 67, a language developed for simulation. SIMULA 67 introduced the concept of **class**, which led to the concept of information hiding in modules. A class is essentially a type, which is a template that defines the structure of data. In fact, the concepts of type in both Pascal and Modula-2 came from class. An **instance** of a class is a data object that can be manipulated. The term *instance* has carried over to expert systems, in which it denotes a fact that matches a pattern. Likewise, a rule is said to be instantiated if its LHS is satisfied. The terms *activated* and *instantiated* in rule-based systems are synonymous.

Another significant concept that came from SIMULA 67 is **inheritance**. In SIMULA 67 a **subclass** could be defined to inherit the properties of classes. For example, one class may be defined to consist of objects that can be used in a stack and another class defined to be complex numbers. A subclass can easily be defined as objects that are complex numbers used in a stack. That is, these objects have inherited properties from both classes above them, called **superclasses**. The concept of inheritance can be extended to organize objects in a hierarchy where objects can inherit from their classes, which can inherit from their classes, and so on. Inheritance is useful because objects can inherit properties from their classes without the programmer having to specify every property. Many expert systems tools in use today such as ART and KEE allow inheritance because it is a powerful tool in constructing large groups of facts.

Logic Programming

One of the first AI applications of computers was in proving logic theorems with the Logic Theorist program of Newell and Simon. This program was first reported at the Dartmouth Conference on AI in 1956 and caused a sensation because electronic computers previously had been used only for numeric calculations. Now a computer was actually reasoning the proofs of mathematical theorems, which had been a task that only mathematicians were thought capable of doing.

In the Logic Theorist and its successor, the General Problem Solver (GPS), Newell and Simon concentrated on trying to implement powerful algorithms that could solve any problem. While the Logic Theorist was meant only for mathematical theorem proving, GPS was designed to solve any kind of logic problem, including games and puzzles such as chess, Tower of Hanoi, Missionaries and Cannibals, and cryptarithmetic. An example of their famous cryptarithmetic (secret arithmetic) puzzle is

```
  DONALD
+ GERALD
  ROBERT
```

where it is known that D = 5. The object is to figure out the arithmetic values of the other letters in the range 0 to 9.

GPS was the first problem-solving program to clearly separate the problem-solving knowledge from the domain knowledge. This paradigm of explicitly separating the problem-solving knowledge from the domain knowledge is now used as the basis of expert systems. In expert systems today, the inference engine decides what knowledge should be used and how it should be applied.

Efforts continued to improve mechanical theorem proving. By the early 1970s it had been discovered that computation is a special case of mechanical logical deduction (Kowalski 1985). When backward chaining was applied to sentences of the form "conclusion if conditions," it was powerful enough for significant theorem proving. The conditions can be thought of as representing patterns to be matched as in production rules discussed earlier. Sentences expressed in this form are called Horn clauses after Alfred Horn, who first investigated them. In 1972 the language PROLOG was created by Kowalski, Colmerauer, and Roussel to implement logic programming by backward chaining using Horn clauses.

Backward chaining can be used both to express the knowledge in a declarative representation and also to control the reasoning process. Typically, backward chaining proceeds by defining smaller **subgoals** that must be satisfied if the initial goal is to be satisfied. These subgoals are then further broken down into smaller subgoals, and so forth.

An example of declarative knowledge is the following classic example:

```
All men are mortal
Socrates is a man
```

which can be expressed in the Horn clauses

```
someone is mortal
    if someone is a man
Socrates is a man
    if (in all cases)
```

For the sentence about Socrates, the *if* condition is true in all cases. In other words, the knowledge about Socrates does not require any pattern to match. Contrast this with the mortal case in which someone must be a man for the pattern of the *if* condition to be satisfied.

Notice that a Horn clause can be interpreted as a procedure that tells how to satisfy a goal. That is, to determine if someone is mortal, it is necessary to determine if someone is a man. As a slightly more complex example,

```
A car needs gas, oil and inflated tires to run
```

can be expressed in a Horn clause as

```
x is a car and runs
    if x has gas and
    if x has oil and
    if x has inflated tires
```

Notice how the problem of determining if a car will run has been reduced to three simpler subproblems or subgoals. Now suppose there is some additional declarative knowledge as follows:

```
The fuel gauge shows not empty if a car has gas
The dipstick shows not empty if a car has oil
```

```
The air pressure gauge shows at least 20 if a car
   has inflated tires
The fuel gauge shows not empty
The dipstick reads empty
The air pressure gauge shows at least 15
```

These can be translated into the following Horn clauses:

```
x has gas
   if the fuel gauge shows not empty
x has oil
   if the dipstick shows not empty
x has inflated tires
   if the air pressure gauge shows at least 20
Fuel gauge is not empty
   if (in all cases)
Dipstick reads empty
Air pressure is at least 15
   if (in all cases)
```

From these clauses a mechanical theorem prover can prove that the car will not run because there is no oil and insufficient air pressure.

One of the advantages of backward chaining systems is that execution can proceed in parallel. That is, if multiple processors were available they could work on satisfying subgoals simultaneously. This parallel operation can greatly speed up the execution of programs and is one of the reasons why the Japanese chose PROLOG as the programming language for their Fifth Generation Computer project (Moto-Oka 1982). This was an ambitious project to develop the next generation of computers for the 1990s with capabilities far surpassing current models. These machines were to be programmed with declarative techniques, but this approach has run into difficulties. The Fifth Generation project was announced by the Japanese in 1981 with a budget of $850 million. The twenty-six initial goals of the project included natural language translation of Japanese to English and vice versa, problem solving and inferencing a thousand times faster than current machines; and the abilities to read handwritten text, understand pictures, access huge databases, and converse in natural language.

PROLOG is more than just a language. At a minimum, PROLOG is a shell because it requires

- an interpreter or inference engine
- a database (facts and rules)
- a form of pattern matching called **unification**
- a **backtracking** mechanism to pursue alternate subgoals if a search to satisfy a goal is unsuccessful.

More elaborate versions of PROLOG such as TurboPROLOG from Borland are tools because of all the enhancements they provide.

As an example of backward chaining, suppose you can pay for the oil to make the car run if you have cash or a credit card. One subgoal is checked to see if you have cash. If there is no fact that you do have cash, the backtracking mechanism will then explore the other subgoal to see if you have a credit card. If you have a credit card, the goal of paying for oil can be satisfied. Notice that the absence of a fact to prove a goal is just as effective, although perhaps less efficient, than a negative fact such as "dipstick reads empty." Either negative facts or missing facts can cause a goal to be unsatisfied.

If the backtracking and pattern-matching mechanisms are not needed by the problem, then the programmer must either work around them or code in a different language. One of the advantages of logic programming is executable specifications. That is, specifying the requirements of a problem by Horn clauses produces an executable program, which differs from conventional programming, in which the requirements document does not look at all like the final executable code. Newer imperative languages such as Ada attempt to circumvent this problem by offering the capability of using Ada itself as the program description language (PDL). The PDL can be used as a skeleton on which to build the rest of the program. If the PDL does not work properly, then neither will the program.

Unlike production rule systems, the order in which subgoals, facts, and rules are entered in a PROLOG program has significant effects. Efficiency—and therefore speed—are affected by the way that PROLOG searches its database. However, there are programs that execute correctly if subgoals, facts, and rules are entered one way but go into an infinite loop or have a run-time error if the order changes (Ghezzi 87, pp. 304–306).

Expert Systems

Expert systems can be considered declarative programming because the programmer does not specify how a program is to achieve its goal at the level of an algorithm. For example, in a rule-based expert system, any rule may become activated and put on the agenda if its LHS matches the facts. The order in which the rules were entered does not affect which rules are activated. Thus, the program statement order does not specify a rigid control flow. Other types of expert systems are based **frames**, discussed in Chapter 2, and **inference nets**, discussed in chapter 4.

There are a number of differences between expert systems and conventional programs. Table 1.13 lists some typical differences.

Characteristic	Conventional Program	Expert System
Control by . . .	Statement order	Inference engine
Control and data	Implicit integration	Explicit separation
Control strength	Strong	Weak
Solution by . . .	Algorithm	Rules and inference
Solution search	Small or none	Large
Problem solving	Algorithm is correct	Rules
Input	Assumed correct	Incomplete, incorrect
Unexpected input	Difficult to deal with	Very responsive
Output	Always correct	Varies with problem
Explanation	None	Usually
Applications	Numeric, file, and text	Symbolic reasoning
Execution	Generally sequential	Opportunistic rules
Program design	Structured design	Little or no structure
Modifiability	Difficult	Reasonable
Expansion	Done in major jumps	Incremental

Table 1.13
Some Typical Differences Between Conventional Programs and Expert Systems

Expert systems are often designed to deal with uncertainty because reasoning is one of the best tools that we have discovered for doing so. The uncertainty may arise in the input data to the expert system and even in the knowledge base itself. At first this may seem surprising to people used to conventional programming. However, much of human knowledge is heuristic, which means that it may only work correctly part of the time. In addition, the input data may be incorrect, incomplete, or inconsistent, or have other errors. Algorithmic solutions are not capable of dealing with such situations because an algorithm guarantees the solution of a problem in a finite series of steps.

Depending on the input data and the knowledge base, an expert system may come up with the correct answer, a good answer, a bad answer, or no answer at all. While this may seem shocking at first, the alternative is no answer all the time. Again, the important thing to keep in mind is that a good expert system will perform no worse than the best problem solver—a human expert—for problems like this and may do better. If we knew an efficient algorithmic method that was better than an expert system, we would use it. The important thing is to use the best, and perhaps only, tool for the job.

Nondeclarative Programming

Nondeclarative paradigms are becoming popular. These new paradigms are being increasingly used for a wide variety of applications. They can be used in stand-alone applications or in conjunction with other paradigms.

Induction-based Programming

An application of AI that is attracting interest is **induction-based** programming. In this paradigm the program learns by example. One application to which this paradigm has been applied is database access. Instead of the user having to type in the specific values for one or more fields for a search, it is only necessary to select one or more appropriate example fields with those characteristics. The database program infers the characteristics of the data and searches the database for a match.

Expert system tools such as 1st-Class and KDS offer induction learning by which they accept examples and case studies and automatically generate rules.

1.13 ARTIFICIAL NEURAL SYSTEMS

A new development in programming paradigms arose in the 1980s called **artificial neural systems** (ANS), based on how the brain processes information. This paradigm is sometimes called **connectionism** because it models solutions to problems by training simulated neurons connected in a network. Many researchers are investigating neural nets. The nets hold great potential as the front-end of expert systems that require massive amounts of input from sensors as well as real-time response.

The Traveling Salesman Problem

ANS has had remarkable success in providing real-time response to complex pattern recognition problems. In one case a neural net running on an ordinary microcomputer obtained a very good solution to the traveling salesman problem in 0.1 seconds compared to the optimum solution that required an hour of CPU time on a mainframe (Port 86). The traveling salesman problem is important because it is the classic problem faced in optimizing the routing of signals in a tele-communications system. Optimizing routing is important in minimizing the travel time, and thus efficiency and speed.

The basic traveling salesman problem is to compute the shortest route through a given list of cities. Table 1.14 shows the possible routes for one to four cities. Notice that the number of routes is proportional to the factorial of the number of cities minus one, $(N - 1)!$.

Number of Cities	Routes
1	1
2	1–2–1
3	1–2–3–1
	1–3–2–1
4	1–2–3–4–1
	1–2–4–3–1
	1–3–2–4–1
	1–3–4–2–1
	1–4–2–3–1
	1–4–3–2–1

Table 1.14 Traveling Salesman Problem Routes

While there are $9! = 362880$ routes for ten cities, there are $29! = 8.8E30$ possible routes for thirty cities. The traveling salesman problem is a classic example of **combinatorial explosion** because the number of possible routes increases so rapidly that there are no practical solutions for realistic numbers of cities. If it takes 1 hour of a mainframe CPU time to solve for thirty cities, it will take 30 hours for thirty-one cities and 330 hours for thirty-two cities. These are actually very small numbers when compared to the thousands of tele-communications switches and cities that are used in the routing of data packets and real items.

A neural net can solve the ten-city case just as fast as the thirty-city case whereas a conventional computer takes much longer. For the ten-city case the neural net came up with one of the two best routes and for the thirty -city case, it came up with one of the best 100,000,000 routes. This is more impressive if it is realized that this route is in the top 1E-22 of the best solutions. Although neural nets may not always give the optimum answer, they can provide a best guess in real-time. In many cases, a 99.999999999999999999 percent correct answer in one millisecond is better than a 100 percent correct answer in thirty hours.

Elements of an ANS

An ANS is basically an analog computer that uses simple processing elements connected in a highly parallel manner. The processing elements perform simple Boolean or arithmetic functions on their inputs. The key to the functioning of an ANS is the **weights** associated with each element. It is the weights that represent the information stored in the system.

A typical artificial neuron is shown in Figure 1.10. The neuron may have multiple inputs but only one output. The human brain contains about 10^{10} neurons and one neuron may have thousands of connections to another. The input signals to the neuron are multiplied by the weights and are summed to yield the total neuron input, I. The weights can be represented as a matrix and identified by subscripts.

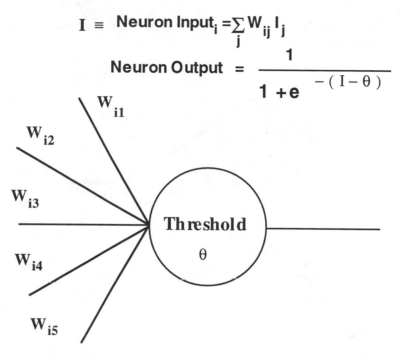

$$I \equiv \text{Neuron Input}_i = \sum_j W_{ij} I_j$$

$$\text{Neuron Output} = \frac{1}{1 + e^{-(I - \theta)}}$$

W_{i1}

W_{i2}

W_{i3}

Threshold

θ

W_{i4}

W_{i5}

Figure 1.10 Neuron Processing Element

The neuron output is often taken as a **sigmoid function** of the input. The sigmoid is representative of real neurons, which approach limits for very small and very large inputs. The sigmoid is called an *activation function*; and a commonly used function is $(1 + e^{-x})^{-1}$. Each neuron also has an associated **threshold value**, θ, which is subtracted from the total input, I. Figure 1.11 shows an ANS that can compute the **exclusive-OR (XOR)** of its inputs using a technique called back-propagation. The XOR gives a true output only when its inputs are not all true or not all false. The number of nodes in the hidden layer will vary depending on the application and the design.

Neural nets are not programmed in the conventional sense. There are about thirteen known neural net learning algorithms, such as **counter-propagation** and back-propagation, to train nets. The programmer "programs" the net simply by supplying the input and corresponding output data. The net learns by automatically adjusting weights in the network that connect the neurons. The weights and the threshold values of neurons determine the propagation of data through the net and thus its correct response to the training data. Training the net to the correct responses may take hours or days, depending on the number of patterns that the net must learn, the hardware, and the software. However, once the learning is accomplished, the net responds quickly.

If software simulation is not fast enough, ANS can be fabricated in chips for real-time response. Once the network has been trained and the weights determined, a chip can be constructed. AT&T and other companies are fabricating experimental neural net chips containing hundreds of neurons. In the next few years, it is very likely that chips will be fabricated containing thousands of neurons.

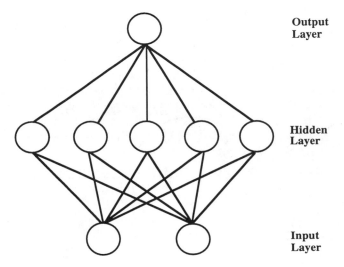

Figure 1.11 A Back-propagation Net

Characteristics of ANS

ANS architecture is very different from conventional computer architecture. In a conventional computer it is possible to correlate discrete information with memory cells. For example, a Social Security number could be stored as ASCII code in a contiguous group of memory cells. By examining the contents of this contiguous group the Social Security number could be directly reconstructed. This reconstruction is possible because there is a one-to-one relationship between each character of the Social Security number and the memory cell that contains the ASCII code of that character.

ANSs are modeled after current brain theories, in which information is represented by the weights. However, there is no direct correlation between a specific weight and a specific item of stored information. This distributed representation of information is similar to that of a hologram, in which the lines of the hologram act as a diffraction grating to reconstruct the stored image when laser light is passed through.

A neural net is a good choice when there is considerable empirical data and no algorithm exists to provide sufficient accuracy and speed. ANS offers several advantages compared to the storage of conventional computers.

- *Storage is **fault tolerant**.* Portions of the net can be removed and there is only a degradation in the quality of the stored data. This occurs because the information is stored in a distributed manner.
- *The quality of the stored image degrades gracefully in proportion to the amount of net removed.* There is no catastrophic loss of information. The storage and quality features are also characteristic of holograms.

- *Data are naturally stored in the form of **associative memory**.* An associative memory is one in which partial data are sufficient to recall the complete stored information. This contrasts with conventional memory, in which data are recalled by specifying the address of that data. A partial or noisy input may still elicit the complete original information.
- *Nets can extrapolate and interpolate from their stored information.* Training teaches a net to look for significant features or relationships in the data. After, the net can extrapolate to suggest relationships on new data. In one experiment (Hinton 86), a neural net was trained on the family relationships of twenty-four hypothetical people. Afterward, the net could also correctly answer relationships about which it had not been trained.
- *Nets have **plasticity**.* Even if a number of neurons are removed, the net can be retrained to its original skill level if enough neurons remain. This is also a characteristic of the brain, in which portions can be destroyed and the original skill levels can be relearned in time.

These characteristics make ANS attractive for robot spacecraft, oil field equipment, underwater devices, process control, and other applications that need to function a long time in a hostile environment without repair. Besides the issue of reliability, ANS offers the potential of low maintenance costs because of plasticity. Even if hardware repair can be done, it will probably be more cost effective to reprogram the neural net than to replace it.

ANSs are generally not well suited for applications that require number-crunching or an optimum solution. Also, if a practical algorithmic solution exists, an ANS is not a good choice.

Developments in ANS Technology

The origins of ANS started with the mathematical modeling of neurons by McCulloch and Pitts in 1943 (McCulloch 43). An explanation of learning by neurons was given by Hebb in 1949 (Hebb 49). In Hebbian learning, a neuron's efficiency in triggering another neuron increases with **firing**. The term *firing* means that a neuron emits an electrochemical impulse that can stimulate other neurons connected to it. There is evidence that the conductivity of connections between neurons at their connections, called **synapses**, increases with firing. In ANS, the weight of connections between neurons is changed to simulate the changing conductance of natural neurons.

In 1961 Rosenblatt published an influential book dealing with a new type of artificial neuron system he had been investigating called a **perceptron** (Rosenblatt 61). The perceptron was a remarkable device that showed capabilities for learning and pattern recognition. It basically consisted of two layers of neurons and a simple learning algorithm. The weights had to be manually set, in contrast to modern ANSs, which set the weights themselves based on training. Many researchers entered the field of ANS and began studying perceptrons during the 1960s.

The early perceptron era came to an end in 1969 when Minsky and Papert published a book, *Perceptrons*, which showed the theoretical limitations of perceptrons as a general computing machine (Minsky 69). They pointed out a deficiency of the perceptron in being able to compute only fourteen of the sixteen basic logic functions, which means that a perceptron is not a general-purpose computing device. In particular, they proved that a perceptron could not recognize the exclusive-OR. Although they had not seriously investigated multiple-layer ANSs, they expressed the pessimistic view that multiple layers would probably not be able to solve the XOR problem. Government funding of ANS research ceased in favor of the symbolic approach to AI using languages such as LISP and algorithms. New methods of representing symbolic AI information by frames, invented by Minsky, became popular during the 1970s. Further work on perceptrons has continued with new types able to overcome Minsky's objections (Reece 87). Because of their simplicity, perceptrons and other ANSs are easy to construct with modern integrated circuit technology.

ANS research continued on a small scale in the 1970s. However, the field finally entered a renaissance starting with the work of Hopfield in 1982 (Hopfield 82). He put ANS on a firm theoretical foundation with the two-layer Hopfield Net and demonstrated how ANS could solve a wide variety of problems. The general structure of a Hopfield Net is shown in Figure 1.12. In particular, Hopfield showed how an ANS could solve the traveling salesman problem in constant time as compared to the combinatorial explosion encountered by conventional algorithmic solutions. An electronic circuit form of an ANS could solve the traveling salesman problem in 1 micro-second. Other combinatorial optimization problems can easily be done by ANS, such as the four-color map, the Euclidean match (Hopfield 86b), and the transposition code (Tank 85).

An ANS that can easily solve the XOR problem is the **back-propagation** net, also known as the **generalized delta rule** (Rumelhart 86). The back-propagation net is commonly implemented as a three-layer net, although additional layers can be specified. The layers between the input and the output layers are called **hidden layers** because only the input and the output layers are visible to the external world. Another popular type of ANS is counterpropagation, invented by Hecht-Nielsen in 1986 (Hecht-Nielsen 90). An important theoretical result from mathematics, the Kolmogorov Theorem, can be interpreted as proving that a three-layer network with n inputs and $2n + 1$ neurons in the hidden layer can map any continuous function (Hecht-Nielsen 87).

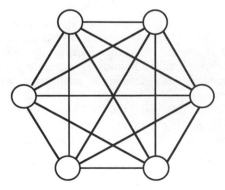

Figure 1.12 Hopfield Artificial Neural Net

Applications of ANS Technology

A significant example of learning by back-propagation was demonstrated by a neural net that learned the correct pronunciations of words from text (Sejnowski 86). The ANS was trained by correcting its output using a DEC text-to-speech device called DECTalk. It required twenty years of linguistic research to devise the rules for correct pronunciation used by DECTalk. The ANS taught itself equivalent pronunciation skills overnight simply by listening to the correct pronunciation of speech from text. No linguistic skills were programmed into the ANS.

Investigations of the ANS are underway for recognition of radar targets by electronic and optical computers (Farhat 86). New implementations of neural nets using optical components promise optical computers with speeds millions of times faster than electronic ones. Optical implementation of ANS is attractive because of the inherent parallelism of light. That is, light rays do not interfere with one another as they travel. Huge numbers of photons can easily be generated and manipulated by optical components such as mirrors, lenses, high-speed programmable spatial light modulators, arrays of optical bistable devices that can function as optical neurons, and diffraction gratings. Optical computers designed as ANSs appear to be complementary to one another. Future developments in ANS appear to be promising (Giarratano 90a). In particular, ANSs are useful in control systems in which conventional approaches are not satisfactory (Giarratano 91b).

Commercial Developments in ANS

A number of new companies and existing firms have been organized to develop ANS technology and products. Nestor markets an ANS product called NestorWriter that can recognize handwritten input and convert it to text using a PC. Other companies such as TRW, SAIC, HNC, Synaptics, Neural Tech, Revelations Research, and Texas Instruments market a variety of ANS simulators and hardware accelerator boards to speed up learning. One of the best bargains for getting started in neural computing is volume three of Rumelhart's books on parallel distributed processing (available from the MIT Press). The book describes a half dozen ANS simulators and also includes a diskette with software for an IBM-PC compatible machine for $27.50. By purchasing an accelerator card, the user can have a very powerful system for ANS at low cost.

1.14 CONNECTIONIST EXPERT SYSTEMS AND INDUCTIVE LEARNING

It is possible to build expert systems using ANS. In one system the ANS is the knowledge base constructed by training examples from medicine for disease (Gallant 88). In this system the expert system tries to classify a disease from its symptoms into one of the known diseases on which the system has been trained. An inference engine called MACIE (Matrix Controlled Inference Engine) was designed that uses the ANS knowledge base. The system uses forward chaining to make inferences and backward chaining to query the user for any additional data needed to produce a solution. Although an ANS by itself cannot explain why its weights are set to certain values, MACIE can interpret the ANS and generate IF...THEN rules to explain its knowledge.

An ANS expert system such as this uses **inductive learning**. That is, the system **induces** the information in its knowledge base by example. Induction is the process of inferring the general case from the specific. Besides ANS, there are a number of commercially available expert systems shells that explicitly generate rules from examples. The goal of inductive learning is to reduce or eliminate the knowledge acquisition bottleneck. By placing the burden of knowledge acquisition on the expert system, the development time may be reduced and the reliability may be increased if the system induces rules that were not known by a human. Expert systems have been combined with ANS (Giarratano 90b).

1.15 SUMMARY

In this chapter we have reviewed the problems and developments that have led to expert systems. The problems for which expert systems are used are generally not solvable by conventional programs because they lack a known or an efficient algorithm. Because expert systems are knowledge-based, they can be effectively used for real-world problems that are ill-structured and difficult to solve by other means.

The advantages and disadvantages of expert systems were also discussed in the context of selecting an appropriate problem domain for an expert system application. Criteria for selecting appropriate applications were given.

The essentials of an expert system shell were discussed with reference to rule-based expert systems. The basic recognize-act inference engine cycle was described and illustrated by a simple rule example. Finally, the relationship of expert systems to other programming paradigms was described in terms of the appropriate domain of each paradigm. The important point of all this is the concept that expert systems should be viewed as another programming tool that is suitable for some applications and unsuitable for others. Later chapters will describe the features and suitability of expert systems in more detail.

The best source for current information about artificial intelligence is the newsgroup comp.ai on the Internet and Usenet. A huge amount of information and software is available. Other newsgroups are concerned with fuzzy logic, neural nets, expert system shells, and many other topics. In addition to the information and software, these newsgroups allow users to post questions and receive answers from others.

PROBLEMS

1.1   Identify a person other than yourself who is considered either an expert or very knowledgeable. Interview this expert and discuss how well this person's expertise would be modeled by an expert system in terms of each criterion in the section "Advantages of Expert Systems" pages 4 and 5.

1.2   (a)   Write ten nontrivial rules expressing the knowledge of the expert in problem 1.

(b)   Write a program that will give your expert's advice. Include test results to show that each of the ten rules gives the correct advice. For ease of programming, you may allow the user to provide input from a menu.

1.3   (a)   In Newell and Simon's book *Human Problem Solving* they mention the nine-dot problem. Given nine dots arranged as follows, how can you draw four lines through all the dots without (a) lifting your pencil from the paper and (b) crossing any dot? (Hint: you can extend the line past the dots.)

• • •
• • •
• • •

(b)   Explain your reasoning (if any) in finding the solution and discuss whether an expert system or some other type of program would be a good paradigm to solve this type of problem.

1.4 Write a program that can solve cryptarithmetic problems. Show the result for the following problem, where D = five.

      DONALD
+ GERALD
      ROBERT

1.5 Write a set of production rules to extinguish five different types of fire such as oil, chemical, and so forth, given the type of fire.

1.6 (a) Write a set of production rules to diagnose three types of poison based on symptoms.
     (b) Modify the program so that it will also recommend a treatment once the poison has been identified.

1.7 Write a report on three different applications of expert systems that were not discussed in this chapter. Include your sources of information.

1.8 Give ten heuristic IF . . . THEN-type rules that save you time.

1.9 Give ten IF . . . THEN-type heuristic rules for buying a used car.

1.10 Give ten IF . . . THEN-type heuristic rules for planning your class schedule.

1.11 Give ten IF . . . THEN-type heuristic rules for buying a motorcycle.

1.12 Give ten IF . . . THEN-type heuristic rules for buying a three-wheeled vehicle.

1.13 Give ten IF . . . THEN-type heuristic rules for excuses for a late assignment.

1.14 Write a report on XCON, XSEL, and all the other expert systems for sales and manufacturing used by Digital Equipment Corp. In particular, discuss how all the expert systems cooperate to work together. Use the two most recent articles for reference and include a copy of the articles with your report.

1.15 Answer the following questions about one of the classic expert systems referenced in the historical bibliography by looking up at least three appropriate papers or other references. Include a copy of all references with your answers.

    (a) What were the purposes in developing it?
    (b) How successful was it for research purposes?
    (c) Was it ever commercially successful or put into routine use?
    (d) What other expert systems, if any, were an outgrowth of it?
    (e) What new concepts did it develop?

BIBLIOGRAPHY

(Buchanan 78). Buchanan, B. G. and Mitchell, T., "Model-directed Learning of Production Rules," Waterman, D. A., and Hayes-Roth, F., eds., *Pattern Directed Inference Systems*, Academic Press, pp. 297-312, 1978.

(Buchanan 78). Bruce G. Buchanan and Edward A. Feigenbaum, "Dendral and Meta-Dendral: Their Applications Dimension," *Artificial Intelligence*, **11**, (1), pp. 5-24, 1978.

(Chase 73). W. G. Chase and Herbert A. Simon, "The Mind's Eye in Chess," *Visual Information Processing*, W. G. Chase, ed., Academic Press, 1973.

(Elson 73). Mark Elson, *Concepts of Programming Languages*, Science Research Associates, p. 290, 1973.

(Ennis 86). R. L. Ennis, *et al.*, "A Continuous Real-time Expert System for Computer Operations," *IBM J. Res. Develop.*, **30**, (1), pp. 14-28, 1986.

(Farhat 86). N. H. Farhat, *et al.*, "Optical Analog of Two-Dimensional Neural Networks and Their Application in Recognition of Radar Targets," *Proceedings of the Neural Networks for Computing Meeting*, Snowbird, UT, pp. 146-152, 1986.

(Feigenbaum 81). Edward A. Feigenbaum, *Handbook of Artificial Intelligence*, Heuris Tech Press/William Kaufman, Inc., 1981-2.

(Feigenbaum 82). Edward A. Feigenbaum, "Knowledge Engineering in the 1980s," Dept. of Computer Science, Stanford University, Stanford, CA, 1982.

(Forgy 82). Charles Forgy, "Rete: A Fast Algorithm for the Many Pattern/Many Object Pattern Match Problem," *Artificial Intelligence*, **19**, pp. 17-37, 1982.

(Gallant 88). Stephen L. Gallant, "Connectionist Expert Systems," *Comm. of the ACM*, **31**, (2), pp. 152-169, Feb. 1988.

(Gersting 82). Judith L. Gersting, *Mathematical Structures for Computer Science*, W. L. Freeman and Co., pp. 64-67, 1982.

(Ghezzi 87). Carlo Ghezzi and Mehdi Jazayeri, *Programming Language Concepts*, John Wiley and Sons, Inc., p. 293, 1987.

(Giarratano 90a). Joseph Giarratano, *et al.*, "Future Impacts of Artificial Neural Systems on Industry," *ISA Transactions*, pp. 9-14, Jan. 1990.

(Giarratano 90b). Joseph Giarratano, *et al.*, "The State of the Art for Current and Future Expert System Tools," *ISA Transactions*, pp. 17-25, Jan. 1990.

(Giarratano 91a). Joseph Giarratano, *et al.*, "An Intelligent SQL Tutor," 1991 Conference on Intelligent Computer-Aided Training (ICAT '91), pp. 309-316, 1991.

(Giarratano 91b). Joseph Giarratano, *et al.*, "Neural Network Techniques in Manufacturing and Automation Systems," in *Control and Dynamic Systems*, Vol. 49, ed. by C.T. Leondes, Academic Press, pp. 37-98, 1991.

(Harmon 85). Paul Harmon and David King, *Expert Systems*, John Wiley and Sons, Inc., p. 21, 1985.

(Hayes-Roth 85). Frederick Hayes-Roth, "Rule-based Systems," *Communications of the ACM*, **28**, (9), pp. 921-932, Sept. 1985.

(Hebb 49). D. O. Hebb, *Organization of Behavior*, John Wiley and Sons, Inc., 1949.

(Hecht-Nielsen 87). Robert Hecht-Nielsen, "Kolmogorov's Mapping Neural Network Existence Theorem," *Proceedings of the First International Conference on Networks*, **III**, pp.11-14, June 1987.

(Hecht-Nielsen 90). Robert Hecht-Nielsen, *Neurocomputing*, Addison-Wesley Pub. Co., pg. 147, 1990.

(Hinton 86). Geoffrey E. Hinton, "Learning Distributed Representations of Concepts," *Proceedings 8th Annual Conference of the Cognitive Science Society*, Lawrence Erlbaum Assoc., 1986.

(Hopfield 82). J. J. Hopfield, "Neural Networks and Physical Systems with Emergent Collective Computational Abilities," *Proceedings of the National Academy of Sciences*, USA, **79,** (8), pp. 2554-2558, 1982.

(Hopfield 86a). John J. Hopfield and David W. Tank, "Computing with Neural Circuits: A Model," *Science*, **233**, pp. 625-633, 1986.

(Hopfield 86b). John J. Hopfield and David W. Tank, *Disordered Systems and Biological Organization*, Springer-Verlag, 1986.

(Hugh 88). Dafydd Ab Hugh, "The Future of Flying," *AI Expert*, pp. 66-69, Jan. 1988.

(Kerschberg 86). Larry Kerschberg, ed., *Expert Database Systems: Proceedings from the First International Workshop*, Benjamin/Cummings Publishing Co., 1986.

(Kowalski 1985). Robert Kowalski, "Logic Programming," *Byte*, p. 161, August 1985.

(Markov 54). A. A. Markov, *A Theory of Algorithms*, National Academy of Sciences, USSR (in English), 1954.

(McCulloch 43). Warren S. McCulloch and Walter Pitts, "A Logical Calculus of the Ideas Immanent in Nervous Activity," *Bulletin of Mathematical Biophysics*, **5**, pp. 115-137, 1943.

(McDermott 84). John McDermott and Judith Bachant, "R1 Revisited: Four Years in the Trenches," *AI Magazine*, **V**, (3), pp. 21-32, Fall 1984.

(Michie 73). D. Michie, "Knowledge Engineering," *Cybernetics*, **2**, pp. 197-200, 1973.

(Minsky 69). *Perceptrons—An Introduction to Computational Geometry*, MIT Press, 1969. *Note:* a second edition was published in 1988 containing some handwritten corrections and an additional chapter criticizing the modern ANS algorithms such as back-propagation.

(Moto-Oka 1982). Moto-Oka, T., ed., *Fifth Generation Computer Systems,* Elsevier, 1982.

(Newell 72). Allen Newell and Herbert A. Simon, *Human Problem Solving*, Prentice-Hall, 1972.

(Parrello 88). Bruce Parrello, "Car Wars: The (Almost) Birth of an Expert System," *AI Expert*, pp. 60-64, Jan. 1988.

(Post 43). Emil L. Post, "Formal Reductions of the General Combinatorial Decision Problem," *American Journal Of Mathematics*, **65**, pp. 197-215, 1943.

(Reece 87). Peter Reece, "Perceptrons & Neural Nets," *AI Expert*, pp. 50-57, Jan. 1987. *Note*: this article includes a listing in BASIC for a perceptron.

(Riley 87). David D. Riley, *Data Abstraction and Structures*, Boyd & Fraser, pp. 305-349, 1987.

(Rosenblatt 61). F. Rosenblatt, *Principles of Neurodynamics*, Sparten Books, 1961.

(Rumelhart 86). David E. Rumelhart, James L. McClelland, *et al.*, "Learning Internal Representations by Error Propagation," *Parallel Distributed Processing*, **1**, MIT Press, 1986.

(Schur 88). Stephen Schur, "The Intelligent Data Base," *AI Expert*, pp. 26-34, Jan. 1988.

(Scown 85). Susan B. Scown, *The Artificial Intelligence Experience: An Introduction*, Digital Equipment Corp., p. 78, 1985.

(Sejnowski 86). Terence J. Sejnowski and Charles R. Rosenberg, "NETtalk: A Parallel Network that Learns to Read Aloud," *Technical Report JHU/EECS-86/01*, Johns Hopkins University, 1986.

(Tank 85). David W. Tank and John J. Hopfield, *IEEE Circuits Systems* , **CAS-33**, p. 533, 1985.

(Waldrop 87). M. Mitchell Waldrop, *Man-Made Minds*, Walker and Co., p. 35, 1987.

(Waterman 86). Donald A. Waterman, *A Guide to Expert Systems*, Addison-Wesley Pub. Co., pp. 41-48, 1986.

A BRIEF HISTORICAL BIBLIOGRAPHY OF EXPERT SYSTEMS

AGE   Knowledge Engineering Assistance

Nii, H. P., and Aiello, N., "AGE (Attempt to Generalize): A Knowledge-based Program for Building Knowledge-based Programs," IJCAI, pp. 645-655, 1979.

AL/X   Expert System Shell Based on MYCIN and PROSPECTOR

Reiter, J., "AL/X: An Expert System Using Plausible Inference," Intelligent Terminals, Ltd., Oxford, 1980.

CASNET   Management of Glaucoma Treatment

Weiss, S. *et al.*, "A Model-based Method for Computer-aided Medical Decision Making.," *Artificial Intelligence*, **11**, pp. 145-172, 1978.

CENTAUR   Analyzes Pulmonary (Lung) Tests

Aikins, J. S., "Prototypes and Production Rules: An Approach to Knowledge Representation for Hypothesis Formation," IJCAI , pp. 1-3, 1979.

CRYSALIS   Uses X-ray Data to Determine Protein Structure

Englemore, R., and Terry, A., "Structure and Function of the CRYSALIS System," IJCAI, pp. 250-256, 1979.

DENDRAL   Identifies Organic Compounds from Mass Spectrometer Data

Buchanan, B. G. and Feigenbaum, E. A, "DENDRAL and Meta-DENDRAL: Their Applications Dimension," *Artificial Intelligence*, **11**, pp. 5-24, 1978.

EMYCIN   Expert System Shell Developed from MYCIN

Van Melle, W., "A Domain-independent Production Rule System for Consultation Programs," IJCAI, pp. 923-925, 1979.

GUIDON   Intelligent Tutor for EMYCIN-Based Systems

Clancey, W. J., "Dialogue Management for Rule-based Tutorials," IJCAI, pp. 155-161, 1979.

INTERNIST   Diagnose Internal Medicine Problems

Pople, H. E., Myers, J. D. and Miller, R. A., "DIALOG: A Model of Diagnostic Logic for Internal Medicine," IJCAI , pp. 848-855, 1975.

MACSYMA   Solves Math Problems of Algebra, Trigonometry, and Calculus

Genesereth, M. R., "The Role of Plans in Automated Consultation," IJCAI, pp. 311-319, 1979.

META-DENDRAL   Induces Rules of Molecular Structure from Mass Spectrometer Data

Buchanan, B. G., and Mitchell, T., "Model-directed Learning of Production Rules," Waterman, D. A., and Hayes-Roth, F., eds., Pattern Directed Inference Systems, Academic Press, pp. 297-312, 1978.

MOLGEN   Plans Experiments on Molecular Genetics

Marin, N., *et al.*, "Knowledge-based Management for Experiment Planning in Molecular Genetics," IJCAI, pp. 882-887, 1977.

MYCIN   Diagnosis and Treatment of Meningitis and Certain Other Blood Diseases.

Davis, R., Buchanan, B. G., and Shortliffe, E. H., "Production Systems as a Representation for a Knowledge-based Consultation Program,"*Artificial Intelligence*, **8**, (1), pp. 15-45, 1977.

PROSPECTOR   Identifcation of Minerals and Selection of Drilling Sites

Duda, R., Gaschnig, J., and Hart, P., "Model Design in the PROSPECTOR Consultant System for Mineral Exploration," D. Michie, ed., *Expert Systems in the Micro-Electronic Age,* Edinburgh University Press, pp. 153-167, 1979.

PUFF   Analyzes Pulmonary (Lung) Tests

Kunz, J. C. *et al.*, "A Physiological Rule-based System for Interpreting Pulmonary Function Test Rules," Heuristic Programming Memo HPP-78-19, Stanford University, Stanford, CA.

XCON/R1   Configures VAX Computer Systems

McDermott, J., and Bachant, J., "R1 Revisited: Four Years in the Trenches," *AI Magazine,* **V**, (3), pp. 21-32, Fall 1984.

SACON   Structural Engineering

Bennett, J. S. and Engelmore, R. S., "SACON: A Knowledge-based Consultant for Structural Analysis," IJCAI, pp. 47-49, 1979.

SU/X   Signal Interpretation

Nii, H. P., and Feigenbaum, E. A., "Rule-based Understanding of Signals," Waterman, D. A., and Hayes-Roth, F., eds., *Pattern Directed Inference Systems*, Academic Press, pp. 483-501, 1978.

TEIRESIAS   Knowledge Acquisition Program Developed for MYCIN

Davis, R., "Interactive Transfer of Expertise: Acquisition of New Inference Rules," *Artificial Intelligence*, **12**, (2), pp. 121-158, 1979.

CHAPTER 2
The Representation of Knowledge

2.1 INTRODUCTION

In this chapter we will discuss some of the commonly used representations of knowledge for expert systems. Knowledge representation is of major importance in expert systems for two reasons. First, expert system shells are designed for a certain type of knowledge representation such as rules or logic. Second, the way in which an expert system represents knowledge affects the development, efficiency, speed, and maintenance of the system. In Chapter 3, we will discuss how inferences are made.

2.2 THE MEANING OF KNOWLEDGE

Knowledge, like *love*, is one of those words that everyone knows the meaning of, yet finds hard to define. Like love, knowledge has many meanings. Other words such as *data, facts*, and *information* are often used interchangeably with *knowledge*.

The study of knowledge is **epistemology** (Angeles 81). It is concerned with the nature, structure, and origins of knowledge. Figure 2.1 illustrates some of the categories of epistemology. Besides the philosophical kinds of knowledge expressed by Aristotle, Plato, Descartes, Hume, Kant, and others, there are two special types, called **a priori** and **a posteriori**. The term *a priori* comes from the Latin and means "that which precedes." *A priori* knowledge comes before and is independent of knowledge from the senses. As an example, the statements "everything has a cause" and "all triangles in a plane have 180 degrees" are examples of *a priori* knowledge. *A priori* knowledge is considered to be universally true and cannot be denied without contradiction. Logic statements, mathematical laws, and the knowledge possessed by teenagers are examples of *a priori* knowledge.

The opposite of *a priori* knowledge is knowledge derived from the senses, or *a posteriori* knowledge. The truth or falsity of *a posteriori* knowledge can be verified using sense experience, as in the statement "the light is green." However, because sensory experience may not always be reliable, *a posteriori* knowledge can be denied on the basis of new knowledge without the necessity of contradictions. For example, if you saw someone with brown eyes, you would believe that person's eyes were brown. However, if you later saw that person removing brown contact lenses to reveal blue eyes, your knowledge would have to be revised.

Knowledge can be further classified into **procedural knowledge**, **declarative knowledge**, and **tacit knowledge**. The procedural and declarative knowledge types correspond to the procedural and declarative paradigms discussed in Chapter 1.

Procedural knowledge is often referred to as knowing how to do something. An example of procedural knowledge is knowing how to boil a pot of water. Declarative knowledge refers to knowing that something is true or false. It is concerned with knowledge expressed in the form of declarative statements such as "Don't put your fingers in a pot of boiling water."

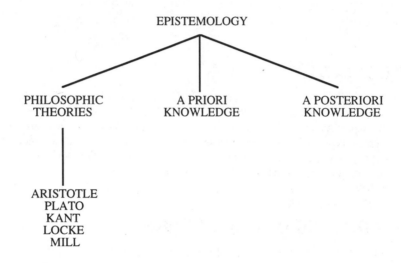

Figure 2.1 Some Categories of Epistemology

Tacit knowledge is sometimes called ***unconscious knowledge*** because it cannot be expressed by language. An example is knowing how to move your hand. On a gross scale, you might say that you move your hand by tightening or relaxing certain muscles and tendons. But at the next lower level, how do you *know* how to tighten or relax the muscles and tendons? Other examples are walking or riding a bicycle. In computer systems ANS is related to tacit knowledge because normally the neural net cannot directly explain its knowledge, but may be able to if given an appropriate program (see Section 1.14).

Knowledge is of primary importance in expert systems. In fact, an analogy to Wirth's classic expression

```
Algorithms + Data Structures = Programs
```

for expert systems is

```
Knowledge + Inference = Expert Systems
```

As used in this book, *knowledge* is part of a hierarchy, illustrated in Figure 2.2. At the bottom is noise, consisting of items that are of little interest and that obscure data. The next higher level is data, which are items of potential interest. Information, or processed data that are of interest are on the third level. Next is knowledge, which represents very specialized information. In Chapter 1, knowledge in rule-based expert systems was defined as the rules that were activated by facts to produce new facts or conclusions. This process of *inferencing* is the second essential part of an expert system. The term inferencing is generally used for mechanical systems such as expert systems. *Reasoning* is generally used in human thinking.

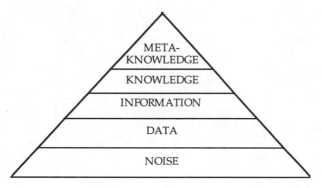

Figure 2.2 The Hierarchy of Knowledge

The term *facts* can mean either data or information. Depending on how they are written, expert systems may draw inferences using data or information. Expert systems may also (1) separate data from noise, (2) transform data into information, or (3) transform information into knowledge.

As an example of these concepts, consider the following sequence of 24 numbers:

```
137178766832525156430015
```

Without knowledge, this entire sequence may appear to be noise. However, if it is known that this sequence is meaningful, then the sequence is data. Determining what is data and what is noise is like the old saying about gardening, "a weed is anything that grows that isn't what you want."

Certain knowledge may exist to transform data into information. For example, the following algorithm processes the data to yield information.

```
Group the numbers by twos.
Ignore any two-digit numbers less than 32.
Substitute the ASCII characters for the two-digit
numbers.
```

Application of this algorithm to the previous 24 numbers yields the information

```
GOLD 438+
```

Now knowledge can be applied to this information. For example, there may be a rule

```
IF gold is less than 500
   and the price is rising (+)
THEN
   buy gold
```

Although not explicitly shown in Figure 2.2, *expertise* is a specialized type of knowledge that experts have. Expertise is not commonly found in public sources of information such as books and papers. Instead, expertise is the implicit knowledge of the expert that must be extracted and made explicit so it can be encoded in an expert system. Above knowledge is **metaknowledge.** One meaning of the prefix **meta** is "above." Metaknowledge is knowledge about knowledge and expertise. An expert system may be designed with knowledge about several different domains. Metaknowledge would specify which knowledge base was applicable. For example, an expert system could have knowledge bases about car repair of 1988 Chevrolets, 1985 Fords, and 1989 Cadillacs. Depending on what car needed repair, the appropriate knowledge base would be used. It would be inefficient in terms of memory and speed for all of the knowledge bases to be working at once. In addition, there could be conflicts as the expert system tried to decide the applicable rules from all knowledge bases at once. Metaknowledge may also be used within one domain to decide which group of rules in the domain is most applicable.

In a philosophical sense, **wisdom** is the peak of all knowledge. Wisdom is the metaknowledge of determining the best goals of life and how to obtain them. A rule of wisdom might be

```
IF I have enough money to keep my spouse happy
THEN I will retire and enjoy life
```

However, due to the extreme scarcity of wisdom in the world, we shall restrict ourselves to knowledge-based systems and leave wisdom-based systems to politicians.

2.3 PRODUCTIONS

A number of different knowledge representation techniques have been devised. These include rules, semantic nets, frames, scripts, knowledge-representation languages such as KL-1 (Woods 83) and KRYPTON (Brachman 83), conceptual graphs (Sowa 84), and others (Brachman 80). As described in Chapter 1, production rules are commonly used as the knowledge base in expert systems because their advantages greatly outweigh their disadvantages.

One formal notation for defining productions is the Backus-Naur form (BNF; McGettrick 80). This notation is a **metalanguage** for defining the **syntax** of a language. Syntax defines the form, whereas **semantics** refers to meaning. A metalanguage is a language for describing languages. The prefix *meta* means "above," and so a metalanguage is "above" normal language.

There are many types of languages: natural languages, logic languages, mathematical languages, and computer languages. The BNF notation for a simple English language rule that a sentence consists of a noun and a verb followed by punctuation is the following production rule:

```
<sentence> ::= <subject> <verb> <end-mark>
```

where the **angle brackets**, **<>**, and **::=** are symbols of the metalanguage and not of the language being specified. The symbol "::=" means "is defined as" and is the BNF equivalent of the arrow, → used in Chapter 1 with production rules. In order to avoid confusion with the Pascal assignment operator, :=, we will use the arrow.

The terms within angle brackets are called ***nonterminal*** *symbols* or simply *nonterminals*. A nonterminal is a variable in that it represents another term. The other term may be either a nonterminal or a **terminal**. A terminal cannot be replaced by anything else and so is a constant.

The nonterminal <sentence> is special because it is the one **start symbol** from which the other symbols are defined. In the definition of programming languages, the start symbol is usually named <program>. The production rule

```
<sentence> → <subject> <verb> <end-mark>
```

states that a sentence is composed of a subject followed by a verb, followed by an end-mark. The following rules complete the nonterminals by specifying their possible terminals. The **bar** means "or" in the metalanguage.

```
<subject> → I | You | We
<verb> → left | came
<end-mark> → . | ? | !
```

All possible sentences in the language, the productions, can be produced by successively replacing each nonterminal by its right-hand-side nonterminals or terminals until all nonterminals are eliminated. The following are some productions:

```
I left.
I left?
I left!
You left.
You left?
You left!
We left.
We left?
We left!
```

A set of terminals is called a ***string*** of the language. If the string can be derived from the start symbol by replacing nonterminals by their definition rules, then the string is called a *valid **sentence***. For example "We," "WeWe," and "leftcamecame" are all valid strings of the language, but are not valid sentences.

A **grammar** is a complete set of production rules that defines a language unambiguously. Although the previous rules do define a grammar, it is a very restricted one because there are so few possible productions. For example, a more elaborate grammar could also include direct objects, as in the productions

```
<sentence> → <subject> <verb> <object> <end-mark>
<object> → home | work | school
```

Although this is a valid grammar, it is too simple for practical use. A more practical grammar is the following in which the end-mark has been left out for simplicity:

```
<sentence> → <subject phrase> <verb> <object phrase>
<subject phrase> → <determiner> <noun>
<object phrase> → <determiner> <adjective> <noun>
<determiner> → a | an | the | this | these | those
<noun> → man | eater
<verb> → is | was
<adjective> → dessert | heavy
```

The <determiner> is used to indicate a specific item. Using this grammar, sentences such as

```
the man was a dessert eater
an eater was the heavy man
```

can be generated.

A **parse tree** or **derivation tree** is a graphic representation of a sentence decomposed into all the terminals and nonterminals used to derive the sentence. Figure 2.3 shows the parse tree for the sentence "the man was a heavy eater." However, the string "man was a heavy eater" is not a valid sentence because it lacks the determiner in the subject phrase. A compiler creates a parse tree when it tries to determine whether statements in a program conform to the valid syntax of a language.

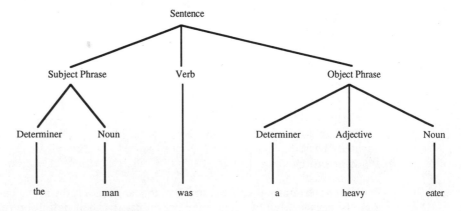

Figure 2.3 Parse Tree of a Sentence

The tree in Figure 2.3 shows that the sentence "the man was a heavy eater" can be derived from the start symbol by applying appropriate productions. The steps in this process are shown below; the **double arrow, =>**, means apply the productions shown.

```
<sentence> => <subject phrase> <verb>
              <object phrase>
<subject phrase> => <determiner> <noun>
<determiner> => the
<noun> => man
<verb> => was
<object phrase> => <determiner> <adjective> <noun>
<determiner> => a
<adjective> => heavy
<noun> => eater
```

An alternative way of using productions is to generate valid sentences by substituting all the appropriate terminals for nonterminals, as discussed previously. Of course, not all productions, such as "the man was the dessert," will make much sense.

2.4 SEMANTIC NETS

A **semantic network**, or net, is a classic AI representation technique used for propositional information (Stillings 87). A semantic net is sometimes called a *propositional net*. As discussed before, a proposition is a statement that is either true or false, such as "all dogs are mammals" and "a triangle has three sides." Propositions are forms of declarative knowledge because they state facts. In mathematical terms, a semantic net is a labeled, directed graph. A proposition is always true or false and is called **atomic** because its truth value cannot be further divided. Here the term *atomic* is used in the classic sense of an indivisible object. In contrast, the fuzzy propositions that will be discussed in Chapter 5 usually need only be true or false.

Semantic nets were first developed for AI as a way of representing human memory and language understanding (Quillian 68). Quillian used semantic nets to analyze the meanings of words in sentences. Since then semantic nets have been applied to many problems involving knowledge representation.

The structure of a semantic net is shown graphically in terms of **nodes** and the **arcs** connecting them. Nodes are often referred to as *objects* and the arcs as *links* or *edges*.

The links of a semantic net are used to express relationships. Nodes are generally used to represent physical objects, concepts, or situations. Figure 2.4 (a) shows an ordinary net, actually a directed graph, in which the links indicate airline routes between cities. Nodes are the circles and links are the lines connecting the nodes. The arrows show the directions in which planes can fly, hence the term directed graph. In Figure 2.4 (b) the links show the relationship between members of a family. Relationships are of primary importance in semantic nets because they provide the basic structure for organizing knowledge. Without relationships, knowledge is simply a collection of unrelated facts. With relationships, knowledge is a cohesive structure about which other knowledge can be inferred. For example, in Figure 2.4 (b) it can be inferred that Ann and Bill are the grandparents of John even though there is no explicit link labeled "grandfather-of."

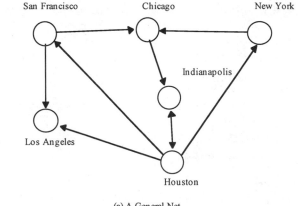

(a) A General Net

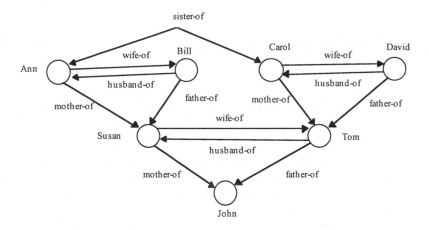

(b) A Semantic Net

Figure 2.4 Two Types of Nets

Semantic nets are sometimes referred to as ***associative nets*** because nodes are associated or related to other nodes. In fact, Quillian's original work modeled human memory as an associative net in which concepts were the nodes and links formed the connections between concepts. According to this model, as one concept node is stimulated by reading words in a sentence, its links to other nodes are activated in a spreading pattern. If another node receives sufficient activation, the concept would be forced into the conscious mind. For example, although you know thousands of words, you are only thinking of the specific words in this sentence as you read it.

Certain types of relationships have proved very useful in a wide variety of knowledge representations. Rather than defining new relationships for different problems, it is customary to use these standard types. The use of common types makes it easier for various people to understand an unfamiliar net.

Two types of commonly used links are **IS-A** and **A-KIND-OF**, which are sometimes written as **ISA** and **AKO** (Winston 84). Figure 2.5 is an example of a semantic net using these links. In this figure the IS-A means "is an instance of" and refers to a specific member of a class. A **class** is related to the mathematical concept of a set in that it refers to a group of objects. Although a set can have elements of any type, the objects in a class have some relation to one another. For example, it is possible to define a set consisting of

```
{ 3, eggs, blue, tires, art }
```

However, members of this set have no common relationship. In contrast, planes, trains, and automobiles in one class are related because they are all types of transportation.

The link AKO is used here to relate one class to another. The AKO is not used to relate a specific individual because that is the function of IS-A. The AKO relates an individual class to a parent class of classes of which the individual is a child class.

From another viewpoint, the AKO relates **generic** nodes to generic nodes whereas the IS-A relates an instance or an **individual** to a generic class. Notice in Figure 2.5 that the more general classes are at the top and the more specific classes are at the bottom. The more general class that an AKO arrow points to is called a **superclass**. If a superclass has an AKO pointing to another node, then it is also a class of the superclass the AKO points to. Another way of expressing this is that an AKO points from a **subclass** to a class. The link **ARE** is sometimes used for AKO, and ARE is read as the ordinary verb "are."

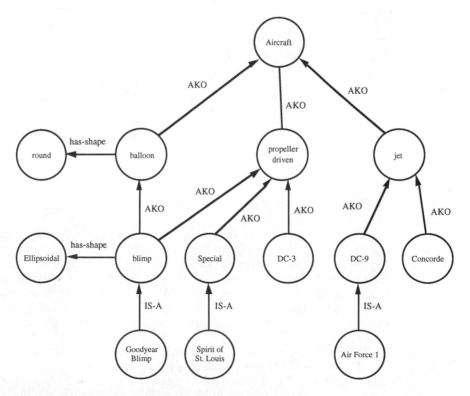

Figure 2.5 A Semantic Net with IS-A and A-Kind-Of (AKO) Links

The objects in a class have one or more **attributes** in common and each attribute has a **value**. The combination of attribute and value is a **property**. For example, a blimp has attributes of size, weight, shape, color, and so forth. The value of the shape attribute is ellipsoidal. In other words, a blimp has the property of an ellipsoidal shape. Because the Goodyear Blimp is a blimp and blimps have ellipsoidal shape, it follows that the Goodyear Blimp is ellipsoidal. Other types of links may also be found in semantic nets. The **IS** link defines a value. For example, whatever aircraft the President is on is Air Force 1. If the President is on a DC-9, then Air Force 1 is a DC-9. The **CAUSE** link expresses causal knowledge. For example, hot air CAUSES a balloon to rise.

The duplication of one node's characteristics by a descendent is called **inheritance**. Unless there is more specific evidence to the contrary, it is assumed that all members of a class will inherit all the properties of their superclasses. For example, balloons have a round shape. However, since the blimp class has a link pointing to the ellipsoidal shape, this takes precedence. Inheritance is a very useful tool in knowledge representation because it eliminates the necessity of repeating common characteristics. Links and inheritance provide a very efficient means of knowledge representation because many complex relationships can be shown with a few nodes and links.

2.5 OBJECT-ATTRIBUTE-VALUE TRIPLES

One problem with using semantic nets is that there is no standard definition of link names. For example, some books use IS-A for both generic and individual relations (Barr 81; Staugaard 87). The IS-A is then used in the sense of the ordinary words "is a" and is also used for AKO. In the expert system tool ART, IS-A relates two classes of objects and INSTANCE-OF relates an individual to a class.

Another common link is HAS-A, which relates a class to a subclass. HAS-A points opposite AKO and is often used to relate an object to a part of the object. For example,

```
car HAS-A engine
car HAS-A tires
car IS-A ford
```

More specifically, IS-A relates a value to an attribute whereas a HAS-A relates an object to an attribute.

The three items of object, attribute, and value occur so frequently that it is possible to build a simplified semantic net using just them. An **object-attribute-value triple (OAV)**, or **triplet**, can be used to characterize all the knowledge in a semantic net and was used in the expert system MYCIN for diagnosing infectious diseases. The OAV triple representation is convenient for listing knowledge in the form of a table and thus for translating the table into computer code by rule induction. An example of an OAV triple table is shown in Table 2.1.

OAV triples are especially useful for representing facts and the patterns to match the facts in the antecedent of a rule. The semantic net for such a system consists of nodes for objects, attributes, and values connected by HAS-A and IS-A links. If only a single object is to be represented and inheritance is not required, an even simpler representation called *attribute-value pairs*, or simply *AV*, may suffice.

Object	Attribute	Value
apple	color	red
apple	type	mcintosh
apple	quantity	100
grapes	color	red
grapes	type	seedless
grapes	quantity	500

Table 2.1 An OAV Table

2.6 PROLOG and Semantic Nets

Semantic nets are easy to translate into PROLOG. For example,

```
is_a(goodyear_blimp,blimp).
is_a(spirit_of_st_louis,special).
has_shape(blimp,ellipsoidal).
has_shape(balloon,round).
```

are PROLOG statements that express some of the relationships in the semantic net of Figure 2.5. A period marks the end of a statement.

Essentials of PROLOG

Each of the statements above is a PROLOG **predicate expression**, or simply a predicate, because it is based on predicate logic. However, PROLOG is not a true predicate logic language because it is a computer language with executable statements. In PROLOG a predicate expression consists of the predicate name, such as is_a, followed by zero or more arguments enclosed in parentheses and separated by commas. Some examples of PROLOG predicates and comments, preceeded by semicolons, follow:

```
color(red).              ; red is a color
father_of(tom,john).     ; tom is the father of john
mother_of(susan,john).   ; susan is the mother of john
parents(tom,susan,john). ; tom and susan are
                         ;   parents of john
```

Predicates with two arguments are more easily understood if you consider the predicate name following the first argument. The meanings of predicates with more than two arguments must be explicitly stated, as the parents predicate illustrates. Another difficulty is that semantic nets are primarily useful for representing binary relationships because a drawn line has only two ends, of course. It's not possible to draw the parents predicate as a single directed edge because there are three arguments. The idea of drawing Tom and Susan together in one parents node and John at the other leads to a new complication. It is then impossible to use the parents node for other binary relationships, such as mother-of, since it would also involve Tom.

Predicates can also be expressed with relations such as the IS-A and HAS-A.

```
is_a(red,color).
has_a(john,father).
has_a(john,mother).
has_a(john,parents).
```

Notice that the has_a predicates do not express the same meaning as previously because John's father, mother, and parents are not explicitly named. In order to name them, some additional predicates must be added.

```
is_a(tom,father).
is_a(susan,mother).
is_a(tom,parent).
is_a(susan,parent).
```

Even these additional predicates do not express the same meaning as the original predicates. For example, we know that John has a father and that Tom is a father, but this does not provide the information that Tom is the father of John.

All of the preceding statements actually describe facts in PROLOG. Programs in PROLOG consist of facts and rules in the general form of **goals**:

$$p \;\; :- \;\; p_1, p_2, \ldots p_N.$$

in which p is the rule's head and the p_i are the **subgoals**. Normally this expression is a Horn clause, which states that the head goal, p, is satisfied if and only if all of the subgoals are satisfied. The exception is when the special predicate for failure is used. A failure predicate is convenient because it's not easy to prove negation in classical logic, and PROLOG is based on classical logic. Negation is viewed as the failure to find a proof, which can be a very long and involved process if there are many potential matches. The **cut** and special failure predicate make the negation process more efficient by reducing the search for a proof.

The commas separating the subgoals represent a logical AND. The symbol, :-, is interpreted as an IF. If only the head exists and there is no right-hand-side, as in

```
p.
```

then the head is considered true. That is why predicates such as the following are considered facts and thus must be true.

```
color(red).
has_a(john,father).
```

Another way of thinking about facts is that a fact is an unconditional conclusion that does not depend on anything else and so the IF, :- is not necessary. In contrast, PROLOG rules require the IF because they are conditional conclusions whose truth depends on one or more conditions. As an example, the parent rules are as follows:

```
parent(X,Y)  :- father(X,Y).
parent(X,Y)  :- mother(X,Y).
```

which means that X is the parent of Y if X is the father of Y or if X is the mother of Y. Likewise, a grandparent can be defined as:

```
grandparent(X,Y) :- parent(X,Z),parent(Z,Y).
```

and an ancestor can be defined as:

```
(1) ancestor(X,Y) :- parent(X,Y).
(2) ancestor(X,Y) :- ancestor(X,Z),ancestor(Z,Y).
```

where (1) and (2) are used for our identification purposes only.

Searching in PROLOG

A system for executing PROLOG statements is generally an interpreter, although some systems can generate compiled code. The general form of a PROLOG system is shown in Figure 2.6. The user interacts with PROLOG by entering predicate queries and receiving answers. The **predicate database** contains the rule and fact predicates that have been entered and so forms the knowledge base. The interpreter tries to determine whether a query predicate that the user enters is in the database. The answer returned is yes if it is in the database or no if it is not. If the query is a rule, the interpreter will try to satisfy the subgoals by conducting a depth-first search, as shown in Figure 2.7. For contrast, a breadth-first search is also shown, although this is not the normal mode of PROLOG. In a **depth-first search**, the search goes down as far as possible and then back up. In PROLOG the search also goes from left to right. A **breadth-first search** proceeds one level at a time before descending to the next lower level.

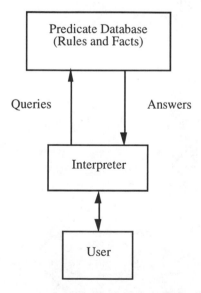

Figure 2.6 General Organization of a PROLOG System

As an example of goal searching in PROLOG, consider the ancestor rules defined as (1) and (2). Assume the following facts are now input.

```
(3) parent(ann,mary).
(4) parent(ann,susan).
(5) parent(mary,bob).
(6) parent(susan,john).
```

Now suppose PROLOG is queried to determine whether Ann is the ancestor of Susan

```
:-ancestor(ann,susan).
```

where the absence of a head indicates a **query**, which is a condition to be proved by PROLOG. Facts, rules, and queries are the three types of Horn clauses of PROLOG. A condition can be proved if it is the conclusion of an instance of a clause. Of course, the clause itself must be provable, which is done by proving the conditions of the clause.

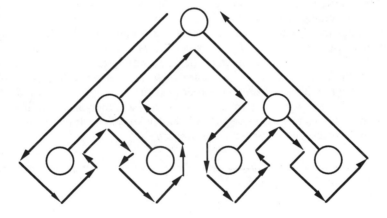

(a) Depth-first Search

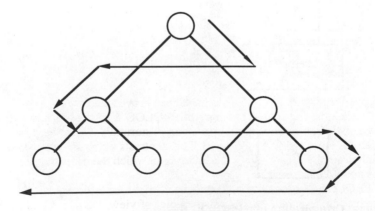

(b) Breadth-first Search

Figure 2.7 Depth-first and Breadth-first Searches for an Arbitrary Tree

On receipt of this input PROLOG will start searching for a statement whose head matches the input pattern of ancestor(ann,susan). This is called *pattern matching,* just like the pattern matching to facts in the antecedent of a production rule. The search starts from the first statement that was entered (1), the **top,** and goes to the last statement (6), the **bottom.** There is a possible match with the first ancestor rule (1). The variable X matches ann and the variable Y matches susan. Since the head matches, PROLOG will now try to match the body of (1), yielding the subgoal parent(ann,susan). PROLOG now tries to match this subgoal against clauses and eventually matches with the fact (4) parent(ann,susan). There are no more goals to match and PROLOG answers "yes" because the original query is true.

As another example, suppose the query is

```
:-ancestor(ann,john).
```

The first ancestor rule (1) matches and X is set to ann andY is set to john. PROLOG now tries to match the body of (1), parent(ann,john) with every parent statement. None match and so the body of (1) cannot be true. Because the body of (1) is not true, the head cannot be true.

Because (1) cannot be true, PROLOG then tries the second ancestor statement (2). X is set to ann and Y is set to john. PROLOG tries to prove the head of (2) is true by proving both subgoals of (2) are true. That is, ancestor(ann,Z) and ancestor(Z,john) must be proved true. PROLOG tries to match the subgoals in a left-to-right manner starting with ancestor(ann,Z). Starting from the top, this first matches statement (1) and so PROLOG tries to prove the body of (1), parent(ann,Z). Starting to search from the top again, this body first matches statement (3) and so PROLOG sets Z to mary. Now PROLOG tries to match the second subgoal of (2) as ancestor(mary,john). This matches (1) and so PROLOG tries to satisfy its body, parent(mary,john). However, there is no parent(mary,john) in statements (3) through (6) and so this search fails.

PROLOG then reconsiders its guess that Z should be mary. Since this choice did not work, it tries to find another value that will work. Another possibility arises from (4) by setting Z to susan. This technique of going back to try a different search path when one path fails is called backtracking, and is often used for problem solving.

With the choice of Z as susan, PROLOG attempts to prove ancestor(susan,john) is true. By (1), the body parent(susan,john) must be proved true. Indeed, the fact (3) does match and so the query

```
:-ancestor(ann,john).
```

is proved true since its conditions have been proved true.

Notice that the control structure of PROLOG is of the Markov algorithm type, in which searching for pattern matching is normally determined by the order in which the Horn clauses are entered. This contrasts with rule-based expert systems, which normally follow the Post paradigm, in which the order that rules are entered does not affect the search.

PROLOG has many other features and capabilities not mentioned in this brief introduction. From an expert systems point of view, the backtracking and pattern matching are very useful. The declarative nature of PROLOG is also very useful because a program specification is an executable program.

2.7 DIFFICULTIES WITH SEMANTIC NETS

Although semantic nets can be very useful in representing knowledge, they have limitations, such as the lack of link name standards discussed previously. This makes it difficult to understand what the net is really designed for and whether it was designed in a consistent manner. A complementary problem to naming links is the naming of nodes. If a node is labeled "chair," does it represent

a specific chair
the class of all chairs
the concept of a chair
the person who is the chair of a meeting

or something else? For a semantic net to represent **definitive knowledge**—that is, knowledge that can be defined—the link and node names must be rigorously defined. Of course, the same problems may occur in programming languages.

Another problem is the combinatorial explosion of searching nodes, especially if the response to a query is negative. For a query to produce a negative result, many or all of the links in a net may have to be searched. As shown in the traveling salesman problem in Chapter 1, the number of links is the factorial of the number of nodes minus one if they are all connected. Although not all representations will require this degree of connectivity, the possibility of a combinatorial explosion exists.

Semantic nets were originally proposed as models of human associative memory in which one node has links to others and information retrieval occurs due to a spreading activation of nodes. However, other mechanisms must also be available to the human brain for the reason that it does not take a long time for a human to answer the query—is there a football team on Pluto? There are about 10^{10} neurons in the human brain and about 10^{15} links. If all knowledge was represented by a semantic net, it would take a very, very long time to answer negative queries like the football question because of all the searching involved with 10^{15} links.

Semantic nets are logically inadequate because they cannot define knowledge in the way that logic can. A logic representation can specify a certain chair, some chairs, all chairs, no chairs, and so forth, as will be discussed later in this chapter. Another problem is that semantic nets are heuristically inadequate because there is no way to embed heuristic information in the net on how to efficiently search the net. A **heuristic** is a rule of thumb that may help in finding a solution but that is not guaranteed in the way an algorithm is guaranteed to find a solution. Heuristics are very important in AI because typical AI problems are so hard that an algorithmic solution does not exist or is too inefficient for practical use. The only standard control strategy built into a net that might help is inheritance, but not all problems may have this structure.

A number of approaches have been tried to correct the inherent problems of semantic nets. Logic enhancements have been made and heuristic enhancements have been tried by attaching procedures to nodes. The procedures will be executed when the node becomes activated. However, the resulting systems gained little in capability at the expense of the natural expressiveness of semantic nets. The conclusion of all this effort is that like any tool, semantic nets should be used for those things they do best, showing binary relationships, and not be distorted into a universal tool.

2.8 SCHEMATA

A semantic net is an example of a **shallow knowledge structure**. The shallowness occurs because all the knowledge in the semantic net is contained in the links and nodes. The term *knowledge structure* is analogous to a data structure in that it represents an ordered collection of knowledge rather than just data. A **deep** knowledge structure has causal knowledge that explains why something occurs. For example, it is possible to build a medical expert system with shallow knowledge as follows:

```
IF a person has a fever
THEN take an aspirin
```

But these systems do not know the fundamental biochemistry of the body and why aspirin decreases fever. The rule could have been defined:

```
IF a person has a pink monkey
THEN take a refrigerator
```

In other words, the expert system's knowledge is shallow because it is based on syntax rather than semantics, where any two words could be substituted for X and Y in the following rule

```
IF a person has a (X)
THEN take a (Y)
```

Note that (X) and (Y) are not variables in this rule, but represent any two words. Doctors have causal knowledge because they have taken many courses and have experience treating ill people. If a treatment is not working right, doctors can reason about it to find an alternative. In other words, an expert knows when to break the rules.

Many types of real world knowledge cannot be represented by the simple structure of a semantic net. More complex structures are needed to better represent complex knowledge structures. In AI, the term *schema* (plural *schemas* or *schematas*) is used to describe a more complex knowledge structure than the semantic net. The term *schema* comes from psychology, in which it refers to the continual organizing of knowledge or responses by a creature due to stimuli. That is, as creatures learn the relationship between a cause and its outcome, they will try to repeat the cause if pleasurable or avoid the cause if painful.

For example, the acts of eating and drinking are pleasurable **sensorimotor** schematas that involve coordinating information from the senses with the required motor (muscle) movements to eat and drink. A person does not have to think about this tacit knowledge to know to do these acts, and it is very difficult to explain exactly how it is done down to the level of controlling muscles. An even more difficult schema to explain is how to ride a bicycle. Try explaining the sense of balance!

Another type of schema is the **concept schema**. For example, everyone has a concept of *animal*. Most people who were asked to explain an animal would probably describe it in terms of something that has four legs and fur. Of course, the concept of *animal* differs depending on whether the person grew up on a farm, in a city, near a river, and so forth. However, we all have **stereotypes** in our minds of concepts. Although the term *stereotype* may have a negative meaning in casual language, in AI it means a typical example. Thus a stereotype of an animal to many people might be something like a dog.

A conceptual schema is an abstraction in which specific objects are classified by their general properties. For example, if you see a small red, roundish object with a green stem under a sign that says "Artificial Fruit," you will probably recognize it as an artificial apple. The object has the properties of applehood that you associate with the conceptual schema of apple, except for being a real apple, of course.

The conceptual schema of a real apple will include general properties of apples such as sizes, colors, tastes, uses, and so on. The schema will not include details of exactly where the apple was picked, the truck by which it was transported to the supermarket, the name of the person who put it on the shelf, and so forth. These details are not important to the properties that comprise your abstract concept of an apple. Also, note that a person who is blind may have a very different concept schema of an apple in which texture is most important.

By focusing on the general properties of an object, it is easier to reason about them without becoming distracted by irrelevant details. Customarily, schemas have an internal structure to their nodes whereas semantic nets do not. The label of a semantic net is all the knowledge about the node. A semantic net is like a data structure in computer science, in which the search key is also the data stored in the node. A schema is like a data structure in which nodes contain records. Each record may contain data, records, or pointers to other nodes.

2.9 FRAMES

One type of schema that has been used in many AI applications is the **frame** (Minsky 75). Another type of schema is the **script**, which is essentially a time-ordered sequence of frames (Schank 77). Proposed as a method for understanding vision, natural language, and other areas, frames provide a convenient structure for representing objects that are typical to a given situation such as stereotypes. In particular, frames are useful for simulating commonsense knowledge, which is a very difficult area for computers to master. Semantic nets are basically two-dimensional representations of knowledge; frames add a third dimension by allowing nodes to have structures. These structures can be simple values or other frames.

The basic characteristic of a frame is that it represents related knowledge about a narrow subject that has much default knowledge. A frame system would be a good choice for describing a mechanical device such as an automobile. Components of the car such as the engine, body, brakes, and so forth would be related to give an overall view of their relationships. Further detail about the components could be obtained by examining the structure of the frames. Although individual brands of cars will vary, most cars have common characteristics such as wheels, engine, body, transmission, and so forth. The frame contrasts with the semantic net, which is generally used for broad knowledge representation. Just as with semantic nets, there are no standards for defining frame-based systems. A number of special-purpose languages have been designed for frames, such as FRL, SRL, KRL, KEE, HP-RL, and frame enhancement features to LISP such as LOOPS and FLAVORS (Finin 86).

A frame is analogous to a record structure in a high-level language such as Pascal or an atom with its property list in LISP. Corresponding to the fields and values of a record are the **slots** and slot **fillers** of a frame. A frame is basically a group of slots and fillers that defines a stereotypical object. An example of a frame for a car is shown in Figure 2.8. In OAV terms, the car is the object, the slot name is the attribute, and the filler is the value.

Slots	Fillers
manufacturer	General Motors
model	Chevrolet Caprice
year	1979
transmission	automatic
engine	gasoline
tires	4
color	blue

Figure 2.8 A Car Frame

Most frames are not as simple as that shown in Figure 2.8. The utility of frames lies in hierarchical frame systems and inheritance. By using frames in the filler slots and inheritance, very powerful knowledge representation systems can be built. In particular, frame-based expert systems are very useful for representing causal knowledge because their information is organized by cause and effect. By contrast, rule-based expert systems generally rely on unorganized knowledge that is not causal.

Some frame-based tools such as KEE allow a wide range of items to be stored in slots. Frame slots may hold rules, graphics, comments, debugging information, questions for users, hypotheses concerning a situation, or other frames.

Frames are generally designed to represent either generic or specific knowledge. Figure 2.9 illustrates a generic frame for the concept of property.

Slots	Fillers
name	property
specialization_of	a_kind_of object
types	(car, boat, house)
	if-added: Procedure ADD_PROPERTY
owner	default: government
	if-needed: Procedure FIND_OWNER
location	(home, work, mobile)
status	(missing, poor, good)
under_warranty	(yes,no)

Figure 2.9 A Generic Frame for Property

The fillers may be values, such as property in the name slot, or a range of values, as in the types slot. The slots may also contain procedures attached to the slots, called *procedural attachments*. These are generally of three types. The **if-needed** types are procedures to be executed when a filler value is needed but none is initially present or the **default** value is not suitable. Defaults are of primary importance in frames because they model some aspects of the brain. Defaults correspond to the expectations of a situation that we build up based on experience. When we encounter a new situation, the closest frame is modified to help us adjust to the situation. People do not start from scratch in every new situation. Instead, the defaults or other fillers are modified. Defaults are often used to represent commonsense knowledge. Commonsense knowledge can be considered to be the knowledge that is generally known. We use commonsense when no more situation specific knowledge is available.

The **if-added** type is run for procedures to be executed when a value is to be added to a slot. In the types slot, the if-added procedure executes a procedure called ADD-PROPERTY to add a new type of property, if necessary. For example, this procedure would be run for jewelry, TV, stereo, and so forth since the types slot does not contain these values.

An **if-removal** type is run whenever a value is to be removed from a slot. This type of procedure would be run if a value was obsolete.

Slot fillers may also contain relations, as in the specialization_of slots. The a-kind-of and is-a relations are used in Figures 2.9, 2.10, and 2.11 to show how these frames are hierarchically related. The frames of Figures 2.9 and 2.10 are generic frames whereas that of Figure 2.11 is a specific frame because it is an instance of the car frame. We have adopted the convention here that a-kind-of relations are generic and is-a relations are specific.

Slots	Fillers
name	car
specialization_of	a-kind-of property
types	(sedan, sports, convertible)
manufacturer	(GM, Ford, Chrysler)
location	mobile
wheels	4
transmission	(manual, automatic)
engine	(gasoline, diesel)

Figure 2.10 Car Frame—A Generic Subframe of Property

Frame systems are designed so more generic frames are at the top of the hierarchy. It is assumed that frames can be customized for specific cases by modifying the default cases and creating more specific frames. Frames attempt to model real-world objects by using generic knowledge for the majority of an object's attributes and specific knowledge for special cases. For example, we commonly think of birds as creatures that can fly. Yet certain types of birds such as penguins and ostriches cannot fly. These types represent more specific classes of birds and their characteristics would be found lower in a frame hierarchy than birds like canaries or robins. In other words, the top of the bird frame hierarchy specifies things that are more true of all birds and the lower levels reflect the fuzzy boundaries between real-world objects. The object that has all of the typical characteristics is called a *prototype*, which literally means the first type.

Slots	Fillers
name	John's car
specialization_of	is_a car
manufacturer	GM
owner	John Doe
transmission	automatic
engine	gasoline
status	good
under_warranty	yes

Figure 2.11 An Instance of a Car Frame

Frames may also be classified by their applications. A **situational frame** contains knowledge about what to expect in a given situation, such as a birthday party. An **action frame** contains slots that specify the actions to be performed in a given situation. That is, the fillers are procedures to perform some actions, such as removing a defective part from a conveyer belt. An action frame represents procedural knowledge. The combination of situational and action frames can be used to describe cause-and-effect relationships in the form of **causal knowledge frames**.

Very sophisticated frame systems have been built for a variety of tasks. Two of the most impressive systems that have demonstrated the power of frames can creatively discover mathematical concepts (Lenat 77) and describe mathematical understanding in domains such as that of linear algebra (Rissland 78). In these systems the slots were used as generators of tasks such as questions to answer. The AM system of Lenat would make conjectures of interesting new concepts and explore them.

2.10 DIFFICULTIES WITH FRAMES

Frames were originally conceived as a paradigm for representing stereotyped knowledge. The important characteristic of a stereotype is that it have well-defined features so that many of its slots have default values. Mathematical concepts are good examples of stereotypes well suited to frames. The frame paradigm has an intuitive appeal because frames' organizcd representation of knowledge is generally easier to understand than either logic or production systems with many rules (Jackson 86). However, major problems have appeared in frame systems that allow unrestrained alteration or cancellation of slots (Brachman 85). The classic example of this problem is illustrated with a frame describing elephants in Figure 2.12.

name	elephant
specialization_of	a-kind-of mammal
color	grey
legs	4
trunk	a cylinder

Figure 2.12 Elephant Frame

At first sight the elephant frame seems like a reasonable generic description of elephants. However, suppose there exists a three-legged elephant called Clyde. Clyde may have lost a leg due to a hunting accident or may simply have lied about losing a leg to get his name in this book. The significant thing is that the elephant frame claims that an elephant has four legs, not three. Thus we cannot consider the elephant frame to be a definition of an elephant.

Of course, the frame could be modified to allow three-legged, two-legged, one-legged, or even legless elephants as exceptions. However, this does not provide a very good definition. Additional problems may arise with the other slots. Suppose Clyde gets a bad case of jaundice and his skin turns yellow. Is he then no longer an elephant?

An alternative to viewing a frame as a definition is to consider it as describing a typical elephant. However, this leads to other problems because of inheritance. Notice that the elephant frame says that an elephant is a-kind-of mammal. Because we are interpreting frames as typical, our frame system says that a typical elephant is a typical mammal. Although an elephant is a mammal, it is probably not a typical mammal. On the basis of quantity, people, cows, sheep, or rats are probably more representative of typical mammals.

Most frame systems do not provide a way of defining unalterable slots. Any slot can be changed, so the properties a frame inherits can be altered or cancelled anywhere in the hierarchy. This means that every frame is really a primitive frame and because there is no guarantee that properties are common and each frame makes up its own rules. Nothing is really certain in such an unrestrained system, and so it is impossible to make universal statements such as those made in defining an elephant. Also, from simpler definitions such as that for an elephant, it is impossible to reliably build composite objects such as elephant-with-three-legs. The same types of problems apply to semantic nets with inheritance. If the properties of any node can be changed, then nothing is certain.

2.11 LOGIC AND SETS

In addition to rules, frames, and semantic nets, knowledge can be represented by the symbols of **logic**, which is the study of the rules of exact reasoning. An important part of reasoning is inferring conclusions from premises. The application of computers to perform reasoning has resulted in **logic programming** and the development of logic-based languages such as PROLOG. Logic is also of primary importance in expert systems in which the inference engine reasons from facts to conclusions. In fact, a descriptive term for logic programming and expert systems is **automated reasoning systems**.

The earliest formal logic was developed by the Greek philosopher Aristotle in the fourth century B.C. Aristotelian logic is based on the **syllogism**, of which he invented fourteen types. Five more were invented in medieval times. Syllogisms have two **premises** and one **conclusion**, which is inferred from the premises. The following is the classic example of a syllogism:

```
Premise:    All men are mortal
Premise:    Socrates is a man
Conclusion: Socrates is mortal
```

In a syllogism the **premises** provide the evidence from which the conclusion must necessarily follow. A syllogism is a way of representing knowledge. Another way is a **Venn diagram**, shown in Figure 2.13.

The outer circle represents all mortal creatures. The inner circle representing man is drawn entirely within the mortal circle to indicate that all men are mortal. Since Socrates is a man, the circle representing him is drawn entirely within the second circle. Strictly speaking, the circle representing Socrates should be a point, since a circle implies a class, but for readability we'll use circles for all. The conclusion that Socrates is mortal is a consequence of the fact that his circle is within that of mortal creatures and so he must be mortal.

In mathematical terms, a circle of the Venn diagram represents a set, which is a collection of objects. The objects within a set are called its **elements**. Some examples of sets are

```
A = {1,3,5}
B = {1,2,3,4,5}
C = {0,2,4,...}
D = {...,-4,-2,0,2,4,...}
E = {airplanes,balloons,blimps,jets}
F = {airplanes,balloons}
```

where the dots, ... , called ellipses, indicate that the terms continued on indefinitely.

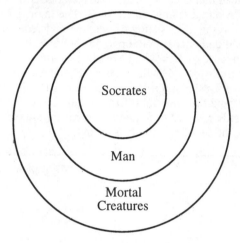

Figure 2.13 Venn Diagram

The Greek letter epsilon, $\in$, indicates that an element is a member of a set. For example, $1 \in A$, means that the number 1 is an element of the set A defined previously. If an element is not a member of a set, the symbol $\notin$ is used, as in $2 \notin A$.

If two arbitrary sets, such as X and Y, are defined so that every element of X is an element of Y, then X is a **subset** of Y and is written in the mathematical form X $\subset$ Y or Y $\supset$ X. From the definition of a subset it follows that every set is a subset of itself. A subset that is not the set itself is called a **proper subset**. For example, the set X defined previously is a proper subset of Y. In discussing sets it is useful to consider the sets as subsets of a **universal set**. The universal set changes as the topic of discussion changes. Figure 2.14 illustrates a subset formed as the **intersection** of two sets in the universe of all cars. In discussing numbers the universe would be all numbers. The universe is drawn as a rectangle surrounding its subsets. Universal sets are not used just for convenience. The indiscriminate use of conditions to define sets can result in logical paradoxes.

If we let A be the set of all blue cars, B the set of all cars with manual transmissions, and C the set of all blue cars with manual transmissions, we can write

```
C = A ∩ B
```

in which the symbol $\cap$ represents the intersection of sets. Another way of writing this is in terms of elements x as follows

$$C = \{x \in U \mid (x \in A) \wedge (x \in B)\}$$

where

U represents the universe set.
| is read as "such that" (a colon, :, is sometimes used instead of |).
$\wedge$ is the **logical AND**.

The expression for C is read that C consists of those elements x in the universe such that x is an element of A and x is an element of B. The logical AND comes from Boolean algebra. An expression consisting of two operands connected by the logical AND operator is true if and only if both operands are true. If A and B have no elements in common, then $A \cap B = \emptyset$ in which the Greek letter phi, $\emptyset$, represents the **empty set** or **null set**, { }, which has no elements. Sometimes the Greek letter lambda, Λ, is used for the null set. Other notations for the universe set are sometimes the numeral 1 and the numeral 0 for the null set. Although the null set has no elements, it is still a set. An analogy is a restaurant with a set of customers. If nobody comes, the set of customers is empty.

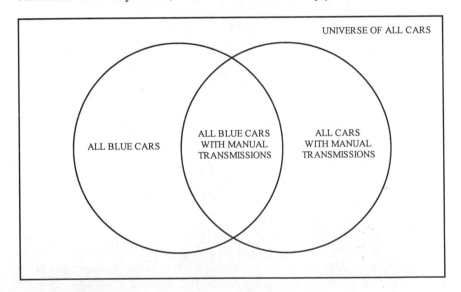

Figure 2.14 Intersecting Sets

Another set operation is **union**, which is the set of all elements in either A or B. This is represented as

$$A \cup B = \{x \in U \mid (x \in A) \vee (x \in B)\}$$

where

$\cup$ is the set operator for **union**
$\vee$ is the **logical OR** operator.

The **complement** of set A is the set of all elements not in A.

$$A' = \{x \in U \mid \sim(x \in A)\}$$

where

    the prime, ´, means complement of a set
    the tilde, ~, is the **logical NOT** operator

The Venn diagrams for these basic operations are shown in Figure 2.15.

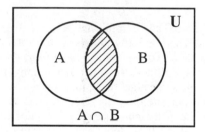

(a) INTERSECTION OF SETS

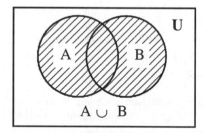

(b) UNION OF SETS

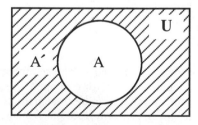

(c) COMPLEMENT OF A SET

Figure 2.15 Basic Set Operations

2.12 PROPOSITIONAL LOGIC

The oldest and one of the simplest types of **formal logic** is the syllogism. The term *formal* means that the logic is concerned with the form of logical statements rather than their meaning. In other words, formal logic is concerned with the syntax of statements rather than their semantics. Although the term *formal logic* may make it sound intimidating, it is no more difficult than algebra. In fact, algebra is really a formal logic of numbers. For example, suppose you were asked to solve the following problem: A school has 25 computers with a total of 60 memory boards. Some of the computers have two memory boards, and some have four. How many computers of each type are there? The solution can be written algebraically as follows:

```
25 = X + Y
60 = 2X + 4Y
```

which can easily be solved for $X = 20$ and $Y = 5$.

Now consider this problem. There are 25 animals with a total of 60 legs in a barnyard. Some of the animals have two legs, others have four. (Note: Clyde our three-legged elephant is in Africa, not the barnyard.) How many animals of each type are there? As you can see, the same algebraic equations apply whether we are talking about computers, animals, or anything else. In the same way that algebraic equations let us concentrate on the mathematical manipulation of symbols without regard to what they represent, formal logic lets us concentrate on the reasoning without becoming confused by the objects we are reasoning about.

As an example of formal logic, consider the syllogism with the nonsense words *squeeg* and *moof.*

```
Premise:    All squeegs are moofs
Premise:    John is a squeeg
Conclusion: John is a moof
```

Although the words *squeeg* and *moof* are nonsense and have no meaning, the *form* of this argument is still correct. That is, the argument is **valid** no matter which words are used because the syllogism has a valid form. In fact any syllogism of the form

```
Premise:    All X are Y
Premise:    Z is a X
Conclusion: Z is a Y
```

is valid no matter what is substituted for X, Y, and Z. This example illustrates that meanings do not matter in formal logic. Only the form or appearance is important. This concept of separating the form from the meaning or semantics is what makes logic such a powerful tool. By separating the form from the semantics, the validity of an argument can be considered objectively, without prejudice caused by semantics. This is like algebra, in which the correctness of expressions such as $X + X = 2X$ holds whether X is an integer, apples, airplanes, or anything.

Aristotelian syllogisms were the foundations of logic until 1847, when the English mathematician George Boole published the first book describing **symbolic logic**. Although Leibnitz had developed his own version of symbolic logic in the seventeenth century, it never achieved general use. One of the new concepts that Boole proposed was a modification of the Aristotelian view that the subject have existence, called *existential import*. According to the classic Aristotelian view, a proposition such as "all mermaids swim well" could not be used as either a premise or a conclusion because mermaids don't exist. The Boolean view, now called the *modern view*, relaxes this restriction. The importance of the modern view is that empty classes can now be reasoned about. For example, a proposition such as "all disks that fail are cheap" could not be used in an Aristotelian syllogism unless there was at least one disk that had failed.

Another contribution by Boole was the definition of a set of **axioms** consisting of symbols representing both objects and classes and algebraic operations to manipulate the symbols. Axioms are the fundamental definitions from which logical systems such as mathematics and logic itself are built. Using only the axioms, theorems can be constructed. A theorem is a statement that can be proved by showing how it is derived from the axioms. Between 1910 and 1913, Whitehead and Russell published their monumental 2000-page, three-volume work *Principia Mathematica*, which showed a formal logic as the basis of mathematics. This was hailed as a great milestone because it appeared to put mathematics on a firm foundation rather than appealing to intuition by totally eliminating the meaning of arithmetic, and instead concentrating on forms and their manipulation. Because of this, mathematics has been described as a collection of meaningless marks on paper. However, in 1931 Gödel proved that formal systems based on axioms could not always be proved internally consistent and thus free from contradictions.

Propositional logic, sometimes called *propositional calculus*, is a symbolic logic for manipulating propositions. In particular, propositional logic deals with the manipulation of **logical variables**, which represent propositions. Although most people think of calculus in terms of the calculus invented by Newton and Leibnitz, the word has a more general meaning. It comes from the Latin word *calculus*, a little stone used for calculations. The general meaning of calculus is a special system for manipulating symbols. Other terms used for propositional logic are **statement calculus** and **sentential calculus**. Sentences are generally classified as one of four types, as illustrated in Table 2.2.

Type	Example
Imperative	Do what I tell you!
Interrogative	What is that?
Exclamatory	That's great!
Declarative	A square has four equal sides.

Table 2.2 Types of Sentences

Propositional logic is concerned with the subset of declarative sentences that can be classified as either true or false. A sentence such as "A square has four equal sides" has a definite truth value of true, whereas the sentence "George Washington was the second president" has a truth value of false. A sentence whose truth value can be determined is called a *statement* or *proposition*. A statement is also called a *closed sentence* because its truth value is not open to question.

If I put a preface to this book stating "everything in these pages is a lie," that statement cannot be classified as either true or false. If it is true then I told the truth in the preface—which I cannot do. If it is untrue, then every word written must be true, so I lied—which also cannot be true. Statements of this type are known as the Liar's Paradox. Statements that cannot be answered absolutely are called **open sentences**. The sentence "Spinach tastes wonderful" is also an open sentence because it is true for some people and not true for others. The sentence "He is tall" is called an open sentence because it contains a variable "He." Truth values cannot be assigned to open sentences until we know the specific person or instance referred to by the variable. Another difficulty with this sentence is the meaning of the word "tall." What's tall to some people is not tall to others. Although this ambiguity of "tall" cannot be handled in the propositional or predicate calculus, it can be easily dealt with in fuzzy logic, described in Chapter 5.

A **compound statement** is formed by using logical connectives on individual statements. The common logical connectives are shown in Table 2.3.

Connective	Meaning
∧	AND; **conjunction**
∨	OR; **disjunction**
~	NOT; **negation**
→	if . . . then; **conditional**
↔	if and only if; **biconditional**

Table 2.3 Some Logical Connectives

Strictly speaking, the negation is not a connective because it is a unary operation that applies to the one operand following, so it doesn't really connect anything. The negation has higher precedence than the other operators and so it is not necessary to put parentheses around it. That is, a statement like ~p ∧ q means the same as (~p) ∧ q.

The conditional is analogous to the arrow of production rules in that it is expressed as an if . . . then form. For example

```
if it is raining then carry an umbrella
```

can be put in the form

```
p → q
```

where

```
p = it is raining
q = carry an umbrella
```

Sometimes the ⊃ is used for →. Another term for the conditional is *material implication*.

The biconditional, p ↔ q, is equivalent to

```
(p → q) ∧ (q → p)
```

and is true only when p and q have the same truth values. That is, p ↔ q is true only when p and q are both true or when they are both false. The biconditional has the following meanings:

```
p if and only if q
q if and only if p
if p then q, and if q then p
```

A **tautology** is a compound statement that is always true, whether its individual statements are true or false. A **contradiction** is a compound statement that is always false. A **contingent** statement is one that is neither a tautology nor a contradiction. Tautologies and contradictions are called analytically true and analytically false, respectively, because their truth values can be determined by their forms alone. For example, the truth table of p ∨ ~ p shows it is a tautology, whereas p ∧ ~ p is a contradiction.

If a conditional is also a tautology then it is called an *implication* and has the symbol ⇒ in place of →. A biconditional that is also a tautology is called a *logical equivalence* or *material equivalence* and is symbolized by either ⇔ or ≡. Two statements that are logically equivalent always have the same truth values. For example, p ≡ ~ ~p.

Unfortunately, this is not the only possible definition for implication, since there are sixteen possible truth tables for two variables that can take on true and false values. In fact, one paper has reviewed eleven different definitions of the implication operator used in expert systems (Whalen 85).

The conditional does not mean exactly the same as the IF . . . THEN in a procedural language or a rule-based expert system. In procedural and expert systems, the IF . . . THEN means to execute the actions following the THEN *if* the conditions of the IF are true. In logic, the conditional is defined by its truth table. Its meaning can be translated into natural language in a number of ways. For example, if

    p → q

where p and q are any statements, this can be translated as

    p implies q
    if p then q
    p, only if q
    p is sufficient for q
    q if p
    q is necessary for p

As an example, let p represent "you are 18 or older" and q represent "you can vote." The conditional p → q can mean

    you are 18 or older implies you can vote
    if you are 18 or older then you can vote
    you are 18 or older, only if you can vote
    you are 18 or older is sufficient for you can vote
    you can vote if you are 18 or older
    you can vote is necessary for you are 18 or older

In some cases, a change of wording is necessary to make these grammatically correct English sentences. The last example says if q does not occur, then neither will p. It is expressed in proper English as "Being able to vote requires that you be 18 or older."

Values for the binary logical connectives are shown in Table 2.4. These are binary connectives because they require two operands. The negation connective, ~, is a unary operator on the one operand that follows it, as shown in Table 2.5.

A set of logical connectives is **adequate** if every truth function can be represented using only the connectives from the adequate set. Examples of adequate sets are { ~, ∧, ∨ }, { ~, ∧ }, {~, ∨ }, and {~, → }.

A single element set is called a **singleton**. There are two adequate singleton sets. These are the NOT-OR (**NOR**) and the NOT-AND (**NAND**). The NOR set is { ↓ } and the NAND set is { | }. The " | " operator is called a **stroke** or **alternative denial**. It is used to deny that both p and q are true. That is, p | q affirms that at least one of the statements, p or q, is true. The **joint denial operator**, "↓", denies that either p or q is true. That is, p ↓ q affirms that both p and q are false.

p	q	p ∧ q	p ∨ q	p → q	p ↔ q
T	T	T	T	T	T
T	F	F	T	F	F
F	T	F	T	T	F
F	F	F	F	T	T

Table 2.4 Truth Table of the Binary Logical Connectives

p	~p
T	F
F	T

Table 2.5 Truth Table of Negation

2.13 THE FIRST ORDER PREDICATE LOGIC

Although propositional logic is useful, it does have limitations. The major problem is that propositional logic can deal only with complete statements. That is, it cannot examine the internal structure of a statement. Propositional logic cannot even prove the validity of a syllogism such as

```
All humans are mortal
All women are humans
Therefore, all women are mortal
```

In order to analyze more general cases, **predicate logic** was developed. Its simplest form is the **first order** predicate logic, the basis of logic programming languages such as PROLOG. In this section we will use the term *predicate logic* to refer to first order predicate logic. Propositional logic is a subset of predicate logic.

Predicate logic is concerned with the internal structure of sentences. In particular, it is concerned with the use of special words called *quantifiers*, such as "all," "some," and "no." These words are very important because they explicitly quantify other words and so make sentences more exact. All the quantifiers are concerned with "how many" and thus permit a wider scope of expression than does propositional logic.

2.14 THE UNIVERSAL QUANTIFIER

A universally quantified sentence has the same truth value for all replacements in the same domain. The **universal quantifier** is represented by the symbol $\forall$ followed by one or more arguments for the **domain variable**. The symbol $\forall$ is interpreted as "for every" or "for all." For example, in the domain of numbers

$$(\forall x) \ (x \ + \ x \ = \ 2x)$$

states that for every x (where x is a number), the sentence x + x = 2x is true. If we represent this sentence by the symbol p, then it can be expressed even more briefly as

$$(\forall x) \ (p)$$

As another example, let p represent the sentence "all dogs are animals," as in

$$(\forall x) \ (p) \ \equiv (\forall x) \ (if \ x \ is \ a \ dog \ \rightarrow \ x \ is \ an \ animal)$$

The opposite statement is "no dogs are animals" and is written as

$$(\forall x) \ (if \ x \ is \ a \ dog \ \rightarrow \ \sim x \ is \ an \ animal)$$

It may also be read as

```
Every dog is not an animal
All dogs are not animals
```

As another example, "all triangles are polygons" is written as follows.

$$(\forall x) \ (x \ is \ a \ triangle \ \rightarrow \ x \ is \ a \ polygon)$$

and is read "for all x, if x is a triangle, then x is a polygon." A shorter way of writing logic statements involving predicates is using **predicate functions** to describe the properties of the subject. The above logic statement can also be written

$$(\forall x) \ (triangle(x) \ \rightarrow \ polygon(x))$$

Predicate functions are usually written in a briefer notation using capital letters to represent the predicates. For example, let T = triangle and P = polygon. Then the triangle statement can be written even more briefly as

$$(\forall x) \ (T(x) \ \rightarrow \ P(x)) \quad or \quad (\forall y) \ (T(y) \ \rightarrow \ P(y))$$

Note that any variables could be used in place of the dummy variables x and y. As another example, let H be the predicate function for *human* and M be the function for *mortal*. Then the statement that all humans are mortal can be written as

$$(\forall x) \ (H(x) \ \rightarrow \ M(x))$$

and is read that for all x, if x is human, then x is mortal. This predicate logic sentence can also be represented as a semantic net, as shown in Figure 2.16. It can also be expressed in terms of rules as

```
IF x is human
THEN x is mortal
```

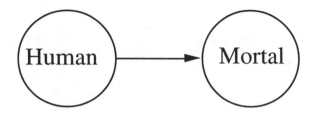

Figure 2.16 Semantic Net Representation of a Predicate Logic Statement

The universal quantifier can also be interpreted as a conjunction of predicates about instances. As mentioned earlier, an instance is a particular case. For example, a dog named Sparkler is a particular instance of the class of dogs and could be written as

```
Dog(Sparkler)
```

where Dog is the predicate function and Sparkler is an instance.
    A predicate logic sentence such as

$$(\forall x)\ P(x)$$

can be interpreted in terms of instances a_1 as

$$P(a_1)\ \wedge\ P(a_2)\ \wedge\ P(a_3)\ \wedge\ \ldots\ P(a_N)$$

where the ellipses indicate that the predicates extend on to all members of the class. This statement says that the predicate applies to all instances of the class.
    Multiple quantifiers can be used. For example, the commutative law of addition for numbers requires two quantifiers, as in

$$(\forall x)\ (\forall y)\ (x + y = y + x)$$

which states that "for every x and for every y, the sum of x and y equals the sum of y and x."

2.15 THE EXISTENTIAL QUANTIFIER

Another type of quantifier is the **existential quantifier**. An existential quantifier describes a statement as being true for at least one member of the domain. This is a restricted form of the universal quantifier that says that a statement is true for all members of the domain. The existential quantifier is written as $\exists$ followed by one or more arguments. For example

```
(∃ x) (x · x = 1)
(∃ x) (elephant(x) ∧ name(Clyde))
```

The first sentence above states that there is some x whose product with itself equals 1. The second statement says there is some elephant with the name Clyde.

The existential quantifier may be read in a number of ways, such as

```
there exists
at least one
for some
there is one
some
```

As another example,

```
(∀ x) (elephant(x) → four-legged(x))
```

says that all elephants are four-legged. However, the statement that some elephants are three-legged is written with the logical AND and existential quantifier as follows.

```
(∃ x) (elephant(x) ∧ three-legged(x))
```

Just as the universal quantifier can be expressed as a conjunction, the existential quantifier can be expressed as a disjunction of instances, a_1.

```
P(a₁) ∨ P(a₂) ∨ P(a₃) ∨  ... P(aₙ)
```

Quantified statements and their negations for the example in which P represents "elephants are mammals" are shown in Table 2.6. The numbers in parentheses are just to identify the examples for the following discussion.

Example		Meaning
(1 a)	(∀ x) (P)	All elephants are mammals.
(1 b)	(∃ x) (~P)	Some elephants are not mammals.
(2 a)	(∃ x) (P)	Some elephants are mammals.
(2 b)	(∀ x) (~P)	No elephants are mammals.

Table 2.6 Examples of Negated Quantifiers

Examples (1 a) and (1 b) are negations of each other, as are (2 a) and (2 b). Notice that the negation of a universally quantified statement of (1 a) is an existentially quantified statement of the negation of P as shown by (1 b). Likewise, the negation of an existentially quantified statement of (2 a) is the universally quantified statement of the negation of P as shown by (2 b).

2.16 QUANTIFIERS AND SETS

Quantifiers may be used to define sets over a universe, U, as shown in Table 2.7.

The relation that A is a proper subset of B, written as $A \subset B$, means that while all elements in A are in B, there is at least one element in B that is not in A. Letting E represent elephants and M represent mammals, the set relation

$$E \subset M$$

states that all elephants are mammals, but not all mammals are elephants. Letting G = grey and F = four-legged, all grey, four-legged elephants are mammals is written

$$(E \cap G \cap F) \subset M$$

Set Expression	Logical Equivalent
$A = B$	$\forall x \, (x \in A \leftrightarrow x \in B)$
$A \subseteq B$	$\forall x \, (x \in A \rightarrow x \in B)$
$A \cap B$	$\forall x \, (x \in A \wedge x \in B)$
$A \cup B$	$\forall x \, (x \in A \vee x \in B)$
A'	$\forall x \, (x \in U \mid \sim(x \in A))$
U (Universe)	T (True)
$\emptyset$ (empty set)	F (False)

Table 2.7 Some Set Expressions and Their Logical Equivalents

Using the following definitions, some examples of quantified sentences are shown:

```
E = elephants
R = reptiles
G = grey
F = four-legged
D = dogs
M = mammals

No elephants are reptiles
E ∩ R = Ø
Some elephants are grey
E ∩ G ≠ Ø
No elephants are grey
E ∩ G = Ø
Some elephants are not grey
E ∩ G′ ≠ Ø
All elephants are gray and four-legged
E ⊂ (G ∩ F)
All elephants and dogs are mammals
(E ∪ D) ⊂ M
Some elephants are four-legged and are grey
(E ∩ F ∩ G) ≠ Ø
```

As another analogy of sets and logic forms, de Morgan's laws are shown in Table 2.8, where the equivalence symbol, $\equiv$, the (biconditional) means that the statement on the left has the same truth value as the statement on the right. That is, the statements are equivalent.

Set	Logic
$(A \cap B)' \equiv A' \cup B'$	$\sim(p \wedge q) \equiv \sim p \vee \sim q$
$(A \cup B)' \equiv A' \cap B'$	$\sim(p \vee q) \equiv \sim p \wedge \sim q$

Table 2.8 Set and Logic Forms of de Morgan's Laws

2.17 LIMITATIONS OF PREDICATE LOGIC

Although predicate logic is very useful in many situations, there are some types of statements that cannot even be expressed in predicate logic using the universal and existential quantifiers (Rescher 64). For example, the following statement cannot be expressed in predicate logic:

```
Most of the class received As
```

In this statement the quantifier *Most* means more than half.

The *Most* quantifier cannot be expressed in terms of the universal and existential quantifiers. To implement *Most*, a logic must provide some predicates for counting, as in fuzzy logic, described in Chapter 5. Another limitation of predicate logic is in expressing things that are sometimes but not always true. This problem can also be solved by fuzzy logic. However, introducing counting also introduces more complications into the logic system and makes it more like mathematics.

2.18 SUMMARY

In this chapter we reviewed the elements of the theory of knowledge and techniques for representing knowledge. Knowledge representation is of major importance in expert systems. Knowledge can be classified in a number of ways such as *a priori*, *a posteriori*, procedural, declarative, and tacit. Production rules, semantic nets, schemata, frames, and logic are common methods by which knowledge is represented in expert systems. Each of these paradigms has advantages and disadvantages. Before designing an expert system you should decide which is the best paradigm for the problem to be solved. Rather than trying to use one tool for all problems, pick the best tool for that particular problem.

PROBLEMS

2.1 Draw a semantic net for computers using AKO and IS-A links. Consider the classes of microcomputer, minicomputer, mainframe, supercomputer, computing system, dedicated, general purpose, board-level, computer-on-a-chip, single processor, and multi processor. Include specific instances.

2.2   Draw a semantic net for computer communications using AKO and IS-A links. Consider the classes of local area net, wide area net, token ring, star, centralized, decentralized, distributed, modems, telecommunications, bulletin boards, and electronic mail. Include specific instances.

2.3   Draw a frame system for the building in which you are attending classes. Consider offices, classrooms, laboratories, and so forth. Include instances with filled slots for one type of each frame such as office and classroom.

2.4   Draw an action frame system explaining what to do in case of hardware failure for your computer system. Consider disk crash, power supply, CPU, and memory problems.

2.5   Draw the Venn diagram and write the set expression for the following:

    (a)   the exclusive-OR of two sets, A and B, consists of all elements that are in one, but not both sets. The exclusive-OR is also called the *symmetric set difference* and is symbolized by the "/ ". For example,

$$\{1,2\} / \{2,3\} = \{1,3\}$$

    (b)   the **set difference** of two sets, symbolized by "–", consists of all the elements in the first set that are not also in the second. For example,

$$\{1,2\} - \{2,3\} = \{1\}$$

where $\{1,2\}$ is the first set and $\{2,3\}$ is the second.

2.6   Write the truth tables and determine which of the following are tautologies, contradictions, or **contingent statements**, and which are neither. For (a) and (b), first express the statements with logic symbols and connectives.

    (a)   If I pass this course and make an 'A' then
        I pass this course or I make an 'A'.
    (b)   If I pass this course then I make an 'A'
        and
        I pass this course and I do not make an 'A'.
    (c) $((A \wedge {\sim}B \rightarrow (C \wedge {\sim}C)) \rightarrow (A \rightarrow B)$
    (d) $(A \rightarrow B) \wedge ({\sim}B \vee C) \wedge (A \wedge {\sim}C)$
    (e) $A \rightarrow {\sim}B$

2.7   Two sentences are logically equivalent if and only if they have the same truth value. Thus if A and B are any statements, the biconditional statement $A \leftrightarrow B$, or the equivalence, $A \equiv B$ will be true in every case, giving a tautology. Determine (a) whether the two sentences below are logically equivalent by writing them using logical symbols and (b) whether the truth table of their biconditional is a tautology.

If you eat a banana split, then you cannot eat a pie.
If you eat a pie, then you cannot eat a banana split.

2.8   Write the logical equivalent corresponding to set difference and symmetric set difference.

2.9   Show that the following are identities for any sets A, B, and C and $\emptyset$ as the null set.

(a) $(A \cup B) \equiv (B \cup A)$
(b) $(A \cup B) \cup C \equiv A \cup (B \cup C)$
(c) $A \cup \emptyset \equiv A$
(d) $A \cap B \equiv B \cap A$
(e) $A \cap A' \equiv \emptyset$

2.10   Write the following in quantified form:

(a) All dogs are mammals.
(b) No dog is an elephant.
(c) Some programs have bugs.
(d) None of my programs have bugs.
(e) All of your programs have bugs.

2.11   The **power set**, P(S), of a set S is the set of all elements that are subsets of S. P(S) will always have at least the null set, $\emptyset$, and S as members.

(a) Find the power set of A = {2, 4, 6}.
(b) For a set with N elements, how many elements does the power set have?

2.12   (a) Write the truth table for the following:

Meaning	Definition
either p or q	$(p \vee q) \wedge {\sim}(p \wedge q)$
neither p nor q	${\sim}(p \vee q)$
p unless q	${\sim}q \rightarrow p$
p because q	$(p \wedge q) \wedge (q \rightarrow p)$
no p is q	$p \rightarrow {\sim}q$

(b) Show that $(p \vee q) \wedge {\sim}(p \wedge q) \equiv p/q$ where "/" is the exclusive OR.

2.13   (a) Write the NOR and NAND truth tables.
(b) Prove that $\{\downarrow\}$ and $\{\,|\,\}$ are adequate sets by expressing ${\sim}$, $\wedge$, and $\vee$ in terms of $\downarrow$ and then in terms of $|$ by constructing truth tables to show the logical equivalences as follows.

$${\sim}{\sim}p \equiv p$$
$$(p \wedge q) \equiv (p \downarrow p) \downarrow (q \downarrow q)$$
$${\sim}p \equiv p \,|\, p$$
$$(p \vee q) \equiv (p \,|\, p) \,|\, (q \,|\, q)$$

(c) Since $p \rightarrow q \equiv {\sim}(p \wedge {\sim}q)$, express $p \rightarrow q$ in terms of $\downarrow$.
(d) What are the advantages and disadvantages of using adequate singleton sets in terms of (i) notation and (ii) construction of chips for electronic circuits?

2.14   What are the advantages and disadvantages of designing an expert system with knowledge about several domains?

BIBLIOGRAPHY

(Angeles 81). Peter A. Angeles, *Dictionary of Philosophy,* Barnes & Noble Books, 1981.

(Barr 81). Arron Barr and Edward A. Feigenbaum, eds., *The Handbook of Artificial Intelligence, Vol. 1,* William Kaufmann, Inc., 1981.

(Brachman 80). R. J. Brachman and B. C. Smith, eds., *SIGART Newsletter, Special Issue on Knowledge Representation*, **70**, Feb. 1980.

(Brachman 83). R. J. Brachman, R. E. Fikes, and H. L. Levesque, "KRYPTON: A Functional Approach to Knowledge Representation," *IEEE Computer*, **16**, p. 67, 1983.

(Brachman 85). Ronald J. Brachman, "I Lied about the Trees," *AI Magazine,* **6**, (3), pp. 80-93, Fall 1985.

(Finin 86). Tim Finin, "Understanding Frame Languages, Part I," *AI Expert*, pp. 44-50, Nov. 1986.

(Jackson 86). Peter Jackson, *Introduction to Expert Systems*, Addison-Wesley Pub., 1986.

(Lenat 77). Doug B. Lenat, "Automated Theory Formation in Mathematics," *Proceedings of the Fifth International Joint Conference on Artificial Intelligence*, 1977.

(McGettrick 80). Andrew D. McGettrick, *The Definitions of Programming Languages,* Cambridge University Press, 1980.

(Minsky 75). Marvin Minsky, "A Framework for Representing Knowledge," in *The Psychology of Computer Vision*, Patrick Winston, ed., McGraw-Hill, pp. 211-217, 1975.

(Quillian 68). M. R. Quillian, "Semantic Memory," *Semantic Information Processing*, Marvin Minsky, ed., MIT Press, pp. 227-270, 1968.

(Rescher 64). Nicholas Rescher, *Introduction to Logic*, St. Martin's Press, pp. 258-259, 1964.

(Rissland 78). E. L. Rissland, "Understanding Understanding Mathematics," *Cognitive Science*, **2**, pp. 361-383, 1978.

(Schank 77). Roger C. Shank and R. P. Abelson, *Scripts, Plans, Goals, and Understanding*, Lawrence Erlbaum, 1977.

(Sowa 84). J. F. Sowa, *Conceptual Structures: Information Processing in Mind and Machine*, Addison-Wesley Pub., 1984.

(Staugaard 87). Andrew C. Staugaard, Jr., *Robotics and AI: An Introduction to Applied Machine Intelligence*, Prentice-Hall, 1987.

(Stillings 87). Neil A. Stillings, *et al.*, *Cognitive Science: An Introduction*, MIT Press, 1987.

(Whalen 85). Thomas Whalen and Brian Schott, "Alternative Logics for Approximate Reasoning in Expert Systems: A Comparative Study," *Int. J. Man-Machine Studies*, **22**, pp. 327-346, 1985.

(Winston 84). Patrick Henry Winston, *Artificial Intelligence*, 2nd ed., Addison-Wesley Pub., 1984.

(Woods 83). W. A. Woods, "What's Important about Knowledge Representation?" *IEEE Computer*, **16**, p. 22, 1983.

CHAPTER 3
Methods of Inference

3.1 INTRODUCTION

In this chapter we will discuss various methods of reasoning or inference. This topic is particularly important in expert systems because reasoning is the standard technique by which expert systems solve problems. Expert systems are commonly used when an inadequate algorithm or no algorithmic solution exists and reasoning offers the only possibility of a solution.

3.2 TREES, LATTICES, AND GRAPHS

A **tree** is a hierarchical data structure consisting of **nodes,** which store information or knowledge, and **branches,** which connect the nodes. Branches are sometimes called *links* or *edges* and nodes are sometimes called *vertices*. Figure 3.1 shows a general binary tree, which has zero, one, or two branches per node. In an **oriented tree** the **root node** is the highest node in the **hierarchy** and the **leaves** are the lowest. A tree can be considered a special type of semantic net in which every node except the root has exactly one **parent** and zero or more **child** nodes. For the usual type of binary tree there is a maximum of two children per node, and the right child nodes are distinguished from the left.

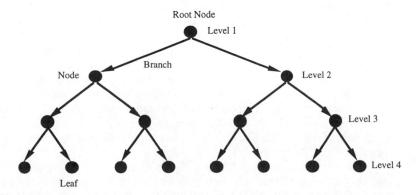

Figure 3.1 Binary Tree

If a node has more than one parent it is in a network. In Figure 3.1, notice that there is only one sequence of edges or **path** from the root to any node because it is not possible to move against an arrow. In oriented trees the arrows all point downward.

Trees are a special case of a general mathematical structure called a **graph**. The terms *network* or simply *net* are often used synonymously with *graph* when describing a particular example of a graph such as a telephone network. A graph can have zero or more links between nodes and no distinction between parents and children. A simple example of a graph is a map, in which the cities are the nodes and the links are the roads. The links may have arrows or directions associated with them and a **weight** to characterize some aspect of the link. An analogy is one-way streets with weight limits on how much trucks can carry through the streets. The weights in a graph can be any type of information. If the graph represents an airline route, the weights can be miles between cities, cost of flying, fuel consumption, and so forth.

An artificial neural system is another example of a graph with cycles; because during training there is feedback of information from one layer of the net to another, which modifies the weights. A simple graph has no links that come immediately back on the node itself, as shown in Figure 3.2 (a). A **circuit** or **cycle** is a path through a graph that begins and ends on the same node, as does the path ABCA in Figure 3.2 (a). An **acyclic** graph has no cycles. A **connected graph** has links to all its nodes. A graph with directed links, called a **digraph,** and a **self-loop** are shown in Fig. 3.2 (c). A directed acyclic graph is a **lattice**, and an example is shown in Figure 3.2 (d). A tree with only a single path from the root to its one leaf is a **degenerate tree**. The degenerate binary trees of three nodes are shown in Figure 3.2 (e). Generally in a tree, the arrows are *not* explicitly shown because they are assumed to be pointing down.

Trees and lattices are useful for classifying objects because of their hierarchical nature, with parents above children. An example is a family tree, which shows the relationships and ancestry of related people. Another application of trees and lattices is making decisions; these are called *decision trees* or *decision lattices*. We will use the term *structure* to refer to both trees and lattices. A decision structure is both a knowledge representation scheme and a method of reasoning about its knowledge. An example of a decision tree for classifying animals is shown in Figure 3.3. This example is for the classic game of twenty questions. The nodes contain questions, the branches "yes" or "no" responses to the questions, and the leaves contain the guesses of what the animal is.

A small portion of a decision tree to classify raspberries is shown in Figure 3.4. Unlike Computer Science trees, classification trees may be drawn with the root down. Not shown is the root, which has a branch to the "Leaves Simple" node and another branch to the "Leaves Compound" node. The decision process starts at the bottom by identifying gross features, such as whether the leaves are simple or compound. More specific details requiring closer observation are used as we travel up the tree. That is, larger sets of alternatives are examined first and then the decision process starts narrowing down the possibilities to smaller sets. This is a good way of organizing the decisions in terms of the time and effort to carry out more detailed observations.

If the decisions are binary, then a binary decision tree is both easy to construct and very efficient. Every question goes down one level in the tree. One question can decide one of two possible answers. Two questions can decide one of four possible answers. Three questions can decide one of eight possible answers and so on. If a binary tree is constructed such that all the leaves are answers and all the nodes leading down are questions, there can be a maximum of 2^N answers for N questions. For example, ten questions can classify one of 1,024 animals whereas twenty questions can classify one of 1,048,576 possible answers.

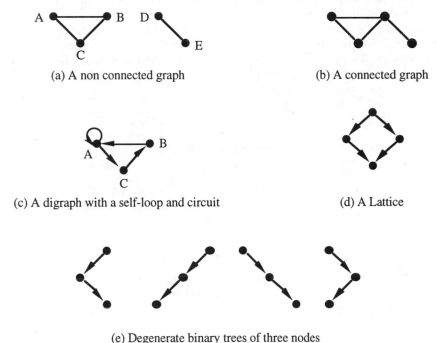

(a) A non connected graph   (b) A connected graph

(c) A digraph with a self-loop and circuit   (d) A Lattice

(e) Degenerate binary trees of three nodes

Figure 3.2 Simple Graphs

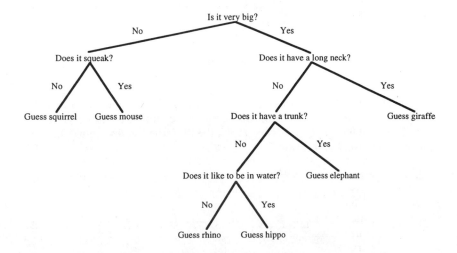

Figure 3.3 Decision Tree Showing Knowledge about Animals

Another useful feature of decision trees is that they can be made **self-learning**. If the guess is wrong, a procedure can be called to query the user for a new, correct classification question and the answers to the "yes" and "no" responses. A new node, branches, and leaves can then be dynamically created and added to the tree. In the original Animals program written in BASIC, knowledge was stored in DATA statements. When the user taught the program a new animal, automatic learning took place as the program generated new DATA statements containing information about the new animal. In Pascal and other languages with pointer capability, the animal knowledge can be stored in trees. Using the expert system tool CLIPS new rules can be built automatically as the program learns new knowledge (Giarratano 92). This **automated knowledge acquisition** is very useful because it can circumvent the knowledge acquisition bottleneck described in Chapter 1.

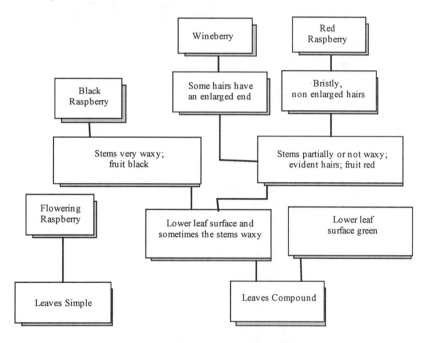

Figure 3.4 Portion of a Decision Tree for Species of Raspberries

Decision structures can be mechanically translated into production rules. This can easily be done by a breadth-first searching of the structure and by generating IF...THEN rules at every node. For example, the decision tree in Figure 3.3 could be translated into rules as follows

```
IF QUESTION = "IS IT VERY BIG?" AND RESPONSE = "NO"
      THEN  QUESTION := "DOES IT SQUEAK?"

IF QUESTION = "IS IT VERY BIG?" AND RESPONSE = "YES"
      THEN  QUESTION := "DOES IT HAVE A LONG NECK?"
```

and so forth for the other nodes. A leaf node would generate an ANSWER response rather than a question. Appropriate procedures would also query the user for input and would then construct new nodes if wrong.

Although decision structures are powerful classification tools, they are limited because they cannot deal with variables, as an expert system can. Expert systems are general purpose tools rather than simply classifiers.

3.3 STATE AND PROBLEM SPACES

Graphs can be applied to many practical problems. A useful method of describing the behavior of an object is to define a graph called the **state space**. A *state* is a collection of characteristics that can be used to define the status or **state** of an object. The state space is the set of states showing the **transitions** between states that the object can experience. A transition takes an object from one state to another.

Examples of State Spaces

As a simple example of state spaces, consider the purchase of a soft drink from a machine. As you put coins into the machine, it makes a transition from one state to another. Figure 3.5 illustrates the state space assuming that only quarters and nickels are available and that 55¢ is required for a drink. Adding other coins such as dimes and fifty-cent pieces makes the diagram more complicated and is not shown here.

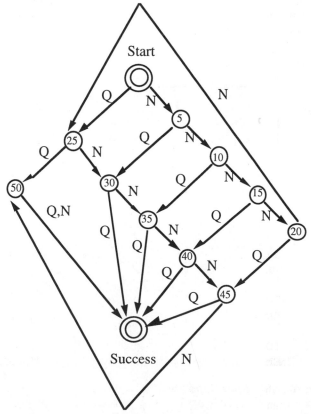

Figure 3.5
State Diagram for a Soft Drink Vending Machine Accepting Quarters (Q) and Nickels (N)

The start and success states are drawn as double circles to make them easier to identify. The states are shown as circles and the possible transitions to other states are drawn as arrows. Notice that this diagram is a weighted digraph, in which the weights are the possible coins that can be input to the machine in every state.

This diagram is also called a **finite state machine** diagram because it describes the finite number of states of a machine. The term *machine* is used in a very general sense. The machine can be a real object, an algorithm, a concept, and so forth. Associated with every state are the actions that drive it to another state. At any time, the machine can be in only one state. As the machine accepts input to a state, it progresses from that state to another. If the correct inputs are given, the machine will progress from the start to the success or final state. If a state is not designed to accept a certain input, the machine will become hung up in that state. For example, the soft drink machine has no provision to accept dimes. If someone puts a dime in the machine, the response is undefined. A good design will include the possibility of invalid inputs from every state and provide for transitions to an error state. The error state is designed to give appropriate error messages and take whatever action is necessary.

Finite state machines are often used in compilers and other programs to determine the validity of an input. For example, Figure 3.6 shows part of a finite state machine to test input strings for validity. Characters of the input are examined one at a time. Only the character strings WHILE, WRITE, and BEGIN will be accepted. Arrows are shown from the BEGIN state for successful input and also for erroneous input going to the error state. For efficiency, some states, such as the one pointed to by "L" and "T," are used for testing both WHILE and WRITE.

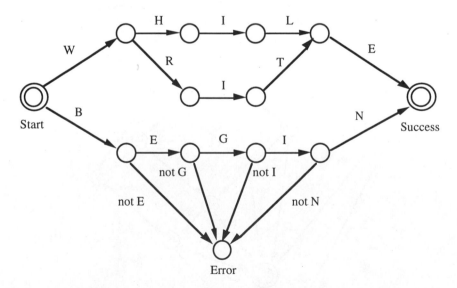

Figure 3.6 Part of a Finite State Machine for Determining Valid Strings WHILE, WRITE, and BEGIN.
Note:*Only some of the error state transitions are shown*

State diagrams are also useful in describing solutions to problems. In these kinds of applications we can think of the state space as a **problem space**, in which some states correspond to intermediate stages in problem solving and some states correspond to answers. In a problem space there may be multiple success states corresponding to possible solutions. Finding the solution to a problem in a problem space involves finding a valid path from start (problem statement) to success (answer). The animal decision tree can be viewed as a problem space where the yes/no responses to questions determine the state transition.

Another example of a problem space occurs in the classic Monkey and bananas problem shown in Figure 3.7. The problem is to give instructions to a monkey telling it how to retrieve some bananas hanging from the ceiling. The bananas are out of reach. Inside the room are a couch and a ladder. The initial starting configuration is typically with the monkey on the couch. Instructions might be

```
jump off couch
move to ladder
move ladder under bananas' position
climb ladder
grab bananas
```

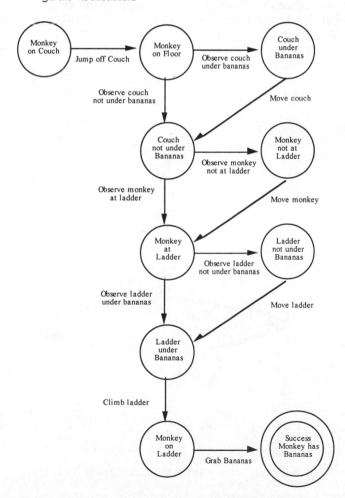

Figure 3.7 The State Space for the Monkey and Bananas Problem

The instructions will vary depending on the initial configuration of monkey, couch, and ladder. Because there are a number of initial start states, the special double circle for the start is not shown. For example, another possible starting state is with the monkey on the couch under the bananas. The monkey will then have to push the couch out of the way before moving the ladder under the bananas. In the simplest starting state, the monkey is already on the ladder under the bananas.

Although this problem seems obvious to a human, it involves a considerable amount of reasoning. A practical application of a reasoning system like this is giving instructions to a robot concerning the solution of a task. Rather than assuming that all objects in the environment are fixed in place, a general solution is a reasoning system that can deal with a variety of situations. A rule-based solution to the monkeys and bananas problem is distributed with the CLIPS disks.

Another useful application of graphs is exploring paths to find a problem's solution. Figure 3.8 (a) shows a simple net for the traveling salesman problem. In this example, assume the problem is to find a complete path from node A that visits all other nodes. As usual in the traveling salesman problem, no node can be visited twice. Figure 3.8 (b) shows all the possible paths starting from node A in the form of a tree. The correct paths ABDCA and ACDBA are shown as thick lines in this graph.

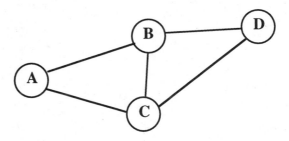

(a) Graph of a Traveling Salesman Problem

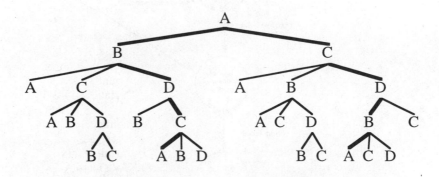

(b) Search Paths (optimal path shown by thick edges)

Figure 3.8 A Traveling Salesman Problem

Depending on the search algorithm, the exploration of paths to find the correct one may involve a considerable amount of backtracking. For example, the path ABA may first be searched unsuccessfully and then backtracked to B. From B, the paths CA, CB, CDB, and CDC will be unsuccessfully searched. Next the path BDB will be unsuccessfully searched until the first correct path ABDCA is found.

Ill-structured Problem Spaces

A useful application of state spaces is in characterizing ill-structured problems (Pople 82). In Chapter 1 an ill-structured problem was defined to have uncertainties associated with it. These uncertainties can be specified more precisely by a problem space.

As an example of an ill-structured problem, let's consider again the case of a person who is thinking about traveling and visits a travel agent, as discussed in Chapter 1. Table 3.1 lists some characteristics of this ill-structured problem as a problem space, indicated by the person's responses to the travel agent's questions.

If you compare Table 3.1 to Table 1.10 (page 19), you'll see that the concept of a problem space lets us specify more precisely the characteristics of an ill-structured problem. It is essential to characterize these parameters precisely to determine if a solution is feasible, and if so, what is needed for a solution. A problem is not necessarily ill-structured just because it has one, some, or even all of these characteristics since much depends on the severity. For example, all theorem-proving problems have an infinite number of potential solutions, but this does not make theorem proving an ill-structured problem.

As you can see from Table 3.1, there are many uncertainties, and yet travel agents cope with them everyday. While not all cases may be as bad as this, it indicates why an algorithmic solution would be very difficult.

Characteristic	Response
Goal not explicit	I'm thinking about going somewhere
Problem space unbounded	I'm not sure where to go
Problem states not discrete	I just like to travel; the destination is not important
Interediate states difficult to achieve	I don't have enough money to go
State operators unknown	I don't know how to get the money
Time constraint	I must go soon

Table 3.1 Example of an Ill-structured Problem for Travel

A well-formed problem is one in which we know the explicit problem, goal, and operators that can be applied to go from one state to another. A well-formed problem is **deterministic** because when an operator is applied to a state, we are sure of the next state. The problem space is bounded and the states are discrete. This means that there are a finite number of states and that each state is well-defined.

In the travel problem the states are unbounded because there are infinite possible destinations that a traveler might choose. An analogous situation occurs with an analog meter, which may indicate an infinite number of possible readings. If we consider each reading of the meter to be a state, then there are an infinite number of states and they are not well defined because they correspond to real numbers. Since there are an infinite number of real numbers between any two real numbers, the states are not discrete because the next state differs only infinitesimally. In contrast, the readings of a digital meter are bounded and discrete.

3.4 AND-OR TREES AND GOALS

Many types of expert systems use backward chaining to find solutions to problems. PROLOG is a good example of a backward chaining system that tries to solve a problem by breaking it up into smaller subproblems and solving them individually. Solving a problem is considered by optimists as a goal to be achieved. In order to reach a goal, zero or more subgoals may need to be accomplished.

One type of tree or lattice that is useful in representing backward chaining problems is the AND-OR tree. Figure 3.9 shows a simple example of an AND-OR lattice to solve the goal of obtaining a college degree. To accomplish this goal, you can attend a college either in person or through correspondence courses. With correspondence courses, work can be performed either by mailing assignments or electronically using a home computer and modem.

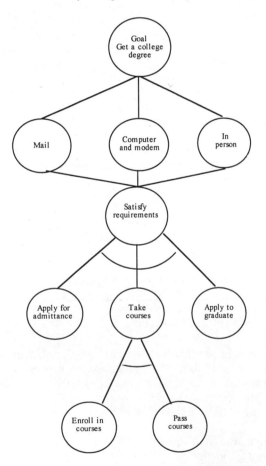

Figure 3.9 AND-OR Lattice Showing How to Obtain a College Degree

In order to satisfy requirements for the degree, three subgoals must be accomplished: (1) apply for admittance, (2) take courses, and (3) apply to graduate. Notice that there is an arc through the edges from the satisfy requirements goal to these three subgoals. The arc through the edges indicates that satisfy requirements is an AND-node that can only be satisfied if all three of its subgoals are satisfied.

Goals without the arc such as mail, computer and modem, and in person are OR-nodes in which accomplishing any of these subgoals satisfies its parent goal of get a college degree.

This diagram is a lattice because the satisfy requirements subgoal has three parent nodes: (1) mail, (2) computer and modem, and (3) in person. Notice that it would be possible to draw this diagram as a tree by simply duplicating the subgoal satisfy requirements and its subtree of goals for the mail, computer and modem, and in person goals. However, since the Satisfy Requirements subgoal is the same for each of its parents there is no real advantage, and it uses more paper to draw the tree.

As another simple example, Figure 3.10 shows an AND-OR tree for the problem of getting to work by different possible ways. For completeness, this could also be converted into a lattice. For example, an edge could be added from the node drive to train station to the car node and from walk to train station to the walk node. Figure 3.11 shows an AND-exclusive OR-type lattice.

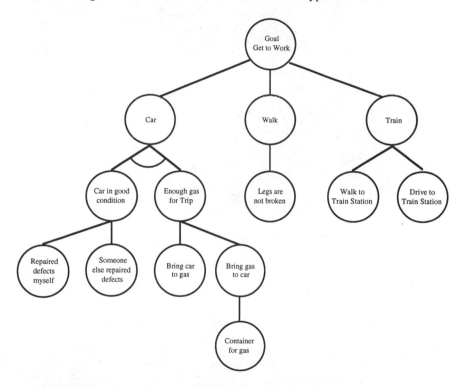

Figure 3.10 A Simple AND-OR Tree Showing Methods of Getting to Work

Another way of describing problem solutions is an AND-OR-NOT lattice, which uses logic gate symbols instead of the AND-OR tree-type notation. The logic gate symbols for AND, OR, and NOT are shown in Figure 3.12. These gates implement the truth tables for AND, OR, and NOT discussed in Chapter 2. Figure 3.13 shows Figure 3.9 implemented with AND and OR gates.

AND-OR trees and decision trees have the same basic advantages and disadvantages. The main advantage of AND-OR-NOT lattices is their potential implementation in hardware for fast processing speeds. These lattices can be custom designed for fabrication as integrated circuits. In practice, one type of logic gate such as the NOT-AND or NAND is used for reasons of manufacturing economy rather than separate AND, OR, and NOT gates. From logic it can be proved that any logic function can be implemented by a NAND gate. An integrated circuit with one type of device is cheaper to manufacture than one with multiple types of logic gates.

A chip using forward chaining can compute the answer quickly as a function of its inputs because processing proceeds in parallel. Chips like this can be used for real-time monitoring of sensor data and make an appropriate response depending on the inputs. The main disadvantage is that like other decision structures, a chip designed for logic cannot handle situations it was not designed for. However, an ANS implemented on a chip can handle unexpected inputs.

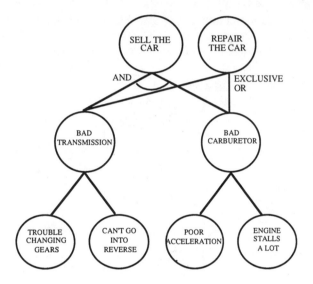

Figure 3.11 AND-OR Lattice for Car Selling/Repair Decision

Figure 3.12 AND, OR, and NOT Logic Gate Symbols

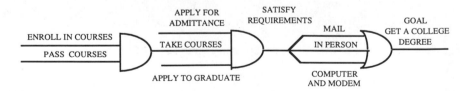

Figure 3.13 AND-OR Logic Gate Representation for Figure 3.9

3.5 DEDUCTIVE LOGIC AND SYLLOGISMS

In Chapter 2 we discussed the representation of knowledge by logic. Now you will see how inferences are made to derive new knowledge or information. In the remainder of this chapter we will discuss different methods of inference. Figure 3.14 is an overview of the methods of inference. A brief summary follows:

- *Deduction*. Logical reasoning in which conclusions must follow from their premises.
- *Induction*. Inference from the specific case to the general.
- *Intuition*. No proven theory. The answer just appears, possibly by unconsciously recognizing an underlying pattern. Expert systems do not implement this type of inference yet. ANSs may hold promise for this type of inference since they can extrapolate from their training rather than just provide a conditioned response or interpolation. That is, a neural net will always give its best guess for a solution.
- *Heuristics*. Rules of thumb based on experience.
- *Generate and test*. Trial and error. Often used with planning for efficiency.
- *Abduction*. Reasoning back from a true conclusion to the premises that may have caused the conclusion.
- *Default*. In the absence of specific knowledge, assume general or common knowledge by default.
- *Autoepistemic*. Self-knowledge.
- *Nonmonotonic*. Previous knowledge may be incorrect when new evidence is obtained.
- *Analogy*. Inferring a conclusion based on the similarities to another situation.

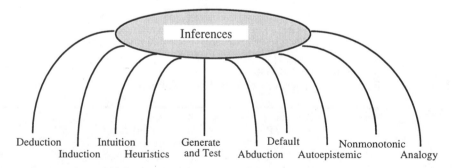

Figure 3.14 Types of Inference

Although not explicitly shown in Figure 3.14, **commonsense knowledge** may be a combination of any of these types. Commonsense reasoning is what people use in ordinary situations, and is very difficult for computers to master. The application of fuzzy logic to commonsense reasoning is discussed in Chapter 5.

One of the most frequently used methods of drawing inferences is **deductive logic**, which has been used since ancient times to determine the validity of an **argument**. Although people commonly use the word *argument* to describe an angry "exchange of views," it has a very different meaning in logic. A logical argument is a group of statements in which the last is claimed to be justified on the basis of the previous ones in the **chain of reasoning**. One type of logical argument is the syllogism, which was discussed briefly in Chapter 2. As an example of a syllogism:

```
Premise:     Anyone who can program is intelligent
Premise:     John can program
Conclusion:  Therefore, John is intelligent
```

In an argument the premises are used as evidence to support the conclusions. The premises are also called the **antecedent** and the conclusion is called the **consequent**. The essential characteristic of deductive logic is that the true conclusion *must* follow from true premises. A line is customarily drawn to separate the premises from the conclusion, as shown above, so that it is not necessary to explicitly label the premises and conclusion.

The argument could have been written more briefly as

```
Anyone who can program is intelligent
John can program
∴ John is intelligent
```

where the three dots, ∴, mean "therefore."

Let's take a closer look at syllogistic logic now. The main advantage of studying syllogisms is that it is a simple, well-understood branch of logic that can be completely proven. Also, syllogisms are often useful because they can be expressed in terms of IF . . . THEN rules. For example, the previous syllogism can be rephrased as

```
IF   Anyone who can program is intelligent and
     John can program
THEN John is intelligent
```

In general, a syllogism is any valid deductive argument having two premises and a conclusion. The classic syllogism is a special type called a **categorical syllogism**. The premises and conclusions are defined as categorical statements of the following four forms, as shown in Table 3.2.

Form	Schema	Meaning
A	All S is P	universal affirmative
E	No S is P	universal negative
I	Some S is P	particular affirmative
O	Some S is not P	particular negative

Table 3.2 Categorical Statements

Note that in logic, the term *schema* specifies the logical form of the statement. This also illustrates another use of the word schema, which is different from its AI use, discussed in Chapter 2. In logic, the word schema is used to show the essential form of an argument. Schemata may also specify the logical form of an entire syllogism as in

```
All M is P
All S is M
∴ All S is P
```

The subject of the conclusion, S, is called the *minor term* while the predicate of the conclusion, P, is called the *major term*. The premise containing the major term is called the *major premise* and the premise containing the minor term is called the *minor premise*. For example

```
Major Premise:    All M is P
Minor Premise:    All S is M
Conclusion: All S is P
```

is a syllogism said to be in **standard form**, with its major and minor premises identified. The **subject** is the object that is being described and the **predicate** describes some property of the subject. For example, in the statement

```
All microcomputers are computers
```

the subject is "microcomputers" and the predicate is "computers." In the statement

```
All microcomputers with 8 megabytes
are computers with a lot of memory
```

the subject is "microcomputers with 8 megabytes" and the predicate is "computers with a lot of memory."

The forms of the categorical statements have been identified since ancient times by the letters A, E, I, and O. The A and I indicate affirmative and are thought to come from the first two vowels of the Latin word "a̲f̲firmo" (I affirm); whereas E and O come from "n̲e̲go" (I negate). The A and I forms are said to be **affirmative in quality** by affirming that the subjects are included in the predicate class. The E and O forms are **negative in quality** because the subjects are excluded from the predicate class.

The verb *is* is called the *copula*, from the Latin which means "to connect". The copula connects the two parts of the statement. In the standard categorical syllogism, the copula is the present tense form of the verb *to be*. So another version is

```
All S are P
```

The third term of the syllogism, M, is called the *middle term* and is common to both premises. The middle term is essential because a syllogism is defined such that the conclusion cannot be inferred from either of the premises alone. So the argument

```
All A is B
All B is C
∴ All A is B
```

is not a valid syllogism because it follows from the first premise alone.

The **quantity** or **quantifier** describes the portion of the class included. The quantifiers *All* and *No* are **universal** because they refer to entire classes. The quantifier *Some* is called **particular** because it refers to just part of the class.

The **mood** of a syllogism is defined by the three letters that give the form of the major premise, minor premise, and conclusion, respectively. For example, the syllogism

```
All M is P
All S is M
∴ All S is P
```

is an AAA mood.

There are four possible patterns of arranging the S, P, and M terms, as shown in Table 3.3. Each pattern is called a **figure,** with the number of the figure specifying its type.

	Figure 1	Figure 2	Figure 3	Figure 4
Major Premise	M P	P M	M P	P M
Minor Premise	S M	S M	M S	M S

Table 3.3 Patterns of Categorical Statements

So the previous example is completely described as an AAA-1 syllogism type. Just because an argument has a syllogistic form does not mean that it is a valid syllogism. Consider the AEE-1 syllogism form:

```
All M is P
No S is M
∴ No S is P
```

is not a valid syllogism, as can be seen from the example

```
All microcomputers are computers
No mainframe is a microcomputer
∴ No mainframe is a computer
```

Rather than trying to think up examples to prove the validity of syllogistic arguments, there is a **decision procedure** that can be used. A decision procedure is a method of proving validity and is some general mechanical method or algorithm by which the process of determining validity can be automated. Although there are decision procedures for syllogistic logic and propositional logic, Church showed in 1936 that there is none for predicate logic. Instead, people must apply creativity to generate proofs.

The decision procedure for propositions is simply constructing a truth table and examining it for tautology. The decision procedure for syllogisms can be done using Venn diagrams with three overlapping circles representing S, P, and M, as shown in Figure 3.15 (a). For the syllogism form AEE-1:

```
All M is P
No S is M
∴ No S is P
```

the major premise is illustrated in Figure 3.15 (b). The lined section of M indicates that there are no elements in that portion. In (c) the minor premise is included by lining its portion with no elements. From (c) it can be seen that the conclusion of AEE-1 is false because there is some S in P.

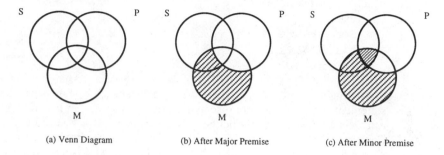

| (a) Venn Diagram | (b) After Major Premise | (c) After Minor Premise |

Figure 3.15 Decision Procedure for Syllogism AEE-1

As another example, the following EAE-1 is valid as can be seen from Figure 3.16 (c).

```
No M is P
All S is M
∴ No S is P
```

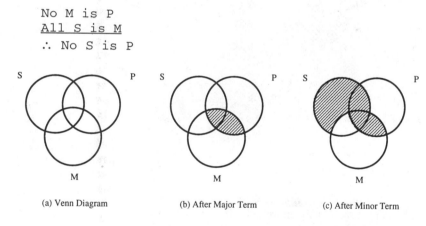

| (a) Venn Diagram | (b) After Major Term | (c) After Minor Term |

Figure 3.16 Decision Procedure for Syllogism EAE-1

Venn diagrams that involve "some" quantifiers are a little more difficult to draw. The general rules for drawing categorical syllogisms under the Boolean view that there may be no members in the A and E statements are:

1. If a class is empty, it is shaded.
2. Universal statements, A and E, are always drawn before particular ones.
3. If a class has at least one member, mark it with an *.
4. If a statement does not specify in which of two adjacent classes an object exists, place an * on the line between the classes.
5. If an area has been shaded, no * can be put in it.

As an example,

```
Some computers are laptops
All laptops are transportable
∴ Some transportables are computers
```

which can be put in IAI-4 type

```
Some P are M
All M are S
∴ Some S are P
```

Following the rules 2 and 1 for Venn diagrams, we start with the universal statement for the minor premise and shade it, as shown in Figure 3.17 (a). Next, rule 3 is applied to the particular major premise and a * is drawn, as shown in Figure 3.17 (b). Since the conclusion "Some transportables are computers" is shown in the diagram, it follows that the argument IAI-4 is a valid syllogism.

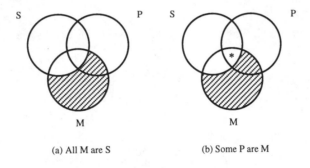

(a) All M are S   (b) Some P are M

Figure 3.17 Syllogism of IAI-4 Type

3.6 RULES OF INFERENCE

Although Venn diagrams are a decision procedure for syllogisms, the diagrams are inconvenient for more complex arguments because they become more difficult to read. However, there is a more fundamental problem with syllogisms because they address only a small portion of the possible logical statements. In particular, categorical syllogisms only address categorical statements of the A, E, I, and O form.

Propositional logic offers another means of describing arguments. In fact, we often use propositional logic without realizing it. For example, consider the following propositional argument:

```
If there is power, the computer will work
There is power
∴ The computer will work
```

This argument can be expressed in a formal way by using letters to represent the propositions as follows:

```
A = There is power
B = The computer will work
```

and so the argument can be written as

```
A → B
A
∴ B
```

Arguments like this occur often. A general schema for representing arguments of this type is

```
p → q
p
∴ q
```

where p and q are logical variables that can represent any statements. The use of logical variables in propositional logic allows more complex types of statements than the four syllogistic forms A, E, I, and O. Inference schema of this propositional form is called by a variety of names: **direct reasoning**, *modus ponens*, **law of detachment,** and **assuming the antecedent**.

Notice that this example can also be expressed in the syllogistic form

```
All computers with power will work
This computer has power
This computer will work
```

which demonstrates that *modus ponens* is really a special case of syllogistic logic. *Modus ponens* is important because it forms the basis of rule-based expert systems. The compound proposition $p \rightarrow q$ corresponds to the rule and the p corresponds to the pattern that must match the antecedent for the rule to be satisfied. However, as discussed in Chapter 2, the conditional $p \rightarrow q$ is not exactly equivalent to a rule because the conditional is a logical definition defined by a truth table and there are many possible definitions of the conditional.

Generally we will follow the convention of logic theory of using capital letters such as A, B, C . . . to represent constant propositions such as "There is power." Lowercase letters such as p, q, r . . . will represent logical variables, which can stand for different constant propositions. Note that this convention is opposite to that of PROLOG, which uses capital letters for variables.

This *modus ponens* schema could also have been written with differently named logical variables as

```
r → s
r
∴ s
```

and the schema would still mean the same.

Another notation for this schema is

```
r, r → s; ∴ s
```

where the comma is used to separate one premise from another and the semicolon indicates the end of the premises. Although so far we have only looked at arguments with two premises, a more general form of an argument is

$$P_1, \quad P_2, \quad \ldots \quad P_N; \quad \therefore \quad C$$

where the capital letters P_i represent premises such as r, r $\rightarrow$ s, and C is the conclusion. Notice how this resembles the goal satisfaction statement of PROLOG discussed in Chapter 2.

$$p \quad :- \quad p_1, \quad p_2, \quad \ldots \quad p_N.$$

The goal, p, is satisfied if all the subgoals $p_1, p_2, \ldots p_N$ are satisfied. An analogous argument for production rules can be written in the general form

$$C_1 \wedge C_2 \wedge \ldots C_N \rightarrow A$$

which means that if each condition, C_i, of a rule is satisfied, then the action, A, of the rule is done. As discussed previously, a logical statement of the form above is not strictly equivalent to a rule because the logical definition of the conditional is not the same as a production rule. However, this logical form is a useful intuitive aid in thinking about rules.

The notation of the logic operators AND and OR have different forms in PROLOG compared to the usual $\wedge$ and $\vee$. The comma between subgoals in PROLOG means a conjunction, $\wedge$, and the disjunction, $\vee$, is indicated with a semicolon. For example,

$$p \quad :- \quad p_1; \quad p_2.$$

means that p is satisfied if p_1 or p_2 is satisfied. Conjunctions and disjunctions can be mixed. For example,

$$p \quad :- \quad p_1, \quad p_2; \quad p_3, \quad p_4.$$

is the same as the two PROLOG statements

$$p \quad :- \quad p_1, \quad p_2.$$
$$p \quad :- \quad p_3, \quad p_4.$$

In general, if the premises and conclusion are all schemata, the argument

$$P_1, \quad P_2, \quad \ldots \quad P_N; \quad \therefore \quad C$$

is a formally valid deductive argument if and only if

$$P_1 \wedge P_2 \wedge \ldots P_N \rightarrow C$$

is a tautology. As an example,

$$(p \wedge q) \rightarrow p$$

is a tautology because it is true for any values, T or F, of p and q. You can verify this by constructing the truth table.

The argument of *modus ponens*

$$
\begin{array}{l}
p \ \rightarrow \ q \\
\underline{p } \\
\therefore \ q
\end{array}
$$

is valid because it can be expressed as a tautology.

$$(p \ \rightarrow \ q) \ \wedge \ p \ \rightarrow \ q$$

Note that we are assuming that the arrow has lower precedence than conjunction and disjunction. This saves writing additional parentheses such as

$$((p \ \rightarrow \ q) \ \wedge \ p) \ \rightarrow \ q$$

The truth table for *modus ponens* is shown in Table 3.4. It is a tautology because the values of the argument, shown in the rightmost column, are all true no matter what the values of its premises. Notice that in the third, fourth, and fifth columns, the truth values are written under certain operators such as the $\rightarrow$ and $\wedge$. These are called the **main connectives** because they connect the two main parts of a compound proposition.

p	q	$p \rightarrow q$	$(p \rightarrow q) \wedge p$	$(p \rightarrow q) \wedge p \rightarrow q$
T	T	T	T	T
T	F	F	F	T
F	T	T	F	T
F	F	T	F	T

Table 3.4 Truth Table for *Modus Ponens*

Although this method of determining valid arguments works, it does require checking every row of the truth table. The number of rows is 2^N, where N is the number of premises, and so the rows increase rapidly with the number of premises. For example, five premises would require 32 rows to be checked while ten premises require 1024 rows. A shorter method of determining a valid argument is to consider only those rows of the truth table in which the premises are all true. The equivalent definition of a valid argument states that it is valid if and only if the conclusion is true for each of these rows. That is, the conclusion is tautologically implied by the premises. For *modus ponens*, the $p \rightarrow q$ premise and p premise are both true only in the first row, and so is the conclusion. Hence, *modus ponens* is a valid argument. If there were any other row in which the premises were all true and the conclusion false, then the argument would be invalid.

The shorter way of expressing the truth table for *modus ponens* is shown in Table 3.5, in which all the rows are explicitly shown. In practice, only those rows that have true premises, such as the first row, need be considered.

The truth table for *modus ponens* shows that it is valid because the first row has true premises and a true conclusion, and there are no other rows that have true premises and a false conclusion.

		Premises		Conclusion
p	q	p → q	p	q
T	T	T	T	T
T	F	F	T	F
F	T	T	F	T
F	F	T	F	F

Table 3.5 Alternate Short-form Truth Table for *Modus Ponens*

Arguments can be deceptive. To show this, first consider the following valid example of *modus ponens*.

```
If there are no bugs, then the program compiles
There are no bugs
∴ The program compiles.
```

Compare this with the following argument that somewhat resembles *modus ponens*.

```
If there are no bugs, then the program compiles
The program compiles
∴ There are no bugs
```

Is this a valid argument? The schema for arguments of this type is

$$p \rightarrow q$$
$$\underline{q}$$
$$\therefore p$$

and its short-form truth table is shown in Table 3.6.

		Premises		Conclusion
p	*q*	*p → q*	*q*	*p*
T	T	T	T	T
T	F	F	F	T
F	T	T	T	F
F	F	T	F	F

Table 3.6 Short-form Truth Table of p → q, q; ∴ p

Notice that this argument is not valid. Although the first row does show that the conclusion is true if all the premises are true, the third row shows that if the premises are true, the conclusion is false. Thus this argument fails the if and only if criterion of a valid argument. Although many programmers wish arguments like this were true, logic (and experience) proves it a **fallacy**, or invalid argument. This particular fallacious argument is called the ***fallacy of the converse***.

As another example, the argument schema

$$p \rightarrow q$$
$$\underline{\sim q}$$
$$\therefore \sim p$$

is because Table 3.7 shows the conclusion is true only when the premises are true.

		Premises		Conclusion
p	*q*	*p → q*	*~q*	*~p*
T	T	T	F	F
T	F	F	T	F
F	T	T	F	T
F	F	T	T	T

Table 3.7 Short-form Truth Table of p → q, ~q; ∴ ~p

This particular schema is called by a variety of names: *indirect reasoning, modus tollens*, and *law of contraposition*.

Modus ponens and *modus tollens* are **rules of inference**, sometimes called *laws of inference*. Table 3.8 shows some of the laws of inference.

The Latin name *modus* means "way," while *ponere* means "assert," and *tollere* means to "deny." The real names of the *modus* rules and their literal meanings are shown in Table 3.9. *Modus ponens* and *modus tollens* are short for the first two types (Stebbing 50). The rule of inference numbers correspond to those in Table 3.8.

The rules of inference can be applied to arguments with more than two premises. For example, consider the following argument:

```
Chip prices rise only if the yen rises.
The yen rises only if the dollar falls and
    if the dollar falls then the yen rises.
Since chip prices have risen,
    the dollar must have fallen.
```

Let the propositions be defined as follows.

```
C = chip prices rise
Y = yen rises
D = dollar falls
```

Recall from Section 2.12 that one of the meanings of the conditional is "p, only if q." A proposition such as "The yen rises only if the dollar falls" has this meaning and so is represented as C → Y. The entire argument has the following form.

```
C → Y
(Y → D) ∧ (D → Y)
C
∴ D
```

The second premise has an interesting form that can be further reduced by using a variant of the conditional. The conditional p → q has several variants, which are the **converse**, **inverse**, and **contrapositive**. These are listed with the conditional, for completeness, in Table 3.10.

Law of Inference	Schemata	
1. Law of Detachment	$p \rightarrow q$ $\underline{p}$ $\therefore q$	
2. Law of the Contrapositive	$\underline{p \rightarrow q}$ $\therefore \sim q \rightarrow \sim p$	
3. Law of *Modus Tollens*	$p \rightarrow q$ $\underline{\sim q}$ $\therefore \sim p$	
4. Chain Rule (Law of the Syllogism)	$p \rightarrow q$ $\underline{q \rightarrow r}$ $\therefore p \rightarrow r$	
5. Law of Disjunctive Inference	$p \vee q$ $\underline{\sim p}$ $\therefore q$	$p \vee q$ $\underline{\sim q}$ $\therefore p$
6. Law of the Double Negation	$\underline{\sim(\sim p)}$ $\therefore p$	
7. De Morgan's Law	$\underline{\sim(p \wedge q)}$ $\therefore \sim p \vee \sim q$	$\underline{\sim(p \vee q)}$ $\therefore \sim p \wedge \sim q$
8. Law of Simplification	$\underline{p \wedge q}$ $\therefore p$	$\underline{\sim(p \vee q)}$ $\therefore q$
9. Law of Conjunction	p $\underline{q}$ $\therefore p \wedge q$	
10. Law of Disjunctive Addition	$\underline{p}$ $\therefore p \vee q$	
11. Law of Conjunctive Argument	$\sim(p \wedge q)$ $\underline{p}$ $\therefore \sim q$	$\sim(p \wedge q)$ $\underline{q}$ $\therefore \sim p$

Table 3.8 Some Rules of Inference for Propositional Logic

Rule of Inference Number	Name	Meaning "mood which by . . ."
1	*modus ponendo ponens*	affirming, affirms
3	*modus tollendo tollens*	denying, denies
5	*modus tollendo ponens*	denying, affirms
11	*modus ponendo tollens*	affirming, denies

Table 3.9 The Modus Meanings

conditional	$p \rightarrow q$
converse	$q \rightarrow p$
inverse	$\sim p \rightarrow \sim q$
contrapositive	$\sim q \rightarrow \sim p$

Table 3.10 The Conditional and Its Variants

As usual, it is assumed that the negation operator has a higher priority than the other logical operators and so no parentheses are used around ~p and ~q.

If the conditional $p \rightarrow q$ and its converse $q \rightarrow p$ are both true, then p and q are equivalent. That is $p \rightarrow q \wedge q \rightarrow p$ is equivalent to the biconditional $p \leftrightarrow q$ or equivalence $p \equiv q$. In other words, p and q always take the same truth values. If p is T then q is true and if p is F then q is F. The argument becomes

(1) C → Y
(2) Y ≡ D
(3) C
∴ D

where numbers are now used to identify the premises. Since Y and D are equivalent from (2), we can substitute D for Y in (1) to yield

(4) C → D

where (4) is an inference made on the basis of (1) and (2). Premises (3) and (4) and the conclusion are:

(4) C → D
(3) C
∴ D

which can be recognized as a schema of *modus ponens*. Hence the argument is valid.

The substitution of one variable that is equivalent to another is a rule of inference called the **rule of substitution**. The rules of *modus ponens* and substitution are two basic rules of deductive logic.

A formal logic proof is usually written by numbering the premises, conclusion, and inferences as shown in the following:

```
1. C → Y
2. (Y → D) ∧ (D → Y)
3. C                        / ∴ D
4. Y ≡ D                    2 Equivalence
5. C → D                    1 Substitution
6. D                        3,5 Modus Ponens
```

Lines 1, 2, and 3 are the premises and conclusion and 4, 5, and 6 are the inferences obtained. The right hand column lists the rule of inference and line numbers used to justify the inference.

3.7 LIMITATIONS OF PROPOSITIONAL LOGIC

Consider our familiar classic argument.

```
All men are mortal
Socrates is a man
Therefore, Socrates is mortal
```

We know that this is a valid argument since it is a valid syllogism. Can we prove its validity using propositional logic? To answer this question, let's first write the argument as a schema.

```
p = All men are mortal
q = Socrates is a man
r = Socrates is mortal
```

and so the argument schema is

```
p
q
∴ r
```

Notice that there are no logical connectives in the premises or conclusions and so each premise and each conclusion must have a different logical variable. Also, propositional logic has no provision for quantifiers and so there is no way to represent the quantifier "all" in the first premise. The only representation of this argument in propositional logic is thus the schema above of three independent variables.

To determine whether this is a valid argument, consider the truth table of three independent variables for all possible combinations of T and F, shown in Table 3.11. The second row of this truth table shows the argument to be invalid because the premises are true but the conclusion is false.

The invalidity of this argument should *not* be interpreted as meaning the conclusion is incorrect. Any person would recognize this as a correct argument. The invalidity simply means that *the argument cannot be proved under propositional logic*. The argument can be proved valid if we examine the internal structure of the premises. For example, we would have to attribute some meaning to "all" and recognize "men" as the plural of "man." However, syllogisms and the propositional calculus do not allow the internal structure of propositions to be examined. This limitation is overcome by predicate logic; and this argument is a valid argument under predicate logic. In fact, all of syllogistic logic is a valid subset of first order predicate logic and can be proved valid under it.

p	q	∴r
T	T	T
T	T	F
T	F	T
T	F	F
F	T	T
F	T	F
F	F	T
F	F	F

Table 3.11 Truth Table for the Schema p, q; ∴ r

The only valid syllogistic form of the proposition is

```
If Socrates is a man, then Socrates is mortal.
Socrates is a man.
Therefore, Socrates is mortal.
```

Let

```
p = Socrates is a man
q = Socrates is mortal
```

The argument becomes

```
p → q
p
∴ q
```

which is a valid syllogistic form of *modus ponens*.

As another example, consider the following classic argument.

```
All horses are animals
Therefore, the head of a horse is the head of an
animal
```

We know that this argument is correct and yet it cannot be proved under propositional logic, although it can be proved under predicate logic (see problem 3.12).

3.8 FIRST ORDER PREDICATE LOGIC

Syllogistic logic can be described completely by predicate logic. Table 3.12 shows the four categorical statements and their representation in predicate logic.

Type	Schema	Predicate Representation
A	All S is P	$(\forall x)\ (S(x) \rightarrow P(x))$
E	No S is P	$(\forall x)\ (S(x) \rightarrow \sim P(x))$
I	Some S is P	$(\exists x)\ (S(x) \wedge P(x))$
O	Some S is not P	$(\exists x)\ (S(x) \wedge \sim P(x))$

Table 3.12 Representation of the Four Categorical Syllogisms Using Predicate Logic

In addition to the rules of inference previously discussed, predicate logic has rules that deal with quantifiers.

The Rule of Universal Instantiation essentially states that an individual may be substituted for a universal. For example, if ϕ is any proposition or **propositional function**,

$$\frac{(\forall\ x)\ \ \phi(x)}{\therefore\ \ \phi(a)}$$

is a valid inference, where *a* is an instance. That is, *a* refers to a specific individual while x is a variable that ranges over all individuals. For example, this can be used to prove that Socrates is human:

$$\frac{(\forall\ x)\ \ H(x)}{\therefore\ \ H(Socrates)}$$

where H(x) is the propositional function that says x is a human. The above states that for every x, that x is human, and so by inference Socrates is human.

Other examples of the Rule of Universal Instantiation are:

$$\frac{(\forall\ x)\ \ A(x)}{\therefore\ \ A(c)}$$

$$\frac{(\forall\ y)\ \ (B(y)\ \vee\ C(b)}{\therefore\ \ B(a)\ \vee\ C(b)}$$

$$\frac{(\forall\ x)\ \ [A(x)\ \wedge\ (\exists\ x)\ \ (B(x)\ \vee\ C(y))]}{\therefore\ \ A(b)\ \wedge\ (\exists\ x)\ \ (B(x)\ \vee\ C(y))}$$

In the first example, the instance *c* is substituted for x. In the second example, notice that the instance *a* is substituted for *y* but not for *b* because *b* is not included in the **scope** of the quantifier. That is, a quantifier such as $\forall$ x applies only to x variables. The variables such as x and y used with quantifiers are called ***bound*** and the others are called ***free***. In the third example, the quantifier x has as its scope only A(x). That is, $\forall$ x does not apply to the existential quantifier $\exists$ x and its scope over B(x) $\vee$ C(y). The convention of nested quantifiers such as this is that the scope ends when a new quantifier is used, even if it uses the same variable, such as x. The formal proof of the syllogism

```
All men are mortal
Socrates is a man
∴ Socrates is mortal
```

is shown following, where H = man, M = mortal, and s = Socrates.

```
1. (∀ x) (H(x) → M(x))
2. H(s)                    /∴ M(s)
3. H(s) → M(s)             1 Universal Instantiation
4. M(s)                    2,3 Modus Ponens
```

3.9 LOGIC SYSTEMS

A logic system is a collection of objects such as rules, axioms, statements, and so forth organized in a consistent manner. The logic system has several goals.

The first goal is to specify the forms of arguments. Since logical arguments are meaningless in a semantic sense, a valid form is essential if the validity of the argument is to be determined. Thus, one important function of a logic system is to determine the **well-formed formulas** (**wffs**) that are used in arguments. Only wffs can be used in logic arguments. For example, in syllogistic logic,

```
All S is P
```

could be a wff, but

```
All
All is S P
Is S all
```

are not wffs. Although the symbols of the alphabet are meaningless, the sequence of symbols that make up the wff is meaningful.

The second goal of a logic system is to indicate the rules of inference that are valid. The third goal of a logic system is to extend itself by discovering new rules of inference and thus extend the range of arguments that can be proved. By extending the range of arguments, new wffs, called *theorems*, can be proved by a logic argument.

When a logic system is well developed it can be used to determine the validity of arguments in a way that is analogous to calculations in systems such as arithmetic, geometry, calculus, physics, and engineering. Logic systems have been developed such as the Sentential or Propositional Calculus, the Predicate Calculus, and so forth. Each system relies on formal definitions of its **axioms** or **postulates**, which are the fundamental definitions of the system. From these axioms people (and sometimes computer programs such as AM), try to determine what can be proved. Anyone who has studied Euclidian geometry in high school is familiar with axioms and the derivation of geometric theorems. Just as geometric theorems can be derived from geometric axioms, so can logic theorems be derived from logic axioms.

An axiom is simply a fact or **assertion** that cannot be proved from within the system. Sometimes we accept certain axioms because they make "sense" by appealing to common sense or observation. Other axioms, such as "parallel lines meet at infinity," do not make intuitive sense because they appear to contradict

Euclid's axiom of parallel lines as never meeting. However, this axiom about parallel lines meeting at infinity is just as reasonable from a purely logical viewpoint as Euclid's and is the basis of one type of non-Euclidean geometry.

A formal system requires the following:

1. An alphabet of symbols.
2. A set of finite strings of these symbols, the wffs.
3. Axioms, the definitions of the system.
4. Rules of inference, which enable a wff, A, to be deduced as the conclusion of a finite set, G, of other wffs where G= {A1, A2 ... An}. These wffs must be axioms or other theorems of the logic system. For example, a propositional logic system can be defined using only *modus ponens* to derive new theorems.

If the argument

$$A_1, A_2, \ldots A_N; \quad \therefore \quad A$$

is valid, then A is said to be a **theorem** of the formal logic system and is written with the symbol $\vdash$. For example, $\Gamma \vdash A$ means that A is a theorem of the set of wffs, Γ. A more explicit schema of a proof that A is a theorem is the following:

$$A_1, A_2, \ldots A_N \vdash A$$

The symbol $\vdash$, which indicates that the following wff is a theorem, is not a symbol of the system. Instead, $\vdash$ is a **metasymbol,** because it is used to describe the system itself. An analogy is a computer language such as Pascal. Although programs can be specified using Pascal's syntax, there is no syntax in Pascal for indicating a valid program.

A rule of inference in a formal system specifies exactly how new assertions, the theorems, can be obtained from axioms and previously derived theorems. An example of a theorem is our syllogism about Socrates, written in predicate logic form:

$$(\forall \ x) \ (H(x) \ \to \ M(x)), \ H(s) \ \vdash \ M(s)$$

where H is the predicate function for man and M is the predicate function for mortal. Because M(s) can be proved from its axioms on the left, it is a theorem of these axioms. However, note that M(Zeus) would not be a theorem since Zeus, the Greek god, is not a man, and there is no alternative way of showing M(Zeus).

If a theorem is a tautology, it follows that Γ is the null set since the wff is always true and so does not depend on any other axioms or theorems. A theorem which is a tautology is written with the symbol $\vDash$, as in $\vDash A$. For example, if Aip $\vee \sim p$, then $\vDash p \vee \sim p$ states that $p \vee \sim p$ is a theorem, which is a tautology. Notice that whatever values are assigned to p, either T or F, the theorem $p \vee \sim p$ is always true. An assignment of truth values is an **interpretation** of a wff. A **model** is an interpretation in which the wff is true. For example, a model of $p \to q$ is p = T and q = T. A wff is called *consistent* or *satisfiable* if there is an interpretation that makes it true, and *inconsistent* or *unsatisfiable* if the wff is false in *all* interpretations. An example of an inconsistent wff is p ∧ ~p.

A wff is **valid** if it is true in all interpretations; otherwise it is **invalid**. For example, the wff p ∨ ~p is valid, whreas p → q is an invalid wff since it is not true for p = T and q = F. A wff is **proved** if it can be shown to be valid. All propositional wffs can be proved by the truth table method since there is only a finite number of interpretations for wffs and so the propositional calculus is **decidable**. However, the predicate calculus is not decidable because there is no general method of proof like truth tables for all predicate calculus wffs.

One example of a valid predicate calculus wff that can be proved is that for any predicate B,

$$(\exists\ x)\ B(x)\ \rightarrow\ \sim\ [(\forall\ x)\ \sim\ B(x)]$$

which shows how the existential quantifier can be replaced by the universal quantifier. This predicate calculus wff is therefore a theorem.

There is a big difference between an expression like ⊢ A and ⊨ B. The A is a theorem and so can be proved from the axioms by the rules of inference. The B is a wff and there may be no known proof to show its derivation. While propositional logic is decidable, predicate logic is not. That is, there is no mechanical procedure or algorithm for finding the proof of a predicate logic theorem in a finite number of steps. In fact, there is a theoretical proof that there is no decision procedure for predicate logic. However, there are decision procedures for subsets of predicate logic like syllogisms and propositional logic. Sometimes predicate logic is referred to as **semidecidable** because of this.

As a very simple example of a complete formal system, define the following:

Alphabet : The single symbol "1"
Axiom : The string "1" (which happens to be the same as the symbol 1)
Rule of Inference : If any string $ is a theorem, then so is the string $11. This rule can be written as a Post production rule,

$ → $11.
    If $ = 1 then this rule gives $11 = 111.
    If $ = 111 then the rule gives $11 = 11111 and in general
            1, 111, 11111, 1111111, . . .

The strings above are the theorems of this formal system (Minsky 67).

Although such as like 11111 do not look like the types of theorems we are used to seeing, they are perfectly valid logic theorems. These particular theorems also have a semantic meaning because they are the odd numbers expressed in a **unary number system** of the single symbol 1. Just as the binary number system has only the alphabet symbols 0 and 1, the unary number system has only the single symbol 1. Numbers in the unary and decimal systemsare expressed as

Unary	Decimal
1	1
11	2
111	3
1111	4
11111	5

and so forth.

Notice that because of our rule of inference and axiom, the strings 11, 1111, and so forth cannot be expressed in our formal system. That is, 11 and 1111 are certainly strings from our formal alphabet, but they are not theorems or wffs because they cannot be proved using only the rule of inference and the axiom. This formal system allows only the derivation of the odd numbers, not the even numbers. The axiom "11" must be added in order to be able to derive the even numbers.

Another property of a formal system is **completeness**. A set of axioms is **complete** if every wff can be either proved or **refuted**. The term *refute* means to prove that some assertion is false. In a complete system, every logically valid wff is a theorem. However, since predicate logic is not decidable, coming up with a proof depends on our luck and cleverness. Of course, another possibility is writing a computer program that will try to derive proofs and let it grind away.

A further desirable property of a logical system is that it be **sound**. A sound system means that every theorem is a logically valid wff. In other words, a sound system will not allow a conclusion to be inferred that is not a logical consequence of its premises. No invalid arguments will be inferred as valid.

There are different **orders** of logic. A **first order** language is defined so that the quantifiers operate on objects that are variables such as ∀ x. A **second order** language would have additional features such as two kinds of variables and quantifiers. In addition to the ordering variables and quantifiers, the second order logic can have quantifiers that range over function and predicate symbols. An example of second order logic is the **equality axiom**, which states that two objects are equal if all predicates of them are equal. If P is any predicate of one argument, then

$$x = y \equiv (\forall\ P)\ [P(x) \leftrightarrow P(y)]$$

is a statement of the equality axiom using a second order quantifier, ∀ P, which ranges over all predicates.

3.10 RESOLUTION

The very powerful **resolution** rule of inference introduced by Robinson in 1965 is commonly implemented in theorem-proving AI programs (Robinson 65). In fact, resolution is the primary rule of inference in PROLOG. Instead of many different inference rules of limited applicability, such as *modus ponens*, *modus tollens*, merging, chaining, and so forth, PROLOG uses the one general purpose inference rule of resolution. This application of resolution makes automatic theorem provers such as PROLOG practical tools for solving problems. Instead of having to try different rules of inference and hoping one succeeds, the single rule of resolution can be applied. This approach can greatly reduce the search space.

As a way of introducing resolution, let's first consider the syllogism about Socrates expressed in PROLOG as follows, where comments are shown with a percent sign:

```
mortal(X) :- man(X).      % All men are mortal
man(socrates).            % Socrates is a man
:- mortal(socrates).      % Query - is Socrates mortal?
yes                       % PROLOG answers yes
```

PROLOG uses a **quantifier-free** notation. Notice that the universal quantifier, $\forall$, is implied in the statement that all men are mortal.

PROLOG is based on first-order predicate logic. However, it also has a number of extensions to make it easier for programming applications. These special programming features violate pure predicate logic and are called *extralogical features*: input/output, cut (which alters the search space) and assert/retract (to alter truth values without any logical justification).

Before resolution can be applied, the wff must be in a **normal** or standard form. The three main types of normal forms are **conjunctive normal form**, clausal form, and its Horn clause subset. The basic idea of normal form is to express wffs in a standard form that uses only the $\wedge$, $\vee$, and possibly $\sim$. The resolution method is then applied to normal form wffs in which all other connectives and quantifiers have been eliminated. This conversion to normal form is necessary because resolution is an operation on pairs of disjuncts, which produces new disjuncts, which simplifies the wff.

The following illustrates a wff in conjunctive normal form, which is defined as the conjunction of disjunctions, which are **literals**.

$$(P_1 \vee P_2 \vee \ldots) \wedge (Q_1 \vee Q_2 \vee \ldots) \wedge \ldots (Z_1 \vee Z_2 \vee \ldots)$$

Terms such as P_1 must be literals, which means that they contain no logical connectives such as the conditional and biconditional, or quantifiers. A literal is an atomic formula or a negated atomic formula. For example, the following wff

$$(A \vee B) \wedge (\sim B \vee C)$$

is in conjunctive normal form. The terms within parentheses are clauses.

$$A \vee B \text{ and } \sim B \vee C$$

As will be shown later, any predicate logic wff, which includes propositional logic as a special case, can be written as clauses. The full **clausal form** can express any predicate logic formula but may not be as natural or readable for a person (Kowalski 79). The syntax of PROLOG is the Horn clause subset, which makes mechanical theorem proving by PROLOG much easier and more efficient to implement than standard predicate logic notation or full clausal form. As mentioned in Chapter 1, PROLOG allows only one head. A full clausal form expression is generally written in a special form called Kowalski clausal form

$$A_1, A_2, \ldots A_N \rightarrow B_1, B_2, \ldots B_M$$

which is interpreted as saying that if all the subgoals $A_1, A_2, \ldots A_N$ are true, then one or more of B_1 or $B_2 \ldots$ or B_M are true also. Note that sometimes the direction of the arrow is reversed in this notation. This clause, written in standard predicate notation, is

$$A_1 \wedge A_2 \ldots A_N \rightarrow B_1 \vee B_2 \ldots B_M$$

This can be expressed in **disjunctive form** as the disjunction of literals using the equivalence

$$p \rightarrow q \equiv \sim p \vee q$$

so

$$A_1 \wedge A_2 \ \ldots \ A_N \rightarrow B_1 \vee B_2 \ \ldots \ B_M$$
$$\equiv \sim(A_1 \wedge A_2 \ \ldots \ A_N) \vee (B_1 \vee B_2 \ \ldots \ B_M)$$
$$\equiv \sim A_1 \vee \sim A_2 \ \ldots \ \sim A_N \vee B_1 \vee B_2 \ \ldots \ B_M$$

where de Morgan's law

$$\sim(p \wedge q) \equiv \sim p \vee \sim q$$

is used to simplify the last expression.

As discussed in Chapter 1, PROLOG uses a restricted type of clausal form, the Horn clause, in which only one head is allowed:

$$A_1, A_2, \ \ldots \ A_N \rightarrow B$$

which is written in PROLOG syntax as

$$B \ :- \ A_1, A_2, \ \ldots \ A_N$$

The problem with trying to prove a theorem directly is the difficulty of deducing it using only the rules of inference and axioms of the system. It may take a very long time to derive a theorem or we may not be clever enough to derive it at all. To prove a theorem is true the classical method of ***reductio ad absurdum***, or method of contradiction, is used. In this method we try to prove the negated wff is a theorem. If a contradiction results, then the original nonnegated wff is a theorem.

The basic goal of resolution is to infer a new clause, the **resolvent**, from two other clauses, called *parent clauses*. The resolvent will have fewer terms than the parents. By continuing the process of resolution, eventually a contradiction will be obtained or the process will be terminated because no progress is being made. A simple example of resolution is shown in the following argument.

$$A \vee B$$
$$\underline{A \vee \sim B}$$
$$\therefore \ A$$

One way of seeing how the conclusion follows is by writing the premises as

$$(A \vee B) \wedge (A \vee \sim B)$$

One of the axioms of distribution is

$$p \vee (q \wedge r) \equiv (p \vee q) \wedge (p \vee r)$$

Applying this to the premises gives

$$(A \vee B) \wedge (A \vee \sim B) \equiv A \vee (B \wedge \sim B) \equiv A$$

where the last step follows since $(B \wedge \sim B)$ is always false. This follows from the Law of the Excluded Middle, which states that something cannot be both true and false. In fuzzy logic, discussed in Chapter 5, we'll see that this law does not hold. Another way of writing this uses the term **nil** or **null**, which means empty, nothing, or false. For example, a nil pointer in Pascal points to nothing, and the Law of the Excluded Middle states $(B \land \sim B) \equiv nil$.

The example of resolution shows how the parent clauses $(A \lor B)$ and $(A \lor \sim B)$ can be simplified into the resolvent A. Table 3.13 summarizes some basic parent clauses and their resolvents in clause notation, where the comma separating clauses means $\land$.

Parent Clauses	Resolvent	Meaning
$p \to q, p$ or $\sim p \lor q, p$	q	*Modus Ponens*
$p \to q, q \to r$ or $\sim p \lor q, \sim q \lor r$	$p \to r$ or $\sim p \lor r$	Chaining or Hypothetical Syllogism
$\sim p \lor q, p \lor q$	q	Merging
$\sim p \lor \sim q, p \lor q$	$\sim p \lor p$ or $\sim q \lor q$	TRUE (a tautology)
$\sim p, p$	nil	FALSE (a contradiction)

Table 3.13 Clauses and Resolvents

3.11 RESOLUTION SYSTEMS AND DEDUCTION

Given wffs $A_1, A_2, \ldots A_N$ and a logical conclusion or theorem C, we know that

$$A_1 \land A_2 \ldots A_N \vdash C$$

is equivalent to stating

$$(1) \quad A_1 \land A_2 \ldots A_N \to C \qquad \equiv \sim(A_1 \land A_2 \ldots A_N) \lor C$$
$$\equiv \sim A_1 \lor \sim A_2 \ldots \sim A_N \lor C$$

is valid. Suppose we take the negation as follows:

$$\sim [A_1 \land A_2 \ldots A_N \to C]$$

Now

$$p \to q \equiv \sim p \lor q$$

and so the above becomes

$$\sim [A_1 \wedge A_2 \ldots A_N \to C] \equiv \sim [\sim (A_1 \wedge A_2 \ldots A_N) \vee C]$$

From de Morgan's laws,

$$\sim (p \vee q) \equiv \sim p \wedge \sim q$$

and so the above becomes

$$(2) \quad \sim [A_1 \wedge A_2 \ldots A_N \to C] \quad \equiv [\sim\sim (A_1 \wedge A_2 \ldots A_N) \wedge \sim C]$$
$$\equiv A_1 \wedge A_2 \ldots A_N \wedge \sim C$$

Now if (1) is valid, then its negation (2) must be invalid. In other words, if (1) is a tautology then (2) must be a contradiction. Formulas (1) and (2) represent two equivalent ways of proving that a formula C is a theorem. Formula (1) can be used to prove a theorem by checking to see if it is true in all cases. At the same time, formula (2) can be used to prove a theorem by showing (2) leads to a contradiction.

As mentioned in the previous section, proving a theorem by showing its negation leads to a contradiction is proof by *reductio ad absurdum*. The primary part of this type of proof is the **refutation**. To refute something means to prove it false. Resolution is a sound rule of inference that is also **refutation complete** because the empty clause will always be the eventual result if there is a contradiction in the set of clauses. Essentially this means that **resolution refutation** will terminate in a finite number of steps if there is a contradiction. Although resolution refutation can't tell us how to *produce* a theorem, it will definitely tell us if a wff *is* a theorem.

As a simple example of proof by resolution refutation, consider the argument

$$A \to B$$
$$B \to C$$
$$\underline{C \to D}$$
$$\therefore A \to D$$

To prove that the conclusion $A \to D$ is a theorem by resolution refutation, first convert it to disjunctive form using the equivalence

$$p \to q \equiv \sim p \vee q$$

So

$$A \to D \equiv \sim A \vee D$$

and its negation is

$$\sim (\sim A \vee D) \equiv A \wedge \sim D$$

The conjunction of the disjunctive forms of the premises and the negated conclusion gives the conjunctive normal form suitable for resolution refutation.

$$(\sim A \vee B) \wedge (\sim B \vee C) \wedge (\sim C \vee D) \wedge A \wedge \sim D$$

The resolution method can now be applied to the premises and conclusion. Figure 3.18 shows a method of representing resolution refutation in the form of a **resolution refutation tree** diagram, where clauses on the same level are resolved. The root, which is the final resolvent, is nil, as can be verified from the last row of Table 3.13 for ~p, p, and so the original conclusion A → D is a theorem.

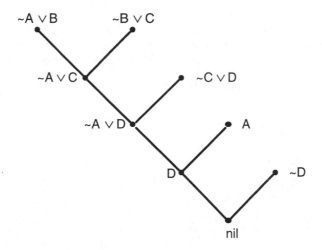

Figure 3.18 Resolution Refutation Tree

3.12 SHALLOW AND CAUSAL REASONING

Resolution systems and production rule systems are two popular paradigms for proving theorems. Although most people think of a theorem in the mathematical sense, we have seen that a theorem is actually the conclusion of a valid logical argument. Now consider an expert system that uses an inference chain. In general, a longer chain represents more causal or deep knowledge, while shallow reasoning commonly uses a single rule or a few inferences. Besides the length of the inference chain, the quality of knowledge in the rules is also a major factor in determining deep and shallow reasoning. Sometimes another definition of shallow knowledge is used, called **experiential knowledge**, which is knowledge based on experience.

The conclusion of an inference chain is a theorem because it is proved by the chain of inference, as demonstrated by the previous example.

$$A \rightarrow B, \ B \rightarrow C, \ C \rightarrow D \vdash A \rightarrow D$$

In fact, expert systems that use an inference chain to establish a conclusion are really using theorems. This result is very important because otherwise we could not use expert systems for causal inference. Instead, expert systems would be restricted to shallow inferences of single rules with no chaining.

Let's look at some rules now in order to better contrast shallow and deep reasoning. As a first example, consider the following rule in which the number in parentheses is for identification purposes only:

```
(1)   IF a car has
         a good battery
         good spark plugs
         gas
         good tires
      THEN the car can move
```

This is a perfectly good rule that could be used in an expert system.

One of the important features of an expert system is the explanation facility, as discussed in Chapter 1. Rule-based expert systems make it easy for the system to explain its reasoning. In this case, if the user asked how the car can move, the expert system could respond by listing its conditional elements:

```
a good battery
good spark plugs
gas
good tires
```

This is an elementary type of explanation facility because the system lists only the conditional elements of the rule. More sophisticated explanation facilities can be designed to list previous rules that have fired and resulted in the current rule firing. Other explanation facilities may allow the user to ask "what if" type questions to explore alternative reasoning paths.

This rule is also an example of **shallow reasoning**. That is, there is little or no understanding of cause and effect in shallow reasoning because there is little or no inference chain. The previous rule is essentially a heuristic in which all the knowledge is contained in the rule. The rule becomes activated when its conditional elements are satisfied and not because there is any understanding by the expert system of what function the conditional elements perform. In shallow reasoning there is little or no **causal chain** of cause and effect from one rule to another. In the simplest case, the cause and effect are contained in one with no relationship to any other rule. If you think of rules in terms of the chunks of knowledge discussed in Chapter 1, shallow reasoning makes no connections between chunks and so is like a simple reflex reaction.

The advantage of shallow reasoning compared to causal reasoning is ease of programming. Easier programming means the development time is shorter and the program is smaller, faster, and costs less to develop.

Frame and semantic nets are two useful models for causal or **deep reasoning**. The term *deep* is often used synonymously for causal reasoning to imply a deep understanding of the subject. However, a deep understanding implies that in addition to understanding the causal chain by which a process occurs, you also understand the process in an abstract sense.

One classic expert system using frames and having a causal understanding is the Steamer system built by the U.S. Navy to teach the operation of ship propulsion plants (Hollan 84). A deep expert system is the LISP Tutor, which is designed to act as an intelligent tutor for teaching students LISP (Reiser 85).

We can add simple causal reasoning to our rule by defining additional rules such as

```
(2)   IF the battery is good
      THEN there is electricity

(3)   IF there is electricity
         and the spark plugs are good
      THEN the spark plugs will fire

(4)   IF the spark plugs fire
         and there is gas
      THEN the engine will run

(5)   IF the engine runs
         and there are good tires
      THEN the car will move
```

Notice that with causal reasoning the explanation facility can give a good explanation of what each car component does since each element is specified by a rule. Such a causal system also makes it easier to write a diagnostic system to determine what effect a bad component will have. Causal reasoning may be used for an arbitrary refinement of the operation of a system limited by the speed of execution, memory size, and increasing development cost.

Causal reasoning can be used to construct a **model** of the real system that behaves in all respects like the real thing. Such a model can be used for simulation to explore hypothetical reasoning of the "what if" type of queries. However, causal models are neither always necessary nor desirable. For example, the MUD system serves as a consultant to drilling fluid or mud engineers (Kahn 85). Drilling fluid, called *mud* because of its resemblance to mud, is an important aid in drilling for a number of reasons, such as cooling and lubrication of the bit. MUD diagnoses problems with the mud and suggests treatments.

A causal system would not be of much use because the drilling engineer cannot normally observe the causal chain of events occurring far below the ground. Instead, the engineer can only observe the symptoms on the surface and not the unobservable intermediate events of potential diagnostic significance.

The situation is very different in medicine, where physicians have a wide range of diagnostic tests that can be used to verify intermediate events. For example, if a person complains of feeling ill, the physician can check for fever. If there is a fever, there may be an infection and so a blood test may be done. If the blood test reveals a tetanus infection, the physician may check the person for recent cuts by a rusty object. In contrast, if the drilling fluid becomes salty, the drilling engineer may suspect the drill has gone through a salt dome. However, there is no simple way to check this since it's not possible to go into the hole, and a seismic test is expensive and not always reliable. Because drilling engineers cannot normally test intermediate hypotheses the way that physicians can, they do not approach diagnostic problems the way that physicians do, and MUD reflects this approach.

Another reason for not using causal reasoning in MUD is that there is a limited number of diagnostic possibilities and symptoms. Most of the relevant tests used by MUD are conducted routinely and input in advance. There is little advantage in an interactive query session with an engineer to explore alternate diagnostic paths if the system knows all the relevant tests and diagnostic paths. If there were many possible diagnostic paths to follow with a verifiable intermediate hypothesis there would be an advantage to causal knowledge because the engineer could work with the system to prune the search to likely paths.

Because of the increased requirements for causal reasoning, it may become necessary to combine certain rules into a shallow reasoning one. The resolution method with refutation can be used to prove that a single rule is a true conclusion of multiple rules. The single rule is the theorem that will be proved by resolution.

As an example, suppose we want to prove that rule (1) is a logical conclusion of rules (2) through (5). Using the following propositional definitions, the rules can be expressed as follows.

```
B = battery is good          C = car will move
E = there is electricity     F = spark plugs will fire
G = there is gas             R = engine will run
S = spark plugs are good     T = there are good tires
```

```
(1)  B ∧ S ∧ G ∧ T → C
(2)  B → E
(3)  E ∧ S → F
(4)  F ∧ G → R
(5)  R ∧ T → C
```

The first step in applying resolution refutation is to negate the conclusion or goal rule.

$$(1') \sim(B \wedge S \wedge G \wedge T \to C) = \sim[\sim(B \wedge S \wedge G \wedge T) \vee C]$$
$$= \sim[\sim B \vee \sim S \vee \sim G \vee \sim T \vee C]$$

Now each of the other rules is expressed in disjunctive form using equivalences such as

$$p \to q \equiv \sim p \vee q \text{ and } \sim(p \wedge q) \equiv \sim p \vee \sim q$$

to yield the following new versions of (2) through (5).

```
(2')  ~B ∨ E
(3')  ~(E ∧ S) ∨ F = ~E ∨ ~S ∨ F
(4')  ~(F ∧ G) ∨ R = ~F ∨ ~G ∨ R
(5')  ~(R ∧ T) ∨ C = ~R ∨ ~T ∨ C
```

As described in the previous section, a convenient way of representing the successive resolvents of (1') - (5') is with a resolution refutation tree, as shown in Figure 3.19. Starting at the top of the tree, the clauses are represented as nodes, which are resolved to produce the resolvent below. For example,

$$\sim B \vee E \text{ and } \sim E \vee \sim S \vee F$$

are resolved to infer

$$\sim B \vee \sim S \vee F$$

which is then resolved with

$$\sim F \ \lor \ \sim G \ \lor \ R$$

to infer

$$\sim B \ \lor \ \sim S \ \lor \ \sim G \ \lor \ R$$

and so forth. For simplicity in drawing, the last resolvents are implied, rather than drawing in every single one.

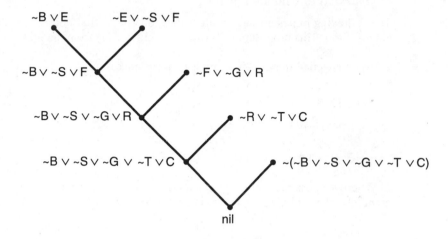

Figure 3.19 Resolution Refutation Tree for the Car Example

Since the root of the tree is nil, this resolution is a contradiction. By refutation, the original conclusion

$$B \ \land \ S \ \land \ G \ \land \ T \ \rightarrow \ C$$

is a theorem since its negation leads to a contradiction. Thus rule (1) does logically follow from rules (2) through (5).

3.13 RESOLUTION AND FIRST ORDER PREDICATE LOGIC

The resolution method is also used with the first order predicate logic. In fact, it is the primary inference mechanism of PROLOG. However, before resolution can be applied, a wff must be put in clausal form. As an example,

```
Some programmers hate all failures
No programmer hates any success
∴ No failure is a success
```

Define the following predicates:

```
P(x) = x is a programmer
F(x) = x is a failure
S(x) = x is a success
H(x,y) = x hates y
```

The premises and negated conclusion are written as

```
(1)  (∃ x)  [P(x) ∧ (∀ y)  (F(y) → H(x,y))]
(2)  (∀ x)  [P(x) → (∀ y)  (S(y) → ~H(x,y))]
(3)  ~(∀ y)  (F(y) → ~S(y))
```

where the conclusion has been negated in preparation for resolution.

Conversion to Clausal Form

The following nine steps are an algorithm to convert first order predicate wffs to clausal form. This procedure is illustrated using wff (1) from the previous page.

1. Eliminate conditionals, →, using the equivalence

$$p \rightarrow q \equiv {\sim}p \lor q$$

so the wff(1) becomes

```
(∃ x)  [P(x) ∧ (∀ y)  (~F(y) ∨ H(x,y))]
```

2. Wherever possible, eliminate negations or reduce the scope of negation to one atom. Use the equivalences shown in Appendix A such as

```
~~p ≡ p
~(p ∧ q) ≡ ~p ∨ ~q
~(∃ x)  P(x) ≡ (∀ x)  ~P(x)
~(∀ x)  P(x) ≡ (∃ x)  ~P(x)
```

3. Standardize variables within a wff so that the bound or dummy variables of each quantifier have unique names. Note that the variable names of a quantifier are dummies. That is,

```
(∀ x)  P(x) ≡ (∀ y)  P(y) ≡ (∀ z)  P(z)
```

and so the standardized form of

```
(∃ x)  ~P(x) ∨ (∀ x)  P(x)
```

is

```
(∃ x)  ~P(x) ∨ (∀ y)  P(y)
```

4. Eliminate existential quantifiers, ∃, using **Skolem functions**, named after the Norwegian logician, Thoralf Skolem. Consider the wff

```
(∃ x)  L(x)
```

where $L(x)$ is defined as the predicate, which is true if x is < 0. This wff can be replaced by

```
L(a)
```

where a is a constant such as −1 that makes L(a) true. The a is called a Skolem constant, which is a special case of the Skolem function. For the case in which there is a universal quantifier in front of an existential one,

$$(\forall \ x) \ (\exists \ y) \ L(x,y)$$

where L(x,y) is true if the integer x is less than the integer y. This wff means that for every integer x there is an integer y which is greater than x. Notice that the formula does not tell how to compute *y* given a value for x. Assume a function f(x) exists which produces a y greater than x. So the above wff becomes Skolemized as

$$(\forall \ x) \ L(x,f(x))$$

The Skolem function of an existential variable within the scope of a universal quantifier is a function of all the quantifiers on the left. For example,

$$(\exists \ u) \ (\forall \ v) \ (\forall \ w) \ (\exists \ x) \ (\forall \ y) \ (\exists \ z) \ P(u,v,w,x,y,z)$$

is Skolemized as

$$(\forall \ v) \ (\forall \ w) \ (\forall \ y) \ P(a,v,w,f(v,w),y,g(v,w,y))$$

where a is some constant and the second Skolem function, g, must be different from the first function, f. Our example wff becomes

$$P(a) \ \wedge \ (\forall \ y) \ (\sim F(y) \ \vee \ H(a,y))$$

5. Convert the wff to **prenex form,** which is a sequence of quantifiers, Q, followed by a **matrix**, M. In general, the quantifiers can be either $\forall$ or $\exists$. However, in this case step 4 has already eliminated all existential quantifiers and so the Q can only be $\forall$. Also, because each $\forall$ has its own dummy variable, all the $\forall s$ can be moved to the left of the wff and the scope of each $\forall$ can be the entire wff.

Our example becomes

$$(\forall \ y) \ [P(a) \ \wedge \ (\sim F(y) \ \vee \ H(a,y)]$$

where the matrix is the term in brackets.

6. Convert the matrix to conjunctive normal form, which is a conjunctive of clauses. Each clause is a disjunction. Our example is already in conjunctive normal form where one clause is P(a) and the other is $(\sim F(y) \ \vee \ H(a,y))$. If necessary, the following distributive rule can be used as necessary to put the matrix in conjunctive normal form:

$$p \ \vee \ (q \ \wedge \ r) \ \equiv \ (p \ \vee \ q) \ \wedge \ (p \ \vee \ r)$$

7. Drop the universal quantifiers as unnecessary since all the variables in a wff at this stage must be bound. The wff is now the matrix. Our example wff becomes

```
P(a) ∧ (~F(y) ∨ H(a,y))
```

8. Eliminate the ∧ signs by writing the wff as a set of clauses. Our example is

```
{ P(a), ~F(y) ∨ H(a,y) }
```

which is usually written without the braces as the clauses

```
P(a)
~F(y) ∨ H(a,y)
```

9. Rename variables in clauses, if necessary, so that the same variable name is only used in one clause. For example, if we had the clauses

```
P(x) ∧ Q(x) ∨ L(x,y)
~P(x) ∨ Q(y)
~Q(z) ∨ L(z,y)
```

these could be renamed as

```
P(x1) ∧ Q(x1) ∨ L(x1,y1)
~P(x2) ∨ Q(y2)
~Q(z) ∨ L(z,y3)
```

   If we carry out the procedure to convert to clausal form the second premise and the negated conclusion of our example, we finally obtain the clauses

```
(1a)  P(a)
(1b)  ~F(y) ∨ H(a,y)
(2a)  ~P(x) ∨ ~S(y) ∨ ~H(x,y)
(3a)  F(b)
(3b)  S(b)
```

where the numbers refer to the original premises and negated conclusion. Thus, premises (1) and (3) are converted to two clauses with suffixes (a) and (b), while premise (2) is converted to the single clause (2a).

Unification and Rules

Once the wffs have been converted to clausal form, it is usually necessary to find appropriate **substitution instances** for the variables. That is, clauses such as

```
~F(y) ∨ H(a,y)
F(b)
```

cannot be resolved on the predicate F until the arguments of F match. The process of finding substitutions for variables to make arguments match is called **unification**.

   Unification is one feature that distinguishes expert systems from simple decision trees. Without unification, the conditional elements of rules could only match constants. This means that a specific rule would have to be written for every possible fact. For example, suppose someone wanted to sound a fire alarm if a sensor indicated smoke. If there are N sensors, you would need a rule for each sensor as follows:

```
IF sensor 1 indicates smoke THEN sound fire alarm 1
IF sensor 2 indicates smoke THEN sound fire alarm 2
...
IF sensor N indicates smoke THEN sound fire alarm N
```

However, with unification, a variable called ?N can be used for the sensor identifier so that one rule can be written as follows.

```
IF sensor ?N indicates smoke
THEN sound fire alarm ?N
```

When two complementary literals are unified, they can be eliminated by resolution. For the two preceding clauses, the substitution of y by b gives

```
~F(b) ∨ H(a,b)
F(b)
```

The predicate F has now been unified and can be resolved into

```
H(a,b)
```

A substitution is defined as the simultaneous replacement of variables by terms that differentiate from the variables. The terms may be constants, variables, or functions. The substitution of terms for variables is indicated by the set

$$\{ \ t_1/v_1, \ t_2/v_2 \ ... \ t_N/v_N \ \}$$

If θ is such a set and A an argument, then $A\theta$ is defined as the substitution instance of A. For example, if

```
θ = { a/x, f(y)/y, x/z }
A = P(x) ∨ Q(y) ∨ R(z)
```

then

```
Aθ = P(a) ∨ Q(f(y)) ∨ R(x)
```

Notice that the substitution is simultaneous, so that we get R(x) and not R(a).

Suppose there are two clauses, C_1 and C_2, defined as

```
C₁ = ~P(x)
C₂ = P(f(x))
```

One possible unification of P is

```
C₁' = C₁ { f(x)/x } = ~P(f(x))
```

Another possible unification for P is the two substitutions using the constant a

```
C₁'' = C₁ { f(a)/x } = ~P(f(a))
C₂' = C₂ { a/x } = P(f(a))
```

Notice that P(f(x)) is more general than P(f(a)) because there are an infinite number of instances of P(f(x)) that can be produced by substituting a constant for x. A clause like C_1 is called the **most general clause**.

In general, a substitution θ is called a ***unifier*** for a set of clauses { A_1, A_2, . . . A_n } if and only if $A_1θ = A_2θ = . . . A_nθ$. A set which has a unifier is called ***unifiable***. The **most general unifier** (**mgu**) is that from which all the other unifiers are instances. This can be expressed more formally by stating that θ is the most general unifier if and only if for each unifier, α, of a set, there is a substitution β such that

$$α = θβ$$

where θβ is the compound substitution created by applying first θ and then β. The **unification algorithm** is a method of finding the most general unifier for a finite unifiable set of arguments (Chang 73; Nilsson 80).

For our example with clauses (1a) through (3b), the results of substitution and unification are shown in the resolution refutation tree of Figure 3.20. Since the root is nil, the negated conclusion is false and so the conclusion is valid that "no failure is a success."

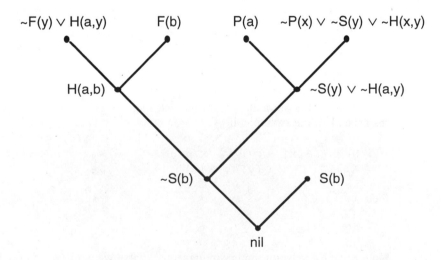

Figure 3.20 Resolution Refutation Tree to Prove No Failure Is a Success

The examples used so far are simple and their resolution is straightforward, although tedious for a human. However, in many other situations the resolution process may lead to a dead end and so backtracking is necessary to try alternative clauses for resolution. Although resolution is very powerful and is the basis of PROLOG, it may be inefficient for some problems. One of the problems with resolution is that it has no efficient built-in search strategy and so the programmer must supply heuristics, such as the PROLOG cut, for efficient searching.

A number of modified versions of resolution have been investigated. such as **unit preference**, **input resolution**, **linear resolution**, and **set of support** (Amble 87). The main advantage of resolution is that it is a single powerful technique that is adequate for many cases. This makes it easier to build mechanical system such as PROLOG than a system that attempts to implement many different rules of inference. Another advantage of resolution is that when it is successful, resolution automatically provides a proof by showing the sequence of steps to a nil.

3.14 FORWARD AND BACKWARD CHAINING

A group of multiple inferences that connects a problem with its solution is called a **chain**. A chain that is searched or traversed from a problem to its solution is called a forward chain. Another way of describing forward chaining is reasoning from facts to the conclusions that follow from the facts. A chain that is traversed from a hypothesis back to the facts that support the hypothesis is a backward chain. Another way of describing a backward chain is in terms of a goal which can be accomplished by satisfying subgoals. As this shows, the terminology used to describe forward and backward chaining depends on the problem being discussed.

Chaining can be easily expressed in terms of inference. For example, suppose we have rules of the *modus ponens* type:

$$p \rightarrow q$$
$$\underline{p}$$
$$\therefore \quad q$$

that form a chain of inference, such as the following:

```
elephant(x) → mammal(x)
mammal(x) → animal(x)
```

These rules may be used in a causal chain of forward inference that deduces that Clyde is an animal, given that Clyde is an elephant. The inference chain is illustrated in Figure 3.21. Notice that the same diagram also illustrates backward chaining.

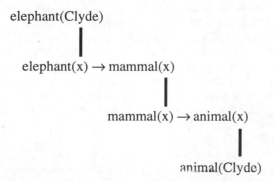

elephant(Clyde)

elephant(x) → mammal(x)

mammal(x) → animal(x)

animal(Clyde)

Figure 3.21 Causal Forward Chain

In Figure 3.21 the causal chain is represented by the sequence of bars, connecting the consequent of one rule to the antecedent of the next. A bar also indicates the unification of variables to facts. For example, the variable x in the predicate elephant(x) must first be unified with the fact elephant(Clyde) before the elephant rule can be applied. The causal chain is really a sequence of implications and unifications, as shown in Figure 3.22.

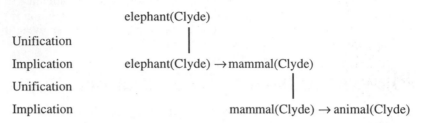

Figure 3.22 Explicit Causal Chain

Backward chaining is the reverse process. Suppose we want to prove the hypothesis animal(Clyde). The central problem of backward chaining is to find a chain linking the evidence to the hypothesis. The fact elephant(Clyde) is called the **evidence** in backward chaining to indicate it is used to support the hypothesis, in the same way evidence in a court is used to prove the guilt of the defendant.

As a simple example of forward and backward chaining, suppose you are driving and suddenly see a police car with flashing light. By forward chaining, you may infer that the police want you or someone else to stop. That is, the initial facts support two possible conclusions. If the police car pulls up right in back of you or the police wave at you, a further inference is that the officer wants you rather than someone else. Adopting this as a working hypotheses, you can apply backward chaining to reason why.

Some possible intermediate hypotheses are littering, speeding, malfunctioning equipment, and driving a stolen vehicle. Now you examine the evidence to support these intermediate hypotheses. Was it the beer bottle that you threw out the window, going 100 in a 30 mile per hour speed zone, the broken tail lights, or the license plates identifying the stolen car you're driving? In this case, each piece of evidence supports an intermediate hypothesis and so they are all true. Any or all of these intermediate hypotheses are possible reasons to prove the working hypothesis that the police want you.

It's helpful to visualize forward and backward chaining in terms of a path through a problem space in which the intermediate states correspond to intermediate hypotheses under backward chaining or intermediate conclusions under forward chaining. Table 3.14 summarizes some of the common characteristics of forward and backward chaining. Note that the characteristics in this table are meant only as a guide. It is certainly possible to diagnose in a forward chaining system and planning in a backward chaining one. In particular, explanation is facilitated in backward chaining because the system can easily explain exactly what goal it is trying to satisfy. In forward chaining explanation is not so easily facilitated because the subgoals are not explicitly known until discovered.

Figure 3.23 illustrates the basic concept of forward chaining in a rule-based system. Rules are triggered by the facts that satisfy their antecedent or left-hand-sides (LHS). For example, to be activated the rule R_1 must be satisfied by facts B and C. However, only fact C is present, so R_1 is not activated. Rule R_2 is activated by facts C and D, which are present, and so R_2 produces the intermediate fact H. Other satisfied rules are R_3, R_6, R_7, R_8, and R_9. The execution of rules R_8 and R_9 produces the conclusions of the forward chaining process. These conclusions may be other facts, output, and so forth.

Forward Chaining	Backward Chaining
Planning, monitoring, control	Diagnosis
Present to future	Present to past
Antecedent to consequent	Consequent to antecedent
Data driven, bottom-up reasoning	Goal driven, top-down reasoning
Work forward to find what solutions follow from the facts	Work backward to find facts that support the hypothesis
Breadth-first search facilitated	Depth-first search facilitated
Antecedents determine search	Consequents determine search
Explanation not facilitated	Explanation facilitated

Table 3.14 Some Characteristics of Forward and Backward Chaining

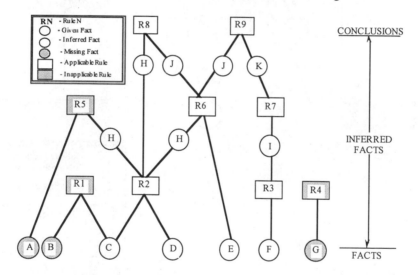

Figure 3.23 Forward Chaining

Forward chaining is called **bottom-up reasoning** because it reasons from the low-level evidence, facts, to the top-level conclusions that are based on the facts. Bottom-up reasoning in an expert system is analogous to bottom-up conventional programming, that was discussed in Chapter 1. Facts are the elementary units of the knowledge-based paradigm because they cannot be decomposed into any smaller units that have meaning. For example, the fact "duck" has definite meanings as a noun and as a verb. However, if it is broken down any further, the result is the letters d, u, c, and k which have no special meaning. In conventional programs the basic units of meaning are data.

By custom, higher-level constructs that are composed of lower-level ones are put at the top. So reasoning from the higher-level constructs such as hypotheses down to the lower-level facts which may support the hypotheses is called **top-down reasoning** or backward chaining. Figure 3.24 illustrates the concept of backward chaining. In order to prove or disprove hypothesis H, at least one of the intermediate hypotheses, H_1, H_2, or H_3, must be proved. Notice that this diagram is drawn as an AND-OR tree to indicate that in some cases, such as H_2, all its lower-level hypotheses must be present to support H_2. In other cases, such as the top-level hypothesis, H, only one lower-level hypothesis is necessary. In backward chaining the system will commonly elicit evidence from the user to aid in proving or disproving hypotheses. This contrasts with a forward chaining system, in which all the relevant facts are usually known in advance.

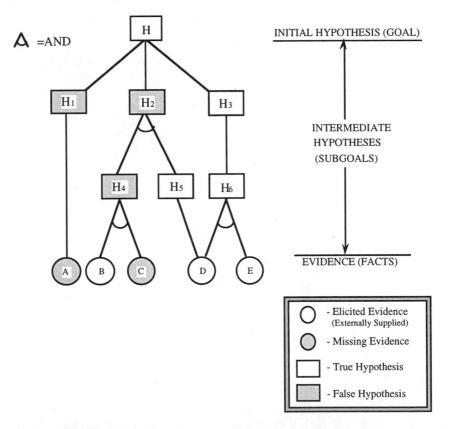

Figure 3.24 Backward Chaining

If you look back at Figure 3.4 (page 100), you will see that the decision net is well organized for backward chaining. The top-level hypotheses are the different types of raspberries such as flowering raspberry, black raspberry, wineberry, and red raspberry. The evidence to support these hypotheses is lower down. The rules to identify a raspberry can be easily written. For example,

```
IF the leaves are simple THEN flowering raspberry
```

One important aspect of eliciting evidence is asking the right questions. The right questions are those that improve the efficiency in determining the correct answer. One obvious requirement for this is that the expert system should only ask questions that deal with the hypotheses that it is trying to prove. While there may be hundreds or thousands of questions that the system could ask about, there is a cost in time and money to obtain the evidence to answer the questions. Also, accumulating certain types of evidence such as medical test results may be uncomfortable and possibly hazardous to the patient (in fact, it's difficult to think of a pleasurable medical test).

Ideally the expert system should also allow the user to volunteer evidence even if the system has not asked for it. Allowing the user to volunteer evidence speeds up the backward chaining process and makes the system more convenient for the user. The volunteered evidence may let the system skip some links in the causal chain or pursue a completely new approach. The disadvantage is that more complex programming of the expert system is involved since the system may not follow a chain link by link.

Good applications for forward and backward chaining are shown in Figure 3.25. For simplicity these diagrams are drawn as trees instead of a general network. A good application for forward chaining occurs if the tree is wide and not very deep. This is because forward chaining facilitates a breadth-first search. That is, forward chaining is good if the search for conclusions proceeds level by level. In contrast, backward chaining facilitates a depth-first search. A good tree for depth-first search is narrow and deep.

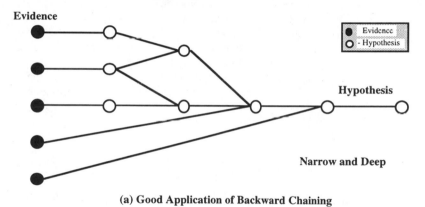

(a) Good Application of Backward Chaining

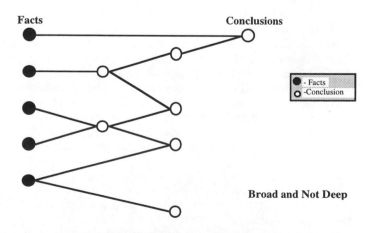

(b) Good Application of Forward Chaining

Figure 3.25 Backward and Forward Chaining

Notice that the structure of the rules determines the search for a solution. That is, the activation of a rule depends on the patterns that the rule is designed to match. The patterns on the LHS determine whether a rule can become activated by facts. The actions on the RHS determine the facts that are asserted and deleted and so affect other rules. An analogous situation exists for backward chaining except that hypotheses rather than rules are used. Of course, an intermediate hypothesis may simply be a rule that is matched on its consequent instead of its antecedent.

As a very simple example, consider the following IF...THEN-type rules:

```
IF  A  THEN  B
IF  B  THEN  C
IF  C  THEN  D
```

If fact A is given and the inference engine is designed to match facts against antecedents, then the intermediate facts B and C will be asserted and conclusion D will be reached. This process corresponds to forward chaining.

In contrast, if the fact (actually hypothesis) D is asserted and the inference engine matches facts against consequents, the result corresponds to backward chaining. In systems designed for backward chaining, such as PROLOG, the backward chaining mechanism includes a number of features, such as automatic back-tracking, to facilitate backward chaining.

Backward chaining can be accomplished in a forward chaining system and vice versa by a redesign of the rules. For example, the previous rules for forward chaining can be rewritten as

```
IF  D  THEN  C
IF  C  THEN  B
IF  B  THEN  A
```

Now C and B are considered subgoals or intermediate hypotheses that must be satisfied to satisfy the hypothesis D. The evidence A is the fact that indicates the end of the generation of subgoals. If there is a fact A, then D is supported and considered true under this chain of backward inference. If there is no A, then the hypothesis D is unsupported and considered false.

One difficulty with this approach is efficiency. A backward chaining system facilitates depth-first search whereas a forward chaining system facilitates breadth-first search. Although you can write a backward chaining application in a forward chaining system and vice versa, the system will not be as efficient in its search for a solution. The second difficulty is a conceptual one. The knowledge elicited from the expert will have to be altered to meet the demands of the inference engine. For example, a forward chaining inference engine matches the antecedent of rules and a backward chaining one matches the consequent. That is, if the expert's knowledge is naturally backward chaining, it will have to be completely restructured to cast it in a forward chaining mode, and vice versa.

3.15 OTHER METHODS OF INFERENCE

A number of other types of inference are sometimes used with expert systems. Although these methods are not as general purpose as deduction, they are very useful.

Analogy

Besides deduction and induction, another powerful inference method is **analogy**. The basic idea of reasoning by analogy is to try to relate old situations as guides to new ones. Most living creatures are very good at applying analogical reasoning in their lives, which is essential because of the tremendous number of new situations that are encountered in the real world. Rather than treat every new situation as unique, it's often helpful to try to relate the new situation to those with which you are familiar. Analogic reasoning is related to induction. Whereas induction makes inferences from the specific to the general of the same situation, analogy tries to make inferences from situations that are not the same. Analogy cannot make formal proofs as deduction can. Instead, analogy is a heuristic reasoning tool that may sometimes work.

An example of reasoning by analogy is medical diagnosis. When you see a doctor because of a medical problem, the doctor will elicit information from you and note the symptoms. If your symptoms are identical or strongly similar to those of other people with problem X, the doctor may infer by analogy that you have problem X. Of course, backward chaining may also be used.

Notice that this diagnosis is not a deduction, because you are unique. Just because someone else with the same problem shows certain symptoms doesn't mean that you will exhibit those symptoms. Instead, the doctor assumes that your symptoms make you analogous to a person with the same symptoms and known problem. This initial diagnosis is a hypothesis that medical tests may either prove or disprove. It's important to have an initial working hypothesis because it narrows down the thousands of potential problems. It would be prohibitively expensive and time-consuming to start giving you every possible test without an initial hypothesis.

As an example of the utility of reasoning by analogy, suppose two people play a game called the 15 Game (Fischler 87). They take turns in picking numbers from 1 to 9 with the constraint that the same number cannot be used twice. The first person whose numbers add up to 15 wins. Although at first this seems like a game that requires some thinking, an analogy can make it easy to play.

Consider the tic-tac-toe board with values assigned to each cell as shown below.

```
 6 │ 1 │ 8
───┼───┼───
 7 │ 5 │ 3
───┼───┼───
 2 │ 9 │ 4
```

This is a **magic square** because the sum of the values in the rows, columns, and diagonals is a constant 15. The tic-tac-toe board with the magic square values can be considered an analogy to the 15 Game. Playing the 15 Game is now very easy if you think in terms of tic-tac-toe and then translate the winning strategy to the 15 Game.

This particular magic square is called the **standard square** of **order** 3. The term order refers to the number of rows or columns in a square. There is only one square of order 3. Other magic squares can be created by rotating or reflecting the standard square. Another way to construct magic squares is by adding the same constant to each cell. Knowing this information allows us to deduce the winning strategies for the 18 Game, where the numbers must be selected from the set

$$\{2, \ 3, \ 4, \ 5, \ 6, \ 7, \ 8, \ 9, \ 10\}$$

or the 21 Game, using the set

$$\{3, \ 4, \ 5, \ 6, \ 7, \ 8, \ 9, \ 10, \ 11\}$$

We can now use induction to infer the winning strategy for the 15 + 3N Game, where N is any natural number 1, 2, 3, . . . by thinking of the game as analogous to a tic-tac-toe board, which is analogous to a magic square of values:

$$\{1+N, \ 2+N, \ 3+N, \ 4+N, \ 5+N, \ 6+N, \ 7+N, \ 8+N, \ 9+N\}$$

Using the analogy of the order 3 square for games of three moves, by induction we can infer that magic squares of a higher order can be used for games involving more than three moves. For example, the magic square of order 4

16	3	2	13
5	10	11	8
9	6	7	12
4	15	14	1

allows you to play the winning strategy of the four move-34 Game by thinking of it in terms of tic-tac-toe. In contrast to the one standard order 3 square, there are 880 standard squares of order 4, which allow considerably more games (Smith 84).

Reasoning by analogy is an important part of common sense reasoning, which is very difficult for computers (and children). Other applications of analogy have been to learning (Carbonell 82).

Generate and Test

Another method of inference is the classic AI strategy of **generate and test**, sometimes called generation and test, which involves the generation of a likely solution and then tests it to see if the proposed solution meets all the requirements. If the solution is satisfactory, then quit, else generate a new solution, test again, and so forth. This method was used in the first expert system, DENDRAL, conceived in 1965, to aid in identifying organic molecular structures (Buchanan 78). Data from an unknown sample are supplied by a mass spectrometer and input in DENDRAL, which generates all the potential molecular structures that could produce the unknown spectrogram. DENDRAL then tests the most likely candidate molecules by simulating their mass spectrograms and comparing it to the original unknown. Another program that uses generate and test is the AM (Artificial Mathematician) program, which infers new mathematical concepts (Lenat 82).

In order to reduce the enormous number of potential solutions, generate-and-test is normally used with a planning program to limit the likely potential solutions for generation. This variation is called **plan-generate-test** and is used for efficiency in many systems. For example, the medical diagnosis expert system MYCIN also has the capability of planning a therapeutic drug treatment after a patient's disease has been diagnosed (Chancey 85). A **plan** is essentially finding chains of rules or inferences that connect a problem with a solution, or goal, with the evidence to support it. Planning is most efficiently done by simultaneously searching forward from the facts and backward from the goal.

The MYCIN planner first creates a prioritized list of therapeutic drugs to which the patient is sensitive. In order to reduce undesirable drug interactions, it's best to limit the number of drugs that a patient receives, even if the patient is thought to be suffering from several different infections. The generator takes the prioritized list from the planner and generates sublists of one or two drugs if possible. These sublists are then tested for efficacy against the infections, the patient's allergies, and other considerations before a decision is made to administer them to the patient.

Generate and test can also be considered the basic inference paradigm of rules. If the conditional elements of a rule are satisfied, it generates some actions such as new facts. The inference engine tests these facts against the conditional elements of rules in the knowledge base. Those rules that are satisfied are put on the agenda and the top priority rule generates its actions, which are then tested, and so on. Thus generate and test produces an inference chain that may lead to the correct solution.

Abduction

Inference by **abduction** is another method that is commonly used in diagnostic problem solving. The schema of abduction resembles *modus ponens*, but is actually very different, as shown in Table 3.15.

Abduction	Modus ponens
$p \rightarrow q$	$p \rightarrow q$
q	p
$\therefore \ p$	$\therefore \ q$

Table 3.15 Comparison of Abduction and *Modus Ponens*

Abduction is another name for a fallacious argument that we discussed in Section 3.6, as the Fallacy of the Converse. Although abduction is not a valid deductive argument, it is a useful method of inference and has been used in expert systems. Like analogy, which also is not a valid deductive argument, abduction may be useful as a heuristic rule of inference. That is, when we have no deductive method of inference, abduction may prove useful, but is not guaranteed to work. Neither analogy, nor generate and test, nor abduction is deductive, and guaranteed to work all the time. From true premises, these methods cannot prove true conclusions. However, these techniques are useful in reducing the search space by generating reasonable hypotheses that can then be used with deduction.

Abduction is sometimes referred to as reasoning from observed facts to the best explanation (Reggia 85). As an example of abduction, consider the following:

```
IF x is an elephant THEN x is an animal
IF x is an animal THEN x is a mammal
```

If we know that Clyde is a mammal, can we conclude that Clyde is an elephant?

The answer to this question depends on whether we are talking about the real world or our expert system. In the real world we could not make this conclusion with any degree of certainty. Clyde could be a dog, cat, cow, or any other kind of animal that is a mammal but not an elephant. In fact, considering how many species of animals there are, without knowing any more information about Clyde, the probability of Clyde being an elephant is rather low.

However, in an expert system with only the preceding rules, we could say by abduction with 100 percent certainty that if Clyde is a mammal, then Clyde is an elephant. This inference follows from a **closed world assumption** in which we have assumed that nothing else exists outside the closed world of our expert system. Anything that cannot be proved is assumed false in a closed world. Under the closed world assumption, all the possibilities are known. Since the expert system consists of only these two rules and only an elephant can be a mammal, then if Clyde is a mammal, he must be an elephant.

Suppose we add a third rule, as follows:

```
IF x is a dog THEN X is an animal
```

We can still operate our expert system under the closed world assumption. However, we can no longer conclude with 100 percent certainty that Clyde is an elephant. All we can be sure of is that Clyde is either an elephant or a dog. In order to decide between the two, more information is needed. For example, if there is another rule,

```
IF x is a dog THEN x barks
```

and evidence that Clyde barks, the rules can be revised as follows.

```
(1)  IF x is an animal THEN x is a mammal
(2)  IF x barks THEN x is an animal
(3)  IF x is a dog THEN x barks
(4)  IF x is an elephant THEN x is an animal
```

Now a backward chain of abductive inference using rules (1), (2), and (3) can be made to show that Clyde must be a dog.

A backward chain of abduction is not the same as the customary meaning of backward chaining. The term *backward chaining* means that we are trying to prove a hypothesis by looking for evidence to support it. Backward chaining would be used in trying to prove that Clyde is a mammal. Of course, for our small system there are no other possibilities. However, other classifications could be added for reptiles, birds, and so forth.

If it's known that Clyde is a mammal, abduction could be used to determine whether Clyde is an elephant or a dog. Forward chaining would be used if it is known that Clyde is an elephant and we wanted to know if he is a mammal. As you can see, the choice of inference method depends on what is to be determined. Because forward chaining is deductive, only its conclusions are guaranteed to be valid. Table 3.16 summarizes the purpose of each of the three inference techniques.

A number of AI and expert systems have used frame-based abduction for diagnostic problem-solving (Basili 85; Miller 82; Pople 82; Reggia 83). In these systems the knowledge base contains **causal associations** between disorders and symptoms. Inferences are made using generate and test of hypotheses for the disorders.

Inference	Start	Purpose
Forward chaining	Facts	Conclusions that must follow
Backward chaining	Uncertain conclusion	Facts to support the conclusion
Abduction	True conclusion	Facts that may follow

Table 3.16   Summary of the Purpose of Forward Chaining, Backward Chaining, and Abduction

Nonmonotonic Reasoning

Normally the addition of new axioms to a logic system means that more theorems can be proved because there are more axioms from which theorems can be derived. This property of increasing theorems with increasing axioms is is known as *monotonicity* and systems such as deductive logic are called *monotonic systems*.

However, a problem can occur if a newly introduced axiom partially or completely contradicts a previous axiom. In this case, the theorems that had been proved may no longer be valid. Thus, in a **nonmonotonic system**, the theorems do not necessarily increase as the numbers of axioms increase.

The concept of nonmonotonicity has an important application to expert systems. As new facts are generated—which is analogous to theorems being proved—a monotonic expert system would keep building up facts. A major problem can occur if one or more facts become false because a monotonic system cannot deal with changes in the truth of axioms and theorems. As a very simple example, suppose there is a fact that asserts the time. As soon as time changes by one second, the old fact is no longer valid. A monotonic system would not be capable of dealing with this situation. As another example, suppose a fact was asserted by an aircraft identification system that a target was hostile. Later, new evidence proves the target is friendly. In a monotonic system, the original identification of hostile could not be changed. A nonmonotonic system allows the retraction of facts.

As another application, suppose you wanted to write an explanation facility for an expert system that would allow a user to go back to previous inferences and explore alternate inference paths of "*What if*" type questions. All inferences made after the desired previous one must be retracted from the system. Besides facts, rules may also have been excised from the system and so must be put back in the knowledge base for nonmonotonicity. Further complications arise in systems such as OPS5 in which rules can be created automatically on the RHS of rules during execution. For nonmonotonicity, any inferred rules made after the previous desired inference would have to be excised from the system. Keeping track of all inferences made can consume a lot of memory and significantly slow down the system.

In order to provide for nonmonotonicity, it is necessary to attach a justification or dependency to each fact and rule that explains the reason for belief in it. If a nonmonotonic decision is made, then the inference engine can examine the justification of each fact and rule to see if it is still believed, and also to possibly restore excised rules and retracted facts that are believed again.

The problem of justifying facts was first pointed out in the **frame problem**, which is not the same concept as the frames discussed in Chapter 2 (McCarthy 69). The frame problem is a descriptive term named after the problem of identifying what has or has not changed in a movie frame. Motion pictures are photographed as a succession of still pictures, called frames. When played back at 24 frames per second or faster, the human eye cannot distinguish the individual frames and so the illusion of motion results. An AI frame problem is to recognize changes in an environment over time. As an example, consider the monkey and bananas problem (Figure 3.7). Suppose the monkey must step on a red box to reach the bananas and so the action is "push red box under bananas." Now the frame problem is how do we know the box is still red after the action? Pushing the box should not change the environment. However, other actions such as "paint the box blue" *will* change the environment. In some expert system tools an environment is called a ***world*** and consists of a set of related facts (Filman 88). An expert system may keep track of multiple worlds to do hypothetical reasoning simultaneously. The problem of maintaining the correctness or truth of a system is called ***truth maintenance*** (Doyle 79). Truth maintenance, or a variation called ***assumption-based truth maintenance***, is essential for keeping each world pure by retracting unjustified facts (de Kleer 86).

As a simple example of nonmonotonic reasoning, let's consider the classic example of Tweety bird. In the absence of any other information, we would assume that since Tweety is a bird, Tweety can fly. This is an example of **default reasoning**, much like the defaults used in frame slots. Default reasoning can be considered as a rule that makes inferences about rules, a **metarule** that states

```
IF X is not known for certain, and
      there is no evidence contradicting X
THEN tentatively conclude Y
```

Metarules are discussed more extensively in the next section.
In our case the metarule has the more specific form

```
X is the rule "All birds can fly," and
      fact "Tweety is a bird"
Y is the inference "Tweety can fly"
```

In terms of production rules, this can be expressed as a rule in our knowledge base, which says

```
IF X is a bird THEN X can fly
```

and the fact that exists in working memory

```
Tweety is a bird
```

Unifying the fact with the antecedent of the rule gives the inference that Tweety can fly.

Now comes the problem. Suppose an additional fact is added to working memory that says that Tweety is a penguin. We know that penguins cannot fly and so the inference that Tweety can fly is incorrect. Of course, there must be a rule in the system that also states this knowledge or else the fact will be ignored.

In order to maintain the correctness of our system, the incorrect inference must be removed. However, this may not be sufficient if other inferences were based on the incorrect inference. That is, other rules may have used the incorrect inference as evidence to draw additional inferences, and so on. This is a problem of truth maintenance. The inference that Tweety can fly was a **plausible inference** that is based on default reasoning. (The term *plausible* means "not impossible", and will be discussed further in Chapter 4.)

One way of allowing for nonmonotonic inference is by defining a sentential operator M, which can be informally defined as "is consistent" (McDermott 82). For example,

$$(\forall \ x) \ [\texttt{Bird(x)} \ \wedge \ \texttt{M(Can\_fly(x))} \rightarrow \texttt{Can\_fly(x)}]$$

can be stated as "For every x, if x is a bird and it is consistent that a bird can fly, then x can fly." A more informal way of stating this is "Most birds can fly." The term "is consistent" means that there are no contradictions with other knowledge. However, this interpretation has been criticized as really stating that the only birds that cannot fly are those that have been inferred not capable of flying (Moore 85). This is an example of **autoepistemic reasoning**, which literally means reasoning about your own knowledge. Both default and autoepistemic reasoning are used in **common sense reasoning**, which humans generally do quite well but is very difficult for computers.

Autoepistemic reasoning is reasoning about your own knowledge as distinct from knowledge in general. Generally, you can do this very well because you know the limits of your knowledge. For example, suppose a total stranger came up to you and stated you were his or her spouse. You would immediately know (unless you had amnesia) that this was not true because you had no knowledge of that stranger. The general metarule of autoepistemic reasoning is

```
IF I have no knowledge of X
THEN X is false
```

Notice how autoepistemic reasoning relies on the closed world assumption. Any fact that is not known is assumed to be false. In autoepistemic reasoning, the closed world is your self-knowledge.

Autoepistemic and default reasoning are both nonmonotonic. However, the reasons are different. Default reasoning is nonmonotonic because it is **defeasible**. The term *defeasible* means that any inferences are tentative and may have to be withdrawn as new information becomes available. However, pure autoepistemic reasoning is not defeasible because of the closed world assumption that declares all true knowledge is already known to you. For example, since married people know who is their spouse (unless they want to forget), a married person would not accept that a total stranger was his or her spouse if they were told that. Because most people recognize that they have imperfect memories, they do not adhere to pure autoepistemic reasoning. Of course, computers do not have this problem.

Autoepistemic reasoning is nonmonotonic because the meaning of an autoepistemic statement is **context sensitive**. The term *context sensitive* means that the meaning changes with the context. As a simple example of context sensitivity, consider how the word "read" is pronounced in the two sentences

```
I have read the book
I will read the book
```

The pronunciation of "read" is context sensitive.

Now consider a system consisting of the following two axioms.

```
(∀ x) [Bird(x) ∧ M(Can_fly(x))→ Can_fly(x)]
Bird(Tweety)
```

In this logic system, Can_fly(Tweety) is a theorem derived by unification of Tweety with the variable x and implication.

Now suppose a new axiom is added that states that Tweety cannot fly and thus contradicts the previously derived theorem.

```
~Can_fly(Tweety)
```

The M-operator must change its operation on its argument because now M(Can_fly(Tweety)) is not consistent with the new axiom. In this new context of three axioms, the M-operator would not give a TRUE result for Can_fly(Tweety) because it conflicts with the new axiom. The returned value by the M-operator must be FALSE in this new context, and so the conjunction is FALSE. Thus there is no implication to produce the theorem Can_fly(Tweety) and no conflict.

One way of implementing this by rules is as follows:

```
IF x is a bird AND x is typical
THEN x can fly
IF x is a bird AND x is nontypical
THEN x cannot fly

Tweety is a bird
Tweety is nontypical
```

Notice that this system does not invalidate the conclusion Can_fly(Tweety), but rather prevents the incorrect rule from firing at all. This is a much more efficient method of truth maintenance than if we had one rule and the special axiom ~Can_fly(Tweety). Now we have a more general system that can easily handle other nonflying birds such as ostriches without our having to continually add new inferences, which is what the system is supposed to do.

3.16 METAKNOWLEDGE

The Meta-DENDRAL program uses induction to infer new rules of chemical structure. Meta-DENDRAL is an attempt to overcome the knowledge bottleneck of trying to extract molecular structural rules from human experts. Meta-DENDRAL has been very successful in rediscovering known rules and inferring new ones.

As an example, the following metarule is taken from the TEIRESIAS knowledge acquisition program for MYCIN, the expert system to diagnose blood infections and meningitis (Feigenbaum 79).

```
METARULE 2
IF
The patient is a compromised host, and
There are rules which mention in their premise
    pseudomonas, and
There are rules which mention in their premise
    klebsiellas
```

```
THEN
    There is suggestive evidence (.4) that the former
        should be done before the latter
```

(The number .4 in the action of the rule is a degree of certainty and will be discussed in a later chapter.)

TEIRESIAS acquires knowledge interactively from an expert. If an incorrect diagnosis has been made by MYCIN, then TEIRESIAS will lead the expert back through the chain of incorrect reasoning until the expert states where the incorrect reasoning started. While going back through the reasoning chain, TEIRESIAS will also interact with the expert to modify incorrect rules or acquire new rules.

Knowledge about new rules is not immediately put into MYCIN. Instead, TEIRESIAS checks to see if the new rule is compatible with similar rules. For example, if the new rule describes how an infection enters the body and other accepted rules have a conditional element stating the portal of entry to the body, then the new rule shouldhave the same. If the new rule does not state the portal of entry, then TEIRESIAS will query the user about this discrepancy. TEIRESIAS has a **rule model** pattern of similar rules that it knows about, and trics to fit the new rule into its rule model. In other words, the rule model is the knowledge that TEIRESIAS has about its knowledge. An analogous situation for a human would occur if you went to a car dealer to buy a new car and the dealer tried to sell you a car with three wheels.

The metaknowledge of TEIRESIAS is of two types. The METARULE 2, described previously, is a control strategy that tells how rules are to be applied. In contrast, the rule model type of metaknowledge determines whether the new rule is in the appropriate form to be entered in the knowledge base. In a rule-based expert system, determining if the new rule is in the correct form is called *verification* of the rule. Determining that a chain of correct inferences leads to the correct answer is called *validation*. Validation and verification are so interdependent that the acronym **V&V** is commonly used to refer to both. A more colloquial definition of the terms from software engineering is (Boehm 84):

```
Verification:   "Am I building the product right?"
Validation:     "Am I building the right product?"
```

V&V will be discussed in more detail in a later chapter.

3.17 SUMMARY

In this chapter the commonly used methods of inferencing for expert systems have been discussed. Inferencing is particularly important in expert systems because it is the technique by which expert systems solve problems. The application of trees, graphs, and lattices to the representation of knowledge was discussed. The advantages of these structures to inferences were illustrated.

Deductive logic was covered starting with simple syllogistic logic. Next, the propositional and first-order predicate logic was discussed. Truth tables and rules of inference were described as ways of proving theorems and statements. The characteristics of logical systems such as completeness, soundness, and decidability were mentioned.

The resolution method of proving theorems was discussed for propositional logic and first-order predicate logic. The nine steps involved in converting a well-formed formula to clausal form were illustrated by an example. Skolemization, the prenex-normal form, and unification were all discussed in the context of converting a wff to clausal form.

Another powerful method of inferences, analogy, was discussed. Although not widely used in expert systems because of the difficulty in implementing it, analogy is often used by people and should be considered in the design of expert systems. Generate and test was also discussed with an example of its use in MYCIN. The application of metaknowledge in TEIRESAS was described and its relationship to verification and validation of expert systems.

PROBLEMS

3.1   Write a decision tree program that is self-learning. Teach it the animal knowledge of Figure 3.3.

3.2   Write a program that will automatically translate the knowledge stored in a binary decision tree into IF . . . THEN-type rules. Test it with the animal decision tree of Problem 3.1.

3.3   Draw a semantic net containing the raspberries knowledge of Figure 3.4.

3.4   Draw the state diagram showing a solution to the classic problem of the farmer, fox, goat, and cabbage. In this problem a farmer, a fox, a goat, and a cabbage are on one bank of a river. A boat must be used to transport them to the other side. However, the boat can only hold two at a time (and only the farmer can row). If the fox is left with the goat and the farmer is not present, tthe fox will eat the goat. If the goat is left alone with the cabbage, the goat will eat the cabbage.

3.5   Draw a state diagram for a well-structured travel problem having

   (a)   three methods of payment: cash, check, or charge
   (b)   traveler's interests: sun, snow
   (c)   four possible destinations depending on the traveler's interests and money
   (d)   three types of transportation

   Write IF . . . THEN rules to advise a traveler where to go depending on money and interests. Pick real destinations and find out the costs to get there from your location.

3.6   Determine whether the following are valid or invalid arguments.

   (a) $p \rightarrow q, \sim q \rightarrow r, r; \therefore p$
   (b) $\sim p \vee q, p \rightarrow (r \wedge s), s \rightarrow q; \therefore q \vee r$
   (c) $p \rightarrow (q \rightarrow r), q; \therefore p \rightarrow r$

3.7   Using the Venn diagram decision procedure, determine whether the following are valid or invalid syllogisms.

   (a)   AEE-4
   (b)   AOO-1
   (c)   OAO-3
   (d)   AAI-1
   (e)   OAI-2

3.8   Prove whether the following are fallacies or rules of inference. Give an example of each.

(a)   Complex Constructive Dilemma

$p \rightarrow q$
$r \rightarrow s$
$\underline{p \vee r}$
$\therefore q \vee s$

(b)   Complex Destructive Dilemma

$p \rightarrow q$
$r \rightarrow s$
$\underline{\sim q \vee \sim s}$
$\therefore \sim p \vee \sim r$

(c)   Simple Destructive Dilemma

$p \rightarrow q$
$p \rightarrow r$
$\underline{\sim q \vee \sim r}$
$\therefore \sim p$

(d)   Inverse

$p \rightarrow q$
$\underline{\sim p}$
$\therefore \sim q$

3.9   Draw the conclusion from the following premises, taken from Lewis Carroll, author of *Alice's Adventures in Wonderland*.

(a)   All the dated letters in this room are written on blue paper.
(b)   None of them are in black ink, except those that are written in the third person.
(c)   I have not filed any of them that I can read.
(d)   None of them, that are written on one sheet, are undated.
(e)   All of them, that are not crossed, are in black ink.
(f)   All of them, written by Brown, begin with "Dear Sir,"
(g)   All of them, written on blue paper, are filed.
(h)   None of them, written on more than one sheet, are crossed.
(i)   None of them, that begin with "Dear Sir," are written in the third person.

Hint: Use the law of contrapositives and define

A = beginning with "Dear Sir"	B = crossed	C = dated
D = filed	E = in black ink	F = in third person
G = letters that I can read	H = on blue paper	I = on one sheet
J = written by Brown		

3.10   Give a formal proof using predicate logic for the following syllogism:

No software is guaranteed
All programs are software
∴. No programs are guaranteed

3.11   Use the following to write quantified first order predicate logic formulas.

$P(x)$ = x is a programmer
$S(x)$ = x is smart
$L(x,y)$ = x loves y

(a)   All programmers are smart.
(b)   Some programmers are smart.
(c)   No programmers are smart.
(d)   Someone is not a programmer.
(e)   Not everyone is a programmer.
(f)   Everyone is not a programmer.
(g)   Everyone is a programmer.
(h)   Some programmers are not smart.
(i)   There are programmers.
(j)   Everyone loves someone.

Hint: Use Appendix B.

3.12   Consider the following predicate logic argument:

A horse is an animal

Therefore, the head of a horse is the head of an animal. Define the following:

$H(x,y)$ = x is the head of y
$A(x)$ = x is an animal
$S(x)$ = x is a horse

The premise and conclusion are

$(\forall x) (S(x) \rightarrow A(x))$
$(\forall x) \{[(\exists y) (S(y) \wedge H(x,y))] \rightarrow [(\exists z) (A(z) \wedge H(x,z))]\}$

Prove the conclusion using resolution refutation. Show all nine steps in clausal conversion for the conclusion.

3.13   (a)   Obtain information from your bank or savings and loan on the criteria for obtaining a car loan. Write a backward chaining system of rules to determine if an applicant should get a car loan. Be as specific as possible.

      (b)   Obtain information on qualifying for a home mortgage. Give the modifications of your car loan program to handle home loans as well as car loans.

      (c)   Obtain information on qualifying for a business loan. Give the modifications to the car–mortgage program to handle business loans.

3.14   Write a production system of causal rules to simulate the operation of the carburetor of your car. You may obtain this information from the repair guide for your car. Be as detailed as possible.

3.15   Using the repair guide for your car, write a production system that can diagnose and remedy carburetor problems for your car , given symptoms.

3.16   If a conclusion is false and you want to determine the facts that followed, would you use abduction or another method of inference? Explain.

3.17   Write IF . . . THEN rules to identify raspberries using the portion of the decision tree shown in Figure 3.4

3.18   A parent and two children are on the left bank of a river and wish to cross to the right side. The parent weighs 200 pounds and each child weighs 100 pounds. One boat is available with a capacity of 200 pounds. At least one person is required to row the boat. Draw the decision tree showing all the possibilities for crossing the river and indicate the successful path through the tree so that they all get across. Assume the following operators in labeling your tree:

SL–Single child crosses from left to right
SR–Single child crosses from right to left
BL–Both children cross from left to right
BR–Both children cross from right to left
PL–Parent crosses from left to right
PR–Parent crosses from right to left

3.19   (a)   Draw a logic diagram version of the AND-exclusive-OR car decision of Figure 3.11. Note that you will have to implement the exclusive-OR using standard AND, OR, and NOT elements.

      (b)   Write forward chaining IF THEN rules to determine which hypothesis to follow— i.e., sell or repair.

BIBLIOGRAPHY

(Amble 87). Tore Amble, *Logic Programming and Knowledge Engineering*, Addison-Wesley Pub., 1987, pp. 41-42, 1987.

(Basili 85). V. Basili and C. Ramsey, "ARROWSMITH-P: A Prototype Expert System for Software Engineering Management," in K. Karna, ed. *Proc. Expert Systems in Government Symposium*, 1985.

(Boehm 84). Barry W. Boehm, "Verifying and Validating Software Requirements and Design Specifications," *IEEE Software J.*, Jan. 1984.

(Buchanan 78). Bruce G. Buchanan and Edward A. Feigenbaum, "Dendral and Meta-Dendral: Their Applications Dimension," *Artificial Intelligence*, **11**, (1), pp. 5-24, 1978.

(Carbonell 82). James G. Carbonell, "Learning by Analogy: Formulating and Generalizing Plans from Past Experience," in *Machine Learning*, R. S. Michalski, J. G. Carbonell, and T. M. Mitchell, eds., Tioga Pub. Co., 1982.

(Chancey 85). William J, Chancey, "Details of the Revised Therapy Algorithm," in *Rule-based Expert Systems*, Bruce G. Buchanan and Edward H. Shortliffe, eds., pp. 133-146, 1985.

(Chang 73). Chin-Liang Chang and Richard Char Tung Lee, *Symbolic Logic and Mathematical Theorem Proving*, Academic Press, p. 77, 1973.

(de Kleer 86). J. de Kleer, "An Assumption-based Truth Maintenance System," *Artif. Intell.*, **28**, (2), pp. 127-162, Jan. 1986.

(Doyle 79). J. Doyle, "A Truth Maintenance System," *Artificial Intelligence*, **12**, (3), pp. 231-272, 1979.

(Feigenbaum 79). Edward A. Feigenbaum, "Themes and Case Studies of Knowledge Engineering," in *Expert Systems in the Micro-Electronic Age*, Donald Michie, ed., pp. 3-25, 1979.

(Filman 88). Robert E. Filman, "Reasoning with Worlds and Truth Maintenance in a Knowledge based Programming Environment," *C. ACM*, **31**, (4), pp. 382-401, April 1988.

(Fischler 87). Martin A. Fischler and Oscar Firschein, *The Eye, the Brain, and the Computer*, Addison-Wesley Pub., p. 65, 1987.

(Giarratano 92). Joesph Giarratano, *CLIPS User's Guide, Vol. 1, Rules,* NASA, Version 5.1 of CLIPS, 1992.

(Hollan 84). James D. Hollan, *et al.*, "Steamer: An Interactive Inspectable Simulation-based Training System," *AI Magazine*, **5**, (2), pp. 15-27, Summer 1984.

(Kahn 85). Gary Kahn, "On When Diagnostic Systems Want to Do Without Causal Knowledge," in *Advances in Artificial Intelligence*, T. O'Shea, ed., Elsevier Science Publishers, pp. 41-50, 1985.

(Kowalski 79). Robert Kowalski, "Algorithm = Logic + Control," *Comm. ACM*, **22**, (7), pp. 424-436, 1979.

(Lenat 82). Douglas B. Lenat, "AM: An Artificial Intelligence Approach to Discovery in Mathematics as Heuristic Search," in *Knowledge based Systems in Artificial Intelligence*, R. Davis and D. B. Lenat, eds., McGraw-Hill, 1982.

(McCarthy 69). J. McCarthy and P. Hayes, " Some Philosophical Problems from the Standpoint of Artificial Intelligence," in *Machine Intelligence*, **4**, B. Meltzer and D. Michie, eds., Edinburgh Univ. Press, pp. 463-502, 1969.

(McDermott 82). D. McDermott, "Nonmonotonic Logic II: Nonmonotonic Modal Theories," *J. ACM*, **29** (1), pp. 33-57, 1982.

(Miller 82). R. Miller, H. Pople, and J. Myers, "INTERNIST-1, An Experimental Computer-based Diagnostic Consultant for General Internal Medicine," *New England J. of Medicine*, **307**, pp. 468-476, 1982.

(Minsky 67). Marvin Minsky, *Computation: Finite and Infinite Machines*, Prentice-Hall, p. 228, 1967.

(Moore 85). Robert C. Moore, "Semantic Considerations on Nonmonotonic Logic," *Artificial Intelligence*, **25**, pp. 75-95, 1985.

(Nilsson 80). Nils J. Nilsson, *Principles of Artificial Intelligence,* Tioga Publishing Co., pp. 142-143, 1980.

(Pople 82). H. Pople, "Heuristic Methods for Imposing Structure on Ill-structured Problems: The Structure of Medical Diagnostics," P. Szolovits, ed., *Artificial Intelligence in Medicine*, pp. 119-190, 1982.

(Reggia 83). J. Reggia, D. Nau, and P. Wang, "Diagnostic Expert Systems Based on a Set Covering Model," *Int. J. of Man-Machine Studies*, pp. 437-460, 1983.

(Reggia 85). J. Reggia, "Abductive Inference," in *Proc. of Expert Systems in Government Symposium*, K. Karna, ed., *IEEE Press*, pp. 484-489, 1985.

(Reiser 85). B. J. Reiser, *et al.*, "Dynamic Student Modelling in an Intelligent Tutor for LISP Programming," *IJCAI*, pp. 8-14, 1985.

(Robinson 65). J. A. Robinson, "A Machine-Oriented Logic Based on the Resolution Principle," *J. ACM*, **12**, (1), pp. 23-41, Jan. 1986.

(Smith 84). Karl J. Smith, *The Nature of Mathematics*, 4th ed., Brooks/Cole, p. 12, 1984.

(Stebbing 50). L. S. Stebbing, *A Modern Introduction to Logic*, Methuen & Co. Ltd., 7th ed., pp. 104-105, 1950.

CHAPTER 4
Reasoning Under Uncertainty

4.1 INTRODUCTION

In this chapter various methods of reasoning under **uncertainty** will be discussed. This topic is very important in expert systems since many expert system applications involve uncertain information.

4.2 UNCERTAINTY

Uncertainty can be considered as the lack of adequate information to make a decision. Uncertainty is a problem because it may prevent us from making the best decision and may even cause a bad decision to be made. In medicine uncertainty may overlook the best treatment for a patient or contribute to an incorrect therapy. In business uncertainty may mean financial loss instead of profit.

A number of theories have been devised to deal with uncertainty. These include classical probability, Bayesian probability, Hartley theory based on classical sets (Hartley 1928), Shannon theory based on probability (Shannon 1948), Dempster-Shafer theory (Shafer 1976), and Zadeh's fuzzy theory (Zadeh 1965). In particular, the Shannon theory has proved very popular in telecommunications and also has been applied to many diverse areas such as biology, psychology, music, and physics.

All living creatures are experts at dealing with uncertainty or they could not survive in the real world. In particular, human beings are used to uncertainty about traffic, weather, jobs, school, and so forth. After a while, we all become experts at driving under various traffic conditions, treating a cold, choosing easy classes, and so on. Dealing with uncertainty requires reasoning under uncertainty.

The deductive method of reasoning described in Chapter 3 is called *exact reasoning* because it deals with exact facts and the exact conclusions that follow from those facts. Recall that in a deductive argument the conclusion must follow from the premises. When uncertain facts are involved, the number of possible conclusions may greatly increase the difficulty in finding the best conclusions.

Unfortunately, determining the "best" conclusion may not be easy. A number of different methods have been proposed for dealing with uncertainty and aid in choosing the best conclusion. It is the responsibility of the expert systems designer to choose the most appropriate method, depending on the application. Although there are expert system tools that incorporate mechanisms for reasoning under uncertainty, they are not generally flexible in allowing other methods to be used.

Although there are many expert systems applications that can be done with exact reasoning, many others require **inexact reasoning** involving uncertain facts, rules, or both. Classic examples of successful expert systems that deal with uncertainty are MYCIN for medical diagnosis and PROSPECTOR for mineral exploration.

In the MYCIN and PROSPECTOR systems conclusions are arrived at even when all the evidence needed to absolutely prove the conclusion is not known. Although it is possible to arrive at a more reliable conclusion by performing more tests, there are problems with the increasing time and cost of performing the tests. These constraints of time and money are particularly important in the case of medical treatment. Delaying treatment for more tests adds considerable cost; in the meantime, the patient may die. In the case of mineral exploration, the cost of additional tests is also a significant factor. It may be more cost effective to start drilling when you are 95 percent certain of success than to spend hundreds of thousands of dollars to be 98 percent certain.

4.3 TYPES OF ERROR

Many different types of **error** can contribute to uncertainty. Different theories of uncertainty attempt to resolve some or all of these to provide the most reliable inference. Figure 4.1 illustrates a simplified classification scheme for errors.

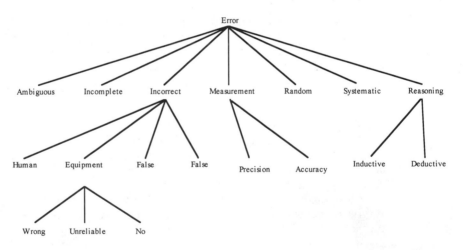

Figure 4.1 Types of Error

This figure should strictly be drawn as a lattice since there may be interconnections among many of the different types of error. For example, human error could be linked to ambiguity, measurement, reasoning, and so on. Table 4.1 gives examples of these errors.

The first type of error shown is **ambiguity**, in which something may be interpreted in more than one way. The second type of error is **incompleteness** where some information is missing. A third type of error is **incorrectness**, in which the information is wrong. Possible causes of incorrectness are human error, such as the accidental misreading of a dial or data, lying or misinformation, and malfunctioning equipment.

Example	Error	Reason .
Turn the valve off	Ambiguous	What valve?
Turn valve-1	Incomplete	Which way?
Turn valve-1 off	Incorrect	Correct is on
Valve is stuck	False positive	Valve is not stuck
Valve is not stuck	False negative	Valve is stuck
Turn valve-1 to 5	Imprecise	Correct is 5.4
Turn valve-1 to 5.4	Inaccurate	Correct is 9.2
Turn valve-1 to 5.4 or 6 or 0	Unreliable	Equipment error
Valve-1 setting is 5.4 or 5.5 or 5.1	Random error	Statistical fluctuation
Valve-1 setting is 7.5	Systematic error	Miscalibration
Valve-1 is not stuck because it's never been stuck before	Invalid induction	Valve is stuck
Output is normal and so valve-1 is in good condition	Invalid deduction	Valve is stuck in open position

Table 4.1 Examples of Common Types of Error

An **hypothesis** is an assumption to be tested. The **null hypothesis** is the assumption initially made, such as "the valve is stuck." One type of incorrect information is called *false positive* that means acceptance of a hypothesis when it is not true. Likewise, a **false negative** means rejection of a hypothesis when it is true. Thus if the valve is not really stuck, then accepting the hypothesis that it is stuck is a false positive. In statistics this is called a *Type I error*. Likewise, if the valve is really stuck and the hypothesis "the valve is stuck" is rejected, this is a false negative or **Type II error**.

The next two types of error shown in Table 4.1 are **errors of measurement**. These are errors of **precision** and **accuracy**. Although these terms are sometimes used synonymously, they are very different. Consider two rulers, one of which is graduated in millimeters and the other graduated in centimeters. Obviously the millimeter ruler is more precise than the centimeter ruler. However, suppose the graduations of the millimeter ruler were incorrectly made. In that case the millimeter ruler is inaccurate and its measurements cannot be trusted unless a correction factor is known. Thus accuracy corresponds to the truth while precision corresponds to how well the truth is known. For the two rulers, the millimeter ruler measures precision ten times more precisely than the centimeter ruler.

Another type of error is **unreliability**. If the measuring equipment supplying the facts is unreliable, the data are **erratic**. An erratic reading is one that is not constant but fluctuates. Sometimes it may be correct, and sometimes not.

A reading that fluctuates may be caused by the basic random nature of the system being studied, such as the decay of radioactive atoms. Because the cause of the decay is a quantum mechanics phenomenon, the rate of decay fluctuates randomly about a mean value. The random fluctuations about the mean constitute a **random error** and lead to uncertainty of the mean. Other types of random error may be caused by Brownian motion, electronic noise due to thermal effects, and so forth. However, erratic readings may also be caused by a loose connection.

A **systematic error** is one that is not random but instead is introduced because of some bias. For example, the miscalibration of a ruler so that its graduations are smaller than normal gives a systematic error that indicates readings are higher than normal.

4.4 ERRORS AND INDUCTION

The next type of error is an **invalid induction**: "the valve is not stuck because it's never been stuck before." The process of **induction** is the opposite of deduction. While deduction proceeds from the general to the specific, as in

```
All men are mortal
Socrates is a man
```

to deduce the specific conclusion

```
Socrates is mortal
```

induction tries to generalize from the specific to the general, as in

```
My disk has never crashed
∴ My disk will never crash
```

where the symbol s stands for the inductive "therefore," in contrast to the deductive ∴ "therefore."

Except for mathematical induction, inductive arguments can never be proven correct. Instead, inductive arguments can only provide some degree of confidence that the conclusion is correct. We would not have much confidence in the preceding inductive argument. The following is a stronger argument:

```
The fire alarm goes off
∴ There is a fire
```

An even stronger argument is

```
The fire alarm goes off
I smell smoke
∴ There is a fire
```

Although this is a strong argument, it is not proof that there is a fire. The smoke could be coming from hamburgers cooking on a grill and the fire alarm could have been set off accidentally. The following is proof of a fire:

```
The fire alarm goes off
I smell smoke
My clothes are burning
∴ There is a fire
```

Notice that this is a deductive argument because you can see the flames.

Expert systems may consist of deductive and inductive rules, where the inductive rules are of an heuristic nature. Induction has also been applied to the automatic generation of rules, as you will see in a later chapter on knowledge acquisition.

Besides uncertainty with facts, the rules of an expert system may have uncertainty if they are based on heuristics. An heuristic is commonly called a *rule of thumb* because it is based on experience. Sometimes experience is a good guide. However, it may not be applicable to 100 percent of the cases since experience is heuristic. For example, you would expect that everyone who jumps off a fifty-story building would be killed. However, people can jump off a fifty-story building and not be killed—if they wear a parachute.

One of the interesting characteristics of human experts is that they reason well under uncertainty. Even if there is a great deal of uncertainty, experts can usually make good judgments, or they won't be considered experts for long.

Another characteristic is that experts can easily revise their opinions if it turns out that some of the original facts were wrong. This is *nonmonotonic reasoning*, as discussed in Chapter 3. It is more difficult to program expert systems to backtrack their reasoning processes because all the intermediate facts need to be saved and a history of rule firings kept. Human experts appear to revise their reasoning with little effort.

Besides inductive errors, there may also be deductive errors or fallacies, as described in Chapter 3. An example of a fallacious schema discussed in Chapter 3 is

$$
\begin{array}{l}
p \rightarrow q \\
\underline{q} \\
\therefore p
\end{array}
$$

For example,

```
If the valve is in good condition,
   then the output is normal
The output is normal
∴ The valve is in good condition
```

is a fallacious argument. The valve may be stuck in the open position so that the output is normal. However, if it is necessary to close the valve, the problem will show up. This can be very serious if the valve needs to be closed quickly, as in the case of an emergency shutdown of a nuclear reactor.

In contrast to the previous errors we have discussed, inductive and deductive errors are errors of reasoning. These types of errors lead to the incorrect formulation of rules.

Generally, humans do not seem to process uncertain information in the best possible way (Hink 87). Even experts are not immune to making mistakes, especially under uncertainty. This can be a major problem in knowledge acquisition, when the expert's knowledge must be quantified in rules. Inconsistencies, inaccuracy, and all the other possible errors of uncertainty may show up. Experts will then have to correct their knowledge, which can delay completion of the expert system.

4.5 CLASSICAL PROBABILITY

An old but still very important tool in AI problem solving is **probability** (Farley 1983). Probability is a quantitative way of dealing with uncertainty that originated in the seventeenth century when some French gamblers asked for help from the leading mathematicians such as Pascal, Fermat, and others. Gambling had become very popular; and because large amounts of money were involved, gamblers wanted methods to aid in calculating the odds of winning.

The theory of **classical probability** was first proposed by Pascal and Fermat in 1654 (Parratt 61). Since then much work has been done with probability and several new branches have been developed. Many applications of probability have been shown in science, engineering, business, economics, and virtually every other field.

The Definition of Classical Probability

Classical probability is also called a priori *probability* because it deals with ideal games or systems. As discussed in Chapter 2, the term *a priori* means "before," that is, without regard to the real world. *A priori* probability considers games such as dice, cards, coins, or whatever, as ideal systems that do not become worn out.

Ideal systems do not exhibit the real world characteristics of wear-and-tear because then they would not have precisely reproducible characteristics. That is, a real die (plural dice) may exhibit a bias toward some particular numbers after one side becomes worn down after numerous throws. Also, depending on the manufacture, a real die may exhibit a preference toward higher numbers because more pips (small colored holes) are drilled in higher numbers. This bias was determined by analyzing data from 1,000,000 throws of a real die. A new die was used every 20,000 throws to avoid bias caused by uneven wearing of the faces. The fraction of times different numbers came up is shown in Table 4.2 (Shafer 76).

Number	1	2	3	4	5	6
Fraction	.155	.159	.164	.169	.174	.179

Table 4.2 Results of 1,000,000 Throws of a Die

In an ideal system all numbers occur equally, which makes analysis much easier.

The fundamental formula of classical probability is defined as the probability

$$P = \frac{W}{N}$$

where W is the number of wins and N is the number of equally possible **events**, which are the possible outcomes of an experiment or **trial**. For example, if you throw a die once, there are six possible events from this single trial. The die may come to rest with its top showing either a 1, 2, 3, 4, 5, or 6. Under classical probability it is assumed that any of these six events is equally possible and so the probability of rolling a 1, $P(1)$, is

$$P(1) = \frac{1}{6}$$

Likewise,

$$P(2) = \frac{1}{6}$$

and so forth.

The probability of losing, Q, is

$$Q = \frac{N - W}{N} = 1 - P$$

The fundamental formula for P is an *a priori* definition because the probability is calculated *before* the game is played. The term *a priori* means "that which precedes" or "before the event" when discussing probabilities. An *a priori* probability assumes that all possible events are known and that each event is equally likely to happen.

For example, in rolling a die, the possible spots on each face are known as 1, 2, 3, 4, 5, and 6. Also, if the die is **fair**—not loaded—then each side is equally likely to come up. Likewise, in a fair deck of cards, all 52 cards are known and equally likely to be drawn under a fair shuffle. The probability of any one face of the die coming up is 1/6 and for any card it is 1/52.

When repeated trials give exactly the same result, the system is **deterministic**. If it is not deterministic, it is **nondeterministic** or random. In some types of expert system shells nondeterminism is used to prevent bias in rule firings. When the patterns of multiple rules are satisfied and there is no explicit preference as to which rule should be executed, the inference engine makes an arbitrary choice of the rule to be executed. This prevents a bias in which one rule, say the first one entered, is fired.

Sample Spaces

The result of a trial is a **sample point** and the set of all possible sample points defines a **sample space**. For example, if a single die is rolled, any one of the sample points 1, 2, 3, 4, 5, or 6 can occur. Figure 4.2(a) shows the sample space for the roll of a single die. The sample space is the set { 1, 2, 3, 4, 5, 6 }.

An **event** is a subset of the sample space. For example, the event { 1 } occurs if the die comes up with a 1. A **simple event** has only one element and a **compound event** has more than one, as shown in Figure 4.2(b).

(a) Sample Space for a Single Die   (b) A Simple {5} and a Compound Event {3,6}

Figure 4.2 Sample Space and Events

A graphic way of determining the sample space is to construct an **event tree**. As a simple example, suppose there are two computers that either work, *W*, or don't work, *D*. Figure 4.3 shows the event tree and Table 4.3 shows a table form of the sample space. Note that the compound events are listed in the order {computer1, computer2}. The sample space is { *WW*, *WD*, *DW*, *DD* }.

This type of event tree is a binary tree since only binary probabilities are involved. That is, either the computer works or it doesn't. Many other cases have this type of tree. For example, the toss of coins leads to a binary event tree since there are only two possible outcomes for every throw.

Probability and statistics are fields that make extensive use of each other's theories. Statistics is concerned with collecting and analyzing data about **populations**, a set from which samples are drawn. One goal of statistics is to make inferences about the parent population from which the sample population is drawn. A typical example of statistical inference is to infer what proportion of registered voters favors a certain candidate based on a telephone poll.

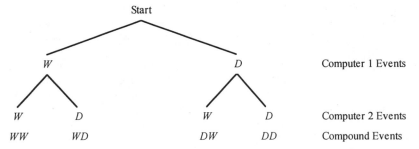

Figure 4.3 Event Tree for Compound Event

		Computer 2	
		W	D
Computer 1	W	WW	WD
	D	DW	DD

Table 4.3 Sample Space of Binary Events

One application of probability theory is to deduce whether the sample of voters is really representative of all voters, or whether it may be biased in favor of a certain party. Although this example relates to real objects such as people (other populations such as the possible number of coin tosses, is hypothetical). Every coin toss is a sample of the hypothetical population of all coin tosses.

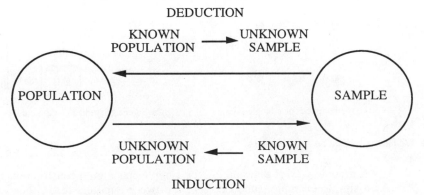

Figure 4.4 Deductive and Inductive Reasoning about Populations and Samples

Deduction and induction are the basis of reasoning about populations, as shown in Figure 4.4. Given a known population, deduction lets us make inferences about the unknown sample. Correspondingly, given a known sample, induction lets us make inferences about the unknown population.

Theory of Probability

A formal theory of probability can be made using three axioms:

$$axiom\ 1:\quad 0 \le P(E) \le 1$$

This axiom defines the range of probability to be the real numbers from 0 to 1. Negative probabilities are not allowed. A **certain event** is assigned probability 1 and an **impossible event** is assigned probability 0.

$$axiom\ 2:\quad \sum_i P(E_i) = 1$$

This axiom states that the sum of all events that do not affect each other, called *mutually exclusive events*, is 1. Mutually exclusive events have no sample point in common. For example, a computer cannot be both working correctly and not working correctly at the same time.

As a corollary of this axiom

$$P(E) + P(E') = 1$$

where E' is the complement of event E. This corollary means that the probability of an event occurring plus the probability of it not occurring is 1. That is, the occurrence and nonoccurrence of an event is a mutually exclusive and complete sample space.

$$axiom\ 3:\quad P(E_1 \cup E_2) = P(E_1) + P(E_2)$$

where E_1 and E_2 are mutually exclusive events. This axiom means that if E_1 and E_2 cannot both occur simultaneously (mutually exclusive events) then the probability of one or the other occurring is the sum of their probabilities.

From these axioms, theorems can be deduced concerning the calculation of probabilities under other situations, such as nonmutually exclusive events, as we shall see later. While these axioms form the basis for a theory of probability, notice that they *do not specify the basic probabilities* P(E), since the basic probabilities of events are determined by other methods such as *a priori*.

These axioms put probability on a sound theoretical basis. In fact, the axiomatic theory is also called the *objective theory of probability*. These particular axioms were devised by Kolmogorov. An equivalent theory using axioms of conditional probability was created by Renyi (Lindley 65).

4.6 EXPERIMENTAL AND SUBJECTIVE PROBABILITIES

Other than ideal games with equal likelihood, classical probability cannot answer questions like what is the probability of your disk drive crashing tomorrow or what is the life expectancy of a 25-year-old male.

In contrast to the *a priori* approach, **experimental probability** defines the probability of an event, P(E), as the limit of a frequency distribution:

$$P(E) = \lim_{N \to \infty} \frac{f(E)}{N}$$

where f(E) is the frequency of outcomes of an event for N observed total outcomes. This type of probability is also called a posteriori *probability*, which means "after the event." Another term for *a posteriori* is the **posterior probability**. The idea of *a posteriori* is to measure the frequency with which an event occurs for a large number of trials and from this induce the experimental probability.

For example, to determine the experimental probability of your disk drive crashing, you could take a poll of other people with your type of drive. The results of a hypothetical poll are shown in Table 4.4.

Total Percent Crashed	Hours Used
10	100
25	250
50	500
75	750
99	1000

Table 4.4 Hypothetical Time for a Disk Drive to Crash

If your drive has been used for 750 hours, then you could induce that there is a 75 percent probability of it crashing tomorrow. Notice that this 75 percent figure is an induction rather than a deduction. Unlike an ideal game, your disk drive is not exactly the same as others. There may be differences in the materials used, quality control, environmental conditions, and use that affect the drive and its longevity. It is much easier to produce simple devices such as dice or cards with much finer tolerances than a complex piece of equipment like a disk drive.

Another type of experimental probability can be induced from mortality tables used by life insurance companies that show the probability of a person dying as a function of age and sex. Calculating the odds of *your* mortality based on these tables is an induction since you are unique. An analogous situation holds for house insurance. Unless your house burns down a lot so that the individual experimental probability can be calculated, the experimental probabilities used will be based on similar types of houses.

There is also a type of probability called **subjective probability**. Suppose you were asked the probability that automobiles using superconducting electric motors would cost $10,000 by the year 2020. Since there is no data on the cost of these cars, there is no way to extrapolate the costs to see if $10,000 is reasonable.

Subjective probability deals with events that are not reproducible and have no historical basis on which to extrapolate, such as drilling an oil well at a new site. However, a subjective probability by an expert is better than no estimate at all and is usually very accurate (or the expert won't be an expert for long) (Sioshansi 1983).

A subjective probability is actually a belief or opinion expressed as a probability rather than a probability based on axioms or empirical measurement. Beliefs and opinions of an expert play important roles in expert systems, as we shall see in this chapter. Table 4.5 summarizes the different types of probabilities.

Names	Formula	Characteristics
a priori (classical, theoretical, mathematical, symmetric, equiprobable, equal likelihood)	$P(E) = \dfrac{W}{N}$ where W is the number of outcomes of event E for a total of N possible outcomes	Repeatable events Equally likely outcomes Exact math form known Not based on experiment All possible events and outcomes known
a posteriori (experimental, empirical, scientific, relative frequency, statistical) $P(E) \approx \dfrac{f(E)}{N}$	$P(E) = \lim\limits_{N \to \infty} \dfrac{f(E)}{N}$ where f(E) is the frequency, f, that event, E, is observed for N total outcomes	Repeatable events based on experiments Approximated by a finite number of experiments Exact math form unknown
subjective (personal)	See Section 4.12	Nonrepeatable events Exact math form unknown Relative frequency method not possible Based on expert's opinion experience, judgment, belief

Table 4.5 Types of Probabilities

4.7 COMPOUND PROBABILITIES

The probabilities of compound events can be computed from their sample spaces. As a simple example, consider the probability of rolling a die such that the outcome is an even number and a number divisible by three. This can be expressed in terms of a Venn diagram for the sets

```
A = { 2, 4, 6 }    B = { 3, 6 }
```

in the sample space of the die, as shown in Figure 4.5.

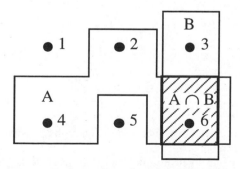

Figure 4.5 Compound Probability of Rolling a Single Die to Give an Even Number and a Number Divisible by Three

Notice that the intersection of the sets A and B is

$$A \cap B = \{\ 6\ \}$$

The compound probability of rolling an even number and a number divisible by three is

$$P(A \cap B) = \frac{n(A \cap B)}{n(S)} = \frac{1}{6}$$

where n is the number of elements in the sets and S is the sample space.

Events that do not affect each other in any way are called *independent events*. For two independent events A and B, the probability is simply the product of the individual probabilities. Events A and B are said to be *pairwise independent*.

$$P(A \cap B) = P(A)\ P(B)$$

Two events are called *stochastically independent* **events** if—and only if—the above formula is true. The term *stochastic* comes from the Greek and means "guess." It is commonly used as a synonym for *probability, random*, or *chance*. Thus a stochastic experiment has a random outcome, in contrast to the nonrandom outcome of a deterministic experiment.

For three events you might assume that independence is

$$P(A \cap B \cap C) = P(A)\ P(B)\ P(C)$$

Unfortunately, life and probability are not that simple. The formula for the **mutual independence** of N events requires that 2^N equations be satisfied. This requirement is summarized by the following equation, in which the asterisks mean that every combination of an event and its complement must be satisfied:

$$P(A^*_1 \cap A^*_2\ \cdots\ \cap A^*_N) = P(A^*_1)\ P(A^*_2)\ \cdots\ P(A^*_N)$$

For three events, the above equation for mutual independence requires that *all* the following equations be satisfied.

$$P(A \cap B \cap C) = P(A)\ P(B)\ P(C)$$
$$P(A \cap B \cap C') = P(A)\ P(B)\ P(C')$$
$$P(A \cap B' \cap C) = P(A)\ P(B')\ P(C)$$
$$P(A \cap B' \cap C') = P(A)\ P(B')\ P(C')$$
$$P(A' \cap B \cap C) = P(A')\ P(B)\ P(C)$$
$$P(A' \cap B \cap C') = P(A')\ P(B)\ P(C')$$
$$P(A' \cap B' \cap C) = P(A')\ P(B')\ P(C)$$
$$P(A' \cap B' \cap C') = P(A')\ P(B')\ P(C')$$

The pairwise independence of every two events is not enough to guarantee mutual independence as shown in Problem 4.6.

For our die, the events of an even number and a number divisible by three definitely affect each other and so it is *not* a stochastic experiment. The probability of an even number on one die and a number divisible by three on another *is* stochastic,

$$P(A \cap B) = P(A)\ P(B) = \frac{3}{6} \cdot \frac{2}{6} = \frac{1}{6}$$

Now let's consider the case of the union of events, $P(A \cup B)$. Define n as a function that returns the number of elements of a set. If we add the number of elements in A to those in B and divide by the total elements in the sample space $n(S)$,

$$(1)\quad P(A \cup B) = \frac{n(A) + n(B)}{n(S)} = P(A) + P(B)$$

then the result will be too big if the sets overlap. If you look at Figure 4.5, applying this formula gives

$$P(A \cup B) = \frac{3 + 2}{6} = \frac{5}{6}$$

but you can easily see that there are only four elements in the union because

$$A \cup B = \{\ 2,\ 3,\ 4,\ 6\ \}$$

The problem is that just adding $n(A)$ to $n(B)$ is counting the set intersection $\{\ 6\ \}$ twice since it belongs to both A and B.

The correct formula simply requires subtracting the extra probability of set intersection

$$(2)\quad P(A \cup B) = P(A) + P(B) - P(A \cap B)$$

which for our die reduces to

$$P(A \cup B) = \frac{3}{6} + \frac{2}{6} - \frac{1}{6} = \frac{4}{6} = \frac{2}{3}$$

Formula (1) holds when the sets are disjoint and so have no elements in common. It is a special case of formula (2), which is called the *Additive Law*. The Additive Law can also be derived as a theorem using the three axioms of probability discussed earlier. The Additive Law for three events is:

$$P(A \cup B \cup C) = P(A) + P(B) + P(C)$$
$$- P(A \cap B) - P(A \cap C) - P(B \cap C)$$
$$+ P(A \cap B \cap C)$$

Other laws for neither A nor B and the exclusive-OR of A and B can also be derived from the axioms. The value of these laws for compound probabilities is that (1) experiments do not have to be made for each possible combination of probabilities and (2) the individual elements of large sample spaces do not have to be counted.

4.8 CONDITIONAL PROBABILITIES

Events that are not mutually exclusive influence one another. Knowing that one event has occurred may cause us to revise the probability that another event will occur.

Multiplicative Law

The probability of an event A, given that event B occurred, is called a **conditional probability** and is indicated by P (A | B). The conditional probability is defined as

$$P(A \mid B) = \frac{P(A \cap B)}{P(B)} \quad \text{for} \quad P(B) \neq 0$$

The probability P(B) is the *a priori* or prior probability before any information is known. When used in association with a conditional probability, the prior probability is sometimes called an ***unconditional probability*** or an ***absolute probability***.

This definition of conditional probability can be intuitively explained if you look at the example of Figure 4.6, which is a sample space of eight events. From Figure 4.6 the probabilities can be calculated as the ratios of the number of events, n(A) or n(B), to the total number in the sample space n(S). That is,

$$P(A) = \frac{n(A)}{n(S)} = \frac{4}{8}$$

$$P(B) = \frac{n(B)}{n(S)} = \frac{6}{8}$$

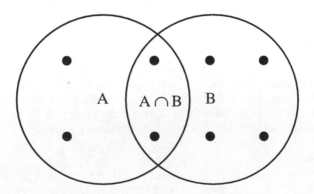

Figure 4.6 Sample Space of Two Intersecting Events

If we know that event B has occurred, the reduced sample space is just that of B:

$$n(S) = 6$$

Since B occurred, only the events in A that are associated with B are considered:

$$P(A \mid B) = \frac{n(A \cap B)}{n(B)} = \frac{2}{6}$$

To express the result in terms of probabilities, just divide the numerator and denominator of the above by n(S):

$$P(A \mid B) = \frac{\dfrac{n(A \cap B)}{n(S)}}{\dfrac{n(B)}{n(S)}}$$

$$= \frac{P(A \cap B)}{P(B)} \qquad \text{for } P(B) \neq 0$$

The **Multiplicative Law** of probability for two events is then defined as:

$$P(A \cap B) = P(A \mid B) \; P(B)$$

which is equivalent to the following;

$$P(A \cap B) = P(B \mid A) \; P(A)$$

The Multiplicative Law for three events is the following:

$$P(A \cap B \cap C) = P(A \mid B \cap C) \; P(B \mid C) \; P(C)$$

and the **Generalized Multiplicative Law** is:

$$P(A_1 \cap A_2 \cap \ldots \cap A_N) = P(A_1 \mid A_2 \cap \ldots \cap A_N) \cdot$$
$$P(A_2 \mid A_3 \cap \ldots \cap A_N) \cdot$$
$$\ldots P(A_{N-1} \mid A_N) \; P(A_N)$$

As an example of probabilities, Table 4.6 shows hypothetical probabilities of a disk crash using a Brand X drive within one year.

	Brand X	Not Brand X′	Total of Rows
Crash C	0.6	0.1	0.7
No crash C′	0.2	0.1	0.3
Total of Columns	0.8	0.2	1.0

Table 4.6 Hypothetical Probabilities of a Disk Crash Within One Year

The probabilities of 0.6, 0.1, 0.2, and 0.1 in the middle of the table are called *interior probabilities* and represent the intersection of events. The sums of the rows and columns are displayed as *totals*, and are called *marginal probabilities* because they lie on the margin of the table.

Tables 4.7 and 4.8 show the set and probability meanings in more detail. Figure 4.7 shows the Venn diagram of the sample space intersection. From Table 4.8 you can see that the sum of total row probabilities and total column probabilities is 1.

	X	X′	Total of Rows
C	C∩X	C∩X′	C = (C∩X) ∪ (C∩X′)
C′	C′∩X	C′∩X′	C′ = (C′∩X) ∪ (C′∩X′)
Total of Columns	X = (C′∩X) ∪ (C∩X)	X′ = (C′∩X′) ∪ (C∩X′)	S (Sample Space)

Table 4.7 Set Interpretation

	X	X′	Total of Rows
C	$P(C∩X)$	$P(C∩X′)$	$P(C)$
C′	$P(C′∩X)$	$P(C′∩X′)$	$P(C′)$
Total of Columns	$P(X)$	$P(X′)$	1.0

Table 4.8 Probability Interpretation of Two Sets

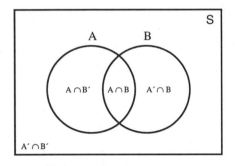

Figure 4.7 The Sample Space Interpretation of Two Sets

Using Table 4.8, the probabilities of all events can be calculated. Some probabilities are:

(1) The probability of a crash for both Brand X and not Brand X (the sample space) is

$$P(C) = 0.7$$

(2) The probability of no crash for the sample space is

$$P(C') = 0.3$$

(3) The probability of using Brand X is

$$P(X) = 0.8$$

(4) The probability of not using Brand X is

$$P(X') = 0.2$$

(5) The probability of a crash while using Brand X is

$$P(C \cap X) = 0.6$$

(6) The probability of a crash, given that Brand X is used, is

$$P(C \mid X) = \frac{P(C \cap X)}{P(X)} = \frac{0.6}{0.8} = 0.75$$

(7) The probability of a crash, given that Brand X is not used, is

$$P(C \mid X') = \frac{P(C \cap X')}{P(X')} = \frac{0.1}{0.2} = 0.50$$

Probabilities (5) and (6) may appear to have similar meanings when you read their descriptions. However (5) is simply the intersection of two events, whereas (6) is a conditional probability. The meaning of the intersection, (5), is the following.

> If a disk drive is picked randomly, then 0.6 of the time it will be Brand X and have crashed.

In other words, we are just picking samples from the population of disk drives. Some of those drives are Brand X and have crashed (0.6), some are not Brand X and have crashed (0.1), some are Brand X and have not crashed (0.2), and some are not Brand X and have not crashed (0.1).

In contrast, the meaning of the conditional probability (6) is very different:

> If a Brand X drive is picked, then 0.75 of the time it will have crashed.

Notice that in the conditional probability we are picking those items (Brand X) of interest to us and considering them as the new sample space.

If any of the following equations are true, then events A and B are **independent.**

$$P(A \mid B) = P(A) \text{ or}$$
$$P(B \mid A) = P(B) \text{ or}$$
$$P(A \cap B) = P(A) \ P(B)$$

If any one of these equations are true, then the others are also true.

Bayes' Theorem

The conditional probability, $P(A \mid B)$, states the probability of event A given that event B occurred. The inverse problem is to find the **inverse probability** that states the probability of an earlier event given that a later one occurred. This type of probability occurs often, as in the case of medical or equipment diagnosis in which symptoms appear and the problem is to find the most likely cause. The solution to this problem is **Bayes' Theorem**, also sometimes called Bayes' Formula, Bayes' Rule or Bayes' Law, named after the eighteenth-century British clergyman and mathematician Thomas Bayes.

As an example of Bayes' theorem, let's see how it applies to the disk drive crashes. From the conditional probability (6), there is a 75 percent probability a Brand X drive will crash within one year, while based on (7), the probability of a non-Brand X drive crash within one year is 50 percent. The inverse question is, suppose you have a drive and don't know its brand, what is the probability that if it crashes, it is Brand X? non-Brand X?

A situation like this, in which you don't really know the drive, occurs all the time since computer manufacturers seldom make their own drives. Instead many buy drives from an original equipment manufacturer (OEM) and repackage the drives to sell under their own label. Depending on what OEM offers the lowest cost, the drive may vary from year to year with only the computer manufacturer's label remaining the same.

Given that a drive crashed, the probability of it being Brand X can be stated using conditional probability and the results (1), (5).

$$P(X \mid C) = \frac{P(C \cap X)}{P(C)} = \frac{0.6}{0.7} = \frac{6}{7}$$

Alternatively, using the Multiplicative Law on the numerator and (1), (3), (6)

$$P(X \mid C) = \frac{P(C \mid X) \; P(X)}{P(C)} = \frac{(0.75)\;(0.8)}{0.7} = \frac{0.6}{0.7} = \frac{6}{7}$$

The probability $P(X \mid C)$ is the **inverse** or *a posteriori* probability, which states that if the drive crashed, it was Brand X. Figure 4.8 shows a decision tree for the disk crashes. The square symbol indicates an **act** or decision, and the circle indicates an **event** or occurrence. The prior probabilities are those determined before the experiments of measuring crashes. The posterior or inverse probabilities are those determined after the completion of the experiments. The posterior probabilities allow us to revise the prior probabilities to obtain more accurate results.

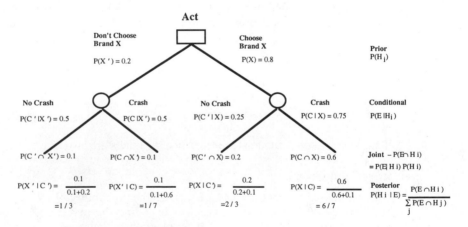

Figure 4.8 Decision Tree for the Disk Crashes

The general form of Bayes' Theorem can be written in terms of events, E, and hypotheses (assumptions), H, in the following alternative forms:

$$P(H_i \mid E) = \frac{P(E \cap H_i)}{\sum_j P(E \cap H_j)}$$

$$= \frac{P(E \mid H_i) \ P(H_i)}{\sum_j P(E \mid H_j) \ P(H_j)}$$

$$= \frac{P(E \mid H_i) \ P(H_i)}{P(E)}$$

4.9 HYPOTHETICAL REASONING AND BACKWARD INDUCTION

Bayes' Theorem is commonly used for decision tree analysis of business and the social sciences. The method of **Bayesian decision making** is also used in the PROSPECTOR expert system to decide favorable sites for mineral exploration. PROSPECTOR has achieved a great deal of fame as the first expert system to discover a valuable molybdenum deposit worth $100,000,000.

As an example of Bayesian decision making under conditions of uncertainty, let's look at the problem of oil exploration. Initially, the prospector must decide what the chances are of finding oil. If there is no evidence either for or against oil, the prospector may assign the subjective prior probabilities for oil, O, of

$$P(O) = P(O') = 0.5$$

With no evidence, an assignment of probabilities that are equally weighted between possible outcomes is said to be made **in desperation**. The term *in desperation* does not mean that the prospector is (necessarily) in desperate need. It is a technical term for the unbiased prior assignment of probabilities. The prospector believes that there is better than a 50-50 chance of finding oil, and assumes the following:

$$P(O) = 0.6 \qquad P(O') = 0.4$$

A very important tool in oil and mineral exploration is the **seismic survey**. In this technique, dynamite or machinery creates sound pulses that travel through the earth. The sound waves are detected by microphones at various locations. By observing the arrival time of pulses and the distortion of the sound waveform, it is possible to determine geologic structures and the possibility of oil and minerals. Unfortunately seismic tests are not 100 percent accurate. The sound waves may be affected by some types of geologic structures causing the test to report the presence of oil when there really is none (false positive). Likewise, the test may report the absence of oil when there really is oil (false negative). Assume that the past history of the seismic test has given the following conditional probabilities, in which + is a positive outcome and − is a negative outcome. Note that these are conditional probabilities because the cause (oil or no oil) must have occurred before the effect (test result). A posterior probability would be from an effect (test result) back to the cause (oil or no oil). Generally, a conditional probability is forward in time whereas a posterior probability is backward in time.

```
P(+ | O)  = 0.8              P(- | O)  = 0.2 (false -)
P(+ | O') = 0.1 (false +)    P(- | O') = 0.9
```

Using the prior and conditional probabilities, we can construct the initial probability tree as shown in Figure 4.9. Also shown are the joint probabilities, which are calculated from the prior and conditional probabilities.

The Addition Law is then used to calculate the total probability of a + and a − test.

$$P(+) = P(+ \cap O) + P(+ \cap O') = 0.48 + 0.04 = 0.52$$
$$P(-) = P(- \cap O) + P(- \cap O') = 0.12 + 0.36 = 0.48$$

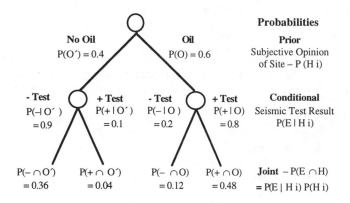

Figure 4.9 Initial Probability Tree for Oil Exploration

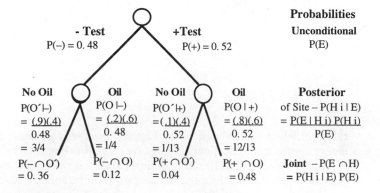

Figure 4.10 Revised Probability Tree for Oil Exploration

The P(+) and P(−) are unconditional probabilities that can now be used to calculate the posterior probabilities at the site, as shown in Figure 4.10. For example, the P(O ′ | −) is the posterior probability for no oil at the site based on a negative test. The joint probabilities are then computed. Notice that the joint probabilities of Figure 4.10 are the same as in Figure 4.9. The revision of probabilities is necessary to give good results when experimental information, such as the seismic test results, occurs after the initial probability estimates (or guess).

Figure 4.11 shows the initial Bayesian decision tree using the data from Figure 4.10. The **payoffs** at the bottom of the tree are positive if money is made and negative if money is lost. The assumed amounts are shown in Table 4.9.

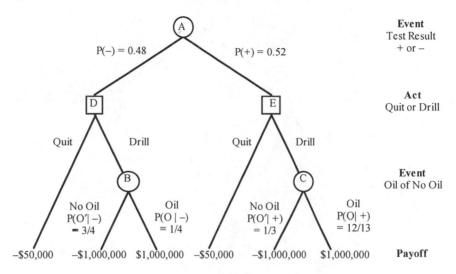

Figure 4.11 Initial Bayesian Decision Tree for Oil Exploration

Oil lease, if successful	$1,250,000
Drilling expense	–$200,000
Seismic survey	–$50,000

Table 4.9 Payoff Table for the Oil Exploration Problem

Thus, if oil is found the payoff is $1,250,000 – $200,000 – $50,000 = $1,000,000 whereas a decision to quit after the seismic test result gives a payoff of –$50,000.

In order for the prospector to make the best decision, the **expected payoff** must be calculated at event node A. The expected payoff is the amount the prospector can make by following the best course of action. To compute the expected payoff at the start, A, we must work backward from the leaves. In probability theory this process is called **backward induction**. That is, in order to achieve the expected payoff or goal that we want, we must reason backward to find the causes that will lead us to the goal.

The expected payoff from an event node is the sum of the payoffs times the probabilities leading to the payoffs.

```
Expected payoff at node C
$846,153 = ($1,000,000) (12/13) - ($1,000,000) (1/13)


Expected payoff at node B
-$500,000 = ($1,000,000) (1/4) - ($1,000,000) (3/4)
```

At action node E we must decide between an expected payoff of –$50,000 by quitting or $846,153 by drilling. Since $846,153 is greater than –$50,000, we will induce that this is the better action and write it over node E. The path to quitting will be **pruned** or **poisoned** by breaking it with a "=" symbol to indicate this path will not be followed, as in Figure 4.12. Likewise at action node D, the best choice between a payoff of -$50,000 and a payoff of –$500,000 is –$50,000 and so this is written at D.

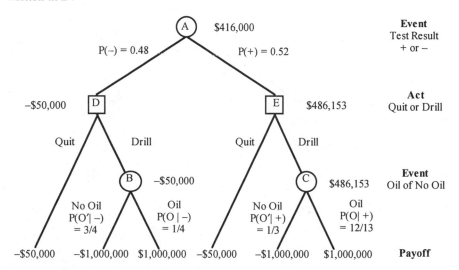

Figure 4.12
Complete Bayesian Decision Tree for Oil Exploration Using Backward Induction

Finally, the expected payoff at the beginning is computed as follows:

```
Expected payoff at node A
$416,000 = ($846,153)(0.52) - ($50,000)(0.48)
```

and this value is written at node A. No path can be pruned at node A because we have already decided to do the seismic test. To decide on a seismic test, the decision tree would have to be extended backward before node A. Notice that in backward induction, we are reasoning back in time so that our actions in the future will be optimal.

The decision tree is an example of hypothetical reasoning or "What if" type situations. By exploring alternate paths of action, we can prune paths that do not lead to optimal payoffs. Some types of expert system tools such as ART, from the Inference Corp., have elaborate mechanisms for hypothetical reasoning and poisoning.

The decision tree in Figure 4.12 shows the optimal strategy for the prospector. If the seismic test is positive, the site should be drilled. If the seismic test is negative, the site should be abandoned. Although this is a very simple example of Bayesian decision making, it does illustrate the type of reasoning involved in dealing with uncertainty. In more complex cases, such as deciding to use a seismic test, the decision trees may grow much larger (Lapin 78).

4.10 TEMPORAL REASONING AND MARKOV CHAINS

Reasoning about events that depend on time is called *temporal reasoning* and is something that humans do fairly easily. However, it is difficult to formalize **temporal events** so that a computer can make temporal inferences. Yet expert systems that reason about temporal events such as aircraft traffic control could be very useful. Expert systems that reason over time have been developed in medicine. These include the VM system (Fagan 1979) for ventilator management of patients on respirators, to help them breathe. Other systems are CASNET for eye glaucoma treatment (Weiss 78) and the digitalis therapy advisor for heart patients (Gorry 78).

Except for VM, the other medical systems mentioned above have a less difficult problem with temporal reasoning compared to an aircraft control system, which must operate in **real time**. Most expert systems cannot operate in real time because of the inference engine design and the large amounts of processing required. An expert system that does a lot of temporal reasoning to explore multiple hypotheses in real time is very difficult to build. Different temporal logics have been developed based on different axioms (Turner 84). Different theories are based on the ways certain questions are answered. Does time have a first and last moment? Is time continuous or discrete? Is there only one past but many possible futures?

Depending on how these questions are answered, many different logics can be developed (McDermott 82; Allen 81). Temporal logic is also useful in conventional programs, such as in the synthesis and the synchronization of processes in concurrent programs (Manna and Wolper 84).

Another approach to temporal reasoning is with probabilities. We can think of a system moving from one state to another as evolving over time. The system can be anything that is probabilistic such as stocks, voters, weather, business, disease, equipment, genetics, and so forth. The system's progression through a sequence of status is called a ***stochastic process*** if it is probabilistic.

It is convenient to represent a stochastic process in the form of a transition matrix. For the simple case of two states, S_1 and S_2, the transition matrix is

$$
\begin{array}{cc}
 & \text{Future} \\
 & \begin{array}{cc} S_1 & S_2 \end{array} \\
\text{Present} \begin{array}{c} S_1 \\ S_2 \end{array} & \begin{bmatrix} P_{11} & P_{12} \\ P_{21} & P_{22} \end{bmatrix}
\end{array}
$$

where P_{mn} is the probability of a transition from state m to state n.

As an example, assume that 10 percent of all people who now use Brand X drives will buy another Brand X drive when needed. Also, 60 percent of the people who don't use Brand X now will buy Brand X when they need a new drive (the only good thing about Brand X is its advertising). Over a long period of time, how many people will use Brand X?

The transition matrix, T, is

$$
T = \begin{array}{cc}
 & \begin{array}{cc} X & X' \end{array} \\
\begin{array}{c} X \\ X' \end{array} & \begin{bmatrix} 0.1 & 0.9 \\ 0.6 & 0.4 \end{bmatrix}
\end{array}
$$

where the sum of each row must add up to 1. A vector whose components are not negative and add up to 1 is called a ***probability vector***. Each row of T is a probability vector. One way of interpreting the transition matrix is in terms of a state diagram, as shown in Figure 4.13. Notice that there is a 0.1 probability of remaining in state X, a 0.4 probability of remaining in state X′, a 0.9 probability of going from X to X′, and a 0.6 probability of going from X′ to X.

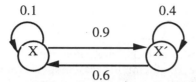

Figure 4.13 State Diagram Interpretation of a Transition Matrix

Suppose initially that 80 percent of the people use Brand X. Figure 4.14 (a) shows a probability tree for a few state transitions, where the states are labeled by state number and drive owned. Notice how the tree is starting to grow. If there were ten transitions, the tree would have $2^{10} = 1024$ branches. An alternate way of drawing the tree, as a lattice, is shown in Figure 4.14 (b). The advantage of the lattice representation is that it doesn't need as many links connecting the states.

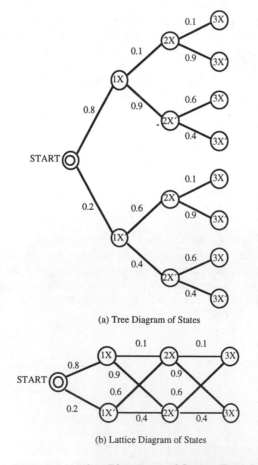

(a) Tree Diagram of States

(b) Lattice Diagram of States

Figure 4.14 Tree and Lattice Diagrams of States Evolving over Time

The probability of the system being in a certain state can be represented as a row matrix called the *state matrix*.

$$S = \begin{bmatrix} P_1 & P_2 & \ldots & P_N \end{bmatrix}$$

where $P_1 + P_2 + \ldots + P_N = 1$

Initially, with 80 percent of the people owning Brand X, the state matrix is

$$S_1 = \begin{bmatrix} 0.8 & 0.2 \end{bmatrix}$$

As time goes on, these numbers will change depending on which drives people buy.

In order to calculate the number of people in state 2 having Brand X and not Brand X, just multiply the state matrix times the transition matrix using the ordinary laws of matrix multiplication:

$$S_2 = S_1 \, T$$

which gives

$$S_2 = \begin{bmatrix} 0.8 & 0.2 \end{bmatrix} \begin{bmatrix} 0.1 & 0.9 \\ 0.6 & 0.4 \end{bmatrix}$$

$$= \begin{bmatrix} (0.8)(0.1)+(0.2)(0.6) & (0.8)(0.9)+(0.2)(0.4) \end{bmatrix}$$

$$= \begin{bmatrix} 0.2 & 0.8 \end{bmatrix}$$

Multiplying this second state by the transition matrix gives

$$S_3 = S_2 \, T$$

$$= \begin{bmatrix} 0.2 & 0.8 \end{bmatrix} \begin{bmatrix} 0.1 & 0.9 \\ 0.6 & 0.4 \end{bmatrix}$$

$$S_3 = \begin{bmatrix} 0.5 & 0.5 \end{bmatrix}$$

Multiplying this third state by the transition matrix gives

$$S_4 = S_3 \, T$$

$$= \begin{bmatrix} 0.5 & 0.5 \end{bmatrix} \begin{bmatrix} 0.1 & 0.9 \\ 0.6 & 0.4 \end{bmatrix}$$

$$S_4 = \begin{bmatrix} 0.35 & 0.65 \end{bmatrix}$$

The next states are

$$S_5 = \begin{bmatrix} 0.425 & 0.575 \end{bmatrix}$$

$$S_6 = [\ 0.3875 \quad 0.6125\ ]$$

$$S_7 = [\ 0.40625 \quad 0.59375\ ]$$

$$S_8 = [\ 0.396875 \quad 0.602125\ ]$$

Notice that the states are converging on

$$[\ 0.4 \quad 0.6\ ]$$

which is called a *steady-state matrix*. The system is said to be in equilibrium when it is in the steady state because it does not change. It's interesting that the steady-state values do not depend on the initial state. If any initial probability vector had been used, the steady-state values would be the same.

A probability vector S is a steady-state matrix for the transition matrix T if

(1) $S = S\ T$

If T is a **regular transition matrix**, which has some power with only positive elements, then a unique steady-state S exists (Kemeny 59). The fact that the transition matrix elements are positive means that, at some time, it is possible to be in any state no matter what the initial state had been. That is, every state is potentially accessible.

A **Markov chain process** is defined as having the following characteristics:

(1) A finite number of possible states.
(2) The process can be in one and only one state at a time.
(3) The process moves or **steps** successively from one state to another over time.
(4) The probability of a move depends only on the immediately preceding state.

For example, given a finite set of states {A,B,C,D,E,F,G,H}, then if the next state that the process goes to after H is I, the conditional probability is the following.

$$P(I\ |\ H) = P(I\ |\ H \cap G \cap F \cap E \cap D \cap C \cap B \cap A)$$

Notice how the lattice diagram of Figure 4.14 (b) resembles a chain.

The disk drive case is a Markov chain process and the steady-state matrix can be found by applying equation (1). Assume some arbitrary vector S with components X and Y and apply equation (1) as follows:

$$[\ X \quad Y\ ] \begin{bmatrix} 0.1 & 0.9 \\ 0.6 & 0.4 \end{bmatrix} = [\ X \quad Y\ ]$$

Multiplying the left side and setting its elements equal to the corresponding elements on the right side gives

```
0.1 X + 0.6 Y = X
0.9 X + 0.4 Y = Y
```

which is a dependent system of equations. Solving for X in terms of Y gives

$$X = \frac{0.6}{0.9} \ Y = \frac{2}{3} \ Y$$

To completely solve for X and Y, we'll make use of the fact that the sum of the probabilities equals 1. That is

```
X + Y = 1
```

and so

$$X = 1 - Y = \frac{2}{3} \ Y$$

and therefore

$$X = \frac{2}{5} \qquad Y = \frac{3}{5}$$

so the steady-state matrix is

```
[ 0.4   0.6 ]
```

which is what our trial values were indeed converging to.

4.11 THE ODDS OF BELIEF

So far we have been concerned with probabilities as measures of repeatable events of ideal systems. However, humans are experts at calculating the probabilities of many nonrepeatable events such as medical diagnoses and mineral exploration because each patient and site is unique. In order to make expert systems in areas like this, we must expand the scope of events to deal with propositions, which are statements that are true or false. For example, an event may be

```
"The patient is covered with red spots"
```

and the proposition is

```
"The patient has measles"
```

Given that A is a proposition, the conditional probability

```
P(A | B)
```

is not necessarily a probability in the classic sense if the events and propositions cannot be repeated or have a mathematical basis. Instead, P(A | B) can be interpreted as the **degree of belief** that A is true, given B.

If $P(A \mid B) = 1$, then we believe that A is certainly true. If $P(A \mid B) = 0$, then we believe A is certainly false while other values, $0 < P(A \mid B) < 1$, mean that we are not entirely sure that A is true or false. From statistics the term **hypothesis** is used for some proposition whose truth or falseness is not known for sure on the basis of some **evidence**. The conditional probability is then referred to as the **likelihood**, as in $P(H \mid E)$, which expresses the likelihood of a hypothesis, H, based on some evidence, E.

Although $P(H \mid E)$ has the form of a conditional probability, it actually means something different—the likelihood or degree of belief. *Probability* refers to repeatable events and *likelihood* refers to our degree of belief in nonrepeatable events. Since expert systems are models of human experts, $P(H \mid E)$ is generally the expert's degree of belief that some hypothesis is true given some evidence, E. Of course, if the events are repeatable, then $P(H \mid E)$ is simply the probability.

If we agree that $P(H \mid E)$ means the likelihood or degree of belief, then what does a value such as 50 percent or 95 percent mean? For example, suppose you are 95 percent sure that your car will start the next time it's started. One way of interpreting this likelihood is in terms of the **odds** of a bet. The odds on A against B given some event C are

$$odds = \frac{P(A \mid C)}{P(B \mid C)}$$

If $B = A'$

$$odds = \frac{P(A \mid C)}{P(A' \mid C)} = \frac{P(A \mid C)}{1 - P(A \mid C)}$$

defining

$$P = P(A \mid C)$$

gives

$$odds = \frac{P}{1 - P} \quad \text{and} \quad P = \frac{odds}{1 + odds}$$

In terms of gambling odds, we can interpret P as wins and $1 - P$ as losses, so

$$odds = \frac{wins}{losses}$$

Knowing the odds allows the probability or likelihood to be calculated and vice versa.

The likelihood of P = 95 percent is thus equivalent to

$$odds = \frac{.95}{1 - .95} = 19 \text{ to } 1$$

that you believe the car will start. That is, you should be **indifferent** to a bet of odds at 19 to 1 that the car will start. If someone offers a $1 bet that the car won't start, you will pay $19 if it doesn't start. Whenever a degree of belief is stated as a probability, you can interpret it in terms of a bet at equivalent odds. In other words, you should be indifferent to the real situation with its degree of belief or the equivalent odds of a bet.

Probabilities are generally used with deductive problems in which a number of different events, E_i, may occur, given the same hypothesis. For example, given that a die rolls an even number, there are three possible events:

```
P(2 | even)
P(4 | even)
P(6 | even)
```

In probability, we are generally interested in $P(E_i \mid H)$ where E_i are the possible events from a common hypothesis. In statistics and inductive reasoning, we know the event that has occurred and want to find the likelihood of the hypothesis that can cause E, which is $P(E \mid H_i)$. Probability is naturally forward chaining or deductive whereas likelihood is backward chaining and inductive. Although we use the same symbolism, $P(X \mid Y)$, for probability and likelihood, the applications are different. Normally we refer to the likelihood of a hypothesis or the probability of an event.

One theory that has been developed using degrees of belief is **personal probability** (Savage 54). In personal probability, **states** are the possible hypotheses and the **consequences** are the results of actions based on the beliefs.

4.12 SUFFICIENCY AND NECESSITY

Bayes' Theorem is

$$(1) \quad P(H \mid E) = \frac{P(E \mid H) \ P(H)}{P(E)}$$

and for the negation of H becomes

$$(2) \quad P(H' \mid E) = \frac{P(E \mid H') \ P(H')}{P(E)}$$

Dividing (1) by (2) gives

$$(3) \quad \frac{P(H \mid E)}{P(H' \mid E)} = \frac{P(E \mid H) \ P(H)}{P(E \mid H') \ P(H')}$$

Defining the prior odds on H as

$$O(H) = \frac{P(H)}{P(H')}$$

and the posterior odds as

$$O(H \mid E) = \frac{P(H \mid E)}{P(H' \mid E)}$$

and finally defining the **likelihood ratio**

$$(4) \quad LS = \frac{P(E \mid H)}{P(E \mid H')}$$

then (3) becomes

$$(5) \quad O(H \mid E) = LS \; O(H)$$

Equation (5) is known as the **odds-likelihood form** of Bayes' Theorem. It is a more convenient form of Bayes' Theorem to work with than equation (1).

The factor LS is also called the *likelihood of sufficiency* because if LS = ∞, then the evidence E is logically sufficient for concluding that H is true. If E is logically sufficient for concluding H, then $P(H \mid E) = 1$ and $P(H \mid E') = 0$. Equation (5) can be used to solve for LS as follows:

$$(6) \quad LS = \frac{O(H \mid E)}{O(H)} = \frac{\dfrac{P(H \mid E)}{P(H' \mid E)}}{\dfrac{P(H)}{P(H')}}$$

Now $P(H) / P(H')$ is some constant, C, and so equation (6) becomes

$$LS = \frac{\dfrac{1}{0}}{C} = \infty$$

Equation (4) also shows in this case that H is sufficient for E. Table 4.10 summarizes the meanings of other values of LS.

The likelihood of necessity, LN, is defined similarly to LS as

$$(7) \quad LN = \frac{O(H \mid E')}{O(H)} = \frac{P(E' \mid H)}{P(E' \mid H')} = \frac{\dfrac{P(H \mid E')}{P(H' \mid E')}}{\dfrac{P(H)}{P(H')}}$$

$$(8) \quad O(H \mid E') = LN \; O(H)$$

If LN = 0, then $P(H \mid E') = 0$. This means that H must be false when E' is true. Thus if E is not present then H is false, which means that E is necessary for H.

Table 4.11 shows the relationship between LN, E, and H. Notice that it is the same as Table 4.10 except "evidence" is replaced by "absence of evidence."

The likelihood values LS and LN must be provided by a human expert in order to compute the posterior odds. The form of equations (5) and (8) is simple for people to understand. The LS factor shows how much the prior odds are changed when the evidence is present. The LN factor shows how much the prior odds are changed when the evidence is absent. These forms make it easier for a human expert to then specify the LS and LN factors.

As an example, in the PROSPECTOR expert system there is a rule that specifies how evidence of a certain mineral supports a hypothesis.

```
IF there are quartz-sulfide veinlets
THEN there is a favorable alteration
     for the potassic zone
```

This particular intermediate hypothesis provides support for other hypotheses leading to the top-level hypothesis that copper is present. The LS and LN values for this rule are

```
LS = 300
LN = 0.2
```

which means that observation of quartz-sulfide veinlets is very favorable while not observing the veinlets is mildly unfavorable. If LN were << 1, then the absence of quartz-sulfide veinlets would strongly suggest the hypothesis is false. An example is the rule

```
IF glassy limonite
THEN best mineralization favorability
```

with

```
LS = 1000000
LN = 0.01
```

LS	Effect on Hypothesis
0	H is false when E is true or E′ is necessary for concluding H
small (0 < LS << 1)	E is unfavorable for concluding H
1	E has no effect on belief of H
large (1 << LS)	E is favorable for concluding H
∞	E is logically sufficient for H or Observing E means H must be true

Table 4.10 Relationship between Likelihood Ratio, Hypothesis, and Evidence

LN	Effect on Hypothesis
0	H is false when E is absent or E is necessary for H
small (0 < LN << 1)	Absence of E is unfavorable for concluding H
1	Absence of E has no effect on H
large (1 << LN)	Absence of E is favorable for H
∞	Absence of E is logically sufficient for H

Table 4.11 Relationship between Likelihood of Necessity, Hypothesis, and Evidence

4.13 UNCERTAINTY IN INFERENCE CHAINS

Uncertainty may be present in rules, evidence used by the rules, or both. In this section you will see some real-world problems of uncertainty and how probability provides an answer.

Expert Inconsistency

From equation (4) of the preceding section,

```
if LS > 1 then P(E | H´) < P(E | H)
```

Subtracting each side from 1 reverses the inequality:

```
1 - P(E | H´) > 1 - P(E | H)
```

Since $P(E' | H) = 1 - P(E | H)$, and $P(E' | H') = 1 - P(E | H')$, then (7) becomes

$$LN = \frac{1 - P(E | H)}{1 - P(E | H´)} < 1$$

The constraints on the values of LN and LN are summarized as the following:

```
Case 1: LS > 1 and LN < 1
```

From equations (4) and (7), the other cases are

```
Case 2: LS < 1 and LN > 1
```

```
Case 3: LS = LN = 1
```

Although these three cases are mathematically rigorous constraints on the values of LS and LN, they don't always work out in the real world. For the expert system PROSPECTOR, used for mineral exploration, it was not uncommon for experts to specify an $LS > 1$ and $LN = 1$, which is not one of these three cases. That is, the expert is saying that the observation of evidence is important but the absence of the evidence is unimportant.

This last case shows that the likelihood theory based on Bayesian probability theory is incomplete for the mineral exploration problem. That is, the Bayesian likelihood theory is only an approximation to a theory that can also deal with the case that $LS > 1$ and $LN = 1$. For domains in which expert opinions satisfy one of the first three cases, the Bayesian likelihood theory is satisfactory.

Uncertain Evidence

In the real world we are seldom absolutely sure of anything except death and taxes. Although so far we have concentrated on uncertain hypotheses, the more general and realistic situation is uncertain hypotheses *and* uncertain evidence.

For the general case, assume that the degree of belief in the **complete evidence**, E, is dependent on the **partial evidence**, e, by

```
P(E | e)
```

The complete evidence is the total evidence, which represents all possible evidence, and hypotheses, which comprise E. The partial evidence, e, is the portion of E that we know. If we do know all the evidence, then $E = e$ and

```
P(E | e) = P(E)
```

where $P(E)$ is the prior likelihood of the evidence E. The likelihood $P(E \mid e)$ is our belief in E given our imperfect knowledge, e, of the complete evidence E.

As an example, suppose that people in your neighborhood who started drilling for oil in their kitchens have become rich. You may consider a hypothesis and evidence

```
H = I'm going to get rich
E = there is oil under my kitchen
```

as expressed in the rule

```
IF there is oil under my kitchen
THEN I'm going to get rich          P(H | E) = 1
```

At this initial stage you do not know for certain that there is oil under your kitchen. Conclusive evidence would be drilling a test well, but this is rather expensive. So you consider the partial evidence, e, in support of E as follows:

- Other people in the neighborhood have struck it rich.
- There is some black substance always seeping up around the kitchen stove (which until now your spouse has blamed on your cooking and cleaning).
- A stranger came to the door and offered $20,000,000 for your house because she said that she liked the view.

Based on this partial evidence, you may decide that the likelihood of oil under your kitchen is rather high, $P(E \mid e) = 0.98$.

In a probabilistic or likelihood type of inference chain, if H depends on E and E is based on some partial evidence e, then $P(H \mid e)$ is the likelihood that H depends on e. By the rule for conditional probability,

$$P(H \mid e) = \frac{P(H \cap e)}{P(e)}$$

Figure 4.15 illustrates how H can be considered to be made up of E and e. So the above becomes

$$P(H \mid e) = \frac{P(H \cap E \cap e) + P(H \cap E' \cap e)}{P(e)}$$

Using the rule of conditional probability gives

$$P(H \mid e) = \frac{P(H \cap E \mid e) \cdot P(e) + P(H \cap E' \mid e) \, P(e)}{P(e)}$$

$$(1) \quad P(H \mid e) = P(H \cap E \mid e) + P(H \cap E' \mid e)$$

Another way of expressing (1) follows since

$$P(H \cap E \mid e) = \frac{P(H \cap E \cap e)}{P(e)}$$

$$(2) \quad P(H \cap E \mid e) = \frac{P(H \mid E \cap e) \; P(E \cap e)}{P(e)}$$

and since

$$P(E \mid e) = \frac{P(E \cap e)}{P(e)}$$

then (2) becomes

$$P(H \cap E \mid e) = P(H \mid E \cap e) \; P(E \mid e)$$

Likewise

$$P(H \cap E' \mid e) = P(H \mid E' \cap e) \; P(E' \mid e)$$

and (1) becomes

$$(3) \quad P(H \mid e) = P(H \mid E \cap e) \; P(E \mid e) \; + \\ P(H \mid E' \cap e) \; P(E' \mid e)$$

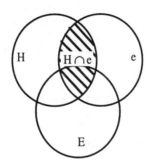

$$H \cap e = H \cap E \cap e + H \cap E' \cap e$$

Figure 4.15 The Intersection of H and e

Normally we do not know the probabilities $P(H \mid E \cap e)$ and $P(H \mid E' \cap e)$. However, if we assume these can be approximated by $P(H \mid E)$ and $P(H \mid E')$, then (3) simplifies to

$$(4) \quad P(H \mid e) = P(H \mid E) \; P(E \mid e) \\ + P(H \mid E') \; P(E' \mid e)$$

Equation (4) is essentially a linear interpolation of $P(H \mid e)$ versus $P(E \mid e)$. The end points are

$$(i) \quad E \text{ is true and so } P(H \mid e) = P(H \mid E).$$
$$(ii) \quad E \text{ is false and so } P(H \mid e) = P(H \mid E').$$

The problem with equation (4) shows up when P(E | e) equals the prior probability P(E). If the system obeys pure Bayesian probability, then

(5) P(H | e) = P(H | E) P(E) + P(H | E´) P(E´)
(6) P(H | e) = P(H)

which is correct.

However, in the real world, experience has shown that human experts give subjective probabilities that are almost certain to be inconsistent. For example, if the expert uses the inconsistent case of LS > 1 and LN = 1, then

O(H | E´) = LN O(H) = O(H)

and since

$$O = \frac{P}{1 - P}$$

then

(7) P(H | E´) = P(H)

Using (7) in (5) gives

P(H | e) = P(H | E) P(E) + P(H) P(E´)

= P(H | E) P(E) + P(H) (1 - P(E))

(8) P(H | e) = P(H) + P(H | E) P(E) - P(H) P(E)

Now

O(H | E) = LS O(H)

If LS = 1 then

O(H | E) = O(H)
P(H | E) = P(H)

Since the human expert has specified LS > 1, then P(H | E) > P(H) and so the term

P(H | E) P(E) - P(H) P(E)

in equation (8) will be > 0, where 0 is the lower bound when LS = 1. So from (8)

P(H | e) > P(H)

when LS > 1 and LN = 1. This contradicts the fact that P(H | e) should equal P(H) when P(E | e) = P(E). Since P(H | e) > P(H), the probability is greater than it should be and may become magnified further as the inference from one rule is used by another in an inference chain.

Correcting Uncertainty

One way of correcting this problem is to assume that P(H | e) is a piecewise linear function (Duda 76). This is an *ad hoc* assumption that worked well with PROSPECTOR but is not based on traditional probability theory. The linear function is chosen for simplicity in calculations.

The function matches the constraints at the three points in Figure 4.16. The formula for P(H | e) is calculated using linear interpolation as follows:

$$P(H \mid e) = \begin{cases} P(H \mid E') + \dfrac{P(H) - P(H \mid E')}{P(E)} \; P(E \mid e) \\[1em] \qquad \text{for } 0 \le P(E \mid e) < P(E) \\[1.5em] P(H) + \dfrac{P(H \mid E) - P(H)}{1 - P(E)} \; [P(E \mid e) - P(E)] \\[1em] \qquad \text{for } P(E) \le P(E \mid e) \le 1 \end{cases}$$

Using this formula, the inconsistent case discussed earlier of LS > 1 and LN = 1 can be satisfied. Now the value of P(H | e) remains the same if P(E | e) < P(E) and increases if P(E | e) ≥ P(E). The reason for choosing this piecewise rather than in a single straight line, is to ensure that when P(E | e) = P(E), then P(H | e) = P(H).

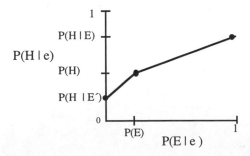

Figure 4.16
Piecewise Linear Interpolation Function for Partial Evidence in PROSPECTOR

4.14 THE COMBINATION OF EVIDENCE

The simplest type of rule is of the form

        IF E THEN H

where E is a single piece of known evidence from which we can conclude that H is true. Unfortunately, not all rules may be this simple, so compensation for uncertainty is necessary.

Classifications of Uncertain Evidence

More complex situations arise if there is uncertainty about the rule. This uncertainty can be expressed as a probability or a likelihood depending on whether we are dealing with reproducible events or subjective probabilities. For simplicity, we'll use the term *probability* for uncertainties.

The different situations can be classified on whether the evidence is certain or uncertain and whether there is **simple evidence** or **compound evidence**. Simple evidence consists of a single piece of evidence such as

```
IF the transmission is bad
THEN repair the car
```

whereas compound evidence consists of multiple pieces of evidence usually linked by AND connections, as in

```
IF the transmission is bad AND
    the carburetor is bad
THEN sell the car
```

or expressed formally:

```
IF E₁ and E₂ then H
```

We may assign a probability to this rule such as $P(H \mid E_1 \cap E_2) = 0.80$, which means we are 80 percent sure the car should be sold on the basis of this evidence.

A further refinement of the evidence is determining its probability. For example, the probability of the transmission's being bad may depend on two symptoms:

(a) Transmission fluid is leaking
(b) The car won't go into reverse

These observations lead to a probability of the transmission evidence. For example, on the basis of symptoms (a) and (b), we may decide

```
P(E | e) = 0.95

where E = transmission is bad
      e = symptoms (a) and (b) above
```

Now let's examine in more detail the probabilities associated with the different situations.

Situation 1: One piece of known evidence concludes H

This is the simplest case with rules of the form

```
IF E THEN H
```

Before any evidence is known the prior probability of H is $P(H)$. After the evidence is known the probability of H changes by Bayes' Theorem:

$$P(H \mid E) = \frac{P(H \cap E)}{P(E)} = \frac{P(H \cap E)}{P(E \cap H) + P(E \cap H')}$$

$$P(H \mid E) = \frac{P(H \mid E) \ P(H)}{P(E \mid H) \ P(H) + P(E \mid H') \ P(H')}$$

where $P(E)$ is the probability of observing E.

Situation 2: Two pieces of known evidence conclude H

This is a more complex case than situation 1 and corresponds to rules of the form

IF E_1 and E_2 then H

After E_1 and E_2 are observed, the probability of H changes from the prior $P(H)$ to

$$P(H \mid E_1 \cap E_2) \quad = \frac{P(H \cap E_1 \cap E_2)}{P(E_1 \cap E_2)}$$

$$= \frac{P(H \cap E_1 \cap E_2)}{P(E_1 \cap E_2 \cap H) + P(E_1 \cap E_2 \cap H')}$$

(1) $P(H \mid E_1 \cap E_2)$

$$= \frac{P(E_1 \cap E_2 \mid H) \ P(H)}{P(E_1 \cap E_2 \mid H) \ P(H) + P(E_1 \cap E_2 \mid H') \ P(H')}$$

This formula cannot be reduced further unless a simplifying assumption is made. If the evidence E_1 and E_2 are assumed conditionally independent of each other, then

$$P(E_1 \cap E_2 \mid H) = P(E_1 \mid H) \ P(E_2 \mid H)$$
$$P(E_1 \cap E_2 \mid H') = P(E_1 \mid H') \ P(E_2 \mid H')$$

and so (see problem 4.12 for conditional independence)

(2) $P(H \mid E_1 \cap E_2)$

$$= \frac{P(E_1 \mid H) \ P(E_2 \mid H)}{P(E_1 \mid H) \ P(E_2 \mid H) + O(H') \ P(E_1 \mid H') \ P(E_2 \mid H')}$$

Equation (2) is a major simplification of equation (1); the probabilities are now all expressed in terms of the individual probabilities rather than the joint ones such as $P(E_1 \cap E_2 \mid H')$. There are problems with this assumption of conditional independence will be discussed later.

While (2) is a simplification, it still does require knowledge of the prior probabilities $P(E_1)$ and $P(E_2)$. It's usually difficult for experts to state prior probabilities because they don't reason that way. For example, if a person goes to see a doctor, the doctor does not assume that the person has a cold *a priori*, because that is the most common disease and so its probability is highest.

The major problem in assigning prior probabilities is the difficulty of determining them for likelihoods. For probabilities involving reproducible events such as throwing dice, it's easy to acquire the probabilities by empirical or theoretical studies. However, when dealing with events such as finding a major mineral deposit, it's impossible to determine exactly the prior likelihoods. For example, what's the prior likelihood that your house sits on land with a major gold deposit under it? Is it 0.0000001, 0.00000001, or some other number? These are unique situations in which the prior probabilities cannot be determined.

Situation 3: N pieces of uncertain evidence conclude H

This is the general case of uncertainty in the evidence and in the rule that depends on the evidence. As the number of pieces of evidence increases, it becomes impossible to determine all the joint and prior probabilities or likelihoods. Different approximations have been used to account for the general case of N pieces of evidence.

Combining Evidence by Fuzzy Logic

Conjunction of Evidence

Suppose a rule

```
IF E THEN H
```

has E as the conjunction of evidence, as in

```
IF E₁ AND E₂ AND ... Eₙ THEN H
```

All E_i must be true with some probability for the antecedent to be true. In the general case, each piece of evidence is based on partial evidence e. The probability of the evidence is

$$P(E \mid e) = P(E_1 \cap E_2 \cap \ldots E_N \mid e)$$

$$= \frac{P(E_1 \cap E_2 \cap \ldots E_N \cap e)}{P(e)}$$

If the evidence, E_i, is all conditionally independent, then the joint probability becomes the product of the individual probabilities. This follows from the Generalized Multiplicative Law. As an example, for two pieces of evidence

$$P(E_1 \cap E_2 \mid e) = \frac{P(E_1 \cap E_2 \cap e)}{P(e)}$$

$$= \frac{P(E_2 \mid E_1 \cap e) \; P(E_1 \mid e) \; P(e)}{P(e)}$$

Using the assumption of independence,

$$P(E_2 \mid e) = P(E_2 \mid E_1 \cap e)$$

because the evidence E_1 does not contribute any knowledge toward E_2. So

$$P(E_2 \cap E_1 \mid e) = P(E_2 \mid e) \, P(E_1 \mid e)$$

and in general

$$P(E_1 \cap E_2 \cap \ldots E_N \mid e) = \prod_{i=1}^{N} P(E_i \mid e)$$

Although this formula is correct in a theoretical sense, there are two difficulties in applying it to real-world problems. First, the individual $P(E_i \mid e)$ are not usually independent in the real world. Second, the multiplication of many factors leads to a product that is generally far too small for $P(E \mid e)$.

An approximate solution to this problem is the use of **fuzzy logic** to calculate $P(E \mid e)$ as follows.

$$P(E \mid e) = \min \, [P(E_i \mid e)]$$

where the **min function** returns the minimum value of all the $P(E_i \mid e)$. In the PROSPECTOR system this formula was satisfactory. Once $P(E \mid e)$ is determined, it can be used with the piecewise linear formula for $P(H \mid e)$.

The main problem with the fuzzy logic formula is that it makes $P(E \mid e)$ insensitive to any $P(E_i \mid e)$ except the minimum. This means that even if all the other probabilities increase and the minimum remains the same, no change in $P(E \mid e)$ will be effected. That is, the minimum $P(E_i \mid e)$ blocks other probability changes from propagating through the inference chain. An advantage of the fuzzy logic formula is that it is computationally simple.

Disjunction of Evidence

If the rule is a disjunction of evidence

IF E_1 OR E_2 OR $\ldots$ E_N THEN H

then it can be shown (see Problem 4.13) that assuming independence of the evidence gives

$$P(E \mid e) = 1 - \prod_{i=1}^{N} [1 - P(E_i \mid e)]$$

The problem with this formula is that the calculated probability is much too high. The formula used by PROSPECTOR as an alternative to this is based on fuzzy logic:

$$P(E \mid e) = \max \, [P(E_i \mid e)]$$

where the **max function** returns the maximum $P(E_i \mid e)$.

Logical Combination of Evidence

If the antecedent is a logical combination of evidence, then the fuzzy logic and negation rules can be used to combine evidence. For example,

```
IF E₁ AND (E₂ OR E₃´) THEN H
```

then

```
E = E₁ AND (E₂ OR E₃´)
E = min {P(E₁ | e), max [P(E₂ | e), 1 - P(E₃ | e)]}
```

Although these formulas from fuzzy logic have been successfully used by a number of systems, other functions for combining evidence may be defined. For example, the following is an alternative to the max function of disjunction (Quinlan 86):

$$P(E_1 \cup E_2 \mid H) = \min [1, P(E_1 \mid H) + P(E_2 \mid H)]$$

Effective Likelihoods

For the general case, multiple rules with uncertain evidence and inconsistent prior probabilities may conclude a specific hypothesis. Assuming conditional independence of the evidence and all E_i contributing to H are true, then

$$O(H \mid E_1 \cap E_2 \cap \ldots E_N) = \left[\prod_{i=1}^{N} LS_i \right] O(H)$$

where LS_i is defined as

$$LS_i = \frac{P(E_i \mid H)}{P(E_i \mid H´)}$$

and a similar formula holds if all the evidence contributing to H is false.

$$O(H \mid E_1´ \cap E_2´ \cap \ldots E_N´) = \left[\prod_{i=1}^{N} LN_i \right] O(H)$$

where

$$LN_i = \frac{P(E_i´ \mid H)}{P(E_i´ \mid H´)}$$

In the general case of inconsistent prior probabilities and uncertain evidence, the **effective likelihood ratio**, LE, is defined as

$$LE_i = \frac{O(H \mid e_i)}{O(H)}$$

where e_i is the ith partial evidence contributing to H. The updating of H based on uncertain and inconsistent evidence is analogous to the previous case:

$$O(H \mid e_1 \cap e_2 \cap \ldots e_N) = \left[\prod_{i=1}^{N} LE_i \right] O(H)$$

For an expert system using uncertain evidence and inconsistent prior probabilities, this formula can be used in the following way:

(a) Store the prior odds of each rule and the LE from each contribution to the rule.
(b) Whenever $P(E_i \mid e_i)$ is updated, compute the new LE_i and posterior odds.

Difficulties with Conditional Independence

Although the assumption of conditional independence is useful in simplifying the Bayes' Theorem, there are a number of problems. The assumption is mainly useful in the initial phases of building up an expert system, when the general behavior of the system is more important than correct numerical results. Initially, a knowledge engineer may be more interested in developing correct inference chains than in the correct numbers. That is, in some system, intermediate hypothesis 10 should be activated by evidence 23 and 34. Hypothesis 10 and evidence 8 should then activate hypotheses 52 and 96. Hypothesis 15 should *not* be activated by evidence 23 and 24, and so on.

As shown by equation (2) of this section, under conditional independence only five probabilities are required to compute $P(H \mid E_1 \cap E_2)$. These are

$$P(E_1 \mid H), \ P(E_2 \mid H), \ P(E_1 \mid H'), \ P(E_2 \mid H'), \ P(H)$$

The other probability $P(H')$ needed to compute $O(H')$ is not independent of the others since

$$P(H') = 1 - P(H)$$

Another formula for $P(H \mid E_1 \cap E_2)$ is shown in Problem 4.12 (b). This formula involves four other probabilities:

$$P(H \mid E_1), \ P(H \mid E_2), \ P(H' \mid E_1), \ P(H' \mid E_2)$$

Thus, there are a total of nine probabilities that can be used to calculate $P(H \mid E_1 \cap E_2)$ but only five are really needed to be specified. Given the five, the other four can be calculated.

This constraint on the number of independent probabilities becomes a real problem as the expert system matures. Once the inference chains function correctly, the knowledge engineer must ensure that the correct numbers are output. Because of the conditional independence assumption, the knowledge engineer does not have complete freedom to tune all nine probabilities by adjusting their values to yield the desired results.

The conditional independence assumption fixes the joint probability $P(E_1 \cap E_2)$ since

$$P(E_1 \cap E_2) =$$

$$P(E_1)P(E_2) \left[\frac{P(H \mid E_1)P(H \mid E_2)}{P(H)} + \frac{P(H' \mid E_1)P(H' \mid E_2)}{P(H')} \right]$$

This means that the prior probabilities $P(E_1)$, $P(E_2)$, and $P(H)$ now constrain $P(E_1 \cap E_2)$. This runs contrary to the knowledge of the human experts who may know $P(E_1)$, $P(E_2)$, and $P(E_1 \cap E_2)$ separately. Conditional independence thus restricts applying all the human expert's knowledge.

Although the assumption of conditional independence appears reasonable, it does depend on the real situation being modeled by the expert system and so may not hold in all cases. One paper went beyond this and claimed that the conditional independence is usually false (Szolovits 78). Another paper claimed that conditional independence implies strict independence and this proves that the evidence is irrelevant to updating hypotheses (Pednault 81)! However, this claim has been disproved by another paper (Glymour 85).

Another method of applying subjective Bayesian probabilities shows how the assumption of conditional independence can be weakened so the strict independence is no longer implied (Pearl 82).

4.15 INFERENCE NETS

Up to this point, the examples of forward and backward chaining you have seen have been very small, consisting of a few rules. For real-world problems, the number of inferences required to support a hypothesis or reach a conclusion is much larger. In addition, many or all of these inferences are made under uncertainty of the evidence and rules themselves. Probabilistic reasoning and Bayes' Theorem have been used successfully in real-world systems such as this.

An inference net is a good architecture for expert systems that rely on a taxonomy of knowledge. A taxonomy is a classification and is commonly used in the natural sciences such as geology and biology. You have already seen a simple taxonomy in the figure classifying the different kinds of blackberries in the Chapter 2 problems.

A taxonomy is useful for two purposes. It helps to organize knowledge about a subject by classifying objects and showing their relationships to other objects. Important features such as inheritance of properties are made clear by taxonomies.

A second reason that taxonomies are useful is that they can guide the search for proof of a hypothesis, such as "there is copper ore at this site." This aids in proving or disproving hypotheses is very important in areas such as mineral exploration since there is rarely any direct evidence of valuable ore at the surface. Before deciding to invest the time and money for drilling, a geologist tries to gather evidence to support this hypothesis.

PROSPECTOR

The classic expert system that uses probabilistic reasoning is PROSPECTOR (Duda 79) which is designed to aid exploration geologists in determining whether a site is favorable for ore deposits of certain types. The basic idea of PROSPECTOR is to encode the expert economic geologists' knowledge of different ore **models** in the system. A geologic model is a group of evidence and hypotheses that support a certain type of mineral's being present at a site. Besides aiding in identifying minerals, PROSPECTOR could also recommend the best location to drill on the site. As more models are created, the capabilities of PROSPECTOR increase.

The data for each model are organized as an **inference net**. Figure 4.17 summarizes the types of nets discussed so far and shows a very simple inference net in (d). Inference net nodes can represent evidence to support other nodes that represent the hypotheses such as the type of mineral present. In 1983 there were 22 mineral models in PROSPECTOR, of which a few are summarized in Table 4.12.

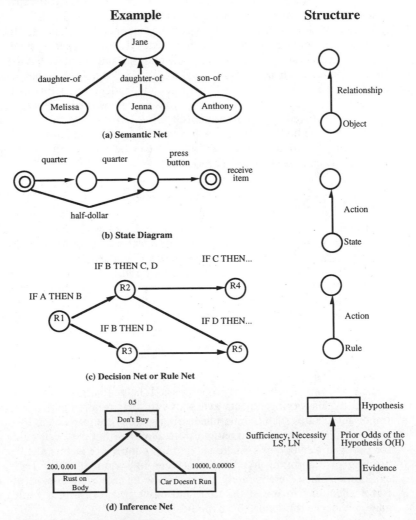

Figure 4.17 Some Types of Networks

Model Name	Model Description	Number of Nodes	Number Askable	Number of Rules
PCD	Porphyry Copper	200	97	135
RFU	Roll-front Uranium	185	147	169
SPB	Sandstone-hosted Lead	35	21	32

Table 4.12 Some PROSPECTOR Models

In Table 4.12 the number of nodes is the total number in the model. The **askable nodes** are those that ask questions of the user to obtain observable evidence. The number of rules in the table are probabilistic inference rules. As you can see, there is much uncertainty in the models, and probability is important in supporting hypotheses.

Inference Networks

Each model for PROSPECTOR is encoded as a network of connections or relations between evidence and hypotheses. Thus an inference net is a type of semantic net. Observable facts, such as the type of rock formations obtained from field exploration, comprise the evidence to support the intermediate hypotheses. Groups of intermediate hypotheses are used to support the **top-level hypothesis**, which is what we want to prove. If it's not important to distinguish between evidence and hypotheses, the term *assertion* is used for either one. A small portion of the inference net for the top-level hypothesis of the porphyry copper model is shown in Figure 4.18.

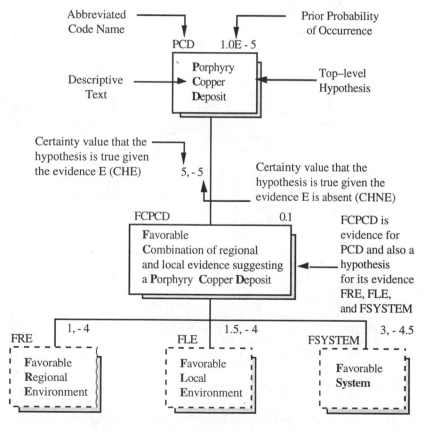

Dashed boxes indicate the node contains other nodes (and is defined elsewhere)

Figure 4.18
The Top-level Porphyry Copper Hypothesis of PROSPECTOR Expressed Using Certainty Factors

The **certainty factors** CHE and CHNE are used in PROSPECTOR because experience has shown that experts find it difficult to specify posterior probabilities or likelihood ratios. Similar experiences were found in the MYCIN system for diagnosing blood diseases, in which physicians did not like to specify probabilities, and certainty factors were used. As in MYCIN, certainty factors are ranked on an 11-point scale from –5 to +5 in which –5 means "definitely not" and +5 means "definitely yes."

PROSPECTOR is not a pure probabilistic system because it uses fuzzy logic and certainty factors for combining evidence. Certainty factors and fuzzy logic will be discussed in more detail in Chapter 5.

Figure 4.19 shows the FRE node expanded in more detail.

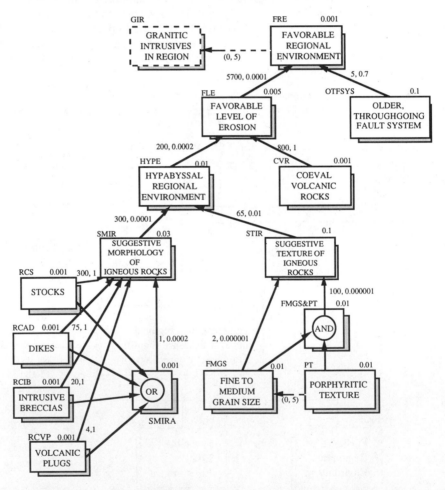

Figure 4.19 A Small Part of the PROSPECTOR Inference Net for Porphyry Copper

This particular diagram has two numbers above nodes which are the likelihood ratio, LS, and necessity measure, LN, separated by commas. For example the LS, LN values for the node labeled RCIB at the left bottom is 20,1. The acronym of each node stands for its description, such as RCIB for "the region contains intrusive breccias." Also shown at the top of each node is the single number of the prior probability, such as 0.001 for RCIB.

Inference Relations

Evidence supporting or disproving a hypothesis is directed up the inference net. For example, RCS, RCAD, RCIB, RCVP, and SMIRA all support or disprove the intermediate hypothesis SMIR. The intermediate hypothesis SMIR is also evidence for its hypothesis HYPE, which is evidence for FLE, and so on.

Evidence can be combined in two general ways to yield the relationships desired by the geologist in the definition of the model:

- **Logical combinations** such as by AND and OR nodes. As mentioned in the previous section, fuzzy logic can be used to calculate the result at these logical nodes.
- **Weighted combinations** using the likelihood ratios, LS, and necessity ratios, LN. The posterior odds are calculated from

$$O(H \mid E) = LS\ O(H)$$

when the evidence E is known to be true and

$$O(H \mid E') = LN\ O(H)$$

when E is known to be false. If E is not known for certain, then $P(H \mid E)$ can be calculated by linear interpolation, as discussed in the previous section.

The term *weighted combination* arises because of the general case in which multiple pieces of evidence contribute to a hypothesis. As shown in the previous section,

$$O(H \mid E_1 \cap E_2 \cap \dots E_N) = \left[\prod_{i=1}^{N} LS_i \right] O(H)$$

The log of this is

$$\log O(H \mid E_1 \cap E_2 \cap \dots E_N) = \log O(H) + \sum_{i=1}^{N} \log LS_i$$

which can be interpreted as each LS_i casting $\log Ls_i$ "votes" for the hypothesis. Each $\log LS_i$ is a weight that affects the hypothesis.

Although PROSPECTOR is sometimes called a *rule-based system* because weighted combinations correspond to rules such as

```
IF E₁ AND E₂ AND ... Eₙ THEN H
```

it is not as flexible as a true production system based on rules. One limitation is the lack of a full mechanism to bind variables. PROSPECTOR is a custom-designed system that emphasizes efficiency and control for geological applications rather than the generality of a production system.

The weighted combinations are also an example of **plausible relations**. The term *plausible* means that there is some evidence for believability. PROSPECTOR is an example of a system that uses plausible inference for or against a hypothesis.

The plausible inferences of PROSPECTOR are based on Bayesian probabilities with the LS and LN values supplied by human experts.

Plausible and other different degrees of belief are illustrated in the fuzzy graph Figure 4.20. The terms have the following general meanings as shown in Table 4.13.

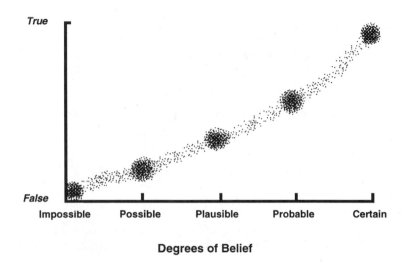

Figure 4.20 Relative Meanings of Some Terms Used to Describe Evidence

Term	Evidence Relative to Hypothesis
impossible	definitely known against
possible	not definitely disproved
plausible	some evidence exists
probable	some evidence for
certain	definitely known supporting

Table 4.13 Some Terms Used with Evidence

The graph in Figure 4.20 is purposely drawn fuzzy to illustrate the vague nature of these terms and the vagueness in progression from one to another. In Figure 4.20, notice how our belief in a hypothesis increases from "impossible" to "certain." A **certain belief** means that the belief is true and an **impossible belief** means that it is false. There is no uncertainty involved with certain and impossible beliefs. These beliefs are equivalent to logical true and logical false. The term *certain evidence* is sometimes used in an ambiguous way. Certain evidence is logically true or false. That is, there is no uncertainty associated with certain evidence. This means that certain evidence corresponds to either certain belief (logically true) or an impossible belief (logically false).

A **possible belief** means that no matter how remote, the hypothesis cannot be ruled out. For example, before scientific analysis of the moon's surface, it was possible, but very, very, very remote that the moon was made of green cheese. This possibility existed because no definite proof was available.

A **plausible belief** means that more than a possibility exists. The term *plausible* is often used in legal cases to mean reasonable, but without hard evidence to back up the belief. Thus, even before scientific studies, it was not plausible that the moon was made of green cheese.

A **probable belief** means that there is some evidence favoring the hypothesis but not enough to definitely prove it.

Without field evidence, such as observation of RCIB, the relations in Figure 4.19 for a particular site are merely plausible. As evidence accumulates, the plausible relations may become *probable* and then *definite*.

A third type of relation in inference nets is **contexts**, which block the propagation of information until it is appropriate. The use of contexts enables or disables portions of the inference net until certain portions are known to be present, absent, or unknown. One purpose of contexts is to avoid having the system ask the user for questions about some evidence until it is established that the evidence is needed.

The basic idea of contexts is to control the order in which assertions are pursued by the system. Contexts state a required condition that must be proved before an assertion can be used. Contexts are indicated by a dashed arrow with a certainty range under it, as in the case of FMGS and PT. The PT node is blocked unless there is evidence with certainty values in the range 0 to +5 that there are fine to medium grain sizes of **porphyritic** rocks. Porphyritic rocks are igneous rocks whose **texture** or appearance consists of small crystals embedded within the rock holding it, the **matrix**. Igneous rocks are those formed by the solidification of molten rock, called magma, from deep within the earth. Certain types of igneous rocks that extend above ground, called *intrusive breccias*, are evidence of mineral formations such as porphyry copper.

Thus, porphyry copper consists of small copper crystals embedded within a rock matrix that holds the crystals. Porphyry copper is the most commonly occurring form of copper. Unless there are at least small crystals of fine to medium grain size present, it's not worth asking about porphyritic texture; the expert system should therefore be intelligent enough not to ask this question. An expert system that asks unnecessary questions is inefficient and will quickly annoy the user.

The certainty range of 0 to +5 for the context means that the PT node will not be pursued unless the user indicates absence of evidence corresponding to a certainty factor of 0 or some positive amount ranging up to +5 for "definitely present."

All three methods of combining or permitting evidence are really relations between nodes. They all specify how a change in the probability of one assertion affects others.

Inference Net Architecture

Formally, an **inference net** can be defined as a directed acyclic graph in which the nodes are assertions and the arcs are measures of uncertainty such as LS and LN. Figure 4.21 (a), (b), and (c) could be used as valid inference net architectures because they have no cycles. Note that in the inference tree the arrows point toward the hypothesis, in contrast to the arrows pointing away from the root in a data structure tree. As described in Chapter 3, in an acyclic graph there is no way to return to the starting point by following the arrows. In (d) there is a cycle involving four nodes. The reason for prohibiting cycles is to prevent circular reasoning in establishing a hypothesis. A valid exception in rule-based systems is to establish a loop by having two rules trigger each other until a terminating condition is satisfied.

Figure 4.21 (c) is an undesirable type of graph for an inference net. The problem is that when many pieces of evidence contribute to a single hypothesis, there is a greater chance of undesirable interactions between the evidence. It's generally better to restructure this type into a more tree-like structure with intermediate hypotheses.

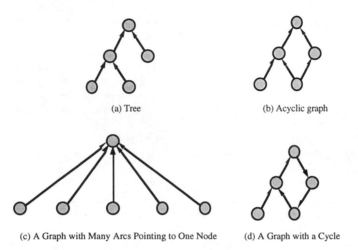

(a) Tree

(b) Acyclic graph

(c) A Graph with Many Arcs Pointing to One Node

(d) A Graph with a Cycle

Figure 4.21 Some Types of Graphs

The PROSPECTOR inference net is also a **partitioned semantic net** to group portions of the net into meaningful units. Partitioned semantic nets were developed by Hendrix to allow power of predicate calculus such as quantification, implication, negation, disjunction, and conjunction (Hendrix 79). Recall from Chapter 2 that ordinary semantic nets are really designed to express descriptive knowledge through relations. While frames are better for causal knowledge, they are difficult to use in expressing logical relationships.

The basic idea of a partitioned semantic net is to group sets of nodes and arcs in abstract **spaces** that define the scope of their relationships. A familiar analogy to a space is the scope of a module or package in a structured language. For example, the Figure 4.18 FRE node can be considered a space with the structure shown in Figure 4.19.

The power of semantic nets comes in modeling statements. In fact, Hendrix first developed them for expressing natural language in his doctoral dissertation. Statements are like the propositions of evidence and hypotheses that make up the nodes of inference nets. As a simple example of a partitioned semantic net for a statement, consider "there is a computer with a color screen." Notice that this is an existential statement because of the "there is" quantifier.

Figure 4.22 shows the partitioned semantic net expression of this statement using three spaces. SPACE-1 consists of some general related concepts about computers. SPACE-2 consists of the particular computer we are talking about, which has been given the identifier COMPUTER-1. SPACE-3 consists of the specific relation COMPONENTS-OF-1, which has as its object the specific COLOR-SCREEN-1 that we are concerned about. Each arc labeled *element* shows that one state is an element of another. The arc labeled *entity* shows which specific computer is the entity with the specific color screen.

The advantage of a partitioned semantic net is shown by a portion of a PROSPECTOR rule for STIR using FMGS evidence as shown in Figure 4.23. The rule can be stated as "If there is an entity named E-1 whose cardinality is ABUNDANT and is composed of INTRUSIVE ROCKS then the consequent is the rule of Suggestive Texture of Igneous Rocks." Note that the diagram has been simplified by not including the requirement that the antecedent also have a fine to medium grain size.

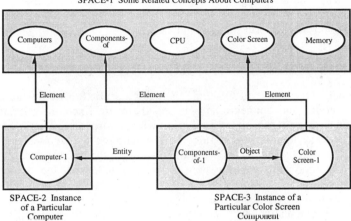

Figure 4.22 A Simple Partitioned Semantic Net about a Computer

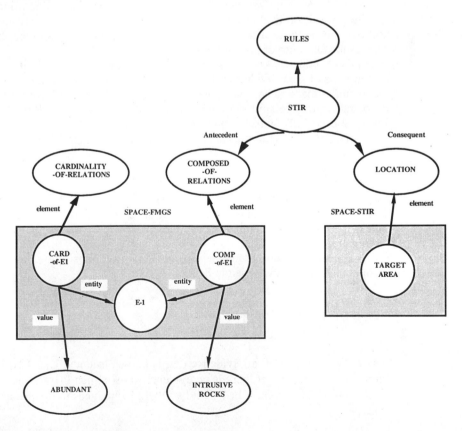

Figure 4.23
Simplified Portion of the PROSPECTOR Partitioned Semantic Net for the STIR Rule Using FMGS Evidence

Notice that in Figure 4.23 one partitioned semantic net makes up the antecedent of the rule and one net makes up the consequent. Although the consequent of this rule is trivial, other rules will have more complex structures (Duda 78). The advantage of the partitioned semantic nets is that the system can infer relationships between nodes that are indirectly linked. Thus the knowledge of the system is deeper than shallow knowledge.

4.16 THE PROPAGATION OF PROBABILITIES

Inference nets such as PROSPECTOR have a **static knowledge structure**. That is, the nodes and connections between them are fixed in order to retain the relationships between nodes in the knowledge structure. This contrasts with a rule-based system in which rules whose patterns match facts are put on the agenda, conflict resolution is performed, and then the top priority rule is executed. Thus a common rule-based system is a **dynamic knowledge structure** because there are no fixed connections between rules as there are between nodes in an inference net.

Although the structure of an inference net is static, the probabilities associated with each hypothesis node change as evidence is obtained. In fact, this change of probabilities is the *only* thing that does change in an inference net. The basic characteristic of an inference net is the change of probabilities from prior probabilities to posterior probabilities as evidence is accumulated. This change of probabilities moves upward to ultimately support or disprove a top-level hypothesis such as the existence of porphyritic copper, PCDA.

Let's examine some of the stages in the propagation of probabilities for PCDA on the basis of some evidence. This will serve as an explicit example of many of the formulas that you have seen. Referring back to Figure 4.19, we will follow the propagation of probabilities from the evidence node the "Region Contains Intrusive Breccias", with acronym RCIB.

If the user says that intrusive breccias are certainly present, then

$$P(E \mid e) = P(RCIB \mid e) = 1$$

From Figure 4.19, notice that the LN values for the other evidence of SMIR are all 1. That is, if the user makes no comment about evidence for stocks, dikes, and volcanic plugs, these make no contribution to SMIR and so can be ignored in the propagation of probabilities.

The reason all this evidence can be ignored comes from the formula for compound evidence discussed in Section 4.14:

$$O(H \mid e) = \left[\prod_{i=1}^{N} L_i \right] O(H)$$

where the $L_i = LS_i$ for all evidence that is known true and $L_i = LN_i$ is used for known false evidence. If there is no evidence known, then $P(E_i \mid e)$ reduces to the prior odds of the evidence, $P(E_i)$, and so $P(H \mid E_i)$ reduces to the prior odds $P(H)$. Thus

$$L_i = \frac{O(H \mid e_i)}{O(H)} = \frac{O(H)}{O(H)} = 1$$

and these L_i make no contribution to $O(H \mid E)$. For example, when only RCIB is known true, the odds of SMIR are

$$O(H \mid E) = LS_{RCVP} \, LS_{RCAD} \, LS_{RCS} \, LS_{SMIRA} \, LS_{RCIB}$$

$$= 1 \cdot 1 \cdot 1 \cdot 1 \cdot 20$$

$$O(SMIR \mid RCIB) = 20$$

Another interesting feature of the SMIR evidence is the OR node called SMIRA. Notice that all the evidence for SMIR also goes to SMIRA. If there is any evidence contributing to SMIR such as RCS, RCAD, RCIB, or RCVP, then the OR node of SMIRA contributes nothing to SMIR, since LS for SMIRA is 1. However, if there is no evidence of RCS, RCAD, RCIB, and RCVP, then the LN value of 0.0002 of SMIRA makes the probability of SMIR essentially zero. Basically this means that although the absence of one or more of the evidences for SMIR is unimportant (LS = 1), the absence of all evidence is very important in ruling out SMIR.

The addition of OR nodes, AND nodes, and LS and LN values lets the model designer manipulate the way in which evidence affects a hypothesis. However, in some complex cases, the addition of many OR and AND nodes to suit the evidence requirements will obscure the inference net so that it is difficult for a person to understand. The addition of these extra nodes also requires more testing of the model.

From Figure 4.20, LS = 20 for intrusive breccias, RCIB, and P(SMIR) = 0.03. Since

$$odds = O = \frac{P}{1 - P}$$

then the prior odds of SMIR are

$$O(SMIR) = \frac{0.03}{1 - 0.03} = 0.0309$$

If the evidence E is certain, then the posterior odds are

$$O(H \mid E) = LS \, O(H)$$

$$O(SMIR \mid RCIB) = 20 \cdot 0.0309 = 0.618$$

and the posterior probability is calculated from the fundamental odds formula.

$$P = \frac{O}{1 + O}$$

$$P(H \mid E) = \frac{O(H \mid E)}{1 + O(H \mid E)}$$

$$P(H \mid E) = \frac{0.618}{1 + 0.618} = 0.382$$

and so the posterior probability of SMIR, given certain evidence of RCIB, is

$$P(SMIR \mid RCIB) = 0.382$$

The HYPE prior odds are

$$O(HYPE) = \frac{0.01}{1 - 0.01} = 0.0101$$

At this point it would be tempting to use

$$O(H \mid E) = LS \; O(H)$$

$$O(HYPE \mid SMIR) = LS_{SMIR} \; O(SMIR)$$

$$= 300 \cdot \frac{0.0101}{1 + 0.0101} = 3.00$$

as the odds of HYPE due to SMIR, but it would be wrong. The formula

$$O(H \mid E) = LS \; O(H)$$

is true when the evidence $\dot{E}$ is certain. This formula expresses the change in the hypothesis's probability assuming that the evidence is certain. However, SMIR is not known for certain. In fact, the probability of SMIR, given certain intrusive breccias, is

$$P(SMIR \mid RCIB) = 0.382$$

which means that the likelihood of our belief is 38.2 percent that SMIR is true.

What we really need is the probability of the HYPE hypothesis based on the uncertain evidence of SMIR, which is P(HYPE | RCIB). One way of calculating this uses the formula for P(H | e), discussed in Section 4.14, as

$$P(H \mid e) = \begin{cases} P(H \mid E') + \dfrac{P(H) - P(H \mid E')}{P(E)} \; P(E \mid e') \\[1em] \qquad \text{for } 0 \leq P(E \mid e) < P(E) \\[2em] P(H) + \dfrac{P(H \mid E) - P(H)}{1 - P(E)} \; [P(E \mid e) - P(E)] \\[1em] \qquad \text{for } P(E) \leq P(E \mid e) \leq 1 \end{cases}$$

where the uncertainty in the SMIR evidence is

$$P(E \mid e) = P(SMIR \mid RCIB) = 0.382$$

and the probability we want is

$$P(H \mid e) = P(HYPE \mid SMIR)$$

where all we know is

$$P(H \mid E) = \frac{O(H \mid E)}{1 + O(H \mid E)} = \frac{3.00}{1 + 3.00} = 0.75$$

and the prior odds from Figure 4.19 are

$$P(H) = P(HYPE) = 0.01$$

$$P(E) = P(SMIR) = 0.03$$

Since $P(E \mid e) > P(E)$, we will use the formula for $P(E) \le P(E \mid e) \le 1$ to compute $P(H \mid E)$ as follows:

$$P(H \mid e) = 0.01 + \frac{(0.75 - 0.01) \; (0.382 - 0.03)}{1 - 0.03}$$

$$P(HYPE \mid RCIB) = 0.279$$

which is the posterior probability of HYPE.

This propagation of probabilities continues up the inference net. Now the probability $P(HYPE \mid RCIB)$ is the uncertain evidence of FLE. The posterior probability $P(FLE \mid RCIB)$ is calculated using the same formula with values adjusted for FLE.

$$P(E) = P(HYPE) = 0.01$$

$$P(E \mid e) = P(HYPE \mid RCIB) = 0.279$$

$$P(H) = P(FLE) = 0.005$$

$$O(H \mid E) = O(FLE \mid HYPE) = LS_{HYPE} \; O(FLE)$$

$$= 200 \cdot 0.005 = 1$$

$$P(H \mid E) = P(FLE \mid HYPE)$$

$$= O/(1 + O)$$

$$= 1/(1 + 1)$$

$$= 0.5$$

$$P(H \mid e) = P(FLE \mid RCIB)$$

$$= 0.005 + \frac{(0.5 - 0.005) \; (0.279 - 0.01)}{1 - 0.01}$$

$$P(FLE \mid RCIB) = 0.140$$

4.17 SUMMARY

In this chapter we started by discussing the basic concepts of reasoning under uncertainty and the possible types of errors caused by uncertainty. The elements of classical probability theory was reviewed. The differences between classical theory and other theories of probability such as experimental and subjective probabilities was discussed. Methods of combining probabilities and Bayes' Theorem was covered. The relationship of belief to probability and the meaning of likelihood was described. The classic expert system PROSPECTOR was analyzed to illustrate how these concepts of probability were used in a real system. The PROSPECTOR system was also used to introduce inference nets and partitioned semantic nets.

PROBLEMS

4.1 (a) Using only the three axioms of probability, prove the Additive Law of probability.

$$P(A \cup B) = P(A) + P(B) - P(A \cap B)$$

(Hint: Any event $X \cup Y$ can be written in the form $X \cup (X' \cap Y)$ where X and $X' \cap Y$ are mutually exclusive. Also, write B as the union of two mutually exclusive sets.)

(b) Given two computers that either work correctly or do not, what is the probability, using the Additive Law, that at least one works correctly?

4.2 Given events A and B that may overlap, derive the probability in terms of sets using the axioms of probability for

(a) neither A nor B.
(b) either A or B, but not both (exclusive–OR).

4.3 Three bins contain some working and some defective components as follows:

Bin	Good	Bad
1	8	2
2	3	1
3	2	2

Over a long period of time, 20 percent of components are drawn from bin 1, 30 percent from bin 2, and 50 percent from bin 3.

(a) Draw a probability tree.
(b) If a defective part is drawn, what are the probabilities it came out of each bin? Write the probability table showing the outcomes and prior, conditional, joint, and posterior probabilities.

4.4 Fred is considering the purchase of a disk drive and is trying to decide among three brands. The following table shows his preferences and the probability of drive crashes within one year (preferences are a function of cost, speed, capacity, and reliability):

Brand	Probability of Choosing	Probability of a Crash
X	0.3	0.1
Y	0.5	0.3
Z	0.2	0.6

(a) Create a probability table showing outcomes and prior, conditional, joint, and posterior probabilities.

(b) What is the probability of each drive crashing within one year?

(c) What is the probability of any drive crashing within one year?

(d) For a crash within one year, what is the probability it is Brand X, Y, or Z?

4.5 A screening test is a low-cost way of checking large groups of people for a disease. A more costly but more accurate test shows that 1 percent of all people have the disease. The screening test indicates the disease (test positive) in 90 percent of those who have it and in 20 percent of those who do not it (false positive).

(a) Make a table showing the outcomes and prior, conditional, joint, and posterior probabilities.

(b) What percentage of people who test positive don't have the disease (false +)?

(c) What percentage of people who test negative do have the disease (false –)?

4.6 To show that pairwise independence does not necessarily mean mutual independence, define the following events for the toss of two dice.

A = even first die
B = even second die
C = even sum

(a) Draw the sample space of the two dice. Draw A, B, and $A \cap B$.

(b) Write the elements of $A \cap B$, C, $A \cap C$, and $B \cap C$.

(c) What is P(C)?

(d) Show the pairwise independence.

$$P(A \cap B) = P(A)\,P(B)$$
$$P(A \cap C) = P(A)\,P(C)$$
$$P(B \cap C) = P(B)\,P(C)$$

(e) Show

$$P(A \cap B \cap C) = P(A \cap B) \neq P(A \cap B)\,P(C)$$

which proves that pairwise independence does not mean mutual independence.

4.7 For mutually exclusive sets A and B

(a) What is $P(A \mid B')$ expressed in terms of A and B (not expressed in terms of A and B')?

(b) What is the numeric value of $P(A' \mid B)$?

(c) What is the numeric value of $P(A \mid B)$?

(d) What is $P(A' \mid B')$ expressed in terms of A and B (not expressed in terms of A' and B')?

(e) What is

    (i) $P(A \mid B) + P(A' \mid B)$

    (ii) $P(A \mid B') + P(A' \mid B')$

4.8 (a) Prove that

$$P(A \cap B \cap C) = P(A \mid B \cap C) \, P(B \mid C) \, P(C)$$

(b) Prove that

$$P(A \cap B \mid C) = P(A \mid B \cap C) \, P(B \mid C)$$

4.9 A disk drive may malfunction with either fault F_1 or F_2, but not both. The possible symptoms are

$A = \{ \text{ bad writes, bad reads } \}$

$B = \{ \text{ bad reads } \}$

and F_2 is three times as likely to occur as F_1. For this type of drive

$P(A \mid F_1) = 0.4 \quad P(B \mid F_1) = 0.6$

$P(A \mid F_2) = 0.2 \quad P(B \mid F_2) = 0.8$

What are the probabilities of a disk drive with fault F_1? F_2?

4.10 Given the transition matrix for switching brands of disk drives in a year:

Next Year

		X	Y	Z
	X	.5	.5	0
This Year	Y	.25	.5	.25
	Z	0	.5	.5

(a) Assuming that initially 50 percent of the people use drive X, 25 percent use drive Y, and 25 percent use drive Z, what percent will be using each drive in 1, 2, and 3 years?

(b) Determine the steady-state matrix.

4.11 (a) Given N people selected at random, what is the probability that no two have the same birthday?

(b) What is the probability for 30 people?

4.12 Under conditional independence of E_1 and E_2, show that for a rule involving the conjunction of known evidence

IF E_1 AND E_2 THEN H

that

(a)

$$P(H \mid E_1 \cap E_2) =$$

$$\frac{P(E_1 \mid H) \, P(E_2 \mid H)}{P(E_1 \mid H) \, P(E_2 \mid H) + O(H') \, P(E_1 \mid H') \, P(E_2 \mid H')}$$

(b)

$$P(H \mid E_1 \cap E_2) =$$

$$\frac{P(H \mid E_1) \, P(H \mid E_2)}{P(H \mid E_1) \, P(H \mid E_2) + O(H) \, P(H' \mid E_1) \, P(H' \mid E_2)}$$

4.13 Given a rule with a disjunction of evidence

IF E_1 OR E_2 OR ... E_N THEN H

show that on the basis of probability theory and assuming conditional independence of the evidence

$$P(E \mid e) = 1 - \prod_{i=1}^{N} (1 - P(E_i \mid e))$$

where E is the evidence and e is the relevant observations toward E.

4.14 Given the following evidence as the antecedent of

IF E THEN H

write the fuzzy logic expressions for $P(E \mid e)$.

(a) $E = E_1$ OR $(E_2$ AND $E_3')$
(b) $E = (E_1$ AND $E_2)$ OR $(E_3$ AND $E_4)$
(c) $E = (E_1'$ AND $E_2')$ OR E_3
(d) $E = E_1'$ AND $(E_2'$ OR $E_3)$
(e) $E = E_1'$ OR $(E_2$ AND $E_3)$

4.15 For the inference net of porphyritic copper, assume RCS is known true and RCAD is known false. What is the updated probability of FRE?

BIBLIOGRAPHY

(Allen 81). J. F. Allen, "An Internal-based Representation of Temporal Knowledge," *Proc. 7th IJCAI*, pp. 221-226, 1981.

(Duda 76). Richard O. Duda, Peter E. Hart, and Nils J. Nilsson, "Subjective Bayesian Methods for Rule-based Inference Systems," *National Computer Conference* (AFIPS Conference Proceedings vol. 45), pp. 1075-1082, 1976.

(Duda 78). Richard O. Duda, *et al.*, "Semantic Network Representations in Rule-based Inference Systems," in *Pattern-directed Inference Systems*, D. A. Waterman and Frederick Hayes-Roth, eds., Academic Press, pp. 203-221, 1978.

(Duda 79). Richard Duda, Hohn Gaschnig, and Peter Hart, "Model Design in the PROSPECTOR Consultant System for Mineral Exploration," in *Expert Systems in the Micro-electronic Age*, Donald Michie, ed., Edinburgh University Press, pp. 153-167, 1979.

(Duda 84). Richard O. Duda and René Reboh, "AI and Decision Making: The PROSPECTOR Experience," *Artificial Intelligence for Business*, ed., Walter Reitman, Ablex Pub. Corp, p. 136, 1984.

(Fagan 79). L. M. Fagan, J. C. Kunz, E. A. Feigenbaum, and J. J. Osborn, "Representation of Dynamic Clinical Knowledge: Measurement Interpretation in the Intensive Care Unit," *Proc. 6th IJCAI*, pp. 260-262, 1979.

(Farley 83). Arthur M. Farley, "A Probabilistic Model for Uncertain Problem Solving," *IEEE Transactions on Systems, Man, and Cybernetics*, **SMC-13**, (4), pp. 568-579, July/August 1983.

(Glymour 85). Clark Glymour, "Independence Assumptions and Bayesian Updating," *Artificial Intelligence*, **25**, pp. 95-99, 1985.

(Gorry 78). G. A. Gorry, H. Silverman, and S. G. Pauker, "Capturing Clinical Expertise: A Computer Program That Considers Clinical Responses to Digitalis," *Amer. J. Med.*, **64**, pp. 452-460, 1978.

(Hartley 28). R. V. L. Hartley, "Transmission of Information," *The Bell System Technical Journal*, **7**, pp. 535-563, 1928.

(Hendrix 79). Gary Hendrix, "Encoding Knowledge in Partitioned Networks" in *Associative Networks*, N. Findler, ed., Academic Press, pp. 51-92, 1979.

(Hink 87). Robert F. Hink and David L. Woods, "How Humans Process Uncertain Knowledge: An Introduction for Knowledge Engineers," *AI Magazine*, **8**, (3), pp. 41-53, Fall 1987.

(Kemeny 59). John G. Kemeny, *et al.*, *Finite Mathematical Structures*, Prentice-Hall, p. 399, 1959.

(Lapin 78). Lawrence Lapin, *Statistics for Modern Business Decisions*, 2nd ed., Harcourt Brace Jovanovich, p. 704, 1978.

(Lindley 65). D. V. Lindley, *Introduction to Probability and Statistics from a Bayesian Viewpoint, Part 1, Probability*, Cambridge University Press, p. xi, 1965.

(Manna and Wolper 84). Z. Manna and P. Wolper, "Synthesis of Communicating Processes from Temporal Logic," *ACM Trans. on Programming Languages and Systems*, **6**, (1), pp. 68-93, 1984.

(McDermott 82). D. McDermott, "A Temporal Logic for Reasoning about Plans and Actions," *Cognitive Science*, **6**, pp. 101-155, 1982.

(Parrat 86). Lyman G. Parratt, *Probability and Experimental Errors in Science,* John Wiley and Sons, Inc., p. 6, 1986.

(Pearl 82). Judea Pearl, "Reverend Bayes on Inference Engines: A Distributed Hierarchical Approach," *Proceedings AAAI*, **2**, pp. 133-136, 1982.

(Pednault 81). E. D. P. Pednault, S. W. Zucker, and L. V. Muresan, "On the Independence Assumption Underlying Subjective Bayesian Inference," *Artificial Intelligence*, **16**, pp. 213-222, 1981.

(Quinlan 86). J. Ross Quinlan, "INFERNO: A Cautious Approach to Uncertain Inference," in *Expert Systems*, Phillip Klahr and Donald Waterman, eds., pp. 350-390, 1986.

(Savage 54). L. J. Savage, *The Foundations of Statistics*, John Wiley and Sons, Inc., 1954.

(Shafer 76). Glenn Shafer, *A Mathematical Theory of Evidence,* Princeton University Press, p. 10, 1976.

(Shannon 48). Claude Shannon, "The Mathematical Theory of Communication," *The Bell System Technical Journal*, **27**, pp. 379-423; 623-656, 1948.

(Sioshansi 83). F. Perry Sioshansi, "Subjective Evaluation Using Expert Judgement: An Application," *IEEE Transactions on Systems, Man, and Cybernetics*, **SMC-13**, (3), pp. 391-397, May/June 1983.

(Stebbing 50). L.S. Stebbing, *A Modern Introduction to Logic,* London, 7th ed., Methuen & Co. Ltd., pp. 104-105, 1950.

(Szolovits 78). P. S. Szolovits and S. G. Pauker, "Categorical and Probabilistic Reasoning in Medical Diagnosis," *Artificial Intelligence*, **11**, pp. 115-144, 1978.

(Turner 84). Raymond Turner, *Logics for Artificial Intelligence*, chapter 6, Ellis Horwood, Ltd., 1984.

(Weiss 78). S. Weiss, C. Kulikowski, S. Amarel, and A. Safir, "A Model-Based Method for Computer-Aided Medical Decision Making," *Artificial Intelligence* **11**, pp. 145-172, 1978.

(Zadeh 65). Lotfi A. Zadeh, "Fuzzy Sets," *Information and Control*, **8**, pp. 338-353. June 1965.

CHAPTER 5
Inexact Reasoning

5.1 INTRODUCTION

This chapter continues the discussion of reasoning under uncertainty begun in Chapter 4. The main paradigm for reasoning under uncertainty was probabilistic reasoning and Bayes' Theorem. In this chapter we shall examine several other approaches to dealing with uncertainty.

Probability theory can be considered as a theory of **reproducible uncertainty**. As described in Chapter 4, probability was originally developed for ideal games of chance in which the same experiment could be reproduced indefinitely. While the subjective probability theory described in Chapter 4 has been successfully used with PROSPECTOR, there are many other applications that are better served by other theories. These alternative theories were specifically developed to deal with human belief rather than the classic frequency interpretation of probability. All these theories are examples of **inexact reasoning** in which the antecedent, the conclusion, and even the meaning of the rule itself is uncertain to some extent.

5.2 UNCERTAINTY AND RULES

This section provides an overview of rules and uncertainty. Later sections will cover specific methods of dealing with uncertainty in rules.

Sources of Uncertainty in Rules

Figure 5.1 illustrates a high-level view of uncertainty in rule-based systems. This uncertainty may come from the individual rules, conflict resolution, and incompatibilities among the consequents of rules. The goal of the knowledge engineer is to minimize or eliminate these uncertainties, if possible.

Minimizing the uncertainties of individual rules is part of the verification of the rule. As mentioned in Section 3.15, verification is concerned with the correctness of the system's building blocks. For a rule-based system, the building blocks are the rules.

Just because the individual rules are correct doesn't mean the system will give a correct answer. Due to incompatibilities among rules, the inference chains may not be correct and so validation is necessary. For a rule-based system, part of validation is minimizing uncertainty in the inference chains. Verification can be viewed as minimizing the local uncertainties whereas validation minimizes the global uncertainty of the entire expert system. As a rough analogy to civil engineering, verification would ask if a bridge is being built properly in terms of good materials and assembly. Validation would ask if the bridge can handle the required traffic load and, most important, is the bridge being built at the right location? Both verification and validation are necessary to insure a quality expert system, as will be discussed further in Chapter 6.

Figure 5.1 Major Uncertainties in a Rule-based Expert System

The top-level view of uncertainties in individual rules of Figure 5.1 is expanded in more detail in Figure 5.2. Besides the possible errors involved in the creation of rules, as described in Section 4.3, there are uncertainties associated with the assignment of likelihood values. For probabilistic reasoning, as described in Chapter 4, these uncertainties are with the sufficiency, LS, and necessity, LN, values. Since the LS and LN values are based on estimates from humans, there is uncertainty in them. There is also an uncertainty with the likelihood of the consequent. For probabilistic reasoning, this was written as P(H | E) for certain evidence and P(H | e) for uncertain evidence.

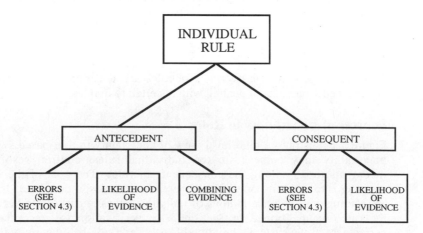

Figure 5.2 Uncertainties in Individual Rules

Another source of uncertainty is the combining of the evidence. Should the evidence be combined

as E_1 AND E_2 AND E_3

or as E_1 AND E_2 OR E_3

or as E_1 AND NOT E_2 OR E_3

or in some other possible way of logical combination using AND, OR, and NOT?

Lack of Theory

As mentioned in Chapter 4, the *ad hoc* introduction of formulas such as fuzzy logic to a probabilistic system introduces a problem. The expert system does not then have a sound theoretical foundation based on classical probability, and so represents an *ad hoc* method that works for a limited case. The danger of *ad hoc* methods is that there is no complete theory to guide the application or warn of inappropriate situations.

Another example of an *ad hoc* method that you have seen is the use of LS and LN factors with inference networks. Theoretically, an inference net with N nodes is a probabilistic system with an event space of N possible events. Thus, there are 2^N possible probabilities. In practice, for real-world situations, few of these probabilities are known. Rather than trying to enumerate all the probabilities, the LS and LN factors are used for significant (we hope) arcs between nodes. Use of LS and LN values for significant arcs greatly reduces the complexity of the net.

However, the LS and LN shortcut also has the detrimental effect that there is no theoretical guarantee that the sum of the conditional probabilities for each hypothesis in the net will be unity. This may not matter much to the user if the goal is simply to obtain a relative ranking of all the hypotheses in the net. For example, the user interested in the porphyry copper hypothesis may well be satisfied to know that the node indicating a favorable likelihood of copper is greatest, even if it is not 1. However, the absolute probability is also important. Even though the copper hypothesis is ranked number 1, is it worth drilling if the probability of finding copper is very low, say, 0.00000001?

Rule Interactions

Another source of uncertainty is conflict resolution of uncertainty. If the knowledge engineer specifies the **explicit priority** of rules, there is a potential source of error because the priority may not be optimal or correct. Other problems with conflict resolution occur because of the **implicit priority** of rules.

Conflict resolution is part of a major source of uncertainty caused by the interactions between rules. The interaction of rules depends on conflict resolution, and the **compatibility of rules**, as shown in Figure 5.3. The compatibility of rules has uncertainty from five major causes.

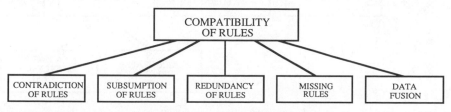

Figure 5.3 Uncertainty Associated with the Compatibilities of Rules

One cause of uncertainty is the potential **contradiction of rules**. Rules may fire with contradictory consequents. This may happen if the antecedents are not specified properly. As a very simple example, assume two rules in the knowledge base:

```
(1) IF there is a fire THEN put water on it
(2) IF there is a fire THEN don't put water on it
```

Rule (1) is applicable to ordinary fires such as wood fires, rule (2) is applicable to oil or grease fires. The problem is that the antecedents are not specified precisely enough for the type of fire. If a fact exists "there is a fire," then both rules will be executed with contradictory consequents and a resulting increase in uncertainty.

A second source of uncertainty is **subsumption of rules**. One rule is subsumed by another if a portion of its antecedent is a subset of another rule. For example, suppose there are two rules that both have the same conclusion:

$$(3)\ \ \text{IF } E_1 \text{ THEN } H$$

$$(4)\ \ \text{IF } E_1 \text{ AND } E_2 \text{ THEN } H$$

If only E_1 is present, then there is no problem since only rule (3) will be activated. However, if both E_1 and E_2 exist, then both rules (3) and (4) will be activated and conflict resolution on them is necessary.

Conflict Resolution

There is uncertainty in conflict resolution regarding priority for firing. This uncertainty depends on a number of factors, as illustrated in Figure 5.4.

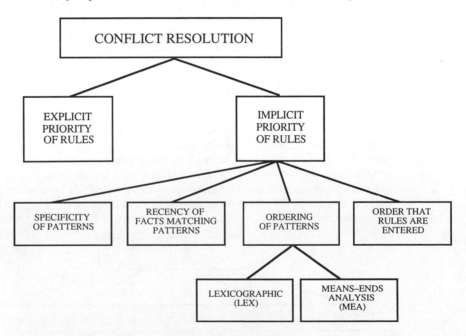

Figure 5.4 Uncertainty Associated with Conflict Resolution

The first factor is the shell or tool used. In OPS5, a rule with more specific patterns has a higher priority. The **specificity** of an OPS5 rule depends on the number of patterns and the internal complexity of each pattern. For example, a pattern

```
(blimp ellipsoidal)
```

is more specific than a pattern

```
(blimp)
```

For our two rules, rule (4) is more specific because it has two patterns in its antecedent and thus has a higher implicit priority. In an OPS5 system, rule (4) is executed first.

However, there are other complications in OPS5. Besides the specificity, there is also the consideration of **recency of facts**. Whenever a fact is entered in the working memory, it receives a unique **timetag** indicating when it was entered. Thus, a rule with the pattern

```
(5)  IF E₃ THEN H
```

would have a higher priority than rule (3) if fact E_3 was entered after E_1.

The ordering of patterns within a rule also makes a difference. OPS5 allows two different **control strategies** called **lexicographic (LEX)** and **means–ends analysis (MEA)**. These strategies determine how the inference engine interprets rule patterns. A control strategy is selected by entering a strategy command to the expert system interpreter. Under LEX, pattern order makes no difference, except possibly in efficiency. Thus, the following two rules are essentially the same under LEX:

```
IF E₁ AND E₂ THEN H

IF E₂ AND E₁ THEN H
```

MEA is the strategy used by Newell and Simon's General Problem Solver, discussed in Chapter 1. The basic idea of MEA is to keep reducing the difference between the starting state and the success state. In the OPS5 implementation of MEA, the first pattern is very important because it acts to control the pattern-matching process. The purpose of MEA is to help the system keep executing a certain task without becoming distracted by very recent facts that have entered working memory. MEA prioritizes rules on the basis of the first pattern, which follows the IF. If one of the rules dominates the others on the basis of the first pattern, then that rule is selected. This domination can be by specificity or recency. If there is more than one dominant rule-first pattern, then MEA orders the rules on the basis of the remaining patterns. Eventually, if there is no dominant rule, an arbitrary choice of a rule is made.

The order in which rules are entered in the expert system may also be a factor in conflict resolution. If the inference engine cannot prioritize rules, an arbitrary choice should be made. However, unless the designers of the inference engine have been careful, the choice may be deterministic in a sense because it depends on the entry of the rule. This may come about because the designers of the inference engine used a stack or queue to store rules on the agenda. For an arbitrary choice of equally prioritized rules, there really should be a random choice from the stack or queue. Instead, the designers may simply take the easy way out and pop the stack or take the next rule from the queue. This selection method is easy but introduces a known artifact into the system because the choice of equally prioritized rules is not arbitrary.

Subsumption and Uncertainty

The problem of subsumption becomes more uncertain if there are likelihoods associated with the rules, as in

(6) IF E$_1$ THEN H with LS$_1$

(7) IF E$_1$ AND E$_2$ THEN H with LS$_2$

For example, consider the following rules:

```
IF the starter motor doesn't work
THEN check the battery with LS₁ = 5
IF the starter motor doesn't work AND
   the lights don't work
THEN check the battery with LS₂ = 10
```

where LS$_2$ is greater than LS$_1$ because of more evidence supporting the conclusion.
From Chapter 4, the posterior odds formula

$$(8) \quad O(H \mid E) = \left[\prod_{i=1}^{N} LS_i \right] O(H)$$

means that the product is $5 \cdot 10 = 50$ if both E$_1$ and E$_2$ are observed.

However, (8) was really meant to describe rules whose evidence combines independently. The antecedents of (6) and (7) are not really independent because they share evidence E$_1$ in common. Thus, E$_1$ AND E$_2$ subsume E$_1$ because E$_1$ alone is a special case of E$_1$ AND E$_2$. The product of the likelihood ratios LS$_1$ and LS$_2$ is thus erroneously high because the antecedents are not independent. A solution is to replace LS$_2$ by the ratio LS$_2$ / LS$_1$ so that when both E$_1$ and E$_2$ exist the correct product LS$_2$ is computed. It may be hard to detect subsumption manually in a large knowledge base.

A third cause of uncertainty is **redundant rules** that have the same consequent and evidence. Generally, these are accidentally entered by the knowledge engineer or accidentally occur when a rule is modified by pattern deletion. For example,

IF E$_1$ AND E$_2$ THEN H

IF E$_2$ AND E$_1$ AND E$_3$ THEN H

are redundant rules if E$_3$ is deleted because the antecedents are the same pattern. Deciding which redundant rule to delete is not necessarily simple. One redundant rule may lead to greater system efficiency if a rare pattern is listed first. The inference engine may not need to check the second pattern for a match if the first pattern fails to match. A further complication arises in expert system shells such as OPS5, in which the order of activation depends on the user-selected control strategy. Like the case of subsumption, redundant rules also give an erroneously high product of the likelihood ratio.

The fourth cause of uncertainty in rule consequents arises from **missing rules**, which occur if the human expert forgets or is unaware of a rule such as

```
IF E₄ THEN H
```

If evidence E_4 is ignored, then H is not concluded with the strength it deserves. One advantage of an inference network such as PROSPECTOR is the explicit nature of the network, which makes it easy to identify hypotheses that are impossible or difficult to achieve. If there are missing rules, the inference net may imply the need for these rules.

The fifth cause of uncertainty occurs because of problems with **data fusion**. This term refers to the uncertainty associated with fusing data from different types of information. For example, in making a diagnosis, a physician may consider evidence from widely different sources such as a physical exam, lab tests, patient history, socioeconomic environment, mental and emotional states, family and job problems, and so forth. These are all different types of evidence that must be fused to support a final hypothesis. The fusion of this evidence from so many different sources is much more difficult than evidence in one domain, such as geology.

Likewise, a business decision may depend on the market for goods, economic conditions, foreign trade, takeover attempts, company politics, personal problems, unions, and many other factors. As with the medical problem, it is very difficult to assign likelihood ratios to all these factors and determine a reasonable combining function.

5.3 CERTAINTY FACTORS

Another method of dealing with uncertainty uses **certainty factors**, originally developed for the MYCIN expert system.

Difficulties with the Bayesian Method

Like the geological problem addressed by PROSPECTOR, medical diagnosis is almost always subject to uncertainty. The major difference is that there are a limited number of geologic hypotheses about minerals since there are only 92 natural elements. Possible disease hypotheses are much greater because there are many more microorganisms.

While Bayes' Theorem is useful in medicine, its accurate use depends on knowing many probabilities. For example, Bayes' Theorem may be used to determine the probability of a specific disease, given certain symptoms as

$$P(D_i \mid E) = \frac{P(E \mid D_i) \; P(D_i)}{P(E)} = \frac{P(E \mid D_i) \; P(D_i)}{\sum_j P(E \mid D_j) \; P(D_j)}$$

where the sum over j extends to all diseases, and

D_i is the ith disease,
E is the evidence,
P(E) is the prior probability of the patient having the disease before any evidence is known,
$P(E \mid D_i)$ is the conditional probability that the patient will exhibit evidence E, given that disease D_i is present.

It is usually impossible to determine consistent and complete values for all these probabilities for the general population.

In practice, evidence tends to accumulate piece by piece. This accumulation costs considerable time and expense, especially when medical tests are involved. These factors of time, cost, and potential risk to the patient of the test usually limit the number of tests performed to a minimum required for a good diagnosis (and malpractice protection).

A convenient form of Bayes' Theorem that expresses the accumulation of incremental evidence like this is the following: (see Problem 5.1)

$$P(D_i \mid E) = \frac{P(E_2 \mid D_i \cap E_1) \; P(D_i \mid E_1)}{\sum_j P(E_2 \mid D_j \cap E_1) \; P(D_j \mid E_1)}$$

where E_2 is the new evidence added to the existing body of evidence, E_1, to yield the new evidence

$$E = E_1 \cap E_2$$

Although this formula is exact, all these probabilities are not generally known. Also, the situation grows much worse as more pieces of evidence accumulate and thus more probabilities are required.

Belief and Disbelief

Besides the problem of amassing all the conditional probabilities for the Bayesian method, another major problem that appeared with medical experts was the relationship of belief and disbelief. At first sight this may appear trivial, because obviously disbelief is simply the opposite of belief. In fact, the theory of probability states that

$$P(H) + P(H') = 1$$

and so

$$P(H) = 1 - P(H')$$

For the case of a posterior hypothesis that relies on evidence, E

$$(1) \quad P(H \mid E) = 1 - P(H' \mid E)$$

However, when the MYCIN knowledge engineers began interviewing medical experts, they found that physicians were extremely reluctant to state their knowledge in the form of equation (1).

For example, consider a MYCIN rule such as the following (Shortliffe 85):

```
IF 1) The stain of the organism is gram positive, and
   2) The morphology of the organism is coccus, and
   3) The growth conformation of the organism is chains
THEN There is suggestive evidence (0.7) that the
     identity of the organism is streptococcus
```

In simple terms, this rule says that if a bacterial organism becomes colored when treated with Gram's stain and resembles chains of spheres, then there is a 70 percent likelihood that it is a type named *streptococcus*. This can be written in terms of posterior probability as

$$(2) \quad P(H \mid E_1 \cap E_2 \cap E_3) = 0.7$$

where the E_i correspond to the three patterns of the antecedent.

The MYCIN knowledge engineers found that although experts would agree to equation (2), they became uneasy and refused to agree with the probabilistic result

$$(3) \quad P(H' \mid E_1 \cap E_2 \cap E_3) = 1 - 0.7 = 0.3$$

This reluctance by the expert to agree to equation (3) illustrates again that these numbers such as 0.7 and 0.3 are likelihoods of belief, not probabilities.

In order to fully appreciate this problem of inconsistent belief and disbelief, consider the following example. Suppose this is your last course required for a degree. Assume your grade point average (GPA) has not been too good and you need an A in this course to bring up your GPA. The following formula may express your belief in the likelihood of graduation.

$$(4) \quad P(\text{graduating} \mid A \text{ in this course}) = 0.70$$

Notice that this likelihood is not 100 percent. The reason it's not 100 percent is that a final audit of your courses and grades must be made by the school. There could be problems due to a number of reasons that would still prevent your graduation, such as the following:

1) School catalog changes so that not all your courses counted toward the degree.
2) You forgot to take a required course.
3) Rejection of transfer courses.
4) Rejection of some elective courses you took.
5) Tuition and library fines that you owe and were hoping would be forgotten weren't.
6) Your GPA was lower than you thought and an A still won't raise it up.
7) "They" are out to get you.

Assuming that you agree with (4) (or perhaps your own value for the likelihood) then by equation (1)

$$(5) \quad P(\text{not graduating} \mid A \text{ in this course}) = 0.30$$

Although equation (5) is correct from a probabilistic viewpoint, it somehow seems intuitively wrong. It's just not right that if you really work hard and get an A in this course, then there is a 30 percent chance that you won't graduate. Equation (5) should make you as uneasy as the medical expert who believes

$$P(H \mid E_1 \cap E_2 \cap E_3) = 0.70$$

but won't believe the probabilistic consequence

$$P(H' \mid E_1 \cap E_2 \cap E_3) = 0.30$$

The fundamental problem is that while P(H I E) implies a cause-and-effect relationship between E and H, there may be no cause-and-effect relationship between E and H´. Yet the equation

```
P(H | E) = 1 - P(H´ | E)
```

implies a cause-and-effect relationship between E and H´ if there is one between E and H.

These problems with the theory of probability led Shortliffe to investigate other ways of representing uncertainty. The method that he used with MYCIN was based on **certainty factors** derived from Carnap's theory of confirmation (Carnap 1950). Carnap distinguished two types of probability.

One type of probability is the ordinary probability associated with the frequency of reproducible events. The second type is called *epistemic probability* or the *degree of confirmation* because it confirms a hypothesis based on some evidence. This second type is another example of the degree of likelihood of a belief.

Measures of Belief and Disbelief

In MYCIN, the degree of confirmation was originally defined as the certainty factor, which is the difference between belief and disbelief:

```
CF(H,E) = MB(H,E) - MD(H,E)
```

where

CF is the certainty factor in the hypothesis H due to evidence E
MB is the **measure of increased belief** in H due to E
MD is the **measure of increased disbelief** in H due to E

The certainty factor is a way of combining belief and disbelief into a single number.

Combining the measures of belief and disbelief into a single number has two uses. First, the certainty factor can be used to rank hypotheses in order of importance. For example, if a patient has certain symptoms that suggest several possible diseases, then the disease with the highest CF would be the one that is first investigated by ordering tests.

The measures of belief and disbelief were defined in terms of probabilities by

$$MB(H,E) = \begin{cases} 1 & \text{if } P(H) = 1 \\ \dfrac{\max[P(H \mid E), P(H)] - P(H)}{\max[1,0] - P(H)} & \text{otherwise} \end{cases}$$

$$MD(H,E) = \begin{cases} 1 & \text{if } P(H) = 0 \\ \dfrac{\min[P(H \mid E), P(H)] - P(H)}{\min[1,0] - P(H)} & \text{otherwise} \end{cases}$$

Now max[1,0] is always 1 and min [1,0] is always 0. The reason for writing 1 and 0 in terms of max and min is to show the formal symmetry between MB and MD. The equations for MB and MD differ only in the replacement of max by min and vice versa.

According to these definitions, some characteristics are shown in Table 5.1.

Characteristics	Values
Ranges	$0 \leq MB \leq 1$
	$0 \leq MD \leq 1$
	$-1 \leq CF \leq 1$
Certain True Hypothesis	MB = 1
P(H | E) = 1	MD = 0
	CF = 1
Certain False Hypothesis	MB = 0
P(H′ | E) = 1	MD = 1
	CF = -1
Lack of Evidence	MB = 0
P(H | E) = P(H)	MD = 0
	CF = 0

Table 5.1 Some Characteristics of MB, MD, and CF

The certainty factor, CF, indicates the net belief in a hypothesis based on some evidence. A positive CF means the evidence supports the hypothesis since MB > MD. CF = 1 means that the evidence definitely proves the hypothesis. CF = 0 means one of two possibilities. First, a CF = MB − MD = 0 could mean that both MB and MD are 0. That is, there is no evidence. The second possibility is that MB = MD and both are nonzero. The result is that the belief is cancelled out by the disbelief.

A negative CF means that the evidence favors the negation of the hypothesis because MB < MD. Another way of stating this is that there is more reason to disbelieve a hypothesis than to believe it. For example, a CF = −70 percent means that the disbelief is 70 percent greater than the belief. CF = 70 percent means that the belief is 70 percent greater than the disbelief. Notice that with certainty factors there are no constraints on the individual values of MB and MD. Only the difference is important. For example:

```
CF = 0.70 = 0.70 - 0
          = 0.80 - 0.10
```

and so forth.

Certainty factors allow an expert to express a belief without committing a value to the disbelief. As shown in Problem 5.2,

```
CF(H,E) + CF(H′,E) = 0
```

which means that if evidence confirms a hypothesis by some value CF(H | E) the confirmation of the negation of the hypothesis is not 1 − CF(H | E), which would be expected under probability theory. That is,

$$CF(H,E) + CF(H',E) \neq 1$$

The fact that CF(H | E) + CF(H' | E) = 0 means that evidence supporting a hypothesis reduces support to the negation of the hypothesis by an equal amount so that the sum is always 0.

For the example of the student graduating if an A is given in the course,

$$CF(H,E) = 0.70 \qquad CF(H',E) = -0.70$$

which means

(6) I am 70 percent certain that I will graduate if I get an A in this course.

(7) I am -70 percent certain that I will not graduate if I get an A in this course.

Notice that the –70 percent comes about because certainty factors are defined on the interval

$$-1 \leq CF(H,E) \leq +1$$

where 0 means no evidence. So certainty values greater than 0 favor the hypothesis while certainty factors less than 0 favor the negation of the hypothesis. Statements (6) and (7) are equivalent using certainty factors analogous to the fact that "yes = not no."

The above CF values might be elicited by asking

How much do you believe that getting an A will help you graduate?

if the evidence is to confirm the hypothesis or

How much do you disbelieve that getting an A will help you graduate?

An answer of 70 percent to each question will set CF(H | E) = 0.70 and CF(H' | E) = –0.70. In MYCIN, rather than asking certainties on a percentage scale, the experts were asked to give certainty on a scale of 1 to 10, where 10 was definite. The user could answer UNK for unknown evidence corresponding to CF = 0.

Calculating with Certainty Factors

Although the original definition of CF was

$$CF = MB - MD$$

there were difficulties with this definition because one piece of disconfirming evidence could control the confirmation of many other pieces of evidence. For example, ten pieces of evidence might produce an MB = 0.999 and one disconfirming piece with MD = 0.799 could then give

$$CF = 0.999 - 0.799 = 0.200$$

In MYCIN, a rule's antecedent CF must be > 0.2 for the antecedent to be considered true and activate the rule. This **threshold value** of 0.2 was not done as a fundamental axiom of CF theory, but rather as an *ad hoc* way of minimizing the activation of rules that only weakly suggest a hypothesis. Without a threshold, many rules of little or no value may be activated and greatly reduce the system's efficiency.

The definition of CF was changed in MYCIN in 1977 to be

$$CF = \frac{MB - MD}{1 - \min(MB, MD)}$$

to soften the effects of a single piece of disconfirming evidence on many confirming pieces of evidence. Under this definition with MB = 0.999, MD = 0.799

$$CF = \frac{0.999 - 0.799}{1 - \min(0.999, 0.799)} = \frac{0.200}{1 - 0.799} = 0.995$$

which is very different from the previous definition that gave 0.999 − 0.799 = 0.200 and so did not activate a rule because it was not greater than 0.2. Now the 0.995 will cause the rule to be activated.

The MYCIN methods for combining evidence in the antecedent of a rule are shown in Table 5.2. Notice that these are the same as the PROSPECTOR rules based on fuzzy logic.

Evidence, E	Antecedent Certainty
E_1 AND E_2	$\min[CF(H, E_1), CF(H, E_2)]$
E_1 OR E_2	$\max[CF(H, E_1), CF(H, E_2)]$
NOT E	$-CF(H, E)$

Table 5.2 MYCIN Rules for Combining Antecedent Evidence of Elementary Expressions

For example, given a logical expression for combining evidence such as

$$E = (E_1 \text{ AND } E_2 \text{ AND } E_3) \text{ OR } (E_4 \text{ AND NOT } E_5)$$

the evidence E would be computed as

$$E = \max[\min(E_1, E_2, E_3), \min(E_4, -E_5)]$$

For values

$$E_1 = 0.9 \quad E_2 = 0.8 \quad E_3 = 0.3$$
$$E_4 = -0.5 \quad E_5 = -0.4$$

the result is

$$E = \max[\min(0.9, 0.8, 0.3), \min(-0.5, -(-0.4))]$$
$$= \max[0.3, -0.5]$$
$$= 0.3$$

The fundamental formula for the CF of a rule

```
IF E THEN H
```

is given by the formula

$$(8) \quad CF(H,e) = CF(E,e) \; CF(H,E)$$

where

CF(E,e) is the certainty factor of the evidence E making up the antecedent of the rule base on uncertain evidence e.
CF(H,E) is the certainty factor of the hypothesis assuming that the evidence is known with certainty, when CF(E,e) = 1.
CF(H,e) is the certainty factor of the hypothesis based on uncertain evidence *e*.

Thus, if all the evidence in the antecedent is known with certainty, the formula for the certainty factor of the hypothesis is

```
CF(H,e) = CF(H,E)
```

since CF(E,e) = 1.
As an example of these certainty factors, consider the CF for the streptococcus rule discussed before:

```
IF 1) The stain of the organism is gram positive, and
   2) The morphology of the organism is coccus, and
   3) The growth conformation of the organism is chains
THEN There is suggestive evidence (0.7) that the
        identity of the organism is streptococcus
```

where the certainty factor of the hypothesis under certain evidence is

$$CF(H,E) = CF(H, E_1 \cap E_2 \cap E_3) = 0.7$$

and is also called the ***attenuation factor***.
The attenuation factor is based on the assumption that all the evidence—E_1, E_2 and E_3—is known with certainty. That is,

$$CF(E_1,e) = CF(E_2,e) = CF(E_3,e) = 1$$

where e is the observed evidence that leads to the conclusion that the E_i are known with certainty. These CF values are analogous to the conditional probabilities of the evidence of PROSPECTOR, P(E | e). The attenuation factor expresses the degree of certainty of the hypothesis, given certain evidence.
Just as with PROSPECTOR, a complication occurs if not all the evidence is known with certainty. With PROSPECTOR, the interpolation formula P(H | e) was used for uncertain evidence. In the case of MYCIN, the fundamental formula (8) must be used to determine the resulting CF value since CF(H,$E_1 \cap E_2 \cap E_3$) = 0.7 is no longer valid for uncertain evidence.

For example, assuming

```
CF(E₁,e) = 0.5
CF(E₂,e) = 0.6
CF(E₃,e) = 0.3
```

then

```
CF(E,e) = CF(E₁ ∩ E₂ ∩ E₃,e)
        = min[CF(E₁,e),CF(E₂,e),CF(E₃,e)]
        = min[0.5,0.6,0.3]
        = 0.3
```

Since the CF of the antecedent, CF(E,e) > 0.2, the antecedent is considered true and so the rule is activated. The certainty factor of the conclusion is

```
CF(H,e) = CF(E,e) CF(H,E)
        - 0.3 · 0.7
        = 0.21
```

Suppose another rule also concludes the same hypothesis, but with a different certainty factor. The certainty factors of rules concluding the same hypothesis are calculated from the **combining function** for certainty factors defined as

$$(9)\ \ CF_{COMBINE}(CF_1,CF_2) = \begin{cases} CF_1 + CF_2\ (1 - CF_1) & \text{both} > 0 \\[2mm] \dfrac{CF_1 + CF_2}{1 - \min(|CF_1|,|CF_2|)} & \text{one} < 0 \\[2mm] CF_1 + CF_2\ (1 + CF_1) & \text{both} < 0 \end{cases}$$

where the formula for CF$_{COMBINE}$ used depends on whether the individual certainty factors are positive or negative. The combining function for more than two certainty factors is applied incrementally. That is, the CF$_{COMBINE}$ is calculated for two CF values, and then the CF$_{COMBINE}$ is combined using formula (9) with the third CF value, and so forth. Figure 5.5 summarizes the calculations with certainty factors for two rules based on uncertain evidence and concluding the same hypothesis. Note that this is *not* an AND/OR tree because CF$_{COMBINE}$ has nothing to do with AND and OR goals.

In our example, if another rule concludes streptococcus with certainty factor $CF_2 = 0.5$, then the combined certainty using the first formula of (9) is

```
CF COMBINE(0.21,0.5)  = 0.21 + 0.5 (1 - 0.21) = 0.605
```

Suppose a third rule has the same conclusion, but with a $CF_3 = -0.4$. Then the second formula of (9) is used to give

$$CF_{COMBINE}(0.605,-0.4) = \frac{0.605 - 0.4}{1 - \min(|0.605|,|-0.4|)}$$

$$= \frac{0.205}{1 - 0.4} = 0.34$$

The $CF_{COMBINE}$ formula preserves the commutativity of evidence. That is,

$$CF_{COMBINE}(X,Y) = CF_{COMBINE}(Y,X)$$

and so the order in which evidence is received does not affect the result.

Rather than storing separate MB and MD values for each hypothesis, MYCIN stored the current $CF_{COMBINE}$ with each hypothesis and combined it with new evidence as it became available.

$$CF_{COMBINE}(CF_1, CF_2) = \begin{cases} CF_1 + CF_2 (1 - CF_1) & \text{both} > 0 \\[2ex] \dfrac{CF_1 + CF_2}{1 - \min(|CF_1|, |CF_2|)} & \text{one} < 0 \\[2ex] CF_1 + CF_2 (1 + CF_1) & \text{both} < 0 \end{cases}$$

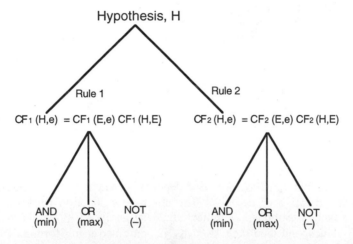

Figure 5.5 CFs of Two Rules with the Same Hypothesis Based on Uncertain Evidence

Difficulties with Certainty Factors

Although MYCIN was successful in diagnosis, there were difficulties with the theoretical foundations of certainty factors. While certainty factors had some basis in both probability theory and confirmation theory, the CFs were also partly *ad hoc*. The major advantage of CF was the simple computations by which uncertainty could be propagated in the system. The CFs were also easy to understand and clearly separated belief from disbelief.

However, there were problems with CFs. One problem was that the CF values could be the opposite of conditional probabilities. For example, if

$$\begin{array}{llll} P(H_1) & = 0.8 & P(H_2) & = 0.2 \\ P(H_1 \mid E) & = 0.9 & P(H_2 \mid E) & = 0.8 \end{array}$$

then

$$CF(H_1, E) = 0.5 \text{ and } CF(H_2, E) = 0.75$$

Since one purpose of CFs is to rank hypotheses in terms of likely diagnosis, it is a contradiction for a disease to have a higher conditional probability P(H | E) and yet have a lower certainty factor, CF(H,E).

The second major problem with CFs is that in general

$$P(H \mid e) \neq P(H \mid i) \ P(i \mid e)$$

where i is some intermediate hypothesis based on evidence e, and yet the certainty factor of two rules in an inference chain is calculated as independent probabilities by

$$CF(H, e) = CF(H, i) \ CF(i, e)$$

The above formula is only true in the special case that the statistical population with property H is contained in the population with property i, and that is contained in the population with property e (Adams 85). The success of MYCIN in spite of these problems is probably due to the short inference chains and simple hypotheses. There could be real problems in applying certainty factors to other domains that did not have short inference chains and simple hypotheses. In fact, Adams demonstrated that the theory of certainty factors is really an approximation to standard probability theory.

5.4 DEMPSTER-SHAFER THEORY

In this section, we will discuss a method of inexact reasoning called the **Dempster-Shafer theory** (or Shafer-Dempster) **theory**. It is based on work done originally by Dempster, who attempted to model uncertainty by a range of probabilities rather than as a single probabilistic number (Dempster 67). Shafer extended and refined Dempster's work in a book published in 1976 called *A Mathematical Theory of Evidence* (Shafer 76). A further extension called *evidential reasoning* deals with information that is expected to be uncertain, imprecise, and occasionally inaccurate (Garvey 81; Lowrance 82). The Dempster-Shafer theory has a good theoretical foundation. Certainty factors can be shown to be a special case of Dempster-Shafer theory, which puts them on a theoretical rather than an *ad hoc* basis (Gordon 85).

Frames of Discernment

The Dempster-Shafer theory assumes that there is a fixed set of mutually exclusive and exhaustive elements called the *environment* and symbolized by the Greek letter Θ.

$$\Theta = \{\theta_1, \ \theta_2, \ \dots \theta_N\}$$

The environment is another term for the universe of discourse in set theory. That is, the environment is the set of objects that are of interest to us. Some examples of environments might be:

```
Θ = {airliner, bomber, fighter}
Θ = {red, green, blue, orange, yellow}
Θ = {barn, grass, person, cow, car}
```

Notice that the elements are all mutually exclusive. For example, an airliner is not a bomber or a fighter, red is not green, grass is not a cow, and so forth. Assume that all possible elements of the universe are in the set and therefore the set is exhaustive. For simplicity in our discussion, assume also that Θ is a finite set. However, work has been done on Dempster-Shafer environments whose elements are continuous variables such as time, distance, velocity, and so forth (Strat 84).

One way of thinking about Θ is in terms of questions and answers. Suppose

```
Θ = {airliner, bomber, fighter}
```

and the question is "Which are the military aircraft?" The answer is the subset of Θ

```
{θ₂, θ₃} = {bomber, fighter}
```

Likewise, the question "Which are the civilian aircraft?" is the set

```
{θ₁} = {airliner}
```

which is called a **singleton set** because it has only one element.

Each subset of Θ can be interpreted as a possible answer to a question. Because the elements are mutually exclusive and the environment is exhaustive, there can be only one correct answer subset to a question. Of course, not all possible questions may be meaningful or interesting to ask. However, the important point to realize is that the subsets of the environment are all possible valid answers in this universe of discourse. Each subset can be considered an implied proposition, such as

```
The correct answer is {θ₁, θ₂, θ₃}
The correct answer is {θ₁, θ₂}
```

and so on for all subsets, in which "The correct answer is" is implied with the subset.

All possible subsets of the aircraft environment are shown in Figure 5.6, with lines drawn to indicate the relationships of the sets. The abbreviations A, B, and F are used for *airliner*, *bomber*, and *fighter*. This diagram is drawn as a hierarchical lattice with Θ at the top and the null set Ø = { } at the bottom. Usually, the null set is not explicitly shown because it always corresponds to the false answer. Since Ø has no elements, its choice as the answer below contradicts the assumption of environment as exhaustive.

```
The correct answer is no element
```

Notice that the figure is a lattice and not a tree because the subset nodes may have more than one parent. The lattice is hierarchical because it is drawn from larger sets to smaller sets. For example, one path from Θ to Ø expresses the hierarchical relation of subsets connecting parent to child, such as

```
Ø ⊂ {A} ⊂ {A,B} ⊂ {A,B,F}
```

As discussed in Section 2.10, a relationship between two sets X and Y, such as

$$X \subseteq Y$$

means that all elements of X are elements of Y, and is written more formally

$$X \subseteq Y = \{x \mid x \in X \rightarrow x \in Y\}$$

This states that if x is an element of set X then this implies x is also an element of set Y. If $X \subseteq Y$, but $X \neq Y$, there is at least one element of Y that is not an element of X and X is called a *proper subset* of Y and is written

$$X \subset Y$$

An environment is called a ***frame of discernment*** when its elements may be interpreted as possible answers and only one answer is correct. The term *discern* means that it's possible to distinguish the one correct answer from all the other possible answers to a question. If the answer is not in the frame, then the frame must be enlarged to accommodate the additional knowledge of elements θ_{N+1}, θ_{N+2}, and so forth. One correct answer requires that the set be exhaustive and that the subsets are disjoint.

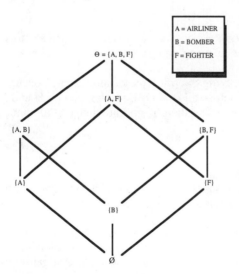

Figure 5.6 All Subsets of the Aircraft Environment

A set of size N has exactly 2^N subsets, including itself, and these subsets define the power set (see Problem 2-11), written as $P(\Theta)$. Thus, for the aircraft environment,

$$P(\Theta) = \{\emptyset, \{A\}, \{B\}, \{F\}, \{A,B\}, \{A,F\}, \{B,F\}, \{A,B,F\}\}$$

The power set of the environment has as its elements all answers to the possible questions of the frame of discernment. This means that there is a one-to-one correspondence between the elements of $P(\Theta)$ and the subsets of Θ.

Mass Functions and Ignorance

In Bayesian theory the posterior probability changes as evidence is acquired. Likewise, in Dempster-Shafer theory the belief in evidence may vary. It's customary in Dempster-Shafer theory to think about the *degree of belief in evidence* as analogous to the **mass** of a physical object. That is, the mass of evidence supports a belief. The **evidence measure**, symbolized by the letter m, is analogous to the amount of mass. Another term for mass is the **basic probability assignment (bpa)** or sometimes simply **basic assignment**, because of an analogy in the form of the equations describing probability densities and mass. However, because of potential confusion with probability theory, we will not use these terms and will simply refer to *mass*. The reason for the analogy with an object of mass is to consider belief as a quantity that can move around, be split up, and combined. It may be helpful to think of the object as composed of clay so that pieces of it can be removed and stuck together again.

A fundamental difference between Dempster-Shafer theory and probability theory is the treatment of **ignorance**. As discussed in Chapter 4, probability theory must distribute an equal amount of probability even in ignorance. For example, if you have no prior knowledge, then you must assume the probability P of each possibility is

$$P = \frac{1}{N}$$

where N is the number of possibilities. As mentioned in Chapter 4, this assignment of P is made *in desperation* or, using a more impressive-sounding term, by using the **principle of indifference**.

The extreme case of applying the principle of indifference occurs when there are only two possibilities, such as oil or no oil, symbolized by H and H′. In cases like this, P = 50 percent even when there is no knowledge at all since probability theory says that

$$P(H) + P(H′) = 1$$

That is, anything that does not support *must* refute, since ignorance is not allowed.

This can lead to some ridiculous consequences if applied without thinking. For example, there either is or is not oil under your house. By the principle of indifference, if you have *absolutely no other knowledge*, there is a 50 percent probability of having oil under your house. If you think about it, a 50 percent chance of oil is very impressive and offers a better chance at getting rich quickly than any legal investment. Since there is a 50 percent chance of oil, should you immediately withdraw all your savings, hire a drilling rig, and start drilling in the kitchen?

Following this same line of reasoning, application of the principle of indifference and probability theory says there is a 50 percent chance of

```
diamonds
a pirate's treasure
fur coats
green cheese
your next homework assignment
```

and anything else you can think of under your house. (In fact, you can probably become rich by just going on TV and telling everyone how *they* can become rich by sending in $9.95 for your book on probability theory. This is also the best reason for never cleaning. If you don't know what's there, it could be anything, and so there's a 50 percent chance of getting rich by discovering something valuable.)

Even if the principle of indifference is not used, the constraint

```
·   P(H) + P(H´) = 1
```

forces the assignment of probability to the negation of the hypothesis even if there is no evidence for this. As discussed in Section 5.3, this is not a good assumption to make with many types of beliefs such as medical knowledge. However, probability theory requires that evidence that does not support a hypothesis must refute it.

The Dempster-Shafer theory does not force belief to be assigned to ignorance or refutation of a hypothesis. Instead, the mass is assigned only to those subsets of the environment to which you wish to assign belief. Any belief that is not assigned to a specific subset is considered **no belief** or **nonbelief** and is just associated with the environment Θ. Belief that refutes a hypothesis is disbelief, which is *not* nonbelief.

For example, suppose that a sensor such as an Identification Friend or Foe (IFF) obtains no response from the transponder of an aircraft (Bogler 87). An IFF is a radio transmitter/receiver that transmits a radio message to an aircraft. If the aircraft is friendly, its transponder should respond by sending back its identification code. Aircraft that do not respond are assumed hostile by default. An aircraft may not respond to IFF for a variety of reasons, such as

- Malfunction in the IFF
- Malfunction in the aircraft transponder
- No IFF on the aircraft
- Jamming of the IFF signal
- Orders to maintain radio silence

Assume that the failure of the IFF to elicit a response indicates a belief in the evidence of 0.7 that the target aircraft is hostile, where hostile aircraft are only considered to be bombers and fighters. Thus, the mass assignment is to the subset {B,F}, and

```
m₁({B,F}) = 0.7
```

where m_1 refers to this first IFF sensor evidence.

The rest of the belief is left with the environment, Θ, as nonbelief.

```
m₁(Θ) = 1 - 0.7 = 0.3
```

Every set in the power set of the environment that has a mass greater than 0 is a **focal element**. The term *focal element* is used because a set X such that m(X) > 0 is a power set element in which the available evidence is focused or concentrated.

The Dempster-Shafer theory has a major difference from probability theory, which would assume that

```
P(hostile) = 0.7
P(non-hostile) = 1 - 0.7 = 0.3
```

In probability theory, if the belief in hostile is 0.7 then the disbelief in hostile must be 0.3. Instead, the 0.3 in Dempster-Shafer theory is held as nonbelief in the environment by m(Θ). This means *neither belief nor disbelief* in the evidence to a degree of 0.3. We believe that the target is hostile to a degree of 0.7 and are reserving judgment of 0.3 in disbelief and the additional belief in hostile. It's very important to realize that the assignment of 0.3 to the environment Θ does not assign *any* value to the subsets of Θ, even though the subsets include the hostile subsets {B, F}, {B}, and {F}.

Going back to the student example of the last section,

```
m(getting an A and graduating) = 0.7
```

would not automatically mean

```
m(getting an A and not graduating) = 0.3
```

unless both of these were assigned values.

A mass has considerably more freedom than probabilities, as Table 5.3 shows.

Dempster-Shafer Theory	Probability Theory
m(Θ) does not have to be 1	$\sum_i P_i = 1$
If X $\subseteq$ Y, it is not necessary that m(X) $\leq$ m(Y)	P(X) $\leq$ P(Y)
No required relationship between m(X) and m(X´)	P(X) + P(X´) = 1

Table 5.3 Comparison of Dempster-Shafer Mass with Probability Theory

Every mass can formally be expressed as a function that maps each element of the power set into a real number in the interval 0 to 1. This simply means that the belief in a subset may take any values from 0 to 1. This mapping is formally stated

```
m: P(Θ) → [0,1]
```

By convention, the mass of the empty set is usually defined as zero:

```
m(∅) = 0
```

and the sum of all the masses for every subset, X, of the power set is 1:

$$\sum_{X \in P(\Theta)} m(X) = 1$$

For example, in the aircraft environment

$$\sum_{X \in P(\Theta)} m(X) = m(\{B,F\}) + m(\Theta) = 0.7 + 0.3 = 1$$

Combining Evidence

Now let's look at the case in which additional evidence becomes available. We would like to combine all the evidence to produce a better estimate of belief in the evidence. To show how this is done, let's first look at an example that is a special case of the general formula for combining evidence.

Suppose that a second type of sensor identifies the target as a bomber with a belief in the evidence of 0.9. The masses of evidence from the sensors are now the following:

$$m_1(\{B,F\}) = 0.7 \quad m_1(\Theta) = 0.3$$

$$m_2(\{B\}) = 0.9 \quad m_2(\Theta) = 0.1$$

where m_1 and m_2 refer to the first and second types of sensors.

This evidence can be combined using the following special form of **Dempster's Rule of Combination** to yield the **combined mass**:

$$m_1 \oplus m_2(Z) = \sum_{X \cap Y = Z} m_1(X) \; m_2(Y)$$

where the sum extends over all elements whose intersection $X \cap Y = Z$. The $\oplus$ **operator** denotes the **orthogonal sum** or **direct sum**, which is defined by summing the mass product intersections on the right side of the rule. Dempster's rule combines masses to produce a new mass that represents a **consensus** of the original, possibly conflicting evidence. The new mass is a *consensus* because it tends to favor agreement rather than disagreement by only including masses in the set intersections. The set intersections represent common elements of evidence. An important point is that the rule should be used to combine evidence having *independent errors*, which is *not* the same as independently gathered evidence.

Table 5.4 shows the masses and product intersections for the aircraft environment arranged in a table. Each set intersection is followed by its numeric mass product.

	$m_2(\{B\}) = 0.9$	$m_2(\Theta) = 0.1$
$m_1(\{B,F\}) = 0.7$	{B} 0.63	{B,F} 0.07
$m_1(\Theta) = 0.3$	{B} 0.27	Θ 0.03

Table 5.4 Confirming Evidence

The entries in the table are calculated by cross-multiplying mass products of rows and columns as follows, where T_{ij} denotes the ith row and jth column of the table:

$$T_{11}(\{B\}) = m_1(\{B,F\}) \; m_2(\{B\}) = (0.7)(0.9) = 0.63$$

$$T_{21}(\{B\}) = m_1(\Theta) \; m_2(\{B\}) = (0.3)(0.9) = 0.27$$

$$T_{12}(\{B,F\}) = m_1(\{B,F\}) \; m_2(\Theta) = (0.7)(0.1) = 0.07$$

$$T_{22}(\Theta) = m_1(\Theta) \; m_2(\Theta) = (0.3)(0.1) = 0.03$$

Once the individual mass products have been calculated, as shown above, then according to Dempster's Rule the products over the common set intersections are added:

$$m_3(\{B\}) \quad = m_1 \oplus m_2(\{B\}) = 0.63 + 0.27$$

$$= 0.90 \qquad\qquad\qquad \text{bomber}$$

$$m_3(\{B,F\}) \quad = m_1 \oplus m_2(\{B,F\})$$

$$= 0.07 \qquad\qquad \text{bomber or fighter}$$

$$m_3(\Theta) \qquad = m_1 \oplus m_2(\Theta)$$

$$= 0.03 \qquad\qquad\qquad \text{nonbelief}$$

The $m_3(\{B\})$ represents the belief that the target is a bomber and *only* a bomber. However, $m_3(\{B,F\})$ and $m_3(\Theta)$ imply additional information. Since their sets include a bomber, it's plausible that their orthogonal sums may contribute to a belief in the bomber. So their $0.07 + 0.03 = 0.1$ may be added to the belief of 0.90 in the bomber set to yield the maximum belief that it could be a bomber—the plausible belief. Instead of restricting belief to a single value, there is a **range of belief** in the evidence. The belief ranges from the minimum 0.9 that is known for the bomber to the maximum plausible $0.90 + 0.1 = 1$ that it *might* be a bomber. The true belief is assumed somewhere in the range 0.9 to 1.

In evidential reasoning the evidence is said to induce an **evidential interval**. The **lower bound** is called the **support** (**Spt**) in evidential reasoning and **Bel** in Dempster-Shafer theory. The **upper bound** is called the **plausibility** (**Pls**). For this example, the evidential interval is [0.90,1], the lower bound is 0.90, and the upper bound is 1. The support is the *minimum belief* based on the evidence, while the plausibility is the *maximum belief* we are willing to give. In general, the ranges of Bel and Pls are $0 \leq \text{Bel} \leq \text{Pls} \leq 1$. In Dempster-Shafer theory, the lower and upper bounds are sometimes called the lower and upper probabilities, based on Dempster's original paper (Dempster 67). Table 5.5 shows some common evidential intervals (Wesley 86).

Evidential Interval		Meaning
[1,1]		Completely true
[0,0]		Completely false
[0,1]		Completely ignorant
[Bel,1]	where 0 < Bel < 1 here	Tends to support
[0,Pls]	where 0 < Pls < 1 here	Tends to refute
[Bel,Pls]	where 0 < Bel ≤ Pls < 1 here	Tends to both support and refute

Table 5.5 Some Common Evidential Intervals

The support or **belief function**, **Bel**, is the *total belief* of a set and *all* its subsets. Bel is all the mass that supports a set, and is defined in terms of the mass.

$$\text{Bel}(X) = \sum_{Y \subseteq X} m(Y)$$

As an example, in the aircraft environment for the first sensor,

```
Bel₁({B,F})  = m₁({B,F}) + m₁({B}) + m₁({F})

       = 0.7 + 0 + 0 = 0.7
```

The Bel function is sometimes called the *belief measure,* or simply *belief.* However, note that the belief function is very different from the mass, which is the belief in the evidence assigned to a *single* set. For example, suppose that you own a Ford and hear that the police are looking for a Ford that was used as the getaway car in a bank robbery. There is a big difference between hearing that the police looking for *a* Ford, and hearing that the police are looking for *your* Ford. Mass is the belief in a set and *not* any of its subsets, while a belief function applies to a set and *all* its subsets. Bel is the *total belief* and so is more global than the *local belief* of mass. Because of the interrelationship of mass and Bel, Dempster-Shafer theory is also called a *theory of belief functions*. In a general sense, Dempster's rule can then be interpreted as a way of combining belief functions. The mass and belief function are related by

$$m(X) = \sum_{Y \subseteq X} (-1)^{|X - Y|} \, Bel(Y)$$

where |X − Y| is the **cardinality** of the set,

$$X - Y = \{x \mid x \in X \text{ and } x \notin Y\}$$

That is, |X - Y| is the number of elements in the set X - Y.

Since belief functions are defined in terms of masses, the combination of two belief functions also can be expressed in terms of orthogonal sums of the masses of a set and all its subsets. For example,

```
Bel₁ ⊕ Bel₂({B}) = m₁ ⊕ m₂({B}) + m₁ ⊕ m₂(∅)

        = 0.90 + 0 = 0.90
```

Normally, the null set mass is not written because it's usually defined to be zero. The total belief for the bomber-fighter subset {B,F}, has more subsets than the above.

```
Bel₁ ⊕ Bel₂({B,F})

   = m₁ ⊕ m₂({B,F}) + m₁ ⊕ m₂({B}) + m₁ ⊕ m₂({F})
       = 0.07 + 0.90 + 0 = 0.97
```

The terms for {B} and {F} are included because they are subsets of {B,F}. From Figure 5.6 you can see that {B,F} has subsets {B} and {F}. Since no mass was given {F}, then m({F}) = 0 and so it does not contribute anything to the sum. In fact, m({F}) and the other masses of value zero never entered into Table 5.4 at all because the result of any cross products with them would be zero. If masses had been assigned to every subset of {A,B,F} except the null set, which is zero, then Table 5.4 would be a $(2^3 − 1)$ $(2^3 − 1) = 7 \cdot 7 = 49$-cell table.

The combined belief function for Θ based on all evidence is the following:

$$\text{Bel}_1 \oplus \text{Bel}_2(\Theta) = m_1 \oplus m_2(\Theta) + m_1 \oplus m_2(\{B,F\}) + \\ m_1 \oplus m_2(\{B\})$$

$$= 0.03 + 0.07 + 0.90 = 1$$

Actually, $\text{Bel}(\Theta) = 1$ in all cases since the sum of masses must always equal 1. The combination of evidence just *redistributes* the masses in different subsets.

The evidential interval of a set S, EI(S), may be defined in terms of the belief:

$$\text{EI}(S) = [\text{Bel}(S), 1 - \text{Bel}(S')]$$

If $S = \{B\}$, then $S' = \{A,F\}$ and

$$\text{Bel}(\{A,F\}) = m_1 \oplus m_2(\{A,F\}) + m_1 \oplus m_2(\{A\}) + \\ m_1 \oplus m_2(\{F\})$$

$$= 0 + 0 + 0 = 0$$

since these are not focal elements and the mass is zero for nonfocal elements. Thus, the evidential interval for $\{B\}$ is the following:

$$\text{EI}(\{B\}) = [0.90, 1 - 0]$$

$$= [0.90, 1]$$

Likewise, if $S = \{B,F\}$, then $S' = \{A\}$ and

$$\text{Bel}(\{A\}) = 0$$

since $\{A\}$ is not a focal element. Also

$$\text{Bel}(\{B,F\}) = \text{Bel}_1 \oplus \text{Bel}_2(\{B,F\}) = 0.97$$

$$\text{EI}(\{B,F\}) = [0.97, 1 - 0] = [0.97, 1]$$

$$\text{EI}(\{A\}) = [0, 1]$$

where the evidential interval [0, 1] reflects our *total ignorance* of $\{A\}$.

The evidential interval of [total belief, plausibility] can be expressed as

[evidence for support, evidence for support + ignorance]

Under probability theory, this interval is the single point

[evidence for support, evidence for support]

since ignorance is not allowed. That is, evidence which does not support must refute.

The plausibility is defined as the degree to which the evidence fails to refute X:

$$Pls(X) = 1 - Bel(X') = 1 - \sum_{Y \subseteq X'} m(X')$$

The plausible belief, Pls, stretches belief to the absolute maximum in which the unassigned belief $m(\Theta)$ may possibly contribute to the belief. While the $m(\Theta)$ could be a bomber, fighter, or airliner, under the assumption of plausibility it is assumed to contribute belief to one of its subsets. Since $\{B\}$ is a subset of Θ, it is plausible that the 0.3 belief of $m_1(\Theta)$ might be assigned to a bomber. Recall from Section 4.15 that a plausible belief is a little stronger than a possible belief, but not necessarily a belief supported by strong evidence. Another point is that Θ isn't the only type of set that stretches the belief of any set X. Any set that intersects X and its complement does it.

The **dubiety (Dbt)** or **doubt** represents the degree to which X is disbelieved or refuted. The **ignorance (Igr)** is the degree to which the mass supports X and X'. These are defined as follows:

$$Dbt(X) = Bel(X') = 1 - Pls(X)$$

$$Igr(X) = Pls(X) - Bel(X)$$

The Normalization of Belief

Suppose a third sensor now reports conflicting evidence of an airliner

$$m_3(\{A\}) = 0.95 \quad m(\Theta) = 0.05$$

Table 5.6 shows how the cross products are calculated.

	$m_1 \oplus m_2(\{B\})$ 0.90		$m_1 \oplus m_2(\{B,F\})$ 0.07		$m_1 \oplus m_2(\Theta)$ 0.03	
$m_3(\{A\}) = 0.95$	$\emptyset$	0.855	$\emptyset$	0.0665	$\emptyset$	0.0285
$m_3(\Theta) = 0.05$	$\{B\}$	0.045	$\{B,F\}$	0.0035	Θ	0.0015

Table 5.6 Combining Additional Evidence, m_3

The null set, $\emptyset$, occurs because $\{A\}$ and $\{B\}$ have no elements in common and neither does $\{A\}$ and $\{B,F\}$. Thus

$$m_1 \oplus m_2 \oplus m_3(\{A\}) = 0.0285$$
$$m_1 \oplus m_2 \oplus m_3(\{B\}) = 0.045$$
$$m_1 \oplus m_2 \oplus m_3(\{B,F\}) = 0.0035$$
$$m_1 \oplus m_2 \oplus m_3(\Theta) = 0.0015$$
$$m_1 \oplus m_2 \oplus m_3(\emptyset) = 0 \quad \text{(by definition of the null set)}$$

Note that for this example, the sum of all the masses is less than 1:

$$\sum m_1 \oplus m_2 \oplus m_3(X) = .0285 + .045 + .0035 + .0015$$
$$= .0785$$

where the sum ranges over all focal elements. However, a sum of 1 is required since the combined evidence, $m_1 \oplus m_2 \oplus m_3$, is a valid mass and the sum over all focal elements must be 1. The fact that the sum is less than 1 presents a problem.

The solution to this problem is a **normalization** of the focal elements by dividing each focal element by

```
1 - κ
```

where κ is defined for any sets X and Y as

$$\kappa = \sum_{X \cap Y = \emptyset} m_1(X)\ m_2(Y)$$

In our example,

```
κ = 0.855 + 0.0665 = 0.9215
```

and so

```
1 - κ = 1 - 0.9215 = 0.0785
```

Dividing each $m_1 \oplus m_2 \oplus m_3$ focal element by $1 - \kappa$ gives the normalized values

```
m₁ ⊕ m₂ ⊕ m₃{A}    = 0.363
m₁ ⊕ m₂ ⊕ m₃{B}    = 0.573
m₁ ⊕ m₂ ⊕ m₃{B,F}  = 0.045
m₁ ⊕ m₂ ⊕ m₃(Θ)    = 0.019
```

Notice that the one evidence of {A} has considerably eroded the belief in {B}, as would be expected.

The total normalized belief in {B} is now

```
Bel({B}) = m₁ ⊕ m₂({B}) = 0.573
```

```
Bel({B}´) = Bel({A,F})
          = m₁ ⊕ m₂ ⊕ m₃({A,F}) +
            m₁ ⊕ m₂ ⊕ m₃({A}) +
            m₁ ⊕ m₂ ⊕ m₃({F})
          = 0 + 0.363 + 0 = 0.363
```

and so the evidential interval is now

```
EI({B}) = [Bel({B}),1 - Bel({B}´)]
        = [0.573,1 - 0.363]
        = [0.573,0.637]
```

Notice that the support and plausibility of {B} has been greatly reduced by the conflicting evidence of {A}.

The general form of Dempster's Rule of Combination is

$$m_1 \oplus m_2(Z) = \frac{\displaystyle\sum_{X \cap Y = Z} m_1(X) \ m_2(Y)}{1 - \kappa}$$

where κ is defined again for convenience. No orthogonal sum is defined if $\kappa = 1$.

$$\kappa = \sum_{X \cap Y = \emptyset} m_1(X) \ m_2(Y)$$

κ indicates the amount of **evidential conflict**. $\kappa = 0$ for complete compatibility and 1 for complete contradiction. Values of $0 < \kappa < 1$ show partial compatibility.

Moving Masses and Sets

The moving mass analogy is helpful in understanding support and plausibility. The main concepts are the following:

- The support is the mass assigned to a set and all its subsets.
- Mass of a set can move freely into its subsets.
- Mass in a set cannot move into its supersets.
- Moving mass from a set into its subset can only contribute to the plausibility of the subset, not its support.
- Mass in the environment, Θ, can move into *any* subset since Θ is outside all.

In Figure 5.7 (a) all the mass is assumed inside set X and so

$$m(X) = 1$$

which means that the support of X is 1. The plausibility of X is also 1 because all the mass is in X and there is no superset that can contribute mass. Thus

$$EI(X) = [1,1]$$

If $m(X) = 0.5$ then $EI(X) = [0.5,0.5]$ and in general, if $m(X) = a$, where *a* is any constant, then $EI(X) = [a,a]$.

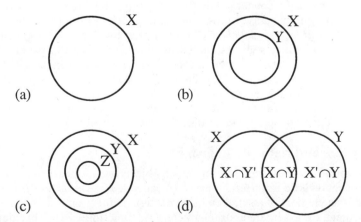

(a) (b) (c) (d)

Figure 5.7 Sets Illustrating Support and Plausibility

In Figure 5.7 (b), assume that m(X) = 0.6 and m(Y) = 0.4, which are also their supports. The plausibility of X is 0.6 since the mass of Y cannot move to X. However, the mass of X can move inside Y since Y is a subset of X and so the plausibility of Y is 0.4 + 0.6 = 1. Thus, the evidential intervals for X and Y are the following:

```
EI({X}) = [0.6,0.6]
EI({Y}) = [0.4,1]
```

Figures 5.7 (c) and (d) are used in Problem 5.4.

Difficulty with the Dempster-Shafer Theory

One difficulty with the Dempster-Shafer theory occurs with normalization and may lead to results that are contrary to our expectations (Zadeh 84a). The problem with normalization is that it ignores the belief that the object being considered does not exist.

An example quoted by Zadeh is the belief by two doctors, A and B, in a patient's illness. The beliefs in the patient's problem are as follows:.

```
mₐ(meningitis)   = 0.99
mₐ(brain tumor) = 0.01
m_B(concussion)   = 0.99
m_B(brain tumor) = 0.01
```

Notice that both doctors think there is a very low chance, 0.01, of a brain tumor but greatly disagree on the major problem. The Dempster rule of combination gives a combined belief of 1 in the brain tumor. This result is very unexpected and against our intuition since both doctors had agreed the brain tumor was very improbable. The same result of 1 for brain tumor would occur no matter what the other probabilities were.

5.5 APPROXIMATE REASONING

In this section we will discuss a theory of uncertainty based on **fuzzy logic**. This theory is primarily concerned with quantifying and reasoning using natural language in which many words have ambiguous meanings such as *tall*, *hot*, *dangerous*, *a little*, *very much*, and so on. Fuzzy logic is a development from the basic theory of fuzzy sets first stated in Lotfi Zadeh's 1965 paper (Zadeh 65). Since then the theory has been extended and applied to many fields, such as automatic camera tracking of an object (Giarratano 91c). Many camcorders and single-lens reflex cameras use fuzzy logic. Table 5.7 (Maiers 85) lists some of the major applications of fuzzy logic. The Maiers paper also includes 450 references, and another book contains over 3000 references (Kandel 82).

Fuzzy Sets and Natural Language

The traditional way of representing which objects are members of a set is in terms of a **characteristic function**, sometimes called a *discrimination function* . If an object is an element of a set, then its characteristic function is 1. If an object is not an element of a set, then its characteristic function is 0. This definition is summarized by the following characteristic function:

$$\mu_A(x) = \begin{cases} 1 & \text{if x is an element of set A} \\ 0 & \text{if x is not an element of set A} \end{cases}$$

where the objects x are elements of some universe X.

The characteristic function can also be defined in terms of a functional mapping (see Section 1.10 on functional programming):

$$\mu_A(x) : X \rightarrow \{0,1\}$$

which states that the characteristic function maps a universal set X to the set consisting of 0 and 1. This definition simply expresses the classical concept that an object is either in a set or not in a set. Sets to which this applies are called *crisp sets*, in contrast to fuzzy sets. This type of thinking dates from the Aristotelian view of **bivalent** or **two-valued logic**, in which true and false are the only possibilities.

Control algorithms
Medical diagnosis
Decision making
Economics
Engineering
Environmental
Literature
Operations research
Pattern recognition
Psychology
Reliability
Security
Science

Table 5.7 Some Applications of Fuzzy Theory

The problem with this bivalent logic is that we live in an analog, not a digital world. In the real world things are generally not in one state or another. It is only in conventional computer architecture using digital logic that bivalent logic holds. The development of analog theories of computation such as artificial neural systems and fuzzy theory more accurately represents the real world.

In fuzzy sets an object may partially belong to a set. The degree of membership in a fuzzy set is measured by a generalization of the characteristic function called the **membership** or **compatibility function** and defined as

$$\mu_A(x) : X \rightarrow [0,1]$$

Although this definition looks superficially like the definition of the characteristic function, it is actually very different. The characteristic function maps all elements of X into one of exactly two elements: 0 or 1. In contrast, the membership function maps X into the codomain of real numbers defined in the **interval** from 0 to 1 inclusive and symbolized by [0,1]. That is, the membership function is a real number

$$0 \leq \mu_A \leq 1$$

where 0 means no membership and 1 means full membership in the set. A particular value of the membership function, such as 0.5, is called a **grade of membership**.

Although it may seem strange at first to talk about an element being only partially in a set, it is actually more natural than the classical two-valued sets. Although many people wish it were, the real world is not just yes or no, black or white, right or wrong, on or off. Just as there are many shades of gray, not just black and white, so too there are many different gradations of meaning in the real world. Only debts and computer source code must be exact.

Using the membership function, real-world situations can be described. As a very simple example, consider cloudy days. A crisp set description requires an arbitrary decision as to what constitutes a cloudy day. Is a cloudy day one with a few clouds many clouds, totally overcast, partially overcast, or some other definition? Is a rainy day one with 1″ of precipitation, 2″, 3″, or is it a certain rate of precipitation?

Fuzzy sets and concepts are commonly used in natural language, such as:

```
"John is tall"
"The weather is hot"
"Turn the dial a little higher"
"Most tests are hard"
"If the dough is much too thick,
    add a lot of water"
```

where the words in italics refer to fuzzy sets and quantifiers. All these fuzzy sets and quantifiers can be represented and operated on in fuzzy theory. In particular, the "most" quantifier that was pointed out as a major limitation of predicate logic in Section 2.16 can be handled in fuzzy logic, as you will see shortly.

In natural language the terms *vague* and *fuzzy* are sometimes used synonymously. However, there is a major difference between the terms in the context of fuzzy theory. A **fuzzy proposition** contains words such as *tall,* which is the identifier of a fuzzy set TALL. Here we shall follow the convention of using all capitals to label fuzzy sets such as this. In contrast to a classic proposition such as "John is exactly five feet tall," which represents a proposition that is either true or false, a fuzzy proposition may have degrees of truth. For example, the fuzzy proposition "John is tall," may be true to some degree: *A Little True, Somewhat True, Fairly True, Very True,* and so on. A fuzzy truth value is called a **fuzzy qualifier**, and may be used as a fuzzy set or to modify a fuzzy set. Unlike crisp propositions, which are not allowed to have quantifiers, fuzzy propositions may have **fuzzy quantifiers** such as *Most, Many, Usually,* and so on, with no distinction between statements and propositions as in the classical case.

The term *vague* is used in the sense of incomplete information. For example, "John is somewhere" is vague if it does not provide sufficient information for a decision. A fuzzy proposition such as "He is tall" may also be vague if we do not know to whom the pronoun refers. There are also degrees of vagueness. A proposition such as "John is tall" is less vague than "He is tall" but is still vague if we do not know which John.

Many fuzzy words are used in natural language, such as those shown in Table 5.8. The meanings of these words can be defined in terms of fuzzy sets, as you'll see shortly. Compound terms, such as those shown in Table 5.9, can also be defined and manipulated in fuzzy theory.

While it's difficult to think of an object as being only partially in a set, another way is to consider the membership functions as representing the degree to which an object has some attribute. This concept of degree of attribute is expressed by the alternate meaning of the membership function as a compatibility function. The term *compatibility* means how well one object conforms to some attribute and is really better for describing fuzzy sets. However, the term *membership function* is most commonly used in the literature and so we will use it. In thinking about fuzzy sets, you may find it helpful to consider fuzzy elements as an object-attribute-value triplet, as described in Chapter 2. For crisp sets there is only the object-attribute since it is assumed the value is either 0 or 1. That is, in crisp sets, an element is either in a set or not in a set. For fuzzy sets the value may be anywhere in the range from 0 to 1.

---

low
medium
high
very
not
more or less
little
several
few
many
more
most
about
approximately
sort of
a great deal

Table 5.8 Some Fuzzy Terms of Natural Language

---

very low
more or less low
approximately low
not low
not very low
not more or less low
medium to sort of high
higher than slightly low
low to sort of medium
most high

Table 5.9 Compound Fuzzy Natural Language Terms

To illustrate the concept of fuzzy sets, consider the previous example

```
"John is tall."
```

If the person is an adult then one possible membership function is shown in Figure 5.8. Anyone about 7 feet and taller is considered to have a membership function of 1.0. Anyone less than 5 feet is not considered to be in the fuzzy set TALL and so the membership function is 0. Between 5 and 7 feet, the membership function is monotonically increasing with height.

This particular membership function is only one of many possible functions. The membership functions will be very different for the average person, basketball players, jockeys, and so on. For example, a five-foot-tall jockey is considered tall to some degree for a jockey even though the membership function for a five-foot-tall person in Figure 5.8 is 0.

Depending on the application, a membership function may be constructed from one person's opinions or from a group of people. In an expert system the membership function will be constructed from the expert's opinion that is being modeled by the system. Although the opinion of tallness is not likely to be modeled in an expert system, many other opinions may be modeled. Some examples might be credit risk for a loan, hostile intent of an unknown aircraft, quality of a product, suitability of a candidate for a job, and so on. Notice that opinions like these are not simple yes or no ones. Although it's possible to establish threshold values for a yes-or-no decision, there is a real question as to the validity of a crisp threshold. For example, should a person be turned down for a mortgage loan because his or her income is $29,999.99 and the threshold is $30,000.00?

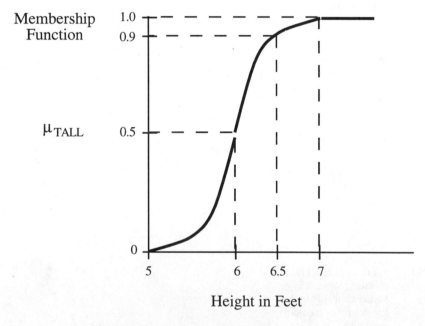

Figure 5.8 A Membership Function for the Fuzzy Set TALL

Intuitively, the membership function for a group of people also may be thought of in terms of an opinion poll. Suppose a group of off-the-street people was asked to specify a minimum value for the word *tall*. Probably no one would say that someone under 5 feet is tall. Likewise probably everyone would say that someone 7 feet and over is tall. In between 5 feet and 7 feet the percentage of people agreeing as to what constitutes *tall* is analogous to the membership function curve shown in Figure 5.8. As the value for tall increases from 5 to 6 feet, more and more people might agree that someone is tall. For this particular membership function, the **crossover point** for tall is 6 feet. A crossover point is where $\mu = 0.5$. In terms of our opinion analogy, 50 percent of the people would agree that someone 6 feet and over is tall. At 6.5 feet, the percentage of people agreeing is 90 percent. From 7 feet up, everyone agrees on tallness, and so the membership function is flat at 1.

It's important to realize that although this example is given in terms of an opinion poll of a group, the membership function is really *not* a frequency distribution. As we discussed in Chapter 4, probabilities are used for repeatable observations of the same or identical objects. Although each person in the group might give a repeatable opinion when asked the question again, the opinions are likelihoods because they express a personal belief.

The **S-function** is a mathematical function that is often used in fuzzy sets as a membership function. It is defined as follows:

$$S(x;\ \alpha, \beta, \gamma) = \begin{cases} 0 & \text{for } x \le \alpha \\ 2\left(\dfrac{x - \alpha}{\gamma - \alpha}\right)^2 & \text{for } \alpha \le x \le \beta \\ 1 - 2\left(\dfrac{x - \gamma}{\gamma - \alpha}\right)^2 & \text{for } \beta \le x \le \gamma \\ 1 & \text{for } x \ge \gamma \end{cases}$$

A plot of the S-function is shown in Figure 5.9.

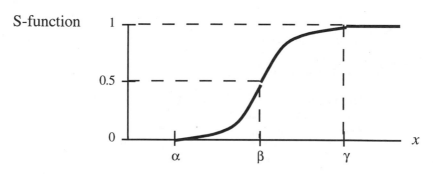

Figure 5.9 The S-function

The S-function can be a valuable tool in defining fuzzy functions such as the word *tall*. Rather than maintain a table of data defining the membership function, all the data may be compactly represented by a formula. In this definition, α, β, and γ are parameters that may be adjusted to fit the desired membership data. Depending on the given membership data, it may be possible to give an exact fit for some values of α, β, and γ, or the fit may only be approximate. Of course, the membership function may simply be defined as an S-function with no reference to any tabular data. Other functions, such as triangular ones, may also be defined depending on the application.

The S-function is flat at a value of 0 for $x \le \alpha$ and at 1 for $x \ge \gamma$. In between α and γ the S-function is a quadratic function of x. As you can see from Figure 5.9, the β parameter corresponds to the crossover point of 0.5 and is $(\alpha + \gamma) / 2$. For the TALL membership function of Figure 5.8, the S-function is the following:

$$(1) \quad S(x; \ 5, \ 6, \ 7) \ = \ \begin{cases} 0 & \text{for } x \leq 5 \\[2em] 2\left(\dfrac{x-5}{7-5}\right)^2 = \dfrac{(x-5)^2}{2} \\ \quad \text{for } 5 \leq x \leq 6 \\[2em] 1 - 2\left(\dfrac{x-7}{7-5}\right)^2 = 1 - \dfrac{(x-7)^2}{2} \\ \quad \text{for } 6 \leq x \leq 7 \\[2em] 1 & \text{for } x \geq 7 \end{cases}$$

A membership function for the fuzzy proposition "X is close to γ" is shown in Figure 5.10. For example, this membership function could represent all numbers close to a specified value γ, as in "X is close to 6," where X could be defined as $\{5.9, 6, 6.1\}$. The membership function may be expressed as

$$\mu_{\text{CLOSE}}(x) \ = \ \frac{1}{1 + \left(\dfrac{x-\gamma}{\beta}\right)^2}$$

with crossover points

$$x = \gamma \pm \beta$$

The parameter β is the **half-width** of the curve at the crossover point, as shown in Figure 5.10. Larger values of β correspond to a wider curve and smaller values correspond to a more narrow curve. A larger β means that numbers must be more close to γ to have a significantly large membership value. Notice that in this definition the membership function only goes to zero at infinity.

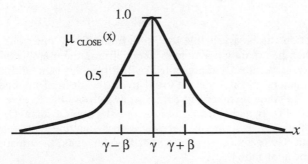

Figure 5.10 A Membership Function for the Fuzzy Proposition "X is close to γ"

A function that also gives a similar curve but does go to zero at specified points is the following:

$$\prod(x;\ \beta,\ \gamma) = \begin{cases} S(x;\ \gamma - \beta,\ \gamma - \beta/2,\ \gamma) & \text{for } x \le \gamma \\ 1 - S(x;\ \gamma,\ \gamma + \beta/2, \gamma + \beta) & \text{for } x \ge \gamma \end{cases}$$

This $\prod$-**function** is plotted in Figure 5.11. Notice that the β parameter is now the **bandwidth** or **total width** at the crossover points. The $\prod$-function goes to zero at the points

$$x = \gamma \pm \beta$$

while the crossover points are at

$$x = \gamma \pm \frac{\beta}{2}$$

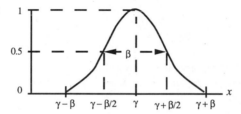

Figure 5.11 The $\prod$-function

Instead of a continuous function, the membership function can be a finite set of elements. For example, in the universe of heights defined as

$$U = \{5, 5.5, 6, 6.5, 7, 7.5, 8\}$$

a fuzzy subset can be defined for a finite set of elements for TALL as follows:

$$\text{TALL} = \{0/5, .125/5.5, .5/6, .875/6.5, 1/7, 1/7.5, 1/8\}$$

In this fuzzy set the symbol "/" separates the membership grades from the numbers corresponding to the heights. Note that the "/" does not mean division in customary fuzzy set notation. The fuzzy set elements for which $\mu(x) > 0$ make up the **support** of the fuzzy set. For TALL, the support is all the elements except 0/5.

A finite fuzzy subset of N elements is represented in standard fuzzy notation as the union of fuzzy singletons μ_i/x_i, where the "+" signs are Boolean union.

$$(2)\quad F = \mu_1/x_1 + \mu_2/x_2 + \ldots \mu_N/x_N$$

$$F = \sum_{i=1}^{N} \mu_i/x_i$$

$$F = \bigcup_{i=1}^{N} \mu_i/x_i$$

In some papers the "/ " symbol is not written and so F can be written in the forms

$$(3) \quad F = \mu_1 x_1 + \mu_2 x_2 + \ldots \mu_n x_N$$

$$F = \sum_{i=1}^{N} \mu_i x_i$$

$$F = \bigcup_{i=1}^{N} \mu_i x_i$$

Both equations (2) and (3) represent finite fuzzy subsets of N elements. Equation (3) is useful for writing fuzzy sets in a compact symbolic form. However, the forms of equation (3) are difficult for people to read when numbers are involved , such as in

$$F = .127 + .385$$

Without the "/" separator, it is impossible to tell if the membership grades are .1 and .3 or .12 and .38, or something else. This is why the notation

$$F = .1/27 + .38/5$$

is better when dealing with numbers.

The **support** of a fuzzy set, F, is a subset of the universe set, X, defined as

$$support(F) = \{x \mid x \in X \text{ and } \mu_F(x) > 0 \}$$

The support set is usually written with the abbreviation **supp**, as in

$$supp(F)$$

for compactness. The advantage of the support is that a fuzzy set F can be written as

$$F = \{ \mu_F(x)/x \mid x \in supp(F) \}$$

which means that only those fuzzy elements whose membership function is greater than zero contribute to F. Thus the TALL set can be written without the 0/5 element since this element is not in the support set.

$$TALL = \{.125/5.5, .5/6, .875/6.5, 1/7, 1/7.5, 1/8\}$$

Although there is only a small savings of one element, the reduction in elements can be significant for fuzzy sets with many elements of membership zero.

A related concept to the support is α–**cuts**. The α-cut of a set is a nonfuzzy set of the universe whose elements have a membership function greater than or equal to some value α.

$$F_\alpha = \{ x \mid \mu_F(x) \geq \alpha \} \qquad \text{for } 0 < \alpha \leq 1$$

Some α-cuts of the TALL set are

$$TALL_{0.1} = \{ 5.5, 6, 6.5, 7, 7.5, 8 \}$$

$$TALL_{0.5} = \{ 6, 6.5, 7, 7.5, 8 \}$$

$$TALL_{0.8} = \{ 6.5, 7, 7.5, 8 \}$$

$$TALL_{1} = \{ 7, 7.5, 8 \}$$

Notice that the α-cuts of a set are subsets of the support. The values of α can be chosen arbitrarily but are usually picked to select desired subsets of the universe.

Another term often used with fuzzy sets is the **height**, which is the maximum membership grade of an element. For our TALL set, the maximum membership grade is 1. If an element in a fuzzy set attains the maximum possible grade, then the set is called ***normalized***. Usually the membership grades are defined in the closed interval [0,1] and so the maximum possible membership grade is 1. However, the grades may be defined in other intervals and so the membership grade may not necessarily be 1.

An arbitrary fuzzy subset of the universe over the **continuum** is written in the form of an integral. The term *continuum* refers to the set of real numbers. The integral represents the union of the fuzzy singletons, $\mu(x) / x$. For example, we could define

$$TALL = \int_X \mu_{TALL}(x) / x$$

$$= \int_5^8 \mu_{TALL}(x) / x$$

$$= \int_5^6 \frac{(x-5)^2}{2} / x + \int_6^7 \left[1 - \frac{(x-7)^2}{2} \right] / x + \int_7^8 1/x$$

using an S-function for TALL. In this formula the "+" signs separating the integrals stand for union, as in Boolean logic notation, rather than arithmetic addition.

There are different types of fuzzy sets. The elementary **type 1 fuzzy subset**, F, of a universe, X, is defined as follows:

$$\mu_F: X \rightarrow [0,1]$$

That is, a type 1 fuzzy subset is simply defined by giving numeric values for its membership function in the closed interval of real numbers from 0 to 1. For example,

$$TALL = .125/5.5 + .5/6 + .875/6.5 + 1/7 + 1/7.5 + 1/8$$

is a type 1 set because its membership grades are all real numbers in [0,1]. Likewise, from equation (1)

$$\mu_{TALL}(x) = S(x; 5, 6, 7)$$

is a type 1 fuzzy subset.

In general, a **type N fuzzy subset** is defined by a mapping for μ_F from a universe to the set of fuzzy subsets of type $N - 1$. For example, a **type 2 fuzzy subset** is defined in terms of a type 1 subset. For heights, a type 2 fuzzy set can be

$$\mu_{TALL}(5) = \text{LESS THAN AVERAGE}$$
$$\mu_{TALL}(6) = \text{AVERAGE}$$
$$\mu_{TALL}(7) = \text{GREATER THAN AVERAGE}$$

where LESS THAN AVERAGE, AVERAGE, and GREATER THAN AVERAGE are all fuzzy subsets of type 1. These might be defined as the following fuzzy subsets:

$$\mu_{\text{LESS THAN AVERAGE}}(x) = 1 - S(x; 4.5, 5, 5.5)$$
$$\mu_{\text{AVERAGE}}(x) = \prod (x; 1, 5.5)$$
$$\mu_{\text{GREATER THAN AVERAGE}}(x) = S(x; 5.5, 6, 6.5)$$

Fuzzy Set Operations

An ordinary crisp set is a special case of a fuzzy set with membership function {0,1}. All the definitions, proofs, and theorems of fuzzy sets must be compatible in the limit as the fuzziness goes to 0 and the fuzzy sets become crisp sets. The theory of fuzzy sets thus has a wider range of applications than crisp sets and so can deal with situations involving subjective opinions. The basic idea of fuzzy sets is to specify fuzzy real world concepts such as TALL by a set of fuzzy elements rather than demanding a sharp binary threshold. Following is a summary of some fuzzy set operators in a universe X.

- **set equality**

$$A = B$$

$$\mu_A(x) = \mu_B(x) \qquad \text{for all } x \in X$$

- **set complement**

$$A'$$

$$\mu_{A'}(x) = 1 - \mu_A(x) \quad \text{for all } x \in X$$

Figure 5.12 illustrates the fuzzy complement of a set. This definition of complementation is justified by Bellman and Giertz (Bellman 1973).

- **set containment**

$$A \subseteq B$$

Fuzzy set A is contained in B or is a **subset** of B if and only if

```
μA(x) ≤ μB(x)      for all x ∈ X
```

Fuzzy set A is a **proper subset** of B if A is a subset of B and the two are unequal.

```
μA(x) ≤ μB(x) and μA(x) < μB(x)
     for at least one x ∈ X
```

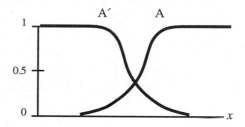

Figure 5.12 Fuzzy Complement

> • **set union**

```
A ∪ B
```

```
μA ∪ B(x) = ∨(μA(x),μB(x))   for all x ∈ X
```

where the **join operator**, ∨, means the maximum of the arguments.

> • **set intersection**

```
A ∩ B
```

```
μA ∩ B(x) = ∧(μA(x),μB(x))   for all x ∈ X
```

where the **meet operator**, ∧, means the minimum of the arguments.

You have already encountered the join and meet operators when discussing the application of fuzzy logic in combining antecedents in PROSPECTOR in Section 4.13, in the subsection "Combining Evidence by Fuzzy Logic." The justification for using the max and min functions for join and meet is given in (Bellman 1973).

With these definitions, the standard laws for crisp sets of commutativity, associativity, and so forth hold for fuzzy sets, with the exception of the Laws of the Excluded Middle and Contradiction. Thus it is possible that for a fuzzy set A

```
A ∪ A´ ≠ U and A ∩ A´ ≠ ∅
```

where ∅ is the empty set and U is the universe. Since fuzzy sets may have no definite boundary, the only constraint on intersection is that

```
A ∩ A´ = min(μA(x),μA´(x)) ≤ 0.5
```

if $\mu(x)$ is defined in the closed range [0,1] and $\mu_{A'}(x) = 1 - \mu_A(x)$.

Likewise, the only constraint on union is

$$A \cup A' = \max(\mu_A(x), \mu_{A'}(x)) \geq 0.5$$

Because fuzzy sets A and A' may overlap, they may not cover the universe completely.

If the Laws of the Excluded Middle and Contradiction is defined to hold for fuzzy sets, then idempotentcy and distribution may not be satisfied. For idempotentcy, this is

$$A \cup A \neq A \qquad A \cap A \neq A$$

Because of the fuzzy nature of sets, it appears more reasonable to accept that the Laws of the Excluded Middle and Contradiction do not hold so that idempotentcy will be satisfied.

- **set product**

$$A\ B$$

$$\mu_{AB}(x) = \mu_A(x)\mu_B(x)$$

- **power of a set**

$$A^N$$

$$\mu_{A^N}(x) = (\mu_A(x))^N$$

- **probabilistic sum**

$$A \mathbin{\hat{+}} B$$

$$\mu_{A\hat{+}B}(x) = \mu_A(x) + \mu_B(x) - \mu_A(x)\mu_B(x)$$

$$= 1 - (1 - \mu_A(x))(1 - \mu_B(x))$$

where the "+" and "−" are ordinary arithmetic operators.

- **bounded sum** or **bold union**

$$A \oplus B$$

$$\mu_{A\oplus B}(x) = \wedge(1, (\mu_A(x) + \mu_B(x)))$$

where the $\wedge$ is the min function and "+" is the arithmetic operator.

• **bounded product** or **bold intersection**

A ℬ B

$$\mu_{A.B}(x) = \vee(0, (\mu_A(x) + \mu_B(x) - 1))$$

where the $\vee$ is the max function and "+" is the arithmetic operator. The bounded sum and product operators do not satisfy idempotentcy, distributivity and absorption, but do satisfy commutativity, associativity, de Morgan's laws, A ⊕ U = U, A ℬØ = Ø, and the Laws of Excluded Middle and Contradiction (see Appendix C for a summary).

• **bounded difference**

A |−| B

$$\mu_{A|-|B}(x) = \vee(0, (\mu_A(x) - \mu_B(x)))$$

where the "−" separating μ_A and μ_B is the arithmetic minus operator. A | − | B represents those elements that are more in A than B. The complement can be written in terms of the universe set, U, and bounded difference as

A′ = U |−| A

• **concentration**

CON(A)

$$\mu_{CON(A)}(x) = (\mu_A(x))^2$$

The CON operation concentrates fuzzy elements by reducing the membership grades more of elements that have smaller membership grades. Figure 5.13 illustrates the CON operation. This operation and the following ones of DIL, NORM, and INT have no counterpart in ordinary set operations. The CON operator can be used to roughly approximate the effect of the linguistic modifier *Very*. That is, for some fuzzy set F,

Very F = F^2

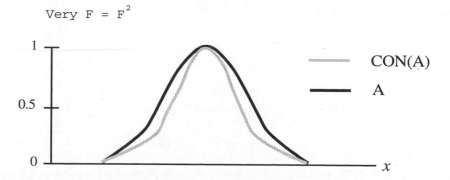

Figure 5.13 Concentration of a Fuzzy Set

For the example of the TALL set,

```
TALL = .125/5 + .5/6 + .875/6.5 + 1/7 + 1/7.5 + 1/8
```

then

```
Very TALL = .016/5 + .25/6 + .76/6.5 +
            1/7 + 1/7.5 + 1/8
```

Notice how the membership grades have decreased for all except those of grade 1. The net effect is to make the Very TALL fuzzy set include fewer small grades.

• dilation

```
DIL(A)
```

$$\mu_{DIL(A)}(x) = (\mu_A(x))^{0.5}$$

The DIL operation dilates fuzzy elements by increasing the membership grade more of elements with smaller membership grades. Figure 5.14 illustrates DIL. Notice that it performs the inverse operation to concentration for these choices of powers 2 and 0.5.

```
A = DIL(CON(A)) = CON(DIL(A))
```

The dilation operator is roughly approximated by the linguistic modifier *More Or Less*. Thus for any fuzzy set F,

```
More Or Less F = F^0.5 = DIL(F)
```

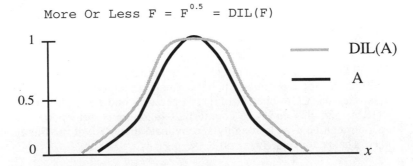

Figure 5.14 Dilation of a Fuzzy Set

• intensification

```
INT(A)
```

$$\mu_{INT(A)}(x) = \begin{cases} 2\,(\mu_A(x))^2 & \text{for } 0 \leq \mu_A(x) \leq 0.5 \\ 1 - 2(1 - \mu_A(x))^2 & \text{for } 0.5 < \mu_A(x) \leq 1 \end{cases}$$

The INT operation is like contrast intensification of a picture. As illustrated in Figure 5.15, the intensification raises the membership grade of those elements within the crossover points and reduces the membership grade of those outside the crossover points. As an electronic analogy, consider the crossover points as defining the bandwidth of a signal. Intensification amplifies the signal within the bandwidth while reducing the "noise" outside the bandwidth. Intensification thus increases the contrast in grade between those elements within the crossover points compared to those outside the crossover points.

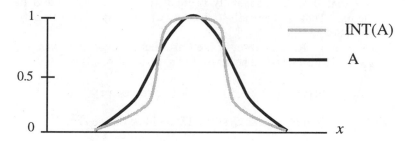

Figure 5.15 Intensification of a Fuzzy Set

• **normalization**

NORM(A)

$\mu_{\text{NORM}(A)}(x) = \mu_A(x)/\max\{\mu_A(x)\}$

where the max function returns the maximum membership grade for all elements x. If the maximum grade is < 1, then all membership grades will be increased. If the max = 1, then the membership grades are unchanged.

Fuzzy Relations

An important concept that can also be modeled by fuzzy sets is that of a **relation**. The intuitive idea of a relation is that of some association between elements. Some examples of relations are

```
Bob and Ellis are friends
Los Angeles and New York are very far apart
1, 2, 3, and 4 are much less than 100
1, 2, and 3 are small numbers
apples and oranges are sort of round fruits
```

where the italicized words are fuzzy.

The **Cartesian product** of N crisp sets is defined as the crisp set whose elements are ordered N-tuples $(x_1, x_2, x_3, \ldots x_N)$, where each x_i is an element of its crisp set X_i. For the two sets A and B,

$$A \times B = \{(a,b) \mid a \in A \text{ and } b \in B\}$$

Defining

```
A = {chocolate, strawberry}
B = {pie, milk, candy}
```

then the Cartesian product is

$$A \times B = \{(\text{chocolate, pie}), (\text{chocolate, milk}),$$
$$(\text{chocolate, candy}), (\text{strawberry, pie}),$$
$$(\text{strawberry, milk}), (\text{strawberry, candy})\}$$

Notice that $B \times A$ is generally unequal to $A \times B$ if A and B have different elements. That is, generally $(a,b) \neq (b,a)$. $A \times B$ is said to define a **binary variable**, (a,b).

A relation, R, is a subset of the Cartesian product. For example, the relation that R = LIKES PIE could be defined as a subset of $A \times B$ by

$$R = \{(\text{chocolate, pie}), (\text{strawberry, pie})\}$$

while the relation R = LIKES SWEETS could be defined as

$$R = \{(\text{chocolate, pie}), (\text{chocolate, candy}),$$
$$(\text{strawberry, pie}), (\text{strawberry, candy})\}$$

A relation is also sometimes called a *mapping* because it associates elements from one domain to another. In $A \times B$, the relation is a mapping from $A \rightarrow B$, where the $\rightarrow$ means a mapping in this context. Chocolate in A is mapped or associated with pie and candy in B, and likewise for strawberry.

If X and Y are universe sets, then

$$R = \{ \mu_R(x,y)/(x,y) \mid (x,y) \subseteq X \times Y\}$$

is a fuzzy relation on $X \times Y$.

A fuzzy relation is fundamentally a fuzzy subset in the Cartesian product universe. Another definition of fuzzy sets is useful when dealing with fuzzy graphs (Zimmerman 85).

The **fuzzy relation** for N sets is defined as an extension of the crisp relation to include the membership grade. That is,

$$R = \{\mu_R(x_1, x_2, \ldots x_N)/(x_1, x_2, \ldots x_N)$$
$$\mid x_i \in X_i, i = 1, \ldots N)\}$$

which associates the membership grade of each N-tuple. For the binary relation of the pie example, another definition could be

$$R = \{.9/(\text{chocolate, pie}), .2/(\text{strawberry, pie})\}$$

as the fuzzy relation to indicate that a person is much more fond of chocolate pie than strawberry pie.

A convenient way of representing a relation is by a matrix. For the relation LIKES SWEETS,

$$M_R = \begin{array}{c} \text{chocolate} \\ \\ \text{strawberry} \end{array} \begin{array}{cc} \text{pie} & \text{candy} \\ \left[\begin{array}{cc} 0.9 & 0.7 \\ 0.2 & 0.1 \end{array}\right] \end{array}$$

where M_R is the matrix representation of the fuzzy relation. Notice that for crisp sets, M_R would consist only of zeros and ones expressing whether you totally like or totally dislike the ordered pairs (flavor, sweet). (This is probably the best proof that the world is truly fuzzy rather than crisp.)

The **composition** of relations is the net effect of applying one relation after another. For the case of two binary relations P and Q, the composition of their relations is the binary relation R.

$$R(A,C) = Q(A,B) \ o \ P(B,C)$$

where

R(A,C) is a relation between A and C
Q(A,B) is a relation between A and B
P(B,C) is a relation between B and C
A, B, and C are sets

and o is the **composition operator**. The relation of R is the same as applying P first followed by Q. In terms of membership grades,

$$R = \{\mu_R(a,c)/(a,c) \ | \ a \in A, \ c \in C\}$$

where μ_R is defined as follows:

$$\mu_R(a,c) = \bigvee_{b \in B} [\mu_Q(a,b) \wedge \mu_P(b,c)]$$

$$= \max_{b \in B} [\min (\mu_Q(a,b), \mu_P(b,c))]$$

This composition is commonly defined by the **max-min matrix product** or simply **max-min**. The max and min functions can be used in place of addition and multiplication for matrix operations. As an example, define

$$Q = \left[\begin{array}{cc} 0.1 & 0.2 \\ 0.3 & 0.4 \end{array}\right] \qquad P = \left[\begin{array}{ccc} 0.1 & 0.3 & 0.5 \\ 0.2 & 0.0 & 0.4 \end{array}\right]$$

then the composition, R, is

$$R = Q \ o \ P = \left[\begin{array}{cc} 0.1 & 0.2 \\ 0.3 & 0.4 \end{array}\right] \ o \ \left[\begin{array}{ccc} 0.1 & 0.3 & 0.5 \\ 0.2 & 0.0 & 0.4 \end{array}\right]$$

$$R = Q \circ P = \begin{bmatrix} \max(0.1,0.2) & \max(0.1,0.0) & \max(0.1,0.2) \\ \max(0.1,0.2) & \max(0.3,0.0) & \max(0.3,0.4) \end{bmatrix}$$

$$= \begin{bmatrix} 0.2 & 0.1 & 0.2 \\ 0.2 & 0.3 & 0.4 \end{bmatrix}$$

Other common relational operator definitions are the **max-product** and **relational join** (Klir 88).

Fuzzy relations have important applications to approximate reasoning, as shown later. The **projection** of a relation is another useful fuzzy set concept. Basically, the projection eliminates specified elements. Before giving the formal definition, let's look at a simple example in Table 5.10.

	y1	y2	y3	1st Projection	
x1	0.2	0.1	0.2	0.2	
x2	0.2	0.3	0.4	0.4	
2nd Projection	0.2	0.3	0.4	0.4	**Total Projection**

Table 5.10 A Relation and Its Projections

Table 5.10 shows the projections of the previous relation for R, where the rows and columns have been given identifiers of x_i and y_i for convenience. Notice that the column labeled *1st Projection* contains the maximum membership grade for the row. Likewise, the row labeled *2nd Projection* contains the maximum membership grade of each column. The cell of value 0.4 at the lower right labeled *Total Projection* is the maximum membership grade of the total relation.

The relation for R can be written in terms of x_i and y_i as the following:

$$R = .2/x_1,y_1 + .1/x_1,y_2 + .2/x_1,y_3 +$$
$$.2/x_2,y_1 + .3/x_2,y_2 + .4/x_2,y_3$$

The 1st projection is denoted by R_1 and is obtained by dropping all except the first point, x_i, of the Cartesian pair, x_i, y_j, where the leftmost element is defined as first.

$$R_1 = .2/x_1 + .1/x_1 + .2/x_1 + .2/x_2 + .3/x_2 + .4/x_2$$

The equation for R_1 is further reduced after the projection because the "+" represents the union operator and so only the maximum fuzzy element is kept.

$$R_1 = .2/x_1 + .4/x_2$$

Likewise, the 2nd projection retains only the second point, y_j, of each Cartesian pair.

$$R_2 = .2/y_1 + .1/y_2 + .2/y_3 + .2/y_1 + .3/y_2 + .4/y_3$$

which reduces to the following upon application of the union operator.

$$R_2 = .2/y_1 + .3/y_2 + .4/y_3$$

In the general case of a relation involving N Cartesian points, drop all components of the N-tuple except those points on which the projection is to be made. For example, if the relation is over N points, then R_{136} would drop all points except the first, third, and sixth.

For a relation over the universe $X \times Y$,

$$R = \{\mu_R(x,y)/(x,y)\} \text{ for all } (x,y) \in X \times Y$$

the 1st projection is defined as

$$\text{proj}(R;X) = R_1$$

where

$$R_1 = \{\max_y \ \mu_R(x,y)/x \mid (x,y) \in X \times Y\}$$

and the max is taken over all y. Likewise,

$$\text{proj}(R;Y) = R_2$$

where

$$R_2 = \{\max_x \mu_R(x,y)/y \mid (x,y) \in X \times Y\}$$

where the max is taken over all x values for R_2.

The **cylindrical extension** of the projection relation is defined as the largest fuzzy relation that is compatible with a projection. The cylindrical projection is somewhat analogous to projection since it expands the projected value (which is max) for all other elements, e.g.,

$$\text{proj}(R;X) = R_1 = .2/x_1 + .4/x2$$

so

$$R_1 = .2/x_1,y_1 + .2/x_1,y_2 + .2/x_1,y_3 \\ + .4/x_2,y_1 + .4/x_2,y_2 + .4/x_2,y_3$$

$$R_2 = .2/y_1,x_1 + .2/y_1,x_2 + .3/y_2,x_1 \\ + .3/y_2,x_1 + .3/y_2,x_2 \\ + .4/y_2,x_1 + .4/y_3,x_2$$

i.e., replace the second variable, $.2/x_1$ {all var} + $.4/x_2$, {all var}. Since the projection gives the $\max_\mu$ then the cylindrical extension is the greatest relation compatible with the projection.

For the previous example,

$$\overline{R_1} = \begin{bmatrix} 0.2 & 0.2 & 0.2 \\ 0.4 & 0.4 & 0.4 \end{bmatrix}$$

$$\overline{R_2} = \begin{bmatrix} 0.2 & 0.3 & 0.4 \\ 0.2 & 0.3 & 0.4 \end{bmatrix}$$

where a bar over a projection symbolizes the cylindrical extension of the projection.

The composition can be defined in terms of projections and cylindrical extensions (Zadeh 75). For the binary relation R defined on the universe set U_1 x U_2, and S defined on U_2 x U_3, the composition is

$$R \ o \ S = proj \ (\ \overline{R} \ \cap \ \overline{S} \ ; \ U_1 \ \times \ U_3)$$

Linguistic Variables

One very important application of fuzzy sets is in **computational linguistics**. The goal is to calculate with natural language statements analogous to the way that logic calculates with logic statements. Fuzzy sets and **linguistic variables** can be used to quantify the meaning of natural language, which can then be manipulated. A linguistic variable is assigned values that are expressions such as words, phrases, or sentences in a natural or an artificial language. Table 5.11 shows some linguistic variables and typical values that might be assigned to them.

Linguistic Variable	Typical Values
height	dwarf, short, average, tall, giant
number	almost none, several, few, many
stage of life	infant, toddler, child, teenager, adult
color	red, blue, green, yellow, orange
light	dim, faint, normal, bright, intense
dessert	pie, cake, ice cream, baked alaska

Table 5.11 Typical Values

Although it's possible to define values, such as the color red, corresponding to these linguistic values, they are very much subjective in nature. For example, the color red corresponds to a range in frequencies that the eye perceives as red, not just a single frequency. Other problems are colors such as aquamarine. Is it blue or green?

Linguistic variables are commonly used in heuristic rules. However, the variables may be implied, as illustrated in the first two rules of Table 5.12.

IF the TV is too dim THEN turn up the brightness
IF it's too hot THEN add some cold
IF the pressure is too high THEN open the relief valve
IF interest rates are going up THEN buy bonds
IF interest rates are going down THEN buy stocks

Table 5.12 Some Heuristic Rules Involving Implied Linguistic Variables

The implied linguistic variables are Picture Quality and Water Temperature.

Some linguistic variables such as Picture Quality may be labels of fuzzy sets of order 2. For example, the values of Picture Quality could be

color, tint, brightness, noise, consistency

in which each of these values may be linguistic variables that can take on values that are fuzzy sets. Thus linguistic variables may be arranged in a hierarchy corresponding to their fuzzy set order. Eventually a fuzzy set of order 1 is reached, such as TALL or BRIGHTNESS, which is defined as a mapping into the closed interval [0,1], and so the linguistic value becomes a numeric range.

The **term-set**, T(L), of a linguistic variable, L, is the set of values it may take. For example,

```
T(PIE) = CHOCOLATE + APPLE + STRAWBERRY + PECAN
```

where each of the terms in T(PIE) is a label of a fuzzy set. These sets may be the union of other sets consisting of subsets. For example,

```
CHOCOLATE = SEMI-SWEET CHOCOLATE + MILK CHOCOLATE +
            DUTCH CHOCOLATE + DARK CHOCOLATE + ...
```

Another definition for the CHOCOLATE fuzzy set may involve **hedges** to modify the meaning of a set. For example, a CHOCOLATE fuzzy set of one type of chocolate could be defined as follows:

```
CHOCOLATE = Very CHOCOLATE + Very Very CHOCOLATE +
            More Or Less CHOCOLATE +
            Slightly CHOCOLATE +
            Plus CHOCOLATE + Not Very CHOCOLATE + ...
```

Standard hedges can be defined in terms of some fuzzy set operators and a fuzzy set, F, as shown in Table 5.13.

Hedge	Operator Definition
Very F	$CON(F) = F^2$
More Or Less F	$DIL(F) = F^{0.5}$
Plus F	$F^{1.25}$
Not F	$1 - F$
Not Very F	$1 - CON(F)$
Slightly F	INT [NORM (PLUS F And NOT (VERY F))]

Table 5.13 Some Linguistic Hedges and Operators

As shown by the "Not Very F " hedge, other compound hedges can be made by combining operators. Notice that the "And" in the "Slightly" hedge is the fuzzy set operator for intersection, $\cap$, acting on the fuzzy sets "Plus F" and "Not (Very F)."

The hierarchy of the linguistic variable "Appetite" is illustrated in Figure 5.16. The LIGHT and HEAVY fuzzy sets are assumed to be S-functions whereas the MODERATE set is taken as a $\prod$-function.

Notice that there is overlap of the fuzzy sets such as LIGHT and MODERATE and even LIGHT and HEAVY. In classical crisp sets there would be no overlap since all these sets would be disjoint. That is, a LIGHT appetite could not be a MODERATE or a HEAVY appetite. However, in fuzzy sets there are usually not (unless defined) sharp boundaries between sets.

The hedged sets are shown as dashed curves within the borders of the fuzzy sets. The hedges, such as *Very*, act as modifiers to the linguistic values to yield the fuzzy sets Very LIGHT, Very MODERATE, and Very HEAVY.

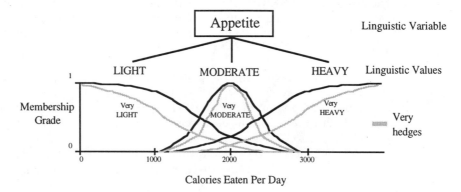

Figure 5.16 The Linguistic Variable "Appetite" and Its Values

A linguistic variable must have a valid syntax and semantics, which can be specified by fuzzy sets or rules. A **syntactic rule** defines the well-formed expressions in T(L). For example, the term-set

$$T(Age) = \{OLD, \ Very \ OLD, \ Very \ Very \ OLD, \ ...\}$$
can be generated recursively using the following syntactic rule (Zadeh 73).

$$T^{i+1} = \{OLD\} \ \cup \ \{Very \ T^i\}$$

For example,

$$T^0 = \emptyset \ (the \ null \ set)$$

$$T^1 = \{OLD\}$$

$$T^2 = \{OLD, \ Very \ OLD\}$$

$$T^3 = \{OLD, \ Very \ OLD, \ Very \ Very \ OLD\}$$

The **semantic rule** associated with T(L) defines the **meaning** of a term, L_i, in L, by a fuzzy set. For example, the semantic rule for Very OLD could be defined as

$$Very \ OLD = \mu_{OLD}^2$$

where the membership function could be defined as the following S-function:

$$\mu_{OLD}(X) = S(x; \ 60, \ 70, \ 80)$$

A **primary term** is a term such as YOUNG, OLD, CHOCOLATE, STRAWBERRY, and so on, whose meaning must be defined before a hedge. Hedges modify the meaning of the primary terms to yield other terms in a term set, such as Very YOUNG, Very OLD, Very CHOCOLATE, Slightly

CHOCOLATE, and so forth. The meaning of the hedged fuzzy sets is determined by applying the appropriate fuzzy set operators. For example,

$$\mu_{\text{Very CHOCOLATE}} = \mu^2_{\text{CHOCOLATE}}$$

$$\mu_{\text{Not CHOCOLATE}} = 1 - \mu_{\text{CHOCOLATE}}$$

$$\mu_{\text{More Or Less CHOCOLATE}} = \mu^{0.5}_{\text{CHOCOLATE}}$$

$$\mu_{\text{Not Very CHOCOLATE}} = 1 - \mu_{\text{Very CHOCOLATE}}$$

Just as conventional language grammars can be defined by BNF notation (see Section 2.2), so too can a **fuzzy grammar**. In fact, the grammar described in Section 2.2 used a fuzzy modifier, "heavy," as in

```
<adjective> → heavy
```

to generate the **fuzzy production**

```
an eater was the heavy man
```

In this production, *heavy* is a hedge on the fuzzy set *man*. At first you may not think *man* is a fuzzy set. However, when does a boy become a man? In some cultures a boy becomes a man at age 12 or after a religious ceremony. Some governments define a male as a man at 18 or 21. Newspaper articles appear to have a policy of referring to males ages 17 to 19 as men if accused of committing a crime, but refer to a 17 to 19 year-old as a youth if he has done something commendable. Males in the armed forces are sometimes referred to as boys and sometimes as men, especially in political speeches.

A fuzzy grammar can be specified in BNF notation by adding nonterminals such as

```
<Range Phrase> ::= <Hedged Primary> TO
                   <Hedged Primary>
<Hedged Primary> ::= <Hedge> <Primary> | <Primary>
<Hedge> ::= Very | More Or Less | A Little
<Primary> ::= SHORT | MEDIUM | TALL
```

to generate productions such as

```
Very SHORT TO Very TALL
A Little TALL TO Very SHORT
More Or Less MEDIUM TO TALL
```

A novel application of the linguistic variable concept is the fuzzy car built by Sugeno at the Tokyo Institute of Technology (Zadeh 88). The Sugeno car uses a control system based on fuzzy logic that allows autonomous operation on a rectangular track. The car can park itself at a specified space and also learn from examples. Linguistic variables are used in rules that control the car's movement. Many other types of fuzzy logic control systems have also been built to control devices and industrial processes such as a cement kiln to manufacture cement (Larsen 81).

Extension Principle

The **extension principle** is a very important concept in fuzzy theory. This principle defines how to extend the domain of a given crisp function to include fuzzy sets. By using the extension principle, any ordinary or crisp function from mathematics, science, engineering, business, and so on can be extended to work in a fuzzy domain with fuzzy sets. This principle makes fuzzy sets applicable to all fields.

Let f be an ordinary function that maps from a universe X to Y. If F is a fuzzy subset of X such that

$$F = \int_X \mu_F(x)/x$$

then the extension principle defines the image of the fuzzy set F under a mapping function f(x) as

$$f(F) = \int_X \mu_F(x)/f(x)$$

For example, let f(x) be defined as a crisp function that squares its arguments:

$$f(x) = x^2$$

The extension principle states how to implement a squaring function of fuzzy sets:

$$f(F) = \int_X \mu_F(x)/f(x) = \int_X \mu_F(x)/x^2$$

For example, define the universes X and Y as the closed real interval [0,1000], and the fuzzy set:

$$F = .3/15 + .8/20 + 1/30$$

then the extension principle defines the mapping f(F) as

$$f(F) = \int_X \mu_F(x)/f(x)$$

$$= .3/f(15) + .8/f(20) + 1/f(30)$$

$$f(F) = .3/225 + .8/400 + 1/900$$

Fuzzy Logic

Just as classical logic forms the basis of conventional expert systems, fuzzy logic forms the basis of **fuzzy expert systems**. Besides dealing with uncertainty, fuzzy expert systems are also capable of modeling **commonsense reasoning**, which is very difficult for conventional systems to do.

A basic limitation of classical logic is its restriction to the two values of true and false. As we discussed in Chapters 2 and 3 this restriction has advantages and disadvantages. The main advantage is that systems based on two-valued logic are easy to model deductively and so the inferences can be exact. The main disadvantage is that very little in the real world is really two-valued. The real world is an analog—not a digital world.

The limitations of two-valued logic have been known since the time of Aristotle. Although Aristotle first formulated the syllogistic rules of inference and the Law of the Excluded Middle, he recognized that propositions about future events were neither actually true or actually false until they occurred.

A number of different logic theories based on multiple values of truth have been formulated, including those of Lukasiewicz, Bochvar, Kleene, Heyting, and Reichenbach. Some common types are those based on three values of truth representing TRUE, FALSE, and UNKNOWN. These **trivalent** or **three-valued logics** commonly represent the three truth values of TRUE, FALSE, and UNKNOWN by 1, 0, and 1/2, respectively.

Several generalized logics of N truth values, where N is an arbitrary integer number greater than or equal to two, have been developed. Lukasiewicz developed the first N-valued logic in the 1930s. In an N-valued logic, the set T_N of truth values are assumed evenly divided over the closed interval [0,1].

$$T_N = \left\{ \frac{i}{N-1} \right\} \quad \text{for } 0 \leq i < N$$

For example,

$$T_2 = \{0, 1\} \qquad T_3 = \{0, 1/2, 1\}$$

Some **Lukasiewicz logic operators** for N-valued logic, where $N \geq 2$, are defined in Table 5.14. As shown in Problem 5.13, these reduce to the standard logic values for N = 2. Notice that the minus, min, and max operators are the same as in fuzzy logic.

x'	$= 1 - x$
$x \wedge y$	$= \min(x, y)$
$x \vee y$	$= \max(x, y)$
$x \rightarrow y$	$= \min(1, 1 + y - x)$

Table 5.14 Primitive Lukasiewicz N-valued Logic Operators

Each N-valued Lukasiewicz logic, or **L-logic**, is written as L_N, where N is the number of truth values. L_2 is the classical two-valued logic, while at the other extreme of N = ∞, the L_∞ defines an **infinite-valued logic** with truth values in the set T_∞. While T_∞ is defined on rational numbers, an alternative infinite-valued logic can be defined on the continuum, which is the set of all real numbers. The term *infinite-valued logic* is commonly taken for this alternative logic where the truth values are the real numbers in [0,1], and this logic is called L_1.

However, L_1 is *not* the same as the **unary logic** with N = 1. Unary logic is not a Lukasiewicz logic at all since **L-logics** are only defined for $N \geq 2$. The 1 in L_1 is actually an abbreviation for $Å_1$ (read "aleph 1"), the cardinality of the real numbers. $Å_1$ is not a finite but a **transfinite number**. This theory was first developed by Cantor as a way of computing with infinite numbers. Instead of one infinite number, Cantor defined different orders of infinity. For example, the smallest transfinite number is $Å_0$, which is the cardinality of the natural numbers. $Å_1$ is a higher order infinity than $Å_0$ since there are infinitely many real numbers for each natural number.

Fuzzy logic may be considered an extension of multivalued logic. However, the goals and applications of fuzzy logic are different because fuzzy logic is the logic of **approximate reasoning** rather than exact multivalued reasoning. Essentially, approximate or **fuzzy reasoning** is the inference of a possibly imprecise conclusion from a set of possibly imprecise premises. People are very familiar with approximate reasoning because it is the most common type of reasoning done in the real world and is the basis of many heuristic rules. Some examples of heuristic rules of approximate reasoning are the following:

```
IF the TV picture is rolling vertically
THEN adjust the vertical control

IF the TV picture is too dim
THEN turn up the brightness control

IF the red color in the TV picture looks too green
THEN turn down the tint control

IF you're getting too fat from eating banana splits
and pies and ice cream and cake
THEN reduce the number of bananas
```

Approximate reasoning is concerned with reasoning that is neither exact nor totally inexact, such as a pure guess. Approximate reasoning is particularly concerned with reasoning about natural language statements and the inferences that follow. Fuzzy logic is related to approximate reasoning in the same way that two-valued logic is related to precise reasoning. An example of precise or exact reasoning is deduction and theorem proving, as discussed in Chapter 3.

There are many different types of possible fuzzy set theory, fuzzy logic, and approximate reasoning. The type of fuzzy logic discussed from here on is Zadeh's theory of approximate reasoning, which uses a fuzzy logic whose base is Lukasiewiczs' L_1 logic. In this fuzzy logic truth values are linguistic variables that are ultimately represented by fuzzy sets.

Fuzzy logic operators based on the Lukasiewicz operators of Table 5.14 are defined in Table 5.15. $x(A)$ is a numeric truth value in the range $[0,1]$ representing the truth of the proposition "x is A", which can be interpreted as the membership grade $\mu_A(x)$.

As an example of fuzzy logic operators, assume a fuzzy set called TRUE defined as

```
TRUE = .1/.1 + .3/.5 + 1/.8
```

Using the operators of Table 5.15 gives

```
FALSE = 1 - TRUE

      = (1 - .1)/.1 + (1 - .3)/.5 + (1 - 1)/.8

      = .9/.1 + .7/.5
```

Using the CON operator for the hedge Very gives

```
Very TRUE = .01/.1 + .09/.5 + 1/.8

Very FALSE = .81/.1 + .49/.5
```

$x(A')$	$= x(\text{NOT } A)$	$= 1 - \mu_A(x)$
$x(A) \wedge x(B)$	$= x(A \text{ AND } B)$	$= \min(\mu_A(x), \mu_B(x))$
$x(A) \vee x(B)$	$= x(A \text{ OR } B)$	$= \max(\mu_A(x), \mu_B(x))$
$x(A) \rightarrow x(B)$	$= x(\Lambda \rightarrow B)$	$= x((\sim A) \vee B) = \max[(1 - \mu_A(x)), \mu_B(x)]$

Table 5.15 Some Fuzzy Logic Operators

Fuzzy Rules

As a simple example of fuzzy set operators, consider the problem of pattern recognition. The patterns might represent objects examined for quality control such as manufactured parts or fresh-picked fruit. Other types of important pattern recognition problems are medical images, seismic data from mineral and oil exploration, and others.

Table 5.16 shows some hypothetical data representing the membership grade in fuzzy sets of missile, fighter, and airliner corresponding to some images. These images might be produced from a laser TV system at long range and contain uncertainty due to target motion and orientation, noise, and so forth.

		Membership Grade	
Image	**Missile**	**Fighter**	**Airliner**
1	1.0	0.0	0.0
2	0.9	0.0	0.1
3	0.4	0.3	0.2
4	0.2	0.3	0.5
5	0.1	0.2	0.7
6	0.1	0.6	0.4
7	0.0	0.7	0.2
8	0.0	0.0	1.0
9	0.0	0.8	0.2
10	0.0	1.0	0.0

Table 5.16 Membership Grades for Images

The union of the fuzzy sets for each image represents the total uncertainty in the target identification. Figure 5.17 illustrates the fuzzy set unions for the ten target images of Table 5.16. Of course, in a real situation there would be many other possible images than these ten depending on the system resolution and distance to the target. Besides uncertainty in the system hardware, there is also uncertainty in the primitive fuzzy sets for missile, fighter, and airliner. The membership grades are assigned in a subjective way based on a knowledge of typical missile, fighter, and airliner configurations. In a real situation there are many types of each of these primitive sets.

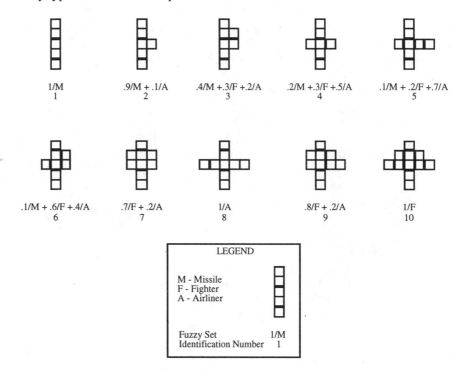

Figure 5.17 Fuzzy Sets for Aircraft Identification

The fuzzy set unions shown in Figure 5.17 can be considered as representing rules such as

```
IF E THEN H
```

where E is the observed image and H is the fuzzy set union. For example,

```
IF IMAGE4 THEN TARGET (.2/M + .3/F + .5/A)
```

where the expression in parentheses is the fuzzy set union of the target. Alternately, the rule could be expressed as

```
IF IMAGE4 THEN TARGET4
```

where

```
TARGET4 = .2/M + .3/F + .5/A
```

Suppose that there is additional time to make another observation of the target and that IMAGE6 is observed. This corresponds to a rule

```
IF IMAGE6 THEN TARGET6
```

where

```
TARGET6 = .1/M + .6/F + .4/A
```

The total elements that have been measured for the target are

```
TARGET = TARGET4 + TARGET6
```

where the "+" denotes set union. Thus,

```
TARGET = .2/M + .3/F + .5/A + .1/M + .6/F + .4/A
```

```
TARGET = .2/M + .6/F + .5/A
```

where only the maximum membership grades for each element are retained in the TARGET fuzzy set.

If the element with maximum grade is interpreted as the most likely target then the target is most likely a fighter, since it has the highest membership grade of 0.6. However, if the airliner membership grade was also 0.6, then all we could say is that the target is equally likely to be a fighter or an airliner.

In general, given N observations and rules,

```
IF E₁ THEN H₁
IF E₂ THEN H₂
        .

        .

        .
IF Eₙ THEN Hₙ
```

where all the H_i bear on some common hypothesis H, then the union of the hypotheses determines the membership grade of H. That is,

$$\mu_H = \max(\mu_{H1}, \mu_{H2}, \ldots \mu_{HN})$$

Notice that this result differs from the Certainty Factors and Dempster-Shafer theories. The μ_H of the hypothesis H is called the ***truth value*** of H.

It is also a reasonable assumption that the truth of a hypothesis can be no greater than the truth of its evidence. In terms of rules, the truth of the consequent can be no greater than the truth of its antecedent. Thus,

$$\mu_H = \max(\mu_{H1}, \mu_{H2}, \ldots \mu_{HN})$$

$$= \max[\min(\mu_{E1}), \min(\mu_{E2}), \ldots \min(\mu_{EN})]$$

where each E_i may be some fuzzy expression. For example, E_1 might be defined as

$$E_1 \ = \ E_A \ \text{AND} \ (E_B \ \text{OR} \ \text{NOT} \ E_C)$$

and the fuzzy logic operators are used to evaluate the expression. That is,

$$\mu_{E_1} \ = \ \min(\mu_{E_A}, \max(\mu_{E_B}, 1 \ - \ \mu_{E_C}))$$

The combined membership grade of the antecedent is called the ***truth value of the antecedent***. This is analogous to the partial evidence of the antecedent in PROSPECTOR rules. In fact, recall that the PROSPECTOR antecedent evidence was combined using fuzzy logic on an *ad hoc* basis. Now you can see that this combination is justified by the fuzzy theory compositional rule of inference.

Max-Min Composition

The equation for H above is the fuzzy logic **max-min compositional rule of inference**. In a simple case of two items of evidence per rule,

$$\text{IF} \ E_{11} \ \text{AND} \ E_{12} \ \text{THEN} \ H_1$$
$$\text{IF} \ E_{21} \ \text{AND} \ E_{22} \ \text{THEN} \ H_2$$

$$.$$
$$.$$
$$.$$

$$\text{IF} \ E_{N1} \ \ \text{AND} \ E_{N2} \ \text{THEN} \ H_N$$

and so the max-min compositional inference rule is

$$\mu_H \ = \ \max[\min(\mu_{E_{11}}, \mu_{E_{12}}), \ \min(\mu_{E_{21}}, \mu_{E_{22}}), \ \ldots$$
$$\min(\mu_{E_{N1}}, \mu_{E_{N2}})]$$

with similar extensions for additional evidence E_{i3}, E_{i4}, and so on.

As another example of the compositional rule of inference, let's see how it is used with a relation. Define the fuzzy relation $R(x,y)$ = APPROXIMATELY EQUAL on the binary relation of people's weights in the range of 120 to 160 pounds of Table 5.17.

x	y 120	130	140	150	160
120	1.0	0.7	0.4	0.2	0.0
130	0.7	1.0	0.6	0.5	0.2
140	0.4	0.6	1.0	0.8	0.5
150	0.2	0.5	0.8	1.0	0.8
160	0.0	0.2	0.5	0.8	1.0

Table 5.17 The Relation APPROXIMATELY EQUAL Defined on Weights

In constructing this table, the membership grades were defined so that the difference from the mean of two values is a decrease of 0.075 / percent. For example, if the x and y values are 150 and 130, then the average is 140. The absolute difference of 150 and 130 from the average is 10/140 = 7.1 percent. This value is multiplied by the constant factor of -.075 / percent to yield −0.5. Thus, the final membership grade for 150, 130 is 1−.5 = 0.5 and this is the table entry. An alternate and computationally simpler definition would be to define any change of 10 as a fixed decrease in the membership grade, such as .3. However, this alternate definition does not yield reasonable results for small weights such as 10 and 20, which would be APPROXIMATELY EQUAL to grade 0.7.

Notice how the relation R(x,y) acts as a **fuzzy restriction** on any two values x and y that have a nonzero membership grade R(x,y). A fuzzy relation acts as an **elastic constraint** by allowing a range of membership grades rather than demanding the rigid constraint of crisp relations. In fact, the term APPROXIMATELY EQUAL could not even be defined in nonfuzzy logic. The rigid constraint of crisp relations would demand that values be either exactly equal or not exactly equal. That is, either x exactly equals y or it does not.

As an example of a fuzzy restriction, consider the proposition, p, as follows:

```
p = X is F
```

in which F is some fuzzy set that acts as a fuzzy restriction on the linguistic variable named X. The following are some examples of fuzzy propositions of the form above.

```
John is tall
Sue is over 21
The concrete mix is too thick
Hitman is friendly
x is a number approximately equal to 100
The pie is fruit
```

In the last example a fuzzy set could be defined as

```
FRUIT = 1/apples + 1/oranges
```

to indicate the types of elements that are considered fruit. Notice that in fuzzy theory you *can* add apples and oranges in a meaningful way.

Let's now define a fuzzy restriction $R_1(x)$. For example, the fuzzy set HEAVY could be defined as

```
R₁(x) = HEAVY = .6/140 + .8/150 + 1/160
```

The compositional rule of inference defines the fuzzy restriction on y values as

```
R₃(y) = R₁(x) o R₂(x,y)
```

where the composition operator, o, is the max-min operation

$$\max_{x} \min(\mu_1(x), \mu_2(x,y))$$

Another way of viewing $R_3(y)$ is by interpreting it as the solution of the relational equations

```
R₁(x)
R₂(x,y)
```

for $R_3(y)$. That is, given the fuzzy restriction of x and the fuzzy restriction on x and y, a fuzzy restriction on *y* can be deduced. Deductions like this comprise the **calculus of fuzzy restrictions**, which is the basis of approximate reasoning.

Using these definitions, $R_3(y)$ can be calculated as follows:

$$R_3(y) = R_1(x) \text{ o } R_2(x,y)$$

$$R_3(y) = [\ 0.0 \quad 0.0 \quad 0.6 \quad 0.8 \quad 1.0 \ ] \text{ o}$$

$$\begin{bmatrix} 1.0 & 0.7 & 0.4 & 0.2 & 0.0 \\ 0.7 & 1.0 & 0.6 & 0.5 & 0.2 \\ 0.4 & 0.6 & 1.0 & 0.8 & 0.5 \\ 0.2 & 0.5 & 0.8 & 1.0 & 0.8 \\ 0.0 & 0.2 & 0.5 & 0.8 & 1.0 \end{bmatrix}$$

where $R_1(x)$ is represented as a row vector. The nonzero elements of $R_3(y)$ are calculated as follows:

$$R_3(120) = \max \min[(.6,.4),(.8,.2)]$$
$$= \max(.4,.2) = .4$$
$$R_3(130) = \max \min[(.6,.6),(.8,.5),(1,.2)]$$
$$= \max(.6,.5,.2) = .6$$
$$R_3(140) = \max \min[(.6,1),(.8,.8),(1,.5)]$$
$$= \max(.6,.8,.5) = .8$$
$$R_3(150) = \max \min[(.6,.8),(.8,1),(1,.8)]$$
$$= \max(.6,.8,.8) = .8$$
$$R_3(160) = \max \min[(.6,.5),(.8,.8),(1,1)]$$
$$= \max(.5,.8,1) = 1$$

and so if $R_1(x)$ is HEAVY, then

$$R_3(y) = .4/120 + .6/130 + .8/140 + .8/150 + 1/160$$

which has the rough linguistic approximation: $R_3(y)$ is MORE OR LESS HEAVY.

The relation $R_3(y)$ is a rough linguistic approximation since the DIL operation of $\mu^{0.5}$ acting on HEAVY actually yields

$$DIL(HEAVY) = .8/140 + .9/150 + 1/160$$

and the terms for 120 and 130 are missing. However, the elements with large membership grades of $\mu \geq .8$ are represented well and this justifies the claim that MORE OR LESS HEAVY is a rough approximation. Thus the compositional inference by max-min has shown the fuzzy linguistic relation

MORE OR LESS HEAVY = HEAVY o APPROXIMATELY EQUAL

Note that these relations depend on the fuzzy set definitions and the linguistic labels of the sets. Thus the above relation is not true in an absolute sense since it depends on the definitions of the fuzzy sets, relations, and labels. However, once these basic definitions are made, fuzzy theory provides a mechanism for manipulating these expressions in a formal and consistent way. This is very important since the linguistic manipulation and meanings of terms are then on a sound theoretical basis and do not depend on an *ad hoc* or intuitive understanding by a person.

Maximum and Moments Methods

The choice of the element with the maximum membership grade is called the ***maximum method*** for deciding the truth of rule consequents. An alternate method, called the ***moments method***, assigns the truth of rule consequents in a way that is analogous to calculating the first moment of inertia of an object. The basic idea of the moments method is to consider the consequents of all rules in a decision rather than just the one maximum. As mentioned before, even the maximum method may lead to ambiguity if the consequents of multiple rules all have the same maximum value.

As a simple example of the moments method, let's first consider the following set of fuzzy production rules for making concrete.

```
R1:   IF MIX IS TOO WET
      THEN ADD SAND AND COARSE AGGREGATE

R2:   IF MIX IS WORKABLE
      THEN LEAVE ALONE

R3:   IF MIX IS TOO STIFF
      THEN DECREASE SAND AND COARSE AGGREGATE
```

Concrete consists of cement, water, sand, and coarse aggregate such as small rocks, mixed in proper proportions. The **mix** is a trial amount of the concrete mixture that is made to determine the optimum proportions for the desired application. General guidelines for the proportions are available depending on the desired concrete strength. However, there is variability due to the local materials used, aggregate sizes, environmental conditions, and other factors. It's a good idea to do a mix before starting a $10,000,000 building.

One common method of determining if the mix is correct or workable is the **slump test**. A trial batch of concrete is put into a cone and the cone is then removed. The distance that the mix slumps after cone removal indicates the condition of the material. Concrete designed for ordinary slabs and beams should have minimum and maximum slumps of 4 and 8 inches, respectively (Adams 79).

The fuzzy sets of Figure 5.18 illustrate possible definitions for the fuzzy concrete mix production rules antecedents. These fuzzy sets may also be defined in a table or as S-functions and $\prod$-functions.

The fuzzy sets used for the fuzzy rule consequents are defined in Figure 5.19. As with the antecedents, there is overlap between these fuzzy consequent actions to provide a workable mix. Note that the limits of –20 and 20 percent for the change in sand and coarse aggregates are defined arbitrarily. Like the fuzzy set antecedents, the consequents may also be defined by S-functions and $\prod$-functions.

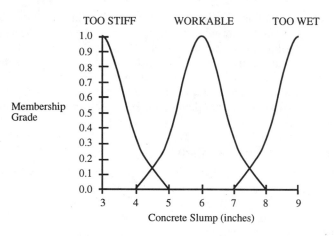

Figure 5.18 Fuzzy Production Rule Antecedents for Concrete Mixture Process Control

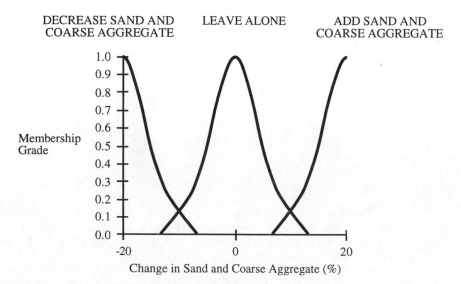

Figure 5.19 Fuzzy Production Rule Consequents for Concrete Mixture Process Control

As an example of how this fuzzy production rule set works, assume that the concrete slump is 6 inches. From Figure 5.18, the membership grade or antecedent truth value for each rule is the following:

$$\mu_{\text{TOO STIFF}}(6) = 0$$
$$\mu_{\text{WORKABLE}}(6) = 1$$
$$\mu_{\text{TOO WET}}(6) = 0$$

so the only rule whose antecedent is satisfied is R_2. This rule is activated and fires with the resulting fuzzy consequent LEAVE ALONE.

Applying the compositional rule of inference gives

$$\mu_{\text{LEAVE ALONE}} = \text{max}[\text{min}(\mu_{\text{WORKABLE}}(6)] = \text{max}[\text{min}(1)] = 1$$

and from Figure 5.19, this translates into a 0 percent change in the sand and coarse aggregate.

Now suppose that the slump is 4.8 inches. From Figure 5.18,

$$\mu_{\text{TOO STIFF}}(4.8) = .05$$
$$\mu_{\text{WORKABLE}}(4.8) = .2$$
$$\mu_{\text{TOO WET}}(4.8) = 0$$

Rules R_1 and R_2 have antecedents that are partially satisfied analogous to the partial evidence satisfaction of probabilistic PROSPECTOR rule antecedents. Since there is some nonzero truth that the mix is too stiff or workable, then both rules R_1 and R_2 will become activated and fire. Notice that in a fuzzy production system, unless there is a threshold on antecedent truth, every rule will fire with a nonzero antecedent truth. Setting a threshold may be desirable to prevent inefficiencies due to many rules with low truth values from becoming activated and firing. Recall that in the MYCIN system, the minimum certainty level of a rule to fire must be greater than 0.2 to improve the expert system's efficiency. A similar threshold on the antecedent truth value of fuzzy sets can be defined.

For the slump of 4.8 inches, there are two rules that become activated. Applying the max-min composition rule gives

$$\mu_{\text{DECREASE SAND AND COARSE AGGREGATE}} = \text{max } [\text{min}(\mu_{\text{TOO STIFF}}(4.8)]$$

$$= .05$$

$$\mu_{\text{LEAVE ALONE}} = \text{max } [\text{min}(\mu_{\text{WORKABLE}}(4.8)] = .2$$

As you can see for a single antecedent term the max and min functions are unnecessary.

Since there are now two rules with nonzero consequents, we must decide on a control action. The maximum method will simply pick the rule with the largest membership grade. In this case, the LEAVE ALONE action is chosen because its grade is .2 compared to .05 of the other rule.

The moments method basically calculates the **center of gravity** of the fuzzy consequent rules. The term *center of gravity* comes from physics, where it represents the point in which, if all the mass of an object were concentrated, the point mass would act the same under the influence of an external force. The definition of the center of gravity, also called the ***first moment of inertia***, I, is

$$I = \frac{\int m(x) x \, d(x)}{\int m(x) \, d(x)}$$

where the integral sign denotes ordinary integration.

Figure 5.20 shows the fuzzy sets for the two rules R_2 and R_3. Notice that the fuzzy sets are truncated at the truth values of their antecedents. This reflects the compositional rule of inference. The truncation is done because, intuitively, it makes sense that the truth value of a consequent cannot exceed that of its antecedent.

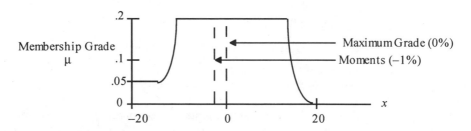

Figure 5.20
Maximum and Moments Methods for the Concrete Process Control Fuzzy Rules

The moment of the consequents is calculated as

$$I = \frac{\int \mu(x) \, x \, d(x)}{\int \mu(x) \, d(x)} \qquad \text{for continuous elements}$$

or

$$I = \frac{\sum_i \mu_i x}{\sum_i \mu_i} \qquad \text{for discrete elements}$$

and is about −1 percent for Figure 5.20. While this is very close to the 0 percent obtained from the maximum method, the difference may become significant for fuzzy sets that are defined with a considerable amount of overlap. Both the maximum and the moments methods have been used in a fuzzy controller for aircraft control (Larkin 85). In this controller the maximum method calculated the arithmetic mean of all the maxima of the fuzzy consequents. Thus, if there were multiple elements with the same maximum value, one crisp control value would still be calculated.

Other approaches besides the maximum and moments methods have been used to solve the **defuzzification problem** of translating a membership grade into a crisp control value, or a linguistic approximation describing the control variable.

However, it is difficult to describe a set of values—the fuzzy set—by a single number or a linguistic phrase.

Possibility and Probability

The term *possibility* has a specific meaning in fuzzy theory. Essentially, *possibility* refers to allowed values. For example, suppose a proposition is defined regarding the throw of two dice in a universe U of their sum, as follows:

```
p = X is an integer in U

U = {2,3,4,5,6,7,8,9,10,11,12}
```

In fuzzy terminology, for any integer *i*,

```
Poss {X = i} = 1    for 2 ≤ i ≤ 12
Poss (X = i} = 0    otherwise
```

where **Poss** {X = i} is short for "The possibility that X may assume the value i." (Zadeh 81). The possibility of the dice showing a value from 2 to 12 is very different from the probability of a value i. That is, the **possibility distribution** is not the same as the **probability distribution**. The probability distribution of the dice is the frequency of expected occurrence of the **random variable** X, the sum. For example, a 7 can occur due to 1 + 6, 2 + 5, and 3 + 4. So the probability of rolling a 7 is

$$\frac{2 \cdot 3}{36} = \frac{1}{6}$$

whereas the probability of rolling a 2 is

$$\frac{1}{36}$$

In contrast, the possibility distribution is a constant value of 1 for fair dice for all integers from 2 to 12. A proposition *p* is said to *induce a possibility distribution*, Π_X. That is, given a fuzzy proposition, *p*, based on a fuzzy set F and a linguistic variable X,

```
p = X is F
```

The proposition is said to be in **canonical form** when expressed this way, in which the term *canonical* means a standard form. The fuzzy set, F, is a **fuzzy predicate**, in contrast to the predicates of ordinary logic. F can also be a fuzzy relation. The possibility distribution induced by p is equal to F and is defined by the following **possibility assignment equation**.

$$\Pi_X = F$$

which means that for all values x in the universe, U

```
Poss (X = x} = μ_F(x)    x ∈ U
```

As an example, given the proposition

```
p = John is tall
```

a linguistic variable, Height, can be defined with a value, John. The canonical form

```
X is F
```

is represented in terms of the variable Height by

```
Height(John) is TALL
```

and so

```
Poss {Height(John) = x} = μ_TALL(x)
```

The proposition, p, can be written as a possibility distribution as follows:

$$\text{John is tall} \rightarrow \Pi_{\text{Height(John)}} = \text{TALL}$$

in which the arrow symbol means "translates into," Height is a linguistic variable, and TALL is a fuzzy set. Note that John is not a linguistic variable.

Although a fuzzy set can be assigned to a possibility distribution, as in $\Pi_X = F$, the two are not really the same. As an example to illustrate the difference, consider the fuzzy set defined for a roll of the dice as follows:

```
ROLL(1) = 1/3 + 1/4
```

This set is defined to mean that a specific roll of the dice, Roll 1, gave a 3 on one die and a 4 on the other. In contrast, the possibility distribution,

$$\Pi_{\text{ROLL}(1)} = 1/3 + 1/4$$

means that the roll gave a 3 *or* a 4, where the "or" is the exclusive-or representing the uncertainty in our knowledge of the roll. There is a possibility of unity that it is a 3 and a possibility of unity that it is a 4. In the fuzzy set it is certain that the dice values were 3 *and* 4. The possibility distribution means that the dice are fair with regard to whether a 3 or a 4 can occur. The fuzzy set tells which values showed after a roll.

As another example, consider the proposition that "Hans ate X eggs for breakfast," where X is any value in the universe, $X = \{1, 2, \ldots 8\}$ (Zadeh 78).

X	1	2	3	4	5	6	7	8
$\Pi_{\text{ATE(Hans)}}(X)$	1.0	1.0	1.0	1.0	0.8	0.6	0.4	0.2
P(X)	0.1	0.8	0.1	0.0	0.0	0.0	0.0	0.0

The possibility distribution $\Pi_{\text{ATE(Hans)}}(X)$ is interpreted as how easily Hans can eat X eggs. The probability distribution, P(X), is determined empirically by asking Hans if you can join him for breakfast for a year to conduct a scientific study.

An important point to realize is that possibility is *nonstatistical* whereas probability is *statistical*. For example, although Hans can eat eight eggs, the empirical study shows that over the period of observation he has never eaten more than three (and kept them down). In this sense, possibility is capability or capacity. A high degree of possibility does not necessarily mean a high degree of probability. That is, there may be no correlation between possibility and probability.

The fuzzy extension to ordinary probability is **fuzzy probability**, which describes probabilities that are known only imprecisely (Zadeh 84b). Some examples of fuzzy probabilities are the **fuzzy qualifiers** *Very Likely*, *Unlikely*, *Not Very Likely*, and so forth. An example of a fuzzy proposition with a fuzzy probability is the following:

```
the battery is BAD is Very Likely
```

Translation Rules

Fuzzy probability is incorporated into the fuzzy logic called **FL** based on Lukasiewicz's L_1 logic (Zadeh 79). One main component of FL is a group of **translation rules** that specify how modified or composite propositions are generated from their elementary propositions.

The translation rules are divided into four categories:

• *Type I* : **modification rules,** such as

```
X is very large

John is much taller than Mike
```

• *Type II* : **composition rules,** such as

conditional composition

```
If X is TALL then Y is SHORT
```

conjunctive composition

```
X is TALL and Y is SHORT
```

disjunctive composition

```
X is TALL or Y is SHORT
```

conditional and conjunctive composition

```
If X is TALL then Y is SHORT
       else Y is Rather SHORT
```

• *Type III* : **quantification rules**, such as

> Most desserts are WONDERFUL
>
> Too Much nutritious food is FATTENING

• *Type IV* : **qualification rules**, such as

> **truth qualification**
>
> chocolate pie is DELICIOUS is Very True
>
> **probability qualification**
>
> chocolate pie is served SOON is Very Likely
>
> **possibility qualification**
>
> chocolate pie is BAD for you is Impossible

The qualification rules are those pertaining to fuzzy probabilities. The quantification rules deal with fuzzy quantifiers such as *Most*, which is not capable of being defined using the classical universal and existential quantifiers.

The translation of a Type I rule is represented by

$$\text{X is F} \rightarrow \prod_x = \text{F}$$

with translated proposition

$$\text{X is } m\text{F} \rightarrow \prod_x = \text{F}^+$$

where m is a modifier such as *Not*, *Very*, *More Or Less*, and so on. F^+ represents the modification of F by m. Some default definitions for m and F^+ are shown in Table 5.18. These are defined in the same way as the linguistic hedges discussed previously. Other definitions for m and F^+ may also be used.

m	**F$^+$**
Not	$F' = \int [1 - \mu_F(x)]/x$
Very	$F^2 = \int \mu_F^2(x)/x$
More or Less	$\sqrt{F} = \int \sqrt{\mu_F(x)} \,/x$

Table 5.18
Values of Translation Parameters for Some Type I Rules
(note that all the integrals are over the universe)

As an example, defining TALL,

$$\text{TALL} = .2/5 + .6/6 + 1/7$$

then the translations are as follows:

```
John is not tall → .8/5 + .4/6 + 0/7
John is very tall → .04/5 + .36/6 + 1/7
John is more or less tall → .45/5 + .77/6 + 1/7
```

The variable X does not have to be a unary variable. Instead, X may be a binary or N-ary relation in general. For example, a proposition such as "Y and Z are F" is subsumed by "X is F." Defining CLOSE as a fuzzy binary relation in U × U,

```
CLOSE = 1/(1,1) + .5/(1,2) + .5/(2,1)
```

then

```
X and Y are close → Π(X,Y) = CLOSE

X and Y are very close → Π(X,Y)
      = CLOSE²
      = 1/(1,1) + .25/(1,2) + .25/(2,1)
```

An example of a type II rule is

$$\text{IF X is F then Y is G} \rightarrow \Pi_{(X,Y)} = \overline{F}' \oplus \overline{G}$$

where $\overline{F}$ and $\overline{G}$ are the cylindrical extensions of F and G in their universes.

$$\overline{F} = F \times V \qquad \overline{G} = U \times G$$

and $\oplus$ is the bounded sum. For this rule

$$\mu_{\overline{F}' \oplus \overline{G}}(x,y) = 1 \wedge [1 - \mu_F(x) + \mu_G(y)]$$

and the min function is $\wedge$. This definition is consistent with implication in L_1 logic, whereas other definitions may not be consistent (Zadeh 79). As an example of a Type II rule, define

```
U = V = {4, 5, 6, 7}

F = TALL = .2/5 + .6/6 + 1/7

G = SHORT = 1/4 + .2/5

IF X is tall then Y is short → Π(X,Y)

      = 1/(5,4)  + 1/(5,5) + 1/(6,4) +
        .6/(6,5) + 1/(7,4) + .2(7,5)
```

where the membership grade of an element such as (5, 4) is calculated as follows:

$$\mu_{\overline{F} \cdot \oplus \overline{G}}(5,4) \ = 1 \wedge [1 - .2 + 1] \ = 1 \wedge [1.8] \ = 1$$

Uncertainty in Fuzzy Expert Systems

When fuzzy probabilities are used in expert systems, there is a difference compared to ordinary probabilistic inference (Zadeh 83). Consider the canonical fuzzy rule

```
If X is F then Y is G (with probability ß)
```

This rule can be written as a conditional probability:

```
P(Y is G | X is F) = ß
```

A conventional expert system using classical probability theory would then assume

```
P(Y is not G | X is F) = 1 - ß
```

However, this is not correct in fuzzy theory if F is a fuzzy set. The valid fuzzy result is weaker

```
P(Y is not G | X is F) + P(Y is G | X is F) ≥ 1
```

because it only sets a lower limit on the probabilities, which may be fuzzy numbers. In general, for fuzzy systems,

P(H | E) is not necessarily equal to 1 – P(H´ | E)

In fuzzy expert systems there may be fuzziness in three areas:
(1) antecedents and/or consequents of rules such as

```
If X is F then Y is G
If X is F then Y is G with CF = α
```

where CF is the certainty factor and α is a numeric value such as 0.5.
(2) partial match between the antecedent and facts that match the antecedent patterns. In nonfuzzy expert systems, a rule does not become activated unless the patterns match the facts exactly. However, in a fuzzy expert system everything is a matter of degree and all rules may be activated to some extent unless a threshold is set.
(3) fuzzy quantifiers such as *Most* and fuzzy qualifiers such as *Very Likely*, *Quite True*, *Definitely Possible*, and so forth.
   Propositions often contain implicit and/or explicit fuzzy quantifiers. As an example, consider the **disposition**

```
d = desserts are WONDERFUL
```

The term *disposition* means a proposition that is usually true, with canonical form

```
Usually(X is R)
```

where *Usually* is an implied fuzzy quantifier and R is a **constraining relation** acting on the constrained variable X to limit the values it may take. Many heuristic rules that people know about are dispositions. In fact, **commonsense knowledge** is basically a collection of dispositions about the real world.

The disposition may be translated into the explicit propositional forms

```
p = Usually desserts are wonderful
p = Most desserts are wonderful
```

which may be expressed as a heuristic rule

```
r = If x is a dessert
      then it is likely that x is wonderful
```

Some rules of inference in fuzzy systems are the following:

- **entailment principle**

```
X is F
F ⊂ G
X is G
```

- **dispositional entailment**: limiting cases where *Usually* becomes *Always*

```
Usually (X is F)
F ⊂ G
Usually (X is G)
```

- **compositional rule**

```
X is F
(X,Y) is R
Y is F o R
```

where R is a binary relation over the binary variable (X,Y) and

$$\mu_{F \circ R}(y) = \sup_{x} [\mu_F(x) \land \mu_R(x,y)]$$

and the **supremum**, symbolized by **sup**, is the **least upper bound**. Generally the supremum is the same as the max function. The difference arises in cases in which there is no maximum value, such as the real number interval of numbers less than 0. Because there is no maximum real number less than 0, the supremum is used to take 0 as the least upper bound.

• **generalized** *modus ponens*

```
X is F
Y is G if X is H
Y is F o (H´ ⊕ G)
```

where H´ is the fuzzy negation of H and the bounded sum is defined

$$\mu_{H´ \oplus G}(x,y) = 1 \wedge [1 - \mu_H(x) + \mu_G(y)]$$

The generalized *modus ponens* does not require that the antecedent "X is H" be identical with the premise "X is F." Notice that this is very different from classical logic, which requires that they match exactly. The generalized *modus ponens* is actually a special case of the compositional rule of inference. Unlike conventional expert systems, in which *modus ponens* is the basic rule of inference, the compositional rule of inference is the basic rule in fuzzy expert systems.

Expert systems using approximate reasoning choose one of two different methods. One method is truth value restriction and the second is compositional inference (Whalen 85). In Whalen's survey of eleven fuzzy expert systems, nearly all used compositional inference.

5.6 THE STATE OF UNCERTAINTY

There is no clear consensus as to the best method of dealing with uncertainty, although a number of techniques have been studied such as classical Bayesian, **convex set Bayesian**, Dempster-Shafer, **Kyburg**, and the possibility theory of fuzzy logic (Thompson 85). In the convex set approach to Bayes theory, the belief state is not a single function of the classical Bayes method. Instead, the belief state is characterized by a set of **convex functions**. This means that any function can be represented as a linear combination of two other functions.

Since the Dempster-Shafer theory was first introduced as a generalization of classical probability there have been rebuttals. For example, Kyburg's paper claims that Dempster-Shafer theory is not a generalization of classical probability, but is actually the other way around. Kyburg believes that Dempster-Shafer theory is included in classical probability and that the Dempster-Shafer intervals are included in the convex set Bayes approach (Kyburg 87). The Dempster-Shafer theory also seems to have difficulties in dealing with beliefs that are close to zero. Very different results are obtained when beliefs are zero compared to results when the beliefs are very small (Dubois 85). Another problem with the Dempster-Shafer theory is the exponential explosion in the number of computations as the number of possible answers to a diagnostic problem increases.

Although the Gordon and Shortliffe approximation avoids the exponential explosion, it may produce poor results in the case of highly conflicting evidence. An alternative approach that is not an approximation and gives good results for hierarchical evidence without the combinatorial explosion has been given (Shafer 87). A number of other papers have attempted to overcome the exponential explosion problem by different generalizations to Dempster-Shafer theory (Liu 86; Yen 86; Lee 87).

The major benefit of all this work has been a reexamination of the foundations of probability theory and widespread interest in methods of dealing with uncertainty.

5.7 SUMMARY

In this chapter, nonprobabilistic theories of uncertainty were discussed. Certainty factors, Dempster-Shafer theory, and fuzzy theory are all ways of dealing with uncertainty in expert systems. Certainty factors are simple to implement and have been used successfully in expert systems such as MYCIN, in which the inference chains are short. However, the theory of certainty factors is an *ad hoc* theory that does not appear to be generally valid for longer inference chains.

Dempster-Shafer theory has a rigorous foundation and holds promise for expert systems. However, at the present time there does not seem to be any clear consensus on how to apply it for general use in expert systems.

Fuzzy theory is the most general theory of uncertainty that has been formulated. It has wide applicability because of the extension principle. Since the first classic paper by Zadeh in 1965, fuzzy theory has been applied to many fields.

PROBLEMS

5.1 Given that evidence E_2 adds to the original evidence E_1, show that

$$P(D_i \mid E_1 \cap E_2) = \frac{P(E_2 \mid D_i \cap E_1) P(D_i \mid E_1)}{\sum_j P(E_2 \mid D_j \cap E_1) P(D_j \mid E_1)}$$

(Hint: use the results of Problem 4.8 (b).)

5.2 Prove that

$$CF(H,E) + CF(H',E) = 0$$

5.3 Given rules

IF E_1 AND E_2 AND E_3
THEN H (CF$_1$)

IF E_4 OR E_5
THEN H (CF$_2$)

where

$CF_1(E_1,e) = 1$ $\qquad$ $CF_1(E_2,e) = 0.5$ $\qquad$ $CF_1(E_3,e) = 0.3$
$CF_2(E_4,e) = 0.7$ $\quad$ $CF_2(E_5,e) = 0.2$
$CF_1(H,E) = 0.5$ $\quad$ $CF_2(H,E) = 0.9$

(a) Draw a tree illustrating how these rules support H.
(b) Calculate the certainty factors $CF_1(H,e)$ and $CF_2(H,e)$.
(c) Calculate $CF_{COMBINE}$ [$CF_1(H,e),CF_2(H,e)$]

5.4 (a) In Figure 5.7 (c) assuming

$m(X) = 0.2$
$m(Y) = 0.3$
$m(Z) = 0.5$

find the evidential intervals of X, Y, and Z using the Dempster-Shafer theory.

(b)   In Figure 5.7 (d) assuming

$m(X) = 0.4$
$m(Y) = 0.6$

find the evidential intervals for

X
$X \cap Y$
Y
$X \cap Y'$
$X' \cap Y$

5.5   Given the rules

Rule 1: IF E THEN H
Rule 2: IF E THEN H'

and assuming

$\Theta = \{H, H'\}$
$m_1(H) = 0.5$ $m_1(\Theta) = 0.5$ for Rule 1
$m_2(H') = 0.3$ $m_2(\Theta) = 0.7$ for Rule 2

(a)   Write the Dempster-Shafer table showing the combination of evidence and calculate the combined belief functions.
(b)   Calculate the plausibilities.
(c)   Calculate the evidential intervals.
(d)   Calculate the dubieties.
(e)   Calculate the ignorances.

5.6   Based on reports from different types of sensors, the following table gives the degrees of belief in the aircraft environment of airliner (H), bomber (B), and fighter (F).

Focal elements	Sensor 1 (m_1)	Sensor 2 (m_2)
Θ	0.15	0.2
A,B	0.3	0.1
A,F	0.1	0.05
B,F	0.1	0.1
A	0.05	0.3
B	0.2	0.05
F	0.1	0.2

(a)   Calculate the initial belief functions, plausibility, evidential intervals, dubieties, and ignorances.
(b)   Calculate these same parameters after the evidence is combined.

5.7 A policeman stops a motorist for speeding. Due to errors in the policeman's radar gun and the motorist's speedometer, the belief functions are as follows:

Policeman	Motorist
$m1(57) = 0.3$	$m2(56) = 0.2$
$m1(56) = 0.5$	$m2(55) = 0.6$
$m1(55) = 0.2$	$m2(54) = 0.2$

(a) Calculate the belief functions, plausibility, evidential intervals, dubieties, and ignorance of each person.

(b) Calculate these parameters after combining the evidences.

(c) Explain why you believe the motorist was or was not speeding, based on the parameters.

5.8 Given the fuzzy sets,

$$A = .1/1 + .2/2 + .3/3 \qquad B = .2/1 + .3/2 + .4/3$$

calculate/explain the following:

(a) Are the sets equal? Explain.
(b) Set complement
(c) Set union
(d) Set intersection
(e) Does the Law of the Excluded Middle hold for each set? Explain.
(f) Set product
(g) Second power of each set
(h) Probabilistic sum
(i) Bounded sum
(j) Bounded product
(k) Bounded difference
(l) Concentration
(m) Dilation
(n) Intensification
(o) Normalization

5.9 Given the fuzzy sets

$$Q = \begin{bmatrix} 0.2 & 0.3 \\ 0.4 & 1.0 \end{bmatrix} \quad \text{defined on } U_1 \times U_2$$

$$P = \begin{bmatrix} 0.1 & 0.5 & 0.3 \\ 0.2 & 0.0 & 0.4 \end{bmatrix} \quad \text{defined on } U_2 \times U_3$$

(a) Calculate the first, second, and total projections for each set.
(b) Calculate the cylindrical extensions of each set.
(c) Show that

$$Q \circ P = \text{proj}(\overline{Q} \cap \overline{P} ; U_1 \times U_3)$$

5.10   Consider the linguistic variable Person as a fuzzy set of order 3.

(a)   Define Person as three fuzzy sets of order 2.
(b)   Define each of the order 2 sets in terms of three fuzzy sets of order 1.
(c)   Define three of the fuzzy order 1 sets in terms of S- and/or $\prod$-functions.

5.11   (a)   Define five linguistic values for the linguistic variable Uncertainty.
(b)   Draw appropriate functions for these values and explain your choices.
(c)   Draw the fuzzy sets for

Not TRUE
More Or Less TRUE
Sort Of TRUE
Pretty TRUE
Rather TRUE
TRUE

assuming TRUE is an S-function. What are the limits of TRUE? Explain.

5.12   (a)   Define at least six values for the linguistic variable Water Temperature.
(b)   Draw the appropriate functions for the fuzzy set values on one graph.
(c)   Give three hedged fuzzy set functions based on FREEZING.

5.13   (a)   Show by truth table for $N = 2$ and $N = 3$ the values of the primitive $L = $ logic operators of Table 5.14.
(b)   derive $x \leftrightarrow y$ in terms of the absolute values of x, and y.

5.14   Given numeric truth values,

$x(A) = .2/.1 + .6/.5 + 1/.9$
$x(B) = .1/.1 + .3/.5 + 1/.9$

calculate the fuzzy logic truth of the following:

(a)   NOT A
(b)   A AND B
(c)   A OR B
(d) $A \rightarrow B$
(e) $B \rightarrow A$

5.15   Define a fuzzy grammar using hedged primaries and range phrases to generate productions such as

IF PRESSURE IS HIGH
THEN TURN VALVE LOWER

IF PRESSURE IS VERY HIGH
THEN TURN VALVE MUCH LOWER

IF PRESSURE IS VERY VERY HIGH
THEN TURN VALVE MUCH MUCH LOWER
IF PRESSURE IS LOW TO MEDIUM
THEN TURN VALVE HIGHER

Assume that (1) the primaries for PRESSURE are only LOW and HIGH, (2) the range phrases involving TO only occur in the antecedent, and (3) the primaries for VALVE in the conclusion are only LOWER and HIGHER.

BIBLIOGRAPHY

(Adams 79). J. T. Adams, *The Complete Concrete, Masonry and Brick Handbook*, Arco Publishing, p. 1059, 1979.

(Adams 85). J. Barclay Adams, "Probabilistic Reasoning and Certainty Factors," in *Rule-based Expert Systems*, Addison Wesley Pub., pp. 263-271, 1985.

(Bellman 73). R. E. Bellman and M. Giertz, "On the Analytic Formalism of the Theory of Fuzzy Sets," *Information Science*, **5**, pp. 149-156, 1973.

(Bogler 87). Philip L. Bogler, "Shafer-Dempster Reasoning with Applications to Multisensor Target Identification Systems," *IEEE Tran. on Systems, Man, and Cybernetics*, **SMC-17**, (6), pp. 968-977, Nov./Dec. 1987.

(Carnap 50). R. Carnap, "The Two Concepts of Probability," in *Logical Foundations of Probability*, University of Chicago Press, pp. 19-51, 1950.

(Dempster 67). A. P. Dempster, "Upper and Lower Probabilities Induced by Multivalued Mappings," *Annals of Math. Stat.*, **38**, pp. 325-329, 1967.

(Dubois 85). Didier Dubois and Henri Prade, "Combination and Propagation of Uncertainty with Belief Functions," *IJCAI '85*, pp. 111-113, 1985.

(Garvey 81). T. D. Garvey, J. D. Lowrance, and M. A. Fischler, "An Inference Technique for Integrating Knowledge from Disparate Sources," *Proc. 7th IJCAI*, pp. 319-325, 1981.

(Giarratano 91c) Joseph Giarratano, *et al.*, "Fuzzy Logic Control for Camera Tracking System," Fifth Annual Workshop on Space Operations Applications and Research (SOAR '91), pp. 94-99, 1991.

(Gordon 85). Jean Gordon and Edward H. Shortliffe. "The Dempster-Shafer Theory of Evidence," in *Rule-based Expert Systems*, Bruce Buchanan and Edward Shortliffe, eds., pp. 272-292, 1985.

(Kandel 82). Abraham Kandel, *Fuzzy Techniques in Pattern Recognition*, John Wiley and Sons, Inc., 1982.

(Klir 88). George J. Klir and Tina A. Folger, *Fuzzy Sets, Uncertainty, and Information*, Prentice-Hall, pp. 75-77, 1988.

(Kyburg 87). Henry E. Kyburg, Jr., "Bayesian and Non-Bayesian Evidential Updating," *Artificial Intelligence*, **31**, (3), pp. 271-293, 1987.

(Larkin 85). L. I. Larkin, "A Fuzzy Logic Controller for Aircraft Flight Control," in *Industrial Applications of Fuzzy Control*, M. Sugeno, ed., North-Holland, pp. 87-103, 1985.

(Larsen 81). P. Martin Larsen, "Industrial Applications of Fuzzy Logic Control," in *Fuzzy Reasoning and Its Applications*, E. H. Mamdani and B. R. Gaines, eds., Academic Press, pp. 335-342, 1981.

(Lee 87). Sunggu Lee and Kang G. Shin, "Uncertain Inference Using Belief Functions," *Proceedings of the Third Conference on Artificial Intelligence Applications*, pp. 238-243, 1987.

(Liu 86). Gerald Shao-Hung Liu, "Causal and Plausible Reasoning in Expert Systems," *AAAI-86*, pp. 220-225, 1986.

(Lowrance 82). J. D. Lowrance and T. D. Garvey, "Evidential Reasoning: A Developing Concept," *Proc. Int. Conf. on Cybernetics and Society*, pp. 6-9, 1982.

(Maiers 85). J. Maiers and Y. S. Sherif, "Applications of Fuzzy Set Theory," *IEEE Transactions on Systems, Man, and Cybernetics*, **SMC-15**, (1), pp. 175-189, Jan./Feb. 1985.

(Shafer 76). Glenn Shafer, *A Mathematical Theory of Evidence*, Princeton University Press, 1976.

(Shafer 87). Glenn Shafer and Roger Logan, "Implementing Dempster's Rule for Hierarchical Evidence," *Artificial Intelligence*, **33**, (3), pp. 271-298, Nov. 1987.

(Shortliffe 85). Edward H. Shortliffe and Bruce G. Buchanan. "A Model of Inexact Reasoning in Medicine," in *Rule-based Expert Systems*, Addison-Wesley Pub., pp. 233-262, 1985.

(Strat 84). Thomas M. Strat, "Continuous Belief Functions for Evidential Reasoning," *Proceedings of the National Conference on AI*, pp. 308-313, 1984.

(Wesley 86). Leonard P. Wesley, "Evidential Knowledge-based Computer Vision," *Optical Eng.*, **25**, (3), pp. 363-379, 1986.

(Whalen 85). Thomas Whalen and Brian Schott, "Alternative Logics for Approximate Reasoning in Expert Systems: A Comparative Study," *Int. J. of Man-Machine Studies*, **22**, pp. 327-346, 1985.

(Yen 86). John Yen, "A Reasoning Model Based on an Extended Dempster-Shafer Theory," *AAAI-86*, pp. 125-131, 1986.

(Zadeh 65). Lotfi A. Zadeh, "Fuzzy Sets," *Information and Control*, pp. 338-353, 1965.

(Zadeh 73). Lotfi A. Zadeh, "The Concept of a Linguistic Variable and Its Application to Approximate Reasoning," *Memorandum ERL-M 411*, University of California at Berkeley, p. 83, October 1973.

(Zadeh 75). Lotfi A. Zadeh, "Calculus of Fuzzy Restrictions," *Fuzzy Sets and Their Applications to Cognitive and Decision Processes*, Academic Press, p. 36, 1975.

(Zadeh 78). Lotfi A. Zadeh, "Fuzzy Sets as a Basis for a Theory of Possibility," *Fuzzy Sets and Systems*, **1**, pp. 3-28, 1978.

(Zadeh 79). Lotfi A. Zadeh, "A Theory of Approximate Reasoning," *Machine Intelligence*, **9**, J. E. Hayes, Donald Michie, and L. I. Mikulich, eds., pp. 149-194, 1979.

(Zadeh 81). Lotfi A. Zadeh, "PRUF —A Meaning Representation Language for Natural Languages," *Fuzzy Reasoning and Its Applications*, E. H. Mamdani and B. R. Gaines, eds., Academic Press, pp. 1-66, 1981.

(Zadeh 83). Lotfi A. Zadeh, "The Role of Fuzzy Logic in the Management of Uncertainty in Expert Systems," *Fuzzy Sets and Systems*, **11**, pp 199-227, 1983.

(Zadeh 84a). Lotfi A. Zadeh, "Review of Books: A Mathematical Theory of Evidence," *The AI Magazine*, pp. 81-83, Fall 1984.

(Zadeh 84b). Lotfi A. Zadeh, "Fuzzy Probabilities," *Information Processing & Management*, **20**, (3), pp. 363-372, 1984.

(Zadeh 88). Lotfi A. Zadeh, "Fuzzy Logic," *IEEE Computer*, pp. 83-93, April 1988.

(Zimmerman 85). H. J. Zimmerman, *Fuzzy Set Theory and Its Applications*, Kluwer-Nijhoff Publishing, pp. 62-63, 1985.

CHAPTER 6
Design of Expert Systems

6.1 INTRODUCTION

In the previous chapters, we have discussed the general concepts and theory of expert systems. This chapter presents general guidelines for building practical expert systems designed for real-world applications, not research prototypes. A **software engineering methodology** is described so that an expert system can be a quality product developed in a cost-effective and timely manner.

6.2 SELECTING THE APPROPRIATE PROBLEM

Before you can build an expert system you must select an appropriate problem, as discussed in Section 1.6. As with any software project, there are a number of general considerations that should be made before a large commitment of people, resources, and time are committed to a proposed expert system. These general considerations are typical of project management concerns in conventional programs, but must be customized for the special requirements of expert systems. A very high-level management view of expert system development is shown in Figure 6.1. The three general stages have more specific considerations, shown below them. These more specific considerations will be discussed as questions-and-answers to serve as guidelines for expert system projects.

Selecting the Appropriate Paradigm

Why are we building an expert system?

This is probably the most important question to be asked of *any* project. While Chapter 1, Section 2 described the general advantages of expert systems, only management authorizes the system and technical personnel needed to implement the need. In particular, the answer to this question must eventually be given to the owners or stockholders funding the development. Before starting, there should be a clear identification of the problem, expert, and users.

Payoff

What is the payoff?

This question is related to the first question. However, this one is more pragmatic in that it is asking for a specific return on investment of people, resources, time, and money. The payoff may be in money, increased efficiency, or any of the other advantages of expert systems described in Chapter 1. It is also important to remember that if no one uses the system, there will be no payoff. Because expert systems is a new technology, it is more difficult and risky to answer this question in relation to conventional programming.

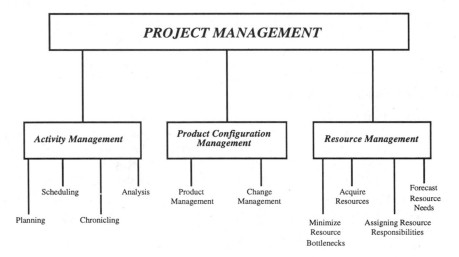

Figure 6.1 Project Management Tasks

Tools

What tools are available to build the system?

There are many expert system tools available today with advantages and disadvantages. Appendix D summarizes the characteristics of some tools. However, this should only be taken as a guide since software tools develop so rapidly. Generally, you can count on a substantial enhancement every year in each tool and a major revision every two to three years.

These enhancements are not limited to the software tools. Many of the state-of-the-art tools that only ran on $50,000 LISP machines in the mid-1980s were later rewritten to run on microcomputers or custom microprocessors. This greatly reduced the cost of hardware to run the tools. Your best guide is to examine current literature and talk to people who have built expert systems.

Cost

How much will it cost?

The cost of building an expert system depends on the people, resources, and time devoted to its construction. In addition to the hardware and software required to run an expert system tool, there may also be considerable cost in training. If your personnel have little or no experience with a tool, it can be costly to train them. For example, training on a state-of-the-art expert system tool may cost $2500/week per person.

6.3 STAGES IN THE DEVELOPMENT OF AN EXPERT SYSTEM

How will the system be developed?

To a large extent, the development of an expert system will depend on the resources provided. However, like any other project, the development will also depend on the how the process is organized and managed.

Project Management

Project management is expected to provide the following—in fact, project management has been the subject of an expert system approach (Sathi 86):

Activity Management
• planning	- define activities
	- specify priority of activities
	- resource requirements
	- milestones
	- durations
	- responsibilities
• scheduling	- assign starting and ending times
	- resolve conflicts in scheduling tasks of equal priority
• chronicling	- monitor project performance
• analysis	- analyze plans, schedules, and chronicled activities

Product Configuration Management
• product management	- manage the different versions of the product
• change management	- manage change proposals and impact evaluations
	- assign personnel to make changes
	- install new product versions

Resource Management
- • forecast needs for resources
- • acquire resources
- • assign responsibilities for optimum use of resources
- • provide critical resources to minimize bottlenecks

For the development of an expert system, the activities are those tasks required to build the system. Figure 6.2 shows a high-level view of the activities required to produce a system in terms of the stages that a system goes through.

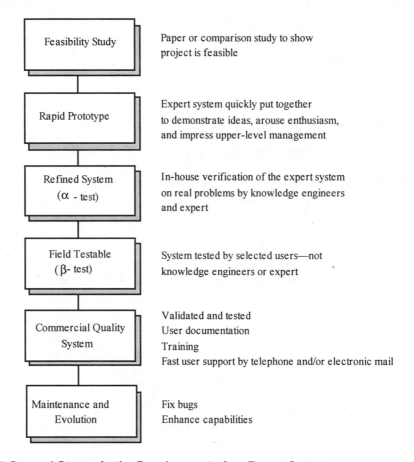

Feasibility Study — Paper or comparison study to show project is feasible

Rapid Prototype — Expert system quickly put together to demonstrate ideas, arouse enthusiasm, and impress upper-level management

Refined System (α - test) — In-house verification of the expert system on real problems by knowledge engineers and expert

Field Testable (β- test) — System tested by selected users—not knowledge engineers or expert

Commercial Quality System — Validated and tested / User documentation / Training / Fast user support by telephone and/or electronic mail

Maintenance and Evolution — Fix bugs / Enhance capabilities

Figure 6.2 General Stages in the Development of an Expert System

The Delivery Problem

How will the system be delivered?

While it is convenient and can minimize development time to use a state-of-the-art workstation, it is often too costly to deliver the system on these workstations. For example, a workstation that has $100,000 worth of hardware and software is rather expensive for use by a thousand or so field offices of a company. In addition, annual maintenance fees can further increase the cost substantially.

Depending on the number of expert systems to be deployed, the **delivery problem** of the developed systems may be a major factor in development. The delivery problem should be considered in the earliest stage of development (Freedman 86).

Ideally, the delivered expert systems should be capable of running on standard hardware. However, some expert system tools require a special LISP microprocessor board, which will substantially increase the cost.

In many cases the expert system must be integrated with other existing programs. Consideration should be given to the communication and coordination of the expert system input/output with these programs. It may also be desirable to call the expert system as a procedure from a conventional programming language, and the system should support this.

Maintenance and Evolution

How will the system be maintained and evolve?

The maintenance and evolution of an expert system is more of an open-ended activity than with conventional programs. Because expert systems are not based on algorithms, their performance is dependent on knowledge. As new knowledge is acquired and old knowledge modified, the performance of the system improves.

In a commercial-quality product there must be a systematic and efficient way to collect bug reports from the users. While the collection and repair of bug reports is not a high priority in research-grade systems, it is a high priority in commercial-quality systems. Good maintenance can be done only if bug reports are acquired.

The enhancement of an expert system after delivery is also more of a concern in a commercial-quality system. The developers of a commercial system want it to be a financial success. This means listening to what the users want and are willing to pay for in improvements. In a very real sense, a commercial expert system may never really be finished—it only keeps getting better.

6.4 ERRORS IN DEVELOPMENT STAGES

The potential major errors of expert system development can be classified by the most likely stages in which they occur, as illustrated in Figure 6.3. These errors include the following:

• **Expert's knowledge errors.** The expert is the **knowledge source** of the expert system. If the expert's knowledge is erroneous, the results may be propagated through the entire development process. As mentioned in Chapter 1, a side benefit of building an expert system is the potential detection of erroneous knowledge when the expert's knowledge is made explicit.

For **mission critical** projects in which human life and property are at risk, it may be necessary to set up formal procedures to certify an expert's knowledge. One approach that NASA has successfully used for space flight is **Flight Technique Panels,** which regularly review problem solutions and the analysis techniques used to develop the solutions (Culbert 87). The panels consist of system users, independent domain experts, system developers, and managers to insure coverage of all areas affecting development.

The advantage of a panel approach is that the expert's knowledge is placed under close scrutiny at the beginning of the development process, when erroneous knowledge is easier to correct. The longer that erroneous knowledge goes undetected, the more expensive it is to correct. If the expert's knowledge is not initially verified, the ultimate test is the validation of the expert system. The final validation of the expert system demonstrates whether the system satisfies requirements, especially correctness and completeness of solutions.

The disadvantage of a panel approach is primarily the cost involved. However, this cost may be offset by the greater efficiency of the development process.

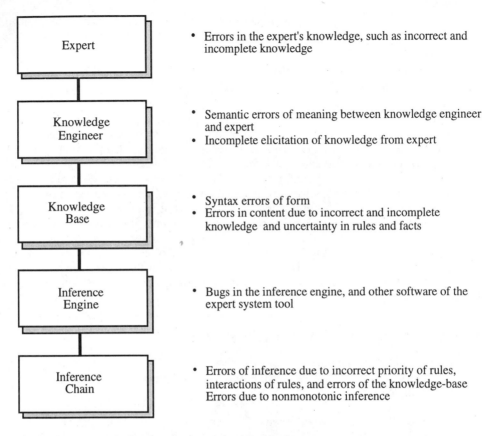

Figure 6.3 Major Errors in Expert Systems and Some Causes

• **Semantic errors**. An error of semantics occurs when the meaning of knowledge is not properly communicated. As a very simple example, suppose an expert says "You can extinguish a fire with water" and the knowledge engineer interprets this as "All fires can be extinguished by water." Semantic errors occur if the knowledge engineer misinterprets the expert's answers, or the expert misinterprets the knowledge engineer's question, or both.

• **Syntax errors**. These are simple errors that occur when the incorrect form of a rule or fact is entered. The expert system tools should flag these errors and an appropriate message issued. Other errors that occur in the knowledge base building phase are due to knowledge source errors that were not detected in the previous stages.

• **Inference engine errors**. Just as with any other piece of software, the inference engine may have bugs. By the time that an expert system tool is released for general use, all of the common bugs should be fixed. However, there may be bugs that only show up in rare circumstances such as having 159 rules on the agenda. Some bugs may be very subtle and only show up in certain pattern-matching operations.

In general, inference engine bugs may show up in pattern matching, conflict resolution, and execution of the actions. These bugs may be difficult to detect if they are not consistent. If the expert system tool is used for mission-critical applications, you should determine how the tool was validated.

The simplest method of checking for tool errors is the classic one of asking other users and the tool vendor. The tool vendor should be willing to supply a list of customers, bug reports, and fixes, and how long the tool has been in use. A user's group is an excellent source of information.

• **Inference chain errors**. These errors may be caused by erroneous knowledge, semantic errors, inference engine bugs, incorrect specification of rule priorities, and unplanned interactions between rules. More complex inference chain errors are due to uncertainty of rules and evidence, the propagation of uncertainty in the inference chain, and nonmonoticity.

The choice of a method for dealing with uncertainty does not automatically resolve all issues dealing with uncertainty. For example, before choosing simple Bayesian inference, you should check to see if the assumption of conditional independence is warranted.

• **Limits of ignorance errors**. A problem that is common to all development stages is specifying the limits of ignorance of the system. As mentioned in Chapter 1, human experts know the extent of their knowledge and their performances degrade gracefully (we hope) at the boundaries of their ignorance. Human experts should be honest enough to admit more uncertainty in their conclusions near the boundaries. However, unless an expert system is specifically programmed to admit uncertainty, it may continue to supply answers even if the inference chain and evidence are weak.

6.5 SOFTWARE ENGINEERING AND EXPERT SYSTEMS

In the previous sections we have discussed the general considerations in using the expert system paradigm. Now let's examine the stages of expert system development from the more technical perspective of the knowledge engineer who actually builds the system.

Since expert systems have moved out of the research stage there is a real need to deliver quality software up to the standards of conventional software. The accepted methodology for developing quality software for commercial, industrial, and government standards is software engineering.

It is important to follow good standards in the development of a product or the product will probably not be of good quality. Expert systems should now be considered a product just as any other software product such as a word processor, payroll program, computer game, and so forth. However, there is a significant difference of **mission** between expert systems and typical consumer products such as word processors and video games. The term *mission* refers to the overall purpose of a project or a technology. Expert systems technology generally has a serious mission of supplying expertise in high-performance and possibly hazardous situations where human life and property are at stake. These are the mission-critical applications mentioned in the previous section.

Mission-critical applications are different from the more relaxed mission of word processors and video games, which is to increase efficiency and provide recreation. No human's life may depend on a bug in a word processor or a video game (or at least it shouldn't).

Expert systems are high-performance systems that must be of high quality or they will be prone to bugs. Software engineering provides methodologies for building quality software, as illustrated in Figure 6.4.

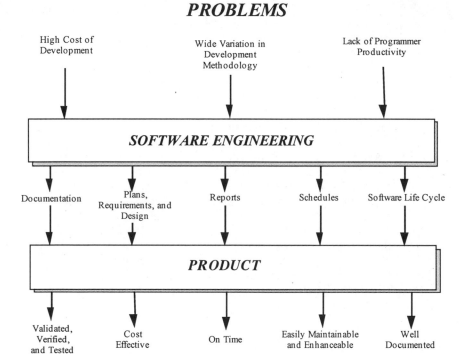

Figure 6.4 The Software Engineering Methodology

Quality is a difficult term to describe in a general sense because it means different things to different people. One way of defining **quality** is as the required or desirable attributes of an object determined on some scale. The term *object* is used here to mean any software or hardware. The attributes and their values are called *metrics* because they are used as measures of an object. For example, the measured reliability of a disk drive is a metric of its quality. One measure of this attribute is the **mean time between failures** (MTBF) of the drive. A reliable drive might have an MTBF of 1000 hours of use between crashes, whereas an unreliable drive might have an MTBF of 100 hours.

Table 6.1 gives a checklist of some metrics that may be used in assessing the quality of an expert system. These metrics should only be taken as a guide since a specific expert system may have more or less of these. However, the important concept is to have a required list of metrics that can be used in describing quality.

A list of metrics allows you to more easily prioritize them since many may be in conflict with others. For example, increasing the testing of an expert system to assure its correctness will increase the cost. Deciding when testing ends is generally a complex decision involving the factors of schedules, cost, and requirements. Ideally, all three of these requirements should be satisfied. In practice, some may be judged more important than others and the constraints of satisfying all factors will be weakened.

Correct outputs given correct input
Complete output given correct input
Consistent output given the same input again
Reliable so that it does not crash (often) due to bugs
Usable for people and preferably user-friendly
Maintainable
Enhanceable
Validated to prove it satisfies the user's needs and requests
Tested to prove correctness and completeness
Cost effective
Reusable code for other applications
Portable to other hardware/software environments
Interfaceable with other software
Understandable code
Accurate
Precise
Graceful degradation at the boundaries of knowledge
Embedded capability with other languages
Verified knowledge base
Explanation facility

Table 6.1 Some Software Quality Metrics for Expert Systems

6.6 THE EXPERT SYSTEM LIFE CYCLE

One of the key methods of software engineering is the **life cycle**. The software life cycle is the period of time that starts with the initial concept of the software and ends with its retirement from use. Rather than thinking of development and maintenance separately, the life cycle concept provides a continuity that connects all stages. Planning for maintenance and evolution early in the life cycle reduces the cost of these stages later.

Maintenance Costs

For conventional software, maintenance typically accounts for about 60 to 80 percent of all software costs and is usually two to four times the original development cost. Although there is little information about the maintenance of expert systems because they are so new, the figures will probably be worse for expert systems. If conventional programs with known algorithms require so much maintenance, then expert systems will probably require more maintenance because they are based on much knowledge that is heuristic and experiential. Expert systems that do a lot of inference under uncertainty should be even more susceptible to high maintenance and evolution costs.

Waterfall Model

A number of different life cycle models have been developed for conventional software. The classic waterfall model, familiar to programmers of conventional software, was the original life cycle model and is illustrated in Figure 6.5 (Boehm 84).

In the waterfall model each stage ends with a verification and validation (V & V) activity to minimize any problems in that stage. Also, notice that the arrows go back and forth only one stage at a time. This represents the iterative development between two adjacent stages in order to minimize the cost compared to the higher cost of iterating development over several stages.

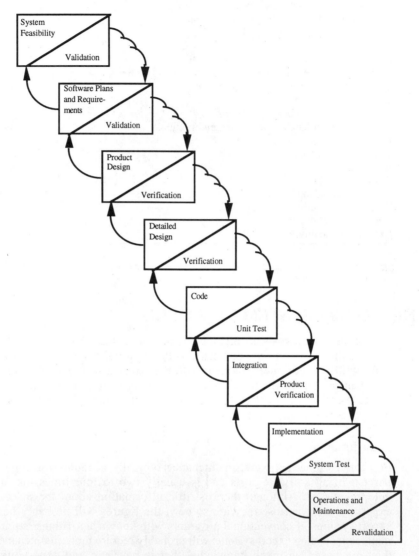

Figure 6.5 The Waterfall Model of the Software Life Cycle

Another term for life cycle is ***process model***, because it is concerned with the two fundamental issues of software development:

(1) What should be done next?
(2) How long should the next stage be performed?

The process model is actually a **metamethodology** because it determines the order and duration in which the common software methods are applied. The common software development methods (or methodologies) show specific methods to accomplish a stage such as

- planning
- requirements
- knowledge acquisition
- testing
- representation of stage products
- documentation
- code
- diagrams

Code-and-Fix Model

A number of process models have been used for software development. The earliest "model" is the infamous **code-and-fix model**, in which some code is written and then fixed when it doesn't work right (Boehm 88). This is usually the method of choice for new programming students both in conventional programming and expert systems.

By 1970 the deficiencies in the code-and-fix approach were so obvious that the waterfall model was developed to provide a systematic methodology that was especially useful for large projects. However, there were difficulties with the waterfall model because it assumed that all the information necessary for a stage was known. In practice, it was often not possible to write the complete requirements until a prototype had been built. This led to the **"do it twice"** concept, in which a prototype was built, the requirements determined, and then the final system was built.

Incremental Model

The **incremental waterfall model** is a refinement of the waterfall and of the standard top-down approach. The basic idea of incremental development is to develop software in increments of functional capability. The incremental model has been used successfully in large conventional software projects. The incremental model is also useful for expert systems development, in which the addition of rules increases the capabilities of the system from assistant to colleague and finally expert level. Thus in an expert system the **major increments** are from assistant, to colleague, and from colleague to expert. The **minor increments** correspond to increments of expertise within each level that offer some significant increase. A **micro increment** is the change in expertise by adding or refining an individual rule.

The primary advantage of the incremental model is that the increases in functional capability are easier to test, verify, and validate than the products of individual stages in the waterfall model. Each functional increment can be tested, verified, and validated immediately with the expert rather than trying to do the entire validation at the end. This decreases the cost of incorporating corrections in the system. In essence, the incremental model is similar to a continuous rapid prototype that extends over the entire development. Rather than just a rapid prototype of the initial stages to determine requirements in the "do it twice" approach, the evolving prototype *is* the system.

Spiral Model

One way of visualizing the incremental model is an adaptation of the conventional **spiral model**, as shown in Figure 6.6. Each circuit of the spiral adds some functional capability to the system. The ending point label "Delivered System" is actually not the end of the spiral. Instead, a new spiral begins with maintenance and evolution of the system. The spiral can be further refined to specify more precisely the general stages of Knowledge Acquisition, Coding, Evaluation, and Planning.

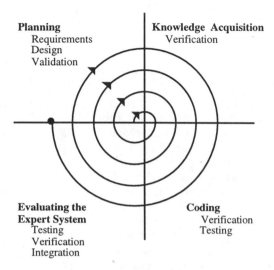

Figure 6.6 A Spiral Model of Expert System Development

6.7 A DETAILED LIFE CYCLE MODEL

A life cycle model that has been successfully used in a number of expert system projects is the **Linear Model,** illustrated in Figure 6.7, adapted from Bochsler (Bochsler 88). This life cycle consists of a number of stages from planning to system evaluation and describes the development of the system to some point at which its functional capabilities will be evaluated. After this, the life cycle repeats this same sequence from planning to system evaluation until the system is delivered for routine use. The life cycle is then used for subsequent maintenance and evolution of the system. Although not explicitly shown, verification and validation proceed in parallel with the stages. Rather than just fixing up some bugs, it is important to follow through with the same sequence of stages to maintain the quality of the expert system. Skipping stages, even to fix one little bug, impairs the quality of the entire system.

The life cycle shown may be considered one circuit of the spiral model. Each stage consists of **tasks**. Not all tasks may be necessary for a stage, especially once the system goes into maintenance and evolution. Instead, the tasks are meant to serve as a composite of all tasks for the entire life cycle, from initial concept to software retirement. The tasks will also depend on the exact type of application being built and so should only be considered as a guide, rather than absolute requirements that must be performed for each stage to be completed.

This life cycle model will be discussed in detail to illustrate the many factors that should be considered for a large quality expert system. For small research type prototypes that are not intended for general use, not all tasks or even stages are necessary. However, it is amazing how much software that is developed for personal or research use gets released to associates and then into general use.

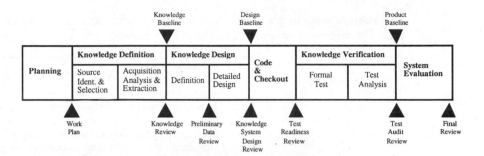

Figure 6.7 The Linear Model of Expert System Development Life Cycle

Planning

The purpose of the planning stage is to produce a formal **work plan** for the expert system development. The work plan is a set of documents that will be used to guide and evaluate development. Table 6.2 illustrates the tasks in this stage.

Task	Objective
Feasibility assessment	Determine if it is worthwhile to build the system and, if so, whether expert system technology should be used.
Resource management	Assess resources of people, time money, software, and hardware required. How to acquire and manage the required resources.
Task phasing	Specify the tasks and their order in the stages.
Schedules	Specify the starting and delivery dates of tasks in the stages.
Preliminary functional layout	Define *what* the system should accomplish by specifying the high-level functions of the system.This task specifies the purpose of the system.
High-level requirements	Describe in high-level terms *how* the functions of the system will be accomplished.

Table 6.2 Planning Stage Tasks

The feasibility assessment is the most important task in the life cycle. The assessment must answer the question of whether the project is worthwhile and the related question of whether an expert system is the appropriate paradigm. The answers to these two questions determine if the project should proceed using an expert systems approach. Many factors are involved in feasibility assessment. As discussed in Section 6.1 these factors include selection of an appropriate expert system domain, cost, payoff, and others.

Knowledge Definition

The object of the **knowledge definition stage** is to define the knowledge requirements of the expert system. The knowledge definition stage consists of two main tasks, as follows:

- knowledge source identification and selection
- knowledge acquisition, analysis, and extraction

Each of these major tasks is composed of other tasks. Table 6.3 describes the tasks involved in source identification and selection.

Task	Objective
Source identification	Who and what are the knowledge sources, without regard to availability.
Source importance	Prioritized list of knowledge sources in order of importance to development.
Source availability	List of knowledge sources ranked in order of availability. Books and other documents are generally much more available than are human experts.
Source selection	Select the knowledge sources based on importance and availability.

Table 6.3 Knowledge Source Identification and Selection Tasks

Acquisition, analysis, and extraction tasks are described in Table 6.4.

Task	Objective
Acquisition strategy	Specify how knowledge will be acquired by methods for interviewing experts, reading documents, rule induction, repertory grids, and so forth.
Knowledge element identification	Pick out the specific knowledge from sources that will be useful in this iteration of the life cycle.
Knowledge classification system	Classify and organize the knowledge to aid in knowledge verification and understanding by developers. Use hierarchical groups whenever possible.
Detailed functional layout	Specify the functional capabilities of the system in detail. This is at a more technical level whereas the preliminary functional layout was at a managerial level.
Preliminary control flow	Describe general phases that the expert system will execute. Phases correspond to logical rules that are activated/deactivated in groups to control execution flow.
Preliminary user's manual	Describes system from user's viewpoint. An often ignored but essential part of the system. It is absolutely important to involve users as soon as possible for feedback. If they don't use the system, it's worthless.
Requirements specifications	Define exactly what the system is supposed to do. The expert system will be validated using these requirements.
Knowledge baseline	Baseline knowledge for the system. Any changes must now be done by a formal change request. The high-level knowledge is now adequate for the next stage of knowledge design.

Table 6.4 Knowledge Acquisition, Analysis and Extraction Tasks

The main objective of the **knowledge acquisition task**, the **knowledge analysis task**, and the **knowledge extraction task** is to produce and verify the knowledge required by the system. By the time that the knowledge is baselined, it should be correct and suitable for the next stage of knowledge design. In addition to the customary method of interviewing experts, other techniques such as

repertory grids or **personal construct theory** may be used to perform automated knowledge acquisition (Boose 84).

Knowledge Design

The objective of the **knowledge design stage** is to produce the detailed design for an expert system. There are two main tasks that comprise this stage:

- knowledge definition
- detailed design

Table 6.5 describes the tasks associated with knowledge definition.

Task	Objective
Knowledge representation	Specify how knowledge will be represented, such as rules, frames, or logic. Dependent upon what the expert system tool will support.
Detailed control structure	Specify three general control structures: (1) If the system is embedded in procedural code, how it will be called. (2) Control of related groups of rules within an executing system. (3) Metalevel control structures for rules.
Internal fact structure	Specify the internal structure of facts in a consistent manner to aid in understanding and good style.
Preliminary user interface	Specify a preliminary user interface. Get feedback from users about the interface.
Initial test plan	Specify how code will be tested. Define test data, test drivers, and how test results will be analyzed.

Table 6.5 Knowledge Definition Tasks

The internal fact structures described in Table 6.5 are discussed in much more detail in the chapters on CLIPS. The basic idea of specifying fact structures is to adapt good style. For example, a fact such as "10" is not very meaningful by itself. What does the "10" represent? If additional information is included with the fact such as "price 10" or, better still, "gold price 10," then the gold price is meaningful. Notice that this form of the fact is in conventional object-attribute-value form and so is convenient for people to read and understand. CLIPS supports this through the deftemplate construct for rules, and also through objects.

In some expert system languages the fields may have **strong typing** so that only certain values are allowed. If a rule tries to specify a value that is not allowed, the inference engine flags this as an error. The **detailed design stage** of knowledge is shown in Table 6.6.

The product of the detailed design stage is the baselined design document from which coding can proceed. The baselined design document undergoes a knowledge system design review as a final check before coding begins.

Task	Objective
Design structure	Specify how knowledge is logically organized in the knowledge base and what is in the knowledge base.
Implementation strategy	Specify how the system is to be implemented.
Detailed user interface	Specify the detailed user interface after receiving user feedback from the preliminary user interface design.
Design specifications and report	Document the design.
Detailed test plan	Specify exactly how the code will be tested and verified.

Table 6.6 Detailed Design of Knowledge Tasks

Code and Checkout

Table 6.7 describes the **code and checkout stage,** which begins the actual code implementation.

Task	Objective
Coding	Implement coding.
Tests	Test code using test data, test drivers, and test analysis procedures.
Source listings	Produce commented, documented source code.
User's manual	Produce working user's manual so experts and users can provide feedback on system.
Installation/operations guide	Document installation/operation of system for users.
System description document	Document overall expert system functionality, limitations, and problems.

Table 6.7 Code and Checkout Tasks

This stage terminates with the **test readiness review,** which determines if the expert system is ready for the next stage of knowledge verification.

Knowledge Verification

The objective of the **knowledge verification stage** is to determine the correctness, completeness, and consistency of the system. This stage is divided into two main tasks:

- formal tests
- test analysis

Table 6.8 describes the **formal test task** of the knowledge verification stage.

Task	Objective
Test procedures	Implement formal test procedures.
Test reports	Document test results.

Table 6.8 Formal Test Tasks of the Knowledge Verification Stage

The **test analysis tasks** are shown in Table 6.9. The test analysis looks for the following major problems:

- incorrect answers
- incomplete answers
- inconsistent answers

and determines if the problem lies in rules, inference chains, uncertainty, or some combination of these three factors. If the problem cannot be pinned down to the expert system, then it is necessary to analyze the expert system tool software for bugs.

Task	Objective
Results Evaluations	Analyze test results.
Recommendations	Document recommendations and conclusions of tests.

Table 6.9 Test Analysis Tasks

System Evaluation

As described in Table 6.10, the final stage in the development life cycle is the **system evaluation stage**. The purpose of this stage is to summarize what has been learned with recommendations for improvements and corrections.

Task	Objective
Results evaluation	Summarize the results of testing and verification..
Recommendations	Recommend any changes to the system.
Validation	Validate that the system is correct with respect to user needs and requirements.
Interim or final report	If the system is complete, issue final report. If not, issue an interim report.

Table 6.10 System Evaluation Stage Tasks

Because an expert system is usually built up in iterations, the report from the system evaluation stage will usually be an interim report describing the increased functionality of the system as new knowledge is added. However, the new system capability must be verified by itself and also as part of the previous knowledge in the system. That is, the system verification must also be performed in conjunction with all the system knowledge, not just the new knowledge. The expert system should also be validated each time at this stage rather than waiting for the final iteration. Automated systems for validation of knowledge bases are also being investigated (Stachowitz 87).

6.8 SUMMARY

In this chapter we discussed a software engineering approach to the construction of expert systems. Now that expert systems technology is being used for solving real-world problems, expert systems *must* be quality products.

A number of factors must be considered in the design of an expert system such as problem selection, cost, and payoff. Both the managerial and technical aspects must be considered in building a successful system.

One very useful concept of software engineering is the life cycle. The life cycle views software development as a series of stages from initial concept to retirement of the software. By consistently following a life cycle, it is possible to build quality software. Several different life cycle models were discussed for expert systems and one was shown in detail.

PROBLEMS

6.1   Consider a simple knowledge-based system for diagnosing problems in an automobile. Describe this proposed system for each stage of the linear model (it is not necessary to do this in terms of each task). Assume there are many people working on the project and consider the coordination of their efforts. Explain any assumptions you make.

6.2   Write a report on an automated tool for knowledge-base validation such as EVA (Stachowitz 87). List all the problems it can detect and all its limitations.

6.3   Explain any changes or differences in the linear model for a large project development with many developers versus a small project with only one person.

BIBLIOGRAPHY

(Bochsler 88). Daniel C. Bochsler, "A Project Management Approach to Expert System Applications," *ISA 88*, pp. 1458-1466, 1988.

(Boehm 84). Barry W. Boehm, "Software Life Cycle Factors," in *Handbook of Software Engineering*, C. R. Vick and C. V. Ramamoorthy, eds., Van Nostrand Reinhold Co., pp. 494-518, 1984.

(Boehm 88). Barry W. Boehm, "A Spiral Model of Software Development and Enhancement," *IEEE Computer*, pp. 61-72, May 1988.

(Boose 84). John H. Boose, "Personal Construct Theory and the Transfer of Human Expertise," *AAAI 84*, pp. 27-33, 1984.

(Culbert 87). Chris Culbert, Gary Riley, and Robert T. Savely, "Approaches to the Verification of Rule-based Expert Systems," NASA Conference Publication 2491, *First Annual Workshop on Space Operations Automation and Robotics (SOAR 87)*, NASA, Houston, Texas, pp. 191-196, 1987.

(Freedman 86). Roy S. Freedman and Robert P. Frail, "OPGEN: The Evolution of an Expert System for Process Planning," *The AI Magazine*, pp. 58-70, Winter 1986.

(Sathi 86). Arvind Sathi, Thomas E. Morton, and Steven F. Roth, "Callisto: An Intelligent Project Management System," *The AI Magazine*, pp. 34-52, Winter 1986.

(Stachowitz 87). R. A. Stachowitz, et al., "Building Validation Tools for Knowledge-based Systems," *First Annual Workshop on Space Operations Automation and Robotics (SOAR 87)*, NASA, Houston, Texas, pp. 209-216, 1987.

CHAPTER 7
Introduction to CLIPS

7.1 INTRODUCTION

This chapter begins the introduction of the practical concepts necessary to build an expert system. Chapters 1 through 6 looked at the background, history, definitions, terminology, concepts, tools, and applications of expert systems. In short, they provided an understanding of what expert systems are and what they can do. This theoretical framework of concepts and algorithms is essential in building expert systems. However, there are many practical aspects to building expert systems that must be learned by doing. Building an expert system is much like writing a program in a procedural language. Knowing how an algorithm works is not the same as being able to write a procedural program to perform that algorithm. Similarly, capturing an expert's knowledge is not the same as building an expert system. For this reason, practical experience in using an expert system tool is invaluable in learning about expert systems.

The expert system language that will be used to demonstrate various concepts in the rest of this book is CLIPS. Three types of programming paradigms are supported by CLIPS: rule-based, object-oriented, and procedural. We will focus primarily on the rule-based programming aspects of CLIPS. The CD-ROM included with this book contains the *CLIPS Basic Programming Guide* and *CLIPS User's Guide* in electronic format. These manuals provide detailed coverage of all CLIPS features including those not discussed in this book. This chapter describes the basic components of a rule-based expert system (as discussed in Chapter 1) that are found within CLIPS. These basic components are:

1. **fact list**: contains the data on which inferences are derived
2. **knowledge base**: contains all the rules
3. **inference engine**: controls overall execution

These three components of CLIPS will provide the focus of this chapter. The first component, facts, will be covered in detail. Adding, removing, modifying, duplicating, displaying, and tracing facts will be discussed, followed by an explanation of how the rules of a CLIPS program interact with facts to make a program execute. Finally, the interaction of multiple rules will be demonstrated.

7.2 CLIPS

CLIPS is a multiparadigm programming language that provides support for rule-based, object-oriented, and procedural programming. The inferencing and representation capabilities provided by the rule-based programming language of CLIPS are similar to, but more powerful than, those of OPS5. Syntactically, CLIPS rules very closely resemble rules in languages such as ART, ART-IM, Eclipse, and Cognate. CLIPS supports only forward chaining rules—it does not support backward chaining.

The object-oriented programming capabilities in CLIPS, collectively referred to as the CLIPS Object-Oriented Language (COOL), are a hybrid combination of features found in other object-oriented languages such as the Common Lisp Object System (CLOS) and SmallTalk in addition to a number of new ideas. The procedural programming language provided by CLIPS has features similar to languages such as C, Ada, and Pascal and is syntactically similar to LISP.

CLIPS, an acronym for C Language Integrated Production System, was designed using the C programming language at NASA/Johnson Space Center with the specific purpose of providing high portability, low cost, and easy integration with external systems. Portions of the CLIPS acronym, however, can be misleading. Originally, CLIPS provided support only for rule-based programming (hence "Production System"). Version 5.0 of CLIPS introduced procedural and object-oriented programming support. The "C Language" portion of the acronym is also misleading since there is one version of CLIPS developed entirely in Ada. The CD-ROM included with this book contains CLIPS 6.05 executables for DOS, Windows 3.1/Windows 95, and MacOS, documentation in electronic format, and the C source code for CLIPS.

Because of its portability, CLIPS has been installed on a variety of computers ranging from PCs to CRAY supercomputers. The majority of examples shown in this and the following chapters should work on any computer on which CLIPS has been installed. It is recommended that CLIPS users have some knowledge of the operating system of the computer on which CLIPS is being used. For example, the method for specifying files tends to vary from one operating system to another. When commands may vary depending on the machine or the operating system, this will be noted.

7.3 NOTATION

This chapter and those following will use the same notation for describing the syntax of various commands and constructs that are introduced. This notation consists of three different types of text to be entered.

The first type of notation is for symbols and characters that are to be entered exactly as shown; this includes anything that is not enclosed by the character pairs < >, [ ], or { }. For example, consider the following syntax description:

```
(example)
```

This syntax description means that *(example)* should be entered as shown. To be exact, the character '(' should be entered first, followed by the character 'e', then 'x', 'a', 'm', 'p', 'l', 'e' and finally the character ')'.

Square brackets, [ ], indicate that the contents of the brackets are optional. For example, the syntax description

```
(example [1])
```

indicates that the 1 found within the brackets is optional. So the following entry would be consistent with the above syntax:

```
(example)
```

as would this entry:

```
(example 1)
```

The less than and greater than characters together, < >, indicate that a replacement is to be made with a value of the type specified by the contents found within the < >. For example, the following within a syntax description

```
<integer>
```

indicates that a substitution should be made with an actual integer value. Following the previous examples, the syntax description

```
(example <integer>)
```

could be replaced with

```
(example 1)
```

or

```
(example 5)
```

or

```
(example -20)
```

or many more entries that contained the characters "(example ", followed by an integer, followed by the character ")". It is important to note that spaces shown in the syntax description should also be included in the entry.

Another notation is indicated with a * following a description. This indicates that the description can be replaced with *zero* or more occurrences of the value specified. Spaces should be placed after each occurrence of a value. For example, the syntax description

```
<integer>*
```

could be replaced with

```
1
```

or

```
1 2
```

or

```
1 2 3
```

or with any number of integers, or with nothing at all.

A description followed by a + indicates that *one* or more of the values specified by the description should by used in place of the syntax description. Note that for this notation, the syntax description

```
<integer>+
```

is equivalent to the syntax description

```
<integer> <integer>*
```

A vertical bar, |, indicates a choice among one or more of the items separated by the bars. For example, the syntax description

```
all | none | some
```

could be replaced with

```
all
```

or

```
none
```

or

```
some
```

7.4 FIELDS

As a knowledge base is constructed, CLIPS must read input from the keyboard and files in order to execute commands and load programs. As CLIPS reads characters from the keyboard or files, it groups them together into **tokens**. Tokens represent groups of characters that have special meaning to CLIPS. Some tokens such as left and right parentheses consist of only one character.

The group of tokens known as **fields** is of particular importance. There are seven types of fields, also called the CLIPS primitive data types: **float, integer, symbol, string, external address, instance name**, and **instance address**.

The first two types of fields, floats and integers, are called *numeric fields* or simply *numbers*. A numeric field consists of three parts: the sign, the value, and the exponent. The sign and the exponent are optional. The sign is either + or −. The value contains one or more digits with a single optional decimal point contained with the digits. The exponent consists of the letter e or E followed by an optional + or − followed by one or more digits. Any number consisting of an optional sign followed by only digits is stored as an **integer**. All other numbers are stored as **floats**.

The following are examples of valid CLIPS floats:

```
1.5
1.0
0.7
9e+1
3.5e10
```

The following are examples of valid CLIPS integers:

```
1
+3
-1
65
```

A **symbol** is a field that starts with a printable ASCII character and is followed by zero or more characters. The end of a symbol is reached when a **delimiter** is encountered. Delimiters include any nonprintable ASCII character (including spaces, tabs, carriage returns, and line feeds), the " (double quotation mark) character, the ((opening parenthesis) character, the) (closing parenthesis) character, the ; (semicolon) character, the & (ampersand) character, the | (vertical bar) character, the ~ (tilde) character, and the < (less than) character. Symbols cannot contain delimiters (with the exception of the < character, which may be the first in a symbol). Also, the **?** and **$?** sequence of characters cannot be placed at the beginning of a symbol since they are used to denote variables (see Section 8.2). In addition, a sequence of characters that does not exactly follow the numeric field format is treated as a symbol.

The following are examples of valid symbols:

```
Space-Station
February
fire
activate_sprinkler_system
notify-fire-department
shut-down-electrical-junction-387
!?#$^*
345B
346-95-6156
```

Notice how the underscore and hyphen characters are used to tie symbols together to make them into a single field.

CLIPS will preserve the uppercase and lowercase letters it finds in tokens. Because it distinguishes between uppercase and lowercase letters, CLIPS is called *case-sensitive*. For example, the following symbols are considered different by CLIPS:

```
case-sensitive
Case-Sensitive
CASE-SENSITIVE
```

The next type of field is a **string**. A string must begin and end with double quotation marks, which are part of the field. There can be zero or more characters of any kind between the double quotes, including characters normally used by CLIPS as delimiters. The following are examples of valid CLIPS strings:

```
"Activate the sprinkler system."
"Shut down electrical junction 387."
"!?#$^"
"John Q. Public"
```

Spaces normally act as delimiters in CLIPS to separate fields (such as symbols) and other tokens. Additional spaces used between tokens are discarded. Spaces included as part of a string, however, are preserved. For example, CLIPS considers the following four distinct strings:

```
"spaces"
"spaces "
" spaces"
" spaces "
```

If the surrounding double quotes were removed, CLIPS would consider each of the lines as containing the same word since spaces other than those used as delimiters would be ignored.

Because double quotes are used to delimit strings, it is not possible to directly place a double quote within a string. For example, the line

```
""three-tokens""
```

would be interpreted by CLIPS as the following three separate tokens following since double quotes act as delimiters:

```
""
three-tokens
""
```

Within a string, double quotes can be included by using the backslash operator, \. For example, the line

```
"\"single-token\""
```

will be interpreted by CLIPS as the string field

```
""single-token""
```

Only a single field is created because the backslash character prevents the following double quotes from acting as a delimiter. The backslash character itself may be placed within a string by using two backslashes in succession. For example, the line

```
"\\single-token\\"
```

will be interpreted by CLIPS as the string field

```
"\single-token\"
```

The remaining three types of fields are **external addresses**, **instance addresses**, and **instance names** and are of limited interest in the exploration of the rule-based programming capabilities of CLIPS. External addresses represent the address of an external data structure returned by a **user-defined function** (a function written in a language such as C or Ada and linked with CLIPS to add additional functionality). Since the value of an external address cannot be specified by a sequence of characters that form a token and the basic unmodified version of CLIPS contains no functions that return external addresses, it is not possible to create this type of field in the basic unmodified version of CLIPS. Instance names and instance addresses are fields used in conjunction with COOL. Instance names are symbols enclosed within left and right square brackets. For example, [pump-1] is an instance name. Instance addresses, like external addresses, can only be obtained as the return value from a function.

A series of zero or more fields contained together is referred to as a **multifield value**. Multifield values are usually created by calling a function (as will be shown in subsequent chapters) or when specifying initial values for facts. When printed, a multifield value is enclosed by left and right parentheses. For example, the zero length multifield would be printed as follows:

```
()
```

and the multifield containing the symbols *this* and *that* would be printed as follows:

```
(this that)
```

7.5 ENTERING AND EXITING CLIPS

CLIPS can be entered by issuing the appropriate run command for the machine on which CLIPS has been installed. The CLIPS prompt should appear as follows:

```
CLIPS>
```

At this point commands can be entered directly to CLIPS; this mode is called the *top level.*

The normal mode of leaving CLIPS is the **exit** command. The syntax of this command is

```
(exit)
```

Notice that the word *exit* is enclosed within matching parentheses. Many rule-based languages draw their origins from LISP, which uses parentheses as delimiters. Since CLIPS is based on a language that was originally developed using LISP machines, it retains these delimiters. The symbol *exit* without enclosing parentheses has quite a different meaning than the symbol *exit* with enclosing parentheses. The parentheses around *exit* indicate that *exit* is a command to be executed and not just the symbol *exit*. We'll see later that parentheses serve as important delimiters for commands.

For now it is important to remember only that each CLIPS command must have a matching number of left and right parentheses and that the parentheses are properly balanced.

The final step in executing a CLIPS command after it has been entered with properly balanced parentheses is to press the return key. The return key may also be pressed before or after any token has been entered. For example, pressing the return key after entering the characters "ex", but before entering the characters "it", would create two tokens: a token for the symbol *ex* and a token for the symbol *it*.

The following command sequence demonstrates a sample session of entering CLIPS, evaluating a constant field value, evaluating a function, and then exiting using the exit command. The example shown is for an IBM PC using MS-DOS in which the CLIPS executable is stored on a disk in drive A and the current drive is also A. The name of the CLIPS executable is assumed to be CLIPS. Output displayed by MS-DOS or CLIPS is shown in regular type. All input that must be typed by the user is shown in bold type. The return key is indicated by the character ↵. Remember that CLIPS is case sensitive, so it is important to type upper- and lowercase letters exactly as they appear.

```
A> CLIPS ↵
          CLIPS (V6.05 09/01/97)
CLIPS> exit ↵
exit
CLIPS> (+ 3 4) ↵
7
CLIPS> (exit) ↵
A>
```

While at the top level, CLIPS will accept input from the user and attempt to evaluate that input to determine the appropriate response. Fields entered by themselves are considered constants and the result of evaluating a constant is the constant itself. So when the symbol *exit* is typed by itself and followed by a carriage return, CLIPS evaluates this input and the symbol *exit* is displayed as the result. A symbol surrounded by parentheses is considered to be a command or function call. Thus the input (+ 3 4) is a call to the + function, which performs addition. Its arguments are the values 3 and 4. The return value of this function call is the value 7 (return values will be discussed in greater detail in Chapter 8). Finally, the input (exit) invokes the *exit* command, which exits CLIPS. The terms *function* and *command* should be thought of interchangeably. Throughout this text, *function* will be used to indicate that a value is returned and *command* will indicate either that no value is returned or that the action is normally performed at the top level prompt.

7.6 FACTS

In order to solve a problem, a CLIPS program must have data or information with which it can reason. A "chunk" of information in CLIPS is called a **fact**. Facts consist of a **relation name** (a symbolic field) followed by zero or more **slots** (also symbolic fields) and their associated values. The following is an example of a fact:

```
(person (name "John Q. Public")
        (age 23)
        (eye-color blue)
        (hair-color black))
```

The entire fact, as well as each slot, is delimited by an opening left parenthesis and a closing right parenthesis. The symbol *person* is the fact's relation name and the fact contains four slots: *name*, *age*, *eye-color*, and *hair-color*. The value of the *name* slot is "John Q. Public," the value of the *age* slot is 23, the value of the *eye-color* slot is *blue*, and the value of the *hair-color* slot is *black*. Note that the order in which slots are specified is irrelevant. The fact

```
(person (hair-color black)
        (name "John Q. Public")
        (eye-color blue)
        (age 23))
```

is treated by CLIPS as identical to the first *person* fact shown.

The Deftemplate Construct

Before facts can be created, CLIPS must be informed of the list of valid slots for a given relation name. Groups of facts that share the same relation name and contain common information can be described using the **deftemplate** construct. **Constructs** form the core of a CLIPS program by adding the programmer's knowledge to the CLIPS environment and are different from functions and commands. The deftemplate construct is analogous to a record structure in a language such as Pascal. The general format of a deftemplate is

```
(deftemplate <relation-name> [<optional-comment>]
   <slot-definition>*)
```

The syntax description <slot-definition> is defined as

```
(slot <slot-name>) | (multislot <slot-name>)
```

Using this syntax, the *person* fact could be described with the following deftemplate:

```
(deftemplate person "An example deftemplate"
   (slot name)
   (slot age)
   (slot eye-color)
   (slot hair-color))
```

Multifield Slots

Slots of a fact that have been specified with the *slot* keyword in their corresponding deftemplates are allowed to contain only one value (these are referred to as *single-field slots*). It is often desirable to place zero or more fields into a given slot. Slots of a fact that have been specified with the **multislot** keyword in their corresponding deftemplates are allowed to contain zero or more values (these are referred to as *multifield slots*). For example, the *name* slot of the *person* deftemplate stores the person's name as a single string value. If the *name* slot were defined using the *multislot* keyword in place of the *slot* keyword, then any number of fields could be stored in it. Thus, the fact

```
(person (name John Q. Public)
        (age 23)
        (eye-color blue)
        (hair-color brown))
```

is illegal if *name* is a single-field slot, but legal if *name* is a multifield slot. A deftemplate can have any combination of single and multifield slots.

Ordered Facts

Facts with a relation name that has a corresponding deftemplate are called ***deftemplate facts***. Facts with a relation name that does not have a corresponding deftemplate are called ***ordered facts***. Ordered facts have a single implied multifield slot that is used to store all values following the relation name. In fact, whenever CLIPS encounters an ordered fact it automatically creates an **implied deftemplate** for that fact (as opposed to an **explicit deftemplate**, created using the deftemplate construct). Since an ordered fact has only one slot, the slot name isn't required when defining a fact. For example, a list of numbers could be represented with the following fact:

```
(number-list 7 9 3 4 20)
```

Essentially this is equivalent to defining the following deftemplate:

```
(deftemplate number-list (multislot values))
```

and then defining the fact as follows:

```
(number-list (values 7 9 3 4 20))
```

Generally, deftemplate facts should be used whenever possible because the slot names make the facts more readable and easier to work with. There are two cases in which ordered facts are useful. First, facts consisting of just a relation name are useful as flags and look identical regardless of whether a deftemplate has been defined. For example, the ordered fact

```
(all-orders-processed)
```

could be used as a flag to indicate when all orders have been processed.

Second, for facts containing a single slot, the slot name is usually synonymous with the relation name. For example, the facts

```
(time 8:45)
(food-groups meat dairy bread
             fruits-and-vegetables)
```

are just as meaningful as

```
(time (value 8:45))
(food-groups (values meat dairy bread
                      fruits-and-vegetables))
```

Figure 7.1 graphically depicts the relationships among the terms introduced in this section.

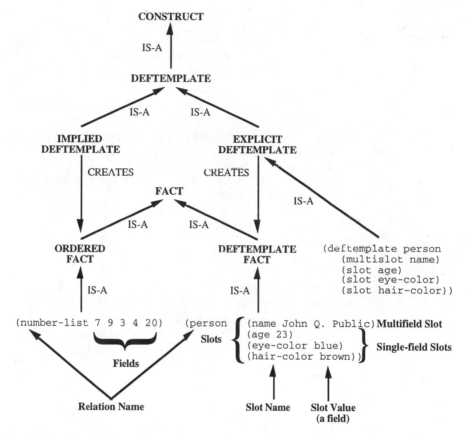

Figure 7.1 Deftemplate Overview

7.7 ADDING AND REMOVING FACTS

The group of all facts known to CLIPS is stored in the fact list. Facts representing information can be added and removed from the fact list. New facts can be added to the fact list using the **assert** command. The syntax of the *assert* command is

```
(assert <fact>+)
```

As an example, let's use the *person* deftemplate to describe some people as facts. Information about John Q. Public can be added to the fact list by using the following commands:

```
CLIPS>
(deftemplate person
    (slot name)
    (slot age)
    (slot eye-color)
    (slot hair-color))↵
CLIPS>
(assert (person (name "John Q. Public")
                (age 23)
                (eye-color blue)
                (hair-color black)))↵
<Fact-0>
CLIPS>
```

Notice that the assert command returns a value, <Fact-0>. The use of return values will be discussed in Chapter 8.

The **facts** command can be used to display the facts in the fact list. The basic syntax of the *facts* command is

```
(facts)
```

For example,

```
CLIPS>  (facts)↵
f-0      (person (name "John Q. Public")
                .(age 23)
                 (eye-color blue)
                 (hair-color black))
For a total of 1 fact.
CLIPS>
```

The term "f-0" is the **fact identifier** assigned to the fact by CLIPS. Every fact that is inserted into the fact list is assigned a unique fact identifier starting with the letter f and followed by an integer called the *fact index*. The fact index 0 was also displayed in the return value, <Fact-0>, from the previous *assert* command. Note that, as shown in this book, extra spaces have been added in the output of the *facts* command between the *(age 23)* and the *(eye-color blue)* slots to improve readibility. Normally CLIPS would only put one space between the slots and would wrap the output from the far left column to the far right column. In other CLIPS examples throughout this book spaces will occasionally be added to CLIPS output to improve readability as long as the addition of spaces does not cause confusion.

Normally CLIPS does not accept duplicate entries of a fact (although this behavior can be changed, as shown in Section 12.2). Therefore, attempting to place a second "John Q. Public" fact with identical slot values into the fact list will have no result. Of course, other facts that do not duplicate existing facts can be easily added to the fact list. For example,

```
CLIPS>
(assert (person (name "Jane Q. Public")
                (age 36)
                (eye-color green)
                (hair-color red)))↵
<Fact-1>
CLIPS> (facts)↵
f-0        (person (name "John Q. Public")
                   (age 23)
                   (eye-color blue)
                   (hair-color black))
f-1        (person (name "Jane Q. Public")
                   (age 36)
                   (eye-color green)
                   (hair-color red))
For a total of 2 facts.
CLIPS>
```

As the syntax of the *assert* command indicates, more than one fact can be asserted using a single *assert* command. For example, the command

```
(assert (person (name "John Q. Public")
                (age 23)
                (eye-color blue)
                (hair-color black))
        (person (name "Jane Q. Public")
                (age 36)
                (eye-color green)
                (hair-color red)))
```

will assert two facts into the fact list.

It is important to realize that identifiers in the fact list are not necessarily sequential. Just as facts can be added to the fact list, there is also a way to remove facts. As facts are removed from the fact list, the deleted fact identifiers will be missing in the fact list, so the fact identifiers may not be strictly sequential as a CLIPS program executes.

Because large numbers of facts can be contained in the fact list, it is often useful to be able to view only a portion of the fact list. This can be accomplished using additional arguments for the *facts* command. The complete syntax for the *facts* command is

```
(facts [<start> [<end> [<maximum>]]])
```

where <start>, <end>, and <maximum> are positive integers. Notice that the syntax of the *facts* command allows from zero to three arguments. If no arguments are specified, all facts are displayed. If the <start> argument is specified, all facts with fact indexes greater than or equal to <start> are displayed. If <start> and <end> are specified, all facts with fact indexes greater than or equal to <start> and less than or equal to <end> are displayed. Finally, if <maximum> is specified along with <start> and <end>, no more than <maximum> facts will be displayed.

Just as facts can be added to the fact list, they can also be removed. Removing facts from the fact list is called ***retraction*** and is done with the **retract** command. The syntax of the *retract* command is

```
(retract <fact-index>+)
```

The fact indices of one or more facts to be retracted are included as the arguments of the *retract* command. For example, John Q. Public can be removed from the fact list with the command

```
(retract 0)
```

Similarly, the command

```
(retract 1)
```

will retract the Jane Q. Public fact.

Attempting to retract a nonexistent fact will produce the following error message (where [PRNTUTIL1] is a key for finding the error message in the *CLIPS Reference Manual*):

```
[PRNTUTIL1] Unable to find fact <fact-identifier>.
```

For example,

```
CLIPS> (retract 1)↵
CLIPS> (retract 1)↵
[PRNTUTIL1] Unable to find fact f-1.
CLIPS>
```

A single *retract* command can be used to retract multiple facts at once. For example, the command

```
(retract 0 1)
```

will retract facts f-0 and f-1.

7.8 MODIFYING AND DUPLICATING FACTS

Slot values of deftemplate facts can be modified using the **modify** command. The syntax of the *modify* command is

```
(modify <fact-index> <slot-modifier>+)
```

where <slot-modifier> is

```
(<slot-name> <slot-value>)
```

For example, if John Q. Public just had a birthday, his age could be changed from 23 to 24 using the modify command.

```
CLIPS> (modify 0 (age 24))↵
<Fact-2>
CLIPS> (facts)↵
f-2      (person (name "John Q. Public")
                 (age 24)
                 (eye-color blue)
                 (hair-color black))
For a total of 1 fact.
CLIPS>
```

The modify command works by retracting the original fact and then asserting a new fact with the specified slot values modified. Because of this, a new fact index is generated for a modified fact.

The **duplicate** command works in the same way with the exception that it does not retract the original fact. Thus, if John's long-lost twin brother Jack is found, he can be added to the fact list by duplicating John's fact and changing the name slot.

```
CLIPS> (duplicate 2 (name "Jack S. Public"))↵
<Fact-3>
CLIPS> (facts)↵
f-2      (person (name "John Q. Public")
                 (age 24)
                 (eye-color blue)
                 (hair-color black))
f-3      (person (name "Jack S. Public")
                 (age 24)
                 (eye-color blue)
                 (hair-color black))
For a total of 2 facts.
CLIPS>
```

The modify and duplicate commands cannot be used with ordered facts.

7.9 THE WATCH COMMAND

The **watch** command is useful for debugging programs. The effect of watching facts will be discussed in this section; the remaining watch items will be discussed in this and later chapters. The syntax of this command is

```
(watch <watch-item>)
```

where <watch-item> is one of the symbols *facts*, *rules*, *activations*, *statistics*, *compilations*, *focus*, or *all*.

These items may be watched in any combination to provide the appropriate amount of debugging information. The *watch* command can be used more than once to watch more than one feature of CLIPS execution. The word *all* can be used to enable all of the watch features. By default, when CLIPS is first started, compilations are watched and the remaining watch items are not watched.

If facts are being watched, CLIPS will automatically print a message indicating that an update has been made to the fact list whenever facts are asserted or retracted. The following command dialog illustrates the use of this debugging command:

```
CLIPS> (facts 3 3)↵
f-3       (person (name "Jack S. Public")
                  (age 24)
                  (eye-color blue)
                  (hair-color black))
For a total of 1 fact.
CLIPS> (watch facts)↵
CLIPS> (modify 3 (age 25))↵
<== f-3       (person (name "Jack S. Public")
                      (age 24)
                      (eye-color blue)
                      (hair-color black))
 ==> f-4      (person (name "Jack S. Public")
                      (age 25)
                      (eye-color blue)
                      (hair-color black))
<Fact-4>
CLIPS>
```

The character sequence <== indicates that the fact is being retracted. The character sequence ==> indicates that the fact is being asserted.

The effects of a *watch* command may be turned off by using the corresponding **unwatch** command. The syntax of the *unwatch* command is

```
(unwatch <watch-item>)
```

7.10 THE DEFFACTS CONSTRUCT

It is often convenient to be able to automatically assert a set of facts instead of typing in the same assertions from the top level. This is particularly true for facts that are known to be true before running a program (i.e., the initial knowledge). Running test cases to debug a program is another instance in which it is useful to automatically assert a group of facts. Groups of facts that represent initial knowledge can be defined using the **deffacts** construct. For example, the following deffacts statement provides initial information about some people we have already encountered:

```
(deffacts people "Some people we know"
    (person (name "John Q. Public") (age 24)
            (eye-color blue) (hair-color black))
    (person (name "Jack S. Public") (age 24)
            (eye-color blue) (hair-color black))
    (person (name "Jane Q. Public") (age 36)
            (eye-color green) (hair-color red)))
```

The general format of a deffacts is

```
(deffacts <deffacts name> [<optional comment>]
   <facts>*)
```

Following the deffacts keyword is the required name of this deffacts construct. Any valid symbol can be used as the name. In this case the name chosen was *people*. Following the name is an optional comment in double quotes. Like the optional comment of a rule, this comment will be retained with the deffacts after it's been loaded by CLIPS. After the name or comment are the facts that will be asserted in the fact list by this deffacts statement.

The facts in a deffacts statement are asserted using the CLIPS **reset** command. The *reset* command removes all facts from the fact list and then asserts the facts from existing deffacts statement. The syntax of the *reset* command is

```
(reset)
```

Assuming that the *people* deffacts had been entered (after the *person* deftemplate), the following dialog shows how the *reset* command adds the facts to the fact list:

```
CLIPS> (unwatch facts) ↵
CLIPS> (reset) ↵
CLIPS> (facts) ↵
f-0     (initial-fact)
f-1     (person (name "John Q. Public")
                (age 24)
                (eye-color blue)
                (hair-color black))
f-2     (person (name "Jack S. Public")
                (age 24)
                (eye-color blue)
                (hair-color black))
f-3     (person (name "Jane Q. Public")
                (age 36)
                (eye-color green)
                (hair-color red))
For a total of 4 facts.
CLIPS>
```

The output shows the facts from the deffacts statement and a new fact generated by the reset command called ***initial-fact***. Upon startup, CLIPS automatically defines the following two constructs:

```
(deftemplate initial-fact)
```

```
(deffacts initial-fact
   (initial-fact))
```

Thus, even if you have not defined any deffacts statements, a reset will assert the fact (initial-fact). The fact identifier of the initial-fact is always f-0. The utility of (initial-fact) lies in starting the execution of a program (as will be discussed in the next section).

7.11 THE COMPONENTS OF A RULE

In order to accomplish useful work, an expert system must have rules as well as facts. Now that fact assertions and retractions have been discussed, it's possible to see how rules work.

Rules can be typed directly into CLIPS or loaded in from a file of rules created by an editor (loading constructs from a file will be discussed in Section 7.17). For all but the smallest programs you'll probably want to use one of the integrated editors provided with CLIPS. Information about the editors for the Windows 3.1, Windows 95, and MacOS executables can be found in the *Interfaces Guide* that is in electronic format on the CD-ROM included with this book. Information about the EMACS editor, which can be used in environments such as UNIX, is described in the *Basic Programming Guide*. The integrated editors allow you to selectively redefine constructs during program development, which can be extremely useful. For example, if you have a typo in a construct that you entered at the top level prompt, you have to retype the entire construct. If you first entered the construct in the editor, then you can correct the typo and redefine the construct with a few keystrokes from within the editor. Initially, the examples shown will be rules entered directly into CLIPS from the top level.

As an example, let's consider the types of facts and rules that might be used to monitor and respond to a range of possible emergencies. One such emergency would be a fire, another would be a flood. The pseudocode for one of the possible rules in the industrial plant monitoring expert system is shown as follows:

```
IF the emergency is a fire
THEN the response is to activate
     the sprinkler system
```

Before converting the pseudocode to a rule, the deftemplates for the types of facts referred to by the rule must be defined. An emergency can be represented by the following deftemplate:

```
(deftemplate emergency (slot type))
```

where the *type* field of the *emergency* fact would contain symbols such as fire, flood, and power outage. Similarly, the response can be represented by the following deftemplate

```
(deftemplate response (slot action))
```

where the *action* field of the *response* fact indicates the response to be taken.

The rule expressed in CLIPS syntax is shown below. The rule can be entered by typing it in after the CLIPS prompt, but you'll have to enter the *emergency* and *response* deftemplates before you can enter the rule. However, before entering any of these constructs, type the command (clear) followed by a return at the top level prompt. This will remove the deftemplates and deffacts created from the previous section. The *clear* command will be fully explained in Section 7.13.

```
(defrule fire-emergency "An example rule"
   (emergency (type fire))
   =>
   (assert (response
            (action activate-sprinkler-system))))
```

If the rule is entered correctly as shown, the CLIPS prompt reappears. Otherwise an error message, most likely indicating a misspelled keyword or misplaced parenthesis, will appear.

The following is the same rule with comments added to match the parts of the rule. Comments begin with a semicolon and continue until a carriage return. They are ignored by CLIPS and will be discussed in Section 7.18.

```
; Rule header
(defrule fire-emergency "An example rule"
   ; Patterns
   (emergency (type fire))
   ; THEN arrow
   =>
   ; Actions
   (assert (response
            (action activate-sprinkler-system))))
```

The general format of a rule is

```
(defrule <rule name> [<comment>]
   <patterns>*   ; Left-Hand Side (LHS) of the rule
   =>
   <actions>*)   ; Right-Hand Side (RHS) of the rule
```

The entire rule must be surrounded by parentheses and each of the patterns and actions of the rule must be surrounded by parentheses. A rule may have multiple patterns and actions. The parentheses surrounding patterns and actions must be properly balanced if they are nested. In the *fire-emergency* rule there is one pattern and one action.

The header of the rule consists of three parts. The rule must start with the **defrule** keyword, followed by the name of the rule. The name can be any valid CLIPS word. If a rule is entered with a rule name that is the same as an existing rule, then the new rule replaces the old rule. In this rule the rule name is *fire-emergency*. Next comes an optional comment string. For this rule the comment is "An example rule." The comment is normally used to describe the purpose of the rule or any other information the programmer desires. Unlike comments beginning with a semicolon, the comment following the rule name is not ignored and can be displayed along with the rest of the rule (using the *ppdefrule* command, which will be introduced in Section 7.13).

After the rule header are zero or more conditional elements (CEs). The simplest type of CE is a **pattern CE** or simply **pattern**. Each pattern consists of one or more constraints intended to match the fields of a deftemplate fact. In the *fire-emergency* rule the pattern is (emergency (type fire)). The constraint for the *type* field indicates that this rule will only be satisfied for *emergency* facts that contain the symbol *fire* in their *type* field. CLIPS attempts to match the patterns of rules against facts in the fact list. If all the patterns of a rule match facts, the rule is **activated** and put on the **agenda**, the collection of activated rules. There may be zero or more rules in the agenda.

The symbol **=>** that follows the patterns in a rule is called an **arrow**. It is formed by typing the equal sign and then the greater than sign. The arrow is a symbol representing the beginning of the THEN part of an IF . . . THEN rule. The part of the rule before the arrow is called the left-hand side (**LHS**) and the part after the arrow is called the right-hand side (**RHS**).

If a rule has no patterns, the special pattern (initial-fact) will be added as a pattern for the rule. Since the *initial-fact* deffacts is automatically defined, any rules with no patterns on their LHSs will be activated when a *reset* command is performed since the (initial-fact) fact will automatically be asserted. Thus any rule without LHS patterns will be placed on the agenda when a reset is performed.

The last part of a rule is the list of actions that will be executed when the rule **fires**. A rule may have no actions. This is not particularly useful, but it can be done. In our example the one action is to assert the fact (response (action activate-sprinkler-system)). The term *fires* means that CLIPS executes the actions of a rule from the agenda. A program normally ceases execution when there are no rules on the agenda. When there are multiple rules on the agenda, CLIPS automatically determines which is the appropriate rule to fire. CLIPS orders the rules on the agenda in terms of increasing priority and fires the rule with the highest priority. The priority of a rule is an integer attribute called *salience*. Salience will be discussed in more detail in Chapter 10.

7.12 THE AGENDA AND EXECUTION

A CLIPS program can be made to run with the **run** command. The syntax of the *run* command is

```
(run [<limit>])
```

where the optional argument <limit> is the maximum number of rules to be fired. If <limit> is not included or <limit> is −1, rules will be fired until none are left on the agenda. Otherwise, execution of rules will cease after <limit> number of rules have fired.

When a CLIPS program is run, the rule with the highest salience on the agenda is fired. If there is only one rule on the agenda, of course that rule will fire. Since the conditional element of the *fire-emergency* rule is satisfied by the fact (emergency (type fire)), the *fire-emergency* rule should fire when the program is run.

Rules become activated whenever all the patterns of the rule are matched by facts. The process of pattern matching is always kept current and occurs regardless of whether facts are asserted before or after a rule has been defined.

Because rules require facts to execute, the *reset* command is the key method for starting or restarting an expert system in CLIPS. Typically, the facts asserted by a reset satisfy the patterns of one or more rules and place activations of these rules on the agenda. Issuing the *run* command then begins execution of the program.

Displaying the Agenda

The list of rules on the agenda can be displayed with the **agenda** command. The syntax of the *agenda* command is

```
(agenda)
```

If no activations are on the agenda, the CLIPS prompt will reappear after the *agenda* command is issued. If the *fire-emergency* rule had been activated by the (emergency (type fire)) fact with a fact index of 1, an *agenda* command would produce the following output:

```
CLIPS> (reset) ↵
CLIPS> (assert (emergency (type fire))) ↵
<Fact-1>
CLIPS> (agenda) ↵
0       fire-emergency: f-1
For a total of 1 activation.
CLIPS>
```

The 0 indicates the salience of the rule on the agenda. That is followed by the name of the rule and then the fact identifiers that match the patterns of the rule. In this case there is only one fact identifier, f-1.

Rules and Refraction

With the *fire-emergency* rule on the agenda, the *run* command will now cause the rule to fire. The fact (response (action activate-sprinkler-system)) will be added to the fact list as the action of the rule, as the following output shows:

```
CLIPS> (run) ↵
CLIPS> (facts) ↵
f-0     (initial-fact)
f-1     (emergency (type fire))
f-2     (response
            (action activate-sprinkler-system))
For a total of 3 facts.
CLIPS>
```

An interesting question occurs at this point: What if the *run* command is issued again? There is a rule and there is a fact that satisfies the rule and so the rule should fire again. However, a *run* command if attempted now will produce no results. Checking the agenda will verify that no rules are fired because there were no rules on the agenda.

The rule didn't fire again because of the way CLIPS is designed. Rules in CLIPS exhibit a property called **refraction**, which means they won't fire more than once for a specific set of facts. Without refraction, expert systems would always be caught in trivial loops. That is, as soon as a rule fired, it would keep on firing on that same fact over and over again. In the real world the stimulus that caused the firing would eventually disappear. For example, the fire would eventually be put out by the sprinkler system or would burn out by itself.

However, in the computer world, once a fact is entered in the fact list, it stays there until explicitly removed.

If necessary, the rule can be made to fire again by retracting the fact (emergency (type fire)) and asserting it again. Basically, CLIPS remembers the fact identifiers that triggered a rule into firing and will not activate that rule again with the exact same combination of fact identifiers. Identical sets of fact identifiers must match one-for-one in both order and fact indices. Examples in Chapter 8 will show how a single fact can match a pattern in more than one way. In this case, several activations with the same set of fact identifiers for a single rule can be placed on the agenda, one for each distinct match.

Alternatively, the **refresh** command can be used to make the rule fire again. The *refresh* command places all activations that have already fired for a rule back on the agenda (with the restriction that the facts that triggered the activation are still present in the fact list). The syntax of the *refresh* command is

```
(refresh <rule-name>)
```

and the following commands show how the *refresh* command could be used to reactivate the *fire-emergency* rule:

```
CLIPS> (agenda) ↵
CLIPS> (refresh fire-emergency) ↵
CLIPS> (agenda) ↵
0       fire-emergency: f-1
For a total of 1 activation.
CLIPS>
```

Watching Activations, Rules, and Statistics

If activations are being watched, CLIPS will automatically print a message whenever an activation has been added to or removed from the agenda. As with facts, the character sequence <== indicates that an activation is being removed from the agenda and the character sequence ==> indicates that an activation is being added to the agenda. After the initial character sequence the activation is printed with the same format used by the *agenda* command. The following command sequence illustrates activations being watched:

```
CLIPS> (reset) ↵
CLIPS> (watch activations) ↵
CLIPS> (assert (emergency (type fire))) ↵
==> Activation 0       fire-emergency: f-1
<Fact-1>
CLIPS> (agenda) ↵
0       fire-emergency: f-1
For a total of 1 activation.
CLIPS> (retract 1) ↵
<== Activation 0       fire-emergency: f-1
CLIPS> (agenda) ↵
CLIPS>
```

If rules are being watched, CLIPS will print a message whenever a rule is fired. The following command sequence illustrates activations and rules being watched:

```
CLIPS> (reset) ↵
CLIPS> (watch rules) ↵
CLIPS> (assert (emergency (type fire))) ↵
==> Activation 0       fire-emergency: f-1
<Fact-1>
CLIPS> (run) ↵
FIRE   1 fire-emergency: f-1
CLIPS> (agenda) ↵
CLIPS>
```

The number following the symbol *FIRE* indicates how many rules have fired since the *run* command was given. For example, if another rule were to fire after the *fire-emergency rule*, it would be preceeded by "FIRE 2." After the firing order is printed the name of the rule is printed, followed by the fact indices that matched the patterns of the rule. Note that watching activations will not cause a message to be displayed when a rule is fired (and hence removed from the agenda).

If statistics are being watched, CLIPS will print informational messages such as the following at the completion of a run:

```
CLIPS> (unwatch all) ↵
CLIPS> (reset) ↵
CLIPS> (watch statistics) ↵
CLIPS> (assert (emergency (type fire))) ↵
<Fact-1>
CLIPS> (run) ↵
1 rules fired       Run time is 0.02 seconds
50.0 rules per second
3 mean number of facts (3 maximum)
1 mean number of instances (1 maximum).
1 mean number of activations (1 maximum)
CLIPS> (unwatch statistics) ↵
CLIPS>
```

When statistics are watched, six statistics are printed out after a *run* command. The total number of rules fired, the amount of time in seconds it took to fire the rules, and the average number of rules fired per second (the first statistics divided by the second statistic) are displayed. In addition, for each cycle of execution, CLIPS keeps statistics on the number of facts, activations, and instances. The mean number of facts is the sum of the total number of facts in the fact list after each rule firing divided by the number of rules fired. The number contained within the parentheses followed by the word *maximum* indicates the largest number of facts contained in the fact list for any one rule firing. Similarly, the mean and maximum numbers of activations statistics indicate the average number of activations per rule firing and the largest number of activations on the agenda for any one rule firing. The mean and maximum numbers of instances display information associated with COOL.

7.13 COMMANDS FOR MANIPULATING CONSTRUCTS

Displaying the List of Members of a Specified Construct

The **list-defrules** command is used to display the current list of rules maintained by CLIPS. Similarly, the **list-deftemplates** and **list-deffacts** commands, respectively, can be used to display the current list of deftemplates or the current list of deffacts. The syntax of these commands is

```
(list-defrules)

(list-deftemplates)

(list-deffacts)
```

For example,

```
CLIPS> (list-defrules) ⏎
fire-emergency
For a total of 1 rule.
CLIPS> (list-deftemplates) ⏎
initial-fact
emergency
response
For a total of 3 deftemplates.
CLIPS> (list-deffacts) ⏎
initial-fact
For a total of 1 deffacts.
CLIPS>
```

Displaying the Text Representation of a Specified Construct Member

The **ppdefrule** (pretty print defrule), **ppdeftemplate** (pretty print deftemplate), and **ppdeffacts** (pretty print deffacts) commands are used to display the text representations of a defrule, a deftemplate, and a deffacts, respectively. The syntaxes of these commands are

```
(ppdefrule <defrule-name>)

(ppdeftemplate <deftemplate-name>)

(ppdeffacts <deffacts-name>)
```

The single argument for each command specifies the name of the defrule, deftemplate, or deffacts to be displayed. When displayed, CLIPS puts different parts of the constructs on different lines for the sake of readability. For example,

```
CLIPS> (ppdefrule fire-emergency) ↵
(defrule MAIN::fire-emergency "An example rule"
   (emergency (type fire))
   =>
   (assert (response
               (action activate-sprinkler-system)))))
CLIPS> (ppdeftemplate response) ↵
(deftemplate MAIN::response
   (slot action))
CLIPS> (ppdeffacts initial-fact) ↵
CLIPS> (deffacts start-fact (start-fact)) ↵
CLIPS> (ppdeffacts start-fact) ↵
(deffacts MAIN::start-fact
   (start-fact))
CLIPS>
```

The symbol MAIN:: preceeding each of the construct names indicates the module in which the constructs have been placed. Modules provide a mechanism for partitioning a knowledge base and will be discussed in greater detail in Chapter 10. Notice that the *initial-fact* deffacts has no text representation (since it is automatically created by CLIPS). However, the *start-fact* deffacts that was entered does have a text representation.

Deleting a Specified Construct Member

The **undefrule**, **undeftemplate**, and **undeffacts** commands are used to delete a defrule, a deftemplate, and a deffacts, respectively. The syntaxes of these commands are

```
(undefrule <defrule-name>)

(undeftemplate <deftemplate-name>)

(undeffacts <deffacts-name>)
```

The single argument for each command specifies the name of the defrule, deftemplate, or deffacts to be deleted. For example,

```
CLIPS> (undeffacts start-fact) ↵
CLIPS> (list-deffacts) ↵
initial-fact
For a total of 1 deffacts.
CLIPS> (undefrule fire-emergency) ↵
CLIPS> (list-defrules) ↵
CLIPS>
```

Notice that the *initial-facts* deffacts and the *initial-facts* deftemplate can be deleted just like any other user-defined construct. If a *reset* command were performed now, the (initial-fact) fact would not be added to the fact list.

If the symbol * is given as an argument to any of the construct deletion commands then all constructs of the appropriate type are deleted. For example, (undefrule *) would delete all defrule constructs. The symbol * can also be used with the *retract* command to remove all facts.

Constructs that are referred to by other constructs cannot be deleted until the referring constructs are deleted. As the following dialog shows, the *initial-fact* deftemplate cannot be deleted until the *initial-fact* deffacts is deleted, the fact (initial-fact) is deleted, and the *example* defrule is deleted (which uses the default *initial-fact* pattern).

```
CLIPS> (defrule example =>) ↵
CLIPS> (undeftemplate initial-fact) ↵
Unable to delete deftemplate initial-fact while
outstanding references to it still exist.
CLIPS> (undeffacts initial-fact) ↵
CLIPS> (undeftemplate initial-fact) ↵
Unable to delete deftemplate initial-fact while
outstanding references to it still exist.
CLIPS> (undefrule example) ↵
CLIPS> (undeftemplate initial-fact) ↵
Unable to delete deftemplate initial-fact while
outstanding references to it still exist.
CLIPS> (retract *) ↵
CLIPS> (undeftemplate initial-fact) ↵
CLIPS>
```

Clearing All Constructs from the CLIPS Environment

The **clear** command can be used to remove all information contained in the CLIPS environment. It removes all constructs currently contained in CLIPS and all facts in the fact list. The syntax of the *clear* command is

```
(clear)
```

After *clearing* the CLIPS environment, the clear command adds the *initial-facts* deffacts to the CLIPS environment:

```
CLIPS> (list-deffacts) ↵
CLIPS> (list-deftemplates) ↵
emergency
response
start-fact
For a total of 3 deftemplates.
CLIPS> (clear) ↵
CLIPS> (list-deffacts) ↵
initial-fact
For a total of 1 deffacts.
CLIPS> (list-deftemplates) ↵
initial-fact
For a total of 1 deftemplate.
CLIPS>
```

7.14 THE PRINTOUT COMMAND

Besides asserting facts in the RHS of rules, the RHS can also be used to print out information using the **printout** command. The syntax of the *printout* command is

```
(printout <logical-name> <print-items>*)
```

where <logical-name> indicates the output destination of the *printout* command and <print-items>* are the zero or more items to be printed by this command.

The following rule demonstrates the use of the *printout* command

```
(defrule fire-emergency
   (emergency (type fire))
   =>
   (printout t "Activate the sprinkler system"
            crlf))
```

It is very important to include the letter t after the *printout* command because this argument indicates the destination of the output. This destination is also referred to as a *logical name*. In this case, the logical name t tells CLIPS to send the output to the **standard output device** of the computer, usually the terminal. This may be redefined so that the standard output device is something else, such as a modem or a printer. The concept of logical names will be fully introduced in Section 8.12.

The arguments following the logical name are items to be printed by the *printout* command. The string

```
"Activate the sprinkler system"
```

will be printed at the terminal without the enclosing quotation marks. The word **crlf** is treated specially by the *printout* command. It forces a carriage return/line feed, which improves the appearance of output by formatting it on different lines.

7.15 USING MULTIPLE RULES

Until now, only the simplest type of program consisting of just one rule has been shown. However, expert systems consisting of only one rule are not particularly useful. Practical expert systems may consist of hundreds or thousands of rules. In addition to the *fire-emergency* rule, the expert system monitoring the industrial plant might include a rule for emergencies in which flooding has occurred. The expanded set of rules now looks like this:

```
(defrule fire-emergency
   (emergency (type fire))
   =>
   (printout t "Activate the sprinkler system"
            crlf))
```

```
(defrule flood-emergency
   (emergency (type flood))
   =>
   (printout t "Shut down electrical equipment"
               crlf))
```

Once these rules have been entered into CLIPS, asserting the fact (emergency (type fire)) and then issuing a *run* command will produce the output "Activate the sprinkler system." Asserting the fact (emergency (type flood)) and issuing a *run* command will produce the output "Shut down the electrical equipment."

Capturing the Real World in a Rule

As long as the fires and floods are the only two emergencies that must be handled, the above rules are sufficient. However, the real world is not quite that simple. For instance, not all fires can be extinguished using water. Some may require chemical extinguishers. What should be done if a fire produces poisonous gases or an explosion occurs? Should an off-site fire department be notified in addition to the on-site firemen? Does it matter which floor of the building the fire is on? Activating the water sprinklers on the second floor might cause water damage to both the first and the second floors. Electrical power to equipment might have to be shut off on both floors. A fire on the first floor may only require that power be shut off to equipment on the first floor. If the building is flooded, are there watertight doors that can be shut to prevent damage? What should be done in case a plant break-in is detected? If all of these situations are included as rules, have all possibilities now been covered?

Unfortunately, the answer is no. In the real world, things don't always operate perfectly. Capturing all pertinent knowledge in an expert system can be quite difficult. In the best case, it may be possible to recognize most major emergencies and to provide rules to allow the expert system to recognize when it doesn't see an emergency.

Rules with Multiple Patterns

Most real-world heuristics are too complicated to be expressed as rules with just a single pattern. For example, activating the sprinkler system for any type of fire might not only be wrong, it could be dangerous. Fires involving ordinary combustibles such as paper, wood, and cloth (class A fires) can be extinguished using water or water-based extinguishers. Fires involving flammable and combustible liquids, greases, and similar materials (class B fires) must be extinguished using a different method, such as a carbon dioxide extinguisher. Rules with more than one pattern could be used to express these conditions. For example,

```
(deftemplate extinguisher-system
   (slot type)
   (slot status))
```

```
(defrule class-A-fire-emergency
   (emergency (type class-A-fire))
   (extinguisher-system (type water-sprinkler)
                        (status off))
   =>
   (printout t "Activate water sprinkler" crlf))

(defrule class-B-fire-emergency
   (emergency (type class-B-fire))
   (extinguisher-system (type carbon-dioxide)
                        (status off))
   =>
   (printout t "Use carbon dioxide extinguisher"
               crlf))
```

Both rules have two patterns. The first pattern would determine that a fire emergency exists and whether the fire was class A or class B. The second pattern determines whether the appropriate extinguisher has been turned on. More rules could be added to shut off the extinguishers (e.g., if the water sprinkler is already on and a class B fire occurs, then shut if off; or if the fire has been extinguished, shut off the extinguishers). Still more rules could be used to determine whether a specific burning material constituted a class A or class B fire.

Any number of patterns can be placed in a rule. The important point to realize is that the rule is placed on the agenda only if *all* the patterns are satisfied by facts. This type of restriction is called an ***and conditional element***. Because the patterns of all rules are implicitly contained within an *and* conditional element, the rule will not fire if only one of the patterns is satisfied. All the facts must be present before the LHS of a rule is satisfied and the rule is placed on the agenda.

7.16 THE SET-BREAK COMMAND

CLIPS has a debugging command called ***set-break*** that allows execution to be halted before any rule from a specified group of rules is fired. A rule that halts execution before being fired is called a ***breakpoint***. The syntax of the set-break command is

```
(set-break <rule-name>)
```

where <rule-name> is the name of the rule for which the breakpoint is set. As an example, consider the following rules (note the use of ordered facts, as described in Section 7.6):

```
(defrule first
   =>
   (assert (fire second)))

(defrule second
   (fire second)
   =>
   (assert (fire third)))
```

```
(defrule third
   (fire third)
   =>)
```

The following command dialog shows execution of the rules without any breakpoints set:

```
CLIPS> (watch rules) ⏎
CLIPS> (reset) ⏎
CLIPS> (run) ⏎
FIRE    1 first: f-0
FIRE    2 second: f-1
FIRE    3 third: f-2
CLIPS>
```

All three rules fire in succession when the *run* command is issued. The following command dialog demonstrates the use of the *set-break* command to halt execution:

```
CLIPS> (set-break second) ⏎
CLIPS> (set-break third) ⏎
CLIPS> (reset) ⏎
CLIPS> (run) ⏎
FIRE    1 first: f-0
Breaking on rule second
CLIPS> (run) ⏎
FIRE    1 second: f-1
Breaking on rule third
CLIPS> (run) ⏎
FIRE    1 third: f-2
CLIPS>
```

In this case execution halts before the rules *second* and *third* are allowed to fire. Notice that at least one rule must be fired by the *run* command before a breakpoint will stop execution. For example, after the rule *second* has halted execution, it does not halt execution again when the *run* command is given.

The **show-breaks** command can be used to list all breakpoints. Its syntax is

```
(show-breaks)
```

The **remove-break** command can be used to remove breakpoints. Its syntax is

```
(remove-break [<rule-name>])
```

If <rule-name> is provided as an argument, only the breakpoint for that rule will be removed. Otherwise, all breakpoints will be removed.

7.17 LOADING AND SAVING CONSTRUCTS

Loading Constructs from a File

A file of constructs made with a text editor can be loaded into CLIPS using the **load** command. The syntax of the *load* command is

```
(load <file-name>)
```

where <file-name> is a string or symbol containing the name of the file to be loaded.

Assuming that the emergency rules and deftemplates were stored in a file called fire.clp on drive B of an IBM PC, the following command would load the constructs into CLIPS:

```
(load "B:fire.clp")
```

Of course, the specification of a file name will be machine dependent, so this example should be taken only as a guide. A problem that may occur in loading is due to the backslash character used on some operating systems as a directory path separator. Since CLIPS interprets the backslash as an escape character, two backslashes must be used to create a single backslash in a string. For example, normally a pathname might be written as

```
B:\usr\clips\fire.clp
```

To preserve the backslash characters, the pathname would have to be written as shown in the following command:

```
(load "B:\\usr\\clips\\fire.clp")
```

Constructs do not all have to be kept in a single file. They can be stored in more than one file and loaded using several load commands. If no errors occur when a file is loaded, the load command will return the symbol *TRUE* (Chapter 8 will go into detail about return values). Otherwise, it will return the symbol *FALSE*.

Watching Compilations

When compilations are watched (by default), an informational message including the construct name is printed for each construct loaded by the load command. For example, assume CLIPS has just been started and the following commands are entered:

```
CLIPS> (load "fire.clp")↵
Defining deftemplate: emergency
Defining deftemplate: response
Defining defrule: fire-emergency +j
TRUE
CLIPS>
```

The messages indicate that two deftemplates were loaded (*emergency* and *response*), followed by the *fire-emergency* rule. The "+j" string at the end of the "Defining defrule" message is information from CLIPS about the internal structure of the compiled rules. This information will be useful for tuning a program and will be discussed in Chapter 11, which deals with efficiency.

If compilations are not being watched, then CLIPS prints a single character for each construct loaded: * for defrules, % for deftemplates, and $ for deffacts. For example:

```
CLIPS>  (clear) ⏎
CLIPS>  (unwatch compilations) ⏎
CLIPS>  (load fire.clp) ⏎
%%*
TRUE
CLIPS>
```

Saving Constructs to a File

CLIPS also provides the opposite of the *load* command. The **save** command allows the set of constructs stored in CLIPS to be saved to a disk file. The syntax of the *save* command is

```
(save <file-name>)
```

For example, the following command will save the fire constructs to a file called *fire.clp* on drive B:

```
(save "B:fire.clp")
```

The *save* command will save all the constructs in CLIPS to the specified file. It is not possible to save specified constructs to a file. Normally if an editor is used to create and modify the constructs there is no need to use the *save* command, since the constructs will be saved while you are using the editor. However, sometimes it is convenient to enter constructs directly at the CLIPS prompt and then save the constructs to a file.

7.18 COMMENTING CONSTRUCTS

It's a good idea to include comments in a CLIPS program. Sometimes constructs can be difficult to understand, and comments can be used to explain to the reader what the constructs are doing. Comments are also used for good documentation of programs and will be helpful in lengthy programs.

A comment in CLIPS is any text that begins with a semicolon and ends with a carriage return. The following is an example of comments in the fire program:

```
;************************************
;*                                  *
;* Programmer: G. D. Riley          *
;*                                  *
;* Title: The Fire Program          *
;*                                  *
;* Date: 10/03/92                   *
;*                                  *
;************************************

; Deftemplates

(deftemplate emergency "template #1"
   (slot type))          ; What type of emergency

(deftemplate response  "template #2"
   (slot action))        ; How to respond

; The purpose of this rule is to activate
; the sprinkler system if there is a fire

(defrule fire-emergency "An example rule" ; IF
   ; There is a fire emergency
   (emergency (type fire))
   =>                                      ; THEN
   ; Activate the sprinkler system
   (assert (response
            (action activate-sprinkler-system))))
```

Loading these constructs into CLIPS and then pretty printing them will demonstrate that every comment starting with a semicolon is eliminated in the CLIPS program. The only comment that is retained is the one in quotes after the construct's name.

7.19 SUMMARY

This chapter introduced the fundamental components of CLIPS. Facts are the first component of a CLIPS system and are made up of fields, which are either symbols, strings, integers, or floats. The first field of a fact is normally used to indicate the type of information stored in the fact and is called a *relation name*. The deftemplate construct is used to assign slot names to specific fields of a fact beginning with a specified relation name. The deffacts construct is used to specify facts as initial knowledge.

Rules are the second component of a CLIPS system. A rule is divided into an LHS and an RHS. The LHS of a rule can be thought of as the IF portion and the RHS can be thought of as the THEN portion. Rules can have multiple patterns and actions.

The third component of CLIPS is the inference engine. Rules that have their patterns satisfied by facts produce an activation that is placed on the agenda. Refraction prevents rules from being constantly activated by old facts.

PROBLEMS

7.1   Convert the following sentences to facts in a deffacts statement. For each group of related facts, define a deftemplate that describes a more general relationship.

```
The father of John is Tom.
The mother of John is Susan.
The parents of John are Tom and Susan.
Tom is a father.
Susan is a mother.
John is a son.
Tom is a male.
Susan is a female.
John is a male.
```

7.2   Define a deftemplate for a fact containing information about a set. The deftemplate should include information about the name or description of the set, the list of elements in the set, and whether it is a subset of another set. Represent the following sets as facts using the format specified by your deftemplate.

```
A = { 1, 2, 3 }
B = { 1, 2, 3, red, green }
C = { red, green, yellow, blue }
```

7.3   A sparsely populated array contains relatively few nonzero elements. It is more efficiently represented as a linked list or tree. How might a sparsely populated array be represented using facts? Describe the deftemplate used for the facts to represent the array. What are the possible disadvantages of representing an array using facts as opposed to using an array data structure in a procedural language?

7.4   Convert the general net representing airline routes as shown in Figure 2.4 (a) on page 64 to a series of facts in a deffacts statement. Use a single deftemplate to describe the facts.

7.5   Convert the semantic net representing a family as shown in Figure 2.4 (b) on page 64 as a series of facts in a deffacts statement. Use several deftemplates to describe the facts produced.

7.6   Convert the semantic net shown in Figure 2.5 on page 65 to a series of facts in a deffacts statement. Use several deftemplates to describe the facts. For example, the IS-A and AKO links should be relation names and each should have its own deftemplate.

7.7   Convert the binary decision tree representing animal classification information in Figure 3.3 on page 99 to a series of facts in a deffacts statement. Show how the links between the nodes can be represented. Do the leaves of the tree require a different representation from the other nodes of the tree?

7.8   Implement the semantic net of Problem 2.1 as a deffacts statement using AKO and IS-A deftemplates.

7.9 Plants require many different types of nutrients for proper growth. Three of the most important plant nutrients that are provided by fertilizer are nitrogen, phosphorus, and potassium. A deficiency in one of these nutrients will produce various symptoms. Translate the heuristics below to rules that determine nutrient deficiency. Assume that the plant is normally green.

```
A plant with stunted growth may have a nitrogen
    deficiency.
A plant that is pale yellow in color may have a
    nitrogen deficiency.
A plant that has reddish-brown leaf edges may have a
    nitrogen deficiency.
A plant with stunted root growth may have a
    phosphorus deficiency.
A plant with a spindly stalk may have a phosphorus
    deficiency.
A plant that is purplish in color may have a
    phosphorus deficiency.
A plant that has delayed in maturing may have a
    phosphorus deficiency.
A plant with leaf edges that appear scorched may have
    a potassium deficiency.
A plant with weakened stems may have a potassium
    deficiency.
A plant with shriveled seeds or fruits may have a
    potassium deficiency.
```

Use deftemplates to describe the facts used in the rules. The input to the program should be made by asserting symptoms as facts. The output should indicate which nutrient deficiencies exist by printing to the terminal. Implement a method so multiple printouts for a single deficiency caused by more than one symptom are avoided. Test your program with the following inputs

```
The plant has stunted root growth.
The plant is purplish in color.
```

7.10 Fires are classified according to the principal burning material. Translate the following information to rules for determining fire class.

```
Type A fires involve ordinary combustibles such as
    paper, wood, and cloth.
Type B fires involve flammable and combustible
    liquids (such as oil and gas), greases,
    and similar materials.
```

Type C fires involve energized electrical equipment.
Type D fires involve combustible metals such as
    magnesium, sodium, and potassium.

The type of extinguisher that should be used on a fire depends on the fire class. Translate the following information to rules.

Class A fires should be extinguished with
    heat-absorbing or combustion-retarding
    extinguishers such as water or water-based liquids
    and dry chemicals.
Class B fires should be extinguished by excluding
    air, inhibiting the release of combustible vapors,
    or interrupting the combustion chain reaction.
    Extinguishers include dry chemicals, carbon
    dioxide, foam, and bromotrifluoromethane.
Class C fires should be extinguished with a
    nonconducting agent to prevent short circuits. If
    possible the power should be cut. Extinguishers
    include dry chemicals, carbon dioxide, and
    bromotrifluoromethane.
Class D fires should be extinguished with smothering
    and heat-absorbing chemicals that do not react
    with the burning metals. Such chemicals include
    trimethoxyboroxine and screened graphitized coke.

Describe the facts used in the rules. The input to the program should be made by asserting the type of burning material as a fact. The output should indicate which extinguishers may be used and other actions that should be taken, such as cutting off the power. Show that your program works for one material from each of the fire classes.

7.11   Write a CLIPS program that aids in the selection process of a suitable shrub for planting. The table below lists several shrubs and indicates whether each shrub possesses certain characteristics, which include tolerance to cold weather, tolerance to shade, tolerance to drought, tolerance to wet soil, tolerance to acidic soil, tolerance to city dwelling (high pollution), tolerance to growth in a container, whether the shrub is easy to care for, and whether the shrub is fast growing. A bullet indicates the shrub has the characteristic. Input to the program should be facts indicating a desired characteristic that the shrub must have, and the output should be a list of the plants having each specified characteristic.

Shrub	Cold	Shade	Dry	Wet Soil	Acid Soil	City	Pot	Easy Care	Grows Fast
French hydrangea		●				●	●		●
Oleander						●	●	●	●
Northern bayberry	●	●	●	●		●		●	●
Box honeysuckle						●	●		●
Gardenia		●			●		●		
Common juniper	●		●		●	●		●	
Sweet pepperbush	●	●		●	●			●	
Tartarian dogwood	●	●		●		●		●	
Japanese aucuba		●	●				●	●	
Swamp azalea		●		●	●		●		

7.12   Low-altitude clouds, those at 6,000 feet or less, include stratus and stratocumulus clouds. Medium-altitude clouds, those between 6,000 and 20,000 feet, include altostratus, altocumulus, and nimbostratus clouds. High-altitude clouds, those at greater than 20,000 feet, include cirrus, cirrostratus, and cirrocumulus clouds. Cumulus and cumulonimbus clouds can extend from low to high altitudes. Stratus, altostratus, cirrostratus, cumulus, and cumulonimbus clouds appear as large rounded piles. Stratus, altostratus, nimbostratus, and cirrostratus clouds appear as smooth even sheets. Cirrus clouds have a wispy appearance, like tufts of hair. Nimbostratus and cumulonimbus clouds are rain clouds and dark gray in color. Write a program to identify cloud types. The input to the program should be facts describing the attributes of the cloud. The program should then print the type of cloud identified.

7.13   Stars can be classified into color groups called *spectral classes*. The classes range from the blue class "O" stars to the yellow class "G" stars to the red class "M" stars. The star's spectral class correlates to its temperature: class "O" stars have a temperature of more than 37,000° F; class "B" temperatures range from 17,001° F to 37,000° F; class "A" temperatures range from 12,501° F to 17,000° F; class "F" temperatures range from 10,301° F to 12,500° F; class "G" temperatures range from 8,001° F to 10,300° F; class "K" temperatures range from 5,501° F to 8,000° F; and class "M" temperatures are 5,500° F or less. Stars can also be classified by their magnitude, which is a measure of their brightness. The lower the magnitude, the brighter the star. Assume that magnitudes can range from –7 to 15. The table belows lists some common brightest stars with their spectral class and magnitude and also their distance from Earth in light-years. Write a program that takes as input two facts representing the spectral class and magnitude of a star. The program should then output the following information in this order: all stars having the specified spectral class, all stars having the specified magnitude, and finally all stars matching both the spectral class and magnitude along with their distance from Earth in light-years.

Star	Spectral Class	Magnitude	Distance
Sirius	A	1	8.8
Canopus	F	–3	98
Arcturus	K	0	36
Vega	A	1	26
Capella	G	–1	46
Rigel	B	–7	880
Procyon	F	3	11
Betelgeuse	M	–5	490
Altair	A	2	16
Aldebaran	K	–1	68
Spica	B	–3	300
Antares	M	–4	250
Pollux	K	1	35
Deneb	A	–7	1630

7.14   The table below lists characteristics of common gems including their hardness (resistance to external stresses as measured by Mohs' scale), density (weight per unit volume in grams per cubic centimeter), and colors. Given three facts representing the hardness, density, and color of a gem, write the rules necessary to determine if the gem is a Chyrsoberyl.

Gem	Hardness	Density	Colors
Diamond	10	3.52	yellow, brown, green, blue, white, colorless
Corundum	9	4	red, pink, yellow, brown, green, blue, violet, black, white, colorless
Chrysoberyl	8.5	3.72	yellow, brown, green
Spinel	8	3.6	red, pink, yellow, brown, green, blue, violet, white, colorless
Topaz	8	3.52–3.56	red, pink, yellow, brown, blue, violet, white, colorless
Beryl	7.5–8.0	2.7	red, pink, yellow, brown, green, blue, white, colorless
Zircon	6–7.5	4.7	yellow, brown, green, violet, white, colorless
Quartz	7	2.65	red, pink, green, blue, violet, white, black, colorless
Tourmaline	7	3.1	red, pink, yellow, brown, green, blue, white, black, colorless
Peridot	6.5–7	3.3	yellow, brown, green
Jadeite	6.5–7	3.3	red, pink, yellow, brown, green, blue, violet, white, black, colorless
Opal	5.5–6.5	2–2.2	red, pink, yellow, brown, white, black, colorless
Nephrite	5–6	2.9–3.4	green, white, black, colorless
Turquoise	5–6	2.7	blue

CHAPTER 8
Pattern Matching

8.1 INTRODUCTION

The types of rules shown in Chapter 7 illustrate simple pattern matching of patterns to facts. This chapter will introduce several concepts that provide powerful capabilities for matching and manipulating facts. The first concept will be the use of variables in pattern matching, the second is field constraints. The use of functions in CLIPS will then be introduced and basic arithmetic will be gone over. A number of functions for performing I/O operations in CLIPS will also be introduced.

8.2 VARIABLES

Just as with other programming languages, CLIPS has **variables** available to store values. Variables in CLIPS are always written in the syntax of a question mark followed by a symbolic field name. Variable names follow the syntax of a symbol, with the exception that they must begin with a character. For good programming style, variables should be given meaningful names. Some examples of variables are

```
?speed
?sensor
?value
?noun
?color
```

There should be no space between the question mark and the symbolic field name. As will be discussed later, a question mark by itself has its own use. Variables are used on the LHS of a rule to contain slot values that can later be compared to other values on the LHS of a rule or accessed on the RHS of a rule. The terms *bound* and *bind* are used to describe the assignment of a value to a variable.

One common use of variables is to bind a variable on the LHS of a rule and then use that value on the RHS of the rule. For example,

```
CLIPS> (clear) ↵
CLIPS>
(deftemplate person
   (slot name)
   (slot eyes)
   (slot hair)) ↵
CLIPS>
(defrule find-blue-eyes
   (person (name ?name) (eyes blue))
   =>
   (printout t ?name " has blue eyes." crlf)) ↵
CLIPS>
(deffacts people
   (person (name Jane)
           (eyes blue) (hair red))
   (person (name Joe)
           (eyes green) (hair brown))
   (person (name Jack)
           (eyes blue) (hair black))
   (person (name Jeff)
           (eyes green) (hair brown)))) ↵
CLIPS> (reset) ↵
CLIPS> (run) ↵
Jack has blue eyes.
Jane has blue eyes.
CLIPS>
```

Both Jane and Jack have blue eyes, so the *find-blue-eyes* rule is activated twice, once each for the facts describing Jane and Jack. When the rule fires, it examines the *name* slot for the fact that activated the rule currently being fired and uses that value for the printout statement.

If a variable is referred to on the RHS of a rule but was not bound on the LHS of the rule, CLIPS will print the following error message (assuming the unbound variable was ?x):

```
[PRCCODE3] Undefined variable x referenced in
           RHS of defrule.
```

8.3 MULTIPLE USE OF VARIABLES

Variables with the same name that are used in multiple places on the LHS of a rule have an important and useful property. The first time a variable is bound to a value, it retains that value within the rule. Other variables with the same name that are bound to a value must be bound to the first variable's value.

Instead of writing a single rule that looks only for people with blue eyes, a fact can be asserted that indicates the specific color of eyes to look for. For example,

```
CLIPS> (undefrule *) ↵
CLIPS> (deftemplate find (slot eyes)) ↵
```

```
CLIPS>
(defrule find-eyes
    (find (eyes ?eyes))
    (person (name ?name) (eyes ?eyes))
    =>
    (printout t ?name " has " ?eyes " eyes." crlf))↵
CLIPS>
```

The *find* deftemplate indicates the eye color; this is specified by the *eyes* slot. The *find-eyes* rule will then retrieve the value from the *eyes* slot in the *find* deftemplate and then look for all person facts for which the value of the *eyes* slot is the same as was bound to the ?eyes variable. The following dialog shows how this works:

```
CLIPS> (reset)↵
CLIPS> (assert (find (eyes blue)))↵
<Fact-5>
CLIPS> (run)↵
Jack has blue eyes.
Jane has blue eyes.
CLIPS> (assert (find (eyes green)))↵
<Fact-6>
CLIPS> (run)↵
Jeff has green eyes.
Joe has green eyes.
CLIPS> (assert (find (eyes purple)))↵
<Fact-7>
CLIPS> (run)
CLIPS>
```

Notice that no rules fire when the (find (eyes purple)) fact is asserted because there are no *person* facts with the value *purple* in the *eyes* slot.

8.4 FACT ADDRESSES

Retraction, modification, and duplication of facts are extremely common operations and are usually done on the RHS of a rule rather than at the top level. Performing these operations on facts at the top level prompt using fact indices has already been demonstrated. Before a fact can be manipulated from the RHS of a rule, however, there must be some way to specify the fact that matched a particular pattern. To accomplish this, a variable can be bound to the **fact address** of the fact matching a pattern on the LHS of a rule by using the **pattern binding** operator, "<-". Once the variable is bound it can be used with the retract, modify, or duplicate commands in place of a fact index. For example, the following dialog shows how to update deftemplate slot values from the RHS of a rule:

```
CLIPS> (clear)↵
CLIPS>
(deftemplate person
    (slot name)
```

```
      (slot address))) ↵
CLIPS>
 (deftemplate moved
   (slot name)
   (slot address)) ↵
CLIPS>
(defrule process-moved-information
  ?f1 <- (moved (name ?name)
                (address ?address))
  ?f2 <- (person (name ?name))
  =>
  (retract ?f1)
  (modify ?f2 (address ?address))) ↵
CLIPS>
(deffacts example
   (person (name "John Hill")
           (address "25 Mulberry Lane"))
   (moved (name "John Hill")
          (address "37 Cherry Lane"))) ↵
CLIPS> (reset) ↵
CLIPS> (watch rules) ↵
CLIPS> (watch facts) ↵
CLIPS> (run) ↵
FIRE    1 process-moved-information: f-2,f-1
<== f-2      (moved (name "John Hill")
                    (address "37 Cherry Lane"))
<== f-1      (person (name "John Hill")
                     (address "25 Mulberry Lane"))
==> f-3      (person (name "John Hill")
                     (address "37 Cherry Lane"))
CLIPS>
```

Two deftemplates are used in this example. The *person* deftemplate is used to store information about a person, in this case just the name of the person and the person's address. Other information, such as age or eye color, could also be stored. The *moved* deftemplate is used to indicate that a person's address has changed. The new address is given in the *address* slot.

The first pattern in the *process-moved-information* rule determines whether an address change needs to be processed, and the second pattern finds the *person* fact for which the address information will need to be changed. The fact address of the *moved* fact is bound to the variable ?f1 so that this fact can be retracted once the change is processed. The fact address of the *person* fact is bound to the variable ?f2, which is later used on the RHS of the rule to modify the value of the *address* slot.

Note that variables bound to values within a fact and variables bound to the fact address of a fact can both be used. In addition, the value of the ?address variable can still be used on the RHS after the fact from which it received its value has been retracted.

Retracting the *moved* fact on the RHS of the *process-moved-information* rule is important for the rule to work correctly. Notice what happens when the *retract* command is removed:

```
CLIPS>
(defrule process-moved-information
  (moved (name ?name) (address ?address))
  ?f2 <- (person (name ?name))
  =>
  (modify ?f2 (address ?address)))↵
CLIPS> (unwatch facts) ↵
CLIPS> (unwatch rules) ↵
CLIPS> (reset) ↵
CLIPS> (watch facts) ↵
CLIPS> (watch rules) ↵
CLIPS> (watch activations) ↵
CLIPS> (run 3) ↵
FIRE    1 process-moved-information: f-2,f-1
<== f-1      (person (name "John Hill")
                    (address "25 Mulberry Lane"))
==> f-3      (person (name "John Hill")
                    (address "37 Cherry Lane"))
==> Activation 0
                process-moved-information: f-2,f-3
FIRE    2 process-moved-information: f-2,f-3
<== f-3      (person (name "John Hill")
                    (address "37 Cherry Lane"))
==> f-4      (person (name "John Hill")
                    (address "37 Cherry Lane"))
==> Activation 0   process-moved-information: f-
2,f-4
FIRE    3 process-moved-information: f-2,f-4
<== f-4      (person (name "John Hill")
                    (address "37 Cherry Lane"))
==> f-5      (person (name "John Hill")
                    (address "37 Cherry Lane"))
==> Activation 0
                process-moved-information: f-2,f-5
CLIPS>
```

The program executes an infinite loop since it asserts a new *person* fact after modifying the fact bound to ?f2, thus reactivating the *process-moved-information* rule. Remember that a *modify* command is treated as a *retract* command followed by an *assert* command. Since the *run* command was told to fire only three rules, that is when the program stopped. If no limit argument had been given to the *run* command, the program would have looped endlessly. The only way to stop an infinite loop like this is by interrupting CLIPS using Control-C, or another appropriate interrupt command for the computer on which CLIPS is running.

8.5 SINGLE-FIELD WILDCARDS

Sometimes it is useful to test for the existence of a field within a slot without actually assigning a value to a variable. This is particularly useful for multifield slots. For example, suppose we want to print the social security number of every person with a specified last name. The deftemplate used to describe each person, a deffacts with some predefined people, and a rule to print the social security numbers of every person with a specified last name are shown here:

```
(deftemplate person
    (multislot name)
    (slot social-security-number))

(deffacts some-people
    (person (name John Q. Public)
            (social-security-number 483-98-9083))
    (person (name Jack R. Public)
            (social-security-number 483-98-9084)))

(defrule print-social-security-numbers
    (print-ss-numbers-for ?last-name)
    (person (name ?first-name ?middle-name
                  ?last-name)
            (social-security-number ?ss-number))
    =>
    (printout t ?ss-number crlf))
```

(assert (print -ss-numbers-for Public))

The *print-social-security-numbers* rule binds the first and middle names of the person to the variables ?first-name and ?middle-name, respectively. These variables, however, are not referred to by actions on the RHS or other pattern or slots on the LHS of the rule. Instead of using a variable, a **single-field wildcard** can be used when a field is required, but the value is not important. A single-field wildcard is represented by a question mark. Using single-field wildcards, the *print-social-security-numbers* rule can be rewritten as follows:

```
(defrule print-social-security-numbers
    (print-ss-numbers-for ?last-name)
    (person (name ? ? ?last-name)
            (social-security-number ?ss-number))
    =>
    (printout t ?ss-number crlf))
```

Note that the *name* slot of a *person* fact must contain exactly three fields for the *print-social-security-numbers* rule to be activated. For example, the fact

```
(person (name Joe Public)
        (social-security-number 345-89-3039))
```

would not satisfy the *print-social-security-numbers* rule.

Notice the importance of not including a space between the question mark and the symbolic name of a variable. The pattern

```
(person (name ?first ?last))
```

expects two fields for the *name* slot, but the pattern

```
(person (name ?first ? last))
```

expects three fields for the *name* slot, and the last field must be the symbol *last*.

When a single-field slot is left unspecified in a pattern, CLIPS automatically adds a single-field wildcard check for that slot to the pattern. For example, the pattern

```
(person (name ?first ?last))
```

is converted to

```
(person (name ?first ?last)
        (social-security-number ?))
```

8.6 BLOCKS WORLD

To demonstrate variable bindings, we will build a program to move blocks in a simple blocks world. This type of program is analogous to the classic blocks world program in which the knowledge domain is restricted to blocks (Firebaugh 88). This is a good example of planning and might be applied to automated manufacturing, where a robot arm manipulates parts.

The second restriction will be that any goal must not already have been achieved. That is, the goal cannot be to move block x on top of block y if block x is already on top of block y. This is a rather simple condition to check; however, the appropriate syntax to test for this condition will not be introduced until Chapter 9.

To begin to solve this problem, it will be useful to set up a configuration of blocks that can be used for testing the program. Figure 8.1 shows the configuration that will be used. There are two stacks in this configuration. The first stack has block A on top of block B on top of block C. The second stack has block D on top of block E on top of block F.

To determine which type of rules would be effective in solving the problem, a step-by-step completion of a blocks world goal is useful. What steps must be taken to move block C on top of block E? The easiest solution for this problem would be to directly move block C on top of block E. However, this rule could only be applied if both block C and block E had no blocks on top of them. The pseudocode for this rule would be

```
RULE MOVE-DIRECTLY
IF   The goal is to move block ?upper on top of
       block ?lower and
     block ?upper is the top block in its stack and
     block ?lower is the top block in its stack,
THEN Move block ?upper on top of block ?lower.
```

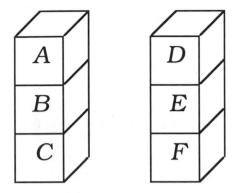

Figure 8.1 Blocks World Initial Configuration

The only things of interest in a blocks world are blocks. A single block may be stacked on another block. The goal of a complex blocks world program is to rearrange the stacks of blocks into a goal configuration with the minimum number of moves. For this example, a number of simplifying restrictions will be made. The first of these restrictions is that only one initial goal is allowed, and this goal can only be to move one block on top of another. With this restriction it is rather trivial to determine the optimal moves to achieve the goal. If the goal is to move block x on top of block y, then move all blocks (if any) on top of block x to the floor and all blocks (if any) on top of block y to the floor and then move block x on top of block y.

The *move-directly* rule cannot be used in this case since blocks A and B are on top of block C, and block D is on top of block E. In order to allow the *move-directly* rule to move block C on top of block E, blocks A, B, and D must be moved to the floor. Since this is the easiest step to take to get them out of the way, that is what happens. The simple blocks world does not require that the blocks be restacked and only a single initial goal is allowed, so there is no need to stack blocks when they are moved out of the way. This rule can be expressed as two pseudocode rules: one rule to clear blocks off the block to be moved and one rule to clear blocks off the block to be stacked on.

```
RULE  CLEAR-UPPER-BLOCK
IF    The goal is to move block ?x and
      block ?x is not the top block in its stack and
      block ?above is on top of block ?x,
THEN  The goal is to move block ?above to the floor

RULE  CLEAR-LOWER-BLOCK
IF    The goal is to move another block on top of
        block ?x and
      block ?x is not the top block in its stack and
      block ?above is on top of block ?x,
THEN  The goal is to move block ?above to the floor
```

The *clear-upper-block* rule will work to clear the blocks off block C. It will first determine that block B needs to be moved to the floor. In order to move block

B to the floor, this same rule will determine that block A needs to be moved to the floor. Similarly, the *clear-lower-block* rule will determine that block D needs to be moved to the floor in order to move something on top of block E.

Now there are subgoals to move blocks A, B, and D to the floor. Blocks A and D can be moved directly to the floor. If written properly, the *move-directly* rule might be able to handle moving blocks on top of the floor as well as on other blocks. Since the floor is really not a block, it may be necessary to treat the floor differently. The following pseudocode rule will handle the special case of moving a block to the floor:

```
RULE MOVE-TO-FLOOR
IF   The goal is to move block ?upper on top of the
         floor and
     block ?upper is the top block in its stack,
THEN Move block ?upper on top of the floor.
```

The *move-to-floor* rule can now move blocks A and D to the floor. Once block A is moved to the floor, the *move-to-floor* rule can be activated to move block B to the floor. With blocks A, B, and D on the floor, blocks C and E are now the top blocks in their stacks and it is possible to use the *move-directly* rule to move block C on top of block E.

Now that the rules have been written using pseudocode, the facts to be used by the rules should be determined. The types of facts needed cannot always be determined without some prototyping. In this case, the pseudocode rules point out several types of facts that will be needed. For example, the information about which blocks are on top of other blocks is crucial. This information could be described with the following deftemplate:

```
(deftemplate on-top-of
   (slot upper)
   (slot lower))
```

and the facts described by this template would be

```
(on-top-of (upper A) (lower B))
(on-top-of (upper B) (lower C))
(on-top-of (upper D) (lower E))
(on-top-of (upper E) (lower F))
```

Since it is also important to know which blocks are at the top and bottom of a stack, it would be useful to include the following facts:

```
(on-top-of (upper nothing) (lower A))
(on-top-of (upper C) (lower floor))
(on-top-of (upper nothing) (lower D))
(on-top-of (upper F) (lower floor))
```

The words *nothing* and *floor* have special meaning in these facts. The facts (on-top-of (upper nothing) (lower A)) and (on-top-of (upper nothing) (lower D)) indicate that A and D are the top blocks in their stacks. Similarly, the facts (on-top-of (upper C) (lower floor)) and (on-top-of (upper F) (lower floor)) indicate that blocks C and F are the bottom blocks in their stacks. Including these facts does not necessarily solve the problem of determining the top and bottom blocks in a stack. If the rules are not written correctly, the words *floor* and *nothing* might be mistaken as the names of blocks. Facts that indicate the names of the blocks might be useful. The following facts using the implied deftemplate *build* can be used to identify the blocks from the special words *nothing* and *floor*:

```
(block A)
(block B)
(block C)
(block D)
(block E)
(block F)
```

Finally, a fact is needed to describe the block-moving goals that are being processed. These goals could be described with the deftemplate

```
(deftemplate goal (slot move) (slot on-top-of))
```

and the initial goal using this deftemplate would be

```
(goal (move C) (on-top-of E))
```

With the facts and deftemplates now defined, the initial configuration of the blocks world can be described by the following deffacts:

```
(deffacts initial-state
    (block A)
    (block B)
    (block C)
    (block D)
    (block E)
    (block F)
    (on-top-of (upper nothing) (lower A))
    (on-top-of (upper A) (lower B))
    (on-top-of (upper B) (lower C))
    (on-top-of (upper C) (lower floor))
    (on-top-of (upper nothing) (lower D))
    (on-top-of (upper D) (lower E))
    (on-top-of (upper E) (lower F))
    (on-top-of (upper F) (lower floor))
    (goal (move C) (on-top-of E)))
```

The *move-directly* rule is written as follows:

```
(defrule move-directly
    ?goal <- (goal (move ?block1)
                   (on-top-of ?block2))
    (block ?block1)
    (block ?block2)
    (on-top-of (upper nothing) (lower ?block1))
```

```
    ?stack-1 <- (on-top-of (upper ?block1)
                           (lower ?block3))
    ?stack-2 <- (on-top-of (upper nothing)
                           (lower ?block2))
    =>
    (retract ?goal ?stack-1 ?stack-2)
    (assert (on-top-of (upper ?block1)
                       (lower ?block2))
            (on-top-of (upper nothing)
                       (lower ?block3)))
    (printout t ?block1 " moved on top of " ?block2
              "." crlf))
```

The first three patterns determine that there is a goal to move a block on top of another block. Patterns two and three ensure that a goal to move a block onto the floor will not be processed by this rule. The fourth and sixth patterns check that the blocks are the top blocks in their stacks. The fifth and sixth patterns match against information necessary to update the stacks that the moving block is being taken from and moved to. The actions of the rule update the stack information for the two stacks and print a message. The block beneath the moved block is now the top block in that stack, and the block being moved is now the top block in the stack to which it was moved.

The *move-to-floor* rule is implemented as follows:

```
(defrule move-to-floor
    ?goal <- (goal (move ?block1) (on-top-of floor))
    (block ?block1)
    (on-top-of (upper nothing) (lower ?block1))
    ?stack <- (on-top-of (upper ?block1)
                         (lower ?block2))
    =>
    (retract ?goal ?stack)
    (assert (on-top-of (upper ?block1)
                       (lower floor))
            (on-top-of (upper nothing)
                       (lower ?block2)))
    (printout t ?block1 " moved on top of floor."
              crlf))
```

This rule is similar to the *move-directly* rule with the exception that it is not necessary to update some information about the floor since it is not a block.

The *clear-upper-block* rule is implemented as follows:

```
(defrule clear-upper-block
    (goal (move ?block1))
    (block ?block1)
    (on-top-of (upper ?block2) (lower ?block1))
    (block ?block2)
    =>
```

```
                    (assert (goal (move ?block2)
                                 (on-top-of floor)))))
```

The *clear-lower-block* rule is implemented as follows:

```
(defrule clear-lower-block
    (goal (on-top-of ?block1))
    (block ?block1)
    (on-top-of (upper ?block2) (lower ?block1))
    (block ?block2)
    =>
    (assert (goal (move ?block2)
                 (on-top-of floor)))))
```

The program is now complete with the *move-directly*, *move-to-floor*, *clear-upper-block*, and *clear-lower-block* rules, the *goal* and *on-top-of* deftemplates, and the *initial-state* deffacts. The following output shows a sample run of this blocks world program:

```
CLIPS> (unwatch all)↵
CLIPS> (reset)↵
CLIPS> (run)↵
A moved on top of floor.
B moved on top of floor.
D moved on top of floor.
C moved on top of E.
CLIPS>
```

Blocks A and B are first moved to the floor to clear block C. Block D is then moved to the floor to clear block E. Finally, block C can be moved on top of block E to solve the initial goal.

This example has demonstrated how to build a program using a step-by-step method. First, pseudorules were written using English-like text. Second, the pseudorules were used to determine the types of facts that would be required. Deftemplates describing the facts were designed, and the initial knowledge for the program was coded using these deftemplates. Finally, the pseudorules were translated to CLIPS rules using the deftemplates as a guide for translation.

The development of an expert system typically requires a great deal more prototyping and iterative development than in this example. It is not always possible to determine the best method for representing facts or the types of rules that will be needed to build an expert system. Following a consistent methodology, however, can aid in the development of an expert system even when a great deal of prototyping and iteration need to be performed.

8.7 MULTIFIELD WILDCARDS AND VARIABLES

Multifield Wildcards

Multifield wildcards and variables can be used to match against zero or more fields of a pattern. The **multifield wildcard** is indicated by a dollar sign followed by a question mark, "**$?**", and represents zero or more occurrences of a field. Note that ordinary variables and wildcards match exactly one field. This is a slight but significant difference. To illustrate the use of multifield wildcards, recall the *print-social-security-numbers* rule described in Section 8.5:

```
(defrule print-social-security-numbers
    (print-ss-numbers-for ?last-name)
    (person (name ? ? ?last-name)
            (social-security-number ?ss-number))
    =>
    (printout t ?ss-number crlf))
```

This rule will only match a name slot that has exactly three fields. The fact

```
(person (name Joe Public)
        (social-security-number 345-89-3039))
```

will not match the rule. However, if the two single-field wildcards are replaced with a single multifield wildcard (as shown below), then the *person* pattern will match any name slot that contains at least one field and has as its last field the specified name.

```
(defrule print-social-security-numbers
    (print-ss-numbers-for ?last-name)
    (person (name $? ?last-name)
            (social-security-number ?ss-number))
    =>
    (printout t ?ss-number crlf))
```

Likewise, when a multifield slot is left unspecified in a pattern, CLIPS automatically adds a multifield wildcard check for that slot to the pattern. For example, the pattern

```
(person (social-security-number ?ss-number))
```

is converted to

```
(person (name $?)
        (social-security-number ?ss-number))
```

Multifield Variables

Just as single-field variables are preceded by a "?", multifield variables are preceeded by a "$?". The following constructs show how to print names of all the children of a specified person:

```
(deftemplate person
    (multislot name)
    (multislot children))
```

```
(deffacts some-people
   (person (name John Q. Public)
           (children Jane Paul Mary))
   (person (name Jack R. Public)
           (children Rick)))

(defrule print-children
   (print-children $?name)
   (person (name $?name)
           (children $?children))
   =>
   (printout t ?name " has children " ?children
                crlf))
```

The first pattern of the *print-children* rule binds the name of the person whose children will be printed to the variable $?name. The second pattern matches the *person* fact with the specified name contained in $?name and then binds the list of that person's children to the variable $?children. This value is then printed from the RHS of the rule.

Notice that when a multifield variable is referred to on the RHS of a rule, it is not necessary to include the $ as part of the variable name. The $ is only used on the LHS to indicate that zero or more fields can be bound to the variable.

The following dialog shows how the *print-children* rule works:

```
CLIPS> (reset) ↵
CLIPS> (assert (print-children John Q. Public)) ↵
<Fact-3>
CLIPS> (run) ↵
(John Q. Public) has children (Jane Paul Mary)
CLIPS>
```

Notice that the multifield values bound to the variables ?name and ?children are surrounded by parentheses when printed.

More than one multifield variable can be used in a single slot. Suppose, for example, that we want to find all the people who have a child with a specific name. The following rule accomplishes this task:

```
(defrule find-child
   (find-child ?child)
   (person (name $?name)
           (children $?before ?child $?after))
   =>
   (printout t ?name " has child " ?child crlf)
   (printout t "Other children are "
                ?before " " ?after crlf))
```

Generally, if we were only interested in the value of the ?child variable, the variables ?before and ?after would have been replaced with multifield wildcards (and the printout statement referring to these variables would be removed). The following dialog shows how the *find-child* rule works:

```
CLIPS> (reset) ↵
CLIPS> (assert (find-child Paul)) ↵
<Fact-3>
CLIPS> (run) ↵
(John Q. Public) has child Paul
Other children are (Jane) (Mary)
CLIPS> (assert (find-child Rick))
<Fact-4>
CLIPS> (run) ↵
(Jack R. Public) has child Rick
Other children are () ()
CLIPS> (assert (find-child Bill)) ↵
<Fact-5>
CLIPS> (run) ↵
CLIPS>
```

When Paul is the child bound to the variable ?child, the variable ?before is bound to (Jane) and the variable ?after is bound to (Mary). Similarly, when Rick is bound to the variable ?child, then the variable ?before is bound to (), a multifield containing zero fields, and the variable ?after is also bound to ().

Matching Patterns in More than One Way

So far we've dealt with situations in which a single fact can match a pattern in only one way. With multifield variables or wildcards, it is possible to match a pattern in more than one way. Suppose that a fact is entered for a person who has named all of his children after himself. For example,

```
CLIPS> (reset) ↵
CLIPS> (assert (person (name Joe Fiveman)
                (children Joe Joe Joe))) ↵
<Fact-3>
CLIPS> (assert (find-child Joe)) ↵
<Fact-4>
CLIPS> (agenda) ↵
0       find-child: f-4,f-3
0       find-child: f-4,f-3
0       find-child: f-4,f-3
For a total of 3 activations.
CLIPS> (run) ↵
(Joe Fiveman) has child Joe
Other children are () (Joe Joe)
(Joe Fiveman) has child Joe
Other children are (Joe) (Joe)
(Joe Fiveman) has child Joe
Other children are (Joe Joe) ()
CLIPS>
```

As the rule firings show, there are three different ways in which the variables ?child, ?before, and ?after can be bound with the fact f-3. In the first case, ?before is bound to (), ?child is bound to *Joe*, and ?after is bound to (Joe Joe). In the second case, ?before is bound to (Joe), ?child is bound to *Joe*, and ?after is bound to (Joe). In the third case, ?before is bound to (Joe Joe), ?child is bound to *Joe*, and ?after is bound to ().

Implementing a Stack

A **stack** is an ordered data structure to which items can be added and removed. Items are added and removed to one "end" of the stack. A new item can be pushed (added) to the stack or the last item added can be popped (removed) from the stack. In a stack the first value added is the last item to be removed and the last item added is the first item to be removed.

A useful analogy for a stack is a set of cafeteria trays. New trays are added (pushed) on top of the trays already in the stack. The last trays added to the top of the stack will be the first trays removed (popped).

It is relatively easy to implement a stack capable of performing push and pop operations using multifield variables. First, an ordered *stack* fact that contains a list of items will be used. The following rule will push a value onto the *stack* fact:

```
(defrule push-value
   ?push-value <- (push-value ?value)
   ?stack <- (stack $?rest)
   =>
   (retract ?push-value ?stack)
   (assert (stack ?value $?rest))
   (printout t "Pushing value " ?value crlf))
```

Two rules are necessary to implement the pop action: one for an empty stack and another if the stack has a value to pop.

```
(defrule pop-value-valid
   ?pop-value <- (pop-value)
   ?stack <- (stack ?value $?rest)
   =>
   (retract ?pop-value ?stack)
   (assert (stack $?rest))
   (printout t "Popping value " ?value crlf))

(defrule pop-value-invalid
   ?pop-value <- (pop-value)
   (stack)
   =>
   (retract ?pop-value)
   (printout t "Popping from empty stack" crlf))
```

These rules could easily be changed to push and pop values to named stacks. For example, the patterns

```
?push-value <- (push-value ?value)
?stack <- (stack $?rest)
```

could be replaced with

```
?push-value <- (push-value ?name ?value)
?stack <- (stack ?name $?rest)
```

where ?name represents the name of the stack.

Blocks World Revisited

The blocks world problem can be reimplemented in a much easier fashion using multifield wildcards and variables. Each stack can be represented by a single fact, as shown below. The operations on moving the blocks are similar to those used in the push/pop example.

```
(deffacts initial-state
    (stack A B C)
    (stack D E F)
    (goal (move C) (on-top-of E))
    (stack))
```

The empty *stack* fact is included to prevent this fact from being added later; for example, when a stack has one block in it and that block is moved on top of another.

The rules for the blocks world program using multifield variables are:

```
(defrule move-directly
    ?goal <- (goal (move ?block1)
                   (on-top-of ?block2))
    ?stack-1 <- (stack ?block1 $?rest1)
    ?stack-2 <- (stack ?block2 $?rest2)
    =>
    (retract ?goal ?stack-1 ?stack-2)
    (assert (stack $?rest1))
    (assert (stack ?block1 ?block2 $?rest2))
    (printout t ?block1 " moved on top of "
              ?block2 "." crlf))

(defrule move-to-floor
    ?goal <- (goal (move ?block1) (on-top-of floor))
    ?stack-1 <- (stack ?block1 $?rest)
    =>
    (retract ?goal ?stack-1)
    (assert (stack ?block1))
    (assert (stack $?rest))
    (printout t ?block1 " moved on top of floor."
              crlf))

(defrule clear-upper-block
    (goal (move ?block1))
    (stack ?top $? ?block1 $?)
```

```
        =>
        (assert (goal (move ?top) (on-top-of floor))))

    (defrule clear-lower-block
        (goal (on-top-of ?block1))
        (stack ?top $? ?block1 $?)
        =>
        (assert (goal (move ?top) (on-top-of floor))))
```

8.8 FIELD CONSTRAINTS

The *Not* Field Constraint

In addition to the elementary pattern-matching capabilities of literal constants and variable bindings, CLIPS has more powerful pattern-matching operators. These additional pattern-matching capabilities will be introduced by reconsidering the problem of determining groups of people with certain hair and eye colors. For example, suppose it is necessary to find all people who do *not* have brown hair. One way to do this is to write rules for each type of hair color. For example, the following rule finds people with black hair (the *person* deftemplate from Section 8.2 is used for the examples in this section):

```
    (defrule black-hair-is-not-brown-hair
        (person (name ?name) (hair black))
        =>
        (printout t ?name " does not have brown hair"
                    crlf))
```

Another rule finds people with blonde hair.

```
    (defrule blonde-hair-is-not-brown-hair
        (person (name ?name) (hair blonde))
        =>
        (printout t ?name " does not have brown hair"
                    crlf))
```

Yet another rule could be written to find people with red hair. The problem with writing the rules in this manner is that the condition being checked is that the hair is not brown. The previous rules attempt to test this condition in a roundabout manner—that is, they determine all the hair colors other than brown and write a rule for each one. If all the colors can be specified, then this technique will work. For this example it would be simpler to assume that hair color could be anything (even purple or green).

One way of handling this problem is to use a **field constraint** to restrict the values a field may have on the LHS. One type of field constraint is called a *connective constraint* (so called because it is used for connecting variables and other constraints). There are three types of connective constraints. The first is called a ***not* constraint**. Its symbol is the **tilde, ~**. The *not* constraint acts on the one constraint or variable that immediately follows it. If the constraint following matched a field, then the *not* constraint fails. If the constraint following failed to match, then the *not* constraint succeeds. Essentially the *not* constraint negates the result of the constraint following.

The rule that looks for people without brown hair can be written much more easily using the *not* constraint:

```
(defrule person-without-brown-hair
    (person (name ?name) (hair ~brown))
    =>
    (printout t ?name " does not have brown hair"
              crlf))
```

By using the *not* constraint this one rule does the work of many others that required specifying each possible hair color.

The *Or* Field Constraint

The second connective constraint is the ***or* constraint**, represented by the bar, |. The *or* constraint is used to allow one or more possible values to match a field of a pattern.

For example, the following rule finds all people with either black or brown hair using the *or* constraint:

```
(defrule black-or-brown-hair
    (person (name ?name) (hair brown | black))
    =>
    (printout t ?name " has dark hair" crlf))
```

Asserting the facts (person (name Joe) (eyes blue) (hair brown)) and (person (name Mark) (eyes brown) (hair black)) would place an activation of this rule for each of the facts on the agenda.

The *And* Field Constraint

The third type of connective constraint is the ***and* constraint**. The *and* constraint is different from the *and* conditional element discussed in Section 7.15. The symbol of the *and* constraint is the ampersand, **&**. The *and* constraint is normally used only with the other constraints; otherwise it's not of much practical use.

One case in which the *and* constraint is useful is in placing additional constraints with the binding instance of a variable. Suppose, for example, that a rule is triggered by a *person* fact with the hair color brown or black. The pattern to find such a fact can be expressed easily using the *or* constraint, as shown in the previous example. However, how can the value of the hair color be identified? The solution is to bind a variable to the color that is matched using the *and* constraint and then print out the variable:

```
(defrule black-or-brown-hair
    (person (name ?name) (hair ?color&brown|black))
    =>
    (printout t ?name " has " ?color " hair" crlf))
```

The variable ?color will be bound to whatever color is matched by the brown|black constraint.

The *and* constraint is also useful with the *not* constraint. For example, the following rule triggers when a person's hair color is neither black nor brown:

```
(defrule black-or-brown-hair
    (person (name ?name)
            (hair ?color&~brown&~black))
    =>
    (printout t ?name " has " ?color " hair" crlf))
```

Combining Field Constraints

Field constraints can be used together with variables and other literal values to provide powerful pattern-matching capabilities. Suppose, for example, that a rule is needed to determine whether two people exist with the fol lowing descriptive conditions. The first person has either blue or green eyes and does not have black hair. The second person does not have the same color eyes as the first person and has either red hair or the same color hair as the first person. The following rule will match these constraints:

```
(defrule complex-eye-hair-match
    (person (name ?name1)
            (eyes ?eyes1&blue|green)
            (hair ?hair1&~black))
    (person (name ?name2&~?name1)
            (eyes ?eyes2&~?eyes1)
            (hair ?hair2&red|?hair1))
    =>
    (printout t ?name1 " has " ?eyes1 " eyes and "
                ?hair1 " hair" crlf)
    (printout t ?name2 " has " ?eyes2 " eyes and "
                ?hair2 " hair" crlf))
```

This example is worth studying in some detail. The constraint ?eyes1&blue|green in the first pattern's *eyes* slot binds the first person's eye color to the variable ?eyes1 if the eye color value of the fact being matched is either blue or green. The constraint ?hair1&~black in the first pattern's *hair* slot binds the variable ?hair1 if the hair color value of the fact being matched is not black.

The constraint ?name2&~?name1 in the second pattern's *name* slot performs a useful operation. It binds the value of the *name* slot of the *person* fact to the variable ?name2 if it is not the same as the value of ?name1. If names are unique identifiers (i.e., no two people in the database have the same name), this will insure that both patterns do not match the same fact. This cannot happen for these two patterns, since the eye color of the second person must be different from the eye color of the first. However, it is a useful technique to understand and has many useful applications. Section 12.2 will show how this same technique can be accomplished using fact addresses to make sure the facts are different. This will allow the rule to work for people with the same names but different hair and eye colors.

The constraint ?eyes2&~?eyes1 in the second pattern's *eyes* slot performs much the same test as the previous constraint. The final constraint, ?hair2&red|?hair1, in the second pattern's *hair* slot binds the hair color value of the second person to the variable ?hair2 if the hair color is either red or the same value as the variable ?hair1. Note that a variable must already be bound if it is used as part of an *or* field constraint.

Variables will be bound only if they are the first condition in a field and only if they occur singly or are tied to the other conditions by an *and* connective constraint. For example, the rule

```
(defrule bad-variable-use
    (person (name ?name) (hair red|?hair))
    =>
    (printout t ?name " has " ?hair " hair " crlf))
```

will produce an error since ?hair is not bound.

As a final note for combining constraints, keep in mind that there are combinations of constraints that perform no useful purpose. For example, using the *and* constraint to tie together literal constants (e.g., black&blue) will always cause the constraint to not be satisfied unless the literals are identical. Similarly, tying together negated literals using the *or* constraint (e.g., ~black|~blue) will always cause the constraint to be satisfied.

8.9 FUNCTIONS AND EXPRESSIONS

Elementary Math Functions

In addition to dealing with symbolic facts, CLIPS can perform calculations. Keep in mind, though, that an expert system language like CLIPS is not designed for number crunching. Although the math functions of CLIPS are powerful, they are primarily meant for modification of numbers that are being reasoned about by the application program. Other languages such as FORTRAN are better for number crunching in which little or no reasoning about the numbers is done. CLIPS provides the elementary arithmetic operators, shown in Table 8.1. (Appendix E contains a list of other mathematical functions provided by CLIPS. The *Basic Programming Guide*, provided in electronic format in the CD-ROM accompanying this book, offers additional details on all of the functions available in CLIPS.)

Arithmetic Operators	Meaning
+	Addition
–	Subtraction
*	Multiplication
/	Division

Table 8.1 CLIPS Elementary Arithmetic Operators

Numeric expressions are represented in CLIPS according to the style of LISP. In LISP and CLIPS, a numeric expression that would customarily be written as 2 + 3 must be written in **prefix form**, (+ 2 3). The customary way of writing numeric expressions is called *infix form* because the math operators are between the **operands** or **arguments**. In the prefix form of CLIPS the operator must go before the operands and parentheses must surround the numeric expression.

It is relatively easy to convert from infix to prefix format. For example, suppose two points are to be checked to see whether they have a positive slope. In the customary infix way, this can be written as

```
(y2 - y1) / (x2 - x1)    >    0
```

Note that the greater than symbol, >, is a CLIPS function that determines if the first argument is greater than the second argument. (The > function is described in Appendix E and in the *Basic Programming Guide*.) In order to write this expression in prefix form it will be useful to start by thinking of the numerator as (Y) and the denominator as (X). So the expression above can be written as

```
(Y) / (X)    >    0
```

The prefix form for division is then

```
(/ (Y) (X))
```

since in prefix the operator comes before the argument. Now the result of the division must be tested to determine whether it is greater than 0. Thus the prefix form is as follows:

```
(> (/ (Y) (X)) 0)
```

In infix form, $Y = y2 - y1$. But the prefix form needs to be used, since a prefix expression is being created. So $(- y2\ y1)$ will be used for (Y) and $(- x2\ x1)$ for (X). Replacing (Y) and (X) by their prefix forms will yield the final expression of whether the two points have a positive slope:

```
(> (/ (- y2 y1). (- x2 x1)) 0)
```

The simplest way to evaluate a numeric expression (as well as any other expression) in CLIPS is to evaluate the expression at the top level prompt. For example, entering (+ 2 2) at the CLIPS prompt would produce the following output:

```
CLIPS> (+ 2 2) ⏎
4
CLIPS>
```

The output shows the correct response, 4. In general, any CLIPS expression to be evaluated can be entered at the top level. Most functions, such as the addition function, have a **return value**. This return value can be an integer, a float, a symbol, a string, or even a multifield value. Other functions, such as the *facts* and *agenda* commands, have no return value. Functions without a return value typically have what is called a ***side effect***. The side effect of the *facts* command is to list the facts in the fact list.

The other arithmetic functions also work at the top level. The following output demonstrates the evaluation of some other expressions:

```
CLIPS> (+ 2 3) ↵
5
CLIPS> (- 2 3) ↵
-1
CLIPS> (* 2 3) ↵
6
CLIPS> (/ 2 3) ↵
0.66666667
CLIPS>
```

Note that the answer for division will probably show a round-off error in the last digit. This result may vary from machine to machine.

The return value of the $+$, $-$, and $*$ functions is an integer if all of the arguments to the function are integers. If one of the arguments to the function is a floating point number, then the return value is a floating point number. The first argument to the / function is always converted to a float, so the return value of this function is always a float. For example,

```
CLIPS> (+ 2 3.0) ↵
5.0
CLIPS> (+ 2.0 3) ↵
5.0
CLIPS> (+ 2 3) ↵
5
CLIPS>
```

Variable Numbers of Arguments

Prefix notation allows variable numbers of arguments to be represented quite simply. Many CLIPS functions accept a variable number of arguments. The arguments in a numeric expression can be extended beyond two for the $+$, $-$, and $*$ functions. The same sequence of arithmetic calculations is performed for more than two arguments. The following examples, entered at the top level, show how three arguments are used. Evaluation proceeds from left to right.

```
CLIPS> (+ 2 3 4) ↵
9
CLIPS> (- 2 3 4) ↵
-5
CLIPS> (* 2 3 4) ↵
24
CLIPS> (/ 2 3 4) ↵
0.16666667
CLIPS>
```

Once again note that the answer for division may vary slightly depending on the machine being used.

Precedence and Nesting Expressions

One important fact about CLIPS and LISP calculations is that there is no built-in precedence of arithmetic operations. In other computer languages multiplication and division rank higher than addition and subtraction and the computer does the higher-ranked operations first. In LISP and CLIPS everything is simply evaluated from left to right, with parentheses determining precedence.

Mixed calculations can be done in prefix notation. For example, suppose the following infix expression is to be evaluated:

```
2 + 3 * 4
```

The customary evaluation is to multiply 3 by 4 and then add the result to 2. However, in CLIPS the precedence must be explicitly written. The expression could be evaluated by entering the following at the top level:

```
CLIPS> (+ 2 (* 3 4)) ↵
14
CLIPS>
```

In this rule the expression in the innermost parentheses is evaluated first, so 3 is multiplied by 4. The result is then added to 2. If the desired evaluation is (2 + 3) * 4, where addition is done first, the top level expression would be

```
CLIPS> (* (+ 2 3) 4) ↵
20
CLIPS>
```

In general, expressions may be freely embedded within other expressions. Thus it is possible to place an expression within an assert command, as the following example shows:

```
CLIPS> (clear) ↵
CLIPS> (assert (answer (+ 2 2))) ↵
<Fact-0>
CLIPS> (facts) ↵
f-0      (answer 4)
For a total of 1 fact.
CLIPS>
```

Also, since function names are also symbols, you can use them as you would other symbols. For example, you could use them as fields in a fact:

```
CLIPS> (clear) ↵
CLIPS> (assert (expression 2 + 3 * 4)) ↵
<Fact-0>
CLIPS> (facts) ↵
f-0      (expression 2 + 3 * 4)
For a total of 1 fact.
CLIPS>
```

However, parentheses are used by CLIPS as delimiters, so it's not possible to use them as you would other symbols. In order to use them in facts or as an argument to a function, you'll need to enclose them in quotation marks to make them strings.

8.10 SUMMING VALUES USING RULES

As a simple example of using functions to perform calculations, consider the problem of summing up the area of a group of rectangles. The heights and widths of the rectangles can be specified using the following deftemplate:

```
(deftemplate rectangle (slot height) (slot width))
```

and the sum of rectangle areas could be specified using an ordered fact such as the following:

```
(sum 20)
```

A deffacts containing sample information is

```
(deffacts initial-information
    (rectangle (height 10) (width 6))
    (rectangle (height 7) (width 5))
    (rectangle (height 6) (width 8))
    (rectangle (height 2) (width 5))
    (sum 0))
```

An initial attempt to produce a rule to sum the rectangle might be

```
(defrule sum-rectangles
    (rectangle (height ?height) (width ?width))
    ?sum <- (sum ?total)
    =>
    (retract ?sum)
    (assert (sum (+ ?total (* ?height ?width)))))
```

This rule, however, will loop endlessly. Retracting the *sum* fact and then reasserting it will produce a loop with a single *rectangle* fact. One solution to solve the problem would be to retract the *rectangle* fact after its area was added to the *sum* fact. This would prevent the rule from firing off the same *rectangle* fact with a different *sum* fact. If the *rectangle* fact needs to be preserved, a different approach is required. A temporary fact containing the area to be added to the sum is created for each *rectangle* fact. This temporary fact can then be retracted, preventing an endless loop. The modified program is as follows:

```
(defrule sum-rectangles
    (rectangle (height ?height) (width ?width))
    =>
    (assert (add-to-sum (* ?height ?width))))
```

```
(defrule sum-areas
   ?sum <- (sum ?total)
   ?new-area <- (add-to-sum ?area)
   =>
   (retract ?sum ?new-area)
   (assert (sum (+ ?total ?area))))
```

The following output shows how these two rules interact to sum the areas of the rectangles:

```
CLIPS> (unwatch all) ↵
CLIPS> (watch rules) ↵
CLIPS> (watch facts) ↵
CLIPS> (watch activations) ↵
CLIPS> (reset) ↵
==> f-0      (initial-fact)
==> f-1      (rectangle (height 10) (width 6))
==> Activation 0      sum-rectangles: f-1
==> f-2      (rectangle (height 7) (width 5))
==> Activation 0      sum-rectangles: f-2
==> f-3      (rectangle (height 6) (width 8))
==> Activation 0      sum-rectangles: f-3
==> f-4      (rectangle (height 2) (width 5))
==> Activation 0      sum-rectangles: f-4
==> f-5      (sum 0)
CLIPS> (run) ↵
FIRE    1 sum-rectangles: f-4
==> f-6      (add-to-sum 10)
==> Activation 0      sum-areas: f-5,f-6
FIRE    2 sum-areas: f-5,f-6
<== f-5      (sum 0)
<== f-6      (add-to-sum 10)
==> f-7      (sum 10)
FIRE    3 sum-rectangles: f-3
==> f-8      (add-to-sum 48)
==> Activation 0      sum-areas: f-7,f-8
FIRE    4 sum-areas: f-7,f-8
<== f-7      (sum 10)
<== f-8      (add-to-sum 48)
==> f-9      (sum 58)
FIRE    5 sum-rectangles: f-2
==> f-10     (add-to-sum 35)
==> Activation 0      sum-areas: f-9,f-10
FIRE    6 sum-areas: f-9,f-10
<== f-9      (sum 58)
<== f-10     (add-to-sum 35)
==> f-11     (sum 93)
FIRE    7 sum-rectangles: f-1
```

```
==> f-12     (add-to-sum 60)
==> Activation 0       sum-areas: f-11,f-12
FIRE    8 sum-areas: f-11,f-12
<== f-11     (sum 93)
<== f-12     (add-to-sum 60)
==> f-13     (sum 153)
CLIPS> (unwatch all) ↵
CLIPS>
```

The *sum-rectangles* rule is activated four times when the *rectangle* facts are asserted as a result of the *reset* command. Each time the *sum-rectangles* rule is fired it asserts a fact that activates the *sum-areas* rule. The *sum-areas* rule adds the area to the running total and removes the *add-to-sum* fact. Since the *sum-rectangles* rule does not pattern match against the *sum* fact, it is not reactivated when a new *sum* fact is asserted.

8.11 THE BIND FUNCTION

It is often useful to store a value in a temporary variable to avoid recalculation, which is crucial when functions produce side effects. The **bind** function can be used to bind the value of a variable to the value of an expression. The syntax of the *bind* function is

```
(bind <variable> <value>)
```

The bound variable, <variable>, uses the syntax of a single field variable. The new value, <value>, should be an expression that evaluates to either a single or a multifield value. For example, the *sum-areas* rule could print out the total sum and the area being added to it for each rectangle.

```
(defrule sum-areas
    ?sum <- (sum ?total)
    ?new-area <- (add-to-sum ?area)
    =>
    (retract ?sum ?new-area)
    (printout t "Adding " ?area " to " ?total crlf)
    (printout t "New sum is " (+ ?total ?area) crlf)
    (assert (sum (+ ?total ?area))))
```

Notice that the expression (+ ?total ?area) is used twice in the RHS of the rule. Replacing the two separate evaluations with one *bind* function would eliminate unnecessary calculations. The rule rewritten with the *bind* function is

```
(defrule sum-areas
    ?sum <- (sum ?total)
    ?new-area <- (add-to-sum ?area)
    =>
    (retract ?sum ?new-area)
    (printout t "Adding " ?area " to " ?total crlf)
    (bind ?new-total (+ ?total ?area))
```

```
(printout t "New sum is " ?new-total crlf)
(assert (sum ?new-total)))
```

In addition to creating new variables for use on the RHS of a rule, the *bind* function can also be used to rebind the value of a variable used in the LHS of a rule.

8.12 I/O FUNCTIONS

The Read Function

Expert systems often require input from the user of the program. CLIPS allows information to be read from the keyboard using the **read** function. The basic syntax of the *read* function requires no arguments, and the following example shows how the *read* function is used to input data:

```
CLIPS> (clear) ↵
CLIPS>
(defrule get-first-name
  =>
  (printout t "What is your first name? ")
  (bind ?response (read))
  (assert (user's-name ?response)))
CLIPS> (reset) ↵
CLIPS> (run) ↵
What is your first name? Gary↵
CLIPS> (facts) ↵
f-0     (initial-fact)
f-1     (user's-name Gary)
For a total of 2 facts.
CLIPS>
```

Notice that the *read* function requires a carriage return before it will read the token entered. The *read* function can only be used to input a single field at a time. All extra characters entered after the first field up to the carriage return are discarded. For example, if the get-first-name rule tried to read both the first name and the last name with the following input,

```
Gary Riley↵
```

only the first field, *Gary*, will be read. To read all of the input, both fields must be enclosed within double quotes. Of course, once the input is within double quotes, it is a single literal field. The individual fields *Gary* and *Riley* cannot easily be accessed.

The read function allows fields that are not symbols, strings, integers, or floats, such as parentheses, to be entered. Such fields are placed within double quotes and treated as strings. The following command line dialog demonstrates this capability:

```
CLIPS> (read) ⏎
(⏎
"("
CLIPS>
```

The Open Function

In addition to keyboard input and terminal output, CLIPS can also read from and write to files. Before a file can be accessed for reading or writing, it must be opened using the **open** function. The number of files that can be open simultaneously depends on the individual operating system and hardware.

The syntax of the *open* function is

```
(open <file-name> <file-ID> [<file-access>])
```

As an example,

```
(open "input.dat" data "r")
```

The first argument of *open*, <file-name>, is a string representing the name of the file on your computer. In the example, the file name "input.dat" is used. The file name may also include path information (the directory in which the file is found). Path specifications typically vary from one operating system to another, so you will have to be somewhat familiar with your computer's operating system in order to specify a path.

The second argument, <file-ID>, is the **logical name** CLIPS associates with the file. The logical name is a global name by which CLIPS can access the file from any rule or the top level prompt. Although the logical name could be the same as the file name, it is good idea to use a different name to avoid confusion. For the example shown, the logical name *data* was used to refer to the "input.dat" file. Other meaningful names, such as input or file-data, could have been used.

One advantage of using a logical name is that a different file name can easily be substituted without making major changes to the program. Since the file name is only used in the *open* function and is later referred to by its logical name, only the *open* function need be changed to read from a different file.

The third argument, <file-access>, is a string representing one of the four possible modes of file access. Table 8.2 lists the file access modes.

Mode	Action
"r"	Read access only
"w"	Write access only
"r+"	Read and write access
"a"	Append access only

Table 8.2 File Access Modes

If <file-access> is not included as an argument, the default value of "r" will be used. Some access modes may not be meaningful to certain operating systems. Most operating systems will support read access (for inputting data) and write access (for outputting data). Read and write access and append access (for appending output data to the end of a file) may not always be available.

It is important to remember that the consequences of opening a file may vary from one machine to another. For example, operating systems that do not support multiple file versions, such as MS-DOS on an IBM PC or UNIX, will replace an existing file if that file is opened using write access. In contrast, VMS on a VAX will create a new version of a file if it already exists and is opened using write access.

The *open* function acts as a predicate function (described in Section 9.4). It returns the symbol *TRUE* if a file was successfully opened; otherwise the symbol *FALSE* is returned. The return value can be used to perform error checking. For example, if the user supplies the name of a file that does not exist and an attempt is made to open the file using read access, the *open* function will return the symbol *FALSE*. The rule that opens the file could detect this and perform the appropriate actions to prompt the user for another file name.

The Close Function

Once access is no longer needed to a file, it should be closed. Unless a file is closed, there is no guarantee that the information written to it will be saved. Further, the longer a file is open, the greater the chances that a power loss or other malfunction would prevent the information from being saved.

The general form of the **close** function is

```
(close [<file-ID>])
```

where the optional argument <file-ID> specifies the logical name of the file to be closed. If <file-ID> is not specified, all open files will be closed. As an example,

```
(close data)
```

will close the file known to CLIPS by the logical file name *data*. The statements

```
(close input)
(close output)
```

will close the files associated with the logical names *input* and *output*. Note that separate statements are necessary to close specific files.

It is important when using files to remember that each opened file should eventually be closed with the *close* function. In particular, if a command is not issued to close a file, the data written to it may be lost. CLIPS will not prompt you to close an open file. The only safeguard built into CLIPS for closing files that have been inadvertently left open is that all open files will be closed when an *exit* command is issued.

Reading and Writing to a File

In the examples thus far, all input has been read from the keyboard and all output has been sent to the terminal. The use of logical names allows input and output to and from other sources. In Chapter 7 the *printout* function used the logical name t to send output to the screen. Other logical names can be used with the *printout* function to send output to destinations other than the screen.

When used as a logical name for an output function, the logical name t writes output to the standard output device, usually the terminal. Similarly, when used as the logical name for an input function, the logical name t reads input from the **standard input device**, normally the keyboard.

The following example illustrates the use of logical names for writing to a file:

```
CLIPS> (open "example.dat" example "w") ↵
TRUE
CLIPS> (printout example "green" crlf) ↵
CLIPS> (printout example 7 crlf) ↵
CLIPS> (close example) ↵
TRUE
CLIPS>
```

First, the file "example.dat" is opened with write access so values may be written to it. The open function has now associated the logical name example with the "example.dat" file. The values *green* and 7 are then written to the file "example.dat" by using the logical name *example* as the first argument to the *printout* function. Once the values have been written to the file, the file is closed using the *close* command.

Now that the values have been written to the file, it can be opened with read access and the values can be retrieved using the *read* function. The general format of the read function is

```
(read [<logical-name>])
```

The *read* function defaults to reading from the standard input device, t, if it is given no arguments. The previous example of the *read* function made use of this default logical name. The following example shows how a logical name can be used with the *read* function to retrieve the values from the "example.dat" file:

```
CLIPS> (open "example.dat" example "r") ↵
TRUE
CLIPS> (read example) ↵
green
CLIPS> (read example) ↵
7
CLIPS> (read example) ↵
EOF
CLIPS> (close example) ↵
TRUE
CLIPS>
```

First the file "example.dat" is opened, but with read access this time. Note that the "r" option did not have to be used for opening the "example.dat" file with the second call to the *open* function since that is the default. Once the file is open, the *read* function is used to retrieve the values *green* and 7 from the file associated with the logical name *example*. Notice that the third call of the *read* function returns the symbol **EOF**. CLIPS returns this value for input functions when an attempt is made to read past the end of the file. By checking the return value of the *read* (or other input) function it is possible to determine when there are no more data left in the file.

The Format Function

There are times when it is desirable to format output from a CLIPS program, such as when arranging data in tables. Although the *printout* function is useful, there is a function specifically designed for formatting, called *format*, that provides a wide variety of formatting styles. The syntax of the *format* function is

```
(format <logical-name> <control-string>
        <parameters>*)
```

The *format* function has several parts. The <logical-name> is the logical name where the output is sent. The default standard output device can be specified with the logical name t. Next comes a **control string**, which must be contained within double quotes. The control string consists of **format flags**, which indicate how the parameters to the *format* function should be printed. Following the control string is a list of parameters. The number of format flags in the control string will determine how many parameters should be specified. Parameters can be either constant values or expressions. The return value of the *format* function is the formatted string. If the logical name nil is used with the format command, then no output is printed (either to the terminal or a file), but the formatted string is still returned.

An example of the *format* function is shown by the following dialog, which creates a formatted string containing a person's name (reserving 15 spaces for the name) followed by the person's age. In the example notice how the names and ages are aligned in columns. The *format* function is useful for displaying columns of data.

```
CLIPS> (format nil "Name: %-15s Age: %3d"
               "Bob Green" 35) ↵
"Name: Bob Green       Age:  35"
CLIPS> (format nil "Name: %-15s Age: %3d"
               "Ralph Heiden" 32) ↵
"Name: Ralph Heiden    Age:  32"
CLIPS>
```

Format flags always begin with a "%" sign. Ordinary strings such as "Name:" can also be put in the control string and will be printed in the output. Some format flags do not format parameters. For example, "%n" is used to put a carriage return/line feed in the output much as the symbol *crlf* is used with the *printout* command.

In this example the format flag "%-15s" is used to print the name in a column that is 15 characters wide. The – sign indicates that the output is to be left justified and the character s indicates that a string or symbol is to be printed. The format flag "%3d" indicates that a number is to be printed right justified as an integer value in a three-character column. If the value 5.25 had been supplied as the parameter for the format flag then the number 5 would have been printed since the fractional part of a number is not allowed in an integer format.

Note that when the *format* function is used on the RHS of a rule, its return value is usually ignored. In these cases the logical name will either be associated with a file or t to send output to the screen. The general specification of a format flag is

```
%-M.Nx
```

where "−" is optional and means to **left justify**. The default is to **right justify**. Justification occurs when the amount of space provided to print a number exceeds the amount of space required to print it. If this situation occurs, left justification of the number will cause it to be printed on the left side of the space provided with unused space to the right filled with character spaces. Right justification causes the number to be printed on the right side of the space provided with unused space to the left filled with character spaces.

M specifies the field width in columns. At least M characters will be output. Spaces are normally used to pad the output to make up the M columns unless M starts with a 0, in which case zeros are used. If the output exceeds M columns, the format function will expand the field as needed.

N is an optional specification of the number of digits past the decimal point that will be printed. The default is six digits past the decimal point for floating-point numbers.

x specifies the display format specification. Table 8.3 gives the display format specifications.

Character	Meaning
d	Integer
f	Floating-point
e	Exponential (in power-of-ten format)
g	General (numeric); display in whatever format is shorter
o	Octal; unsigned number (N specifier not applicable)
x	Hexadecimal; unsigned number (N specifier not applicable)
s	String; quoted strings will be stripped of quotes
n	Carriage return/line feed
%	The "%" character itself

Table 8.3 Display Format Specifications

The Readline Function

The **readline** function can be used to read an entire line of input. Its syntax is

```
(readline [<logical-name>])
```

As with the *read* function, the logical name is optional. If no logical name is provided or if the logical name t is used, input will be read from the standard input device. The *readline* function will return as a string the next line of input from the input source associated with the logical name up to and including the carriage return. The *readline* function will return the symbol *EOF* if the end of the file has been reached. This will only occur when the logical name used by *readline* is associated with a file. The following dialog illustrates the use of the *readline* function:

```
CLIPS> (clear) ↵
CLIPS>
(defrule get-name
```

```
  =>
  (printout t "What is your name? ")
  (bind ?response (readline))
  (assert (user's-name ?response)))
CLIPS> (reset) ⏎
CLIPS> (run) ⏎
What is your name? Gary Riley⏎
CLIPS> (facts) ⏎
f-0       (initial-fact)
f-1       (user's-name "Gary Riley")
For a total of 2 facts.
CLIPS>
```

In this example the name "Gary Riley" is stored in the *user's-name* fact as a single field. Because it's stored as a single field, it's not possible to directly retrieve the first and last names from the field using pattern variables. Using the **explode$** function, which accepts a single string argument and converts it to a multifield value, we can convert the string returned by the *readline* function to a multifield value, which will be asserted as a series of fields in the *user's-name* fact. The following dialog illustrates the use of the *readline* in conjunction with the *explode$* function:

```
CLIPS>
(defrule get-name
   =>
   (printout t "What is your name? ")
   (bind ?response (explode$ (readline)))
   (assert (user's-name ?response))) ⏎
CLIPS> (reset) ⏎
CLIPS>  (run) ⏎
What is your name? Gary Riley
CLIPS> (facts) ⏎
f-0       (initial-fact)
f-1       (user's-name Gary Riley)
For a total of 2 facts.
CLIPS>
```

Appendix E contains a list of other functions that are useful for creating and manipulating strings and multifield values. The *Basic Programming Guide* accompanying this book provides additional details on all of the functions available in CLIPS .

8.13 SUMMARY

This chapter introduced the concept of variables, which are used to retrieve information from facts and to constrain slot values when pattern matching on the LHS of a rule. Variables can store the fact addresses of patterns on the LHS of a rule so that the fact bound to the pattern can be retracted on the RHS of the rule. Single-field wildcards can be used in place of variables when the field to be matched against can be anything and its value is not needed later in the LHS or

RHS of the rule. Multifield variables and wildcards allow matching against more than one field in a pattern.

Field constraints allow the negation and combination of more than one constraint for a given field. The *not* field constraint is used to prevent matching against certain values. The *and* field constraint is used to guarantee that all of a series of matching conditions are true. The *or* field constraint is used to guarantee that at least one of a series of matching conditions is true.

Functions are entered into the CLIPS top level command loop or are used on the LHS or RHS of a rule. Many functions, such as some of the arithmetic functions, can have a variable number of arguments. Function calls can be nested within other function calls. The bind command allows variables to be bound on the RHS of a rule.

CLIPS provides several I/O functions. The *open* and *close* functions can be used to open and close files. Opened files are associated with a logical name. Logical names can be used in most functions that perform input and output to more than one type of physical device. Both *printout* and *read* functions use logical names. The *printout* function can output to the terminal and files. The *read* function can input from the keyboard and files. The *format* and *readline* functions also accept logical names. The *format* function allows more control over the appearance of output. The *readline* function can be used to read an entire line of data. The *explode$* function converts a string to a multifield value.

PROBLEMS

8.1 Given the following deftemplates for facts describing a family tree,

```
(deftemplate father-of (slot father) (slot child))
(deftemplate mother-of (slot mother) (slot child))
(deftemplate male (slot person))
(deftemplate female (slot person))
(deftemplate wife-of (slot wife) (slot husband))
(deftemplate husband-of (slot husband) (slot wife))
```

write rules that will infer the following relations. Describe the deftemplates you use to solve the problem.

(a) Uncle, aunt
(b) Cousin
(c) Grandparent
(d) Grandfather, grandmother
(e) Sister, brother
(f) Ancestor

8.2 An industrial plant has ten sensors with ID numbers 1 through 10. Each sensor has either "good" or "bad" status. Build a deftemplate for representing the sensors and write one or more rules that will print a warning message if three or more sensors have bad status. Test your rules with sensors 3 and 5 bad; sensors 2, 8, and 9 bad; and sensors 1, 3, 5, and 10 bad. What must be done to prevent the warning message from being displayed multiple times?

8.3   Build a CLIPS program based on the IF-THEN rules developed for Problem 3.5 on page 158. The program should ask for the traveler's payment method and travel interests and should output potential trips based on these two inputs.

8.4   In a stack the first value added is the last value removed and the last value added is the first value removed. A queue works in the opposite manner—the first value added is the first value removed and the last value added is the last value removed. Write rules that will add and remove values to a queue. Assume that only one queue exists.

8.5   Write one or more rules that will generate all the permutations of a base fact and print them out. For example, the fact

```
(base-fact red green blue)
```

should generate the output

```
Permutation is (red green blue)
Permutation is (red blue green)
Permutation is (green red blue)
Permutation is (green blue red)
Permutation is (blue red green)
Permutation is (blue green red)
```

8.6   Given a series of facts describing shapes using the following deftemplates

```
(deftemplate square
    (slot id) (slot side-length))
(deftemplate rectangle
    (slot id) (slot width) (slot height))
(deftemplate circle
    (slot id) (slot radius))
```

write one or more rules that will compute the sum of

(a)   the areas of the shapes.
(b)   the perimeters of the shapes.

Test the output of the rules with the following deffacts:

```
(deffacts test-8-8
    (square (id A) (side-length 3))
    (square (id B) (side-length 5))
    (rectangle (id C) (width 5) (height 7))
    (circle (id D) (radius 2))
    (circle (id E) (radius 6)))
```

8.7 Given information about the name, eye color, hair color, and nationality of a person from a group using the following deftemplate,

```
(deftemplate person (slot name)
                    (slot eye-color)
                    (slot hair-color)
                    (slot nationality))
```

write one rule that will identify

(a) anyone with blue or green eyes who has brown hair and is from France.
(b) anyone who does not have blue eyes or black hair and does not have the same color hair and eyes.
(c) two people, the first having brown or blue eyes, not having blond hair, and a German nationality; the second having green eyes, the same hair color as the first person, and any nationality. The second person's eyes may be brown if the first person's hair is brown.

8.8 Convert the following infix expressions to prefix expressions.

(a) `(3 + 4) * (5 + 6) + 7`
(b) `(5 * (5 + 6 + 7)) - ((3 * (4 / 9) + 2) / 8)`
(c) `6 - 9 * 8 / 3 + 4 - (8 - 2 - 3) * 6 / 7`

8.9 Write rules that will take a finite state machine from its present state to its next state given a fact of the form

```
(input <value>)
```

The state machine and its arcs should be represented as facts. The input fact should be retracted when the machine goes to its next state. Test your rules and fact representations on the finite state machines shown in Figures 3.5 and 3.6 on pages 101 and 102.

8.10 Consider the following information about a baseball team. Andy dislikes the catcher. Ed's sister is engaged to the second baseman. The center fielder is taller than the right fielder. Harry and the third baseman live in the same building. Paul and Allen each won $20 from the pitcher at pinochle. Ed and the outfielders play poker during their free time. The pitcher's wife is the third baseman's sister. All the battery (the pitcher and catcher) and infield, except Allen, Harry, and Andy, are shorter than Sam. Paul, Andy, and the shortstop each lost $50 at the racetrack. Paul, Harry, Bill, and the catcher took a trouncing at pool from the second baseman. Sam is undergoing a divorce. The catcher and the third baseman each have two children. Ed, Paul, Jerry, the right fielder, and the center fielder are bachelors; the others are married. The shortstop, the third baseman, and Bill each cleaned up $100 betting on a fight. One of the outfielders is either Mike or Andy. Jerry is taller than Bill. Mike is shorter than Bill. Each of them is heavier than the third baseman. Sam, the catcher, and the third baseman are left handed. Ed, Sam, and the shortstop went to high school together. Write a CLIPS program to determine who plays each position.

8.11   Convert the decision tree shown in Figure 3.3 on page 99 to a series of CLIPS rules. Create patterns to match facts using the following deftemplate:

```
(deftemplate question
    (slot query-string)
    (slot answer))
```

For example, if the answer to the question represented by the root node in the tree was "no," the fact representing this information would be

```
(question (query-string "Is it very big?")
            (answer no))
```

Use the *printout* and *read* functions on the RHS of the rules to ask the questions shown in the figure and assert *question* facts with the user's response.

8.12   Write a CLIPS program that will add two binary numbers without using any arithmetic functions. Represent the binary numbers using the following deftemplate.

```
(deftemplate binary-#
    (multislot name)
    (multislot digits))
```

Given a fact indicating which two named binary numbers are to be added, the program should create a new named binary number containing the sum. For example, the facts

```
(binary-# (name A) (digits 1 0 1 1 1))
(binary-# (name B) (digits 1 1 1 0))
(add-binary-#s (name-1 A) (name-2 B))
```

should cause the following fact to be added to the fact list.

```
(binary-# (name { A + B }) (digits 1 0 0 1 0 1))
```

8.13   Write a CLIPS program that prompts for the blood types of a patient in need of a blood transfusion and a donor. The program should then determine whether the transfusion should proceed based on the blood types. Type O blood can only be transfused with type O blood. Type A blood can be transfused with either type A or type O blood. Type B blood can be transfused with either type B or type O blood. Type AB blood can be transfused with type AB, type A, type B, or type O blood.

8.14   Write a CLIPS program that gives information on either how a specified cut of beef can be cooked or the cuts of beef that can be cooked in a specific way. The program should first prompt whether a cut of beef or a method of cooking is to be selected and then it should prompt for the appropriate selection. Use the following guidelines to determine the appropriate cuts or methods of cooking: rump roast should be braised or roasted; sirloin steak should be broiled, pan-broiled, or pan-fried; T-bone steak should be broiled, pan-broiled, or pan-fried; rib roast should be roasted; ground beef should be roasted, broiled, pan-broiled, pan-fried, or braised; flank steak should be braised; and round steak should be braised.

8.15   Modify the program developed for Problem 7.14 on page 363 so that the input is determined by asking the user a series of questions regarding the necessary characteristics of the shrub. The output of the program should be the same.

8.16   Bacteria can be classified by several characteristics including their basic shapes (spherical, rod, spiral, or filamentous), the results of a laboratory gram stain test (positive, negative, or none), and whether they require oxygen to survive (aerobic or anaerobic). Write a program that identifies the bacterial type based on the information stored in the table below. The program should ask the user for the shape, gram stain, and oxygen requirements of the bacteria. The user should be able to specify that any of the inputs is unknown. The output of the program should be all of the possible bacteria types based on the information from the user.

Type	Shape	Gram Stain	Oxygen Requirements
Actinomycete	rod or filamentous	positive	aerobic
Coccoid	spherical	positive	aerobic and anaerobic
Coryneform	rod	positive	aerobic
Endospore-forming	rod	positive or negative	aerobic and anaerobic
Enteric	rod	negative	aerobic
Gliding	rod	negative	aerobic
Mycobacterium	spherical	none	aerobic
Mycoplasma	spherical	none	aerobic
Pseudomonad	rod	negative	aerobic
Rickettsia	spherical or rod	negative	aerobic
Sheathed	filamentous	negative	aerobic
Spirillum	spiral	negative	aerobic
Spirochete	spiral	negative	anaerobic
Vibrio	rod	negative	aerobic

8.17   Acme Electronics makes a device called the Thingamabob 2000. This device is available in five different models distinguished by the chassis. Each chassis provides a number of bays for optional gizmos and is capable of generating a certain amount of power. The following table summarizes the chassis attributes:

Chassis	Gizmo Bays Provided	Power Provided	Price ($)
C100	1	4	2000.00
C200	2	5	2500.00
C300	3	7	3000.00
C400	2	8	3000.00
C500	4	9	3500.00

Each gizmo that can be installed in the chassis requires a certain amount of power to operate. The following table summarizes the gizmo attributes:

Gizmo	Power Used	Price ($)
Zaptron	2	100.00
Yatmizer	6	800.00
Phenerator	1	300.00
Malcifier	3	200.00
Zeta-shield	4	150.00
Warnosynchronizer	2	50.00
Dynoseparator	3	400.00

Given as input facts representing the chassis and any gizmos that have been selected, write a program that generates facts representing the number of gizmos used, the total amount of power required for the gizmo, and the total price of the chassis and all gizmos selected.

8.18   Using the gem table from Problem 7.13 on page 363, write rules for identifying the following gems: diamond, corundum, chrysoberyl, spinel, quartz, and tourmaline. Include rules to query the user for the hardness, density, and color of the gem. The user should be prompted until he or she responds with one of the colors listed in the table.

BIBLIOGRAPHY

(Firebaugh 88). Morris W. Firebaugh, *Artificial Intelligence: A Knowledge-Based Approach*, Boyd & Fraser Publishing Co., pp. 224-226, 1988.

CHAPTER 9
Advanced Pattern Matching

9.1 INTRODUCTION

This chapter introduces various techniques for controlling the execution of rules. Groups of rules are used to build more powerful and more complex programs than have been shown in previous chapters. Techniques for input, comparing values, and generating loops will be demonstrated, as will techniques for specifying control knowledge using rules. Several other types of conditional elements besides the pattern CE are introduced here. These conditional elements allow a single rule to perform the function of several rules and provide the capability to allow matching against the absence of facts. Finally, a number of useful utility commands will be introduced.

9.2 THE GAME OF STICKS

In this chapter a simple two-player game called Sticks will be used to demonstrate various techniques of control in a rule-based language. The object of Sticks is to avoid being forced to take the last one in a pile of sticks. Each player must take 1, 2, or 3 sticks in turn. The trick (or heuristic) to winning this game is in noticing that you can force your opponent to lose if it is your turn and there are 2, 3, or 4 sticks remaining. A player who has 5 sticks remaining on his or her move has lost. To force the other player to face 5 sticks, always leave 5 sticks plus some multiple of 4 at the end of your turn. That is, at the end of your turn, force the pile to 5, 9, 13, and so on sticks. If you move first and the pile is set to one of the "losing" numbers, you cannot win unless your opponent makes a mistake. If you move first and the pile is not set to a "losing" number, then you can always win.

9.3 INPUT TECHNIQUES

Before it can begin to play Sticks, the program must determine some information. First, because the program will play against a human opponent, it must be determined who will get the first move. In addition, the starting size of the pile must be determined. This information could be placed in a deffacts construct. However, it is quite simple to ask the program's opponent for it by input from the keyboard. The following example shows how the *read* function is used to input data:

```
(deffacts initial-phase
   (phase choose-player))

(defrule player-select
   (phase choose-player)
   =>
   (printout t "Who moves first (Computer: c "
                "Human: h)? ")
   (assert (player-select (read))))

(defrule good-player-choice
   ?phase <- (phase choose-player)
   ?choice <- (player-select ?player&c | h)
   =>
   (retract ?phase ?choice)
   (assert (player-move ?player)))
```

Both rules use the pattern (phase choose-player) to indicate their applicability only when a specific fact is in the fact list. This is called a ***control pattern*** because it is specifically used to control when the rule is applicable. A **control fact** is used to trigger a control pattern. Since the control pattern for these rules contains only literal fields, the control fact must match the pattern exactly. In this case the control fact to trigger these rules must be the fact (phase choose-player). This control fact will be useful for error correction when the input received by the read function does not match the expected values of "c" or "h," for "computer" and "human." By retracting and reasserting the control fact, the *player-select* rule can be retriggered.

The following output shows how the *player-select* and *good-player-choice* rules work to determine who should move first:

```
CLIPS> (unwatch all) ↲
CLIPS> (watch facts) ↲
CLIPS> (reset) ↲
==> f-0      (initial-fact)
==> f-1      (phase choose-player)
CLIPS> (run) ↲
Who moves first (Computer: c Human: h)? c↲
==> f-2      (player-select c)
<== f-1      (phase choose-player)
<== f-2      (player-select c)
==> f-3      (player-move c)
CLIPS>
```

These rules work properly if the correct response of *c* or *h* is entered, but if an incorrect response is entered no error checking is performed. There are many situations in which an input request should be repeated to correct faulty input. One way of programming an input request loop is shown in the next example. The following rule used in conjunction with the *player-select* and *good-player-choice* rules provides error checking.

```
(defrule bad-player-choice
   ?phase <- (phase choose-player)
   ?choice <- (player-select ?player&~c&~h)
   =>
   (retract ?phase ?choice)
   (assert (phase choose-player))
   (printout t "Choose c or h." crlf))
```

Once again, note the use of the control pattern (phase choose-player). It provides the basic control for the input loop and also prevents this group of rules from firing during other phases of execution in the program.

Notice how the two rules, *player-select* and *bad-player-choice*, work together in that each rule supplies the facts necessary to activate the other. If the response to the player question is incorrect, the *bad-player-choice* rule will retract the control fact (phase choose-player) and then reassert it, causing the *player-select* rule to be reactivated.

9.4 PREDICATE FUNCTIONS

A **predicate function** is defined to be any function that returns either the symbol *TRUE* or the symbol *FALSE*. Actually, when dealing with predicate logic, CLIPS treats any value other than the symbol FALSE as the symbol TRUE. A predicate function may also be thought of as having a Boolean return value. Predicate functions may be either **predefined** or **user-defined functions**. Predefined functions are those functions already provided by CLIPS. User-defined or **external functions** are functions other than predefined functions that are written in C or another language and linked with CLIPS. Appendix E contains a list of predefined CLIPS predicate functions for performing Boolean logic operations, comparing values, and testing for a specific type. Some of these functions are shown in the following dialog:

```
CLIPS> (and (> 4 3) (> 4 5))↲
FALSE
CLIPS> (or (> 4 3) (> 4 5))↲
TRUE
CLIPS> (> 4 3)↲
TRUE
CLIPS> (< 6 2)↲
FALSE
CLIPS> (integerp 3)↲
TRUE
CLIPS> (integerp 3.5)↲
FALSE
CLIPS>
```

9.5 THE TEST CONDITIONAL ELEMENT

There are many instances in which it is useful to repeat a calculation or other information processing. The common way of doing this is by setting up a loop. In the previous example a loop was set up to repeat until the user responded correctly to a question. However, there are many situations in which a loop needs to terminate automatically as the result of the evaluation of an arbitrary expression.

The **test conditional element** provides a powerful way to evaluate expressions on the LHS of the rule. Instead of pattern matching against a fact in the fact list, the test CE evaluates an expression. The outermost function of the expression must be a predicate function. If the expression evaluates to any value other than the symbol *FALSE*, the test CE is satisfied. If the expression evaluates to the symbol *FALSE*, the test CE is not satisfied. A rule will be triggered only if all its test CEs are satisfied along with other patterns. The syntax of the test CE is

```
(test <predicate-function>)
```

As an example, suppose it is the human player's turn. If only one stick remains in the pile, the human player has lost. If there is more than one stick, the human player should be asked how many sticks are to be removed from the pile. The rule that asks the human player how many sticks should be removed from the pile needs to check that there is more than one stick remaining in the pile. The > predicate function can be used to express this constraint, as shown in the following test CE, where ?size is the number of sticks remaining in the pile:

```
(test (> ?size 1))
```

Once the human player has stated the number of sticks to be removed the response must be checked to insure that it is valid. The number of sticks taken must be an integer and it must be greater than or equal to one and less than or equal to three. A player cannot take more sticks than are in the pile and must be forced to take the last stick. The *and* predicate function can be used to express all of these constraints, as shown in the following test CE, where ?choice would contain the number of sticks to be taken and ?size is the number of sticks remaining in the pile:

```
(test (and (integerp ?choice)
           (>= ?choice 1)
           (<= ?choice 3)
           (< ?choice ?size)))
```

Likewise, an invalid number of sticks to take would be a value that is not an integer, less than one or greater than three, or greater than or equal to the number of sticks remaining. This can be expressed using the *or* predicate function, as shown in the following test CE, where ?choice would contain the number of sticks to be taken and ?size is the number of sticks remaining in the pile:

```
(test (or  (not (integerp ?choice))
           (< ?choice 1)
           (> ?choice 3)
           (>= ?choice ?size)))
```

The following rules use the preceding test CEs to check that the human player has taken a valid number of sticks. The *pile-size* fact used in these rules stores the information about the number of sticks remaining in the pile.

```
(defrule get-human-move
   (player-move h)
   (pile-size ?size)
   ; Human player only has a choice when there is
   ; more than one stick remaining in the pile
   (test (> ?size 1))
   =>
   (printout t
           "How many sticks do you wish to take? ")
   (assert (human-takes (read))))

(defrule good-human-move
   ?whose-turn <- (player-move h)
   (pile-size ?size)
   ?number-taken <- (human-takes ?choice)
   (test (and (integerp ?choice)
              (>= ?choice 1)
              (<= ?choice 3)
              (< ?choice ?size)))
   =>
   (retract ?whose-turn ?number-taken)
   (printout t "Human made a valid move" crlf))

(defrule bad-human-move
   ?whose-turn <- (player-move h)
   (pile-size ?size)
   ?number-taken <- (human-takes ?choice)
   (test (or  (not (integerp ?choice))
              (< ?choice 1)
              (> ?choice 3)
              (>= ?choice ?size)))
   =>
   (printout t "Human made an invalid move" crlf)
   (retract ?whose-turn ?number-taken)
   (assert (player-move h)))
```

This program will end when a valid choice for the number of sticks taken has been entered. Once again, a control fact is used to retrigger a rule to allow invalid responses to be reentered. The *bad-human-move* rule will reassert the control fact (player-move h) to reactivate the *get-human-move* rule. The human player can then reenter the number of sticks to be taken from the pile.

9.6 THE PREDICATE FIELD CONSTRAINT

The **predicate field constraint**, :, is useful for performing predicate tests directly within patterns. In many ways it is similar to performing a test CE directly after a pattern, although in some cases, as will be discussed in Chapter 11, it is more efficient to use the predicate field constraint than it is to use a test CE. The predicate field constraint can be used just like a literal field constraint. It can stand by itself in a field or be used as one part of a more complex field using the ~, &, and | connective field constraints. The predicate field constraint is always followed by a function for evaluation. As with a test CE, this function should be a predicate function.

As an example, the *get-human-move* rule in the previous section used the following two patterns to check that the pile contained more than one stick:

```
(pile-size ?size)
(test (> ?size 1))
```

These two patterns could be replaced with the following single pattern:

```
(pile-size ?size&:(> ?size 1))
```

The predicate field constraint can be used by itself; however, there are few situations in which this is useful. Typically a variable is bound and then tested using the predicate field constraint. When reading a pattern it is useful to think of the predicate field constraint as meaning *such that*. For example, the field constraint shown previously,

```
?size&:(> ?size 1)
```

could be read as "bind ?size such that ?size is greater than 1."

One application of the predicate field constraint is error checking of data. For example, the following rule checks that a data item is numeric before adding it to a running total:

```
(defrule add-sum
   (data-item ?value&:(numberp ?value))
   ?old-total <- (total ?total)
   =>
   (retract ?old-total)
   (assert (total (+ ?total ?value))))
```

The second field of the first pattern can be read as "bind ?value such that ?value is a number." The following two rules both perform the same kind of error checking and demonstrate the use of the ~ and | connective field constraints with the predicate field constraint:

```
(defrule find-data-type-1
   (data ?item&:(stringp ?item)|:(symbolp ?item))
   =>
   (printout t ?item " is a string or symbol "
                crlf))

(defrule find-data-type-2
   (data ?item&~:(integerp ?item))
   =>
   (printout t ?item " is not an integer " crlf))
```

The rule *find-data-type-1* checks that a data item is either a string or a symbol by using the *stringp* and *symbolp* type predicate functions. The rule *find-data-type-2* checks that a data item is not an integer by using the *integerp* function and then using the ~ connective constraint to negate the value.

9.7 THE RETURN VALUE FIELD CONSTRAINT

The **return value field constraint**, =, allows the return value of a function to be used for comparison inside a pattern. The return value field constraint can be used in conjunction with the ~, &, and | connective field constraints, as well as the predicate field constraint. Like the predicate field constraint, the return value field constraint must be followed by a function. However, the function does not have to be a predicate function. The only restriction is that the function must have a single field return value. The following rule shows how the return value constraint can be used in the Sticks program to determine the number of sticks the computer player should remove from the pile:

```
(deftemplate take-sticks
   (slot how-many)
   (slot for-remainder))

(deffacts take-sticks-information
   (take-sticks (how-many 1) (for-remainder 1))
   (take-sticks (how-many 1) (for-remainder 2))
   (take-sticks (how-many 2) (for-remainder 3))
   (take-sticks (how-many 3) (for-remainder 0)))

(defrule computer-move
   ?whose-turn <- (player-move c)
   ?pile <- (pile-size ?size)
   (test (> ?size 1))
   (take-sticks (how-many ?number)
                (for-remainder =(mod ?size 4)))
   =>
   (retract ?whose-turn ?pile)
   (assert (pile-size (- ?size ?number)))
   (assert (player-move h)))
```

The *computer-move* rule determines the appropriate number of sticks for the computer to take on its turn. The first pattern CE insures that the rule is applicable only when it is the computer's move. The second and third CEs check to see that the remaining number of sticks is greater than one. If there had been only one remaining stick, the computer would be forced to take it and lose. The final pattern works in conjunction with the *take-sticks-information* deffacts to determine the appropriate number of sticks to take. The **mod** (short for modulus) function returns the integer remainder of its first argument divided by its second. When reading a pattern it is useful to think of the return value field constraint as meaning *is equal to*. For example, the field constraint

```
=(mod ?size 4)
```

could be read as "The field is equal to ?size modulus 4."

The computer will try to take enough sticks to set the remainder to one when the total number of sticks is divided by four. If the remainder is one when the computer has begun its move, then it has lost unless its opponent makes a mistake. It only takes one stick in this case to make the game last longer (hoping that the human player will make a mistake). In all other cases the computer can take the appropriate number of sticks to cause its opponent to lose.

To demonstrate how the return value field constraint works in more detail, let's consider a specific example. Assume that the pile size is 7 and that it is the computer's move. The first three CEs of the *computer-move* rule will be satisfied with the last CE remaining. The function expression (mod ?size 4) will have the value 7 substituted for ?size, leaving the expression (mod 7 4), which evaluates to 3. There is only one take-sticks fact with a for-remainder slot value of 3. The how-many slot value for this fact is 2, so the computer will end up taking 2 sticks, leaving a pile size of 5. After the human player's next move, the computer can force a loss.

Note that the = field constraint, which can only be used within a pattern CE, is not the same as the = predicate function, which can be used within a : field constraint, test CE, RHS of rule, or at the top level prompt. Again, as with the predicate field constraint, more complex field constraints can be generated by using the return value constraint with the ~, &, and | connective field constraints.

9.8 THE STICKS PROGRAM

All of the basic techniques needed for completing the Sticks program have been discussed. The complete listing of the Sticks program is in the file *stick.clp*, found on the disk packaged with this book. A sample run of the program after it has been loaded is shown below.

```
CLIPS> (reset) ↵
CLIPS> (run) ↵
Who moves first (Computer: c Human: h)? c↵
How many sticks in the pile? 15↵
Computer takes 2 stick(s).
13 stick(s) left in the pile.
How many sticks do you wish to take? 3↵
10 stick(s) left in the pile.
Computer takes 1 stick(s).
```

```
9 stick(s) left in the pile.
How many sticks do you wish to take? 2↵
7 stick(s) left in the pile.
Computer takes 2 stick(s).
5 stick(s) left in the pile.
How many sticks do you wish to take? 1↵
4 stick(s) left in the pile.
Computer takes 3 stick(s).
1 stick(s) left in the pile.
You must take the last stick!
You lose!
CLIPS>
```

9.9 THE *OR* CONDITIONAL ELEMENT

Thus far all the rules shown have an **implicit *and* conditional element** between the patterns. That is, a rule will not be triggered unless all the patterns are true. CLIPS also provides the capability of specifying both an **explicit *and* conditional element** and an **explicit *or* conditional element** on the LHS.

As an example of an *or* CE, consider the following rules for use by the industrial plant monitoring system (as discussed in Chapter 7) that are first written without an *or* CE. Then you will see how to rewrite them with an *or* CE.

```
(defrule shut-off-electricity-1
   (emergency (type flood))
   =>
   (printout t "Shut off the electricity" crlf))

(defrule shut-off-electricity-2
   (extinguisher-system (type water-sprinkler)
                        (status on))
   =>
   (printout t "Shut off the electricity" crlf))
```

Rather than write two separate rules, they can all be combined into the following rule, using an *or* CE:

```
(defrule shut-off-electricity
   (or (emergency (type flood))
       (extinguisher-system (type water-sprinkler)
                            (status on)))
   =>
   (printout t "Shut off the electricity" crlf))
```

This one rule using the *or* CE is equivalent to the two previous rules. Asserting the two facts matching the patterns of this rule would cause the rule to be triggered twice, once for each of the facts.

Other CEs can be included outside the *or* CE and will be part of the implicit *and* CE for the entire LHS of the rule. For example, the rule

```
(defrule shut-off-electricity
   (electrical-power (status on))
   (or (emergency (type flood))
       (extinguisher-system (type water-sprinkler)
                            (status on)))
   =>
   (printout t "Shut off the electricity" crlf))
```

is equivalent to these two rules:

```
(defrule shut-off-electricity-1
   (electrical-power (status on))
   (emergency (type flood))
   =>
   (printout t "Shut off the electricity" crlf))

(defrule shut-off-electricity-2
   (electrical-power (status on))
   (extinguisher-system (type water-sprinkler)
                        (status on))
   =>
   (printout t "Shut off the electricity" crlf))
```

Since an *or* CE generates the equivalent of multiple rules, it is possible for a rule to be activated more than once by patterns contained with the *or* CE. Thus a natural question to ask is how to prevent the problem of more than one triggering? For example, multiple printouts of "Shut off the electricity" appearing for multiple facts are unnecessary. After all, the power only needs to be shut off once, regardless of the number of reasons to do so.

Perhaps the most appropriate manner to prevent the other rules from firing is to change the rule to update the fact list, indicating that the electricity has been shut off. The modified rule is shown below. (Note that we've been assuming in writing these rules that we have an alert plant operator who's watching the output of the monitoring system and taking action. In the real world the expert system might have direct control to turn various systems on and off or the plant operator might have a mechanism for telling the monitoring system that various actions have been taken.)

```
(defrule shut-off-electricity
   ?power <- (electrical-power (status on))
   (or (emergency (type flood))
       (extinguisher-system (type water-sprinkler)
                            (status on)))
   =>
   (modify ?power (status off)))
   (printout t "Shut off the electricity" crlf))
```

The rule now fires only once because the fact containing information about the electrical power is modified when the rule fires. This will remove other activations of the rule made by the other patterns. If it is also necessary to remove the supporting reason for shutting off the power from the fact list, then the rule would have to be written as follows:

```
(defrule shut-off-electricity
    ?power <- (electrical-power (status on))
    (or ?reason <- (emergency (type flood))
        ?reason <- (extinguisher-system
                        (type water-sprinkler)
                        (status on)))
    =>
    (retract ?reason)
    (modify ?power (status off))
    (printout t "Shut off the electricity" crlf))
```

Notice that all the pattern CEs within the *or* CE are bound to the same variable, ?reason. At first this may appear to be an error, since the same variables are not normally assigned to different patterns of an ordinary rule. But a rule using an *or* CE is different. Since an *or* CE will produce multiple rules, the above rule is equivalent to the following two rules:

```
(defrule shut-off-electricity-1
    ?power <- (electrical-power (status on))
    ?reason <- (emergency (type flood))
    =>
    (retract ?reason)
    (modify ?power (status off))
    (printout t "Shut off the electricity" crlf))

(defrule shut-off-electricity-2
    ?power <- (electrical-power (status on))
    ?reason <- (extinguisher-system
                    (type water-sprinkler)
                    (status on))
    =>
    (retract ?reason)
    (modify ?power (status off))
    (printout t "Shut off the electricity" crlf))
```

By looking at the two rules we can see that the same variable name was necessary to match the (retract ?power ?reason) action on the RHS.

9.10 THE *AND* CONDITIONAL ELEMENT

The *and* CE is opposite in concept to the *or* CE. Instead of any one of several CEs triggering a rule, the *and* CE requires that all of the CEs be satisfied. CLIPS automatically places an implicit *and* CE around the LHS of a rule. A rule such as

```
(defrule shut-off-electricity
   ?power <- (electrical-power (status on))
   (emergency (type flood))
   =>
   (modify ?power (status off))
   (printout t "Shut off the electricity" crlf))
```

could also be written with an explicit *and* CE as

```
(defrule shut-off-electricity
   (and ?power <- (electrical-power (status on))
        (emergency (type flood)))
   =>
   (modify ?power (status off))
   (printout t "Shut off the electricity" crlf))
```

Of course there is no advantage to writing a rule with an explicit *and* CE around the entire LHS. The *and* CE is provided so it can be used with other CEs to make more complex patterns. For example, it can be used with an *or* CE to require groups of multiple conditions to be true, as shown in the following example:

```
(defrule use-carbon-dioxide-extinguisher
   ?system <- (extinguisher-system
                  (type carbon-dioxide)
                  (status off))
   (or (emergency (type class-B-fire))
       (and (emergency (type class-C-fire))
            (electrical-power (status off))))
   =>
   (modify ?system (status on))
   (printout t "Use carbon dioxide extinguisher"
               crlf))
```

This rule will be activated if there is a class B fire emergency (such as burning oil or grease) or if there is a class C fire emergency (involving electrical equipment) and the electrical power has already been shut off. In effect, always use the carbon dioxide extinguisher for a class B fire, but only use it for a class C fire if turning off the electricity didn't extinguish the fire. The *use-carbon-dioxide-extinguisher* is equivalent to the following two rules:

```
(defrule use-carbon-dioxide-extinguisher-1
   ?system <- (extinguisher-system
                  (type carbon-dioxide)
                  (status off))
   (emergency (type class-B-fire))
   =>
   (modify ?system (status on))
   (printout t "Use carbon dioxide extinguisher"
               crlf))
```

```
(defrule use-carbon-dioxide-extinguisher-2
   ?system <- (extinguisher-system
                    (type carbon-dioxide)
                    (status off))
   (emergency (type class-C-fire))
   (electrical-power (status off))
   =>
   (modify ?system (status on))
   (printout t "Use carbon dioxide extinguisher"
                    crlf))
```

9.11 THE *NOT* CONDITIONAL ELEMENT

Sometimes it is useful to be able to activate rules based on the absence of a particular fact in the fact list. CLIPS allows the specification of the absence of a fact in the LHS of a rule using the *not* **conditional element**. As a simple example, the monitoring expert system might have two rules for reporting its status:

```
IF the monitoring status is to be reported and
     there is an emergency being handled
THEN report the type of the emergency

IF the monitoring status is to be reported and
     there is no emergency being handled
THEN report that no emergency is being handled
```

The *not* CE can be conveniently applied to the simple rules above as follows:

```
(defrule report-emergency
   (report-status)
   (emergency (type ?type))
   =>
   (printout t "Handling " ?type " emergency"
                    crlf))

(defrule no-emergency
   (report-status)
   (not (emergency))
   =>
   (printout t "No emergency being handled" crlf))
```

Notice that these two rules are mutually exclusive. That is, they cannot both be on the agenda at the same time because the second pattern in each rule cannot be satisfied simultaneously.

Variables can also be used within a negated pattern to produce some interesting effects. Consider the following rule, which looks for the largest number out of a group of facts representing numbers:

```
(defrule largest-number
   (number ?x)
   (not (number ?y&:(> ?y ?x)))
   =>
   (printout t "Largest number is " ?x crlf))
```

The first pattern will bind to all of the *number* facts, but the second pattern will not allow the rule to become activated for any but the fact with the largest value for ?x.

Note that variables first bound within a *not* CE retain their value only within the scope of the *not* CE. For example, the rule

```
(defrule no-emergency
   (report-status)
   (not (emergency (type ?type)))
   =>
   (printout t "No emergency of type " ?type crlf))
```

will generate an error since the variable ?type is used in the RHS of the rule but is bound only within the *not* CE in the LHS of the rule.

The scope of variables also applies to the LHS of a rule. For example, the following rule determines that there are no known people who have a birthday on a given day:

```
(defrule no-birthdays-on-specific-date
   (check-for-no-birthdays (date ?date))
   (not (person (birthday ?date)))
   =>
   (printout t "No birthdays on " ?date crlf))
```

If the first two CEs are switched as follows,

```
(defrule no-birthdays-on-specific-date
   (not (person (birthday ?date)))
   (check-for-no-birthdays (date ?date))
   =>
   (printout t "No birthdays on " ?date crlf))
```

the rule no longer works correctly. The first CE will be unsatisfied if there are *any* *person* facts at all. The value bound to the variable ?date in the first CE has no effect on the allowed values for the variable ?date in the second CE. This contrasts with the original version of the *no-birthdays-on-specific-date* rule, in which the value bound to the variable ?date in the first CE restricted the search for *person* facts in the second CE to those having a birthday on a specific date. Unlike pattern CEs, the order of placement of a *not* CE on the LHS of a rule can affect the activation of the rule.

The *not* CE can be used in conjunction with other CEs. For example, the following rule determines that there are no two people who have birthdays on the same date:

```
(defrule no-identical-birthdays
   (not (and (person (name ?name)
                     (birthday ?date))
             (person (name ~?name)
                     (birthday ?date))))
   =>
   (printout t
      '"No two people have the same birthday" crlf)
```

The *and* CE is used within the *not* CE because the *not* CE can contain at most one CE. Notice that the variables ?name and ?date are reused within the *not* CE to correctly constrain the search for two people with the same birthday.

Because of the underlying algorithm used by CLIPS, the (initial-fact) pattern is added to the beginning of any *and* CE (implicit or explicit) whose first CE is a *not* CE or a *test* CE. Thus the rule

```
(defrule no-emergencies
   (not (emergency))
   =>
   (printout t "No emergencies" crlf))
```

is converted to the following rule:

```
(defrule no-emergencies
   (initial-fact)
   (not (emergency))
   =>
   (printout t "No emergencies" crlf))
```

Understanding this conversion is useful when examining the output from the *matches* command. Also note that fact indices for *not* CEs are not displayed in partial matches or activations for rules. Thus the activation "f-5,,f-3" indicates that the first CE was matched by the fact with fact index 5, the second CE was a *not* CE that was not matched by any facts and thus is satisfied, and the third CE was matched by the fact with fact index 3.

9.12 THE *EXISTS* CONDITIONAL ELEMENT

The *exists* **conditional element** allows you to pattern match based on the existence of at least one fact that matches a pattern without regard to the total number of facts that actually match the pattern. This allows a single partial match or activation for a rule to be generated based on the existence of one fact out of a class of facts. For example, suppose an informational message should be printed whenever an emergency occurs to indicate to the plant operators that they should be on alert. The rule could be written as follows:

```
(deftemplate emergency (slot type))
(defrule operator-alert-for-emergency
   (emergency)
   =>
   (printout t "Emergency: Operator Alert" crlf)
   (assert (operator-alert)))
```

Notice what happens when more than one *emergency fact* is asserted—the message to the operators is printed more than once:

```
CLIPS> (reset) ↵
CLIPS> (assert (emergency (type fire))) ↵
<Fact-1>
CLIPS> (assert (emergency (type flood))) ↵
<Fact-2>
CLIPS> (run) ↵
Emergency: Operator Alert
Emergency: Operator Alert
CLIPS>
```

The *operator-alert-for-emergency* rule could be modified in the following way to prevent the retriggering of the rule for an additional emergency:

```
(defrule operator-alert-for-emergency
   (emergency)
   (not (operator-alert))
   =>
   (printout t "Emergency: Operator Alert" crlf)
   (assert (operator-alert)))
```

The (not (operator-alert)) CE prevents the rule from being retriggered; however, changing the rule in this manner assumes that if there is already an operator alert, it was triggered by the *operator-alert-for-emergency* rule. It's possible that the operators could be placed on alert for an emergency drill, as the following rule shows:

```
(defrule operator-alert-for-drill
   (operator-drill)
   (not (operator-alert))
   =>
   (printout t "Drill: Operator Alert" crlf)
   (assert (operator-alert)))
```

Notice that if the drill alert rule fires first, the emergency alert rule will not be able to fire later since the *operator-alert* fact will have been asserted. To correct the problem the *operator-alert* fact could be modified to store the cause of the alert; however, excessive use of control facts to prevent rules from firing increases the complexity of rules and decreases the maintainability of rules by adding control dependencies between rules.

Fortunately, the *operator-alert-for-emergency* rule can be modified to use the *exists* CE, which will remove the need for control facts. Regardless of how many facts match the CEs inside the *exists* CE, the *exists* CE will generate only one partial match. Thus if an *exists* CE is the Nth CE of a rule and the previous N – 1 CEs have generated M partial matches, the largest number of partial matches that can be generated by the first N CEs is M. The *operator-alert-for-emergency* rule rewritten to use the *exists* CE is

```
(defrule operator-alert-for-emergency
   (exists (emergency))
   =>
   (printout t "Emergency: Operator Alert" crlf)
   (assert (operator-alert)))
```

This rule will only generate one activation and thus the operator alert message will only be printed once, as the following dialog shows:

```
CLIPS> (reset) ↵
CLIPS> (assert (emergency (type fire))) ↵
<Fact-1>
CLIPS> (assert (emergency (type flood))) ↵
<Fact-2>
CLIPS> (agenda) ↵
0       operator-alert-for-emergency: f-0,
For a total of 1 activation.
CLIPS> (run) ↵
Emergency: Operator Alert
CLIPS>
```

The *exists* CE is implemented by using a combination of *and* CEs and *not* CEs. The CEs within the *exists* CE are enclosed within an *and* CE and then within two *not* CEs. Thus the *operator-alert-for-emergency* rule is converted to the following by surrounding the entire LHS with an *and* CE and then replacing the *exists* CE as stated:

```
(defrule operator-alert-for-emergency
   (and (not (not (and (emergency)))))
   =>
   (printout t "Emergency: Operator Alert" crlf)
   (assert (operator-alert)))
```

Since the *and* CE surrounding the LHS of the rule has a *not* CE as its first CE, the (initial-fact) pattern CE is added to the beginning. Making this addition and removing the extraneous *and* CE around the emergency pattern produces the following rule:

```
(defrule operator-alert-for-emergency
   (and (initial-fact)
        (not (not (emergency))))
   =>
   (printout t "Emergency: Operator Alert" crlf)
   (assert (operator-alert)))
```

The (initial-fact) pattern at the beginning of the rule explains the f-0 fact index that was displayed for the rule when the *agenda* command was issued in the previous dialog. If there are no *emergency* facts, then the innermost *not* CE will be satisfied. If this CE is satisfied, then the outermost *not* CE will not be satisfied and the rule will not be activated. Conversely, if there are emergency facts, the innermost *not* CE will not be satisfied. Since this CE is not satisfied, the outermost *not* CE will be satisfied and the rule will be activated.

9.13 THE *FORALL* CONDITIONAL ELEMENT

The *forall* **conditional element** allows you to pattern match based on a set of CEs that are satisfied for *every* occurrence of another CE. For example, suppose there are a number of locations (such as buildings) at an industrial plant that could be on fire, and we want to determine if every building that's on fire has been evacuated and has a squad of firefighters attempting to extinguish the fire. The *forall* CE can be used to check this. The *emergency* fact will be modified as shown below to contain the location of the emergency in addition to the type of emergency. Two other deftemplates will be used to indicate the location of fire squads and whether a building has been evacuated. The *all-fires-being-handled* rule uses these deftemplates to determine whether the appropriate conditions have been satisfied.

```
(deftemplate emergency
    (slot type)
    (slot location))

(deftemplate fire-squad
    (slot name)
    (slot location))

(deftemplate evacuated
    (slot building))

(defrule all-fires-being-handled
    (forall (emergency (type fire)
                       (location ?where))
            (fire-squad (location ?where))
            (evacuated (building ?where)))
    =>
    (printout t
              "All buildings that are on fire " crlf
              "have been evacuated and" crlf
              "have firefighters on location" crlf))
```

For every fact that matches the (emergency (type fire) (location ?where)) pattern, there must also be facts matching the (fire-squad (location ?where)) pattern and the (evacuated (building ?where)) pattern. When the deftemplates and defrule are initially loaded and the *reset* command is issued the rule should be satisfied since there are no fire emergencies.

```
CLIPS> (watch activations) ↵
CLIPS> (reset) ↵
==> Activation 0      all-fires-being-handled: f-0,
CLIPS>
```

Once an *emergency* fact is asserted, the rule is deactivated until the appropriate *fire-squad* and *evacuated* facts are asserted.

```
CLIPS>
(assert (emergency (type fire)
                   (location building-11))) ↵
<== Activation 0      all-fires-being-handled: f-0,
<Fact-1>
CLIPS>
(assert (evacuated (building building-11))) ↵
<Fact-2>
CLIPS>
(assert (fire-squad (name A)
                    (location building-11))) ↵
==> Activation 0      all-fires-being-handled: f-0,
<Fact-3>
CLIPS>
(assert (fire-squad (name B)
                    (location building-1))) ↵
<Fact-4>
CLIPS>
(assert (emergency (type fire)
                   (location building-1))) ↵
<== Activation 0      all-fires-being-handled: f-0,
<Fact-5>
CLIPS> (assert (evacuated (building building-1))) ↵
==> Activation 0      all-fires-being-handled: f-0,
<Fact-6>
CLIPS>
```

If the *fire-squad* fact for building-1 is removed, then the rule is deactivated. Removing the *emergency* fact for this building will reactivate the rule.

```
CLIPS> (retract 4) ↵
<== Activation 0      all-fires-being-handled: f-0,
CLIPS> (retract 5) ↵
==> Activation 0      all-fires-being-handled: f-0,
CLIPS> (run) ↵
All buildings that are on fire
have been evacuated and
have firefighters on location
CLIPS>
```

The general format of the *forall* CE is shown following.

```
(forall <first-CE>
        <remaining-CEs>+)
```

In order for the *forall* CE to be satisfied, each fact matching the <first-CE> must also have facts that match all of the <remaining-CEs>. The general format of the *forall* CE is replaced with combinations of the *and* and *not* CEs using the following format:

```
(not (and <first-CE>
          (not (and <remaining-CEs>+)))))
```

9.14 THE *LOGICAL* CONDITIONAL ELEMENT

The *logical* **conditional element** allows you to specify that the existence of a fact depends on the existence of another fact or group of facts. The *logical* CE is the facility that CLIPS provides for truth maintenance. As an example, consider the following rule, which indicates that oxygen masks should be used by firefighters when a fire is giving off noxious fumes:

```
(defrule noxious-fumes-present
   (emergency (type fire))
   (noxious-fumes-present)
   =>
   (assert (use-oxygen-masks)))
```

As the following dialog shows, the preceding rule will assert the *use-oxygen-masks* fact whenever there is such a fire emergency:

```
CLIPS> (unwatch all) ↵
CLIPS> (reset) ↵
CLIPS> (watch facts) ↵
CLIPS> (assert (emergency (type fire))
               (noxious-fumes-present))) ↵
==> f-1     (emergency (type fire))
==> f-2     (noxious-fumes-present)
<Fact-2>
CLIPS> (run) ↵
==> f-3     (use-oxygen-masks)
CLIPS>
```

What happens when the fire is extinguished and there are no longer any noxious fumes? As the next dialog shows, retracting the *emergency* fact or *noxious-fumes-present* fact doesn't affect the *use-oxygen-masks* fact.

```
CLIPS> (retract 1 2) ↵
<== f-1     (emergency (type fire))
<== f-2     (noxious-fumes-present)
CLIPS> (facts) ↵
f-0     (initial-fact)
f-3     (use-oxygen-masks)
```

```
For a total of 2 facts.
CLIPS>
```

CLIPS provides a truth maintenance mechanism for creating dependencies between facts; that mechanism is the *logical* CE. Modifying the *noxious-fumes-present* rule as shown below allows a dependency to be created between the facts that match the patterns in the LHS of a rule and the facts that are asserted from the RHS of the rule.

```
(defrule noxious-fumes-present
    (logical (emergency (type fire))
             (noxious-fumes-present))
    =>
    (assert (use-oxygen-masks)))
```

When the *noxious-fumes-present* rule is executed, a link is created between the facts matching the patterns contained within the logical CE in the LHS of a rule and the facts asserted from the RHS of a rule. For this rule, if either the *emergency* fact or the *noxious-fumes-present* fact is retracted, then the *use-oxygen-masks* rule will also be retracted, as the following dialog shows:

```
CLIPS> (unwatch all) ↵
CLIPS> (reset) ↵
CLIPS> (watch facts) ↵
CLIPS> (assert (emergency (type fire))
               (noxious-fumes-present))) ↵
==> f-1      (emergency (type fire))
==> f-2      (noxious-fumes-present)
<Fact-2>
CLIPS> (run) ↵
==> f-3      (use-oxygen-masks)
CLIPS> (retract 1) ↵
<== f-1      (emergency (type fire))
<== f-3      (use-oxygen-masks)
CLIPS>
```

The *use-oxygen-masks* fact receives **logical support** from the *emergency* fact and the *noxious-fumes-present* fact. The *emergency* fact and the *noxious-fumes-present* fact provide logical support to the *use-oxygen-masks* fact. The *use-oxygen-masks* fact is a **dependent** of the *emergency* fact and the *noxious-fumes-present* fact. The *noxious-fumes-present* fact and the *emergency* fact are **dependencies** of the use-oxygen-masks fact.

The *logical* CE does not have to be included around all the patterns on the LHS of a rule. If it is used, however, it must enclose the first CE in the LHS of a rule, and there can be no gaps between CEs enclosed by the *logical* CE. For example, *logical* CEs could not be placed around the second and fourth CEs of a rule or even around the first and third CEs of a rule, since this would leave gaps. This restriction on the *logical* CE is the result of its underlying implementation. It's also possible to make facts dependent on the nonexistence of facts by using the *not* CE within the *logical* CE. Even more complex conditions using the *exists* and *forall* CEs or other combinations of CEs can be used within the logical CE.

Other than creating dependencies between groups of facts, the *logical* CE acts in all other respects like an *and* CE.

In order to modify the *noxious-fumes-present* rule to make the *use-oxygen-masks* fact dependent on only the *noxious-fumes-present* fact it would be necessary to reorder the patterns as shown:

```
(defrule noxious-fumes-present
   (logical (noxious-fumes-present))
   (emergency (type fire))
   =>
   (assert (use-oxygen-masks)))
```

With the rule modified as shown, the *use-oxygen-masks* fact won't be retracted automatically if the *emergency* fact is retracted (which is a safer approach since there may still be noxious fumes even if the fire is extinguished).

Normally, asserting a fact that's already in the fact list has no effect. However, a logically dependent fact that is derived from more than one source is not automatically retracted until the logical support from all of its sources is removed. For example, suppose another rule is added to indicate oxygen masks should be used if gas extinguishers are in use:

```
(defrule gas-extinguishers-in-use
   (logical (gas-extinguishers-in-use))
   (emergency (type fire))
   =>
   (assert (use-oxygen-masks)))
```

Running the system now causes two separate rules to assert the same fact based on different reasons.

```
CLIPS> (unwatch all) ↵
CLIPS> (reset) ↵
CLIPS> (watch facts) ↵
CLIPS> (watch rules) ↵
CLIPS> (assert (emergency (type fire))
               (noxious-fumes-present)
               (gas-extinguishers-in-use)) ↵
==> f-1      (emergency (type fire))
==> f-2      (noxious-fumes-present)
==> f-3      (gas-extinguishers-in-use)
<Fact-3>
CLIPS> (run) ↵
FIRE    1 gas-extinguishers-in-use: f-3,f-1
==> f-4      (use-oxygen-masks)
FIRE    2 noxious-fumes-present: f-1,f-2
CLIPS>
```

Retracting the *noxious-fumes-present* fact isn't sufficient to cause the automatic retraction of the *use-oxygen-masks* fact since there is other logical support for the oxygen masks to be used. The *gas-extinguishers-in-use* fact must also be retracted before the *use-oxygen-masks* fact will be retracted.

```
CLIPS> (retract 2) ↵
<== f-2      (noxious-fumes-present)
CLIPS> (retract 3) ↵
<== f-3      (gas-extinguishers-in-use)
<== f-4      (use-oxygen-masks)
CLIPS>
```

A fact that is asserted from the top level prompt or from the RHS of a rule that does not have any logical CEs in its LHS is **unconditionally supported**. A fact that is unconditionally supported will never be automatically retracted by the retraction of another fact. Any previous logical support for a fact is discarded once it receives unconditional support.

CLIPS provides two commands for viewing the **dependents** and the **dependencies** associated with a fact. The syntax for these commands is

```
(dependents <fact-index-or-address>)
(depedencies <fact-index-or-address>)
```

For the last example, before the *noxious-fumes-present* and *gas-extinguishers-in-use* facts were retracted, these commands would have produced the following output:

```
CLIPS> (facts) ↵
f-0      (initial-fact)
f-1      (emergency (type fire))
f-2      (noxious-fumes-present)
f-3      (gas-extinguishers-in-use)
f-4      (use-oxygen-masks)
For a total of 5 facts.
CLIPS> (dependents 1) ↵
None
CLIPS> (dependents 2) ↵
f-4
CLIPS> (dependents 3) ↵
f-4
CLIPS> (dependents 4) ↵
None
CLIPS> (dependencies 1) ↵
None
CLIPS> (dependencies 2) ↵
None
CLIPS> (dependencies 3) ↵
None
CLIPS> (dependencies 4) ↵
f-2
f-3
CLIPS>
```

9.15 UTILITY COMMANDS

The System Command

The **system** command allows the execution of operating system commands from within CLIPS. The syntax of the system command is

```
(system <expression>+)
```

For example, the following rule will give a directory listing for a specified directory on a machine using the UNIX operating system:

```
(defrule list-directory
   (list-directory ?directory)
   =>
   (system "ls " ?directory))
```

For this example the first argument to the *system* command, "ls", is the UNIX command for listing a directory. Notice that a space is included after the characters. The *system* command simply appends all its arguments together as strings before allowing the operating system to process the command. Any spaces needed for the operating system command must be included as part of an argument in the *system* command call.

The effects of the *system* command may vary from one operating system to another. Not all operating systems provide the functionality for implementing the *system* command, so you cannot rely on this command being available in CLIPS. The *system* command does not return a value, so it is not possible to directly return a value to CLIPS after executing an operating system command.

The Batch Command

The **batch** command allows commands and responses that would normally have to be entered at the top level prompt to be read directly from a file. The syntax of the *batch* command is

```
(batch <file-name>)
```

For example, suppose the following dialog shows the commands and responses that must be entered to run a CLIPS program (remember that the boldface letters indicate keys you enter):

```
CLIPS> (load "rules1.clp") ↵
**************
CLIPS> (load "rules2.clp") ↵
********************
CLIPS> (load "rules3.clp") ↵
**********
CLIPS> (reset) ↵
CLIPS> (run) ↵
```

```
How many iterations? 10↵
Starting value? 1↵
End value? 20↵
Completed
CLIPS>
```

The commands and responses needed to run the program could be stored in a file as shown:

```
(load "rules1.clp")↵
(load "rules2.clp")↵
(load "rules3.clp")↵
(reset)↵
(run)↵
10↵
1↵
20↵
```

If the file with the commands and responses was named "commands.bat", the following dialog shows how the *batch* command can be used (notice again that the boldface letters indicate keys you enter):

```
CLIPS> (batch "commands.bat")↵
CLIPS> (load "rules1.clp")↵
**************
CLIPS> (load "rules2.clp")↵
******************
CLIPS> (load "rules3.clp")↵
***********
CLIPS> (reset)↵
CLIPS> (run)↵
How many iterations? 10↵
Starting value? 1↵
End value? 20↵
Completed
CLIPS>
```

Once all the commands and responses have been read from a batch file, keyboard interaction at the top level prompt is returned to normal.

When run under operating systems that support command line arguments for executables (such as UNIX), CLIPS can automatically execute commands from a batch file on startup. Assuming that the CLIPS executable can be executed by typing "clips," the syntax for executing a batch file on startup is

```
clips -f <file-name>
```

Using the –f option is equivalent to entering the command (batch <file-name>) once CLIPS has been started. Calls to the *batch* command can be nested.

The Dribble-on and Dribble-off Commands

The **dribble-on** command can be used to store a record of all output to the terminal and all input from the keyboard. The syntax of the *dribble-on* command is

```
(dribble-on <file-name>)
```

Once the dribble-on command has been executed, all output sent to the terminal and all input entered at the keyboard will be echoed to the file specified by <file-name>, as well as to the terminal.

The effects of the *dribble-on* command can be turned off with the **dribble-off** command. The syntax of the *dribble-off* command is

```
(dribble-off)
```

9.16 SUMMARY

This chapter introduced various concepts for controlling the flow of execution. The *read* function is used to demonstrate how a simple control loop for input could be created using control facts that are retracted and then asserted again. *Test* CEs along with predicate functions can be used on the LHS of a rule to provide more powerful pattern-matching capabilities. In addition, *test* CEs can be used to maintain a control loop. The predicate field constraint allows predicate tests to be placed directly within a pattern. The equality field constraint is used to compare a field to a value returned by a function. The Sticks program demonstrates several of these control techniques.

There are several other CEs besides the *test* CE. The *or* CE is used to express several rules as a single rule. The *not* CE allows pattern matching against the absence of a fact in the fact list. The *and* CE is used to group CEs together and, in conjunction with the *or* and *not* CEs, can be arbitrarily nested to express complex conditions needed to satisfy a rule. The *exists* CE is used to determine the existence of at least one group of facts that satisfies a CE or a combination of CEs. The *forall* CE is used to determine that a set of CEs is satisfied for *every* occurrence of another CE. The *logical* CE provides a truth maintenance mechanism. The existence of facts can be made dependent on the existence or nonexistence of other facts.

The *system* command allows operating system commands to be executed from within CLIPS. The *batch* command allows a series of commands and responses stored in a file to replace normal keyboard input. The *dribble-on* and *dribble-off* commands allow a record of terminal output to be stored in a file.

PROBLEMS

9.1 Add rules to the Sticks program that will ask if the human player wants to play again after the game has finished.

9.2 Modify the Sticks program to allow two human players to play the game against each other, in addition to the computer playing against a human.

9.3   Rewrite the following rules as a single rule using *and* and *or* CEs.

```
(defrule rule-1
   (fact-a)
   (fact-d)
   =>)

(defrule rule-2
   (fact-b)
   (fact-c)
   (fact-e)
   (fact-f)
   =>)

(defrule rule-3
   (fact-a)
   (fact-e)
   (fact-f)
   =>)

(defrule rule-4
   (fact-b)
   (fact-c)
   (fact-d)
   =>)
```

9.4   Write a program using *and* and *or* CEs for the AND/OR tree of getting to work shown in Figure 3.10 on page 107. Test it for all branches.

9.5   Determine whether the variable x is referenced properly for each of the following rules. Explain your answers.

(a)   ```
(defrule example-1
   (not (fact ?x))
   (test (> ?x 4))
   =>)
```

(b)    ```
(defrule example-2
   (not (fact ?x&:(> ?x 4)))
   =>)
```

(c)   ```
(defrule example-3
   (not (fact ?x))
   (fact ?y&:(> ?y ?x)))
   =>)
```

(d)    ```
(defrule example-4
   (not (fact ?x))
   (fact ?x&:(> ?x 4)))
   =>)
```

9.6 Rewrite the blocks world program in Section 8.6 on page 371 so it can rearrange the blocks from any initial state of stacked blocks to any goal state of stacked blocks. For example, if the initial state of the blocks was

```
(stack A B C)
(stack D E F)
```

One possible goal state might be

```
(stack D C B)
(stack A)
(stack F E)
```

9.7 Write a CLIPS program that will query a user for color values and then print a list of all countries with flags that contain all of the specified colors. The flag colors for various countries are listed below.

Country	Flag Colors
United States	Red, white, and blue
Belgium	Black, yellow, and red
Poland	White and red
Monaco	White and red
Sweden	Yellow and blue
Panama	Red, white, and blue
Jamaica	Black, yellow, and green
Colombia	Yellow, blue, and red
Italy	Green, white, and red
Ireland	Green, white, and orange
Greece	Blue and white
Botswana	Blue, white, and black

9.8 Given the following deftemplate describing a set,

```
(deftemplate set
  (multislot name)
  (multislot members))
```

write one or more rules that will

(a) Compute the union of two specified sets given a fact using the following deftemplate.

```
(deftemplate union
  (multislot set-1-name)
  (multislot set-2-name))
```

(b) Compute the intersection of two specified sets given a fact using the following deftemplate.

```
(deftemplate intersection
  (multislot set-1-name)
  (multislot set-2-name))
```

Note that when computing the union and intersection, duplicate elements should not be allowed to appear in the union or the intersection of the sets. The final result for both (a) and (b) should be a new *set* fact containing the union or intersection of the two specified sets and the *union* and *intersection* facts should be retracted when the operations are complete.

9.9 Write a set of rules for classifying syllogistic forms by mood and figure. For example, the syllogistic form

```
No M is P
Some M is not S
∴ Some S is P
```

is of type EOI-3. The input for the rules should be a single fact representing the major and minor premises and the conclusion. The output should be a printed statement of the mood and figure.

9.10 Write a program that will read a data file containing a list of people's names and ages and create a new file containing the list sorted in ascending order by age. The program should prompt for both input and output files. For example, input file

```
Phyllis Sebesta 37
Robert Delwood 35
Jack Kennedy 36
Glen Steele 34
```

should create the output file

```
Glen Steele 34
Robert Delwood 35
Jack Kennedy 36
Phyllis Sebesta 37
```

9.11 Write a program to compute the value of the thirteen cards in a bridge player's hand using the point count method. Aces count for four points; kings count for three points; queens count for two points; and jacks count for one point. A void suit (no cards of one suit) counts for three points; a singleton suit (one card of a suit) counts for two points; and a doubleton suit (two cards of a suit) counts for one point.

9.12 Write a program that will indicate the action to be taken when someone swallows poison. The program should have knowledge of the following poisons: acids (such as rust remover and iodine), alkalines (such as ammonia and bleach), and petroleum products (such as gasoline and turpentine). All other poisons should be grouped into the category *other*.

In the event of poisoning, a physician or poison control center should be called. For acids, alkalines, and other types of poison (but not petroleum products), dilute the poison by having the victim drink a liquid such as water or milk. Induce vomiting for other types of poison, but do not induce vomiting for acids, alkalines, or petroleum products. Do not give liquids or induce vomiting if the victim is unconscious or is having convulsions.

9.13   Write a program that, when given two points, computes the slope of the line formed by the two points. Your program should check to insure that the points provided contain numbers and that one point is not specified twice. Treat vertical lines as having an infinite slope.

9.14   A scalene triangle has three unequal sides. An isosceles triangle has two sides of the same length. An equilateral triangle has three sides of the sane length. Write a program that, when given the three points forming a triangle, will determine the type of triangle. The program should account for possible roundoff error (assume two sides are equal if the difference between their lengths is less than .00001). Test your program with the following triangles.

(a)   Points (0,0), (2,4), and (6,0).

(b)   Points (1,2), (4,5), and (7,2).

(c)   Points (0,0), (3,5.196152), and (6,0).

9.15   Write a program to solve the Towers of Hanoi problem in which you must move a set of rings from one peg to another peg without ever putting a larger ring on top of a smaller ring. There are three pegs for you to use. The number of rings should be an input to the program. In the initial configuration all the rings are on the first peg in descending size from bottom to top. The initial goal should be to move all of the rings from the first peg to the third peg.

9.16   Write a program to determine the values of the letters that make the following cryptarithmetic problem correct. Each of the letters H, O, C, U, S, P, R, E, and T corresponds uniquely to a digit in the range 0 to 9.

```
  HOCUS
+ POCUS
= PRESTO
```

9.17   Write a program that gives advice on investing in mutual funds. The output of the program should indicate the percentage of money to be invested in fixed-income funds, funds mainly investing in bonds and preferred stocks, and stock funds, funds with a higher risk but greater potential returns. The percentages will be determined by "scoring" the amount of risk the investor is willing to take based on the responses to various questions. If the investor is 29 years old or younger, add 4 to the score; 30 to 39, add 3; 40 to 49, add 2; 50 to 59, add 1; and 60 or more, add 0. If the investor has 0 to 9 years until retirement, add 0; 10 to 14, add 1; 15 to 19, add 2; 20 to 24, add 3; and 25 or more, add 4. If the investor is willing to ride out losses of only 5% or less, add 0 to the score; 6% to 10%, add 1; 11% to 15%, add 2; and 16% or more, add 3. If the investor is very knowledgeable about investments and the stock market, add 4 to the score; if somewhat knowledgeable, add 2 to the score; if not knowledgeable, add 0 to the score. If the investor is willing to take significant risk for higher possible returns, add 4 to the score; if some risk, add 2; and if little risk, add 0. If the investor believes his or her retirement goals will be met given his or her current income and assets, add 4 to the score; if the goals might possibly be met, add 2; if the goals are unlikely to be met, add 0. If the final score is more than 20 points, then 100% of the investments should be in stock funds; if 16 to 20 points, 80% should be in stock funds and 20% in fixed-income funds; if 11 to 15 points, 60% should be in stock funds and 40% in fixed-income funds; if 6 to 10 points, then 40% should be in stock funds and 60% in fixed-income funds; if 0 to 5 points, then 20% should be in stock funds and 80% in fixed-income funds.

9.18   Modify the program developed for Problem 8.15 on page 403 so that only the shrubs having all of the necessary characteristics are listed. For example, if the user specifies that the plant must tolerate cold and drought, then only northern bayberry and common juniper should be listed. If none of the shrubs meet all requirements, then a message should be printed to indicate this.

9.19   Modify the program developed for Problem 7.12 on page 362 so that the information about stars is represented using facts. The program output should be in the same order: all stars having the specified spectral class, all stars having the specified magnitude, and finally all stars matching both the spectral class and magnitude along with their distance from Earth in light-years.

9.20   Modify the program developed for Problem 8.17 on page 403 so that the total price of the configuration is printed. A warning message should be printed if more gizmos are selected than there are available bays or if the power required for the gizmos exceeds the power supplied by the chassis.

9.21   Modify the program developed for Problem 8.18 on page 404 to include the remaining gems found in the gem table in Problem 7.13 on page 363. For gems having a single numerical value for their hardness or density, modify the rules so that any value within .01 of the specified value is acceptable. Include rules to verify and reprompt the user if the hardness is not between 1 and 10 inclusive and the density is not between 1 and 6 inclusive.

CHAPTER 10

Modular Design and Execution Control

10.1 INTRODUCTION

This chapter introduces a number of CLIPS features useful for the development and maintenance of expert systems. Deftemplate attributes allow the enforcement of value constraints for deftemplate slot values. When a rule is loaded, deftemplate constraint attributes can detect semantics errors that prevent the LHS of that rule from being matched. Using salience, which provides a method for prioritizing rules, and facts representing flow of control knowledge, this chapter demonstrates techniques for controlling the execution of a CLIPS program. In addition, it looks at the defmodule construct, which allows a knowledge base to be partitioned and provides a more explicit method for controlling the execution of a system.

10.2 DEFTEMPLATE ATTRIBUTES

CLIPS provides a number of slot attributes that can be specified when a deftemplate's slots are defined. These attributes aid in the development and maintenance of an expert system by providing strong typing and constraint checking. It is possible to define the allowed types and values that can be stored in a slot. For numeric values, the allowed range of numbers can be specified. Multislots can specify the minimum and maximum number of fields they can contain. Finally, the default attribute provides a default slot value to be used for slots that are not specified in an *assert* command.

The Type Attribute

The **type attribute** defines the data types that can be placed in a slot. The general format of the type attribute is (type <type-specification>) where <type-specification> is either ?VARIABLE or one or more of the symbols SYMBOL, STRING, LEXEME, INTEGER, FLOAT, or NUMBER. If ?VARIABLE is used, the slot may contain any data type (which is the default behavior for all slots). If one or more of the symbolic type specifications are used, the slot is restricted to one of the specified types. The type specification LEXEME is equivalent to specifying SYMBOL and STRING. The type specification NUMBER is equivalent to specifying INTEGER and FLOAT.

The following *person* deftemplate restricts the values stored in the *name* slot to symbols and the values stored in the *age* slot to integers:

```
(deftemplate person
    (multislot name (type SYMBOL))
    (slot age (type INTEGER)))
```

Once this deftemplate has been defined CLIPS will automatically enforce the restrictions of any slot attributes. For example, assigning the symbol *four* to the age slot rather than the integer 4 will cause an error as shown:

```
CLIPS> (assert (person (name Fred Smith)
                       (age four)))↵

[CSTRNCHK1] A literal slot value found in the
assert command does not match the allowed types for
slot age.
CLIPS>
```

CLIPS will also check the consistency of variable bindings in the LHS and the RHS of a rule. For example, let's assume there is a rule that updates a person's *age* slot whenever he or she has a birthday. The deftemplate for the control fact that indicates that a person has just had a birthday is

```
(deftemplate had-a-birthday
    (slot name (type STRING)))
```

The allowed types of the name slots for the two deftemplates are inconsistent. An attempt to directly compare the two slots will generate an error, as the following dialog illustrates:

```
CLIPS>
(defrule update-birthday
    ?f1 <- (had-a-birthday (name ?name))
    ?f2 <- (person (name ?name) (age ?age))
    =>
    (retract ?f1)
    (modify ?f2 (age (+ ?age 1))))↵

[RULECSTR1] Variable ?name in CE #2 slot name has
constraint conflicts which make the pattern
unmatchable.

ERROR:
(defrule MAIN::update-birthday
    ?f1 <- (had-a-birthday (name ?name))
    ?f2 <- (person (name ?name) (age ?age))
    =>
```

```
            (retract ?f1)
            (modify ?f2 (age (+ ?age 1))))
CLIPS>
```

The *name* slot for the *had-a-birthday* fact must be a string and the *name* slot for the *person* fact must be a symbol. It is not possible for the variable ?name to satisfy both of these constraints and thus the LHS of the rule can never be satisfied.

Static and Dynamic Constraint Checking

CLIPS provides two levels of constraint checking. The first level, **static constraint checking**, is performed by default when CLIPS parses an expression or a construct and is illustrated by the previous constraint violation examples using the type attribute. Static constraint checking can be disabled by calling the **set-static-constraint-checking** function and passing it the symbol *FALSE*. Conversely, calling this function with the symbol *TRUE* will activate static constraint checking. The value returned by the function is the previous status value (the symbol *FALSE* if it was previously disabled and the symbol *TRUE* otherwise). You can determine the current status of static constraint checking by calling the **get-static-constraint-checking** function (which returns the symbol *TRUE* if static constraint checking is enabled and the symbol *FALSE* otherwise).

It is not always possible to determine all constraint errors at parse time. For example, in the *create-person* rule shown here, the variables ?age and ?name can be bound to illegal values:

```
(defrule create-person
    =>
    (printout t "What is your name? ")
    (bind ?name (explode$ (readline)))
    (printout t "What is your age? ")
    (bind ?age (read))
    (assert (person (name ?name) (age ?age))))
```

The *readline* function is used to input a person's entire name as a string and the *explode$* function then converts it to a multifield value that can be placed in the *name* slot. The *read* function is used to input a person's age, which can be placed in the *age* slot. For both input values it is possible to receive invalid values. For example, the symbol *four* may be input for the person's age, as the following dialog shows:

```
CLIPS> (reset) ↵
CLIPS> (run) ↵
What is your name? Fred Smith↵
What is your age? four↵
CLIPS> (facts) ↵
f-0     (initial-fact)
f-1     (person (name Fred Smith) (age four))
For a total of 2 facts.
CLIPS>
```

Notice that the same *person* fact for Fred Smith that caused a constraint violation before and was not added to the fact list has now been added to it. This is because the second level of constraint checking performed by CLIPS, **dynamic constraint checking**, is disabled by default. Dynamic constraint checking is performed on facts when they are actually asserted, thus catching errors that cannot be detected at parse time.

Dynamic constraint checking can be enabled or disabled using the function **set-dynamic-constraint-checking** and the current status of dynamic constraint checking can be determined with the **get-dynamic-constraint-checking** function. With dynamic constraint checking enabled, the following dialog shows how the constraint violation is handled. The Fred Smith *person* fact is still added to the fact list, but the constraint violation is detected and the execution of rules is halted.

```
CLIPS> (set-dynamic-constraint-checking TRUE) ↵
FALSE
CLIPS> (reset) ↵
CLIPS> (run) ↵
What is your name? Fred Smith↵
What is your age? four↵


[CSTRNCHK1] Slot value (Fred Smith) found in fact
f-1 does not match the allowed types for slot age.
[PRCCODE4] Execution halted during the actions of
defrule create-person.
CLIPS> (facts) ↵
f-0     (initial-fact)
f-1     (person (name Fred Smith) (age four))
For a total of 2 facts.
CLIPS>
```

The Allowed Value Attributes

In addition to restricting allowed types with the type attribute, CLIPS also allows you to specify a list of allowed values for a specific type. For example, if a *gender* slot is added to the *person* deftemplate, the allowed symbols for that slot can be restricted to *male* and *female*:

```
(deftemplate person
    (multislot name (type SYMBOL))
    (slot age (type INTEGER))
    (slot gender (type SYMBOL)
                 (allowed-symbols male female)))
```

There are seven different allowed value attributes provided by CLIPS: **allowed-symbols**, **allowed-strings**, **allowed-lexemes**, **allowed-integers**, **allowed-floats**, **allowed-numbers**, and **allowed-values**. Each of these attributes should be followed either by ?VARIABLE (which indicates that any values of the specified type are legal) or by a list of values of the type following the *allowed-* prefix. For example, the *allowed-lexemes* attribute should by followed either by ?VARIABLE or by a list of symbols and/or strings. The default allowed value attribute for slots is (allowed-values ?VARIABLE).

Note that the allowed value attributes do not restrict the allowed types of a slot. For example, (allowed-symbols male female) does not restrict the type of the *gender* slot to being a symbol. It merely indicates that if the slot's value is a symbol, then it must be one of the two symbols: either *male* or *female*. Any string, integer, or float would be a legal value for the *gender* slot if the (type SYMBOL) attribute were removed.

The allowed-values attribute can be used to completely restrict the set of allowed values for a slot to a specified list. For example, changing the *person* deftemplate to the following effectively limits the allowed types for the *gender* slot to symbols:

```
(deftemplate person
    (multislot name (type SYMBOL))
    (slot age (type INTEGER))
    (slot gender (allowed-values male female)))
```

The Range Attribute

The **range attribute** allows the specification of minimum and maximum numeric values. The general format of the range attribute is (range <lower-limit> <upper-limit>), where <lower-limit> and <upper-limit> are either ?VARIABLE or a numeric value. The <lower-limit> term indicates the minimum value for the slot and the <upper-limit> term indicates the maximum value for the slot. ?VARIABLE indicates that there is either no minimum or no maximum value (depending on whether it is first or second). For example, the *age* slot in the *person* deftemplate can be modified to prevent negative values from being placed in the slot:

```
(deftemplate person
    (multislot name (type SYMBOL))
    (slot age (type INTEGER) (range 0 ?VARIABLE)))
```

If we're willing to assume that no one lives beyond 125 years, then the range attribute could be changed to (range 0 125). As with the allowed value attributes, the range attribute does not restrict the type of a slot value to being numeric. It only restricts the allowed numeric values of a slot to the specified range if the slot's value is numeric. The default range attribute for slots is (range ?VARIABLE ?VARIABLE).

The Cardinality Attribute

The **cardinality attribute** allows the specification of minimum and the maximum number of values that can be stored in a multislot. The general format of the cardinality attribute is (cardinality <lower-limit> <upper-limit>), where <lower-limit> and <upper-limit> are either ?VARIABLE or a positive integer. The <lower-limit> term indicates the minimum number of values the slot can contain and the <upper-limit> term indicates the maximum number of values the slot can contain. ?VARIABLE indicates that there is either no minimum or no maximum number of values the slot can contain (depending on whether it is first or second). The default cardinality attribute for a multislot is (cardinality ?VARIABLE ?VARIABLE). The following deftemplate could be used to represent company volleyball teams, which must have six players and may have up to two alternate players. Note that type, allowed value, and range attributes are applied to every value contained in a multislot.

```
(deftemplate volleyball-team
    (slot name (type STRING))
    (multislot players (type STRING)
                         (cardinality 6 6))
    (multislot alternates (type STRING)
                           (cardinality 0 2)))
```

The Default Attribute

In previous chapters each deftemplate fact that was asserted always had an explicit value stated for every slot. It is often convenient to automatically have a specified value stored in a slot if no value is explicitly stated in an *assert* command. The **default attribute** allows such a default value to be specified. The general format of the default attribute is (default <default-specification>), where <default-specification> is either ?DERIVE, ?NONE, a single expression (for a single-field slot), or zero or more expressions (for a multifield slot).

If ?DERIVE is specified in the default attribute, then a value is derived for the slot that satisfies all of the slot attributes. If the default attribute is not specified for a slot, then it is assumed to be (default ?DERIVE). For a single-field slot, this means that a value is selected that satisfies the type, range, and allowed values attributes for the slot. The derived default value for a multifield slot will be a list of identical values that are the minimum allowed cardinality for the slot (zero by default). If one or more values are contained in the default value for a multifield slot, then each value will satisfy the type, range, and allowed values attributes for the slot. An example of derived values is the following:

```
CLIPS> (clear) ↵
CLIPS>
(deftemplate example
    (slot a)
    (slot b (type INTEGER))
    (slot c (allowed-values red green blue))
    (multislot d)
    (multislot e (cardinality 2 2)
                  (type FLOAT)
                  (range 3.5 10.0))) ↵
CLIPS> (assert (example)) ↵
<Fact-0>
CLIPS> (facts) ↵
f-0      (example (a nil)
                  (b 0)
                  (c red)
                  (d)
                  (e 3.5 3.5))
For a total of 1 fact.
CLIPS>
```

CLIPS only guarantees that the derived default value for a slot satisfies the constraint attributes for the slot. In other words, your programs should not depend on specific derived values (such as the symbol *nil* for for slot *a* or the integer 0 for slot *b* in the previous example) being placed in slots. If your program depends upon a specific default value you should use an expression with the default attribute (which will be explained shortly).

If ?NONE is specified in the default attribute, a value must be supplied for the slot when the fact is asserted. That is, there is no default value. For example,

```
CLIPS> (clear) ↵
CLIPS>
(deftemplate example
    (slot a)
    (slot b (default ?NONE))) ↵
CLIPS> (assert (example)) ↵

[TMPLTRHS1] Slot b requires a value because of its
(default ?NONE) attribute.
CLIPS> (assert (example (b 1))) ↵
<Fact-0>
CLIPS> (facts) ↵
f-0      (example (a nil) (b 1))
For a total of 1 fact.
CLIPS>
```

If one or more expressions are used with the default attribute, the expressions are evaluated when the slot is parsed and this value is stored in the slot whenever the value for the slot is left unspecified in an *assert* command. The default attribute for a single-field slot must contain exactly one expression. If no expressions are specified in the *default* attribute for a multifield slot, then a multifield of length zero is used for the default value. Otherwise, the return values of all of the expressions are grouped together to form one multifield value. The following is an example using expressions with the *default* attribute:

```
CLIPS> (clear) ↵
CLIPS>
(deftemplate example
    (slot a (default 3))
    (slot b (default (+ 3 4)))
    (multislot c (default a b c))
    (multislot d (default (+ 1 2) (+ 3 4)))) ↵
CLIPS> (assert (example)) ↵
<Fact-0>
CLIPS> (facts) ↵
f-0      (example (a 3) (b 7) (c a b c) (d 3 7))
For a total of 1 fact.
CLIPS>
```

The Default-Dynamic Attribute

When the default attribute is used, the default value for a slot is determined when the slot definition is parsed. It's also possible to have the default value generated when the fact that will use the default value is asserted. This is done with the **default-dynamic attribute**. When the value of a slot that uses the default-dynamic attribute is left unspecified in an assert command, the expression specified with the default-dynamic attribute is evaluated and used for the slot's value.

As an example, let's consider the problem of deleting facts after a certain amount of time has transpired. First, we'll need some way of knowing when our facts have been asserted. The **time** function provided by CLIPS will be used to tag the facts with time of creation. It also returns the number of seconds that have elapsed since a system-dependent reference time. By itself, the return value of the time function is not meaningful. It is useful only when compared with other values returned by the function. The following deftemplate will be used for this example. It contains a *creation-time* slot, to store the time of creation, and a *value* slot, to store a value associated with the fact.

```
(deftemplate data
    (slot creation-time (default-dynamic (time)))
    (slot value))
```

Each time a *data* fact is created and the *creation-time* slot is unspecified, the *time* function is called and the value is stored in the *creation-time* slot.

```
CLIPS> (watch facts) ↵
CLIPS> (assert (data (value 3))) ↵
==> f-0      (data (creation-time 12002.45)
                   (value 3))
<Fact-0>
CLIPS> (assert (data (value b))) ↵
==> f-1      (data (creation-time 12010.25)
                   (value b))
<Fact-1>
CLIPS> (assert (data (value c))) ↵
==> f-2      (data (creation-time 12018.65)
                   (value c))
<Fact-2>
CLIPS>
```

Assuming that a *current-time* fact is asserted and updated by other rules to contain the current system time, the following rule will retract *data* facts that were asserted more than one minute ago:

```
(defrule retract-data-facts-after-one-minute
    ?f <- (data (creation-time ?t1))
    (current-time ?t2)
    (test (> (- ?t2 ?t1) 60))
    =>
    (retract ?f))
```

Note that changing the *retract-data-facts-after-one-minute* rule to the following does not produce the same results.

```
(defrule retract-data-facts-after-one-minute
   ?f <- (data (creation-time ?t1))
   (test (> (- (time) ?t1) 60))
   =>
   (retract ?f))
```

The *time* function in the *test* CE will only be checked when the first pattern is matched by a *data* fact. Since the value returned will be approximately the same time as the value in the *creation-time* slot, the rule will not be satisified. CLIPS does not continually recheck *test* CEs to determine whether they evaluate to a different value; they are checked only when changes occur to preceeding CEs. This is why the *current-time* fact in the original version of the rule must be updated so the *test* CE will be periodically rechecked.

Conflicting Slot Attributes

CLIPS does not allow you to specify conflicting attributes for a slot. For example, a slot's default value must satisfy the slot's type, allowed-..., range, and cardinality attributes. If an allowed-... attribute is specified, the type associated with the attribute must satisfy the slot's type attribute. The allowed-numbers, allowed-integers, and allowed-floats attributes may not be used with the range attribute.

10.3 SALIENCE

Up to this point, control facts have been used to indirectly control the execution of programs. CLIPS provides two explicit techniques for controlling the execution of rules: salience and modules. The control of rule execution using modules will be discussed later in this chapter. The use of the keyword **salience** allows the priority of rules to be explicitly specified. Normally the agenda acts like a stack. That is, the most recent activation placed on the agenda is the first to fire. Salience allows more important rules to stay at the top of the agenda, regardless of when the rules were added. Lower salience rules are pushed below higher salience rules on the agenda.

Salience is set using a numeric value ranging from the smallest value of −10,000 to the highest of 10,000. If a rule has no salience explicitly assigned by the programmer, CLIPS assumes a salience of 0. Notice that a salience of 0 is midway between the largest and the smallest salience values. A salience of 0 does not mean that the rule has no salience, but rather that it has an intermediate priority level. A newly activated rule is placed on the agenda before all rules with equal or lesser salience and after all rules with greater salience.

One use of salience is to force rules to fire in a sequential fashion. Consider the following set of rules, in which no salience values are declared:

```
(defrule fire-first
   (priority first)
   =>
   (printout t "Print first" crlf))
```

```
(defrule fire-second
   (priority second)
   =>
   (printout t "Print second" crlf))

(defrule fire-third
   (priority third)
   =>
   (printout t "Print third" crlf))
```

The order in which the rules fire depends on the order in which the facts that satisfy the CEs in the LHS of the rules are asserted. For example, if the rules are entered, the following commands will produce the output shown below:

```
CLIPS> (unwatch all) ↵
CLIPS> (reset) ↵
CLIPS> (assert (priority first)) ↵
<Fact-1>
CLIPS> (assert (priority second)) ↵
<Fact-2>
CLIPS> (assert (priority third)) ↵
<Fact-3>
CLIPS> (run) ↵
Print third
Print second
Print first
CLIPS>
```

Notice the order of output statements. First "Print third" is printed, then "Print second," and finally "Print first." The first fact (priority first) activates the rule *fire-first*. When the second fact is asserted it activates the rule *fire-second*, which is stacked on top of the activation for rule *fire-first*. Finally, the third fact is asserted and its activated rule, *fire-third*, is stacked on top of the activation for rule *fire-second*.

In CLIPS, rules of equal salience that are activated by different patterns are prioritized based on the stack order of facts. Rules are fired from the agenda from the top of the stack down. So rule *fire-third* is fired first because it's on the top of the stack, then rule *fire-second*, and finally rule *fire-first*. If the order in which the facts are asserted is reversed, then the order in which the rules are fired will also be reversed. This is seen in the following output:

```
CLIPS> (reset) ↵
CLIPS> (assert (priority third)) ↵
<Fact-1>
CLIPS> (assert (priority second)) ↵
<Fact-2>
CLIPS> (assert (priority first)) ↵
<Fact-3>
CLIPS> (run) ↵
Print first
```

```
Print second
Print third
CLIPS>
```

One important point is that if two or more rules with the same salience are activated by the same fact, there is no guarantee in which order the rules will be placed on the agenda.

Salience can be used to force the rules to fire in the order *fire-first*, *fire-second*, *fire-third*, despite the order in which the activating facts are asserted. This can be accomplished by declaring salience values:

```
(defrule fire-first
   (declare (salience 30))
   (priority first)
   =>
   (printout t "Print first" crlf))

(defrule fire-second
   (declare (salience 20))
   (priority second)
   =>
   (printout t "Print second" crlf))

(defrule fire-third
   (declare (salience 10))
   (priority third)
   =>
   (printout t "Print third" crlf))
```

Regardless of the order in which the priority facts are asserted, the agenda will always be ordered the same. Performing the *agenda* command after asserting the priority facts would produce the following output:

```
CLIPS> (reset) ↵
CLIPS> (assert (priority second)
               (priority first)
               (priority third)) ↵
<Fact-3>
CLIPS> (agenda) ↵
30      fire-first: f-2
20      fire-second: f-1
10      fire-third: f-3
For a total of 3 activations.
CLIPS>
```

Notice how the salience values have rearranged the priority of rules in the agenda. When the program is run, the order of rule firing will always be *fire-first*, *fire-second*, *fire-third*.

10.4 PHASES AND CONTROL FACTS

The purest concept of a rule-based expert system is one in which the rules act opportunistically whenever they are applicable. However, most expert systems have some procedural aspect to them. The Sticks program, for example, had different rules that were applicable depending on whether it was the human's or the computer's move. The control for this program was handled by facts that indicated whose turn it was. These control facts allow information about the control structure of the program to be embedded in the rules of domain knowledge. This does have a drawback: knowledge about the control of the rules is intermixed with knowledge about how to play the game. This is not a major drawback in the case of the Sticks program because it is small. However, for programs involving hundreds or thousands of rules, the intermixing of domain knowledge and control knowledge makes development and maintenance a major problem.

As an example, consider the problem of performing **fault detection**, **isolation**, and **recovery** of a system such as an electronic device. *Fault detection* is the process of recognizing that the electronic device is not working properly. *Isolation* is the process of determining the components of the device that have caused the fault. *Recovery* is the process of determining the steps necessary to correct the fault, if possible. Typically with this type of problem the expert system will have rules to determine whether a fault has occurred, other rules to isolate the cause of the fault, and still other rules to determine how to recover from the fault. The cycle will then loop back. Figure 10.1 shows an example of control flow in this type of system.

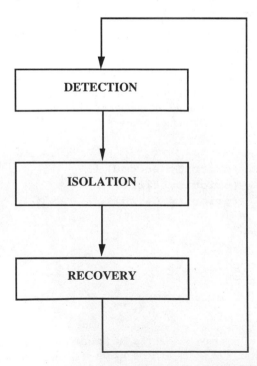

Figure 10.1 Different Phases for Fault Detection, Isolation, and Recovery Problem

Implementing the flow of control in this system can be done in at least four ways. The first three approaches use salience and will be discussed in this section. The fourth approach uses modules and will be discussed later in the chapter.

The first approach to implementing the flow of control is to embed the control knowledge directly into the rules. For instance, the detection rules would include rules indicating when the isolation phase should be entered. Each group of rules would be given a pattern indicating in which phase it would be applicable. This technique has two drawbacks. First, as already mentioned, control knowledge is being embedded into the domain knowledge rules, which makes them more difficult to understand. Second, it is not always easy to determine when a phase is completed. This generally requires writing a rule that is applicable only when all the other rules have fired.

The second approach is to use salience to organize the rules, as shown in Figure 10.2. This approach also has two major drawbacks. First, control knowledge is still being embedded into the rules using salience. Second, this approach does not guarantee the correct order of execution. Detection rules will always fire before isolation rules. However, when the isolation rules begin firing they might cause a detection rule to become activated and immediately fire because of its higher salience.

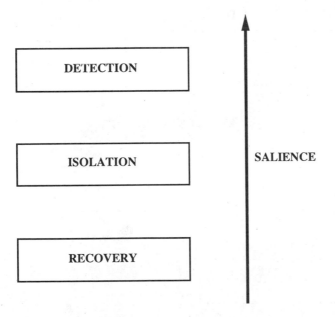

Figure 10.2 Assignment of Salience for Different Phases

A third and better approach in controlling the flow of execution is to separate the control knowledge from the domain knowledge, as shown in Figure 10.3. Using this approach, each rule is given a control pattern that indicates its applicable phase. Control rules are then written to transfer control between the different phases, as shown here:

```
(defrule detection-to-isolation
   (declare (salience -10))
   ?phase <- (phase detection)
   =>
   (retract ?phase)
   (assert (phase isolation)))

(defrule isolation-to-recovery
   (declare (salience -10))
   ?phase <- (phase isolation)
   =>
   (retract ?phase)
   (assert (phase recovery)))

(defrule recovery-to-detection
   (declare (salience -10))
   ?phase <- (phase recovery)
   =>
   (retract ?phase)
   (assert (phase detection)))
```

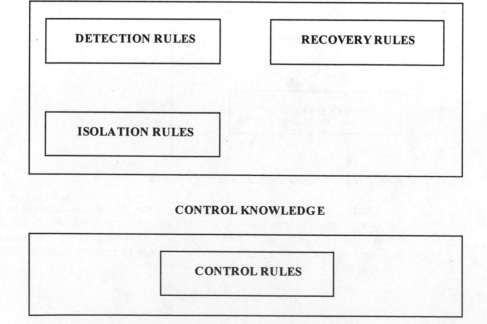

Figure 10.3 Separation of Expert Knowledge from Control Knowledge

Each of the rules applicable for a particular phase is then given a control pattern that confirms that the appropriate control fact is present. For example, a recovery rule might look like this:

```
(defrule find-fault-location-and-recovery
    (phase recovery)
    (recovery-solution switch-device
                         ?replacement on)
    =>
    (printout t "Switch device " ?replacement " on "
              crlf))
```

A **salience hierarchy** is a description of the salience values used by an expert system. Each level in a salience hierarchy corresponds to a specific set of rules whose members are all given the same salience. If the rules for detection, isolation, and recovery are given a default salience of zero, then the salience hierarchy is as shown in Figure 10.4. Notice that while the fact (phase detection) is in the fact list, the *detection-to-isolation* rule will be on the agenda. Since it has a lower salience than the detection rules, it will not fire until all of the detection rules have had an opportunity to fire. The following output shows a sample run of the three previous control rules:

```
CLIPS> (reset) ↵
CLIPS> (assert (phase detection)) ↵
<Fact-1>
CLIPS> (watch rules) ↵
CLIPS> (run 10) ↵
FIRE     1 detection-to-isolation: f-1
FIRE     2 isolation-to-recovery: f-2
FIRE     3 recovery-to-detection: f-3
FIRE     4 detection-to-isolation: f-4
FIRE     5 isolation-to-recovery: f-5
FIRE     6 recovery-to-detection: f-6
FIRE     7 detection-to-isolation: f-7
FIRE     8 isolation-to-recovery: f-8
FIRE     9 recovery-to-detection: f-9
FIRE    10 detection-to-isolation: f-10
CLIPS>
```

Notice that the control rules just keep firing in sequence because there are no domain knowledge rules to be applied during any of the phases. If there were, then the domain knowledge rules would be applied for activated rules during the appropriate phases.

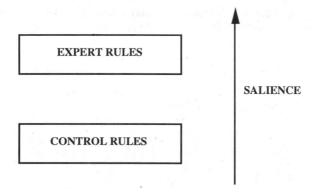

Figure 10.4 Salience Hierarchy Using Expert and Control Rules

The previous control rules could be more generically written with a deffacts construct and a single rule as

```
(deffacts control-information
    (phase detection)
    (phase-after detection isolation)
    (phase-after isolation recovery)
    (phase-after recovery detection))

(defrule change-phase
    (declare (salience -10))
    ?phase <- (phase ?current-phase)
    (phase-after ?current-phase ?next-phase)
    =>
    (retract ?phase)
    (assert (phase ?next-phase)))
```

or they could be written using a sequence of phases to be cycled through as

```
(deffacts control-information
    (phase detection)
    (phase-sequence isolation recovery detection))

(defrule change-phase
    (declare (salience -10))
    ?phase <- (phase ?current-phase)
    ?list <- (phase-sequence ?next-phase
                               $?other-phases)
    =>
    (retract ?phase ?list)
    (assert (phase ?next-phase))
    (assert (phase-sequence ?other-phases
                             ?next-phase)))
```

Additional levels can easily be added to the salience hierarchy. Figure 10.5 shows a hierarchy with two additional levels. The constraint rules represent rules that detect illegal or unproductive states that may occur in the expert system. For example, an expert system scheduling people to various tasks may produce a schedule that violates a constraint. Instead of allowing the lower salience rules to continue working on the schedule, the constraint rules will immediately remove violations in the schedule. As another example, the user may enter in response to a series of questions a series of legal values that result in an illegal value being generated. The constraint rules could be used to detect such violations.

The query rules shown in the diagram represent rules that ask the user particular questions to aid the expert system in determining an answer. These rules have lower salience than the expert rules because it is undesirable to ask the user a question that can be determined by the expert rules. Thus the query rules are only fired when no more information can be derived by the expert rules.

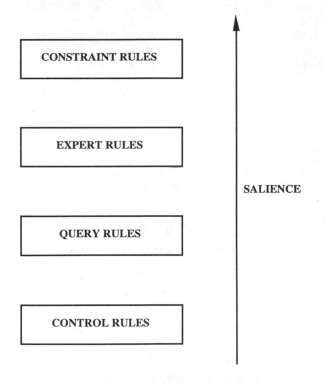

Figure 10.5 Four-Level Salience Hierarchy

10.5 MISUSE OF SALIENCE

Although salience is a powerful tool for controlling execution, it can easily be abused. In particular, people who are just learning rule-based programming tend to overuse salience because it gives them explicit control of execution. It is more like the procedural programming they are used to, in which statements execute sequentially.

Overuse of salience results in a poorly coded program. The main advantage of a rule-based program is that the programmer does not have to worry about controlling execution. A well-designed rule-based program has a natural mode of execution that permits the inference engine to guide rule firings in an optimal manner.

Salience should primarily be used as a mechanism for determining the order in which rules fire. This means that in general a rule that is placed on the agenda is eventually fired. Salience should not be used as a method for selecting a single rule from a group of rules when patterns can be used to express the criteria for selection, nor should it be used as a "quick fix" to get rules to fire in the proper order.

In general, *any* salience value used in a rule should correspond to a level in the salience hierarchy of the expert system. The range of salience values from − 10,000 to 10,000 is somewhat misleading. Rarely should more than seven salience values ever be required for coding an expert system; most well-coded expert systems need no more than three or four salience values. For large expert systems, it is strongly recommended that programmers use modules to control the flow of execution (as discussed in the next section) and that no more than two or three salience values be used.

As an example of how the use of salience can be avoided, the following is a simple set of rules that suggests which squares to mark in a tic-tac-toe game. The rules are listed in the order in which they should be applied.

```
IF a winning square is open, THEN take it.
IF a blocking square is open, THEN take it.
IF a square is open, THEN take it.
```

If the *choose-move* fact indicates the a move should be taken and the *open-square* facts indicate whether a winning, blocking, middle, corner, or side square is open, the following rules will select the appropriate move:

```
(defrule pick-to-win
    (declare (salience 10))
    ?phase <- (choose-move)
    (open-square win)
    =>
    (retract ?phase)
    (assert (move-to win)))

(defrule pick-to-block
    (declare (salience 5))
    ?phase <- (choose-move)
    (open-square block)
    =>
    (retract ?phase)
    (assert (move-to block)))

(defrule pick-any
    ?phase <- (choose-move)
    (open-square ?any&corner|middle|side)
    =>
    (retract ?phase)
    (assert (move-to ?any)))
```

Notice that if more than one type of square is available, all three rules will be placed on the agenda. When rule *pick-to-win*, *pick-to-block*, or *pick-any* is fired, the retraction of the control fact will remove the other rules from the agenda. All three rules are thus very closely interrelated. It is not possible to understand the intent of each of these rules without seeing all the rules together. This violates a basic concept of rule-based programming. As much as possible, a rule should represent a completely expressed heuristic. In this case, salience is used to express an implicit relationship among these rules that could be explicitly stated with additional patterns in the rules. The rules can be rewritten without salience as follows:

```
(defrule pick-to-win
    ?phase <- (choose-move)
    (open-square win)
    =>
    (retract ?phase)
    (assert (move-to win)))

(defrule pick-to-block
    ?phase <- (choose-move)
    (open-square block)
    (not (open-square win))
    =>
    (retract ?phase)
    (assert (move-to block)))

(defrule pick-any
    ?phase <- (choose-move)
    (open-square ?any&corner|middle|side)
    (not (open-square win))
    (not (open-square block))
    =>
    (retract ?phase)
    (assert (move-to ?any)))
```

Adding the additional patterns to the rules explicitly states the conditions under which the rules are applicable. The tight interaction between the rules is removed, allowing the rules to act opportunistically. Rewriting the rules also demonstrates that the original heuristics could have been expressed more clearly.

```
IF a winning square is open, THEN take it.
IF a blocking square is open, and
   a winning square is not open, THEN take it.
IF a corner, middle, or side square is open, and
   a winning square is not open, and
   a blocking square is not open, THEN take it.
```

10.6 THE DEFMODULE CONSTRUCT

Until now, all the defrules, deftemplates, and deffacts have been contained in a single work space. CLIPS uses the **defmodule** construct to partition a knowledge base by defining the various modules. The basic syntax for this construct is

```
(defmodule <module-name> [<comment>])
```

By default CLIPS defines a module called the MAIN module. In previous examples we have seen that the MAIN module name appears with the pretty print representation of the constructs. For example,

```
CLIPS> (clear) ↵
CLIPS> (deftemplate sensor (slot name)) ↵
CLIPS> (ppdeftemplate sensor) ↵
(deftemplate MAIN::sensor
    (slot name))
CLIPS>
```

The :: symbol in the name MAIN::sensor is called the *module separator*. To the right of the module separator is the name of the construct. To the left of the module separator is the name of the module in which the construct is contained. Since all the constructs that have been defined so far have been placed in the MAIN module by default, the MAIN module name appears with the pretty print representation of the constructs.

Now that we know the defmodule syntax, we can define new modules. Using the previous example of a fault detection system, we will define modules that correspond to the phases DETECTION, ISOLATION, and RECOVERY.

```
CLIPS> (defmodule DETECTION) ↵
CLIPS> (defmodule ISOLATION) ↵
CLIPS> (defmodule RECOVERY) ↵
```

Once we've defined more than the MAIN module, the question arises "In which module are new constructs placed?" By default, CLIPS places newly defined constructs in the current module. When CLIPS is initially started or cleared, the current module is automatically the MAIN module. Thus in our previous examples, since there was only one module and that was the current module, all defined constructs were placed in the MAIN module.

Whenever a new module is defined, CLIPS makes it the current module. Because the dialog above last defined the RECOVERY module, that is the current module and a newly defined rule will be placed in it.

```
CLIPS> (defrule example1 =>) ↵
CLIPS> (ppdefrule example1) ↵
(defrule RECOVERY::example1
   =>)
CLIPS>
```

The module in which a construct is placed can be specified in the construct's name. In the name, specify the module first, followed by the module separator, and then the construct's name.

```
CLIPS> (defrule ISOLATION::example2 =>) ↵
CLIPS> (ppdefrule example2) ↵
(defrule ISOLATION::example2
   =>)
CLIPS>
```

The current module is changed when the module name is specified in a construct's name. The current module can be determined with the **get-current-module** function. This function takes no arguments and returns the name of the current module. The function **set-current-module** is used to change the current module. It takes a single argument, the name of the new current module, and returns the name of the previous current module.

```
CLIPS> (get-current-module) ↵
ISOLATION
CLIPS> (set-current-module DETECTION) ↵
ISOLATION
CLIPS>
```

Specifying Modules in Commands

By default, most of the CLIPS commands that operate on constructs work only on the constructs contained in the current module. For example, the *list-defrules* command will produce no output if the current module is the DETECTION module because that module contains no rules:

```
CLIPS> (list-defrules) ↵
CLIPS>
```

If we wanted to see the defrules contained in the ISOLATION module we could set the current module to the ISOLATION module and then execute another *list-defrules* command:

```
CLIPS> (set-current-module ISOLATION) ↵
DETECTION
CLIPS> (list-defrules) ↵
example2
For a total of 1 defrule.
CLIPS>
```

Alternatively, the *list-defrules* command accepts a module name as an optional argument. This argument specifies which module will have its rules listed:

```
CLIPS> (list-defrules RECOVERY) ↵
example1
For a total of 1 defrule.
CLIPS>
```

If the symbol * is passed as an argument to *list-defrules*, then the rules in all of the modules are listed. Each list is preceded by the name of the module followed by the list of the rules contained in that module.

```
CLIPS> (list-defrules *) ↵
MAIN:
DETECTION:
ISOLATION:
    example2
RECOVERY:
    example1
For a total of 2 defrules.
CLIPS>
```

The listing functions *list-deftemplates* and *list-deffacts* work similarly to the list-defrules command. The *show-breaks* command also allows you to specify which module will have its breakpoints displayed. The modified syntax for these functions is

```
(list-defrules [<module-name>])
(list-deftemplates [<module-name>])
(list-deffacts [<module-name>])
(show-breaks [<module-name>])
```

Rules that operate on specific constructs also allow a module to be specified. For example, *ppdefrule* will only search the current module if no module name is specified:

```
CLIPS> (ppdefrule example2) ↵
(defrule ISOLATION::example2
    =>)
CLIPS> (ppdefrule example1) ↵
[PRNTUTIL1] Unable to find defrule example1.
CLIPS>
```

The rule *example2* has its pretty print form displayed since it is contained in the ISOLATION module, but because rule *example1* is not in the ISOLATION module, it is not found by the *ppdefrule* command.

The module in which to search for a construct can be specified by placing the module name, followed by the module separator, in front of the construct's name. For example,

```
CLIPS> (ppdefrule RECOVERY::example1) ↵
(defrule RECOVERY::example1
    =>)
CLIPS>
```

It is possible to have two constructs with the same name in different modules. Using the module specifier before the construct's name allows you to distinguish between the two in a command:

```
CLIPS> (defrule DETECTION::example1 =>) ↵
CLIPS> (list-defrules *) ↵
MAIN:
DETECTION:
    example1
ISOLATION:
    example2
RECOVERY:
    example1
For a total of 3 defrules.
CLIPS> (ppdefrule RECOVERY::example1) ↵
(defrule RECOVERY::example1
    =>)
CLIPS> (ppdefrule DETECTION::example1) ↵
(defrule DETECTION::example1
    =>)
CLIPS>
```

The following commands allow the module to be specified as part of the construct name: *ppdefrule*, *undefrule*, *ppdeftemplate*, *undeftemplate*, *ppdeffacts*, *undeffacts*, *matches*, *refresh*, *remove-break*, and *set-break*.

10.7 IMPORTING AND EXPORTING FACTS

You have learned how to partition constructs by placing them in separate modules. Facts themselves can also be partitioned. Asserted facts are automatically associated with the module in which their corresponding deftemplates are defined. For example,

```
CLIPS>
(deftemplate DETECTION::fault
    (slot component)) ↵
CLIPS> (assert (fault (component A))) ↵
<Fact-0>
CLIPS> (facts) ↵
f-0     (fault (component A))
For a total of 1 fact.
CLIPS>
(deftemplate ISOLATION::possible-failure
    (slot component)) ↵
CLIPS> (assert (possible-failure (component B))) ↵
<Fact-1>
CLIPS> (facts) ↵
f-1     (possible-failure (component B))
For a total of 1 fact.
CLIPS> (set-current-module DETECTION) ↵
ISOLATION
CLIPS> (facts) ↵
f-0     (fault (component A))
```

```
For a total of 1 fact.
CLIPS>
```

Notice that in the ISOLATION module the only fact listed is the *possible-failure* fact, whose corresponding deftemplate is contained in the ISOLATION module. The same is true for the *fault* fact in the DETECTION module.

The *facts* command, like the *list-defrules* and similar commands, can accept a module name as an optional argument. The syntax for the *facts* command is

```
(facts [<module-name>]
       [<start> [<end> [<maximum>]]])
```

As with the *list-defrules* command, specifying a module name lists only the facts contained in the specified module. If * is used for the module name, then all the facts are listed:

```
CLIPS> (facts DETECTION) ↵
f-0     (fault (component A))
For a total of 1 fact.
CLIPS> (facts ISOLATION) ↵
f-1     (possible-failure (component B))
For a total of 1 fact.
CLIPS> (facts RECOVERY) ↵
CLIPS> (facts *) ↵
f-0     (fault (component A))
f-1     (possible-failure (component B))
For a total of 2 facts.
CLIPS>
```

Unlike defrule and deffacts constructs, deftemplate constructs (and all facts using that deftemplate) can be shared with other modules. A fact is "owned" by the module in which its deftemplate is contained, but the owning module can **export** the deftemplate associated with the fact, thus making that fact and all other facts using that deftemplate visible to other modules. It is not sufficient just to export the deftemplate to make a fact visible to another module. In order to use a deftemplate defined in another module, a module must also **import** the deftemplate definition.

Modules that export deftemplates must use the export attribute in their defmodule definition. The export attribute must use one of the following formats:

```
(export ?ALL)
(export ?NONE)
(export deftemplate ?ALL)
(export deftemplate ?NONE)
(export deftemplate <deftemplate-name>+)
```

The first format will export all exportable constructs from a module. Of the constructs discussed in this book, only deftemplates are exportable. Some of the other procedural and object-oriented programming constructs in CLIPS can be exported. The second format indicates that no constructs are exported and is the default for a defmodule. The third format indicates that all deftemplates in a module are exported. For the constructs discussed in this book, this is the same as the first format. Similarly, the fourth format indicates that no deftemplate constructs are exported. The second and fourth formats are provided primarily so the constructs exported by a module can be explicitly stated. Finally, the fifth format gives a specific list of deftemplates exported by a module. The export attribute can be used more than once in a defmodule definition to specify different types of exported constructs, but since deftemplates are the only exportable construct that we have discussed there will be no need to use more than one export attribute statement.

The import attribute also has five possible formats:

```
(import <module-name> ?ALL)
(import <module-name> ?NONE)
(import <module-name> deftemplate ?ALL)
(import <module-name> deftemplate ?NONE)
(import <module-name> deftemplate
                       <deftemplate-name>+)
```

Each of the formats has the same meaning as its export counterpart except that the specified constructs are imported. In addition, the module from which the constructs are being imported must be specified. Like the export attribute, a defmodule definition can have more than one import attribute.

A construct must be defined before it can be specified in an import list, but it does not have to be defined before it can be specified in an export list (in order to place a construct in a module, the module must be defined, so in fact it is not possible to have a construct defined before the module that exports it is defined). Because of this restriction, it is not possible for two modules to mutually import from each other (i.e., if module A imports from module B, it isn't possible for module B to import from module A).

To illustrate importing and exporting facts, let's assume that the RECOVERY module wants to import the *fault* deftemplate from the DETECTION module and the *possible-failure* deftemplate from the ISOLATION module. Unlike other constructs, once defined, a defmodule cannot be redefined. Thus, in order to change the import and export attributes of a defmodule, a clear command must be issued first. There is one exception to the restriction: the MAIN module, which is predefined, may be redefined once to include different import and export attributes (by default the MAIN module exports and imports nothing). *Note* that the default definition of the MAIN module *does not* export the *initial-fact* deftemplate. Recall from Chapter 9 that the (initial-fact) pattern is added to the LHS of a rule under certain circumstances (such as when the first CE is a *not* CE). If such a rule is placed in a module that does not import the *initial-fact* deftemplate from the MAIN module, that rule cannot be activated. Also note that you will not get an error when the rule is defined since the (initial-fact) pattern will cause the creation of an implied *initial-fact* deftemplate in the current module.

The new definitions for the DETECTION, ISOLATION, and RECOVERY modules along with their deftemplates (which should all be entered after a *clear* command) are the following:

```
(defmodule DETECTION
   (export deftemplate fault))
```

```
(deftemplate DETECTION::fault
   (slot component))

(defmodule ISOLATION
   (export deftemplate possible-failure))

(deftemplate ISOLATION::possible-failure
   (slot component))

(defmodule RECOVERY
   (import DETECTION deftemplate fault)
   (import ISOLATION deftemplate possible-failure))
```

With the defmodules and deftemplates defined, it is now possible to assert *fault* facts in the DETECTION and RECOVERY modules and *possible-failure* facts in the ISOLATION and RECOVERY modules.

```
CLIPS>
(deffacts DETECTION::start
   (fault (component A)))⏎
CLIPS>
(deffacts ISOLATION::start
   (possible-failure (component B)))⏎
CLIPS>
(deffacts RECOVERY::start
   (fault (component C))
   (possible-failure (component D)))⏎
CLIPS> (reset)⏎
CLIPS> (facts DETECTION)⏎
f-0     (fault (component A))
f-2     (fault (component C))
For a total of 2 facts.
CLIPS> (facts ISOLATION)⏎
f-1     (possible-failure (component B))
f-3     (possible-failure (component D))
For a total of 2 facts.
CLIPS> (facts RECOVERY)⏎
f-0     (fault (component A))
f-1     (possible-failure (component B))
f-2     (fault (component C))
f-3     (possible-failure (component D))
For a total of 4 facts.
CLIPS>
```

Notice that both the DETECTION and the RECOVERY modules see the *fault* facts asserted by either module. The same holds true for the *possible-failure* facts asserted by the ISOLATION and RECOVERY modules.

10.8 MODULES AND EXECUTION CONTROL

In addition to controlling which deftemplates a module can import and export, the defmodule construct can be used to control the execution of rules. Instead of being part of just one overall agenda, each module defined in CLIPS has its own agenda. Execution can then be controlled by deciding which module's agenda is selected for executing rules. For example, the following defrules should all be activated by the fault and possible-failure facts asserted in the previous example:

```
(defrule DETECTION::rule-1
   (fault (component A | C))
   =>)

(defrule ISOLATION::rule-2
   (possible-failure (component B | D))
   =>)

(defrule RECOVERY::rule-3
   (fault (component A | C))
   (possible-failure (component B | D))
   =>)
```

If the *agenda* command is issued after these rules are loaded, the agenda of the RECOVERY module will be displayed because the last rule defined was placed in that module:

```
CLIPS> (get-current-module) ↵
RECOVERY
CLIPS> (agenda) ↵
0       rule-3: f-0,f-3
0       rule-3: f-0,f-1
0       rule-3: f-2,f-3
0       rule-3: f-2,f-1
For a total of 4 activations.
CLIPS>
```

Like the *list-defrules* and *facts* commands, the agenda command accepts an optional argument that, if specified, indicates the module whose agenda will be listed:

```
CLIPS> (agenda DETECTION) ↵
0       rule-1: f-2
0       rule-1: f-0
For a total of 2 activations.
CLIPS> (agenda ISOLATION) ↵
0       rule-2: f-3
0       rule-2: f-1
For a total of 2 activations.
CLIPS> (agenda RECOVERY) ↵
0       rule-3: f-0,f-3
```

```
0        rule-3:  f-0,f-1
0        rule-3:  f-2,f-3
0        rule-3:  f-2,f-1
For a total of 4 activations.
CLIPS> (agenda *) ↵
MAIN:
DETECTION:
    0        rule-1:  f-2
    0        rule-1:  f-0
ISOLATION:
    0        rule-2:  f-3
    0        rule-2:  f-1
RECOVERY:
    0        rule-3:  f-0,f-3
    0        rule-3:  f-0,f-1
    0        rule-3:  f-2,f-3
    0        rule-3:  f-2,f-1
For a total of 8 activations.
CLIPS>
```

The Focus Command

Now that there are rules on three separate agendas, what happens when a *run* command is issued?

```
CLIPS> (unwatch all) ↵
CLIPS> (watch rules) ↵
CLIPS> (run) ↵
CLIPS>
```

No rules fire! In addition to the current module, which CLIPS uses to determine where new constructs are added and which constructs are used or affected by commands, CLIPS also maintains a **current focus**, which determines which agenda the *run* command uses during execution. The *reset* and *clear* commands automatically set the current focus to the MAIN module. The current focus *does not* change when the current module is changed. Thus, in the current example, when the *run* command is issued, the agenda associated with the MAIN module is used to select rules to execute. Since this agenda is empty, no rules are fired.

The **focus** command is used to change the current focus. Its syntax is

```
(focus <module-name>+)
```

In the simple case in which only one module name is specified, the current focus is set to the specified module. By setting the current focus to the DETECTION module and then issuing a run command, the rules on the DETECTION module's agenda will be fired:

```
CLIPS> (focus DETECTION) ↵
TRUE
CLIPS> (run) ↵
```

```
FIRE    1 rule-1: f-2
FIRE    2 rule-1: f-0
CLIPS>
```

Using the *focus* command not only changes the current focus but also recalls the previous value of the current focus. The current focus is really the top value of a stack data structure called the ***focus stack***. Whenever the *focus* command changes the current focus, it is actually pushing the new current focus onto the top of the focus stack, displacing the previous current focuses. As rules execute, when the agenda of the current focus becomes empty, the current focus is popped (removed) from the focus stack and the next module becomes the current focus. Rules are then executed from the agenda of the new current focus until a new module is focused on or until there are no rules left on the agenda of the current focus. Rules will continue to execute until there are no modules left on the focus stack or the *halt* command is issued.

Continuing the current example, focusing first on the ISOLATION module and then on the RECOVERY module will cause all of the rules on the RECOVERY module's agenda to fire, which will be followed by the firing of rules on the ISOLATION module's agenda. The **list-focus-stack** command (which takes no arguments) is used to display the modules on the focus stack.

```
CLIPS> (focus ISOLATION) ↵
TRUE
CLIPS> (focus RECOVERY) ↵
TRUE
CLIPS> (list-focus-stack) ↵
RECOVERY
ISOLATION
CLIPS> (run) ↵
FIRE    1 rule-3: f-1,f-4
FIRE    2 rule-3: f-1,f-2
FIRE    3 rule-3: f-3,f-4
FIRE    4 rule-3: f-3,f-2
FIRE    5 rule-2: f-4
FIRE    6 rule-2: f-2
CLIPS> (list-focus-stack) ↵
CLIPS>
```

Using two focus commands to push the ISOLATION and RECOVERY modules causes the RECOVERY rules to execute before the ISOLATION rules. However, when more than one module is specified in a single *focus* command, the modules are pushed onto the focus stack from right to left. For example,

```
CLIPS> (focus ISOLATION RECOVERY) ↵
TRUE
CLIPS> (list-focus-stack) ↵
ISOLATION
RECOVERY
CLIPS> (focus ISOLATION) ↵
TRUE
```

```
CLIPS> (list-focus-stack) ↵
ISOLATION
RECOVERY
CLIPS> (focus RECOVERY) ↵
TRUE
CLIPS> (list-focus-stack) ↵
RECOVERY
ISOLATION
RECOVERY
CLIPS>
```

Notice that the same module can be on the focus stack more than once, but focusing on a module that is already the current focus has no effect.

Manipulating and Examining the Focus Stack

CLIPS provides several commands and functions for manipulating the current focus and the focus stack. The **clear-focus-stack** command removes all modules from the focus stack. The **get-focus** function returns the module name of the current focus or the symbol FALSE if the focus stack is empty. The **pop-focus** function removes the current focus from the focus stack (and returns the module name or the symbol FALSE if the focus stack is empty). The **get-focus-stack** function returns a multifield value containing the modules on the focus stack.

```
CLIPS> (get-focus-stack) ↵
(RECOVERY ISOLATION RECOVERY)
CLIPS> (get-focus) ↵
RECOVERY
CLIPS> (pop-focus) ↵
RECOVERY
CLIPS> (clear-focus-stack) ↵
CLIPS> (get-focus-stack) ↵
()
CLIPS> (get-focus) ↵
FALSE
CLIPS> (pop-focus) ↵
FALSE
CLIPS>
```

The *watch* command can be used to see changes to the focus stack by using the keyword *focus* as the command's argument:

```
CLIPS> (watch focus) ↵
CLIPS> (focus DETECTION ISOLATION RECOVERY) ↵
==> Focus RECOVERY
==> Focus ISOLATION from RECOVERY
==> Focus DETECTION from ISOLATION
TRUE
CLIPS> (run) ↵
<== Focus DETECTION to ISOLATION
```

```
<== Focus ISOLATION to RECOVERY
<== Focus RECOVERY
CLIPS>
```

In the event that the *run* command is given and the focus stack is empty, the MAIN module is automatically pushed onto the focus stack. This feature is provided mainly as a convenience for the case in which new activations are added after the program has ended because there are no modules left on the focus stack. For example,

```
CLIPS> (clear) ↵
CLIPS> (watch focus) ↵
CLIPS> (watch rules) ↵
CLIPS> (defrule example-1 =>) ↵
CLIPS> (reset)
<== Focus MAIN
==> Focus MAIN
CLIPS> (run) ↵
FIRE    1 example-1: f-0
<== Focus MAIN
CLIPS> (defrule example-2 =>) ↵
CLIPS> (agenda) ↵
0       example-2: f-0
For a total of 1 activation.
CLIPS> (list-focus-stack) ↵
CLIPS>
```

The rule *example-2* is on the agenda, but there are no modules on the focus stack. Issuing a *run* command, however, places the MAIN module on the focus stack, so rule *example-2* is able to fire anyway.

```
CLIPS> (run) ↵
==> Focus MAIN
FIRE    1 example-2: f-0
<== Focus MAIN
CLIPS>
```

The Return Command

One of the drawbacks of controlling the flow of execution by using control facts to represent phases, as discussed in Section 10.4, is that it is not possible to fire some activations in a particular phase, exit that phase, and then return later to the phase and execute the remaining activations on the agenda. This occurs because once the control fact representing the phase is retracted, all of the activations from that phase are removed from the agenda. When the control fact is later reasserted, *all* of the previous activations for that phase will be reactivated, not just those that didn't fire (this, of course, is assuming that only the control fact and not any other facts were asserted or retracted).

If modules are used to control the flow of execution, it is possible to stop executing the activations from a specific module's agenda prematurely (that is, before the module's agenda is empty). The **return** command can be used to immediately terminate the execution of a rule's RHS and remove the current focus from the focus stack (thus returning control of execution to the next module on the focus stack). When used from the RHS of a rule, the *return* command should be passed no arguments (the *return* command can also used by the procedural programming constructs provided with CLIPS). The following example illustrates the use of the *return* command:

```
CLIPS> (clear) ↵
CLIPS>
(defmodule MAIN
    (export deftemplate initial-fact)) ↵
CLIPS>
(defmodule DETECTION
    (import MAIN deftemplate initial-fact)) ↵
CLIPS>
(defrule MAIN::start
    =>
    (focus DETECTION)) ↵
CLIPS>
(defrule DETECTION::example-1
    =>
    (return)
    (printout t "No printout!" crlf)) ↵
CLIPS>
(defrule DETECTION::example-2
    =>
    (return)
    (printout t "No printout!" crlf)) ↵
CLIPS> (watch rules) ↵
CLIPS> (watch focus) ↵
CLIPS> (reset) ↵
<== Focus MAIN
==> Focus MAIN
CLIPS> (run) ↵
FIRE    1 start: f-0
==> Focus DETECTION from MAIN
FIRE    2 example-1: f-0
<== Focus DETECTION to MAIN
<== Focus MAIN
CLIPS>
```

There are two points worth noting about this example. First, in order for the rules in the DETECTION module to be activated by using the default *initial-fact* pattern, the *initial-fact* deftemplate must be exported by the MAIN module and imported by the DETECTION module. Second, notice that the return command *immediately* halts execution of the rule's RHS. The *printout* command following the *return* command is not executed in the *example-1* rule (or in the *example-2* rule, since it didn't get the opportunity to fire). Note that the functionality of the *return* command is similar to, but not the same as, the *pop-focus* command, which removes the current focus from the focus stack but will allow the execution of the actions of the RHS of a rule to continue. If the *pop-focus* command had been used in place of the *return* command for this example, the string "No printout!" would have been printed when the actions of the *example-1* rule were executed.

The Auto-Focus Feature

In addition to being able to explicitly focus on modules using the *focus* command, it's also possible to automatically focus on a module when specific rules from that module are activated. By default, a rule's module is not automatically focused upon when that rule is activated. This can be changed by using the **auto-focus** attribute. The auto-focus attribute is specified in the declare statement along with the salience attribute. The keyword *auto-focus* is specified followed by either TRUE (to enable the feature) or FALSE (to disable the feature). It's not necessary that all rules in a module have the auto-focus feature enabled in order for some rules in the module to make use of it. Similarly, it's not necessary to declare both the salience attribute and the auto-focus attribute if the declare statement is used for a rule. The following example illustrates the use of the auto-focus feature:

```
CLIPS> (clear) ↵
CLIPS>
(defmodule MAIN
    (export deftemplate initial-fact)) ↵
CLIPS>
(defmodule DETECTION
    (import MAIN deftemplate initial-fact)) ↵
CLIPS>
(defrule DETECTION::example
    (declare (auto-focus TRUE))
    =>) ↵
CLIPS> (watch focus) ↵
CLIPS> (reset) ↵
<== Focus MAIN
==> Focus MAIN
==> Focus DETECTION from MAIN
CLIPS>
```

When the *reset* command is issued the MAIN module is automatically focused on because the focus stack is empty. The *example* rule is activated by the assertion of the *initial-fact* fact. Since the auto-focus attribute is enabled for this rule its module, the DETECTION module, is automatically pushed onto the focus stack. The auto-focus feature is particularly useful for rules that detect constraint violations. Because the constraint rule's module immediately becomes the current focus, it is possible to take action when the violation occurs, rather than having an explicit phase in which violations are detected.

Replacing Phases and Control Facts

Through the use of defmodules, the focus and return commands, and the auto-focus feature it is now possible to replace the use of phases and control fact s with a much more explicit mechanism for controlling the flow of execution of rules.

The constructs described in Section 10.4 for controlling execution can be replaced with the following constructs:

```
(defmodule DETECTION)
(defmodule ISOLATION)
(defmodule RECOVERY)

(deffacts MAIN::control-information
   (phase-sequence DETECTION ISOLATION RECOVERY))

(defrule MAIN::change-phase
   ?list <- (phase-sequence ?next-phase
                               $?other-phases)
   =>
   (focus ?next-phase)
   (retract ?list)
   (assert (phase-sequence ?other-phases
                             ?next-phase)))
```

Control of execution will be cycled from the DETECTION module to the ISOLATION module to the RECOVERY module, and back again. All the rules in each module would fire before allowing the rules in the next module to fire (unless a return command was issued or a new module was focused on as a result of the auto-focus feature).

```
CLIPS> (unwatch all) ↵
CLIPS> (reset) ↵
CLIPS> (watch rules) ↵
CLIPS> (watch focus) ↵
CLIPS> (run 5) ↵
FIRE     1 change-phase: f-1
==> Focus DETECTION from MAIN
<== Focus DETECTION to MAIN
FIRE     2 change-phase: f-2
==> Focus ISOLATION from MAIN
<== Focus ISOLATION to MAIN
FIRE     3 change-phase: f-3
==> Focus RECOVERY from MAIN
<== Focus RECOVERY to MAIN
FIRE     4 change-phase: f-4
==> Focus DETECTION from MAIN
<== Focus DETECTION to MAIN
FIRE     5 change-phase: f-5
==> Focus ISOLATION from MAIN
<== Focus ISOLATION to MAIN
CLIPS>
```

10.9 SUMMARY

This chapter introduced various CLIPS features to assist in the development of robust expert systems. Deftemplate attributes permit enforcement of type and value constraints, which can prevent typographic as well as semantic errors. Constraint checking can be performed statically (when expressions or constructs are defined) or dynamically (when expressions are evaluated). The type attribute allows the legal types allowed for a slot to be constrained. The allowed value attributes allow the legal values of a slot to be restricted to a specified list. The range attribute allows numeric values to be restricted to a specified range. The cardinality attribute allows the minimum and maximum number of fields stored in a multifield slot to be restricted. Two other deftemplate attributes, the default and default-dynamic attributes, don't constrain slot values but allow the initial value of a deftemplate slot to be specified.

Salience provides a mechanism for even more complex control structures. It is used to prioritize rules such that the activated rule with the highest salience is fired first. Salience can be combined with control facts in order to separate expert knowledge from control knowledge.

The defmodule construct allows a knowledge base to be partitioned. By explicitly stating which deftemplates are imported from and exported to other modules, a module can control which facts are visible to it. Using the focus command, the execution of a program can be controlled without the use of salience by partitioning rules into groups and placing them in separate modules.

PROBLEMS

10.1 Modify the Sticks program in Chapter 9 so the control rules are separated from the rules of playing the game. Use salience to give the control rules lower priority.

10.2 Add a rule to the blocks world program in Section 8.6 on page 371 that would remove a move goal if it has already been satisfied.

10.3 Create rules for implementing the decision procedure for determining whether a syllogism is valid. Test your program on the syllogism from Problem 9.9 on page 433.

10.4 Write a program to determine the prime factors of a number. For example, the prime factors of 15 are 3 and 5.

10.5 Given the following distances between cities in Texas, solve the travelling salesman problem (page 43 in Section 1.13) for the cities. Write a program that finds the shortest route that visits all the cities. The input to the program should be the starting city and the list of cities to be visited. To test your program, determine the shortest route, beginning in Houston.

	Houston	Dallas	Austin	Abilene	Waco
Houston	—	241	162	351	183
Dallas	241	—	202	186	97
Austin	162	202	—	216	106
Abilene	351	186	216	—	186
Waco	183	97	106	186	—

10.6 Given the following information, write a program that will ask for the type of clouds visible and the wind direction, and then give a forecast for the chances of rain.

Cumulus clouds indicate good weather, but they may change to nimbostratus clouds if the wind blows from the northeast to the south. Cirrocumulus clouds indicate rain within a day if the wind direction is northeast to south. If the wind blows north to west, then overcast skies are predicted. Stratocumulus clouds may change to cumulonimbus clouds if the wind direction is northeast to south. Stratus clouds indicate a light drizzle. If the wind blows from the northeast to the south, then a long rain may occur. Nimbostratus clouds indicate a short rain if wind direction is southwest to north. A long rain is indicated if the wind blows from the northeast to the south. Cumulonimbus clouds indicate showers if they are visible before noon. Cirrostratus clouds indicate rain within 15 to 24 hours if the wind direction is northeast to south. Altostratus clouds indicate rain within a day if winds are northeast to south, otherwise the skies will be overcast. Altocumulus clouds indicate rain within 15 to 20 hours if winds are from northeast to south.

10.7 Write a program to convert a Morse code message to its equivalent series of alphabetic characters. Look first at the examples of input and output to the program (where the * and – are dots and dashes and the character / is used to delimit the Morse code characters).

```
Enter a message (<CR> to end): * * * / - - - / * * *↵
The message is S O S
Enter a message (<CR> to end): ↵
CLIPS>
```

The codes and their character equivalents are the following:

A	* —	H	* * * *	O	— — —	V	* * * —
B	— * * *	I	* *	P	* — — *	W	* — —
C	— * — *	J	* — — —	Q	— — * —	X	— * * —
D	— * *	K	— * —	R	* — *	Y	— * — —
E	*	L	* — * *	S	* * *	Z	— — * *
F	* * — *	M	— —	T	—		
G	— — *	N	— *	U	* * —		

10.8 Write a program that when given an expression consisting of numbers and units, will convert the units in the expression into a set of base units (such as meters, seconds, kilograms, pennies, and amps). The following are examples of input and output to the program.

```
Enter an expression (<CR> to end): 30 meters / minute↵
Conversion is 0.5 m / s
Enter an expression (<CR> to end): ↵
CLIPS>
```

10.9 Write a program for playing Life (a common program that simulates cellular automata). Given a two-dimensional array of cells in which each cell is either dead or alive, the values for the next generation of cells are based on the following rules. Any living cell that is adjacent to exactly two or three other living cells continues to live. Any living cell that is adjacent to any less than two or any greater than three other living cells will die. Any dead cell that is adjacent to exactly three other living cells comes to life. For example, if the first generation was a five-by-five array with the live cells filled with dots as shown, then the next generation would appear as follows:

Using the initial configuration shown previously, compute the next four generations.

10.10   A quadrilateral is a four-sided figure. A quadrilateral is a kite if it has two distinct pairs of consecutive sides of the same length. A quadrilateral is a trapezoid if it has at least one pair of parallel sides. A quadrilateral is a parallelogram if both pairs of its opposite sides are parallel. A quadrilateral is a rhombus if its four sides are equal in length. A quadrilateral is a rectangle if it has four right angles. A quadrilateral is a square if it has four equal sides and four right angles. Note that a rhombus is a kite and a parallelogram, a parallelogram is a trapezoid, a rectangle is a parallelogram, and a square is a rhombus and a rectangle.

Write a program which, when given the four points forming a quadrilateral will determine the type of quadrilateral. The program should account for possible roundoff error (assume that two sides are equal if the difference between their lengths is less than .00001). Test your program with the following quadrilaterals:

(a)   Points (0,0), (2,4), (6,0), and (3,2).

(b)   Points (0,3), (2,5), (4,3), and (2,0).

(c)   Points (0,0), (3,2), (4,2), and (9,0).

(d)   Points (0,0), (1,3), (5,3), and (4,0).

(e)   Points (0,0), (3,5.196152), (9,5.196152), and (6,0).

(f)   Points (0,0), (0,4), (2,4), and (2,0).

(g)   Points (0,2), (4,6), (6,4), and (2,0).

(h)   Points (0,2), (2,4), (4,2), and (2,0).

Hint: If side 1 contains the points $(x1,y1)$ and $(x2,y2)$ and side 2 contains the points $(x3,y3)$ and $(x4,y4)$, then side 1 is parallel to side 2 if $(x2 - x1) * (y4 - y3)$ is equal to $(x4 - x3) * (y2 - y1)$.

10.11   Write a CLIPS program that can determine if a simple sentence is grammatically correct. The sentence should use the following BNF.

```
<sentence> ::= <verb> <direct-object>
                           [<indirect-object>]
<direct-object> ::= [<determiner>] <adjective>* <noun>
<indirect-object> ::= <preposition> <direct-object>
<determiner> ::= a | an | the
<adjective> ::= red | shiny | heavy
<noun> ::= ball | wrench | gun | pliers
<preposition> ::= with | in | at
<verb> ::= get | throw | shoot
```

For example:

```
Enter a sentence (<CR> to end): shoot the red shiny gun
at the pliers⏎
OK
Enter a sentence (<CR> to end): gun shoot⏎
I don't understand.
Enter a sentence (<CR> to end):
CLIPS>
```

10.12   Modify the program developed for Problem 9-18 on page 435 so that if none of the shrubs meet all requirements, the shrubs meeting the most requirements are listed. The number of requirements satisfied should be printed.

10.13   Given a number of generators supplying power and a number of devices consuming power, write a program to attach devices to generators that minimizes the number of generators used and the amount of unused power for each generator used. For example, if there are four generators supplying 5, 6, 7, and 10 watts of power and four devices consuming 4, 5, 6, and 7 watts of power, attaching the 5-watt device to the 5-watt generator, the 7-watt device to the 7-watt generator, and the 4- and 6-watt devices to the 10-watt generator would minimize both the number of generators used and the unused power. The input and output of the program can be a series of facts. Test your program with the example above and also for the case using the same generators as above but with devices consuming 1, 3, 4, 5, and 9 watts of power.

10.14   Write a program that functions like the operating system of a computer and determines suitable locations in memory to load applications with fixed amounts of memory allocated to them. The input to the program will be a series of facts such as the following:

```
(launch (application word-processor) (memory-needed 2))
(launch (application spreadsheet) (memory-needed 6))
(launch (application game) (memory-needed 1))
(terminate (application word-processor))
(launch (application game) (memory-needed 1))
(terminate (application spreadsheet))
(terminate (application game))
```

Assume the computer has eight megabytes of memory and that the number of megabytes required by an application is an integer. If an exact fit in memory exists for an application, it should be used. For example, if there were two blocks of free memory, one of six megabytes and another of four megabytes, and an application was launched that required four megabytes, then the application should be placed in the four-megabyte free block rather than the six-megabyte free block. When a launch or terminate command is processed, a message should be printed. If there is not a large enough memory block to launch a program, then a message to this effect should be printed. Test your program by asserting the preceding facts and issuing a *run* command after each fact is asserted. The output should be similar to the following:

```
Application word-processor memory location is 1 to 2.
Application spreadsheet memory location is 3 to 8.
Unable to launch application game.
Terminating word-processor.
Application game memory location is 1 to 1.
Terminating spreadsheet.
Terminating game.
```

10.15   Develop a text menu interface that is self-contained within a module and is suitable for reuse in other programs. The menu items should be represented as facts. Two types of actions should be supported for menu items. One is to quit execution of the program. If this item type is selected, the program should halt execution. The other is to assert a fact and focus on a specific module. For this action, the menu-item facts should contain slots that specify the focus module and fact value to be asserted when the item is selected. For example, in the following dialog the result of selecting "Option A" would be to focus on module A and assert the fact (menu-select (value option-a)) where A and *option-a* are the values specified in the *menu-item* fact. Module A contains a rule that matches on the *menu-select* fact causing the "Executing Option A" message to be printed.

```
CLIPS> (run)
Select one of the following options:

     1 -- Option A
     2 -- Option B
     9 -- Quit Program

Your choice: 1

Executing Option A

Select one of the following options:

     1 -- Option A
     2 -- Option B
     9 -- Quit Program

Your choice: 9
CLIPS>
```

10.16   Modify the program developed for Problem 9-19 on page 435 so that the separate modules are used to print the information of all stars having the specified spectral class, all stars having the specified magnitude, and all stars matching both the spectral class and magnitude along with their distance from Earth in light-years.

10.17   Modify the program developed for Problem 9-21 on page 435 to use modules. If no matching gem can be found for the specified color, hardness, and density, the program should indicate this. After identifying a gem, the program should provide the user an opportunity to identify another gem.

10.18   The table below lists available courses at a high school, the name of the instructor, and the class periods during which the course is available. Given as input a fact indicating a class to be scheduled and preferences indicating the instructors and periods that are preferred and not preferred, write a program that suggests an appropriate instructor and period in which to take the class. To determine the "best" instructor and period, score each possible candidate as follows: the starting score is zero; a preferred instructor or period each adds one point to the score; an instructor or period that is not preferred each subtracts one point from the score; no preference for an instructor or period leaves the score unchanged; the instructor and period with the highest score is the "best."

Course	Instructor	Periods Offered
Algebra	Jones	1, 2, 3
Algebra	Smith	3, 4, 5, 6
American History	Vale	5
American History	Hill	1, 2
Art	Jenkins	1, 3, 5
Biology	Dolby	1, 2, 5
Chemistry	Dolby	3, 6
Chemistry	Vinson	6
French	Blake	2, 4
Geology	Vinson	1
Geometry	Jones	5, 6
Geometry	Smith	1
German	Blake	5
Literature	Henning	2, 3, 4, 5, 6
Literature	Davis	1, 2, 3, 4, 5
Music	Jenkins	2, 4
Physical Education	Mack	1, 2, 3, 4, 5
Physical Education	King	1, 2, 3, 4, 6
Physical Education	Simpson	2, 3, 4, 5, 6
Physics	Vinson	2, 3, 5
Spanish	Blake	1, 3
Texas History	Vale	2, 3, 4
Texas History	Hill	5, 6
World History	Vale	2, 3, 4
World History	Hill	4

CHAPTER 11

Efficiency in Rule-Based Languages

11.1 INTRODUCTION

This chapter provides many techniques for increasing the efficiency of a rule-based expert system that uses the Rete Pattern-Matching Algorithm. The reasons for needing an efficient pattern-matching algorithm will be discussed before the Rete Algorithm is explained. Several techniques for writing rules more efficiently will also be discussed.

11.2 THE RETE PATTERN-MATCHING ALGORITHM

Rule-based languages such as CLIPS, ART, OPS5, and OPS83 use a very efficient algorithm for matching facts against the patterns in rules to determine which rules have had their conditions satisfied. This algorithm is called the ***Rete Pattern-Matching Algorithm*** (Forgy 79; Forgy 85; Brownston 85). Writing efficient CLIPS rules does not require an understanding of the Rete Algorithm. However, an understanding of the underlying algorithm used in CLIPS and other rule-based languages makes it easier to understand why writing rules one way is more efficient than writing them another way.

To understand why the Rete Algorithm is efficient, it is helpful to look at the problem of matching facts to rules in general and then to examine other algorithms that are not as efficient. Figure 11.1 shows the problem addressed by the Rete Algorithm.

If the matching process only has to occur once, then the solution to the problem is straightforward. The inference engine can examine each rule and then search the set of facts to determine whether the rule's patterns have been satisfied. If the rule's patterns have been satisfied, then the rule can be placed on the agenda. Figure 11.2 shows this approach.

In rule-based languages, however, the matching process takes place repeatedly. Normally the fact list will be modified during each cycle of execution. New facts may be added to the fact list or old facts may be removed from it. These changes may cause previously unsatisfied patterns to be satisfied or vice versa. The problem of matching now becomes an ongoing process. During each cycle, as facts are added and removed the set of rules satisfied must be maintained and updated.

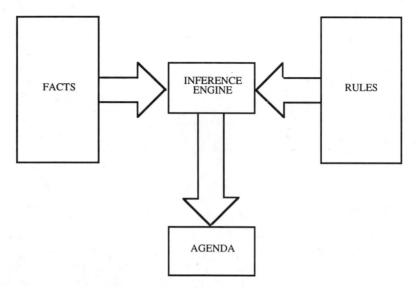

Figure 11.1 Pattern Matching: Rules and Facts

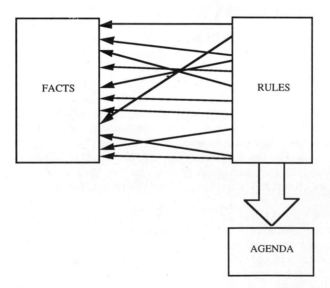

Figure 11.2 Rules Searching for Facts

Having the inference engine check each rule to direct the search for facts after each cycle of execution provides a simple and straightforward technique for solving this problem. The primary disadvantage of such an approach is that it can be very slow. Most rule-based expert systems exhibit a property called ***temporal redundancy***. Typically, the actions of a rule will only change a few facts in the fact list. That is, the facts in the expert system change slowly over time. Each cycle of execution may see only a small percentage of facts either added or removed and so only a small percentage of rules are typically affected by the changes in the fact list. Thus, having the rules drive the search for needed facts requires a lot of unnecessary computation, since most of the rules are likely to find the same facts in the current cycle as were found in the last cycle. The inefficiency of this approach is shown in Figure 11.3. The shaded area represents the changes that have been made to the fact list. Unnecessary recomputation could be avoided by remembering what has already been matched from cycle to cycle and then computing only the changes necessary for the newly added or newly removed facts, as shown in Figure 11.4. The rules remain static and the facts change, so the facts should find the rules, and not the other way around.

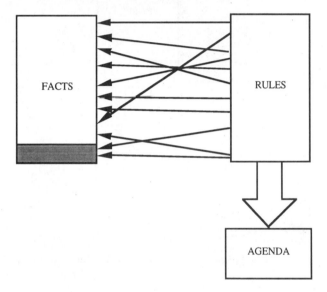

Figure 11.3 Unnecessary Computations When Rules Search for Facts

The Rete Pattern-Matching Algorithm is designed to take advantage of the temporal redundancy exhibited by rule-based expert systems. It does so by saving the state of the matching process from cycle to cycle and recomputing the changes in this state only for the changes that occur in the fact list. That is, if a set of patterns finds two of three required facts in one cycle, it is not necessary for a check to be made in the next cycle for the two facts that have already been found—only the third fact is of interest. The state of the matching process is updated only as facts are added and removed. If the number of facts added and removed is small compared to the total number of facts and patterns, the process of matching will proceed quickly. As a worst case, if all the facts were to be changed, then the matching process would work as if all the facts were to be compared against all the patterns.

If only updates to the fact list are processed, then each rule must remember what has already matched it. That is, if a new fact has matched the third pattern of a rule, information about the matches for the first two patterns must be available to finish the matching process. This type of state information indicating the facts that have matched previous patterns in a rule is called a ***partial match***. A partial match for a rule is any set of facts that satisfy the rule's patterns, beginning with the first pattern of the rule and ending with any pattern up to and including the last. Thus, a rule with three patterns would have partial matches for the first pattern, the first and second patterns, and the first, second, and third patterns. A partial match of all of the patterns of a rule will also be an activation. The other type of state information saved is called a ***pattern match***. A pattern match occurs when a fact has satisfied a single pattern in any rule without regard to variables in other patterns that may restrict the matching process.

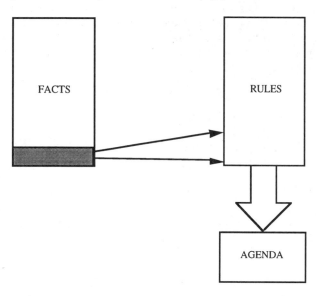

Figure 11.4 Facts Searching for Rules

The primary disadvantage of the Rete Pattern-Matching Algorithm is that it is memory intensive. Simply comparing all the facts to all the patterns requires no memory. Saving the state of the system using pattern matches and partial matches can consume considerable amounts of memory. In general, this tradeoff of memory for speed is worthwhile, however, it is important to remember that a poorly written rule cannot only run slowly, it can use up considerable amounts of memory.

The Rete Algorithm also improves the efficiency of rule-based systems by taking advantage of **structural similarity** in the rules. *Structural similarity* refers to the fact that many rules often contain similar patterns or groups of patterns. The Rete Algorithm uses this feature to increase efficiency by pooling common components so they don't have to be computed more than once.

11.3 THE PATTERN NETWORK

The problem of matching facts to rules can be divided into two steps. First, when facts are added and removed, it must be determined which patterns have been matched. Second, comparison of variable bindings across patterns must be checked to determine the partial matches for a group of patterns.

The process of determining which facts have matched which patterns is performed in the **pattern network**. For brevity we will limit the explanation of pattern matching to single-field slots of deftemplate facts. All matching that does not involve comparison against variables bound in other patterns can be performed in the pattern network. The pattern network is structured like a tree, in which the first slot constraint of all the patterns are the nodes connected to the root of the tree, the second slot constraints of all of the patterns are the nodes connected to those nodes, and so on. The last slot constraints in a pattern are the leaves of the tree. The nodes in the pattern network are called ***one-input nodes*** because each only receives information from the node above it. Nodes in the pattern network are sometimes referred to as ***pattern nodes***. The leaf nodes are also referred to as ***terminal nodes***. Each pattern node contains a specification used for determining whether the slot value of a fact has matched the slot constraint of a pattern. For example, the pattern

```
(data (x 27))
```

would be represented by one node since there is only one slot constraint. The matching specification for the first node would then be the following.

```
The slot x value is equal to the constant 27
```

Actually, determining whether the fact has the appropriate relation name for the pattern also must be checked (e.g., you don't want *foobar* facts to be matching *data* patterns just because they have the same slot names). To perform this test CLIPS maintains separate pattern networks for each deftemplate so the relation name check is performed as the fact is created, but before pattern matching occurs.

Matching specifications include all the information for matching a single slot. Several tests can be performed together. For example, the pattern

```
(data (x ~red&~green))
```

would generate the following matching specification for the *x* slot:

```
The slot x value is not equal to the constant red
            and is not equal to the constant green
```

Normally variable bindings are not checked in the pattern network unless the variable is used more than once in the pattern. For example, the pattern

```
(data (x ?x) (y ?y) (z ?x))
```

would not generate match specifications for either the *x* slot or the *y* slot since the first binding of a variable to a slot value has no effect on whether the pattern is matched by the fact. However, the *z* slot must have the same value as the *x* slot, so the match specification for the *z* slot would be the following:

```
The z slot value is equal to the x slot value
```

Expressions containing variables that are all found within the pattern can be checked within the pattern network. For example, the pattern

```
(data (x ?x&:(> ?x ?y)))
```

would not generate a match specification for the x slot because the variable ?y is not contained within the pattern (assuming, of course, that the variable ?y is defined in a previous pattern). However, the x slot in the pattern

```
(data (x ?x&:(> ?x 4)))
```

would have the match specification

```
The x slot value is greater than the constant 4
```

since the only variable found in the expression, *?x*, is also contained within the pattern.

As stated previously, the pattern network is arranged hierarchically, with the pattern nodes corresponding to the first slot constraints of the patterns at the top. When a fact is asserted the pattern nodes for the first slot constraints in the pattern network are checked. Any pattern node whose matching specification is satisfied will activate the pattern nodes directly below it. This process continues until a terminal node in the pattern network has been reached. The terminal nodes in the pattern network represent the end of a pattern and a successful pattern match. Each terminal node has an **alpha** or **right memory** associated with it. The alpha memory contains the set of all facts that have matched the pattern associated with the terminal node. In other words, the alpha memory stores the set of pattern matches for a particular pattern.

The pattern network takes advantage of structural similarity by sharing common pattern nodes among patterns. Since the pattern nodes are stored hierarchically, two patterns can share their first *N* pattern nodes if the match specifications for their first *N* slot constraints are identical. For example, the patterns

```
(data (x red) (y green))
(data (x red) (y blue))
```

can share common pattern nodes for the *x* slot. Notice that it is the match specifications that must be identical, and not necessarily the slot constraints found in the pattern. For example, the patterns

```
(data (x ?x) (y ?x))
(data (x ?y) (y ?y))
```

can share the pattern node for the *y* slot even though the variables used in the two patterns are different. The *x* slots don't generate a match specification and so are ignored for sharing purposes. However, switching the order of the slots to

```
(data (x ?x) (y ?x))
(data (y ?y) (x ?y))
```

would prevent the patterns from sharing nodes since the first pattern would generate a match specification for the *y* slot and the second pattern would generate a match specification for the *x* slot.

Figure 11.5 shows the pattern network generated by the following rules:

```
(defrule Rete-rule-1
  (match (a red))
  (data (x ?x) (y ?x))
  =>)
```

```
(defrule Rete-rule-2
  (match (a ?x) (b red))
  (data (x ~green) (y ?x))
  (data (x ?x) (y ?x))
  =>)
```

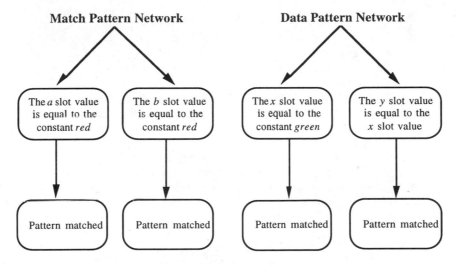

Figure 11.5 Pattern Network for Two Rules

11.4 THE JOIN NETWORK

Once it has been determined which patterns have been matched by facts, comparison of variable bindings across patterns must be checked to insure that variables used in more than one pattern have consistent values. This comparison is performed in the **join network**. Each terminal node in the pattern network acts as an input to a **join**, or **two-input node**, in the join network. Each join contains a matching specification for the matches of the alpha memory associated with its terminal node and for the set of partial matches that have matched previous patterns. The partial matches for previous patterns are stored in the **beta** or **left memory** of the join. A rule with N patterns would then have $N - 1$ joins (although CLIPS actually uses N joins to simplify the Rete algorithm, thus allowing each join to be entered by only one pattern).

The first join compares the first two patterns and the remaining joins compare an additional pattern to the partial matches of the previous join. For example, given the rule *Rete-rule-2* used in the previous example,

```
(defrule Rete-rule-2
  (match (a ?x) (b red))
  (data (x ~green) (y ?x))
  (data (x ?x) (y ?x))
  =>)
```

the first join would contain the match specification

```
The a slot value of the fact
    bound to the first pattern is equal to
the y slot value of the fact
    bound to the second pattern.
```

The second join would receive as input the set of partial matches from the first join and it would contain the following match specification:

```
The x slot value of the fact
    bound to the third pattern is equal to
the y slot value of the fact
    bound to the second pattern.
```

Notice that the variable *?x* in the third pattern could have its value compared to the variable *?x* in the first pattern instead of variable *?x* in the second pattern. The second occurrence of *?x* in the third pattern does not have to be checked in the join network since it can be checked in the pattern network. The pattern and join networks for rule *Rete-rule-2* are shown in Figure 11.6.

The join network takes advantage of structural similarity by sharing joins between rules. Joins in the join network can be shared by two rules if they have identical patterns and join comparisons for two or more patterns, starting with the first pattern. For example, these rules

```
(defrule sharing-1
    (match (a ?x) (b red))
    (data (x ~green) (y ?x))
    (data (x ?x) (y ?x))
    (other (q ?z))
    =>)

(defrule sharing-2
    (match (a ?y) (b red))
    (data (x ~green) (y ?y))
    (data (x ?y) (y ?y))
    (other (q ?y))
    =>)
```

could share all of their patterns in the pattern network and the joins created for their first three patterns in the join network. The join for the fourth pattern cannot be shared in the join network because the match specifications for the two rules are different. The match specification for the fourth pattern of rule *sharing-1* does not have to perform any comparisons because the variable *?z* is not used in other patterns. However, the match specification for the fourth pattern of rule *sharing-2* must compare the variable *?y* to the variable *?y* in another pattern to insure that the variable bindings are consistent. Notice again that the variable names do not have to be identical to take advantage of structural similarity. All that matters is that the match specifications be identical.

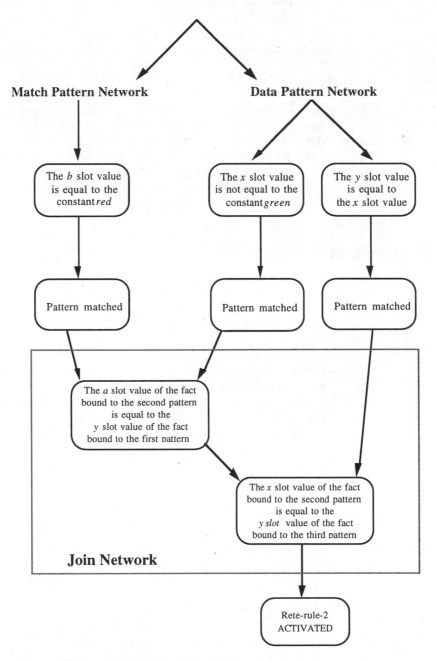

Figure 11.6 Pattern and Join Networks for Rule *Rete-rule-2*

CLIPS provides useful information about join sharing if the *watch compilations* command has been issued. For example, the following commands illustrate how information about sharing is displayed. Assume that rules *sharing-1* and and *sharing-2* are in the file "rules.clp."

```
CLIPS> (watch compilations) ↵
CLIPS> (load "rules.clp") ↵
Defining defrule: sharing-1 +j+j+j+j
Defining defrule: sharing-2 =j=j=j+j
TRUE
CLIPS>
```

The *+j* in the output indicates that a join is being added, whereas *=j* indicates that a join is being shared. Thus when rule *sharing-1* is added four new joins are created. When rule *sharing-2* is added, it shares its first three joins with rule *sharing-1* and creates a new join for its last pattern. Notice that CLIPS has used four joins to represent the rule, as opposed to the three joins that would normally be required. For implementation reasons it is convenient to have only one pattern per join; so instead of using one join for the first two patterns, CLIPS uses two joins.

11.5 THE IMPORTANCE OF PATTERN ORDER

Programmers new to rule-based languages often have misconceptions about the importance of ordering the patterns in rules correctly for both speed and memory efficiency. Since the Rete Algorithm saves the state from one cycle to the next, it is very important to make sure that rules do not generate large numbers of partial matches. For example, consider the following simple program:

```
(deffacts information
   (find-match a c e g)
   (item a)
   (item b)
   (item c)
   (item d)
   (item e)
   (item f)
   (item g))

(defrule match-1
   (find-match ?x ?y ?z ?w)
   (item ?x)
   (item ?y)
   (item ?z)
   (item ?w)
   =>
   (assert (found-match ?x ?y ?z ?w)))
```

This program will reset very quickly. A *watch facts* command followed by a *reset* command will verify this. Now consider the following program:

```
(deffacts information
   (find-match a c e g)
   (item a)
   (item b)
```

```
                (item c)
                (item d)
                (item e)
                (item f)
                (item g))

        (defrule match-2
            (item ?x)
            (item ?y)
            (item ?z)
            (item ?w)
            (find-match ?x ?y ?z ?w)
            =>
            (assert (found-match ?x ?y ?z ?w)))
```

A *watch facts* command followed by a *reset* command for this program will demonstrate a considerably slower reset time. As the reset is performed, the first few facts in the deffacts construct will be asserted quickly. Subsequent facts will require an increasingly longer time to be asserted. Rules *match-1* and *match-2* each have the same patterns, but rule *match-2* takes much longer to reset. In fact, on some computers rule *match-2* may may cause CLIPS to run out of memory. An even greater difference in speed can be demonstrated by adding more item facts to the *information* deffacts (in fact, on some computers it may be necessary to add additional *item* facts to the *information* deffacts in order to see a noticeable difference).

Counting for Rule *match-1*

Counting the pattern matches and partial matches for rule *match-1* provides useful information. The fact ids will be used instead of the entire fact in listing the pattern and partial matches. In addition, partial matches will be enclosed in braces. The fact ids are as follows:

```
        f-1 (find-match a c e g)
        f-2 (item a)
        f-3 (item b)
        f-4 (item c)
        f-5 (item d)
        f-6 (item e)
        f-7 (item f)
        f-8 (item g)
```

Rule *match-1* has the following pattern matches:

```
        Pattern 1: f-1
        Pattern 2: f-2, f-3, f-4, f-5, f-6, f-7, f-8
        Pattern 3: f-2, f-3, f-4, f-5, f-6, f-7, f-8
        Pattern 4: f-2, f-3, f-4, f-5, f-6, f-7, f-8
        Pattern 5: f-2, f-3, f-4, f-5, f-6, f-7, f-8
```

Rule *match-1* has the following partial matches:

```
Pattern   1:   [f-1]
Patterns 1-2: [f-1,f-2]
Pattern  1-3: [f-1,f-2,f-4]
Pattern  1-4: [f-1,f-2,f-4,f-6]
Pattern  1-5: [f-1,f-2,f-4,f-6,f-8]
```

Rule *match-1* has a total of 29 pattern matches and 5 partial matches.

Counting for Rule *match-2*

Rule *match-2* has the following pattern matches:

```
Pattern 1: f-2, f-3, f-4, f-5, f-6, f-7, f-8
Pattern 2: f-2, f-3, f-4, f-5, f-6, f-7, f-8
Pattern 3: f-2, f-3, f-4, f-5, f-6, f-7, f-8
Pattern 4: f-2, f-3, f-4, f-5, f-6, f-7, f-8
Pattern 5: f-1
```

Rules *match-1* and *match-2* have the same number of pattern matches. Now consider only the partial matches for pattern 1:

```
[f-2],[f-3],[f-4],[f-5],[f-6],[f-7],[f-8]
```

Pattern 1 has seven partial matches. This is no surprise since the partial and pattern matches will be the same for the first pattern. The partial matches for patterns 1 and 2, however, are numerous.

```
[f-2,f-2],[f-2,f-3],[f-2,f-4],[f-2,f-5],
          [f-2,f-6],[f-2,f-7],[f-2,f-8],
[f-3,f-2],[f-3,f-3],[f-3,f-4],[f-3,f-5],
          [f-3,f-6],[f-3,f-7],[f-3,f-8],
[f-4,f-2],[f-4,f-3],[f-4,f-4],[f-4,f-5],
          [f-4,f-6],[f-4,f-7],[f-4,f-8],
[f-5,f-2],[f-5,f-3],[f-5,f-4],[f-5,f-5],
          [f-5,f-6],[f-5,f-7],[f-5,f-8],
[f-6,f-2],[f-6,f-3],[f-6,f-4],[f-6,f-5],
          [f-6,f-6],[f-6,f-7],[f-6,f-8],
[f-7,f-2],[f-7,f-3],[f-7,f-4],[f-7,f-5],
          [f-7,f-6],[f-7,f-7],[f-7,f-8],
[f-8,f-2],[f-8,f-3],[f-8,f-4],[f-8,f-5],
          [f-8,f-6],[f-8,f-7],[f-8,f-8]
```

In all there are forty-nine partial matches for patterns 1 and 2 (seven pattern matches for pattern 1 multiplied by seven pattern matches for pattern 2). Space will quickly limit the partial matches that can be listed for the other patterns since there will be 343 partial matches for patterns 1 through 3 and 2401 partial matches for patterns 1 through 4. Just as for rule *match-1*, only one partial match exists for patterns 1 through 5.

```
[f-2,f-4,f-6,f-8,f-1]
```

Notice that although the numbers of pattern matches and activations are the same for rules *match-1* and *match-2*, rule *match-1* has only five partial matches, whereas rule *match-2* has 2801 partial matches, a difference that will continue to grow as more item facts are added. The fact (item h) will create no new partial matches for rule *match-1*; however, it will create 1880 new partial matches for rule *match-2*. This example demonstrates that the number of partial matches created can drastically affect the performance of a program. An efficient set of rules should attempt to minimize not only the creation of new partial matches but the deletion of old partial matches as well. In effect, an attempt should be made to minimize the change of state of the system from one cycle to the next. Specific techniques for minimizing the change of state will be discussed later in this chapter.

The Matches Command

CLIPS has a debugging command called **matches** that will display the pattern matches, partial matches, and activations of a rule. This command is useful for finding rules that generate large numbers of partial matches and for debugging cases in which a rule appears to have all of its patterns satisfied but is nonetheless not activated. The syntax of the *matches* command is

```
(matches <rule-name>)
```

The argument of the *matches* command is the name of the rule for which matches are displayed. The following dialog illustrates the output of the *matches* command:

```
CLIPS> (clear) ↵
CLIPS>
(defrule match-3
   (find-match ?x ?y)
   (item ?x)
   (item ?y)
   =>
   (assert (found-match ?x ?y))) ↵
CLIPS>
(assert (find-match a b)
        (find-match c d)
        (find-match e f)
        (item a)
        (item b)
        (item c)
        (item f)) ↵
<Fact-6>
CLIPS> (facts) ↵
f-0     (find-match a b)
f-1     (find-match c d)
f-2     (find-match e f)
f-3     (item a)
f-4     (item b)
f-5     (item c)
```

```
f-6       (item f)
For a total of 7 facts.
CLIPS> (matches match-3) ↵
Matches for Pattern 1
f-0
f-1
f-2
Matches for Pattern 2
f-3
f-4
f-5
f-6
Matches for Pattern 3
f-3
f-4
f-5
f-6
Partial matches for CEs 1 - 2
f-1,f-5
f-0,f-3
Partial matches for CEs 1 - 3
f-0,f-3,f-4
Activations
f-0,f-3,f-4
CLIPS>
```

The first pattern of rule *match-3* has three pattern matches, one for each *find-match* fact. Similarly, the second and third patterns both have four pattern matches, one for each *item* fact. The first two patterns have two partial matches: one for the facts (find-match c d) and (item c), and another for the facts (find-match c d) and (item c). There is no partial match associated with the fact (find-match e f) since the fact (item e) does not exist. There is only one partial match for all three patterns: the partial match for the facts (fact-match a b), (item a), and (item b). There is also an activation for this partial match. Once the *match-3* rule has fired for this activation it will no longer be displayed by the *matches* command.

Watching the Changing State

The *matches* command provides one useful way of examining partial matches for a rule. Another way to watch partial matches is to consider them partial activations of a rule. If rule *match-1* is considered several separate rules each trying to compute partial matches, the *watch activations* command can be used to see the partial matches as they are generated. The rule *match-1* can be split into several rules as follows:

```
(defrule m1-pm-1
        "Partial matches for pattern 1"
    (find-match ?x ?y ?z ?w)
    =>)
```

```
(defrule m1-pm-1-to-2
        "Partial matches for patterns 1 and 2"
   (find-match ?x ?y ?z ?w)
   (item ?x)
   =>)

(defrule m1-pm-1-to-3
        "Partial matches for patterns 1 to 3"
   (find-match ?x ?y ?z ?w)
   (item ?x)
   (item ?y)
   =>)

(defrule m1-pm-1-to-4
        "Partial matches for patterns 1 to 4"
   (find-match ?x ?y ?z ?w)
   (item ?x)
   (item ?y)
   (item ?z)
   =>)

(defrule match-1 "Activations for the match rule"
   (find-match ?x ?y ?z ?w)
   (item ?x)
   (item ?y)
   (item ?z)
   (item ?w)
   =>
   (assert (found-match ?x ?y ?z ?w)))
```

If the preceding rules and the *information* deffacts are loaded, the partial matches can be watched as they are created using the fol lowing command dialog:

```
CLIPS> (watch activations) ↵
CLIPS> (watch facts) ↵
CLIPS> (reset) ↵
==> f-0      (initial-fact)
==> f-1      (find-match a c e g)
==> Activation 0      m1-pm-1: f-1
==> f-2      (item a)
==> Activation 0      m1-pm-1-to-2: f-1,f-2
==> f-3      (item b)
==> f-4      (item c)
==> Activation 0      m1-pm-1-to-3: f-1,f-2,f-4
==> f-5      (item d)
==> f-6      (item e)
==> Activation 0      m1-pm-1-to-4: f-1,f-2,f-4,f-6
==> f-7      (item f)
==> f-8      (item g)
==> Activation 0      match-1: f-1,f-2,f-4,f-6,f-8
CLIPS>
```

Using this same technique for rule *matches-2* would produce hundreds of partial activations. It should be clear by now that the LHS of a rule cannot be considered as a whole for purposes of efficiency. Each LHS of a rule should be considered several separate rules, each producing a set of partial matches for the rule as a whole. Writing an efficient rule becomes a matter of limiting not just the total number of activations for a rule, but also the partial matches for each of the separate subrules that make up the LHS of the rule.

11.6 ORDERING PATTERNS FOR EFFICIENCY

Several guidelines should be kept in mind when ordering patterns to limit the number of partial matches that are made. Finding the best way to order patterns can be difficult because some guidelines may conflict with others. In general, the guidelines for ordering are used to avoid gross inefficiencies that may appear in a rule-based system. Fine-tuning an expert system can require considerable trial and error in reordering patterns to determine which changes make the system run faster. Often, trying a completely different approach rather than attempting the fine-tuning of patterns may yield much better results.

Most Specific Patterns Go First

The most specific pattern should be placed toward the front of the LHS of a rule. A specific pattern will generally have the smallest number of matching facts in the fact list and will have the largest number of variable bindings that constrain other patterns. The pattern (match ?x ?y ?z ?w) shown in rules *match-1* and *match-2* is specific because it constrains the facts allowed to generate partial matches for the four other patterns of the rule.

Patterns Matching Volatile Facts Go Last

Patterns matching against facts that are frequently added and removed from the fact list should be placed toward the end of the LHS of a rule. This causes the smallest number of changes in the partial matches for the rule. It is important to note that patterns matching volatile facts are often the most specific patterns in the rule. This can create a dilemma in trying to arrange the patterns of the rule for greatest efficiency. For example, it is generally advantageous to place control facts as the beginning pattern of a rule. If the control fact is not present, no partial matches will be generated for the rule. However, if control facts are being asserted and retracted quite frequently and a larger number of partial matches are constantly being recomputed, then it can be more efficient to place the control fact toward the end of a rule.

Patterns Matching the Fewest Facts Go First

Placing patterns that will match very few facts in the fact list near the front of the rule will reduce the number of partial matches that can be generated. Once again, use of this guideline may conflict with other guidelines. A pattern matching that matches very few facts is not necessarily the most specific pattern, or the facts matched by the pattern might be volatile.

11.7 MULTIFIELD VARIABLES AND EFFICIENCY

Multifield wildcards and multifield variables provide powerful pattern-matching capabilities. When used improperly, however, they can lead to inefficiency. Two rules should be applied to the use of multifield wildcards and variables. First, they should not be used unless needed. Second, when they are used, care should be taken to limit the number of multifield wildcards and variables in a single slot of a pattern. The following rule demonstrates that multifield wildcards and variables can be useful, but are also quite expensive:

```
(defrule produce-twoplets
   (list (items $?b $?m $?e))
   =>
   (assert (front ?b))
   (assert (middle ?m))
   (assert (back ?e)))
```

Given a fact such as (list (items a 4 z 2)), this rule will produce facts representing the front, middle, and back parts of the list. The lengths of the various parts will vary from zero to the length of the list. This rule is easy to state using multifield variables; however, it is an extremely expensive pattern-matching operation. Table 11.1 shows all of the matches that were attempted and also that multifield wildcards and variables can perform a great deal of work as part of the pattern-matching process. In general, for N fields contained in the *items* fact, $(N^2 + 3N + 2) / 2$ matches for the *produce-twoplets* rule will occur.

Match attempt	Fields matched by $?b	Fields matched by $?m	Fields matched by $?e
1			a 4 z 2
2		a	4 z 2
3		a 4	z 2
4		a 4 z	2
5		a 4 z 2	
6	a		4 z 2
7	a	4	z 2
8	a	4 z	2
9	a	4 z 2	
10	a 4		z 2
11	a 4	z	2
12	a 4	z 2	
13	a 4 z		2
14	a 4 z	2	
15	a 4 z 2		

Table 11.1 Matching Attempts for Three Multifield Variables

11.8 THE TEST CE AND EFFICIENCY

Any test conditional elements within a rule should be placed as close to the top of the rule as possible. For example, the following rule tests to find three distinct points:

```
(defrule three-distinct-points
   ?point-1 <- (point (x ?x1) (y ?y1))
   ?point-2 <- (point (x ?x2) (y ?y2))
   ?point-3 <- (point (x ?x3) (y ?y3))
   (test (and (neq ?point-1 ?point-2)
              (neq ?point-2 ?point-3)
              (neq ?point-1 ?point-3)))
   =>
   (assert (distinct-points (x1 ?x1) (y1 ?y1)
                            (x2 ?x2) (y2 ?y2)
                            (x3 ?x3) (y3 ?y3))))
```

The test CE that determines that the fact address ?point-1 is not the same as the fact address ?point-2 can be placed immediately after the second pattern. Placing the test CE at this point will reduce the number of partial matches created.

```
(defrule three-distinct-points
   ?point-1 <- (point (x ?x1) (y ?y1))
   ?point-2 <- (point (x ?x2) (y ?y2))
   (test (neq ?point-1 ?point-2))
   ?point-3 <- (point (x ?x3) (y ?y3))
   (test (and (neq ?point-2 ?point-3)
              (neq ?point-1 ?point-3)))
   =>
   (assert (distinct-points (x1 ?x1) (y1 ?y1)
                            (x2 ?x2) (y2 ?y2)
                            (x3 ?x3) (y3 ?y3))))
```

Test CEs on the LHS of a rule are always evaluated when partial matches are being generated in the join network. Expressions used with the predicate or equality field constraint may be evaluated during the pattern-matching process if certain conditions are met. Expression evaluation during the pattern-matching process in the pattern network yields greater efficiency. An expression used by the predicate or return value field constraints will be evaluated during the pattern-matching process if all variables referenced in the expression can be found within the enclosing pattern.

The expression in the following rule will be evaluated during the generation of partial matches because it is within a test CE:

```
(defrule points-share-common-x-or-y-value
   (point (x ?x1) (y ?y1))
   (point (x ?x2) (y ?y2))
   (test (or (= ?x1 ?x2) (= ?y1 ?y2)))
   =>
   (assert (common-x-or-y-value
              (x1 ?x1) (y1 ?y1)
              (x2 ?x2) (y2 ?y2))))
```

Placing the expression within the pattern does not cause evaluation during pattern matching because the variables *?x1* and *?y1* are not contained within the second pattern.

```
(defrule points-share-common-x-or-y-value
   (point (x ?x1) (y ?y1))
   (point (x ?x2) (y ?y2&:(or (= ?x1 ?x2)
                              (= ?y1 ?y2))))
   =>
   (assert (common-x-or-y-value
              (x1 ?x1) (y1 ?y1)
              (x2 ?x2) (y2 ?y2))))
```

Once again, the expression in the following rule will be evaluated during the generation of partial matches because it is within a test CE:

```
(defrule point-not-on-x-y-diagonals ""
   (point (x ?x1) (y ?y1))
   (test (and (<> ?x1 ?y1) (<> ?x1 (- 0 ?y1))))
   =>
   (assert (non-diagonal-point (x ?x1) (y ?y1))))
```

This time, however, placing the expression within the pattern allows it to be evaluated during pattern matching because the two variables *?x1* and *?y1* are both contained within the enclosing pattern of the expression:

```
(defrule point-not-on-x-y-diagonals
   (point (x ?x1)
          (y ?y1&:(and (<> ?x1 ?y1)
                       (<> ?x1 (- 0 ?y1)))))
   =>
   (assert (non-diagonal-point (x ?x1) (y ?y1))))
```

11.9 BUILT-IN PATTERN-MATCHING CONSTRAINTS

The built-in pattern-matching constraints are always more efficient than an equivalent expression that must be evaluated. For example, a rule such as

```
(defrule primary-color
   (color ?x&:(or (eq ?x red)
                  (eq ?x green)
                  (eq ?x blue)))
   =>
   (assert (primary-color ?x)))
```

should not be used when pattern-matching constraints can be used to accomplish the same results, as shown here:

```
(defrule primary-color
   (color ?x&red|green|blue)
   =>
   (assert (primary-color ?x)))
```

11.10 GENERAL RULES VERSUS SPECIFIC RULES

It is not always obvious whether many specific rules will perform more efficiently than fewer, more general rules. Specific rules tend to isolate much of the pattern-matching process in the pattern network, reducing the amount of work in the join network. General rules often provide more opportunity for sharing in the pattern and join networks. A single rule can also be more maintainable than a larger group of specific rules. General rules, though, need to be written carefully. Since they tend to perform the work of several rules, it is much easier to write an inefficient general rule than an inefficient specific rule. To illustrate the difference between the two techniques, consider the following deftemplate and four rules that will update a fact containing the grid coordinates of an object that can move north, south, east, or west. The location fact contains the x and y coordinates of the object. A move north increases the value of the y coordinate; a move east increases the value of the x coordinate.

```
(deftemplate location (slot x) (slot y))

(defrule move-north
   (move north)
   ?old-location <- (location (y ?old-y))
   =>
   (modify ?old-location (y (+ ?old-y 1))))

(defrule move-south
   (move south)
   ?old-location <- (location (y ?old-y))
   =>
   (modify ?old-location (y (- ?old-y 1))))

(defrule move-east
   (move east)
   ?old-location <- (location (x ?old-x))
   =>
   (modify ?old-location (x (+ ?old-x 1))))

(defrule move-west
   (move west)
   ?old-location <- (location (x ?old-x))
   =>
   (modify ?old-location (x (- ?old-x 1))))
```

The four previous rules can be replaced with a single more general rule, an additional deftemplate, and a deffacts construct:

```
(deftemplate direction
   (slot which-way)
   (slot delta-x)
   (slot delta-y))

(deffacts direction-information
   (direction (which-way north)
              (delta-x 0) (delta-y 1))
   (direction (which-way south)
              (delta-x 0) (delta-y -1))
   (direction (which-way east)
              (delta-x 1) (delta-y 0))
   (direction (which-way west)
              (delta-x -1) (delta-y 0)))

(defrule move-direction
   (move ?dir)
   (direction (which-way ?dir)
              (delta-x ?dx)
              (delta-y ?dy))
   ?old-location <- (location (x ?old-x)
                              (y ?old-y))
   =>
   (modify ?old-location (x (+ ?old-x ?dx))
                         (y (+ ?old-y ?dy)))))
```

The variables *?dx* and *?dy* are the delta *x* and delta *y* values, which need to be added to the *x* and *y* values of the old location to obtain the *x* and *y* values for the new location.

This new rule requires more work in creating partial matches to determine the delta *x* and delta *y* values to be added to the current location. However, it provides a level of abstraction that makes it simple to add more directions. To move northeast, southeast, northwest, and southwest would require the addition of four new specific rules. The general example requires only the addition of four new facts in the deffacts construct, as shown:

```
(deffacts direction-information
   (direction (which-way north)
              (delta-x 0) (delta-y 1))
   (direction (which-way south)
              (delta-x 0) (delta-y -1))
   (direction (which-way east)
              (delta-x 1) (delta-y 0))
   (direction (which-way west)
              (delta-x -1) (delta-y 0))
   (direction (which-way northeast)
              (delta-x 1) (delta-y 1))
   (direction (which-way southeast)
              (delta-x 1) (delta-y -1))
```

```
(direction (which-way northwest)
           (delta-x -1) (delta-y 1))
(direction (which-way southwest)
           (delta-x -1) (delta-y -1)))
```

11.11 PROCEDURAL FUNCTIONS

Occasionally it is useful (and more efficient) to perform some operations using a procedural programming paradigm rather than a rule-based programming paradigm. CLIPS provides some functions for controlling the flow of execution of actions on the RHS of a rule. Two of these are the *while* and *if* functions also found as control structures in modern high-level languages such as Ada, Pascal, and C. In addition, the *halt* function allows the execution of rules to be stopped from the RHS of a rule.

CLIPS is designed to be an efficient rule-based language. The *if* and *while* procedural functions are intended for judicious use only. Writing a lengthy procedural program on the RHS of a rule defeats the entire purpose of using a rule-based language. In general, the *if* and *while* functions should be used for performing simple tests and loops on the RHS of a rule. Complex nesting of *if* and *while* functions on the RHS of a rule should be avoided.

The *If* Function

The syntax of the *if* function is

```
(if <predicate-expression>
   then <expression>+
   [else <expression>+])
```

where <predicate-expression> is a single expression (such as a predicate function or variable) and the <expression>+ following the *if* and *then* keywords are the one or more expressions to be evaluated based on the return value of evaluating <predicate-expression>. Notice that the *else* clause is optional.

When an *if* function is evaluated, the condition represented by <predicate-expression> is first evaluated to determine whether the actions of the *then* clause or the *else* clause are executed. If the condition evaluates to any symbol other than FALSE, the actions in the *then* clause of the function are executed. If the condition evaluates to the symbol FALSE, the actions in the *else* clause are executed. If the *else* clause has not been included, then no action is taken on a false condition. Once the *if* function completes execution, CLIPS continues with the next action, if any, on the RHS.

The *if* function can be useful for checking values on the RHS of a rule instead of having other rules perform a test. For example, the following rule could be used to determine whether a program should continue:

```
(defrule continue-check
   ?phase <- (phase check-continue)
   =>
   (retract ?phase)
   (printout t "Continue? ")
   (bind ?answer (read))
```

```
(if (or (eq ?answer y) (eq ?answer yes))
   then (assert (phase continue))
   else (assert (phase halt))))
```

Notice that the *if* function is used to convert the user's yes or no response to a fact indicating the type of action to be taken. In this case the action is either to continue or to halt.

The return value of the *if* function is the last expression evaluated in either the *then* or the *else* portions of the function. If the <predicate-expression> evaluates to FALSE and there is no *then* portion, the symbol FALSE is returned.

The *While* Function

The syntax of the *while* function is

```
(while <predicate-expression> [do]
   <expression>*)
```

where <predicate-expression> is a single expression (such as a predicate function or variable) and the <expression>* following the optional *do* keyword are the zero or more expressions to be evaluated based on the return value of evaluating <predicate-expression>. These expressions comprise the **body** of the loop.

The part of the *while* function represented by <predicate-expression> is evaluated before the actions in the body are executed. If the <predicate-expression> evaluates to any value other than the symbol FALSE, the expressions in the body will be executed. If the <predicate-expression> evaluates to the symbol FALSE, execution continues with the next statement after the *while* function, if any. The condition of the *while* function will be checked each time the body is executed to determine whether it should be executed again.

The *while* function can be used with the *if* function to implement input error checking on the RHS of a rule. The following modification to the rule *continue-check* uses the *while* function to continue looping until an appropriate answer is received:

```
(defrule continue-check
   ?phase <- (phase check-continue)
   =>
   (retract ?phase)
   (printout t "Continue? ")
   (bind ?answer (read))
   (while (and (neq ?answer yes) (neq ?answer no))
      do
      (printout t "Continue? ")
      (bind ?answer (read)))
   (if (eq ?answer yes)
      then (assert (phase continue))
      else (assert (phase halt))))
```

The *Halt* Function

The *halt* function can be used on the RHS of a rule to stop the execution of rules on the agenda. It requires no arguments. When called, no further actions will be executed from the RHS of the rule being fired and control will return to the top level prompt. The agenda will contain any remaining rules that were activated when the *halt* function was called.

As an example, the *continue-check* rule could replace the action

```
(assert (phase halt))
```

with the following action

```
(halt)
```

which would stop the execution of rules.

The *halt* function is particularly useful for halting execution when the user intends to restart execution later using the *run* command. Consider the following modification to the *continue-check* rule:

```
(defrule continue-check
    ?phase <- (phase check-continue)
    =>
    (retract ?phase)
    (printout t "Continue? ")
    (bind ?answer (read))
    (while (and (neq ?answer yes) (neq ?answer no))
       do
       (printout t "Continue? ")
       (bind ?answer (read)))
    (assert (phase continue))
    (if (neq ?answer yes)
       then (halt)))
```

Notice that the rule asserts the fact (phase continue) regardless of the user's response to the continue question. Asserting this fact will place the appropriate rules on the agenda to continue execution. If the reply to the continue question was not yes, execution will be stopped by the *halt* function. The user could then examine the rules and facts, later restarting execution where it had left off by issuing a *run* command.

11.12 SIMPLE RULES VERSUS COMPLEX RULES

Rule-based languages allow many problems to be expressed in a simple yet elegant manner. Although not specifically designed for algorithmic or computational problems, CLIPS can easily be used to find the largest of a group of numbers. The following rule and associated deffacts will assert a group of sample numbers that will be used as test data by the rule that finds the largest number:

```
(deffacts max-num
    (loop-max 100))

(defrule loop-assert
    (loop-max ?n)
```

```
=>
(bind ?i 1)
(while (<= ?i ?n) do
   (assert (number ?i))
   (bind ?i (+ ?i 1))))
```

The simplest way of finding the largest number was demonstrated in Chapter 9. As shown below, one rule can be used to find the largest number:

```
(defrule largest-number
   (number ?number1)
   (not (number ?number2&:(> ?number2 ?number1)))
   =>
   (printout t "Largest number is " ?number1 crlf))
```

This rule, although simple, is not the fastest method for finding the largest number. If N represents the number of facts with the *number* relation, then both the first and second patterns will have a number of pattern matches equal to N. Even though there will only be one partial match for the first two patterns, N-squared comparisons will have to be performed to find that partial match. Increasing the value of the *loop-max* fact to 200, 300, 400, and so on will demonstrate that the time to run the problem is proportional to the square of N.

This type of comparison is extremely inefficient because as each number is added it is compared to *all* other numbers to determine whether it is the largest. For example, if the facts representing the numbers 2 through 100 have already been asserted and the fact representing the number 1 is asserted, 199 comparisons will be made to determine whether 1 is the largest number. The fact (number 1) will match the first pattern, so it will be compared to the 99 facts matching the second pattern to determine whether it is the largest. The first comparison will fail (because any of the numbers between 2 and 100 will be larger), but the remaining numbers will still be compared. Similarly, the fact (number 1) will match the second pattern, so it will be compared to the 100 facts matching the first pattern (which now includes the (number 1) fact as well).

The key to speeding up the program is to prevent unnecessary comparisons from occurring. This can be accomplished by using an additional fact to keep track of the largest number and comparing the *number* facts with it. The following rules show how this is done:

```
(defrule try-number
   (number ?n)
   =>
   (assert (try-number ?n)))

(defrule largest-unknown
   ?attempt <- (try-number ?n)
   (not (largest ?))
   =>
   (retract ?attempt)
   (assert (largest ?n)))
```

```
(defrule largest-smaller
   ?old-largest <- (largest ?n1)
   ?attempt <- (try-number ?n2&:(> ?n2 ?n1))
   =>
   (retract ?old-largest ?attempt)
   (assert (largest ?n2)))

(defrule largest-bigger
   (largest ?n1)
   ?attempt <- (try-number ?n2&:(<= ?n2 ?n1))
   =>
   (retract ?attempt))

(defrule print-largest
   (declare (salience -1))
   (largest ?number)
   =>
   (printout t "Largest number is " ?number crlf))
```

Running this program for *max-loop* values of 100, 200, 300, 400, and so on will demonstrate that the time to run this program is proportional to N. This is even more interesting considering that the first program will fire only two rules whereas the second program will fire approximately $2N$ rules. The second group of rules demonstrates that a rule should try to limit not only the number of partial matches it has, but also the number of comparisons needed for determining the partial matches. As demonstrated by the first rule, if the first pattern has N matches and the second pattern has N matches, then the rule will make N-squared comparisons in determining the partial matches for the first two patterns. Even if no partial matches are generated, the computational time spent will be roughly equivalent to having generated N-squared partial matches. The second group of rules limits the number of comparisons that will be made to N. Since only one *largest* and one *try-number* fact exist at a time, only one partial match can exist at any time for the *largest-unknown*, *largest-smaller*, and *largest-bigger* rules. Since N try-number facts are generated, this will limit the computational time to that of generating N partial matches. At first glance it may appear that it's possible to generate more than one *try-number* fact (thus causing N-squared partial matches). But recall from Section 10.3, that the agenda works like a stack—this means that all of the *try-number* activations placed on the agenda by the *loop-assert* rule will always fire after any activations of the *largest-unknown*, *largest-smaller*, and *largest-bigger* rules. Since these rules always remove the current *try-number* fact, there will never be more than one fact of this type.

This example demonstrates two important concepts. First, the easiest way to code a problem in a rule-based language is not necessarily the best. Second, the number of comparisons performed can often be reduced by using temporary facts to store data. The *largest* fact is used in this problem to store the value for later comparison so that not all the *number* facts have to be searched when comparing.

11.13 LOADING AND SAVING FACTS

The speed of a CLIPS program can be increased by reducing the number of facts in the fact list. One method for reducing the number of facts is to load facts into CLIPS only when they are needed. For example, a program for diagnosing problems with cars might first ask for the make and model of the car and then load information specific for that car. The **load-facts** and **save-facts** functions are provided by CLIPS to allow facts to be loaded from or saved to a file. The syntax of these two functions is

```
(load-facts <file-name>)

(save-facts <file-name>
           [<save-scope> <deftemplate-names>*])
```

where <save-scope> is defined as

```
visible | local
```

The *load-facts* function will load in a group of facts stored in the file specified by <file-name>. The facts in the file should be in the standard format of either an ordered or a deftemplate fact. For example, if the file "facts.dat" contained

```
(data 34)
(data 89)
(data 64)
(data 34)
```

then the command

```
(load-facts "facts.dat")
```

would load the facts contained in that file.

The *save-facts* function can be used to save facts in the fact list to the file specified by <file-name>. The facts are stored in the format required by the *load-facts* function. If <save-scope> is not specified or if it is specified as **local**, then only those facts corresponding to deftemplates defined in the current module would be saved to the file. If <save-scope> is specified as **visible**, then all facts corresponding to deftemplates that are visible to the current module would be saved to the file. If <save-scope> is specified, one or more deftemplate names may also be specified. In this case, only facts corresponding to the specified deftemplates will be saved (however, the deftemplate names must still satisfy the *local* or *visible* specification).

Both load-facts and save-facts return TRUE if the facts file is successfully opened and then loaded or saved; otherwise, FALSE is returned. It is the programmer's responsibility to ensure that the deftemplates corresponding to deftemplate facts in a facts file are visible to the current module in which the *load-facts* command is being executed.

11.14 SUMMARY

This chapter demonstrates the importance of matching facts against rules in an efficient manner. The Rete Algorithm is efficient for this matching process because it takes advantage of the temporal redundancy and structural similarity exhibited by rule-based expert systems.

Rules are converted into data structures in a rule network. This network consists of a pattern network and a join network. The pattern network matches facts against patterns and the join network insures that variable bindings across patterns are consistent. The ordering of patterns can have a significant effect on the performance of a rule. Generally, the most specific patterns and patterns matching the fewest facts should be placed first in the LHS of a rule and volatile patterns should be placed last in the LHS of a rule. The *matches* command is used to display the pattern matches, partial matches, and activations of a rule.

There are several other techniques for improving rule efficiency, including proper use of multifield variables, the positioning of test patterns, and the use of built-in pattern-matching constraints. There are also efficiency tradeoffs associated with writing general versus specific rules and simple versus complex rules.

The *if* and *while* functions can be used for flow of control on the RHS of a rule. The *halt* function can be used to halt the execution of rules. Overuse of these functions on the RHS of a rule is considered poor programming style. The *save-facts* and *load-facts* functions can be used to save facts to and load facts from a file.

PROBLEMS

11.1   List the pattern node specifications generated for the slots of the following patterns.

```
(a)  (blip (altitude 100))
(b)  (blip (altitude ?x&:(> ?x 100)))
(c)  (stop-light (color ~red))
(d)  (balloon (color blue|white))
```

11.2   Draw the pattern network for the following group of patterns.

```
(data (x red) (y ?y) (z ?y))
(data (x ~red))
(item (b ?y) (c ?x&:(> ?x ?y)))
(item (a red) (b blue|yellow))
```

11.3   Draw the pattern and join network for the following rules. List the expressions evaluated at each node.

```
(defrule rule1
   (phase (name testing))
   (data (x ?x) (y ?y))
   (data (x ?y) (y ?x&:(> ?x ?y)))
   =>)
```

```
(defrule rule2
  (phase (name testing))
  (data (x ?x) (y ?y))
  (data (x ?y&~red) (y ?x&~green))
  =>)
```

11.4   Rewrite the following rule to make it more efficient.

```
(defrule bad-rule
  (items (x ?x1) (y ?y1) (z ?z1))
  (items (x ?x2) (y ?y2) (z ?z2))
  (items (x ?x3) (y ?y3) (z ?z3))
  (test (and (or (eq ?x3 green)
                 (eq ?x3 red))
             (eq ?z2 ?y3)
             (> ?y1 ?x1)
             (< ?z1 ?x1)
             (neq ?z3 ?x1)))
  =>)
```

11.5   The figure below shows a fault network for a hypothetical piece of equipment. The arrows indicate the direction in which faults will be propagated. For example, if component A has a fault, then components B and C will also have faults.

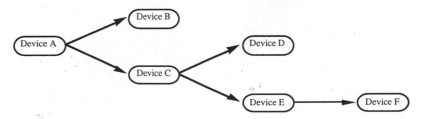

The following rules will propagate faults throughout the network.

```
(defrule propagate-device-A-fault
  (fault device-A)
  =>
  (assert (fault device-B))
  (assert (fault device-C)))

(defrule propagate-device-C-fault
  (fault device-C)
  =>
  (assert (fault device-D))
  (assert (fault device-E)))

(defrule propagate-device-E-fault
  (fault device-E)
  =>
  (assert (fault device-F)))
```

Rewrite these three rules as one general rule and a deffacts construct that will propagate the faults as the three rules do. Explain the changes that must be made for each of these approaches when a new device is added to the fault network.

11.6 Rewrite the following rule into one or more rules that do not use the *if* and *while* functions. Verify that your rules perform the same actions by comparing the output and final fact list of your rules with this rule.

```
(defrule continue-check
    ?phase <- (phase check-continue)
    =>
    (retract ?phase)
    (printout t "Continue? ")
    (bind ?answer (read))
    (while (and (neq ?answer yes) (neq ?answer no)) do
        (printout t "Continue? ")
        (bind ?answer (read)))
    (if (eq ?answer yes)
        then (assert (phase continue))
        else (assert (phase halt))))
```

11.7 Given an $N \times N$ chessboard, where N is an integer, write a program that will place N queens on the chessboard such that no queen can capture another queen. Hint: develop your program using 4 as the number of rows and columns. This is the smallest number for which there is a solution (with the exception of the trivial case of a 1 x 1 board).

11.8 Modify the program developed for Problem 10.12 on page 474 to provide explanation capabilities. After the output for the best matching shrub is printed, the program should prompt the user to determine whether he or she wants an explanation for a specified shrub. If the return key is pressed, the program should stop. If the name of a shrub is entered, the program should list the requirements it satisfied, the requirements it did not satisfy, and other requirements which it could satisfy. Once the explanation is printed, the user should be prompted again to determine whether he or she wants another explanation.

11.9 Combine the programs developed for Problems 10.14 and 10.15 on pages 474 and 475. The resulting program should have a textual menu interface with menu items for launching an application, terminating an application, and quitting the program. When the launch menu item is selected, the user should be prompted for the name and memory requirements of the application. When the terminate menu item is selected, the user should be prompted for the name of the application to terminate.

11.10 Modify the program developed for Problem 10.15 on page 475 to support submenus. For example:

```
CLIPS> (run)

Select one of the following options:

    1 -- Option A
    2 -- Option B
    3 -- Submenu 1
    9 -- Quit Program
```

```
Your choice: 3

Select one of the following options:

   1 -- Option C
   2 -- Option D
   9 -- Previous Menu

Your choice: 9

Select one of the following options:

   1 -- Option A
   2 -- Option B
   3 -- Submenu 1
   9 -- Quit Program

Your choice: 9
CLIPS>
```

11.11   Modify the program developed for Problem 10.18 on page 476 to schedule six courses for a single student. The program should attempt to maximize the overall score (as described in Problem 10.18) for all six courses. The input to the program should be six facts indicating the courses to be scheduled, and the output should be the list of scheduled courses in order from period one to six. Test your program with the following course selections:

Course	Instructors Preferred	Periods Preferred	Instructors Not Preferred	Periods Not Preferred
Texas History	Hill	2, 5	–	1, 3
Algebra	Smith	1, 2	Jones	6
Physical Education	–	–	Mack, King	1
Chemistry	Dolby	5, 6	–	–
Literature	–	3, 4	–	1, 6
German	–	–	–	–

11.12   A poker player has just been dealt five cards. Given as input facts representing these five cards, write a program that will print the type of the player's hand: royal flush, straight flush, four-of-a-kind, full house, flush, straight, three-of-a-kind, two pair, one pair, or nothing.

11.13   Write a program that will simplify an algebraic equation by moving all constants to the right side of the equation and all variables to the left side of the equation and then reducing common terms. For example, the equation

$$2 \ x + y + 5 + 3 \ y - 2 \ z - 8 = 3 \ z - 4 \ y + 4$$

can be simplified to

$$2 \ x + 8 \ y - 5 \ z = 7$$

Since the = symbol has special significance in patterns, you will probably want to represent the equation in a format where the = symbol is implied. For example:

```
(equation (LHS 2 x + y + 5 + 3 y - 2 z - 8)
          (RHS 3 z - 4 y + 4))
```

11.14   Combine the programs developed for Problems 9.20 on page 435 and Problem 11.10 to create a menu driven interface for the configuration program. The main menu options should allow the user to select a chassis, add gizmos to the configuration, remove gizmos from the configuration, and print the cost of the configuration. Submenus should be used to allow the selection of the chassis and to add or remove gizmos to the configuration. After selecting a chassis or adding or removing a gizmo, warning messages should be printed indicating if there are conflicts between the gizmos and the number of bays and power supplied by the chassis. Control should return to the main menu. Selecting the menu option to print the configuration should list the chassis and gizmos selected along with their individual prices and the total price of all added together.

BIBLIOGRAPHY

(Brownston 85). Lee Brownston *et al.*, *Programming Expert Systems in OPS5: An Introduction to Rule-Based Programming*, Addison-Wesley Pub., 1985.

(Forgy 85). Charles L. Forgy, "Rete: A Fast Algorithm for the Many Pattern/Many Object Pattern Match Problem," *Artificial Intelligence*, **19,** pp. 17-37, 1985.

(Forgy 79). Charles L. Forgy, "On the Efficient Implementation of Production Systems," Ph.D. thesis, Carnegie-Mellon University, 1979.

CHAPTER 12
Expert System Design Examples

12.1 INTRODUCTION

This chapter provides several examples of CLIPS programs. The first example demonstrates how uncertainty can be represented in CLIPS. The next two examples demonstrate how other knowledge representation paradigms can be emulated using CLIPS: one shows how decision trees can be represented in CLIPS and the other shows how backward chaining rules can be represented in CLIPS. The fourth and final example builds the framework of a simple expert system that monitors a group of sensors.

12.2 CERTAINTY FACTORS

CLIPS has no built-in capabilities for handling uncertainty. However, it is possible to incorporate uncertainty into CLIPS by placing information dealing with uncertainty directly into facts and rules. As an example, the MYCIN uncertainty mechanism will be emulated using CLIPS. This section will demonstrate how the following MYCIN rule (Firebaugh 88) can be rewritten in CLIPS:

```
IF
    The stain of the organism is gramneg and
    The morphology of the organism is rod and
    The patient is a compromised host
THEN
    There is suggestive evidence (0.6) that the
        identity of the organism is pseudomonas
```

MYCIN represents factual information as object–attribute–value triples. These OAV triples can be represented in CLIPS using the following deftemplate construct (which will be placed in its own module to create a reusable software component):

```
(defmodule OAV (export deftemplate oav))
(deftemplate OAV::oav
    (multislot object (type SYMBOL))
    (multislot attribute (type SYMBOL))
    (multislot value))
```

Using this deftemplate, some of the facts required by the IF portion of the preceding MYCIN rule would be

```
(oav (object organism)
     (attribute stain)
     (value gramneg))

(oav (object organism)
     (attribute morphology)
     (value rod))

(oav (object patient)
     (attribute is a)
     (value compromised host))
```

MYCIN also associates with each fact a certainty factor (CF) that represents a degree of belief in the fact. The certainty factor ranges from −1 to 1; −1 means the fact is known to be false, 0 means no information is known about the fact (complete uncertainty), and 1 means the fact is known to be true.

Since CLIPS does not handle certainty factors automatically, this information must also be maintained. To do this, an additional slot in each fact will be used to represent the certainty factor. The *oav* deftemplate for each fact now becomes

```
(deftemplate OAV::oav
    (multislot object (type SYMBOL))
    (multislot attribute (type SYMBOL))
    (multislot value)
    (slot CF (type FLOAT) (range -1.0 +1.0)))
```

and the examples facts might be

```
(oav (object organism)
     (attribute stain)
     (value gramneg)
     (CF 0.3))

(oav (object organism)
     (attribute morphology)
     (value rod)
     (CF 0.7))

(oav (object patient)
     (attribute is a)
     (value compromised host)
     (CF 0.8))
```

One further modification to CLIPS must be made in order for the *oav* facts to work properly. MYCIN allows the same OAV triple to be derived by separate rules. The OAV triples are then combined to produce a single OAV triple that combines the certainty factors of the two. The current *oav* deftemplate will allow two identical OAV triples to be asserted only if they have different certainty factors (since CLIPS normally does not allow two duplicate facts to be asserted). In order to allow identical OAV triples to be asserted with the same certainty factors, the **set-fact-duplication** command can be used to disable the CLIPS behavior that prevents duplicate facts from being asserted. The command

```
(set-fact-duplication TRUE)
```

will disable the behavior. Similarly, the command

```
(set-fact-duplication FALSE)
```

will prevent duplicate facts from being asserted.

As stated, MYCIN will combine two identical OAV triples into a single OAV triple with a combined certainty. If the certainty factors of the two facts (represented by CF_1 and CF_2) are both greater than or equal to zero, MYCIN uses the following formula to compute the new certainty factor:

```
New Certainty = (CF₁ + CF₂) - (CF₁ * CF₂)
```

For example, assume that the following facts are in the fact list:

```
(oav (object organism)
     (attribute morphology)
     (value rod)
     (CF 0.7))

(oav (object organism)
     (attribute morphology)
     (value rod)
     (CF 0.5))
```

Let CF_1 be 0.7 and CF_2 be 0.5; then the new certainty for the combination of the two facts is computed as

```
New Certainty = (0.7 + 0.5) - (0.7 * 0.5)
              = 1.2 - 0.35
              = 0.85
```

and the new fact to replace the two original facts would then be

```
(oav (object organism)
     (attribute morphology)
     (value rod)
     (CF 0.85))
```

Since CLIPS does not automatically handle certainty factors for facts, it follows that it also does not automatically combine two OAV triples derived from different rules. The combination of OAV triples can easily be handled by a rule that searches the fact list for identical OAV triples to be combined. The following rule demonstrates how this can be accomplished when the certainty factors of both OAV triples are greater than or equal to zero:

```
(defrule OAV::combine-certainties-both-positive
   (declare (auto-focus TRUE))
   ?fact1 <- (oav (object $?o)
                  (attribute $?a)
                  (value $?v)
                  (CF ?C1&:(>= ?C1 0)))
   ?fact2 <- (oav (object $?o)
                  (attribute $?a)
                  (value $?v)
                  (CF ?C2&:(>= ?C2 0)))
   (test (neq ?fact1 ?fact2))
   =>
   (retract ?fact1)
   (bind ?C3 (- (+ ?C1 ?C2) (* ?C1 ?C2)))
   (modify ?fact2 (CF ?C3)))
```

Notice that the fact identifiers *?fact1* and *?fact2* are compared to each other in the *test* CE. This is to insure that the rule does not match using the exact same fact for the first two patterns. The functions *eq* and *neq* are able to compare fact addresses. Also note that the auto-focus attribute for the rule has been enabled. This will insure that two OAV triples are combined before other rules satisfied by both of the triples are allowed to fire.

The next step in implementing certainty factors is to link the certainty factors of the facts that match the LHS of the rule to the certainty factors of the facts asserted by the RHS of the rule. In MYCIN the certainty factor associated with the LHS of a rule is derived using the following formulas:

```
CF(P₁ or P₂)  = max { CF(P₁), CF(P₂) }
CF(P₁ and P₂) = min { CF(P₁), CF(P₂) }
CF(not P)     = - CF(P)
```

where P, P_1, and P_2 represent patterns of the LHS. Additionally, if the certainty factor of the LHS is less than 0.2 the rule is considered inapplicable and will not be fired.

The certainty factor of a fact asserted from the RHS of a rule is derived by multiplying the certainty factor of the assertion by the certainty factor of the LHS of the rule. The following CLIPS rule translation of the MYCIN rule introduced at the beginning of this section demonstrates the computation of LHS and RHS certainty factors. The rule is placed in the *IDENTIFY* module, which imports the *oav* deftemplate from the *OAV* module.

```
(defmodule IDENTIFY (import OAV deftemplate oav))
(defrule IDENTIFY::MYCIN-to-CLIPS-translation
   (oav (object organism)
        (attribute stain)
        (value gramneg)
        (CF ?C1))
   (oav (object organism)
        (attribute morphology)
        (value rod)
        (CF ?C2))
   (oav (object patient)
        (attribute is a)
        (value compromised host)
        (CF ?C3))
   (test (> (min ?C1 ?C2 ?C3) 0.2))
   =>
   (bind ?C4 (* (min ?C1 ?C2 ?C3) 0.6))
   (assert (oav (object organism)
                (attribute identity)
                (value pseudomonas)
                (CF ?C4))))
```

One final step is required for completing the MYCIN certainty factor emulation. The *combine-certainties-both-positive* rule handles only one case of certainty factor combination—the remaining combination cases are the following:

$$\text{New Certainty} = (CF_1 + CF_2) + (CF_1 * CF_2)$$

$$\text{if} \quad CF_1 \leq 0 \text{ and } CF_2 \leq 0$$

$$\text{New Certainty} = \frac{CF_1 + CF_2}{1 - \min \{ \ |CF_1| \ , \ |CF_2| \ \}}$$

$$\text{if} \quad -1 < CF_1 * CF_2 < 0$$

12.3 DECISION TREES

Recall from Chapter 3 that decision trees provide a useful paradigm for solving certain types of classification problems. Decision trees derive solutions by reducing the set of possible solutions with a series of decisions or questions that prune their search space. Problems that are suitable for solution by decision trees are typified by the characteristic that they provide the answer to a problem from a predetermined set of possible answers. For example, a taxonomy problem might require the identification of a gem from the set of all known gems or a diagnosis problem might require the selection of a possible remedy from a set of remedies or the selection of the cause of a failure from a set of possible causes. Because the answer set must be predetermined, in general, decision trees do not work well for scheduling, planning, or synthesis problems—problems that must generate solutions in addition to selecting among them.

Remember that a decision tree is composed of nodes and branches. Nodes represent locations in the tree. Branches connect parent nodes to child nodes when moving from top to bottom and connect child nodes to parent nodes when moving from bottom to top. The node at the top of the tree that has no parent is called the root node. Note that in a tree, every node has only one parent, with the exception of the root node, which has none. Nodes with no children are called leaves.

The leaf nodes of a decision tree represent all the possible solutions that can be derived from the tree. These nodes are referred to as *answer nodes*, and all other nodes in the tree are referred to as *decision nodes*. Each decision node represents a question or decision that when answered or decided, determines the appropriate branch of the decision tree to follow. In simple decision trees this question could be a yes or no question such as "Is the animal warm blooded?" The left branch of the node would represent the path to follow if the answer is yes and the right branch of the node would represent the path to follow if the answer is no. In general, a decision node may use any criteria to select which branch to follow, provided that the selection process always yields only a single branch. Thus, decision nodes may select a branch corresponding to a set or range of values, a series of cases, or functions mapping from the state at the decision node to the branches of the decision node. Sophisticated decision nodes might even allow backtracking or probabilistic reasoning.

To illustrate the operation of a decision tree, consider the following heuristics in selecting the appropriate wine to serve with a meal:

```
IF the main course is red meat
THEN serve red wine

IF the main course is poultry and it is turkey
THEN serve red wine

IF the main course is poultry and it is not turkey
THEN serve white wine

IF the main course is fish
THEN serve white wine.
```

The representation of the wine heuristics as a binary decision tree is shown in Figure 12.1. The decision nodes assume that each question can be answered only yes or no. A default answer node containing the answer "The best color is unknown" has been added to the set of heuristics in the event that the main course is neither red meat, nor poultry, nor fish.

The procedure for traversing the tree to reach an answer node is quite simple. The inferencing process is started by setting the current location in the decision tree to the root node. If the current location is a decision node, then the question associated with the decision node must be answered in some manner (typically by the person consulting the decision tree). If the answer is yes, then the current location is set to the child node connected to the yes (or left) branch of the current location. If the answer is no, then the current location is set to the child node connected to the no (or right) branch of the current location. If at any point an answer node becomes the current location, then the value of the answer node is the answer derived through consultation with the decision tree. Otherwise the procedure for handling a decision node is repeated until an answer node is reached. The pseudocode for this algorithm is

```
procedure Solve_Binary_Tree
    Set the current location in the tree
        to the root node.
    while the current location is a decision node do
        Ask the question at the current node.
        If the reply to the question is yes
            Set the current node to the yes branch.
        else
            Set the current node to the no branch.
        end if
    end do
    Return the answer at the current node.
end procedure
```

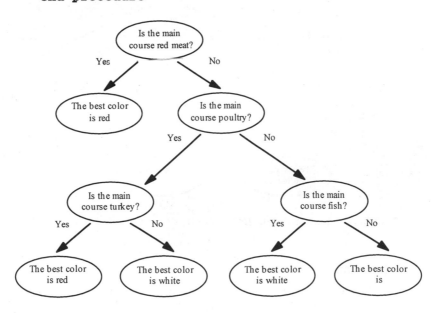

Figure 12.1 Binary Decision Tree

Decision Trees with Multiple Branches

Decision trees that allow only binary branches from a decision node make it difficult to represent a decision that allows for a set of responses or a series of cases. The binary decision tree constructed for the wine example provides a good example of this inefficiency. In the event that the main course is fish, three decisions must be made before it can be determined that the best color is white: the questions "Is the main course red meat?", "Is the main course poultry?", and "Is the main course fish?" must all be asked. A much more direct question that would allow the decision node to be expressed succinctly is "What is the main course?" A decision node capable of handling this question must allow multiple branches, given a series of possible decisions (in this case red meat, poultry, fish, and other). Figure 12.2 shows the modified decision tree of Figure 12.1 now allowing multiple branches achieved through a simple modification in the *Solve_Binary_Tree* algorithm:

```
procedure Solve_Tree
    Set the current tree location to the root node.
    while the current location is a decision node do
        Ask the question at the current node until
            an answer in the set of valid choices
            for this node has been provided.
        Set the current node to the child node of
            the branch associated with the choice
            selected.
    end do
    Return the answer at the current node.
end procedure
```

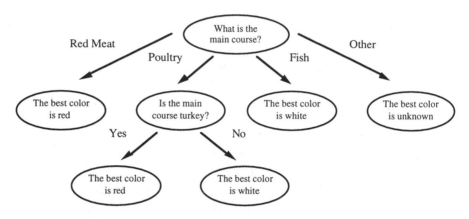

Figure 12.2 Decision Tree with Multiple Branches

Decision Trees That Learn

Occasionally it is useful to add new knowledge to a decision tree as it is learned, as in the commonly used example of the animal identification decision tree. Once the decision tree has reached an answer, it asks whether the answer is correct, and if so, then nothing more is done. If the answer is incorrect, however, the decision tree is modified to accommodate the correct answer. The answer node is replaced with a decision node that contains a question that will differentiate between the old answer that was at the node and the answer that was not correctly guessed. Figure 12.3 shows a decision tree that will classify an animal by characteristics. This decision tree is somewhat naive (it only knows three animals) and is in need of learning.

An example guessing session with the tree might proceed as follows:

```
Is the animal warm-blooded? (yes or no) yes↵
Does the animal purr? (yes or no) no↵
I guess it is a dog
Am I correct? (yes or no) no↵
What is the animal? bird↵
What question when answered yes will distinguish
    a bird from a dog? Does the animal fly?↵
```

```
Now I can guess bird
Try again? (yes or no) no↵
```

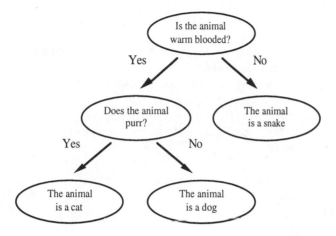

Figure 12.3 Animal Identification Decision Tree

The session can continue on and on, with the decision tree learning more and more information. Figure 12.4 shows the representation of the decision tree after the above session. One drawback to learning in this manner is that the decision tree may not end up being either very hierarchically structured or very efficient in guessing the appropriate animal. An efficient decision tree should have approximately the same number of branches from root to answer nodes for all paths.

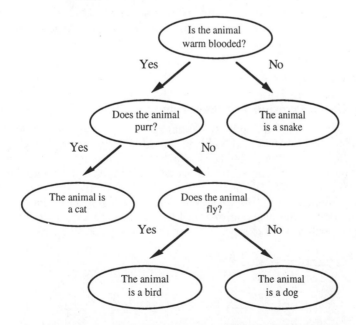

Figure 12.4 Animal Identification Decision Tree After Learning *Bird*

The pseudocode to modify the *Solve_Tree* algorithm to incorporate learning is

```
procedure Solve_Tree_and_Learn
    Set the current location in the tree
        to the root node
    while the current location is a decision node do
        Ask the question at the current node.
        if the reply to the question is yes
            Set the current node to the yes branch.
        else
            Set the current node to the no branch.
        end if
    end do
    Ask if the answer at the current node is
    correct.
    if the answer is correct
        Return the correct answer.
    else
        Determine the correct answer.
        Determine a question which when answered yes
            will distinguish the answer at the current
            node from the correct answer.
        Replace the answer node with a decision node
            that has as its no branch the current
            answer node and as its yes branch an
            answer node with the correct answer.
            The decision node's question should be
            the question which distinguishes the
            two answer nodes.
    end if
end procedure
```

A Rule-Based Decision Tree Program

The first step in determining how a learning decision tree can be implemented in CLIPS is to decide how the knowledge should be represented. Since the decision tree must learn, it will probably be worthwhile to represent the tree as facts instead of rules because facts can easily be added and removed to update the tree as it learns. A set of CLIPS rules can be used to traverse the decision tree by implementing the *Solve_Tree_and_Learn* algorithm using a rule-based approach.

Each node of the decision tree will be represented by a fact. The following deftemplate will be used to represent both answer and decision nodes:

```
(deftemplate node
    (slot name)
    (slot type)
    (slot question)
    (slot yes-node)
    (slot no-node)
    (slot answer))
```

where the *name* slot is the unique name for the node and the *type* slot is the type of the node and contains the value *answer* or *decision*. The *question*, *yes-node*, and *no-node* slots are used only for decision nodes. The *question* slot is the question that is asked when a question node is traversed. The *yes-node* slot is the node to proceed to if the question is answered affirmatively, and the *no-node* slot is the node to proceed to if the question is answered negatively. The *answer* slot is used only by answer nodes and is the answer to the decision tree when an answer node is tranversed.

Because the animal program will learn, it will be necessary to store information about what has been learned from one run of the program to the next. Since the decision tree will be structured as a collection of facts, it will be useful to store them in a file in the *load-facts* command format and assert them using the *load-facts* command when the program begins and save them using the *save-facts* command when the program finishes. For this program the facts will be stored in a file called "animal.dat". If Figure 12.3 is used for the initial decision tree the file "animal.dat" should contain the text below. Notice that the root node has been labeled as such and that each of the other nodes has been given a unique name. Also note that some slots (such as the *decision*, *yes-node*, and *no-node* slots for the answer nodes) remain unspecified, since these will be assigned default values (and our program won't care what values are placed in the slots).

```
(node (name root) (type decision)
      (question "Is the animal warm-blooded?")
      (yes-node node1) (no-node node2))
(node (name node1) (type decision)
      (question "Does the animal purr?")
      (yes-node node3) (no-node node4))
(node (name node2) (type answer) (answer snake))
(node (name node3) (type answer) (answer cat))
(node (name node4) (type answer) (answer dog))
```

Now the rules to traverse the decision tree must be written. The following rule will initialize the learning decision tree program:

```
(defrule initialize
   (not (node (name root)))
   =>
   (load-facts "animal.dat")
   (assert (current-node root)))
```

This *initialize* rule will fire if the root node is not present in the fact list. The actions of the *initialize* rule load the decision tree representation into the fact list and assert a fact indicating that the current node of interest is the root node.

The next rule asks the question associated with a decision node and then asserts a fact containing the answer to the question:

```
(defrule ask-decision-node-question
   ?node <- (current-node ?name)
   (node (name ?name)
         (type decision)
         (question ?question))
```

```
    (not (answer ?))
    =>
    (printout t ?question " (yes or no) ")
    (assert (answer (read))))
```

The second pattern matches against the current node only if it is a decision node. The third pattern checks that the question hasn't already been answered. This pattern will be used in conjunction with the following rule to cause the *ask-decision-node-question* rule to be reactivated if the answer to the question is something other than yes or no:

```
(defrule bad-answer
    ?answer <- (answer ~yes&~no)
    =>
    (retract ?answer))
```

If the answer was yes or no, then one of the following two rules will be fired. The *current-node* fact will be retracted and and then updated with a new assertion that depends on the answer to the question. The answer fact will be retracted so that the *ask-decision-node-question* rule will be activated again.

```
(defrule proceed-to-yes-branch
    ?node <- (current-node ?name)
    (node (name ?name)
          (type decision)
          (yes-node ?yes-branch))
    ?answer <- (answer yes)
    =>
    (retract ?node ?answer)
    (assert (current-node ?yes-branch)))

(defrule proceed-to-no-branch
    ?node <- (current-node ?name)
    (node (name ?name)
          (type decision)
          (no-node ?no-branch))
    ?answer <- (answer no)
    =>
    (retract ?node ?answer)
    (assert (current-node ?no-branch)))
```

The next rule asks whether an answer node has made the correct guess. It acts similarly to the *ask-decision-node-question* rule.

```
(defrule ask-if-answer-node-is-correct
    ?node <- (current-node ?name)
    (node (name ?name) (type answer)
          (answer ?value))
    (not (answer ?))
    =>
```

```
(printout t "I guess it is a " ?value crlf)
(printout t "Am I correct? (yes or no) ")
(assert (answer (read))))
```

If the answer was something other than yes or no, then the bad-answer rule will cause another activation of the *ask-if-answer-node-is-correct* rule. If the answer was yes or no, then one of the two rules below will be fired. If the value of the answer node is verified, then the *ask-try-again* fact is asserted to indicate the user should be asked to continue. If the answer is wrong, then learning will occur and the *replace-answer-node* fact is asserted to indicate the name of the node to be replaced. In either case the *current-node* and *answer* facts are retracted.

```
(defrule answer-node-guess-is-correct
    ?node <- (current-node ?name)
    (node (name ?name) (type answer))
    ?answer <- (answer yes)
    =>
    (assert (ask-try-again))
    (retract ?node ?answer))

(defrule answer-node-guess-is-incorrect
    ?node <- (current-node ?name)
    (node (name ?name) (type answer))
    ?answer <- (answer no)
    =>
    (assert (replace-answer-node ?name))
    (retract ?node ?answer))
```

The following three rules are used to determine whether the user wants to continue. The ask-try-again rule asks the "Try again?" question. Once again, the bad-answer rule will fire if other than a yes or no answer was given. If the answer is yes, the one-more-time rule will reset the current-node fact to the root node to begin the guessing process again. If the answer is no, the facts representing the decision tree are saved to the "animal.dat" file using the *save-facts* command.

```
(defrule ask-try-again
    (ask-try-again)
    (not (answer ?))
    =>
    (printout t "Try again? (yes or no) ")
    (assert (answer (read)))

(defrule one-more-time
    ?phase <- (ask-try-again)
    ?answer <- (answer yes)
    =>
    (retract ?phase ?answer)
    (assert (current-node root)))
```

```
(defrule no-more
   ?phase <- (ask-try-again)
   ?answer <- (answer no)
   =>
   (retract ?phase ?answer)
   (save-facts "animal.dat" local node))
```

Finally, if the answer was wrong the following rule will add a new decision node that allows the decision tree to learn:

```
(defrule replace-answer-node
   ?phase <- (replace-answer-node ?name)
   ?data <- (node (name ?name)
                  (type answer)
                  (answer ?value))
      =>
   (retract ?phase)
   ; Determine what the guess should have been
   (printout t "What is the animal? ")
   (bind ?new-animal (read))
   ; Get the question for the guess
   (printout t "What question when answered yes ")
   (printout t "will distinguish " crlf "    a ")
   (printout t ?new-animal " from a " ?value "? ")
   (bind ?question (readline))
   (printout t "Now I can guess " ?new-animal crlf)
   ; Create the new learned nodes
   (bind ?newnode1 (gensym*))
   (bind ?newnode2 (gensym*))
   (modify ?data (type decision)
                 (question ?question)
                 (yes-node ?newnode1)
                 (no-node ?newnode2))
   (assert (node (name ?newnode1)
                 (type answer)
                 (answer ?new-animal)))
   (assert (node (name ?newnode1)
                 (type answer)
                 (answer ?value)))
   ; Determine if the player wants to try again
   (assert (ask-try-again)))
```

The *replace-answer node* rule asks for the correct identification of the animal and for a question that will distinguish this animal from the animal the decision tree had identified as the correct answer. The old answer node is replaced by a decision node and two answer nodes are created as the answers for the newly learned question. The **gensym*** function (which generates a unique symbol each time it is called) is used to provide a name for each of the two new answer nodes. The *ask-try-again* fact is then asserted to determine whether another run of the program should be made.

A Step-by-Step Trace of the Decision Tree Program

The behavior of the decision tree program can be observed by watching its execution. Assuming that decision tree rules have been loaded and the file "animal.dat" containing the facts representing the initial decision tree has been created, the following dialog shows the state of the system after a *reset* command has been performed:

```
CLIPS> (watch facts) ↵
CLIPS> (watch rules) ↵
CLIPS> (reset) ↵
==> f-0     (initial-fact)
CLIPS> (agenda) ↵
0       initialize:
For a total of 1 activation.
CLIPS>
```

The *initialize* rule has been activated by the absence of the *root node* fact. Allowing the *initialize* rule to fire will load in the decision tree. Note that some of the output in the following traces is indented to improve its readability.

```
CLIPS> (run 1) ↵
FIRE    1 initialize:
==> f-1     (node (name root) (type decision)
            (question "Is the animal warm-blooded?")
               (yes-node node1) (no-node node2)
               (answer nil))
==> f-2     (node (name node1) (type decision)
               (question "Does the animal purr?")
               (yes-node node3) (no-node node4)
               (answer nil))
==> f-3     (node (name node2) (type answer)
               (question nil) (yes-node nil)
               (no-node nil) (answer snake))
==> f-4     (node (name node3) (type answer)
               (question nil) (yes-node nil)
               (no-node nil) (answer cat))
==> f-5     (node (name node4) (type answer)
               (question nil) (yes-node nil)
               (no-node nil) (answer dog))
==> f-6     (current-node root)
CLIPS> (agenda) ↵
0       ask-decision-node-question: f-6,f-1,
For a total of 1 activation.
CLIPS>
```

The *initialize* rule uses the load-facts function to load in the decision tree. The *current-node* fact is set to the *root node* fact. Since the root node is a decision node, the *ask-decision-node-question* rule is activated. Allowing this rule and the associated *proceed-to-yes-branch* rule to fire produces the following dialog:

```
CLIPS> (run 2) ↵
FIRE    1 ask-decision-node-question: f-6,f-1,
Is the animal warm-blooded? (yes or no) yes↵
==> f-7      (answer yes)
FIRE    2 proceed-to-yes-branch: f-6,f-1,f-7
<== f-6      (current-node root)
<== f-7      (answer yes)
==> f-8      (current-node node1)
CLIPS> (agenda) ↵
0       ask-decision-node-question: f-8,f-2,
For a total of 1 activation.
CLIPS>
```

The question associated with the root decision node is "Is the animal warm blooded?" Since the reply to the question is yes, the left node of the decision node (node1) is made the current node by the *proceed-to-yes-branch* rule. Since node1 is also a decision node, the rule *ask-decision-node-question* is activated again. Allowing the next two rules to fire again produces the following dialog:

```
CLIPS> (run 2) ↵
FIRE    1 ask-decision-node-question: f-8,f-2,
Does the animal purr? (yes or no) no↵
==> f-9      (answer no)
FIRE    2 proceed-to-no-branch: f-8,f-2,f-9
<== f-8      (current-node node1)
<== f-9      (answer no)
==> f-10     (current-node node4)
CLIPS> (agenda) ↵
0       ask-if-answer-node-is-correct: f-10,f-5,
For a total of 1 activation.
CLIPS>
```

The question associated with the node1 decision node is "Does the animal purr?" Since the reply to the question is no, the right node of the decision node, node4, is made the current node by the *proceed-to-no-branch* rule. Since node4 is an answer node, the rule *ask-if-answer-node-is-correct* is activated. Allowing this rule and the next to fire produces the following dialog:

```
CLIPS> (run 2) ↵
FIRE    1 ask-if-answer-node-is-correct: f-10,f-5,
I guess it is a dog
Am I correct? (yes or no) no↵
==> f-11     (answer no)
FIRE    2 answer-node-guess-is-incorrect: f-10,f-5,
                                           f-11
```

```
==> f-12    (replace-answer-node node4)
<== f-11    (answer no)
<== f-10    (current-node node4)
CLIPS> (agenda) ↵
0       replace-answer-node: f-12,f-5
For a total of 1 activation.
CLIPS>
```

The guess associated with this answer node is dog. Since the guess is incorrect, the *replace-answer-node* rule is activated to determine the correct answer. Allowing this rule to fire produces the following dialog:

```
CLIPS> (run 1) ↵
FIRE    1 replace-answer-node: f-12,f-5
<== f-12    (replace-answer-node node4)
What is the animal? bird↵
What question when answered yes will distinguish
    a bird from a dog? Does the animal fly? ↵
Now I can guess bird
<== f-5     (node (name node4) (type answer)
                  (question nil)
                  (yes-node nil) (no-node nil)
                  (answer dog))
==> f-13    (node (name node4) (type decision)
                  (question "Does the animal fly?")
                  (yes-node gen1) (no-node gen2)
                  (answer dog))
==> f-14    (node (name gen1) (type answer)
                  (question nil)
                  (yes-node nil) (no-node nil)
                  (answer bird))
==> f-15    (node (name gen2) (type answer)
                  (question nil)
                  (yes-node nil) (no-node nil)
                  (answer dog))
==> f-16    (ask-try-again)
CLIPS> (agenda) ↵
0       ask-try-again: f-16,
For a total of 1 activation.
CLIPS>
```

First, the control fact (replace-answer-node node4) is retracted. The correct guess is then determined along with the question that will determine the correct guess. The incorrect answer node is modified to be a question node and then two answer nodes for the new question node are generated. Finally, the *ask-try-again* control fact is asserted to determine whether another identification is to be made. Allowing the *ask-try-again* rule and then the *no-more* rule to fire produces the following dialog:

```
CLIPS> (run 2) ↵
FIRE    1 ask-try-again: f-16,
Try again? (yes or no) no↵
==> f-17      (answer no)
FIRE    2 no-more: f-16,f-17
<== f-16      (ask-try-again)
<== f-17      (answer no)
CLIPS> (agenda) ↵
CLIPS>
```

The user is asked by the *ask-try-again* rule whether another identification is to be made. Since the reply is no, the *no-more* rule saves the decision tree back to the "animal.dat" file. After this session the final form of the "animal.dat" file is

```
(node (name root) (type decision)
      (question "Is the animal warm-blooded?")
      (yes-node node1) (no-node node2)
      (answer nil))
(node (name node1) (type decision)
      (question "Does the animal purr?")
      (yes-node node3) (no-node node4)
      (answer nil))
(node (name node2) (type answer)
      (question nil)
      (yes-node nil) (no-node nil) (answer snake))
(node (name node3) (type answer)
      (question nil)
      (yes-node nil) (no-node nil) (answer cat))
(node (name node4) (type decision)
      (question "Does the animal fly?")
      (yes-node gen1) (no-node gen2) (answer dog))
(node (name gen1) (type answer)
      (question nil)
      (yes-node nil) (no-node nil) (answer bird))
(node (name gen2) (type answer)
      (question nil)
      (yes-node nil) (no-node nil) (answer dog))
```

The node4 answer node has been replaced with a decision node that refers to two new answer nodes. In addition, the default value *nil*, automatically assigned to some of the deftemplate slots, is now explicitly stated when the facts are saved.

12.4 BACKWARD CHAINING

CLIPS does not directly implement backward chaining as part of its inference engine. However, backward chaining can be emulated using forward chaining CLIPS rules. This section will demonstrate how a simple backward chaining system can be built in CLIPS. It should be noted that CLIPS is designed to be used as a forward chaining language; if a backward chaining approach is most suitable for solving a problem, then a language that directly implements backward chaining within its inference engine, such as PROLOG, should be used.

The CLIPS backward chaining system will be built with the following capabilities and limitations:

- Facts will be represented as Attribute-Value pairs.
- Backward chaining will be started with the assertion of a single initial goal attribute.
- Only the equality of an attribute to a specific value will be tested as a condition in the antecedent of a rule.
- The only action of the antecedent of a rule will be to assign the value of a single attribute.
- If the value of a goal attribute cannot be determined using rules, the backward chainer will ask for the value of the attribute to be supplied. Attributes cannot be assigned an unknown value.
- An attribute may have only a single value. Hypothetical reasoning about different attribute values from different rules will not be supported.
- Uncertainty will not be represented.

An Algorithm for the Backward Chainer

Before writing a backward chaining inference engine and attempting a rule-based approach using CLIPS we should consider a procedural algorithm. The following pseudocode procedure can be used to determine the value of a goal attribute using a backward chaining approach with the capabilities and limitations discussed previously:

```
procedure Solve_Goal(goal)
    goal: the current goal to be solved

    if value of the goal attribute is known
       Return the value of the goal attribute.
    end if

    for each rule whose consequent is the goal
    attribute do
       call Attempt_Rule with the rule
       if Attempt_Rule succeeds then
          Assign the goal attribute the value
          indicated by the consequent of the rule.
          Return the value of the goal attribute.
       end if
    end do

    Ask the user for the value of the goal
    attribute.
    Set the goal attribute to the value supplied
    by the user.
    Return the value of the goal attribute.

end procedure
```

A goal attribute is passed to procedure *Solve_Goal* as an argument. This procedure will determine the value of the goal attribute and return it. Procedure *Solve_Goal* first checks to determine whether the value of the goal attribute is already known. The value may already have been assigned as the consequent of another rule or supplied by the user of the backward chainer. If the value is indeed known, it is returned.

If the attribute value is not known, procedure *Solve_Goal* will attempt to determine the value by finding a rule that assigns the attribute a value as its consequent. Procedure *Solve_Goal* will attempt each rule that assigns a value to the goal attribute as its consequent until one of the rules succeeds. Procedure *Attempt_Rule* (which will be discussed in more detail shortly) is given each of the rules with the desired goal attribute to attempt. If the antecedent of the attempted rule is satisfied the rule will succeed; otherwise it will fail. If the rule succeeds, the attribute value in the consequent of the rule is assigned to the goal attribute and this value is returned by procedure *Solve_Goal*. If the rule does not succeed, then the next rule that assigns a value to the goal attribute as its consequent is attempted.

If none of the rules succeed, the user must be queried to determine the value of the goal attribute. The value supplied by the user is returned by procedure *Solve_Goal*.

Procedure *Attempt_Rule* is used to determine whether the antecedent of a rule is satisfied. If the antecedent is satisfied, the consequent can be used to assign the value of a goal attribute. The pseudocode for this procedure is

```
procedure Attempt_Rule(rule)
    rule: rule to be attempted to solve goal

    for each condition in the antecedent
    of the rule do
        call Solve_Goal with condition attribute
        if the value returned by solve_goal is not
        equal to the value required by the condition
        then
            Return unsuccessful.
        end if
    end for

    Return successful

end procedure
```

Procedure *Attempt_Rule* will start at the first condition of a rule and attempt to prove it before attempting the subsequent conditions of the rule. In order to determine whether a condition is satisfied, procedure *Attempt_Rule* must know the value of the attribute being tested in the condition. To determine the value, procedure *Solve_Goal* is called recursively. If the value returned by procedure *Solve_Goal* is not equal to the value required by the condition, procedure *Attempt_Rule* exits with the return value unsuccessful (remember that only equality is being tested in conditions). Otherwise the next condition of the rule is tested. If all conditions of the rule are satisfied, procedure *Attempt_Rule* exits with the return value successful.

Representing Backward Chaining Rules in CLIPS

Once again, the first step in solving this problem is determining how the knowledge should be represented. Since CLIPS does not automatically perform backward chaining, it will be useful to represent backward chaining rules as facts so the antecedents and consequents can be examined by rules that will act as a backward chaining inference engine. The deftemplate for representing backward chaining rules is shown below. It will be stored in the defmodule *BC* (which will be defined at the end of this subsection once all the deftemplates needed for the backward chaining engine have been identified).

```
(deftemplate BC::rule
    (multislot if)
    (multislot then))
```

The *if* and *then* slots will store the antecedent and the consequent, respectively, of each rule. Each antecedent will contain either a single attribute-value pair of the format

```
<attribute> is <value>
```

or a series of such attribute-value pairs connected by the symbol *and*. The consequent of each rule will be allowed to contain only a single attribute-value pair.

As an example of representing rules using this format, consider the decision tree in Figure 12.2. This tree can easily be converted to rules using AV pairs, as described previously. The pseudocode for the converted rules is

```
IF main-course is red-meat
THEN best-color is red

IF main-course is poultry and
    meal-is-turkey is yes
THEN best-color is red

IF main-course is poultry and
    meal-is-turkey is no
THEN best-color is white

IF main-course is fish
THEN best-color is white
```

The attributes used in the rules are *main-course*, *meal-is-turkey*, and *best-color*. The *main-course* attribute corresponds to the answer determined by the decision tree question "What is the main course?" *The meal-is-turkey* attribute corresponds to the answer determined by the question "Is the main course turkey?" Notice that the branch of the decision tree that determines that the best color is unknown is not represented as a rule, since one of the limitations of our backward chainer is that unknown values are not represented. If the main course is not one of those that produce an answer, in this case the user will be asked the value of the *best-color* attribute.

The following deffacts shows how the wine rules can be represented using the backward chaining rule format. Since these *rule* facts are not an intrinsic part of the backward chaining mechanism, they'll be placed in the *MAIN* module (recall that the *MAIN* module imports from all other modules, so the *rule* deftemplate will be visible to it).

```
(deffacts MAIN::wine-rules
    (rule (if main-course is red-meat)
          (then best-color is red))

    (rule (if main-course is fish)
          (then best-color is white))

    (rule (if main-course is poultry and
              meal-is-turkey is yes)
          (then best-color is red))

    (rule (if main-course is poultry and
              meal-is-turkey is no)
          (then best-color is white)))
```

This representation provides a great deal of flexibility when manipulating the backward chaining rules. For example, if the attribute *main-course* is determined to have the value *poultry*, the facts

```
(rule (if main-course is red-meat)
      (then best-color is red))
```

and

```
(rule (if main-course is fish)
      (then best-color is white))
```

can be removed from the fact list to indicate that these rules are not applicable, and the facts

```
(rule (if main-course is poultry and
          meal-is-turkey is yes)
      (then best-color is red))
```

and

```
(rule (if main-course is poultry and
          meal-is-turkey is no)
      (then best-color is white))
```

can respectively be modified to the facts

```
(rule (if meal-is-turkey is yes)
      (then best-color is red))
```

and

```
(rule (if meal-is-turkey is no)
      (then best-color is white))
```

to indicate that the first condition of these two rules has been satisfied.

As backward chaining proceeds, subgoals will be generated to determine the value of attributes. A fact will be needed to represent information about goal attributes. Ordered facts will be used to represent goal attributes and their format will be

```
(deftemplate BC::goal
   (slot attribute))
```

Initially the goal attribute is *best-color*. This can be represented using a deffacts as shown here:

```
(deffacts MAIN::initial-goal
   (goal (attribute best-color)))
```

When values for attributes are determined they will be need to be stored, which can be done with the following deftemplate:

```
(deftemplate BC::attribute
   (slot name)
   (slot value))
```

Now that all of the deftemplates have been identified we can provide the definition of the *BC* module. Remember that when you are loading a file of constructs the defmodule that will contain other constructs must be defined before the constructs it contains are defined.

```
(defmodule BC
   (export deftemplate rule goal attribute))
```

The CLIPS Backward Chaining Inference Engine

The backward chaining inference engine can be implemented with two sets of rules. The first group will generate goals for attributes and ask the user to supply attribute values when these values cannot be determined by rules. The second group of rules will perform update operations. Update operations include modifying rules when their conditions have been satisfied and removing goals when they have been satisfied. The first set of rules is the following:

```
(defrule BC::attempt-rule
   (goal (attribute ?g-name))
   (rule (if ?a-name $?)
         (then ?g-name $?))
   (not (attribute (name ?a-name)))
   (not (goal (attribute ?a-name)))
   =>
```

```
            (assert (goal (attribute ?a-name)))))

      (defrule BC::ask-attribute-value
         ?goal <- (goal (attribute ?g-name))
         (not (attribute (name ?g-name)))
         (not (rule (then ?g-name $?)))
         =>
         (retract ?goal)
         (printout t "What is the value of "
                      ?g-name "? ")
         (assert (attribute (name ?g-name)
                            (value (read)))))
```

The *attempt-rule* rule searches for rules whose antecedents will supply the attribute value for a goal attribute. The first pattern matches against a *goal* fact. The second pattern searches for all rules whose antecedent assigns a value to the goal attribute. The third pattern checks to see that the value of the goal attribute has not already been determined. The fourth pattern confirms that there is not already a goal to determine the attribute's value. For each rule found, the RHS of the *attempt-rule* rule will assert a goal to determine the value of the attribute tested by the first condition of the rule.

The *ask-attribute-value* rule is quite similar to the *attempt-rule* rule. Its first two patterns are identical. Its third pattern checks that there are no remaining rules that can be used to determine the value of the goal attribute. In this case the user is asked to supply the value of the attribute. A fact representing the attribute's value is asserted and the *goal* fact for the attribute is retracted.

The next four rules are used to update the backward chaining rules and goals that are represented as facts. These rules are given a salience of 100 so that updates will occur before any attempts are made to generate new goals or ask the user for attribute values.

```
      (defrule BC::goal-satisfied
         (declare (salience 100))
         ?goal <- (goal (attribute ?g-name))
         (attribute (name ?g-name))
         =>
         (retract ?goal))

      (defrule BC::rule-satisfied
         (declare (salience 100))
         (goal (attribute ?g-name))
         (attribute (name ?a-name)
                    (value ?a-value))
         ?rule <- (rule (if ?a-name is ?a-value)
                        (then ?g-name is ?g-value))
         =>
         (retract ?rule)
         (assert (attribute (name ?g-name)
                            (value ?g-value))))
```

```
(defrule BC::remove-rule-no-match
    (declare (salience 100))
    (goal (attribute ?g-name))
    (attribute (name ?a-name) (value ?a-value))
    ?rule <- (rule (if ?a-name is ~?a-value)
                   (then ?g-name is ?g-value))
    =>
    (retract ?rule))

(defrule BC::modify-rule-match
    (declare (salience 100))
    (goal (attribute ?g-name))
    (attribute (name ?a-name) (value ?a-value))
    ?rule <- (rule (if ?a-name is ?a-value and
                       $?rest-if)
                   (then ?g-name is ?g-value))
    =>
    (retract ?rule)
    (modify ?rule (if $?rest-if)))
```

The *goal-satisfied* rule removes any goals for which the attribute value has been determined.

The *rule-satisfied* rule searches for any rules that have a single remaining condition. If an attribute exists that satisfies this remaining condition and there is a goal to determine the value of this attribute, then the attribute value of the consequent of the rule is added to the fact list.

The *remove-rule-no-match* rule searches for rules whose antecedents can supply the attribute value for a goal attribute and contain one or more conditions of which the first conflicts with a value assigned to an attribute. If this is the case then the rule is removed from fact list since it is not applicable.

The *modify-rule-match* rule searches for rules whose antecedents can supply the attribute value for a goal attribute and contain two or more conditions of which the first is satisfied by a value assigned to an attribute. If such a rule is found, the first condition is removed from the rule to leave the remaining conditions, which must be tested.

Now that all of the backward chaining rules have been provided, all that is required to start the backward chaining process is to focus on the *BC* module. This can be accomplished by adding the following rule to the *MAIN* module:

```
(defrule MAIN::start-BC
    =>
    (focus BC))
```

A Step-by-Step Trace of the Backward Chainer

The behavior of the CLIPS backward chaining inference engine implemented using rules can be observed by watching its execution. Assuming that the *wine-rules* and *initial-goal* deffacts have been loaded along with the backward chaining inference engine rules, the initial state of the system after a *reset* command is as below (once again, some output has been indented to improve readability):

```
CLIPS> (unwatch all) ↵
CLIPS> (reset) ↵
CLIPS> (facts) ↵
f-0      (initial-fact)
f-1      (goal (attribute best-color))
f-2      (rule (if main-course is red-meat)
             (then best-color is red))
f-3      (rule (if main-course is fish)
             (then best-color is white))
f-4      (rule (if main-course is poultry and
                 meal-is-turkey is yes)
             (then best-color is red))
f-5      (rule (if main-course is poultry and
                 meal-is-turkey is no)
             (then best-color is white))
For a total of 6 facts.
CLIPS> (agenda) ↵
0        start-BC: f-0
For a total of 1 activation.
CLIPS>
```

The *start-BC* rule merely focuses on the *BC* module. Once this rule fires the *BC* module becomes the current focus.

```
CLIPS> (run 1) ↵
CLIPS> (agenda) ↵
0        attempt-rule: f-1,f-5,,
0        attempt-rule: f-1,f-4,,
0        attempt-rule: f-1,f-3,,
0        attempt-rule: f-1,f-2,,
For a total of 4 activations.
CLIPS>
```

Notice that the agenda contains four activations of the *attempt-rule* rule. The starting goal is to determine the value of the *best-color* attribute as specified by fact f-1. Since the consequents of the *rule* facts f-2, f-3, f-4, and f-5 each assign a value to the *best-color* attribute, each of these rules should be attempted to satisfy the *best-color* attribute goal.

The next step in execution is to fire the first activation of the *attempt-rule* rule. The rules and facts watch items are activated before the rule is fired:

```
CLIPS> (watch rules) ↵
CLIPS> (watch facts) ↵
CLIPS> (run 1) ↵
FIRE   1 attempt-rule: f-1,f-5,,
==> f-6      (goal (attribute main-course))
CLIPS> (agenda) ↵
0        ask-attribute-value: f-6,,
For a total of 1 activation.
CLIPS>
```

The *attempt-rule* rule fires based in part on fact f-5, which represents the backward chaining rule shown here:

```
IF main-course is poultry and
   meal-is-turkey is no
THEN best-color is white
```

Before this rule can be applied to assign the value of the *best-color* attribute, the CEs in its antecedents must be satisfied. The first condition requires the value of the attribute main -course. Since this attribute is unknown, a goal is created for it, and is represented by fact f-6. Because there are no rules that assign the value of the *main-course* attribute, the *ask-attribute-value* rule is activated.

Proceeding with execution, the *ask-attribute-value* rule fires to determine the value of the attribute *main-course*.

```
CLIPS> (run 1) ↵
FIRE    1 ask-attribute-value: f-6,,
<== f-6     (goal (attribute main-course))
What is the value of main-course? poultry↵
==> f-7     (attribute (name main-course)
                       (value poultry))
CLIPS> (agenda) ↵
100    remove-rule-no-match: f-1,f-7,f-3
100    remove-rule-no-match: f-1,f-7,f-2
100    modify-rule-match: f-1,f-7,f-5
100    modify-rule-match: f-1,f-7,f-4
For a total of 4 activations.
CLIPS>
```

Since the user is being asked to supply the value of the *main-course* attribute, the goal for this attribute f-6 is removed. The value supplied by the user is asserted as the *attribute* fact f-7. The assertion of this fact causes four new activations to be placed on the agenda. The rules represented by facts f-4 and f-5 each require as the first condition that the *main-course* attribute be *poultry*. Since the value of the *main-course* attribute is *poultry*, both of these *rule* facts must be modified to represent that the first condition has been satisfied. Thus both facts cause activations of the *modify-rule-match* rule. The rules represented by facts f-2 and f-3 both require as the first condition that the *main-course* attribute be something other than *poultry*. Thus neither of these facts is applicable any longer. The rule *remove-rule-no-match* is activated to cause both of them to be removed.

Allowing the two *remove-rule-no-match* activations to fire produces the following output:

```
CLIPS> (run 2) ↵
FIRE    1 remove-rule-no-match: f-1,f-7,f-3
<== f-3     (rule (if main-course is fish)
                  (then best-color is white))
FIRE    2 remove-rule-no-match: f-1,f-7,f-2
```

```
  <== f-2       (rule (if main-course is red-meat)
                      (then best-color is red))
CLIPS> (agenda) ↵
100    modify-rule-match: f-1,f-7,f-5
100    modify-rule-match: f-1,f-7,f-4
For a total of 2 activations.
CLIPS>
```

The facts f-2 and f-3 are removed from the fact list, indicating that the rules represented by these facts are no longer applicable. The *attempt-rule* activations for these facts are removed from the agenda when the facts are removed.

Moving now to the execution of the two *modify-rule-match* activations produces the following output:

```
CLIPS> (run 2) ↵
FIRE    1 modify-rule-match: f-1,f-7,f-5
  <== f-5       (rule (if main-course is poultry and
                          meal-is-turkey is no)
                      (then best-color is white))
  ==> f-8       (rule (if meal-is-turkey is no)
                      (then best-color is white))
FIRE    2 modify-rule-match: f-7,f-4
  <== f-4       (rule (if main-course is poultry and
                          meal-is-turkey is yes)
                      (then best-color is red))
  ==> f-9       (rule (if meal-is-turkey is yes)
                      (then best-color is red))
CLIPS> (agenda) ↵
0      attempt-rule: f-1,f-9,,
0      attempt-rule: f-1,f-8,,
For a total of 2 activations.
CLIPS>
```

The first firing of the *modify-rule-match* rule is based in part on fact f-5, which represents the following backward chaining rule:

```
IF main-course is poultry and
   meal-is-turkey is no
THEN best-color is white
```

The actions of the *modify-match-rule* rule modify this backward chaining rule as

```
IF meal-is-turkey is no
THEN best-color is white
```

The new fact representing the modified rule is f-8. This new fact represents the conditions of the initial rule that remain after the first condition has been satisfied and causes another activation of the *attempt-rule* rule for this backward chaining rule. This new activation will assert a new goal to determine the value of the meal-is-turkey so the consequent of the rule can be applied to assign the value of the best-color attribute.

The second firing of the *modify-rule-match* rule is similar to the first. The fact representing the rule

```
IF main-course is poultry and
   meal-is-turkey is red
THEN best-color is red
```

is modified to the following rule:

```
IF meal-is-turkey is yes
THEN best-color is red
```

which is represented by fact f-9. Similarly, this new fact causes an activation of the *attempt-rule* rule to replace the activation lost when the fact representing the rule was retracted.

Allowing the first *attempt-rule* activation to fire produces the following output:

```
CLIPS> (run 1) ↵
FIRE    1 attempt-rule: f-1,f-9,,
==> f-10    (goal (attribute meal-is-turkey))
CLIPS> (agenda) ↵
0       ask-attribute-value: f-10,,
For a total of 1 activation.
CLIPS>
```

The fact f-10 is asserted representing a goal to determine the value of the *meal-is-turkey* attribute. Since no rule assigns the value of this attribute, the *ask-attribute-value* rule is activated to determine the value.

Allowing the *ask-attribute-value* rule to fire produces the following output:

```
CLIPS> (run 1) ↵
FIRE    1 ask-attribute-value: f-10,,
<== f-10    (goal (attribute meal-is-turkey))
What is the value of meal-is-turkey? yes ↵
==> f-11    (attribute (name meal-is-turkey)
                       (value yes))
CLIPS> (agenda) ↵
100     rule-satisfied: f-1,f-11,f-9
100     remove-rule-no-match: f-1,f-11,f-8
For a total of 2 activations.
CLIPS>
```

An *attribute* fact representing the value of the *meal-is-turkey* attribute is asserted as a result of this rule firing. In addition, the *goal* fact to determine the value of this attribute is removed. The new *attribute* fact causes two activations. The first activation is for the *remove-rule-no-match* rule. Since fact f-8's first condition is inconsistent with the value of the new attribute and the rule represented by the fact is no longer applicable, this fact needs to be removed. The second activation is for the *rule-satisfied* rule. Since fact f-8's remaining condition is satisfied by the new *attribute* fact, the consequent of this fact can be applied.

The remaining rules left to fire finish the backward chaining process.

```
CLIPS> (run) ↵
FIRE    1 rule-satisfied: f-1,f-11,f-9
<== f-9     (rule (if meal-is-turkey is yes)
                   (then best-color is red))
==> f-12    (attribute (name best-color) (value
red))
FIRE    2 goal-satisfied: f-1,f-12
<== f-1     (goal (attribute best-color))
CLIPS> (agenda) ↵
CLIPS> (facts) ↵
f-0     (initial-fact)
f-7     (attribute (name main-course) (value
poultry))
f-8     (rule (if meal-is-turkey is no)
               (then best-color is white))
f-11    (attribute (name meal-is-turkey) (value
yes))
f-12    (attribute (name best-color) (value red))
For a total of 5 facts.
CLIPS>
```

The rule *rule-satisfied* is fired to assign the value of the *best-color* attribute as part of the consequent of the rule represented by fact f-9. The *attribute* fact asserted by this rule satisfies the remaining *goal* fact in the fact list. The rule *goal-satisfied* is activated and then fired to remove the remaining *goal* fact.

The *agenda* command shows that there are no rules remaining to fire. The *facts* command shows the attributes that have been assigned values. Fact f-12 shows that the initial goal attribute *best-color* was assigned the value *red*.

12.5 A MONITORING PROBLEM

This section presents the step-by-step development of a CLIPS program as the solution of a simple problem. The development steps include the initial description of the problem, assumptions made about the nature of the problem, and the initial definitions for representation of problem knowledge, followed by an incremental buildup of the rules to solve the problem.

Problem Statement

The problem to be solved in this section is an example of a simple monitoring system. Monitoring problems tend to be well suited for forward chaining rule-based languages because of their data-driven nature. Typically a set of input or sensor values are read during each program cycle. Inferencing occurs until all possible conclusions that can be derived from the input data are reached. This is consistent with a data-driven approach, in which reasoning occurs from data to the conclusions that can be derived from the data.

For this example the type of monitoring to be performed will be generic in nature. A hypothetical processing plant contains several devices that have to be monitored. Some devices will depend on others for their operation. Each device will have one or more sensors attached to it to provide numeric readings indicating the general health of the device. Each sensor will have low guard line (LGL), low red line (LRL), high guard line (HGL), and high red line (HRL) values. A reading between the low and high guard lines will be considered normal. A reading above the high guard line but below the high red line or below the low guard line but above the low red line will be considered acceptable, although it is an indication that the device may soon become unhealthy. A reading above the high red line or below the low red line will indicate an unhealthy device, which should be shut down. Any device in the guard region should have warnings issued. In addition, any device that remains in a guard region for an excessively long time should be shut down. Table 12.1 summarizes the actions to be taken for given sensor values.

Sensor Value	Action
Less than or equal to low red line	Shut down device
Greater than low red line and less than or equal to low guard line	Issue warning or shut down device
Greater than low guard line and less than high guard line	None
Greater than or equal to high guard line and less than high red line	Issue warning or shut down device
Greater than or equal to high red line	Shut down device

Table 12.1 Actions for Sensor Values

The monitoring program should be able to read in sensor data, evaluate the sensor readings, and issue warnings and shut down devices based on sensor evaluations and trends. Sample output from the monitoring program might look like the following:

```
Cycle 20 - Sensor 4 in high guard line
Cycle 25 - Sensor 4 in high red line
   Shutting down device 4
Cycle 32 - Sensor 3 in low guard line
Cycle 38 - Sensor 1 in high guard line for 6 cycles
   Shutting down device 1
```

For this example Figure 12.5 shows the connections between the devices and sensors to be monitored and Table 12.2 lists the attributes of each of the sensors.

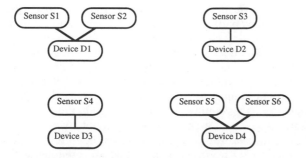

Figure 12.5 Devices and Sensors in a Monitored System

Sensor	Low Red Line	Low Guard Line	High Guard Line	High Red Line
S1	60	70	120	130
S2	20	40	160	180
S3	60	70	120	130
S4	60	70	120	130
S5	65	70	120	125
S6	110	115	125	130

Table 12.2 Sensor Attributes

Part of the solution of this problem involves using the general description of the problem to determine specific details that must be resolved before the implementation of the solution. Typically this process would include iterative consultation with experts knowledgeable about the problem domain but not necessarily able to completely specify the task intended to be captured by an expert system. Prototypes of the problem would be developed to point out details missing in the problem specification. These details would be determined through consultations with experts and another prototype would be developed that may reveal further missing details in the problem specification. Eventually the problem specification would be completely captured through this iterative development programming philosophy.

Many specification details of this problem remain unanswered: How will the information about the sensors and devices be represented? How general or specific should the facts and rules be made? How will the sensor data be retrieved? How long should a sensor be in a guard region before its associated device is shut down? What actions are to be taken when the monitor detects unhealthy devices?

The Details Needed to Begin

One of the major problems encountered in building an expert system is that more often than not the problem is poorly specified. The idea is to emulate an expert, but no one except the expert is sufficiently knowledgeable to specify the details. Typically the expected behavior of the system is known, but the manner in which this behavior is to be generated is not. An expert may have difficulty communicating the exact steps taken in coming to a solution. Because of the iterative development techniques the expert system paradigm naturally supports, it is relatively easy to build expert systems that solve poorly specified problems. This does not mean, however, that the expert systems can solve problems that have never been solved before, or that problems that are not understood can be solved.

Several problem specifications are necessary before an expert system for this monitoring example can be built. First, the expected behavior of the expert system should be specified, including the initial information and the information that the system is to produce. This does not mean that this specification cannot change. Development of the program may indicate that the scope of the problem should be narrowed or perhaps widened, and this would affect the initial inputs and final outputs. Some assumptions must be made and initial details about how the expert system should perform its tasks must be decided. Again, these types of decisions are not permanent. Experts can often demonstrate how they went about solving a problem, but then cannot easily formulate the rules they used. In describing the rules they use, experts may leave out details that are obvious to them or may forget exceptions.

The monitoring problem requires the making of many initial decisions. The first of these is in implementation. Should the solution be specifically geared to the exact details of the problem specification or should it incorporate enough generality to allow it to be easily upgraded or modified? Specific rules could be written for each of the devices to be monitored, or a general rule could be written to monitor all of the devices. For this problem writing general rules appears to be more appropriate because the individual devices and sensors to be modeled have no unique characteristics. This type of generality should allow the easy addition of more devices and sensors.

Details about the flow of control for the system are also missing. For this problem a simple monitoring cycle will be used. Each monitoring cycle will have three phases. During the first phase values will be read from the sensors. During the second phase an analysis will be made of the sensor values. During the third phase any appropriate actions will be taken.

Assumptions must also be made about how the sensor data are to be retrieved. Will they be read directly from sensors? Will it be necessary to handle the simulation of sensor data? Will sensor data always be available when requested? Are the sensor data reliable or are they subject to error? Under normal prototyping situations the experts could be interviewed to determine this information, but for the purposes of this problem assumptions will be made to fill in details.

All of these questions point out gaps that may be encountered in a poorly defined problem. During development a list of assumptions, questions, and possible inconsistencies relating to the problem specification should be maintained. In the iterative development of the program this list should be the focal point of discussion, with experts to ensure that the problem specification matches the expert's view of how the problem is to be solved. The following assumptions begin this list for the monitoring problem:

- Sensor data are always reliable and always available on request.
- Sensor values should be readable directly from sensors. Simulated sensor values should also be supported.
- Sensor values will not be monitored for a machine that has been shut down.
- Actions specified by the monitoring system are assumed to be carried out (i.e., we're assuming that we either have an alert operator or that control of the devices is directly handled by the program).
- The problem will be split into three phases: reading of sensor values, analysis of sensor values, and taking of appropriate actions such as shutting down a device.

In addition to details of problem specification, details of problem implementation must also be decided. These details include how to represent the available information, flow of control, and testing of the expert system.

Knowledge Definitions

Once again, we start solving the problem by determining how the knowledge should be represented. A good start for this problem is to encode the knowledge in Figure 12.5 and Table 12.2. The following deftemplate will be used to describe each of the devices:

```
(defmodule MAIN (export ?ALL))
(deftemplate MAIN::device
   (slot name (type SYMBOL))
   (slot status (allowed-values on off)))
```

where the *name* slot is the name of the device and the *status* slot indicates whether the device is on or off. Using Figure 12.5 and assuming that all devices are initially turned on, we describe the initial state of the devices using the following deffacts:

```
(deffacts MAIN::device-information
   (device (name D1) (status on))
   (device (name D2) (status on))
   (device (name D3) (status on))
   (device (name D4) (status on)))
```

Figure 12.5 also indicates which sensors are associated with which devices. The following deftemplate will be used to represent this relation:

```
(deftemplate MAIN::sensor
   (slot name (type SYMBOL))
   (slot device (type SYMBOL))
   (slot raw-value (type SYMBOL NUMBER)
                   (allowed-symbols none)
                   (default none))
   (slot state (allowed-values low-red-line
                               low-guard-line
                               normal
                               high-red-line
                               high-guard-line)
            (default normal))
   (slot low-red-line (type NUMBER))
   (slot low-guard-line (type NUMBER))
   (slot high-guard-line (type NUMBER))
   (slot high-red-line (type NUMBER)))
```

where the *name* slot is the name of the sensor and the *device* slot is the name of the device with which the sensor is associated. The *raw-value* slot contains the data value read directly from the sensor before it has been processed. The state slot indicates the current state of the sensor (e.g., normal, low guard line, high red line, etc.). The *low-red-line*, *low-guard-line*, *expected-average-value*, *high-guard-line*, and *high-red-line* slots are used to contain the information described in Table 12.2. The following deffacts can be used to describe the sensors in Figure 12.5:

```
(deffacts MAIN::sensor-information
   (sensor (name S1) (device D1)
           (low-red-line 60) (low-guard-line 70)
           (high-guard-line 120)
           (high-red-line 130))
   (sensor (name S2) (device D1)
           (low-red-line 20) (low-guard-line 40)
```

```
          (high-guard-line 160)
          (high-red-line 180))
   (sensor (name S3) (device D2)
          (low-red-line 60) (low-guard-line 70)
          (high-guard-line 120)
          (high-red-line 130))
   (sensor (name S4) (device D3)
          (low-red-line 60) (low-guard-line 70)
          (high-guard-line 120)
          (high-red-line 130))
   (sensor (name S5) (device D4)
          (low-red-line 65) (low-guard-line 70)
          (high-guard-line 120)
          (high-red-line 125))
   (sensor (name S6) (device D4)
          (low red line 110) (low-guard-line 115)
          (high-guard-line 125)
          (high-red-line 130)))
```

Since the monitoring system will be cyclic, a fact will be needed to represent the current cycle. The first cycle can be started at 1 and then be incremented by 1 with each new cycle. The ordered fact format for this information will be

```
(cycle <number>)
```

where <number> is the value of the current cycle. In addition, since sensor values might be read from more than one source (e.g., one source for simulation and another for actual operation), it will be useful to have a fact indicating the sensor data source. This fact can be represented with the following format:

```
(data-source <source>)
```

where <source> is a name representing the source from which data are read. Potential sources could be the sensors, a simulator, a text file, a set of facts, or user input.

A deffacts containing this initial information is

```
(deffacts MAIN::cycle-start
   (data-source user)
   (cycle 0))
```

Notice that the user will supply data for the sensors. For this example entering data from the keyboard will be more convenient than reading data from a file.

Control of Execution

The statement of problem assumptions indicates that there will be three specific phases to the monitoring process. The first phase will read in either user-supplied, simulated, or actual values from the sensors. The second phase will associate guard line and red line conditions for the sensor values and determine any developing trends. Once trends have been established the monitoring system will issue any appropriate warnings, shut down malfunctioning equipment, and restart equipment that can be brought back on line. After appropriate actions have been taken a new cycle will begin by reading new sensor values.

Control of the monitoring expert system will be handled using the techniques similar to those described in Chapter 10. Three separate modules will be created: *INPUT*, *TRENDS*, and *WARNINGS*. Each cycle, the value of the *cycle* fact will be updated and the proceeding modules will be focused on in the appropriate order. The following rule will perform these actions:

```
(defrule MAIN::Begin-Next-Cycle
   ?f <- (cycle ?current-cycle)
   =>
   (retract ?f)
   (assert (cycle (+ ?current-cycle 1)))
   (focus INPUT TRENDS WARNINGS))
```

The *Begin-Next-Cycle* rule reactivates itself, so it will be necessary to use the *halt* command from the RHS of a rule to terminate execution.

Reading the Raw Sensor Values

The next step in building the monitoring system is to read in the sensor values from the sensors. The logical place to read the values is when the current focus is the *INPUT* module. For debugging and testing purposes it will be convenient to be able to read sensor values from several sources. This section will demonstrate how to read values directly from the sensors, from deffacts, from a file, and from the user. The data-source fact described previously is used to indicate the source of data for the monitoring system. Sensor values read as "raw" data will be stored directly in the *raw-value* slot of the *sensor* facts and processing and analysis of this raw value will be performed in the analysis phase.

Under actual operating conditions the values would probably be extracted directly from the sensors, requiring external functions to do this work. Let's assume that the function *get-sensor-value* will return the current sensor value, given an argument representing the sensor id for which the value is desired. (In order to call a function written in C, Ada, FORTRAN, or some other programming language, it's necessary to recompile the CLIPS source code). The rule for directly reading sensor values is the following:

```
(defrule INPUT::Read-Sensor-Values-From-Sensors
   (data-source sensors)
   ?s <- (sensor (name ?name)
                 (raw-value none)
                 (device ?device))
   (device (name ?device) (status on))
   =>
   (modify ?s (raw-value (get-sensor-value ?name))))
```

The first pattern of the rule, (data-source sensors), limits the rule to uses only when the data source is from the sensors. The next two patterns form the major part of the LHS of the rule. The rule will be activated for every sensor fact in the fact list that has a corresponding device that is on. The *none* literal constraint ensures that sensor values will be read only for sensors that have not already obtained a raw value (otherwise the rule would loop endlessly). The *raw-value* slot will have to be set back to value none after analysis of the sensor has occurred. The RHS of the rule then makes an external function call to the function *get-sensor-value* and places the return value in the *raw-value* slot of the *sensor* fact.

This particular rule might be difficult to use during the actual prototyping of the expert system because the program would have to communicate with the actual sensors and devices. One technique for reading the sensor values would be to query the user directly for them. This would allow the maximum flexibility in debugging since the user would be directly queried for each sensor value:

```
(defrule INPUT::Get-Sensor-Value-From-User
   (data-source user)
   ?s <- (sensor (name ?name)
                 (raw-value none)
                 (device ?device))
   (device (name ?device) (status on))
   =>
   (printout t "Input value for sensor " ?name ": ")
   (bind ?raw-value (read))
   (if (not (numberp ?raw-value))
       then (halt)
       else (modify ?s (raw-value ?raw-value))))
```

All the patterns of rule *Get-Sensor-Value-From-User* are identical to the rule *Read-Sensor-Values-From-Sensors* with the exception of the first (data-source user), which limits the rule's activations to scenarios in which the data source is the user. The RHS of the rule is similar, with the exception that the user is queried for the raw value of the sensor. Notice also the *if* expression that follows the binding of the variable *?raw-value*. This expression will halt the program if a nonnumeric slot is returned by the *read* function. This test is a convenient method for the user to halt execution of the program when sensor values are being entered.

For test cases or to avoid a great deal of user input, it might be more desirable to read data from a "script" rather than actually reading from a sensor or questioning the user for every value. One technique for accomplishing this would store the data in facts that the rules could then access. The following deftemplate describes a fact used to store data values:

```
(deftemplate INPUT::fact-data-for-sensor
   (slot name)
   (multislot data))
```

where *name* slot is the name of the sensor associated with the data values and the *data* slot is the actual list of data values for the sensor.

Using this deftemplate, a deffacts containing test values might look like the following:

```
(deffacts INPUT::sensor-fact-data-values
   (fact-data-for-sensor (name S1)
      (data 100 100 110 110 115 120))
   (fact-data-for-sensor (name S2)
      (data 110 120 125 130 130 135))
```

```
(fact-data-for-sensor (name S3)
   (data 100 120 125 130 130 125))
(fact-data-for-sensor (name S4)
   (data 120 120 120 125 130 135))
(fact-data-for-sensor (name S5)
   (data 110 120 125 130 135 135))
(fact-data-for-sensor (name S6)
   (data 115 120 125 135 130 135)))
```

The following rule could be used to access the data values from the *fact-data-for-sensor* facts:

```
(defrule INPUT::Read-Sensor-Values-From-Facts
  (data-source facts)
  ?s <- (sensor (name ?name)
                (raw-value none))
  ?f <- (fact-data-for-sensor
                (name ?name)
                (data ?raw-value $?rest))
  =>
  (modify ?s (raw-value ?raw-value))
  (modify ?f (data ?rest)))
```

This rule is similar to the two previous input rules. Notice, however, that the (device (name ?device) (status on)) pattern that was included in the previous rules has been omitted. This omission allows the *n*th value in a *fact-data-for-sensor* fact to correspond directly to the value for a sensor in the *n*th cycle of monitoring. The last pattern on the LHS also merits comment. The *fact-data-for-sensor* fact contains the data values to be used for the sensor with the name bound to the variable *?name*. The first data value in the fact is bound to the variable *?raw-value* and the remaining values are bound to the variable *?rest*. The first data value is then stored in the *raw-value* slot of the corresponding sensor. The *fact-data-for-sensor* fact is then modified with the just-used data value missing. One problem remains in that the rule will not fire if the *fact-data-for-sensor* fact has no data values. We now make the assumption that if there are no data values left for a sensor, the system should be halted. The following rule handles this situation:

```
(defrule INPUT::No-Fact-Data-Values-Left
  (data-source facts)
  (sensor (name ?name)
          (raw-value none))
  (fact-data-for-sensor (name ?name) (data))
  =>
  (printout t "No fact data for sensor " ?name
              crlf)
  (printout t "Halting monitoring system" crlf)
  (halt))
```

The final input technique to be discussed involves reading the information from a data file. This is more complicated than the previous examples because several issues must be handled. The data file must initially be opened and the data must be read sequentially from the file. The previous input techniques were not dependent on reading the data sequentially, but rather could access the new data values for the sensors in any order. It is also not necessarily known how many sensor values have to be read, and it is desirable to prevent hardcoding of such information in the rules. To add more complexity, an assumption will be made that sensor data values may be left unspecified, in which case they will assume the raw data value of the sensor from the previous cycle.

The first issue that must be handled is to open the data file initially. To indicate that the data file has been opened, a fact will be used to act as a flag. The presence of the fact (data-file-open) will indicate that a data file has been opened using the logical name *data-file*. The absence of this fact will indicate the need to open the data file. The following rule will open the data file if it has not already been opened:

```
(defrule INPUT::Open-File-With-Sensor-Values
  (data-source file)
  (not (data-file-open))
  =>
  (bind ?flag file-closed)
  (while (eq ?flag file-closed)
    (printout t
              "What is the name of the data file? ")
    (bind ?file-name (readline))
    (if (open ?file-name data-file "r")
       then (bind ?flag true)))
  (assert (data-file-open)))
```

This rule has two simple conditions: the data source must be a file and the data file must not already have been opened. If these conditions have been met, then the RHS of the rule will open a data file whose name is supplied by the operator of the monitoring system. The *while* loop, in conjunction with the variable *?flag*, sets up a convenient method for ensuring that the file supplied by the operator has been successfully opened. The operator will be repeatedly queried for the name of a source data file as long as the *open* function is unsuccessful in opening the file supplied. Once a file has been successfully opened, the *data-file-open* fact flag will be asserted.

The next decision involves the file format for storing the sensor data. It is desirable to be able to specify only those sensor values that have changed since the last cycle. Therefore, for a given cycle it is not known how many sensor values are to be read. Also, the order in which sensor values are to be read cannot necessarily be determined beforehand. These assumptions dictate a data format in which the name of the sensor is kept alongside the raw sensor value to be read. Since the number of data values to be read is unknown, the end-of-data values for a cycle will be indicated by the keyword *end-of-cycle*. The data format will look like this:

```
S1 100
S2 110
S3 100
S4 120
S5 110
S6 115
end-of-cycle
S2 120
S3 120
S5 120
S6 120
end-of-cycle
S1 110
S2 125
S3 125
S5 125
S6 125
end-of-cycle
. . .
```

The first rule needed is one to read all the raw values from the data file for the current cycle. The rule to perform this operation is

```
(defrule INPUT::Read-Sensor-Values-From-File
  (data-source file)
  (data-file-open)
  (cycle ?time)
  =>
  (bind ?name (read data-file))
  (if (eq ?name EOF) then (halt))
  (while (and (neq ?name end-of-cycle)
              (neq ?name EOF))
    (bind ?raw-value (read data-file))
    (if (eq ?raw-value EOF) then (halt))
    (assert (raw-sensor-value ?name ?raw-value))
    (bind ?name (read data-file))
    (if (eq ?name EOF) then (halt))))
```

This rule reads all of the data values from the data file until the keyword *end-of-cycle* has been reached. If the end of file is reached, then the monitoring system is halted. The data values read are asserted as facts with the relation name *raw-sensor-value*. The two remaining slots in the fact specify the sensor name for which the data value applies and the raw sensor value.

The following rule will remove the raw data value fact for any sensor whose device has been shut off so that reasoning is limited only to those sensors whose devices are on:

```
(defrule INPUT::Remove-Values-For-Inactive-Sensors
  (data-source file)
  (data-file-open)
  (cycle ?time)
  (sensor (name ?name) (device ?device))
  (device (name ?device) (status off))
  ?data <- (raw-sensor-value ?name ?raw-value)
  =>
  (retract ?data))
```

The following rule stores the raw sensor value read from the file in the *raw-value* slot of the sensors. No action is taken during this phase of execution for the sensors that did not have a change in raw data value.

```
(defrule INPUT::Transfer-Sensor-Values-To-Sensors
  (data-source file)
  ?s <- (sensor (name ?name)
                (raw-value none)
                (device ?device))
  (device (name ?device) (status on))
  ?f <- (raw-sensor-value ?name ?raw-value)
  =>
  (modify ?s (raw-value ?raw-value))
  (retract ?f))
```

Detecting a Trend

The next phase of activity, the *trends* phase, determines the current state of the sensors and calculates trends that may be developing. The current state of the sensor (normal, low or high guard line, or low or high red line) must be determined from the raw sensor value asserted during the *input* phase. The current state of the sensor is stored in the *state* slot of the *sensor* deftemplate. The following rule determines whether a sensor is in the normal state:

```
(defrule TRENDS::Normal-State
  ?s <- (sensor (raw-value ?raw-value&~none)
                (low-guard-line ?lgl)
                (high-guard-line ?hgl))
  (test (and (> ?raw-value ?lgl)
             (< ?raw-value ?hgl)))
  =>
  (modify ?s (state normal) (raw-value none)))
```

The first pattern and following test CE look for any sensors that are in the normal state. The *raw-value* slot in the *sensor* pattern is compared against the value none to ensure that a symbol is not compared to numeric values in the test CE of the rule. The range needed for testing whether a sensor is in a normal state is between the low and high guard line values. The test CE constrains the rule to situations in which the raw sensor value is in the normal state range. The only action of this rule is to assert the derived state of the sensor. The *raw-value* slot is also set to the literal *none* so it will be read in the next *input* phase.

Four more rules are necessary to analyze the remaining four possible states of a sensor. Each of the rules will be similar to the rule *Normal-State*, with the exception of the values retrieved from the *sensor* fact and the test CE used to determine the current state. All five of the state rules could be written as a single rule with an *if* expression on the RHS of the rule to determine the appropriate state of the sensor. This type of coding, however, defeats the purpose of a data-driven system. In addition, further modifications involving actions or conditions or both of a subset of the possible states would be made much more difficult by a single unwieldy rule. The remaining four state analysis rules are as follows:

```
(defrule TRENDS::High-Guard-Line-State
  ?s <- (sensor (raw-value ?raw-value&~none)
                (high-guard-line ?hgl)
                (high-red-line ?hrl))
  (test (and (>= ?raw-value ?hgl)
             (< ?raw-value ?hrl)))
  =>
  (modify ?s (state high-guard-line)
             (raw-value none)))

(defrule TRENDS::High-Red-Line-State
  ?s <- (sensor (raw-value ?raw-value&~none)
                (high-red-line ?hrl))
  (test (>= ?raw-value ?hrl))
  =>
  (modify ?s (state high-red-line)
             (raw-value none)))

(defrule TRENDS::Low-Guard-Line-State
  ?s <- (sensor (raw-value ?raw-value&~none)
                (low-guard-line ?lgl)
                (low-red-line ?lrl))
  (test (and (> ?raw-value ?lrl)
             (<= ?raw-value ?lgl)))
  =>
  (modify ?s (state low-guard-line)
             (raw-value none)))

(defrule TRENDS::Low-Red-Line-State
  ?s <- (sensor (raw-value ?raw-value&~none)
                (low-red-line ?lrl))
  (test (<= ?raw-value ?lrl))
  =>
  (modify ?s (state low-red-line)
             (raw-value none)))
```

The five previous rules determine the state of a sensor for the current cycle. Since detecting trends in the sensors is one of the objectives of the *TRENDS* module, it will be necessary to maintain information about the past state of a sensor. The following deftemplate will be used to store this information. Since both the *TRENDS* and the *WARNINGS* module will use this deftemplate, it will be placed in the MAIN module.

```
(deftemplate MAIN::sensor-trend
    (slot name)
    (slot state (default normal))
    (slot start (default 0))
    (slot end (default 0))
    (slot shutdown-duration (default 3)))
```

The *name* slot is the name of the sensor, the *state* slot corresponds to the most current state of the sensor, the *start* slot is the first cycle during which the sensor was in its current state, the *end* slot is the current cycle, and the *shutdown-duration* slot is the amount of time a sensor must be in a guard line region before its associated device must be shut down.

The rules that update the trend information will depend on a *sensor-trend* fact existing in the fact list for each sensor. For this reason the initial sensor trends will be defined in a deffacts construct.

```
(deffacts MAIN::start-trends
    (sensor-trend (name S1) (shutdown-duration 3))
    (sensor-trend (name S2) (shutdown-duration 5))
    (sensor-trend (name S3) (shutdown-duration 4))
    (sensor-trend (name S4) (shutdown-duration 4))
    (sensor-trend (name S5) (shutdown-duration 4))
    (sensor-trend (name S6) (shutdown-duration 2)))
```

With this information, two rules may be defined to monitor the trends for a sensor. One rule will monitor a trend that has *not* changed since the last cycle and the other will monitor a trend that *has* changed since the last cycle:

```
(defrule TRENDS::State-Has-Not-Changed
    (cycle ?time)
    ?trend <- (sensor-trend (name ?sensor)
                            (state ?state)
                            (end ?end-cycle&~?time))
    (sensor (name ?sensor) (state ?state)
            (raw-value none))
    =>
    (modify ?trend (end ?time)))

(defrule TRENDS::State-Has-Changed
    (cycle ?time)
    ?trend <- (sensor-trend (name ?sensor)
                            (state ?state)
                            (end ?end-cycle&~?time))
    (sensor (name ?sensor)
            (state ?new-state&~?state)
            (raw-value none))
```

```
=>
(modify ?trend (start ?time)
                (end ?time)
                (state ?new-state)))
```

The first pattern of both rules establishes the cycle. The next pattern finds the *sensor-trend* fact for the previous cycle. The constraint on the *end* slot insures that the rules do not endlessly loop. For the rule *State-Has-Not-Changed*, the next pattern checks that the state from the previous cycle is the same as the state for the current cycle. The constraint ?new-state&~?state in the rule *State-Has-Changed* performs exactly the opposite test, making sure that the state has changed from the last cycle. Checking that the *raw-value* slot is the literal *none* prevents the trend from being determined before the present state of the sensor is determined. In both rules the end cycle time is updated. If the state has changed, then the state value and start cycle time must be updated as well.

Issuing Warnings

The final phase of the cycle is the *warnings* phase. Three types of actions must be handled during this phase: sensors that have entered a red line region will have their associated devices shut off, sensors that have stayed in the guard line region for a specified number of cycles will have their associated devices shut off, and sensors that are in the guard line region and did not have their associated devices shut off will have a warning issued.

The following rule shuts off sensors that have entered a red line region:

```
(defrule WARNINGS::Shutdown-In-Red-Region
   (cycle ?time)
   (sensor-trend
      (name ?sensor)
      (state ?state&high-red-line | low-red-line))
   (sensor (name ?sensor) (device ?device))
   ?on <- (device (name ?device) (status on))
   =>
   (printout t "Cycle " ?time " - ")
   (printout t "Sensor " ?sensor " in " ?state crlf)
   (printout t "   Shutting down device " ?device
               crlf)
   (modify ?on (status off)))
```

The state of a sensor is checked using the *sensor-trend* fact. If the sensor is in a red line region, the associated device is turned off. Devices are immediately shut off once one of their sensors enters a red line region, so it serves little purpose to check how long a sensor has been in this state.

The rule *Shutdown-In-Guard-Region* is similar to the previous rule, with the difference that the sensor must have been in the guard line region for a period of time (specified by the shutdown-duration slot of the sensor-trend fact) before it is shut down. The length of time a sensor has been in a particular state can be determined by subtracting the *start* slot from the *end* slot of the *sensor-trend* fact.

```
(defrule WARNINGS::Shutdown-In-Guard-Region
  (cycle ?time)
  (sensor-trend
      (name ?sensor)
      (state ?state&high-guard-line |
                  low-guard-line)
      (shutdown-duration ?length)
      (start ?start) (end ?end))
  (test (>= (+ (- ?end ?start) 1)  ?length))
  (sensor (name ?sensor) (device ?device))
  ?on <- (device (name ?device) (status on))
  =>
  (printout t "Cycle " ?time " - ")
  (printout t "Sensor " ?sensor " in " ?state " ")
  (printout t "for " ?length " cycles "
              crlf)
  (printout t "   Shutting down device " ?device
              crlf)
  (modify ?on (status off)))
```

The addition of the *shutdown-duration* slot in the *sensor-trend* pattern and the associated test CE is the only major difference between this rule and the *Shutdown-In-Red-Region* rule. These two patterns determine whether a sensor has been in a guard region long enough to shut down the device associated with the sensor.

The final rule for the monitoring system will issue a warning for sensors that are in a guard region but that have not been in the region long enough to warrant shutting off their associated devices:

```
(defrule WARNINGS::Sensor-In-Guard-Region
  (cycle ?time)
  (sensor-trend
      (name ?sensor)
      (state ?state&high-guard-line |
                  low-guard-line)
      (shutdown-duration ?length)
      (start ?start) (end ?end))
  (test (< (+ (- ?end ?start) 1) ?length))
  =>
  (printout t "Cycle " ?time " - ")
  (printout t "Sensor " ?sensor " in "
              ?state crlf))
```

This rule acts as the complement of the *Shutdown-In-Guard-Region* rule. The test CE has been modified to check that the sensor has been in the guard line region less than the number of cycles required to shut down its associated device. Since the sensor's associated device does not need to be shut down, the patterns to determine the associated device are not included.

This final rule completes the basis of a very simple monitoring system. Additional rules could cover specific situations that should be monitored or provide a generic model for handling complex monitoring situations and representing sensor/device relationships.

12.6 SUMMARY

This chapter demonstrated a technique for representing MYCIN-style certainty factors in CLIPS. Facts are used to represent Object–Attribute–Value triples. An additional slot in each fact represents the certainty factor of the fact. Rules are used to compute certainty values for newly asserted facts on the RHS of a rule by using the certainty values bound in the LHS of the rule. A rule is then used to combine two occurrences of an OAV triple into a single occurrence with a new certainty factor computed from the certainty factors of the original pair.

Decision trees can also be represented using the forward chaining paradigm of CLIPS. There are several algorithms for traversing decision trees including binary decision trees, multiple-branch decision trees, and learning multiple-branch decision trees. The algorithm for a multiple-branch decision tree that learns is implemented in CLIPS.

CLIPS can also emulate a backward chaining inferencing strategy. A backward chaining inference engine is built using CLIPS rules and is based in part on an algorithm for accomplishing backward chaining in a procedural language. Backward chaining rules are represented as facts and acted on by the CLIPS backward chaining inference rules. A step-by-step trace of a sample backward chaining session demonstrates how this paradigm is represented in CLIPS.

The final example in this chapter is a simple monitoring expert system. An initial statement of the monitoring problem is used to begin the process of writing the expert system. Assumptions are made and additional details are added as more rules are added to the monitoring system. The execution of the monitoring system is split into three phases. The *input* phase gathers raw data values for the sensors. Several different methods for supplying data values are demonstrated. The *trends* phase analyzes the raw sensor values and checks for developing trends. Finally, the *warnings* phase issues warnings and performs appropriate actions based on the analysis of the *trends* phase.

PROBLEMS

12.1   Write CLIPS rules to combine MYCIN certainty factors as shown in Section 12.2 for the following two cases

$$\text{New Certainty} = (CF_1 + CF_2) + (CF_1 * CF_2)$$

$$\text{if} \quad CF_1 \leq 0 \text{ and } CF_2 \leq 0$$

$$\text{New Certainty} = \frac{CF_1 + CF_2}{1 - \min\{\, |CF_1| \,, \, |CF_2| \,\}}$$

$$\text{if} \quad -1 < CF_1 * CF_2 < 0$$

12.2   Show how classical probability could be incorporated into CLIPS using the types of techniques demonstrated in Section 12.2. List possible advantages and disadvantages of using classical probability in rules.

12.3   Implement the *Solve_Tree_and_Learn* algorithm described in Section 12.3 using a procedural language such as LISP, C, or PASCAL. Test your implementation using the animal identification example.

12.4   Implement the *Solve_Goal* and *Attempt_Rule* algorithms described in Section 12.4 using a procedural language such as LISP, C, or PASCAL. Test your implementation using the wine selection example.

12.5   Modify rule *INPUT::Get-Sensor-Value-From-User* so it will only allow numeric input from the user. The rule should cause a halt only if the word *halt* is entered during input.

12.6   Modify rule *INPUT::Get-Sensor-Value-From-User* and add additional rules if necessary to allow the user to use a carriage return to indicate that the previous value of each sensor should be retained. For example, if the previous values for sensors 1 and 2 were 100 and 120, then the following responses

```
What is the value for sensor 1? ↵
What is the value for sensor 2? 130↵
```

should set the raw data value of sensor 1 to 100 and the raw data value of sensor 2 to 130. What assumptions should be made and what actions should be taken if the previous sensor value is unknown?

12.7   Modify the program so a device that has been shut off will continue to have its sensors monitored. If all sensors for the device return to a normal state, then the device should be turned back on.

12.8   The rule *Sensor-In-Guard-Region* will issue a warning for a sensor even if another rule is on the agenda, after it which would shut off its associated device. What change should be made to this rule to prevent it from issuing a warning if another rule in the *WARNINGS* module would turn off its associated device?

12.9   Add rules to print a message in the *warnings* phase to indicate that a sensor has had normal status for at least n cycles, where the number n is specified in a fact. Print the message only every nth cycle.

12.10   How could the backward chaining rules in Section 12.4 be modified to allow forward chaining?

12.11   Modify the program developed for Problem 11.8 on page 506 so that the facts representing the shrubs are loaded from a file using the load-facts function. After explanations are provided, the user should be queried to determine whether another shrub selection is desired, and, if so, the program should be run again.

12.12   Modify the program developed for Problem 11.11 on page 507 so that it can schedule several students. The input to the program should be read from a file. You are free to determine the format of the input data; however, it should contain at least the name of each student, the courses to be scheduled, and the student's preferences for instructors and periods. The output of the program should be written to a file. The output file should contain the name of each student followed by the courses scheduled for that student.

12.13   Modify the program developed for Problem 11.10 on page 506 to demonstrate dynamically reconfigurable menus. For example, selecting menu item 1 in submenu 1 causes two menu items to be displayed in submenu 2, but selecting menu item 2 in submenu 1 causes four menu items to be displayed in submenu 2.

12.14 Using the program developed for Problem 12.13, modify the program developed for Problem 11-14 on page 508 so that only the gizmos that have not been selected are listed in the "Add Gizmo" submenu and only the gizmos that have been selected are listed in the "Remove Gizmo" submenu. In the main menu, the "Add Gizmo" menu choice should appear only if there are unselected gizmos, and the "Remove Gizmo" menu choice should appear only if there are selected gizmos.

12.15 Using the program developed for Problem 11.10 on page 506, modify the program developed for Problem 10.17 on page 476 to use a menu-driven interface. The user should be provided with separate menu options for specifying the color, hardness, and density of the gem being identified. Specification of the color should be done using a submenu containing the valid colors. A menu option should be provided that lists the gems satisfying the currently specified criterion. For example, if the user has only specified that the gem is black, the selection of this menu option will list only gems that can be black. Two other menu options should be provided, one that lists the current values specified for the criterion and another that resets all of the criteria to an unspecified state.

BIBLIOGRAPHY

(Firebaugh 88). Morris W. Firebaugh, *Artificial Intelligence: A Knowledge-Based Approach*, Boyd & Fraser Publishing, p. 309, 1988.

APPENDIX A

Some Useful Equivalences

$\sim\sim p \equiv p$

$p \rightarrow q \equiv \sim p \vee q \equiv \sim q \rightarrow \sim p$

$\sim(p \wedge q) \equiv \sim p \vee \sim q$
$\sim(p \vee q) \equiv \sim p \wedge \sim q$

$p \wedge (q \vee r) \equiv (p \wedge q) \vee (p \wedge r)$
$p \vee (q \wedge r) \equiv (p \vee q) \wedge (p \vee r)$

$(p \wedge q) \wedge r \equiv p \wedge (q \wedge r)$
$(p \vee q) \vee r \equiv p \vee (q \vee r)$

$p \wedge q \equiv q \wedge p$
$p \vee q \equiv q \vee p$

$\sim(\forall x)\ P(x) \equiv (\exists x)\ \sim P(x)$
$\sim(\exists x)\ P(x) \equiv (\forall x)\ \sim P(x)$

$(\forall x)\ P(x) \wedge (\forall x)\ Q(x) \equiv (\forall x)\ (P(x) \wedge Q(x))$
$(\exists x)\ P(x) \vee (\exists x)\ Q(x) \equiv (\exists x)\ (P(x) \vee Q(x))$

Note: The $\forall$ does not distribute over an $\vee$, and $\exists$ does not distribute over $\wedge$, so a new dummy variable, z, is needed in the following two equivalences.

$(\forall x)\ P(x) \vee (\forall x)\ Q(x) \equiv (\forall x)\ P(x) \vee (\forall z)\ Q(z)$
$ \equiv (\forall x)\ (\forall z)\ (P(x) \vee Q(z))$

$(\exists x)\ P(x) \wedge (\exists x)\ Q(x) \equiv (\exists x)\ P(x) \wedge (\exists z)\ Q(z)$
$ \equiv (\exists x)\ (\exists z)\ (P(x) \wedge Q(z))$

APPENDIX B

Some Elementary Quantifiers and Their Meanings

Formula	Meaning
$(\forall x)\,(P(x) \rightarrow Q(x))$	For all x, all P are Q
$(\forall x)\,(P(x) \rightarrow {\sim}Q(x))$	For all x, no P are Q
$(\exists x)\,(P(x) \wedge Q(x))$	For some x, x are P and Q
$(\exists x)\,(P(x) \wedge {\sim}Q(x))$	For some x, x are P and not Q
$(\forall x)\,P(x)$	For all x, x is P
$(\exists x)\,P(x)$	Some x is P (or there are P)
${\sim}(\forall x)\,P(x)$	Not all x are P (or some x are P)
$(\forall x)\,{\sim}P(x)$	All x are not P
$(\forall x)\,(\exists y)\,P(x,y)$	For all x, there is a y such that P
$(\exists x)\,{\sim}P(x)$	Some x is not P

APPENDIX C
Some Set Properties

Commutativity	$A \cup B = B \cup A$ $A \cap B = B \cap A$
Associativity	$A \cup (B \cup C) = (A \cup B) \cup C$ $A \cap (B \cap C) = (A \cap B) \cap C$
Idempotence	$A \cup A = A$ $A \cap A = A$
Distributivity	$A \cup (B \cap C) = (A \cup B) \cap (A \cup C)$ $A \cap (B \cup C) = (A \cap B) \cup (A \cap C)$
Law of the Excluded Middle	$A \cup A' = U$
Law of Contradiction	$A \cap A' = \emptyset$
Identity	$A \cup \emptyset = A$ $A \cap U = A$
Absorption	$A \cup (A \cap B) = A$ $A \cap (A \cup B) = A$
de Morgan's Laws	$(A \cap B)' = A' \cup B'$ $(A \cup B)' = A' \cap B'$
Involution	$(A')' = A$
Equivalence	$(A' \cup B) \cap (A \cup B') = (A' \cap B') \cup (A \cap B)$
Symmetrical Difference	$(A' \cap B) \cup (A \cap B') = (A' \cup B') \cap (A \cup B)$

APPENDIX D

CLIPS Support Information

The CD-ROM included with this book contains CLIPS executables for MS-DOS, Windows 3.1/Windows 95, and Mac OS. Also included on the CD-ROM are all of the CLIPS source code, the three-volume *CLIPS Reference Manual*, and the *CLIPS User's Guide*. Volume I of the *CLIPS Reference Manual*, *The Basic Programming Guide*, provides the definitive description of CLIPS syntax and examples of usage. Volume II, *The Advanced Programming Guide*, provides details on customizing CLIPS, adding new functions to CLIPS, embedding CLIPS, and other advanced features. Volume III, *The Interfaces Guide*, provides information on the environment-specific interfaces for CLIPS. An X Windows version of CLIPS can be created by compiling the X Windows interface and CLIPS source code found on the CD-ROM.

Bug fixes, updates, and other information related to CLIPS can be found at the CLIPS home page at http://www.jsc.nasa.gov/~clips/CLIPS.html or alternatively at http://www.ghg.net/clips/CLIPS.html. Questions regarding CLIPS can be sent via electronic mail to clips@ghg.net. Usenet users can find information and post questions about CLIPS at the comp.ai.shells news group.

An electronic conferencing facility is also available to CLIPS users. Subscribers to this facility may send questions, observations, answers, editorials, and so forth in the form of electronic mail to the conference. All subscribers will have a copy of these messages reflected back to them at their respective email addresses. To subscribe, send a single line message to listserv@cosmic.uga.edu saying SUBSCRIBE CLIPS-LIST (the hyphen is required) YOUR NAME. The subject field is ignored but the address found in the "Reply:", "Reply to:", or "From:" fields will be entered in the distribution list. Upon subscription you will receive a mail message instructing you how to participate in the conference from that point forward. Save this mail message because you may need the instructions later if you wish to unsubscribe from the list server.

Appendix E
CLIPS Commands and Functions Summary

Predicate Functions

`(and <expression>+)`

    Returns TRUE if each of its arguments evaluates to TRUE, otherwise FALSE.

`(eq <expression> <expression>+)`

    Returns TRUE if its first argument is equal in type and value to all its subsequent arguments, otherwise FALSE.

`(evenp <expression>)`

    Returns TRUE if <expression> is an even integer, otherwise FALSE.

`(floatp <expression>)`

    Returns TRUE if <expression> is a float, otherwise FALSE.

`(integerp <expression>)`

    Returns TRUE if <expression> is an integer, otherwise FALSE.

`(lexemep <expression>)`

    Returns TRUE if <expression> is a string or symbol, otherwise FALSE.

`(multifieldp <expression>)`

    Returns TRUE if <expression> is a multifield value, otherwise FALSE.

`(neq <expression> <expression>+)`

    Returns TRUE if its first argument is not equal in type and value to all its subsequent arguments, otherwise FALSE.

`(not <expression>)`

    Returns TRUE if its argument evaluates to FALSE, otherwise TRUE.

```
(numberp <expression>)
```
   Returns TRUE if <expression> is a float or an integer, otherwise FALSE.

```
(oddp <expression>)
```
   Returns TRUE if <expression> is an odd integer, otherwise FALSE.

```
(or <expression>+)
```
   Returns TRUE if any of its arguments evaluate to TRUE, otherwise FALSE.

```
(stringp <expression>)
```
   Returns TRUE if <expression> is a string, otherwise FALSE.

```
(symbolp <expression>)
```
   Returns TRUE if <expression> is a symbol, otherwise FALSE.

```
(= <numeric-expression> <numeric-expression>+)
```
   Returns TRUE if its first argument is equal in numeric value to all its subsequent arguments, otherwise FALSE.

```
(<> <numeric-expression> <numeric-expression>+)
```
   Returns TRUE if its first argument is not equal in numeric value to all its subsequent arguments, otherwise FALSE.

```
(> <numeric-expression> <numeric-expression>+)
```
   Returns TRUE if, for all its arguments, argument $n - 1$ is greater than argument n, otherwise FALSE.

```
(>= <numeric-expression> <numeric-expression>+)
```
   Returns TRUE if, for all its arguments, argument $n - 1$ is greater than or equal to argument n, otherwise FALSE.

```
(< <numeric-expression> <numeric-expression>+)
```
   Returns TRUE if, for all its arguments, argument $n - 1$ is less than argument n, otherwise FALSE.

```
(<= <numeric-expression> <numeric-expression>+)
```
   Returns TRUE if, for all its arguments, argument $n - 1$ is less than or equal to argument n, otherwise FALSE.

Multifield Functions

```
(create$ <expression>*)
```
   Appends zero or more expressions together to create a multifield value.

```
(delete$  <multifield-expression>
          <begin-integer-expression>
          <end-integer-expression>)
```
   Deletes all fields in the specified range (<begin-integer-expression> to <end-integer-expression>) from <multifield-expression> and returns the result.

```
(explode$ <string-expression>))
```
Returns a multifield value created from the fields contained in a string.

```
(first$ <multifield-expression>)
```
Returns the first field of <multifield-expression>.

```
(implode$ <multifield-expression>)
```
Returns a string containing the fields from a multifield value.

```
(insert$ <multifield-expression>
         <integer-expression>
         <single-or-multifield-expression>+)
```
Inserts all the <single-or-multifield-expression> values in the <multifield-expression> before the *n*th value (<integer-expression>) of <multifield-expression>.

```
(length$ <multifield-expression>)
```
Returns the number of fields in a multifield value.

```
(member$ <single-field-expression>
         <multifield-expression>)
```
Returns the position of the first argument in the second argument or FALSE if the first argument is not contained in the second argument.

```
(nth$ <integer-expression> <multifield-expression>)
```
Returns the *n*th field (<integer-expression>) contained in <multifield-expression>.

```
(replace$ <multifield-expression>
          <begin-integer-expression>
          <end-integer-expression>
          <single-or-multifield-expression>+)
```
Replaces the fields in the specified range (<begin-integer-expression> to <end-integer-expression>) in <multifield-expression> with all of the <single-or-multifield-expression> values and returns the result.

```
(rest$ <multifield-expression>)
```
Returns a multifield value containing all but the first field of <multifield-expression>.

```
(subseq$ <multifield-expression>
         <begin-integer-expression>
         <end-integer-expression>)
```
Extracts the fields in the specified range (<begin-integer-expression> to <end-integer-expression>) from <multifield-expression> and returns them in a multifield value.

```
(subsetp <expression>)
```
  Returns TRUE if the first argument is a subset of the second argument, otherwise FALSE.

String Functions

```
(lowcase <string-or-symbol-expression>)
```
  Returns its argument with all uppercase letters replaced with lowercase letters.

```
(str-cat <expression>*)
```
  Returns all of its arguments concatenated as a string.

```
(str-compare <string-or-symbol-expression>
             <string-or-symbol-expression>)
```
  Returns zero if both arguments are equal, otherwise a nonzero value.

```
(str-index <lexeme-expression> <lexeme-expression>)
```
  Returns the integer position of the first argument within the second argument if the first argument is a substring of the second argument, otherwise FALSE.

```
(str-length <string-or-symbol-expression>)
```
  Returns the length of a string in characters.

```
(sub-string <begin-integer-expression>
            <end-integer-expression>
            <string-expression>)
```
  Returns the substring from <string-expression> of the specified range (<begin-integer-expression> to <end-integer-expression>).

```
(sym-cat <expression>*)
```
  Returns all of its arguments concatenated as a symbol.

```
(upcase <string-or-symbol-expression>)
```
  Returns its argument with all lowercase letters replaced with uppercase letters.

I/O Functions

```
(close [<logical-name>])
```
  Closes the file associated with the logical name <logical-name> (or all files if unspecified). Returns TRUE if the file was successfully closed, otherwise FALSE.

```
(format <logical-name> <string-expression>
        <expression>*)
```
Evaluates and prints as formatted output to the logical name <logical-name> zero or more expressions formatted by <string-expression>. See Section 8.12 for details on formatting flags.

```
(open <file-name> <logical-name> [<mode>])
```
Opens the file <file-name> in the specified mode (either "r," "w," "r+," or "a") and associates the logical name <logical-name> with the file. Returns TRUE if the file was successfully opened, otherwise FALSE.

```
(printout <logical-name> <expression>*)
```
Evaluates and prints as unformatted output to the logical name <logical-name> zero or more expressions.

```
(read [<logical-name>])
```
Reads a single field from the specified logical name (*stdin* if unspecified). Returns the field if successful or EOF if no input available.

```
(readline [<logical-name>])
```
Reads an entire line from the specified logical name (*stdin* if unspecified). Returns a string if successful or EOF if no input available.

```
(remove <file-name>)
```
Deletes the file <file-name>.

```
(rename <old-file-name> <new-file-name>)
```
Renames the file <old-file-name> to <new-file-name>.

Basic Math Functions

```
(abs <numeric-expression>)
```
Returns the absolute value of its only argument.

```
(div <numeric-expression> <numeric-expression>+)
```
Returns the value of the first argument divided by each of the subsequent arguments. Division is performed using integer arithmetic.

```
(float <numeric-expression>)
```
Returns its only argument converted to type float.

```
(integer <numeric-expression>)
```
Returns its only argument converted to type integer.

```
(max <numeric-expression> <numeric-expression>+)
```
Returns the value of its largest argument.

```
(min <numeric-expression> <numeric-expression>+)
```
Returns the value of its smallest argument.

```
(+ <numeric-expression> <numeric-expression>+)
```
Returns the sum of its arguments.

```
(- <numeric-expression> <numeric-expression>+)
```
Returns the value of the first argument minus the sum of all subsequent arguments.

```
(* <numeric-expression> <numeric-expression>+)
```
Returns the product of its arguments.

```
(/ <numeric-expression> <numeric-expression>+)
```
Returns the value of the first argument divided by each of the subsequent arguments.

Trigonometric Functions

```
(acos <numeric-expression>)
```
Returns the arccosine of its argument (in radians).

```
(acosh <numeric-expression>)
```
Returns the hyperbolic arccosine of its argument (in radians).

```
(acot <numeric-expression>)
```
Returns the arccotangent of its argument (in radians).

```
(acoth <numeric-expression>)
```
Returns the hyperbolic arccotangent of its argument (in radians).

```
(acsc <numeric-expression>)
```
Returns the arccosecant of its argument (in radians).

```
(acsch <numeric-expression>)
```
Returns the hyperbolic arccosecant of its argument (in radians).

```
(asec <numeric-expression>)
```
Returns the arcsecant of its argument (in radians).

```
(asech <numeric-expression>)
```
Returns the hyperbolic arcsecant of its argument (in radians).

```
(asin <numeric-expression>)
```
Returns the arcsine of its argument (in radians).

```
(asinh <numeric-expression>)
```
Returns the hyperbolic arcsine of its argument (in radians).

```
(atan <numeric-expression>)
```
Returns the arctangent of its argument (in radians).

```
(atanh <numeric-expression>)
```
Returns the hyperbolic arctangent of its argument (in radians).

```
(cos <numeric-expression>)
```
Returns the cosine of its argument (in radians).

```
(cosh <numeric-expression>)
```
Returns the hyperbolic cosine of its argument (in radians).

```
(cot <numeric-expression>)
```
Returns the cotangent of its argument (in radians).

```
(coth <numeric-expression>)
```
Returns the hyperbolic cotangent of its argument (in radians).

```
(csc <numeric-expression>)
```
Returns the cosecant of its argument (in radians).

```
(csch <numeric-expression>)
```
Returns the hyperbolic cosecant of its argument (in radians).

```
(sec <numeric-expression>)
```
Returns the secant of its argument (in radians).

```
(sech <numeric-expression>)
```
Returns the hyperbolic secant of its argument (in radians).

```
(sin <numeric-expression>)
```
Returns the sine of its argument (in radians).

```
(sinh <numeric-expression>)
```
Returns the hyperbolic sine of its argument (in radians).

```
(tan <numeric-expression>)
```
Returns the tangent of its argument (in radians).

```
(tanh <numeric-expression>)
```
Returns the hyperbolic tangent of its argument (in radians).

Conversion Functions

```
(deg-grad <numeric-expression>)
```
Returns the value of its argument converted from units of degrees to units of gradients.

```
(deg-rad <numeric-expression>)
```
Returns the value of its argument converted from units of degrees to units of radians.

```
(exp <numeric-expression>)
```
Returns the value of *e* raised to the power of its only argument.

```
(grad-deg <numeric-expression>)
```
Returns the value of its argument converted from units of gradients to units of degrees.

```
(log <numeric-expression>)
```
Returns the logarithm base *e* of its argument.

```
(log10 <numeric-expression>)
```
Returns the logarithm base 10 of its argument.

```
(mod <numeric-expression> <numeric-expression>)
```
Returns the remainder of the result of dividing its first argument by its second argument.

```
(pi )
```
Returns the value of π.

```
(rad-deg <numeric-expression>)
```
Returns the value of its argument converted from units of radians to units of degrees.

```
(round <numeric-expression>)
```
Returns the value of its argument rounded to the closest integer.

```
(sqrt <numeric-expression>)
```
Returns the square root of its argument.

```
(** <numeric-expression> <numeric-expression>)
```
Returns the value of its first argument raised to the power of its second argument.

Procedural Functions

```
(bind <variable> <value>)
```
Binds a variable to a specified value.

```
(if <predicate-expression>
   then <expression>+ [else <expression>+])
```
Evaluates the expressions contained in the *else* portion of the function if the <predicate-expression> evaluates to the symbol FALSE, otherwise evaluates the expressions contained in the *then* portion of the function.

```
(while <predicate-expression> [do] <expression>*)
```
Evaluates <expression>* as long as the <predicate-expression> does not evaluate to the symbol FALSE.

Miscellaneous Functions

(gensym)

> Returns a sequenced symbol of the form genX where *X* is an integer.

(gensym*)

> Returns a sequenced symbol of the form genX where *X* is an integer. Unlike the gensym function, gensym* produces a unique symbol that does not currently exist within the CLIPS environment.

(random)

> Returns a "random" integer value.

(seed <integer-expression>)

> Sets the seed used by the random number generator for the *random* function.

(setgen <integer-expression>)

> Sets the sequence index used by *gensym* and *gensym**.

(time)

> Returns a floating-point value representing the number of elapsed seconds since a system reference time.

Environment Commands

(apropos <lexeme>)

> Displays all symbols currently defined in the CLIPS environment that contain the specified substring <lexeme>.

(batch <file-name>)

> Allows "batch" processing of CLIPS interactive commands by replacing standard input with the contents of the file <file-name>. Returns TRUE if the file was successfully executed, otherwise FALSE.

(clear)

> Removes all constructs from the CLIPS environment.

(exit)

> Exits from the CLIPS environment.

(get-dynamic-constraint-checking)

> Returns the current value of the dynamic constraint checking behavior.

(get-static-constraint-checking)

> Returns the current value of the static constraint checking behavior.

```
(load <file-name>)
```
Loads the constructs stored in the file specified by <file-name> into the CLIPS environment. Returns TRUE if the file was successfully loaded, otherwise FALSE.

```
(reset)
```
Resets the CLIPS environment.

```
(save <file-name>)
```
Saves all of the constructs in the CLIPS environment to the file specified by <file-name>.

```
(set-dynamic-constraint-checking
    <boolean-expression>)
```
Disables dynamic constraint checking if <boolean-expression> is FALSE, otherwise enables dynamic constraint checking. The old value of the constraint checking behavior is returned.

```
(set-static-constraint-checking
    <boolean-expression>)
```
Disables static constraint checking if <boolean-expression> is FALSE, otherwise enables static constraint checking. The old value of the constraint checking behavior is returned.

```
(system <lexeme-expression>*)
```
Concatenates its arguments together as a string and passes the string as a command to be executed by the operating system.

Debugging Commands

```
(dribble-off)
```
Stops sending output to the trace file opened with the *dribble-on* function. Returns TRUE if the trace file was successfully closed, otherwise FALSE.

```
(dribble-on <file-name>)
```
Sends all output that normally goes to the screen to the trace file <file-name>. Returns TRUE if the trace file was successfully opened, otherwise FALSE.

```
(unwatch <watch-item>)
```
Disables the display of informational messages when certain CLIPS operations occur.

```
(watch <watch-item>)
    <watch-item> ::= activations | all |
                     compilations | facts | focus |
                     rules | statistics
```
Enables the display of informational messages when certain CLIPS operations occur.

Deftemplate Commands

```
(list-deftemplates [<module-name>])
```
Lists the deftemplates in the specified module (or in the current module if <module-name> is unspecified).

```
(ppdeftemplate <deftemplate-name>)
```
Displays the text of the specified deftemplate.

```
(undeftemplate <deftemplate-name>)
```
Deletes the specified deftemplate.

Fact Functions and Commands

```
(assert <RHS-pattern>)
```
Adds one or more facts to the fact list. The fact address of the last fact added is returned.

```
(assert-string <string-expression>)
```
Converts a string to a fact and asserts it. The fact address of the newly asserted fact is returned.

```
(dependencies <fact-index-or-fact-address>)
```
Lists all the partial matches from which the specified fact receives logical support.

```
(dependents <fact-index-or-fact-address>)
```
Lists all facts that receive logical support from the specified fact.

```
(duplicate <fact-index-or-fact-address>
   <RHS-slot>*)
```
Asserts a duplicated copy of a deftemplate fact with one or more slot values changed.

```
(facts [<module-name>]
   [<start-integer-expression>
    [<end-integer-expression>
     [<max-integer-expression>]]])
```
Displays the facts in the fact list. If <module-name> is specified, only those facts visible to the specified module are listed, otherwise facts visible to the current module are listed. Facts with fact indices less than <start-integer-expression> or greater than <end-integer-expression> are not listed. If <max-integer-expression> is specified, then no more facts than that value will be listed.

```
(fact-index <fact-address-expression>)
```
Returns the fact index associated with a fact address.

```
(get-fact-duplication)
```
Returns the current value of the fact duplication behavior.

```
(load-facts <file-name>)
```
Asserts the facts contained in the file <file-name> in the current module. Returns TRUE if successful, otherwise FALSE.

```
(modify <fact-index-or-fact-address> <RHS-slot>*)
```
Changes one or more slot values of a deftemplate fact.

```
(retract <fact-index-or-fact-address>+)
```
Removes one or more facts from the fact list.

```
(save-facts <file-name>
    [visible | local <deftemplate-names>*])
```
Saves the specified facts to the file <file-name>. Returns TRUE if successful, otherwise FALSE.

```
(set-fact-duplication <boolean-expression>)
```
Allows identical facts to be asserted if <boolean-expression> is FALSE, otherwise prevents duplicate facts from being added to the fact list. The old value of the duplication behavior is returned.

Deffacts Commands

```
(list-deffacts [<module-name>])
```
Lists the deffacts in the specified module (or in the current module if <module-name> is unspecified).

```
(ppdeffacts <deffacts-name>)
```
Displays the text of the specified deffacts.

```
(undeffacts <deffacts-name>)
```
Deletes the specified deffacts.

Defrule Commands

```
(list-defrules [<module-name>])
```
Lists the defrules in the specified module (or in the current module if <module-name> is unspecified).

```
(matches <defrule-name>)
```
Displays the list of facts and partial matches that match the patterns of the specified rule.

```
(ppdefrule <defrule-name>)
```
Displays the text of the specified defrule.

```
(refresh <defrule-name>)
```
Refreshes the specified defrule. Activations for the rule that have already fired but are still valid are placed on the agenda.

```
(remove-break [<defrule-name>])
```
Removes a breakpoint for the specified rule. If no rule is specified, all breakpoints are removed.

```
(set-break <defrule-name>)
```
Sets a breakpoint for the specified rule. This will cause rule execution to halt before the rule is fired.

```
(show-breaks [<module-name>])
```
Lists the rules in the specified module that have breakpoints set (or in the current module if <module-name> is unspecified).

```
(undefrule <defrule-name>)
```
Deletes the specified defrule.

Agenda Functions and Commands

```
(agenda [<module-name>])
```
Lists the activations on the agenda of the specified module (or in the current module if <module-name> is unspecified).

```
(clear-focus-stack)
```
Returns all the module names from the focus stack.

```
(focus <module-name>+)
```
Pushes one or more modules onto the focus stack. The specified modules are pushed onto the focus stack in the reverse order from the argument list.

```
(get-focus)
```
Returns the module name of the current focus.

```
(get-focus-stack)
```
Returns all the module names in the focus stack as a multifield value.

```
(halt)
```
Stops the execution of rules.

```
(list-focus-stack)
```
Lists all the module names on the focus stack.

```
(pop-focus-stack)
```
Returns the module name of the current focus and removes the current focus from the focus stack.

```
(run [<integer-expression>])
```
Starts the execution of rules in the current focus. If <integer-expression> is specified then only that number of rules is executed, otherwise execution halts when the agenda is empty.

Defmodule Commands

```
(get-current-module)
```
Returns the current module.

```
(list-defmodules)
```
Lists all defmodules in the CLIPS environment.

```
(ppdefmodule <defmodule-name>)
```
Displays the text of the specified defmodule.

```
(set-current-module <defmodule-name>)
```
Sets the current module to the specified module and returns the previous current module.

APPENDIX F

CLIPS BNF

CLIPS Program

```
<CLIPS-program> ::= <construct>*

<construct>        ::= <deftemplate-construct> |
                       <deffacts-construct> |
                       <defrule-construct> |
                       <defmodule-construct>
```

Deftemplate Construct

```
<deftemplate-construct>  ::= (deftemplate <name>
                                 [<comment>]
                                 <slot-definition>*)

<slot-definition>        ::= <single-slot-definition> |
                             <multislot-definition>

<single-slot-definition> ::= (slot <slot-name>
                                    <slot-attribute>*)

<slot-name>              ::= <symbol>

<multislot-definition>   ::= (multislot <slot-name>
                                    <slot-attribute>*)

<slot-attribute>      ::= <type-attribute> |
                          <allowed-constant-attribute> |
                          <range-attribute> |
                          <cardinality-attribute> |
                          <default-attribute>

<type-attribute>      ::= (type <type-specification>)

<type-specification> ::= <allowed-type>+ | ?VARIABLE
```

```
<allowed-type>          ::= SYMBOL | STRING | LEXEME |
                            INTEGER | FLOAT | NUMBER

<allowed-constant-attribute>
                ::= (allowed-symbols <symbol-list>) |
                    (allowed-strings <string-list>) |
                    (allowed-lexemes <lexeme-list> |
                    (allowed-integers <integer-list>) |
                    (allowed-floats <float-list>) |
                    (allowed-numbers <number-list>) |
                    (allowed-values <value-list>)

<symbol-list>      ::= <symbol>+ | ?VARIABLE

<string-list>      ::= <string>+ | ?VARIABLE

<lexeme-list>      ::= <lexeme>+ | ?VARIABLE

<integer-list>     ::= <integer>+ | ?VARIABLE

<float-list>       ::= <float>+ | ?VARIABLE

<number-list>      ::= <number>+ | ?VARIABLE

<value-list>       ::= <constant>+ | ?VARIABLE

<range-attribute> ::= (range <range-specification>
                             <range-specification>)

<range-specification> ::= <number> | ?VARIABLE

<cardinality-attribute>
          ::= (cardinality <cardinality-specification>
                           <cardinality-specification>)

<cardinality-specification> ::= <integer> | ?VARIABLE

<default-attribute> ::= (default <default-item>) |
                        (default-dynamic <expression>*)

<default-item>      ::= ?DERIVE | ?NONE | <expression>*
```

Deffacts Construct

```
<deffacts-construct> ::= (deffacts <name> [<comment>]
                          <RHS-pattern>*)
```

Defrule Construct

```
<defrule-construct>    ::= (defrule <name> [<comment>]
                            [<declaration>]
                            <conditional-element>*
                            =>
                            <expression>*)

<declaration>          ::= (declare <rule-property>+)

<rule-property>    ::= (salience <integer-expression>) |
                       (auto-focus <boolean-symbol>)

<boolean-symbol>       ::= TRUE | FALSE

<conditional-element> ::= <pattern-CE> |
                          <assigned-pattern-CE> |
                          <test-CE> |
                          <not-CE> |
                          <and-CE> |
                          <or-CE> |
                          <logical-CE> |
                          <exists-CE> |
                          <forall-CE>

<pattern-CE>           ::= <ordered-pattern-CE> |
                          <template-pattern-CE>

<assigned-pattern-CE>
           ::= <single-field-variable> <- <pattern-CE>

<test-CE>                 ::= (test <function-call>)

<not-CE>                  ::= (not <conditional-element>)

<and-CE>                  ::= (and <conditional-element>+)

<or-CE>                   ::= (or <conditional-element>+)

<logical-CE>         ::= (logical <conditional-element>+)

<exists-CE>          ::= (exists <conditional-element>+)

<forall-CE>          ::= (forall <conditional-element>
                                 <conditional-element>+)

<ordered-pattern-CE>  ::= (<symbol> <constraint>+)
```

```
<template-pattern-CE>
                    ::= (<deftemplate-name <LHS-slot>*)

<LHS-slot>              ::= <single-field-LHS-slot> |
                           <multifield-LHS-slot>

<single-field-LHS-slot> ::= (<slot-name> <constraint>)

<multifield-LHS-slot> ::= (<slot-name> <constraint>*)

<constraint>           ::= ? | $? | <connected-constraint>

<connected-constraint>
    ::= <single-constraint> |
        <single-constraint> & <connected-constraint> |
        <single-constraint> | <connected-constraint>

<single-constraint>    ::= <term> | ~<term>

<term>                 ::= <constant> |
                           <variable> |
                           :<function-call> |
                           =<function-call>
```

Fact Specification

```
<RHS-pattern>             ::= <ordered-RHS-pattern> |
                             <template-RHS-pattern>

<ordered-RHS-pattern>    ::= (<symbol> <RHS-field>+)

<template-RHS-pattern>
                    ::= (<deftemplate-name> <RHS-slot>*)

<RHS-slot>               ::= <single-field-RHS-slot> |
                             <multifield-RHS-slot>

<single-field-RHS-slot> ::= (<slot-name> <RHS-field>)

<multifield-RHS-slot>    ::= (<slot-name> <RHS-field>*)

<RHS-field>              ::= <variable> |
                             <constant> |
                             <function-call>

<deftemplate-name>       ::= <symbol>
```

Variables and Expressions

```
<single-field-variable> ::= ?<variable-symbol>
```

```
<multifield-variable>    ::= $?<variable-symbol>

<variable>               ::= <single-field-variable> |
                            <multifield-variable>

<function-call>   ::= (<function-name> <expression>*) |
                      <special-function-call>

<special-function-call>
       ::= (assert <RHS-pattern>+) |
           (modify <expression> <RHS-slot>+) |
           (duplicate <expression> <RHS-slot>+) |
           (bind <single-field-variable> <expression>)

<expression>            ::= <constant> |
                            <variable> |
                            <function-call>
```

Data Types

`<symbol> ::=` *A valid symbol as specified in Section 7.4*

`<string> ::=` *A valid string as defined in Section 7.4*

`<float>  ::=` *A valid float as defined in Section 7.4*

`<integer>`
        `::=` *A valid integer as specified in Section 7.4*

`<number>     ::= <float> | <integer>`

`<lexeme>     ::= <symbol> | <string>`

`<constant>   ::= <number> | <lexeme>`

`<comment>    ::= <string>`

`<variable-symbol> ::=` *A <symbol> beginning with an alphabetic character*

`<function-name>   ::= <symbol>`

`<name>            ::= <symbol>`

Index

= 61
" 87
~ 81, 331, 382
» 80
" 331
"do it twice" 319
$ 358
$? 331, 377
% 358, 396
& 331, 383
(331
() 36
) 331
* 329, 358, 385, 570
** 572
+ 330, 334, 385, 569
+j 358, 486
- 570
/ 385, 570
< 328, 329, 331, 566
<- 367
<= 566
<== 342, 348
<> 61, 566
= 411, 566
==> 342, 348
=> 62, 346
=j 486
> 328, 386, 566
>, 329
>= 566
? 331
?DERIVE 442
?NONE 443
?VARIABLE 437
[328
\ 332
] 328
{ 328

{ } 35
| 35, 86, 330, 331, 383
} 328
´ 81
∏-function 263
∫ 35
≈ operator 249
− 385
Ø 86
Œ 79

"a" 393
a-cuts 264
A-KIND-OF 64
a posteriori 57
a posteriori probability 174
a priori 57
a priori probability 170
abduction 151
abs 569
absolute probability 178
accuracy 167
acos 570
acosh 570
acot 570
acoth 570
acsc 570
acsch 570
act 27, 182
action 334
action frame 77
actions 27
activated 12, 26, 346
activation 480
activation function 45
acyclic 98
Ada 328, 333
Additive Law 177
adequate 86

affirmative in quality 111
agenda 23, 346, 347, 463, 577
AKO 64
algorithm 33
algorithmic programming 33
allowed-strings attribute 440
allowed-symbols attribute 440
allowed-values attribute 440
allowed-floats attribute 440
allowed-integers attribute 440
allowed-lexemes attribute 440
allowed-numbers attribute 440
alpha memory 482
alternative denial 86
ambiguity 166
ampersand 383
analogy 8, 149
and 565
and conditional element 355, 415
and connective constraint 385
and constraint 383
angle brackets 61
ANS 43
antecedent 25, 110
APL 36
application operations 36
approximate reasoning 282
apropos 573
arcs 63
ARE 65
argument. 109
arguments 385, 387
arithmetic operators 385
arrow 346
ART 328, 477
ART-IM 328
artificial neural systems 43
asec 570
asech 570
asin 570
asinh 570
askable nodes 209
assert 337, 437, 575
assert-string 575
assertion 125, 209
association 35
associative memory 46
associative nets 64
assuming the antecedent 115
assumption-based truth maintenance, 154
atan 570
atanh 571

atomic 63
atoms 36
attenuation factor 240
attribute-value pairs 66
Attribute-Value pairs 527
attributes 65
auto-focus attribute 469
autoepistemic reasoning 155
automated knowledge acquisition 100
automated reasoning systems 78
AV 66
axioms 83, 125

back-propagation 45
back-propagation 48
backtracking 41
backward chaining 26, 328, 526
backward induction 185
bandwidth 263
bar 35, 61
basic assignment 246
basic probability assignment 246
batch 428, 573
Bayes' Theorem 181
Bayesian decision making 183
Bel 250
belief function 250
belief measure, 251
beta memory 483
biconditional 84
binary variable 272
bind 365, 391
bivalent logic 257
blocks world 371, 381
body 499
bold intersection 269
bold union 268
bottom 71
bottom-up 35
bottom-up reasoning 145
bound 124, 365
bounded difference 269
bounded product 269
bounded sum 268
bpa 246
branches, 97
breadth-first search 69
breakpoint 355

C 328, 333
calculus of fuzzy restrictions 288
canonical form 293

cardinality 251
cardinality attribute 441
Cartesian product 271
case-sensitive 331
categorical syllogism 110
causal associations 153
causal chain 134
causal knowledge 7
causal knowledge frames 77
CAUSE 66
center of gravity 291
certain event 173
certainty factor 510
certainty factors 210, 233, 236
chain 143
chain of reasoning 110
characteristic function 256
check for halt 27
child 97
chunk 12
circuit 98
class 39, 64
classical probability 170
clausal form 129
clear 344, 352, 573
clear-focus-stack 466, 577
CLIPS 327, 477
CLIPS Object-Oriented Language 328
CLOS 328
close 394, 568
closed sentence 83
closed world assumption 152
code-and-fix model 319
code and checkout stage, 324
codomain 35
Cognate 328
cognition 11
cognitive processor 12
cognitive science 10
combinatorial explosion 44
combined mass 249
command 334
comment 358
Comments 345
Common Lisp Object System 328
commonsense knowledge 109, 299
commonsense reasoning 155, 281
compatibility function 257
compatibility of rules 229
complement 80
complete 128
complete evidence 196

completeness 128
composition 273
composition operator 273
composition rules 295
compositional rule 299
compound event 171
compound evidence 201
compound statement 84
computational linguistics 276
concentration 269
concept schema 73
conclusion 78
conditional 84
conditional and conjunctive composition
    295
conditional composition 295
conditional element 25
conditional part 25
conditional probability 178
configuration 16
conflict resolution 27
conjunction 84
conjunctive composition 295
conjunctive normal form 129
connected graph 98
connectionism 43
connective constraint 382
consensus 249
consequences 193
consequent 27, 110
consistent 127
constraining relation 299
constructs 335
context-sensitive 155
contexts 213
contingent 84
contingent statements 92
continuum 265
contradiction 84
contradiction of rules 229
contrapositive 119
control fact 406, 448, 469, 525
control pattern 406
control strategies 231
control strategy 30
control string 396
control structure 19
converse 119
convex functions 300
convex set Bayesian 300
COOL 328
copula 111

cos 571
cosh 571
cot 571
coth 571
counter-propagation 45
create$ 566
crisp sets, 257
crlf 353
crossover point 260
csc 571
csch 571
curly braces 35
current focus 464
cut 68
cycle 98
cycles 27
cylindrical extension 275

data abstraction 21
data fusion 233
data objects 36
Dbt 253
decidable 127
decision lattices 98
decision procedure 112
decision trees 98
declarative knowledge 58
declarative paradigm 38
deductive logic 109
deep 73
deep knowledge 7
deep reasoning 134
default 75
default attribute 442
default reasoning 154
default-dynamic attribute 444
defeasible 155
deffacts 342
definitive knowledge 72
defmodule 456
defrule 345
deftemplate 335
    explicit 336
    implied 336
defuzzification problem 292
deg-grad 571
deg-rad 571
degenerate tree 98
degree of belief 191
degree of confirmation 236
delete$ 566
delimiter 331

delivery problem 37, 312
Dempster-Shafer theory 243
Dempster's Rule of Combination 249, 254
dependencies 425, 427, 575
dependent 425
dependents 427, 575
depth-first search, 69
derivation tree 62
detailed design stage 323
deterministic 105, 171
digraph, 98
dilation 270
direct reasoning 115
direct sum 249
discrimination function 256
disjunction 84
disjunctive composition 295
disjunctive form 129
disposition 298
div 569
domain 1, 35
domain variable 87
double arrow 62
doubt 253
dribble-off 430
dribble-on 430
dribble-off 574
dribble-on 574
dubiety 253
duplicate 341, 575
dynamic knowledge structure 216

Eclipse 328
edges 63, 97
effective likelihood ratio 205
elastic constraint 287
elements 78
empty list 36
empty set 80
emulates 2
environment 243
EOF 395, 397
epistemic probability 236
epistemology 57
eq 565
equality axiom 128
erratic 167
error 166
errors of measurement 167
evenp 565
event 171, 182
event tree 171

events 170
evidence 144, 192
evidence measure 246
evidential conflict 255
evidential interval 250, 252
evidential reasoning 243
exact reasoning 165
exclusive-OR 45
existential import 82
existential quantifier 88
exists conditional element 419
exit 333, 334, 573
exp 572
expected payoff 185
experiential knowledge 20, 133
experimental probability 173
expert 2
expert systems 1
expert's knowledge errors 313
expertise 2, 3
explanation facility 6, 23
explicit and conditional element 413
explicit or conditional element 413
explicit priority 229
explode$ 398, 567
export 460
expression 385, 388, 391
extension principle 280
external address 330, 333
external functions 407
extralogical features 129

fact 327, 334
    deftemplate 336
    ordered 336, 341
fact address 367
fact addresses 512
fact identifier 338, 339
fact identifiers 512
fact index 338
fact list 327, 337
fact-index 575
facts 338, 575
fair 171
fallacy 118
fallacy of the converse 118
false negative 167
false positive 167
fault detection, isolation, and recovery 448
fault tolerant 46
field constraint 382, 384
fields 330

fillers 74
finite state machine 102
fires 346
firing 26, 47
first moment of inertia 291
first order 86, 128
first$ 567
FL 295
Flight Technique Panels, 313
float 330, 437, 569
floatp 565
focal element 247
focus 464, 577
focus stack 465
forall conditional element 422
formal logic 81
formal test task 324
format 396, 568
format flags 396
forward chaining 26, 328
frame 74
frame of discernment 245
frame problem 154
frames 42
free 124
function 334
functional forms 36
functional programming 34
functions 35
·fuzzy expert systems 280
fuzzy grammar 279
fuzzy logic 204, 256
fuzzy predicate 293
fuzzy probability 295
fuzzy production 279
fuzzy proposition 258
fuzzy qualifier 258
fuzzy qualifiers 295
fuzzy quantifiers 258
fuzzy reasoning 282
fuzzy relation 272
fuzzy restriction 287

General Problem Solver 11
generalized delta rule 48
generalized modus ponens 300
Generalized Multiplicative Law 179
generate-and-test 150
generic 65
gensym 573
gensym* 522, 573
get-static-constraint-checking 439

get-current-module 457, 578
get-dynamic-constraint-checking 440, 573
get-fact-duplication 576
get-focus 466, 577
get-focus-stack 466, 577
get-static-constraint-checking 573
global database 23
goal 38
goals 68
grad-deg 572
grade of membership 258
grammar 61
granularity 13
graph 98

half-width 262
halt 498, 499, 577
hedges 277
height 265
heuristic 72
heuristic knowledge 7
hidden layers 48
hierarchy 97
hypothesis 9, 167, 192
hypothetical reasoning 6

if 498, 572
if-added 76
if-needed 75
if-removal 76
ignorance 246, 253
Igr 253
ill-structured problems 18
images 35
imperative 33
implication 85
implicit and conditional element 413
implicit priority 229
implode$ 567
import 460
impossible belief 212
impossible event 173
in desperation 183
incompleteness 166
inconsistent 127
incorrectness 166
incremental waterfall model 319
incrementally 10
independent 181
independent events 176
indifferent 192
indirect reasoning 119

individual 65
induces 49
induction 168
induction-based 43
inductive learning 49
inexact reasoning 166, 227
inference chain errors 315
inference engine 3, 13, 23, 327
inference engine errors 314
inference net 208, 213
inference nets 42
inferences 4
infinite-valued logic 281
infix form 385
inheritance 39, 66
initial-fact 343, 346, 351, 461
input resolution 143
insert$ 567
instance 39
instance address 330, 333
instance name 330, 333
instantiated 26
integer 330, 437, 569
integerp 565
intensification 270
interior probabilities 179
interpretation 127
interrupt command 369
intersection 79
interval 257
intrusive breccias, 213
invalid 127
invalid induction 168
inverse 119, 182
inverse probability 181
IS 66
IS-A 64
ISA 64
⊢ 126
⊨ 126

Johnson Space Center 328
join 483
join network 483
join operator 267
joint denial operator 86

knowledge-based programming 14
knowledge abstraction 21
knowledge acquisition bottleneck 8
knowledge acquisition facility 23
knowledge acquisition task 322

knowledge analysis task 322
knowledge base 327
knowledge definition stage 321
knowledge design stage 323
knowledge domain 3
knowledge engineer 6
knowledge engineering 6
knowledge extraction task 322
knowledge source 313
knowledge structure 73
knowledge verification stage 324
knowledge-based expert system 2, 6
Kyburg 300

L-logic 281
L-logics 281
L1 281
language 22
lattice 98
law of contraposition 119
law of detachment, 115
laws of inference 119
least upper bound 299
leaves 97
left-hand-side 25
left justify 397
left memory 483
length$ 567
LEX 231
LEXEME 437
lexemep 565
lexicographic 231
LHS 25, 346
life cycle 317
likelihood 192
likelihood of sufficiency 194
likelihood ratio 193
limits of ignorance 7
limits of ignorance errors 315
Linear Model, 320
linear resolution 143
linguistic variables 276
links 63, 97
LISP 328
LISP, 333
list-deffacts 350, 458, 576
list-defmodules 578
list-defrules 350, 457, 576
list-deftemplates 350, 458, 575
list-focus-stack 465, 577
lists 36
literals 129

LN 281
load 357, 574
load-facts 503, 519, 524
local 503
log 572
log10 572
logic 78
logic programming 78
logical AND 80
logical combinations 211
logical conditional element 424
logical equivalence 85
logical name 353, 393
    nil 396
logical NOT 81
logical support 425
logical variables, 83
long-term memory 12
lowcase 568
lower bound 250
Lukasiewicz logic operators 281

magic square 149
main connectives 117
MAIN module 456
major increments 319
major premise 111
major term 111
mapping 272
marginal probabilities 179
Markov algorithm 30
Markov chain process 190
mass 246
match 27
matches 419, 459, 489, 576
material equivalence 85
material implication 84
matrix 139, 213
max 569
max-min 273
max-min compositional rule of inference
    286
max-min matrix product 273
max-product 274
maximum method 289
MEA 231
mean time between failures 316
meaning 278
means-ends analysis 231
measure of increased belief 236
measure of increased disbelief 236
meet operator 267

member$ 567
membership function 257
meta 60
metaknowledge. 60
metalanguage 60
metamethodology 318
metarule 10, 154
metasymbol, 126
metrics 316
mgu 142
micro increment 319
middle term 111
min 569
min function 204
minor increments 319
minor premise 111
minor term 111
missing rules 233
mission 315
mission critical 313
mix 289
mod 412, 572
model 127, 135, 207
modification rules 295
modify 340, 576
modify and duplicate 341
module 351
module separator 456
modus ponens 115
modus tollens 119
moments method 289
monitoring 538
monotonic systems 153
monotonicity 153
mood 112
most general clause 142
most general unifier 142
multifield slots 336
multifield value 333
multifield variables 493
multifield wildcard 376
multifieldp 565
Multiplicative Law 179
multislot 335
mutual independence 176
mutually exclusive events 173
MYCIN 509

naming procedures 36
NAND 86
NASA 328
negation 84

negative in quality 111
neq 565
neuron 26
nil 36, 131
no belief 247
nodes 63
nodes, 97
nonbelief 247
nondeterministic 171
nonmonotonic system 153
nonprocedural 33
nonterminal 61
NOR 86
normal 129
normalization 254, 271
normalized 265
not 565
not conditional element 417
not constraint 382
nth$ 567
null 131
null hypothesis 167
null set 80
null string 30
number 330, 437
numberp 566
numeric field 330

OAV 66
object-attribute-value triple 66
object-oriented design 38
object-oriented programming 38, 327
object-oriented 38
objective theory of probability 173
objects 6
object–attribute–value triples 509
oddp 566
odds 192
odds-likelihood form 194
one-input nodes 481
open 393, 569
open sentence 83
operands 385
OPS5 328, 477
OPS83 477
or 566
or constraint 383
or field constraint 385
order 150
orders 128
oriented tree 97
orthogonal sum 249

pairwise independent 176
paradigm 14
parent 97
parent clauses 130
parse tree 62
partial evidence 196
partial match 479
particular 112
partitioned semantic net 214
Pascal 328, 335
path 98
pattern 25, 345
pattern binding 367
pattern CE 345
pattern match 480
pattern matching, 71
pattern network 480
pattern nodes 481
pattern part 25
payoffs 185
perceptron 47
personal construct theory 323
personal probability 193
pi 572
plan 151
plan-generate-test 151
planning 513
plasticity 47
plausibility 250
plausible belief 212
plausible inference 155
plausible relations 211
Pls 250
poisoned 185
pop-focus 466
pop-focus-stack 577
populations 172
porphyritic 213
portability 328
Poss 293
possibility 293
possibility assignment equation 293
possibility distribution 293
possibility qualification 296
possible belief 212
posterior probability 174
postulates 125
power of a set 268
power set 93
ppdeffacts 350, 459, 576
ppdefmodule 578

ppdefrule 345, 350, 459, 576
ppdeftemplate 350, 459, 575
precedence of arithmetic operations 388
precision 167
predefined functions 407
predicate 111
predicate database 69
predicate expression 67
predicate field constraint 410
predicate function 407, 498
predicate function or variable) 499
predicate functions 87
predicate logic 86
predicates 36
prefix form 385
premises 78
prenex form, 139
primary term 278
primitive data types 330
primitive functions 36
principle of indifference 246
printout 353, 394, 395, 569
probabilistic sum 268
probability 169
probability distribution 293
probability qualification 296
probability vector 187
probable belief 213
problem domain 3
problem space 102
procedural attachments 75
procedural knowledge 58
procedural program 33
procedural programming 327
process model 318
production memory 24
production rules 11, 13
production system 13, 328
prognosis 9
projection 274
PROLOG 527
proper subset 79, 267
property 65
proposition 83
propositional calculus 83
propositional function 124
propositional net 63
prototype 76
proved 127
pruned 185

qualification rules 296

quality 316
quantification rules 296
quantifier-free 129
quantifier 86, 112
quantity 112
query 70

"r" 393
"r+" 393
rad-deg 572
random 573
random error 167
random variable 293
range 35
range attribute 441
range of belief 250
rapid prototyping 10
read 392, 395, 397, 569
readline 397, 569
real time 187
recency of facts 231
recognize-act cycle 27
reductio ad absurdum 130
redundant rules 232
Reference Manual viii
referentially transparent 35
refraction 347
refresh 348, 459, 577
refutation 132
refutation complete 132
refuted 128
regular transition matrix 190
relation 271
relation name 334
relational join 274
remove 569
remove-break 356, 459, 577
rename 569
repertory grids 323
replace$ 567
reproducible uncertainty 227
reset 343, 574
resolution 128
resolution refutation 132
resolution refutation tree 133
resolvent 130
rest$ 567
Rete Algorithm 32
Rete Pattern Matching Algorithm 477
retract 340, 367, 576
retraction 340
return 467

return value 334, 386
return value field constraint 411
rewrite rules 29
RHS 27, 346
right-hand side 27
right justify 397
right memory 482
root node 97
round 572
rule induction 7
rule model 157
rule of substitution 121
rule-based programming 327
rules 5
rules of inference 119
run 346, 467, 578
run command 500

S-function 261
salience 346, 445, 454
salience hierarchy 451
sample point 171
sample space 171
satisfiable 127
save 358, 574
save-facts 503, 519
scheduling 513
schemas 73
schematas 73
scope 124
script 74
search space 513
sec 571
sech 571
second order 128
seed 573
seismic survey 183
select-execute cycle 27
self-learning 99
self-loop 98
semantic errors 314
semantic network 63
semantic rule 278
semantics 60
semidecidable 127
sensorimotor 73
sentence 61
sentential calculus 83
sequential 33
set 35
set-break 355
set-dynamic-constraint-checking 440

set complement 266
set containment 266
set equality 266
set intersection 267
set of support 143
set product 268
set union 267
set-break 459, 577
set-current-module 457, 578
set-dynamic-constraint-checking 574
set-fact-duplication 511, 576
set-static-constraint-checking 439, 574
setgen 573
shallow 73
shallow knowledge 7
shallow reasoning 134
shell 14, 23
short-term memory 12
show-breaks 356
show-breaks 458, 577
side effect 386
sigmoid function 45
simple event 171
simple evidence 201
sin 571
single-field slots 335
single-field wildcard 370
singleton 86
singleton set 244
sinh 571
situation-action cycle 27
situation-response cycle 27
situational frame 77
Skolem functions 138
slot 335
slots 74, 334
slump test 289
SmallTalk 328
software engineering methodology 309
sound 128
space 332, 365
spaces 214
specificity 230
spiral model 319
Spt 250
sqrt 572
stack 380
standard form 111
standard input device 394, 397
standard output device 353
standard square 150
start symbol 61

state 101
state space 101
statement 83
statement-oriented 33
statement calculus 83
states 193
static constraint checking 439
static knowledge structure 216
steady-state matrix 190
steps 190
stereotypes 73
stochastic process 187
stochastically independent events 176
str-cat 568
str-compare 568
str-index 568
str-length 568
string 61, 330, 332, 437
stringp 566
stroke 86
strong typing 323
structural similarity 480
structure 98
sub-string 568
subclass 39, 65
subgoals 40, 68
subject 111
subjective probability 174
subseq$ 567
subset 79, 267
subsetp 568
substitution instances 140
subsumption of rules 230
sup 299
superclass 65
superclasses 39
supp 264
support 250, 263, 264
supremum 299
syllogism 78
sym-cat 568
symbol 330, 331, 437
symbolic expressions 36
symbolic logic 82
symbolp 566
synapses 47
syntactic rule 278
syntax 60
syntax errors 314
synthesis 513
system 428, 574
system evaluation stage 325

systematic error 167

tacit knowledge 58
tan 571
tanh 571
tasks 320
tautology 84
taxonomy 32, 513
temporal events 186
temporal reasoning 186
temporal redundancy 478
term-set 277
terminal 61
terminal nodes 481
test analysis tasks 324
test conditional element 408, 493
test readiness review, 324
texture 213
theorem 125, 126
three-valued logics 281
threshold value 45, 239
time 444, 573
time constraints 8
timetag 27, 231
tokens 330
tool 22
top 71
top-down 34
top-level 28
top level 333, 334
top level prompt 386
top-down reasoning 145
top-level hypothesis 209
total width 263
transitions 101
translation rules 295
tree 97
triplet 66
trivalent 281
truth maintenance 154, 424
truth qualification 296
truth value 285
truth value of the antecedent 286
two-input node 483
two-valued logic, 257
type 1 fuzzy subset 265
type 2 fuzzy subset 266
type attribute 437
Type I error 167
Type II error 167
type N fuzzy subset 266

unary number system 127
uncertainty 165, 509
unconditional probability 178
unconditionally supported 427
unconscious knowledge 58
undeffacts 351, 459, 576
undefrule 351, 459, 577
undeftemplate 351, 459, 575
unifiable 142
unification 41, 140
Unification Algorithm 142
unifier 142
union 80
unit preference 143
universal quantifier 87
universal set 79
unreliability 167
unsatisfiable 127
unwatch 342, 574
upcase 568
upper bound 250
user-defined functions 407
user interface 23
User's Guide ix
user-defined function 333

V&V 157
valid 82, 127
validation 157
value 65
variable 391
variables 365, 376
Venn diagram 78
verification 157
vertices 97
visible 503

"w" 393
warrant 10
watch 341, 466, 574
    activations 341, 348
    all 341
    compilations 341, 357, 485
    facts 341
    focus 341
    rules 341, 349
    statistics 341, 349
weight 98
weighted combinations 211
weights 44
well-formed formulas 125
wffs 125

while 498, 499, 572
wildcards 376
wisdom 60
work plan 321
working memory 23
world 154

XOR 45

About the CD-ROM

The CD-ROM included with this book contains several directories:

- **STARTING**

  The STARTING directory contains ASCII text and Portable Document Format (PDF) files that describe the contents of the CD-ROM and installation instructions for using the CLIPS software and electronic documentation included on the CD-ROM.

- **ACROREAD**

  The ACROREAD directory contains Windows, MacOS, and Unix installers for Adobe Acrobat 3.01, which must be installed to read the documentation on the CD-ROM stored in PDF format.

- **PROGRAMS**

  The PROGRAMS directory contains CLIPS executables for use with DOS, Windows 3.1, Windows 95, and MacOS. A number of example programs are also provided.

- **DOCUMENT**

  The DOCUMENT directory contains the CLIPS Reference Manuals, CLIPS User's Guide, CLIPS conference proceedings, and other documents.

- **SOURCE**

  The SOURCE directory contains the core CLIPS source code, which can be compiled on most operating systems with an ANSI C compiler, in addition to the source code for the Windows, MacOS, and X Windows interfaces for CLIPS.